D0350068

# HARRY
# HOPKINS

*Harry Hopkins, c. 1944*

# HARRY HOPKINS

*Ally of the Poor*
*and*
*Defender of Democracy*

■

**George McJimsey**

Harvard University Press
Cambridge, Massachusetts, and London, England   1987

This book is printed on acid-free paper, and its binding materials
have been chosen for strength and durability.

*Library of Congress Cataloging-in-Publication Data*

McJimsey, George T.
   Harry Hopkins : ally of the poor and defender of
Democracy.

   Includes index.
   1. Hopkins, Harry Lloyd, 1890–1946.   2. Statesmen—
United States—Biography.   3. United States—Foreign
relations—1933–1945.   4. World War, 1939–1945—
Diplomatic history.   I. Title.
E748.H67M35  1987      973.917′092′4  [B]   86-22764
ISBN 0-674-37287-5 (alk. paper)

*For Sandra*

# Preface

This book portrays a man who helped lead the United States through its two greatest crises of the twentieth century: the Great Depression and World War II. Although prominent in his profession of social work, Harry Hopkins was unknown to most Americans at the time he joined Franklin D. Roosevelt's New Deal to manage federal relief for the unemployed. By the end of Roosevelt's first term, Hopkins's Works Progress Administration had become the best known and most effective of the New Deal programs, and Hopkins himself had become one of Roosevelt's most prominent spokesmen. Although failing health denied him further political advancement, Hopkins stayed on to become Roosevelt's personal representative and expediter during World War II. In these roles he confronted problems of wartime grand strategy, shipping, production, finance, and diplomacy. Few individuals, if any, were as important to the U.S. war effort as Harry Hopkins.

 Hopkins's wartime activities were the culmination of his career and are the focus of this biography. The first eight chapters discuss Hopkins's earlier activities as important in their own right while showing the development of the traits and skills that characterized his wartime service.

During the course of the narrative I have defined those traits and skills, but I have refrained from handing down an ultimate verdict on Hopkins's success. Opinions about a person's success or failure derive, I believe, less from the kind of expert knowledge a biographer acquires through years of research and reflection than from the public values we all acquire as we lead our lives as citizens. I do, however, want to influence the reader's judgment in one respect. During his years in government Hopkins operated as a crisis manager, grappling with problems of economic collapse and world war that were unprecedented in American history. We who read in more settled and predictable times need to realize that the dangers Hopkins faced required fast, improvised decisions that often created as many problems as they solved. For Harry Hopkins, then, success meant not only devising means to deal with immediate problems but also coming to grips with the consequences, realizing all the while that failure could mean disaster for his country.

Writing this book has been a small-scale example of the unpredictability of human affairs. I began the project thinking that I would update the information provided by Robert E. Sherwood in his magisterial volume *Roosevelt and Hopkins*, which was first published in 1948. Writing shortly after Hopkins's death, Sherwood had access to Hopkins's voluminous papers and the opportunity to interview people who had known Hopkins. He also had the advantage of having worked with Hopkins when he served as speech writer for President Roosevelt in the 1940s. Sherwood's volume is so detailed that I believed I should concentrate on placing Hopkins's career in the context of the latest published scholarship. I soon realized, however, that I had access to documents that had been unavailable to Sherwood and would have to change course and write a biography primarily based on manuscript sources. Thus as my research proceeded I grew to rely less and less on Sherwood's volume. One result has been that when people have asked me how my book compares with Sherwood's, I have replied that Sherwood wrote his book and I have written mine, always hastening to add that I have great respect and admiration for Sherwood's accomplishment.

Writing the book would have been not only unpredictable but absolutely impossible without the assistance of numerous people. William R. Emerson and his staff at the Frankin D. Roosevelt Library in Hyde Park, New York, have provided an ideal atmosphere for research and have been endlessly helpful in providing materials and answering my questions. Similarly helpful were many individuals in the various branches of the National Archives and Records Service in Washington, D.C. Anyone who has undertaken the wearying task of multiarchival research can appreciate why I offer special thanks to Anthony R. Crawford, former archivist of the George C. Marshall Library in Lexington, Virginia, who picked me up at the bus station in a pouring rain, drove me around town discussing places I might stay, and opened the library for my use on a holiday.

Special thanks go also to the late Dr. James Halsted and Diana Halsted, who generously made available materials on Harry Hopkins's personal life.

I wish also to thanks the staffs of the Manuscript Division of the Library of Congress, the British Public Records Office in Kew, Churchill College in Cambridge, the University of Virginia Library, the Yale University Library, the Houghton Library of Harvard University, the Social Work History Archives in Minneapolis, the Dwight D. Eisenhower Library, the Harry S. Truman Library, the Manuscripts Division and the Oral History Collection of the Butler Library of Columbia University, the New York State Library at Albany, the Community Service Society of New York City, the Lung Association of New York City, the American Red Cross of Washington, D.C., the Burling Library of Grinnell College, and the Parks Library of Iowa State University.

I owe thanks to Robert Hopkins for permission to quote from his father's papers and for granting me an interview during an early stage of my research. I also thank the Right Honorable the Earl of Halifax for permission to quote from the Halifax Papers; the University of Virginia Library for permission to quote from the Edward Stettinius, Jr., Papers; Mrs. Raleigh Hansl, Jr., for permission to quote from the Raymond Clapper Papers; the George C. Marshall Research Foundation for permission to quote from the papers of George C. Marshall; and the Trustees of Columbia University in the City of New York for permission to quote from the oral history interviews of Henry Wallace, John Carmody, Lee Pressman, J. V. Cardon, and Chester Davis.

I would also like to thank Harper and Row, Publishers, Inc., for permission to quote from Robert E. Sherwood, *Roosevelt and Hopkins,* and A. M. Heath and Company Limited for permission to quote from the London edition of Sherwood's book, *The White House Papers of Harry Hopkins.* For permission to reproduce photographs I am grateful to Grinnell College for the photographs on pp. 13, 14, and 16; to Acme Newsphotos, the Bettmann Archive for those on pp. 98 and 147; to *Life* Magazine for the photograph on p. 187 (by Margaret Bourke-White, © 1945 Time Inc.); and to the Franklin D. Roosevelt Library for the photographs on the remaining pages.

I received valuable research support from the Eleanor Roosevelt Institute, which gave me two generous grants to begin this project, and from Iowa State University, which provided grants for summer research and travel and leaves of absence for both research and writing.

My colleagues in the Department of History at Iowa State University have been helpful with their advice about various parts of this manuscript. I am especially grateful to Richard Lowitt, Richard Kirkendall, Hamilton Cravens, Alan Marcus, and Richard Kottman. Frank Freidel of the University of Washington read a draft of the manuscript and offered very useful suggestions for revision. All have provided both intellectual stimulation and the kind of emotional encouragement one needs to complete a project of this scope.

Special thanks go to Aida Donald and Elizabeth Suttell of Harvard University Press. Their efforts and encouragement have made this a better book in numerous ways.

Finally, I want to thank my wife, Sandra, who helped with the research, offered valuable editorial advice, arranged moves to Hyde Park and London, and managed our family finances to provide for the considerable expense of this project. In all these ways she contributed directly to this book, but more important, in her helpfulness to others and her efforts to be a useful citizen, she represents the values for which Harry Hopkins stood. With gratitude and pride I dedicate this book to her.

# Contents

# Illustrations

# HARRY
# HOPKINS

# Prologue:
# 1946 and 1973

The ambassador was amused. Although a few moments of the funeral service had been overly pompous, even for his British taste, for the most part it had been impressive, even moving, attended by people "of all sorts and kinds," a mix that seemed to reflect the deceased's "wide humanity." It was not the service that had amused him but something that happened afterward, when another of the pallbearers had politely remarked to the minister that it had been a fine service and the minister had replied, "Well, anyhow I think we have given him a nice send-off." The ambassador thought that "Harry would have chuckled no end at that."[1]

The funeral took place in February 1946. The deceased's ashes remained in the church until his daughter arranged for them to be interred in the city cemetery in Grinnell, Iowa, in September 1973, where they rest alongside the remains of his parents, one grandmother, and one of his brothers. The grave is marked by a gray marble block inscribed:

Harry Lloyd Hopkins
1890–1946

If you raise your eyes from the marker, you will look toward the graves of Florence and Robert Kerr and Hallie Flanagan, friends and college classmates who played a part in Harry Hopkins's life. About two miles to the north and east are his boyhood home, still intact but somewhat weathered and dilapidated, and the small liberal arts college from which he graduated in 1912. In contrast to his home, the college shows signs of prosperity, including several recent buildings, one of which is perhaps the finest physical education facility at any school of

1

its kind. The building was paid for in part by a federal grant, sponsored by an assistant secretary of the Department of Health, Education and Welfare who had worked for Harry Hopkins and who wanted to do something in his honor. Harry, who loved the college and had wanted to do something for it himself, would, in a different way, have liked that too.[2]

# Chapter 1

# Harness Maker's Son

Harry Lloyd Hopkins grew up in the Middle West, principally in Iowa. His father, David Aldona Hopkins, who liked to be called Al, had moved with his parents from Massachusetts to Sioux City a few years after the Civil War. When Al's father died in 1877, he and his mother moved to the town of Vermillion across the Missouri River in Dakota Territory, where he went to work as a harness maker. There he married Anna Pickett, whose family had moved from Hamilton, Ontario, to homestead. When floods devastated Vermillion, Al, his mother, and Anna began a middle western odyssey through a series of small Nebraska towns—Fremont, North Bend, Schuyler, Cedar Bluffs, Norfolk—as Al tried to make a success as a harness maker. But nothing seemed to work out. Wheat prices were low, rainfall inadequate. Farmers bought on credit and then failed to pay their bills. As the money ran lower, Al's responsibilities multiplied with his growing family. Adah May was born in 1882, followed by Lewis Andrew (1884), Rome Miller (1887), and Etta (born in 1889 and died in infancy). In 1889 the family returned to Sioux City, where Al opened another harness store. It was there, on August 17, 1890, that Harry Lloyd was born.[1]

In 1892 the family resumed their travels, ending up in Chicago. In the process Al gave up trying to succeed as a small businessman and became a traveling salesman for a Milwaukee harness wholesaler.[2] In 1895 their last child, John Emery, was born.

In 1901 the Hopkinses moved to Grinnell, Iowa, a college town chosen by Harry's mother for the children's education. They rented a two-story frame house on the corner of Elm and Sixth streets, a few blocks from downtown and just south of Grinnell College. Al traveled for a few more years, enjoying city entertainments and the chance to indulge what his son Lewis called his "champagne appetites."[3] In 1909 he cut back his traveling and opened a harness shop. The next year he collected $1,550 in damages as a result of a carriage accident in Chicago, invested the money in his store, and stopped traveling.

During these years Al and Anna grew into an oddly matched couple. Al was an outgoing gladhander, a man of many friendships, active in civic organizations, and, beneath his easygoing exterior a fierce competitor. Nothing called forth these qualities more than bowling, a game he mastered and labored to popularize in central Iowa, once bowling in Des Moines against Adrian ("Cap") Anson, an Iowa native and the star pitcher for the Chicago White Sox baseball team. None of these traits suggested any compatibility with Anna, who was prim, self-disciplined, and devoutly religious. Just as Al's instincts led him to the bowling alleys, Anna's led her, and her children, to services at the Methodist church—five each Sunday. The product of her upbringing, Anna's religious faith had been stiffened during the years of raising the children while Al was traveling, and while his mother continued to live with them. Anna coped with her situation by establishing an iron rule over the household. Outside the door, Al was free to argue good-naturedly with his cronies, hustle bets at the bowling alleys, and play the role of the town character; but at home he had to conform to Anna's standards.[4]

Something about this family situation bothered Harry. Perhaps it was that his mother was particularly close to Adah, though she felt that she had tried to give Harry her love and understanding too. Although one might imagine a small-town Methodist household to be dominated by Bible reading and sober conversation, Harry's childhood seems not to have been particularly confining. Life in the Elm Street house was proper but not grim. The children entertained their friends and classmates at home and enjoyed the usual pastimes. If not the standard of behavior, then, perhaps it was his father's lack of authority around the house that bothered Harry. When Al came home one night with $500 he had won at the bowling lanes, he had to take Harry to the basement, safely out of Anna's hearing, to tell him about it. Whatever the reason, Harry drew away from his mother, and eventually left home feeling that he had been surrounded by "conservative narrow-mindedness." He would speak reproachfully of "the good Methodists back in Iowa."[5] Harry returned for occasional visits but showed little warmth toward his parents and, apart from Adah, not much toward his siblings.

Actually, Harry's parents had set a more wholesome example than he seemed to realize. In their different and even contradictory ways they represented the egalitarian neighborliness of small-town America. Anna demonstrated this in the home missionary work she undertook for the Methodist Church and the patient sympathy which she showed those who came to her for advice, and Al in his friendliness (college students who patronized his store called him "Dad"), his optimism, and his delight in deflating pomposity.

As he matured, Harry turned his parents' example to positive use. He showed much of his father's good-natured friendliness, enthusiasm for advertising his projects, love of competition, and optimism in defeat. And although he forsook his mother's strict religious practices, he shared much of her moral courage and capacity for self-sacrifice. He synthesized his parents' example into a lack of pretense and concern for social position, a neighborly sociability, and a satisfaction in beating the pompous and self-important at their own game.

Harry's family provided him with an even more positive example in his sister Adah. Almost all the Hopkins children absorbed their mother's missionary impulse, but Adah became a professional social worker. She nurtured her commitment at Grinnell College, where she was active in YWCA work. In 1905 she denounced child labor to a commencement audience as "the Curse of Childhood" and declared that the "high ideals that the four years of receiving which we experience here places us in obligation to spend our lives in giving to the good of the world." Adah was more than a campus gadfly; she was a leader. She held top student offices, managed the college literary magazine and annual, and was chosen to wear her class mantle as the outstanding senior. Her speech condemning child labor won first prize in an oratorical contest in which she was the only female entrant.[6]

After graduating in 1905, Adah worked for social welfare agencies in the East. She returned to Grinnell in 1912, when her mother was hospitalized briefly for tuberculosis, and in addition to looking after the household, she managed welfare activities in Poweshiek County. Combining jobs in public and private welfare, she became the county's overseer of the poor and the secretary of the private Social Service League. She taught classes in sociology at Grinnell College, organized an employment service, held physical training classes, supervised the Camp Fire Girls, and organized the townswomen to vote for a one-mill tax levy for playgrounds. She served as a truant officer and a guardian of the mentally retarded. She organized town clean-up days and promoted health care programs for schoolchildren, unwed mothers, and the tubercular poor. By investigating applications to determine eligibility, in her first year she reduced the number of people on permanent relief by 25 percent, cut relief expenditures in half, and increased allowances to the needy. The county board of supervisors was ecstatic. Neighboring counties inquired about the Grinnell plan so that they could copy it. Adah was invited to conferences around the state. She had demonstrated the value of trained professionalism. "That she has been successful," observed the *Grinnell Herald,* "is putting it mildly."[7]

Adah described her technique as prevention. "All emphasis and effort," she told the Social Service League, "should be directed toward prevention rather than cure and there should be developed in our midst a stronger feeling of democracy and of community interest." Elsewhere, others were calling her approach "organized neighborliness."[8]

To Harry, Adah attractively personified his mother's values. Her graceful self-assurance won respect and admiration. Her energy and executive drive were tremendous, and she balanced her ideals with sociability and a sense of humor. Adah and Harry even looked alike, with their mother's sharp features and large, dark eyes. In later years Adah played down her influence on Harry, claiming that he had entered social work only to get to New York.[9] This comment shows her inclination to see Harry as just a frivolous and irresponsible kid brother, a view for which she accumulated some fairly convincing evidence but which failed to give Harry credit for emulating her choice of a career and keeping up friendly relations with her during their years in New York.

Above all, Harry's family background determined his politics. Al Hopkins's people were New England Democrats. During the Civil War his grandfather Marcellus Emery had been branded a Copperhead and his newspaper press smashed when he attacked the Lincoln administration. Instead of moderating his partisanship, Marcellus repaired the damage and sued his assailants. Twenty years later Al Hopkins found a suitable object for his Democratic loyalties in a Nebraska congressman named William Jennings Bryan. Around the Hopkins table only reverence for Bryan competed with the Scriptures. Al's loyalty, however, was partisan rather than ideological. Bryan preached agrarianism, the virtues of farming and the value of agriculture to

America. Destroy the farms, Bryan would say, and grass would grow in the streets of the cities; but destroy the cities and leave the farms, and the cities would spring up again as if by magic. This may have comforted some inhabitants of rural America but not Al Hopkins. To him Grinnell was just a "dead country village" and farmers were customers who didn't pay their bills.[10]

When young Harry Hopkins was growing up in Grinnell, there was still a lot of country in the town. Grinnell, with a population of four thousand, was a market center fifty miles east of Des Moines, the state capital. Outdoor toilets were common, and residents kept chickens, cows, and pigs, creating unsanitary conditions that led to a serious outbreak of typhoid fever in the summer of 1910. Popular entertainments included a yearly agricultural fair, high school and college athletic events, and such special occasions as an exhibition by a champion roller skater. When a tarantula—the *Herald* called it "a grizzly looking creature"—was discovered in the bananas at the Ideal Grocery, it was displayed in a glass case for the whole town to see.

In other ways, however, Grinnell appealed to more sophisticated tastes. Traveling New York theater companies performed Shakespearean plays and contemporary drama at the Colonial Theater. The Grinnell College chapel was the scene of recitals and concerts by world-famous opera singers, musicians, and symphony orchestras.[11]

Harry seems to have avoided Grinnell's extremes of rusticity and sophistication. He delivered papers, entertained friends at home and traveled with them out of town, joined a local boys club (the Stars), had a steady girlfriend, and enjoyed after-school snacks of bread and jam. He acquired enough poise to keep his composure when the younger sister of Hallie Ferguson (later Hallie Flanagan of the Federal Theater Project) accidentally dumped stuffed tomato salad on his new blue serge suit during a dinner party. He took up athletics, playing football with a neighborhood club until he broke his leg so badly that a friend had to carry him to school. From then on he concentrated on baseball, tennis, and especially basketball, which he played well enough to be considered a good prospect for the college team. In the summer he worked at a brickyard and a nearby farm. The summer after he graduated from high school he worked as an office clerk in the railroad yard at Laurel, Montana, and played on the local baseball team.[12]

If Harry was a typical American small-town boy, he was also a typical Hopkins. He enjoyed poking fun at authority and deflating the self-important. In his junior year he arranged to elect an undistinguished student class president over the astonished and indignant objections of the school authorities. On another occasion Harry and his friends broke up a party some junior girls were giving for seniors by "kidnapping" one of the guests. A classmate confided years later that she had been "tickled pink" by the kidnapping. "She was such a snob," she wrote of the victim. "I know from following your career all these years you've hated snobbery. While I haven't always agreed with the way you've carried out a lot of your policies . . . at least I feel you've been sincere and have raised the standard of living of the underdog."[13]

If Harry shared his father's taste for discomfiting snobs, he balanced it with his mother's sympathy for the unfortunate and helpless. In junior high school Harry and his classmates unmercifully teased Dwight Bradley, the son of the new college president. Dwight and his brother had been raised "to be little quasi-Lord Fauntleroys." One day the boys tied Dwight to a telephone pole and, declaring they were going to burn him at the stake, lighted a grass fire near his feet. Terrified and choked with the smoke, Bradley was completely helpless. Before the prank could go too far, Harry rushed forward and cut Dwight loose with his jackknife. Harry and Dwight thereafter became friends and members of the Stars Club. When the college was playing baseball, they would get in free by carrying the catcher's equipment. The Bradleys left Grinnell in 1906, two years before Harry enrolled at the college.[14]

Harry Hopkins later recalled his years at Grinnell College as "the very happiest and best days of my life," adding that "one of the best things in college is to have fun." Considering his many campus activities, his popularity with his classmates, and his uneven academic record, this attitude seems to have summed up his college years. Still, Grinnell gave Harry more than a chance to sharpen his social skills. He acquired values there that influenced him throughout his life.[15]

From its early years Grinnell College had been a center of social reform. In 1846 Congregational ministers had founded Iowa College in Davenport. Thirteen years later it had moved west in an arrangement with Josiah Bushnell Grinnell, a Congregational minister, antislavery radical, and temperance advocate who had founded a town in his name as a Christian temperance community. The school attracted a capable faculty that included a few nationally distinguished scholars and gained recognition as a good liberal arts college with particular strengths in history, philosophy, and the social sciences. In the 1890s it became a center of Social Gospel Christianity under the leadership of President George A. Gates and Professor of Applied Christianity George D. Herron.

Gates and Herron believed that people had an obligation to sacrifice themselves for Christian ideals, a major one of which was democracy. True Christians trusted the people and worked for the common good. The greatest sin was selfishness, as exemplified by plutocratic power, which used wealth for its own ends. Businesses that refused to work for the common good, Gates argued, should be taken over by the public. In all of this there was a sense of righteous inevitability. Gates and Herron preached that democracy was sweeping the world. Informing this confidence was evolutionary thinking built on the writings of Charles Darwin. Unlike many who saw evolutionary science as a threat to biblical teachings, Gates and Herron welcomed Darwin's message. "Evolution and redemption," Herron prophesied, "are coming to be synonymous terms for one human revelation and destiny, one final strifeless progress."[16]

By the time Harry Hopkins entered Grinnell, both Gates and Herron were gone, but their influence remained. The Grinnell faculty considered Darwin's scientific method a new key to truth. In the same manner that Christian righteousness lifted one above narrow self-interest, Darwin's systematic, painstaking observations directed one toward objective truth. "The righteous man," declared Professor of Political Science Jesse Macy, "is one who keeps an open mind to all truth. The modern scientific spirit is simply the Christian spirit realized in a limited field of experience." This spirit could solve social problems. Professor of Philosophy John D. Stoops declared that the social significance of Christ's teachings was that he placed human experience at the center of all social problems. The way to understand the labor problem was to learn about the workingman; the way to understand crime was to learn about the criminal. President John H. T. Main declared that nature invited and challenged persons to make its "unused forces . . . instruments of social improvement." Professor of Sociology Garret P. Wyckoff argued that the social sciences would become truly scientific only when they applied themselves to the "problems of social life."[17]

The scientific spirit also called for direct observation and immediate action. Macy sent his students out to learn how Grinnell's city government worked. Professor of History Charles E. Payne taught that history was to be found not only in books but also in the daily newspapers. Professor Wyckoff held various offices in the Iowa State Conference of Charities and Correction, and Professor of Applied Christianity Edward A. Steiner taught courses in settlement house work and served on the board of a New York settlement house.[18]

The essential value and goal of social reform, as these scholars saw it, was democracy. Professor Steiner urged his students to "see to it that the democratic spirit be preserved in Grinnell." That spirit found expression in acceptance of others. Macy noted that in seventeenth-century England the same persons advocated religious toleration and democratic government. Steiner advised students who had outgrown their youthful faith that the church prevented many communities "from losing their democracy" because religion created "truly liberal" persons who were "tolerant with the intolerant." President Main declared that the human race was becoming "one family," requiring schools to foster a worldwide educational community. In his autobiography, written during Harry Hopkins's years at Grinnell, Steiner declared, "My great aim now is to teach intelligent and religious men and women how . . . to break through prejudice so that the emotions are not conquered by hate, how to be able to stand in this conglomerate of races and nationalities which flow into our nation and be able to say without cant: We the People."[19]

Not surprisingly, Grinnell College welcomed the reforms of Progressivism, the movement by middle-class white Americans to break corrupt alliances between party bosses and business interests, to dispense a paternal social justice to the poor, to establish rights for labor, and to return government to "the people." In Congress, Progressive representatives were fighting to pare down the power of the conservative Speaker and to defeat the high-tariff policies of President William Howard Taft and his Old Guard Republican supporters. In the 1910 elections insurgent congressmen in the Middle West, led by "Fighting Bob" La Follette of Wisconsin, battled successfully against Old Guard challengers. In New Jersey a former college president named Woodrow Wilson was breaking with the conservative Democrats who had elected him governor and bringing his state into the Progressive mainstream.

No other Grinnell professor welcomed Progressivism more warmly than Jesse Macy. One of the founders of academic political science and later president of the American Political Science Association, Macy had taken up the study of government in the 1870s, when corrupt government, whether in Ulysses S. Grant's White House, Roscoe Conkling's customhouse, or "Boss" Tweed's City Hall, seemed the order of the day. As one who believed that honest men made honest government, Macy championed civil service reform, which aimed at breaking the stranglehold of political bosses by taking away their patronage power. If government jobs went only to people who scored well on competitive examinations, the reformers reasoned, the bosses would be defeated, and honest, capable men would run the government. Macy, in his textbook *Our Government,* published in 1886, stated that patronage was "bribery pure and simple."[20]

It is difficult to say precisely how these ideas and teachers influenced Harry Hopkins. He spoke infrequently about his college years and died before he could compose his memoirs. Although his friends and relatives have offered several candidates for the role of most influential professor, the only evidence that comes directly from Harry himself suggests that he held a special regard for Macy. In 1937 he had the Works Progress Administration staff compile a chronology of Macy's life and a bibliography of his writings, and in a 1939 Grinnell talk he referred to Macy as "a great man . . . a very great man."[21]

More influential than any one person was the college itself. Grinnell taught Harry that one was morally obligated to accept others and to work to improve their lives and the condition of society. It also taught him that systematic observation would deepen one's understanding and help solve problems. In this it reinforced Adah's example as a professional social worker.

Most important, Grinnell inspired a dedication to democracy. The campus newspaper, the *Scarlet and Black,* declared that Grinnell students had "a help-each-other spirit," founded on self-sacrifice, friendship, and the "broadening" influence of a liberal education. "Quality of character" counted for more than social or economic status. Campus life followed these democratic ideals. No fraternities or sororities were allowed. Student organizations maintained a conventional distinction between the sexes but otherwise were open to all. Student voices were heard on campus issues and could modify faculty decisions. Senior men in the class of 1910 said that Grinnell had made them "liberal, broad and fair-minded," given them "a deeper appreciation of the things most worth while," "a sense of the unity which exists among all people of whatever type or position," "discrimination and toleration, and [the ability] to think for ourselves." One regretted that he had "limited my friendships too much to my own class, and have not, during my upper-class years, been of as much service to others as I should have been."[22]

Two of Harry Hopkins's college contemporaries looked back on Grinnell in much the same way. Chester Davis, who later joined Harry as a New Deal administrator, saw Grinnell "as a great experience in democracy" with "a very real sense of brotherhood and helpfulness [and] a minimum of class distinction." Florence Kerr, who also became a New Deal administrator, expressed it more concretely: "We all knew each other at Grinnell. It wasn't dating or anything special—we were together all the time. We went to classes together, ate together—about the only thing we didn't do was room together. I don't think there were very many left out people at Grinnell then. Everybody knew everybody."[23]

One of the students everyone knew better than most was Harry Hopkins. During his four years at Grinnell, Harry was a member of the social committee of his freshman class; secretary of his sophomore class; permanent president of his senior class; auditor and treasurer of the YMCA; member of the staff of the college annual; associate editor, assistant sports editor, and business manager of the *Scarlet and Black*; musical director and vice president of the men's literary society; and vice chairman of the College Council. Minor efforts at drama won him a role in a YMCA minstrel show and the leading role in the senior play. In 1911 he organized the Woodrow Wilson club to boost the New Jersey governor's presidential prospects and arranged for Wilson to appear briefly when his campaign train stopped at Grinnell and for the college band to appear for the occasion. He later served as permanent chairman of the student Democratic convention.[24]

Harry was even better known for his athletic achievements. He played on the college tennis team and occasionally played right field on the baseball team, but his best sport was basketball. During his first two years in college he played for his class in round robin tournaments against the other classes, and in his junior and senior years he participated in intercollegiate competition. He was a gritty player, and although his teammates called him "Dirty" Hopkins, it was probably because of his intense, dogged efforts and not his rough play.[25]

If anything distinguished Hopkins's play, it was his ability to rise to

*Hopkins (front row, third from left) with Grinnell College classmates Robert
Kerr (second row, fourth from right) and future Assistant Secretary of
Agriculture Paul Appleby (second row, third from left), 1912*

the level of his competition. This he showed on February 22, 1911,
when Grinnell played Kansas University. Four days earlier Kansas had
won the Missouri Valley Conference championship. The students and
fans who packed Grinnell's tiny gymnasium on the central campus
yelled themselves hoarse during the tense, exciting contest. In those
days players passed the ball deliberately and milled around the court in
what resembled a mob scene. Well-played games usually wound up
with scores in the tens and twenties. This one started even more
slowly, with Grinnell leading 4-3 at halftime thanks to two free throws
by center James Slutz and a field goal by Hopkins. Early in the second
half Harry fired in two more goals as Grinnell surged to an eight-point
lead. He seemed to be all over the floor, dogging his man on defense
without fouling and quarterbacking the offense. Eventually he wore
down and the coach took him out in the last minutes as Kansas fought
back to tie the score at 15-15. With four minutes to play, Grinnell
scored from the side to make it 17-15. Kansas could add only one free
throw. Grinnell walked off the court with a 17-16 victory over the
champions and Hopkins with honors as the game's "bright and shining
light."[26]

Harry's many activities, offices, and honors reveal some of the success he enjoyed in his college years. His was not the awe-inspiring
success of the Big Man on Campus but the friendly, good-natured
popularity won with a wave and a smile, lighthearted quips, and conscientious hard work. He achieved academic success as well. He had
entered college poorly prepared and somewhat aimless, and during his

*Hopkins and Chester Davis at Grinnell College in 1935*

first two years he ranked near the bottom of his class. But in his junior and senior years he blossomed, earning A's and B's. Professor Macy assigned him the research topic that went to his best senior student and gave him an A in the course.[27]

It is impossible to say why he succeeded to such a degree. Perhaps college gave him a chance to escape the tension he felt at home or the dull routine of small-town life. Such speculation aside, the results of his success are clear enough. For the rest of his life Harry loved Grinnell College. If someone had done well at Grinnell, he believed that he or she would do well anywhere. He hired Professor Wyckoff to assist with civilian relief in the Gulf states and brought in his fellow students Hallie Flanagan and Florence Kerr to administer programs in the Works Progress Administration (WPA). He also served as a trustee of the college, taking no active role in college affairs but keeping up his correspondence with Presidents John S. Nollen and Samuel N. Stevens. One of the thrilling moments of his New Deal years came when he returned to the college to receive an honorary degree.

Although many honors were to come his way, Harry Hopkins never forgot his small-town upbringing. After his first visit to Moscow, in 1941, when he set in motion American Lend-Lease aid to Russia, he told a friend that as he walked up the staircase of the Kremlin, he asked himself, "What are *you* doing here, Hopkins, you—son of a harness maker from Sioux City—?" His friend pointed out that the Kremlin had probably seen its quota of harness makers' sons and that Hopkins was there as a representative of the president of the United States.[28] Still, at the height of his prominence, Hopkins could not resist calling himself a harness maker's son, for nothing else would have conveyed so vividly the image of middle western rural simplicity out of which he had risen.

But Hopkins was not merely bragging about his rise from humble origins. His years as a professional social worker and a federal relief administrator had impressed upon him the role of chance in human affairs. Wasn't it possible, he asked himself, that he might just as easily have become one of society's victims instead of one of its successes? As he put it in an impromptu speech to members of a WPA arts project in 1936, "It's just an 'Act of God' that you are sitting on one side of the table and I *happen* to be sitting on the other."[29] From time to time this feeling came over him again, as he visited the White House, No. 10 Downing Street, the Kremlin, Casablanca, Tehran, Yalta, and other seats of prominence and power: a sense of wonder that Harry Hopkins should be there.

In calling himself a harness maker's son, Hopkins was also paying tribute to the values of his Grinnell years. He linked his personal success to the workings of democracy. One night in 1940, after he had resigned as secretary of commerce, he declared to a gathering of friends in a New York hotel room: "Maybe it's all over now, but REMEMBER

*Harry Hopkins's graduation picture, 1912*

. . . the son of an Iowa harness maker *did* make the Cabinet of Franklin D. Roosevelt. That's one thing they can't take away from me. And it's a pretty good answer to those who say democracy doesn't work!"[30]

Grinnell convinced Harry that democracy worked and that people had to work for democracy. About a month before his graduation he addressed the YMCA on the topic "Application of Ideals." He declared that it was not enough to have ideals but that all must carry them out; that every man had the spark of Christianity in him but all were obliged to help him kindle it; and that Grinnell was not the most democratic school, but with the cooperation of the faculty and the students it could be more democratic. These words showed that he was ready to put his ideals into action. He had chosen a career that would give him plenty of opportunity to test those values and his commitment to them. Before graduation day the *Scarlet and Black* had asked seniors about their plans. "Harry Hopkins," it reported, "will do social settlement work in New York City."[31]

# Chapter 2

# Innovative
# Social Worker

Harry Hopkins had various reasons for going to New York City in the summer of 1912. Adah was there, working as registrar of the School of Philanthropy, and Lewis was attending medical school and serving with welfare organizations. Harry had visited New York before and had inherited his father's taste for the bright lights. The specific reason that brought him east was that he had had an offer to direct junior boys' programs at Northover Camp near Bound Brook, New Jersey. Although the camp was administered by Christadora House, a New York City social settlement whose director was well acquainted with Adah, the offer had come through a Grinnell professor of philosophy, Louis D. Hartson, who had worked at the camp two previous summers. He arranged for the job when Harry told him that he had decided to go into social work.

The job would not start until a few weeks after commencement, but Harry was eager to move on, so he and Hartson left town soon after the ceremonies. They traveled to New York, on to Washington, and then to Baltimore, where the Democratic national convention was in session. Harry had boosted Woodrow Wilson on the Grinnell campus, and he now spoke up for his hero in more high-powered precincts, buttonholing New York delegates who were supporting a favorite son. After the convention, which resulted in Wilson's nomination, Hartson and Hopkins traveled to Philadelphia to see Independence Hall and from there to Bound Brook.[1] When the summer job ended, Hopkins moved to New York City to begin social work in earnest at Christadora House.

Harry took in all that the city had to offer, and he loved it. He joined opera claques, cheering for such stars as Enrico Caruso and Geraldine Farrar in return for a seat. When his Grinnell friends Florence and Robert Kerr visited New York, he took them on an all-night tour beginning at the police station to see streetwalkers and other people of the night, then to St. Patrick's Cathedral, and to Greenwich Village for an international festival.

He tackled his job with the same enthusiasm and curiosity. Christadora House employed him as a district visitor to investigate requests for aid. He entered the homes of the poor, saw how they lived, and tried to understand their condition. Not everything made sense. The vast poverty of New York confounded his small-town experience. Nor could he fathom why the boys in the youth club he supervised should stand in silence to honor four murderers on the day of their execution. His reaction was both judgmental and inquisitive. He was shocked at the boys' behavior, but he also wanted to understand it.[2]

While Harry sought answers to such puzzles, he found something else he had been seeking: love. Ethel Gross had been born in Hungary. After her father died when she was quite young, her mother moved the family to New York. There her brothers went into business; she took secretarial jobs and became active in the women's suffrage movement. When Harry first arrived in New York, Ethel was living in Paris and working as secretary to the founder of the Equal Suffrage Association. In December 1912 she was given a furlough to visit her family. The director of Christadora persuaded her to take on a special project and gave her a desk on the same floor as Harry's.[3]

It was love at first sight. Only a few weeks after they met, Harry was talking of marriage. "I love you if I ever loved anybody in my life," he told her, and she responded, "The thought of you keeps singing in my heart until this seems a beautiful world and the part that makes me happiest is that I know you care."[4]

For Harry, Ethel represented a healthy break with his small-town past. "We have lived absolutely different lives up till now," he wrote her. "While you have been working, I have been playing at school— you were brought up in a city where you could follow your natural inclinations, I have been surrounded by conservative narrowminded- ness—we have been somewhat separated socially and it would be hard for you to come down to my means." News of their engagement, he predicted, would "rock the very foundations of [his parents'] dining room" and give them—"the poor old dears"—enough conversation for a week. The reason was simple enough: Ethel was Jewish.

Harry tried to make light of the situation, but Ethel took it seriously, especially after her older sister warned her that Harry could not have escaped his parents' prejudices. Although Ethel was not strictly religious herself, she took the warning seriously enough to question Harry about his true feelings. This was a mature step to take, but it was a shock to Harry—free from his parents, reveling in the life of the city, and smitten beyond reason. Ethel's practical attitude deflated his romantic balloon, but in the end he concluded that he loved her all the more for her "honesty and frankness."[5]

The episode showed that Harry had not left his past as far behind as he liked to think. He was still a small-town romantic, believing that love conquers all. Naive as he may have been, though, even Harry realized that poverty could be a powerful impediment to love. The letters which he wrote to Ethel during their courtship frequently mentioned money. After formally proposing, he sent her a note outlining a budget for living on $160 a month. "Now if we can't live on that," he wrote, "we had better stop," surely not a serious suggestion but one that shows his concern about money matters. He was, after all, the impecunious son of an indifferent provider, and he feared that marrying him would be a financial step down for Ethel.[6]

In this earnest spirit he set out to make enough money to marry on. Shortly after he and Ethel were engaged, Harry took a new job in the employment bureau of the Association for Improving the Condition of the Poor (AICP), New York's oldest and most respected social welfare agency. For $40 a month he worked in a waterfront district which was thought unsafe for female workers. Still, the pay fell short of his goal, so Harry asked his supervisor for a better job at a higher salary. Surprised, the man told Harry that he did not have another job available but would raise his pay to $60 a month. "Oh boy," Harry exclaimed, "now I can get married after all." In October 1913 he and Ethel exchanged vows at the Ethical Culture Society.[7]

The supervisor whose generosity opened the doors to matrimony was John A. Kingsbury, general agent for the AICP, and this incident marked the start of an important friendship. Kingsbury had grown up in the Pacific Northwest, served as superintendent of schools in Seattle, and moved to New York in 1906, entering social work and making his mark as an innovator in public health and child care and as a skilled promoter. His knack for public relations enabled him to persuade politicians that social welfare could win votes. He became a staunch Progressive and advised Theodore Roosevelt on the social welfare planks in the Bull Moose party platform of 1912. He also served on the city and state party committees.[8]

In Hopkins, Kingsbury saw qualities he admired—perhaps a youthful version of his own energetic personality. He made Hopkins his friend and protégé. As a result, Hopkins's career advanced rapidly. He joined the AICP in April of 1913. By February of 1914 he was making $1,260 a year, and by the fall he had risen to supervisor of relief on the Lower East Side at $1,440. The following year he left to become supervisor of the AICP's Fresh Air Hospital, a tuberculosis clinic, at $1,680.

Hopkins's marriage and his association with social workers like Kingsbury introduced him to New York's left-wing political culture. He and Ethel attended plays and lectures that pleaded the cause of the poor and the working classes. He registered as a voter with the Socialist party and for several years referred to himself as a socialist. By all indications, however, his socialism was of a mild variety. In the 1913 mayoral election he supported the Progressive John Purroy Mitchel. In 1917 he voted for the Socialist Morris Hillquit, who represented a moderate faction committed to peaceful change and representative government. He also followed those few party members who supported the party's stand against U.S. entry into World War I but supported the war effort once the United States entered the conflict. "One's actions," he wrote, "cannot be governed by what he thinks, but rather by what the majority agrees to, unless he be an out and out anarchist." All that remained of his socialist thinking was a desire to finance the war effort by progressive taxation that would confiscate all income over $50,000. As he wrote his Grinnell classmates, "Aside from unhorsing the capitalist class, I know of no pleasanter duty than driving Kaiser Bill into Dante's retreat for autocrats."[9]

Harry's career as a professional social worker began in earnest at the AICP. He was assigned to study unemployment in the city to discover why relief applications had increased dramatically. After reviewing questionnaires sent to large employers, labor unions, employment agencies, and charitable institutions, he concluded that the principal cause was a decrease in the number of available jobs aggravated by an influx of unskilled workers who had come to New York looking for construction work. Although the public commonly thought of the unemployed as homeless vagrants, Hopkins estimated that no more than 6 percent fell into that category. Taking up proposals that had been under discussion in recent years, he recommended creating local, state, and national labor exchanges (employment offices) to classify people for jobs and to refer unemployables to the settlement houses.

Hopkins also recommended city relief pensions for widows with dependent children in order to take them out of the labor market and limiting workdays to eight hours in order to spread employment. He also believed that state and city governments should provide jobs during periods of high unemployment. That winter he administered a small public works project in which the AICP paid men to work at the Bronx Zoo under the supervision of park officials.

In the process he concluded that the AICP was doing a poor job as an employment agency. Its visitors did not know how to help their clients find work, and there was no procedure for checking to see whether people sent to prospective employers took the job or, if they did, tried to maintain a good work record. Because 37 percent of the families the AICP had aided in the previous year had suffered from unemployment, the agency desperately needed an effective employment program to get potentially productive workers off welfare.

Hopkins's recommendations combined the traditional prevention standard that separated the deserving from the undeserving poor with a sensitive awareness of the psychology of unemployment. "Pressed by penury," Hopkins wrote, the unemployed man desperately answers one advertisement after another, only to find that "fifty other applicants" have arrived ahead of him. At last he becomes "discouraged" and "despairing," abandons his self-respect, retreats into the belief that the world owes him a living, and becomes dependent on welfare. Because Hopkins concluded that unemployment and not personal character cause dependence on relief, he proposed that employment exchanges free themselves "from any association or stigma of charity" and concentrate on assuring the applicant that they have "no interest whatever in [his] private affairs . . . outside of determining his fitness for the position which he is applying for."[10]

Although he wanted to help the unemployed and to correct the public's misunderstanding of their character, Hopkins was not inclined to encourage romantic ideas about them. "The day you issue a call for [applicants for work relief projects]," he told a *New York Times* reporter, "you will have as many unemployed men available as you care to put to work. They will represent for the greater part, men who are willing to do just as little as possible to keep their places. If there are industrious men among them, the industrious will be demoralized. Each year these [lazy and demoralized] men will try to gain subsistence by doing the relief work and in the end the city will find that kind of

labor more costly. [Under work relief] the idler will be given preference over the industrious worker."[11]

Hopkins's ambition kept pace with his growing experience,
motivated in part by family responsibilities. In October 1914 Ethel
gave birth to their first child, a boy whom they named David after
Harry's father. The chance to advance came shortly afterward, when
Mayor Mitchel appointed Kingsbury commissioner of public charities.
Hopkins dashed off a letter at once, declaring that while he was
satisfied with the AICP, he would welcome "any opportunity for advancement in social work." Kingsbury filed it with his "preferred applications."[12] In the fall of 1915, when Mitchel appointed a Board of
Child Welfare to give relief to mothers with dependent children at
home, Hopkins was chosen the board's executive secretary at a salary
of $200 a month.

Building a welfare organization from scratch was the perfect chance
for Hopkins to show what his experience had taught him. He recruited
and supervised the office staff, handled correspondence with city
officials, attended state and national conventions, and oversaw state
legislative proceedings. He encouraged his staff, praising those who
worked overtime, pressing for salary increases for efficient workers,
and filing complaints about his crowded, airless accommodations.
Most important, he held weekly conferences to discuss problems and
techniques and to encourage investigators to do their best for their
clients. He advised his staff to help clients deal with their problems and
not simply to limit themselves to routine. Their investigations provided information which he used to advise the board on policy questions.

He made sure that need and not political influence determined
awards. Once when the mayor's office inquired about a particular applicant, he replied that she would have to wait her turn, and because
she already had a small income could "probably wait her turn better
than most." He was not blind, however, to public relations. He objected to a board decision not to count the earnings of widows' children because he considered it "unfair to the taxpayers." Similarly he
rooted out people who abused the system and praised those who
turned them in as "citizens interested in a decent administration of the
law."[13]

Hopkins built good relations with private charities. He discussed the
board's program and plans with those agencies and arranged interim

financing for widows while the board carried out its investigation. He referred ineligible cases to private agencies and relied on them to certify mothers and children for tuberculosis treatment and to supplement pensions he thought too meager. He hoped that his work would set standards for the private charities. He even turned down a chance for a better-paying job in Connecticut, saying that he wanted to stay on and establish "a widows' pension system second to none in the United States."[14]

In the end, however, his ambitions fatally collided with politics. As applications piled up, Hopkins applied to the board for ten additional investigators and three supervisors. The board gave him the investigators, but the issue of the supervisors became entangled in a struggle between Kingsbury and William H. Matthews, Hopkins's former colleagues at the AICP, and a faction headed by Sophie Irene Loeb, a reporter for the *New York World* with connections to the Hearst papers. In 1916 Loeb forced Kingsbury from the board. The next year Mayor Mitchel lost his bid for reelection to a Tammany Hall Democrat supported by the *World*. At that point several board members including Matthews resigned, and that December in an act of solidarity Hopkins followed suit.

Hopkins had been thinking about other job possibilities, but he had not seriously considered any and had no firm offers. His precipitate action meant that he had to find another job quickly. When he learned that the American Red Cross was looking for people to help provide for the families of servicemen, he sent in his name, saying that he was willing to take a temporary assignment and to work anywhere.[15] He was looking for a job to carry him through a brief transitional period. What he found lasted nearly five years.

Hopkins hoped for a post with the Red Cross's newly created Division of Civilian Relief, established to aid the families of servicemen by making loans and cash grants to compensate for the absence of a breadwinner. This was similar to the family relief work he had been carrying out with the Board of Child Welfare. When he arrived at Red Cross headquarters in Washington, however, things were in such confusion that he was assigned to direct disaster relief in the Gulf division (Alabama, Mississippi, and Louisiana). His move to division headquarters in New Orleans was briefly complicated by a notice from his New York draft board to report for a physical examination. The Red Cross asked that his induction be deferred, and in the end he was rejected because of defective vision owing to a detached retina. When he arrived in New Orleans in February 1918 he may have wondered if getting his deferment had been worth the effort. If disaster were to strike the city, it would most likely come from flooding along the Mississippi, and he noted with grim amusement that his office was within sight of the river. The disaster director, he remarked, would be "of very little service if the river breaks here!"[16]

The river did not break, but responsibilities flooded in. After a few months the head of civilian relief left for military service. For two months Hopkins and two others managed the office until mid-June, when he was appointed acting director of civilian relief. The next month he was promoted to associate manager of the division, still in charge of civilian relief but with overall responsibility for the field staff.

Thus Hopkins once again had to create a social welfare organization. It was a titanic job, since neither the Red Cross nor other welfare agencies were well established in the region, and many Red Cross chapters were merely paper organizations. Undaunted, he reduced the number of chapters, established training programs for volunteers, hired new clerical staff and field supervisors, and streamlined office procedures. To run the training institutes he hired his Grinnell sociology professor, Garrett Wyckoff, and his classmate Florence Kerr. He established friendly relations with the public welfare agencies, holding conferences in which he pinpointed areas where the Red Cross could supplement the agencies' work and thus assured them that he did not intend to supplant them. The results were astonishing. By the time of the armistice in November 1918, home service, as civilian relief was called, was serving ten to fifteen thousand families a month with a staff of two hundred professionals and volunteers. In New Orleans it was handling more families each month than the private charities handled in a year. When the Red Cross decided to continue the program during peacetime, Hopkins's division established 104 sections, compared to 29 for the next highest division and an average of 12 for the rest.[17] Almost overnight, he had brought professional social work to the lower South.

All of this he accomplished in a way that showed his particular genius for administration. He had clearly mastered the professional social worker's skills of organizing and processing, and he had enriched them with the intuition and personality traits of the successful executive. More than anything else, he showed a strong sense of purpose.

His job was to deliver services, and he directed all his energies to that end. Reorganizing and consolidating departments in his central office saved money, but his real objective was better communication with investigators in the field. His idea of management was to help those who were actually helping clients. He told directors to avoid recommending new projects unless they were sure that the chapters could handle them. He instructed his professional supervisors to write "very personal" letters to the volunteers in their sections, to visit them and give inspiration and encouragement as well as information, and to remain as long as needed to get the chapter functioning. He held efficiency contests to boost morale and urged the chapters to report their activities "even to the point of [causing] indifferent . . . workers to resign."[18]

Hopkins's greatest skill was his ability to inspire. Working with volunteers, many of them women who had never handled administrative responsibility, he believed that he had to bolster their confidence as well as train them to be skillful. Years later one of the home service volunteers recalled how she had hesitated when Hopkins asked her to take over relief for the families of navy and marine enlistees in addition to her work for the army. Seeing her fear, he "half closed those eyes of his" and asked: "Did you know any more about the Army when you took it over?"

She shook her head, and he smiled. "You learned it didn't you? Well, you can learn this too." Then he stretched his hand out and said simply, "I am behind you."

She took the job, "and because Harry Hopkins was behind me I was able to do it."[19]

In smaller ways his sympathy and encouragement touched those around him. He assured employees who were ill that their jobs would be waiting for them when they returned to work. He went out of his way to provide special favors for those in need. He seemed able to notice even the smallest detail. One colleague at the AICP remembered how, as "a very green young man, fresh from the country," he was hired to become Hopkins's assistant. "Within half an hour," he recalled, Hopkins "had marched into . . . the Cashier for an advance on salary which somehow [he] had sensed was badly needed."[20]

To his coworkers he conveyed his loyalty, hard work, and optimism. Even in a profession in which workers commonly put in long hours, others noted his "work horse proclivities." But hard work seems less a

burden when people know that they can accomplish their goal. Hopkins never admitted that any task was impossible. "It is a real problem,"
he declared in a discussion of helping servicemen with serious health
difficulties, but "as far as the Red Cross is concerned we are going to
omit nothing to help disabled men to get back on their feet!"[21]

Hopkins's ultimate method of achieving success was through cooperation. He set up channels of communication to create a community
inspired to achieve a common goal. As an administrator he tailored
structures to people and to collective ends. He was willing to trust
others because he had confidence that he could give them the training,
supervision, and inspiring leadership they needed. When R. J. Colbert
arrived in New Orleans to take over educational programs, he realized
that Hopkins had been waiting for him so that they could work together. Within three weeks Hopkins had called a series of conferences
with his department heads to establish a sound system. "The spirit
manifested in these conferences," Colbert reported, "was, in the main,
most cordial and cooperative, indicating clearly that most of the staff
recognized the urgent need for better correlation of effort and team
play. The genuine interest and appreciation of Educational Service
thus shown by the Manager and his staff made possible an early development of an educational program upon which all could agree and
lend their support."[22]

Hopkins's talents inevitably attracted attention. At one time he was
considered as a replacement for the director of civilian relief in the
central district, with headquarters in Chicago. The move would have
meant nearly a 40 percent increase in salary (from $3,600 to $5,000).
But the division manager, Leigh Carroll, argued that Hopkins's experience, contacts, and reputation made him indispensable where he was.
In the end it was arranged for him to stay on as associate manager with
responsibilities for home service, nursing, first aid, junior membership,
and publicity at a salary of $4,500. In the fall of 1919 Red Cross
officials assisting the League of Nations requested that he be transferred to direct relief activities in Poland and Czechoslovakia, but the
Red Cross decided that he could not be spared.[23]

Ultimately he realized that further advancement was necessary if he
was to continue with the Red Cross. In the spring of 1920 he arranged
with the national office to be named division manager, replacing Carroll, who was asked to stay on as the head of an advisory committee.[24]
The move was made in anticipation of the Gulf division's merger with

the southeastern division (Florida, Georgia, North Carolina, South Carolina, Tennessee, and Virginia). When the two were joined later in the year, to create a southern division, with headquarters in Atlanta, Hopkins was named manager.

Thus shortly before his thirty-first birthday Hopkins entered the upper ranks of social work administration. His success resulted mostly from his abilities, though perhaps the nature of social work magnified them somewhat. He had entered a profession founded principally by women, but which in a male-dominated society was quick to reward the talents of the comparatively few men who entered it. This was particularly true of the Red Cross, where men held all the top management jobs. To Florence Kerr, who knew Hopkins from college and then worked with him in the Gulf division and later in the WPA, it seemed that as "an active, vigorous personality boy in the social work field . . . he just naturally went up to the top very fast. . . . He was an outstanding *male* social worker." Contemporary evidence supports her estimate to an extent. Hopkins made his friendships and sought his opportunities for professional advancement among other male social workers such as John Kingsbury and William H. Matthews. Matthews remembered that Hopkins once cornered him on a stairway to ask if he was coming back from a trip to California because he "did not want to stay . . . all alone with all those ladies."[25]

To be sure, he had other advantages. His rise was helped considerably by conditions in the Gulf region, where competing social welfare agencies were too weak to interfere with his drive to establish home service, where excellent volunteer talent was available, and at a time when wartime patriotism inspired many to help the families of servicemen. In getting to the top, Hopkins did not shoulder women aside; he treated them with respect and cooperation. Both women and men commented favorably on his leadership. During the New Deal his work relief agencies would place more women in executive positions than any other government department.

Hopkins's success left him with some ambivalent feelings. When he conferred with the general manager, Frederick C. Munroe, about replacing Leigh Carroll as division manager, Hopkins suggested that Munroe ask Carroll to stay on as an adviser to the division, on the grounds that he, Hopkins, was "a little overambitious" and needed "a steady hand."[26]

Hopkins's remarks suggest a number of things. Aside from indicating his uneasiness at his rapid rise, his flattering others at his own expense indicates a willingness to manipulate people by telling them what they wanted to hear. At the same time his words point to a more wholesome trait, suggesting an immature version of the capacity for self-criticism that those who later worked with him in government service found especially attractive. He seldom hesitated to state his opinions, but when pressed by determined counterargument he would smile and say that he did not know all the answers. By that time he had become one of the most powerful men in Washington; his opinions were taken seriously. That he continued to express his ideas in such a modest and accommodating way showed how much he valued consensus and cooperation over the blunt exercise of authority. Munroe sensed this spirit of accommodation and redrafted Hopkins's statement to applaud his ambition ("He is an ambitious young man and very properly so. I should not want him to be otherwise") and to stress Hopkins's regard and affection for Carroll.[27]

Hopkins's career as division manager did not turn out as he had hoped. With the end of the war home service was dismantled, and the Red Cross ceased to expand. Because of the underdeveloped nature of social service in the division, he had to spend over half his time visiting the chapters. This aggravated an already strained family situation. Harry had originally left for New Orleans so hurriedly that Ethel was unable to follow until several months later. While they were in New Orleans she gave birth to a daughter, Barbara, who fell victim to an epidemic of whooping cough and died within a month. The loss of one child encouraged a desire for another, and in May 1920 Harry and Ethel welcomed their second son, whom they named Robert after Harry's Grinnell classmate and friend Robert Kerr. With his family growing, Harry's travels became increasingly burdensome, and he was soon looking for an opportunity to change jobs.[28]

Harry knew, however, that he wanted more than merely to lead a more settled life. He jumped at the chance to apply for a position with one agency that had "rather ambitious plans ahead." That job did not materialize, but early in 1922 he received an offer that seemed almost as promising. During Hopkins's years in the South his friend and benefactor John Kingsbury had become director of the Milbank Fund in New York, a foundation established early in the century to support public health. With his usual energy and skill at public relations, Kingsbury planned to establish a major project that would employ the latest techniques and the services of public and private health agencies in a selected area of New York City. Smaller-scale projects had been tried some years before in the city, and the recent success of a tuberculosis prevention project in Framingham, Massachusetts, had rekindled interest. Kingsbury had hoped that his old agency, the AICP, would supervise the project, and he persuaded the AICP director, Bailey B. Burritt, to establish a department of health activities for this purpose. Believing that the only way to attract money from the foundations was to have a big program with a high-powered head, he next looked for a person of "conspicuous leadership" to run the department. When his first choices turned him down, he persuaded Burritt to offer the job to Hopkins.[29]

Although the offer had obviously attractive features—a return to New York and involvement with a major project—Hopkins responded cautiously. He wanted to be sure that he would be his own boss and that his salary would be high. Negotiations dragged on for months, but in September 1922 he finally accepted a position as assistant director of the AICP at $8,000 a year.[30]

Up to this point Hopkins had operated social welfare programs from a position of strength; his agency had dominated the field. Organizing the AICP project gave him his first taste of institutional rivalry. With characteristic energy he was rounding up support when Dr. Louis I. Harris of the city's Health Department proposed turning over the project's major activities to his Bureau of Preventable Diseases.

This was a serious blow to Hopkins, who had come to New York expecting that the AICP would manage the project. Even Kingsbury was considering administering the project through an executive board on which the AICP would be only one voice. Approaching the situation cautiously, Hopkins discussed with Harris the AICP's proposal to manage the project and also tried to persuade the project's technical board to accept it. When he found that, apart from the issue of control, Harris was enthusiastic about the project and that the board was unprepared to address the issue, he decided to avoid stirring up difficulties and let the subject ride. Fortunately for him, events soon fell his way. The New York Tuberculosis Association formally complained about Harris's trying to take over the project and asked the Health Department to name another representative. Hopkins decided to let the Tuberculosis Association "carry on the scrap with Harris without implicating [the AICP] in any way." Indeed, he now thought that he might assume a mediator's role, and he began contemplating "a scheme . . . by which the whole [project] could be given some kind of official recognition on the part of the Health Department." He had a moment's pause when the Tuberculosis Association seemed to want to press its own organizational plan, but he soon assured himself that the director "recognizes our prior interest and natural claim to act as the advisory and sponsoring organization."[31] Discussions continued for several months until the various parties finally decided to organize the project "as a supplement and aid to the Health Department." Harris eventually became health commissioner, and Hopkins headed a committee that nominated him chairman of the project.

By this time, however, Hopkins had left the AICP. Unable to work with Burritt, who wanted to be the AICP's principal representative on the project, he resigned in the summer of 1923 to become general director of the New York Tuberculosis Association. There he pioneered innovative programs in health administration by offering his services to various independent agencies, enabling them to employ more trained personnel to deal with the public. As the organization extended its reach, it became the New York Tuberculosis and Health Association. In accepted administrative thinking, this approach was called centralization, but Hopkins saw it more as managing discrete but interrelated parts. Each of the departments served specific health needs, and to this degree they were separate. The association brought them together by providing unified administrative services.[32]

This was the thinking that Hopkins brought to the health project, which he continued to promote, and which in 1924 was inaugurated as the Bellevue-Yorkville Health Demonstration. Designed as a laboratory for public health education and preventive treatment, the project was based in east central Manhattan and involved that segment of the city's social, economic, and ethnic population with high incidences of disease and mortality. Its administrative strategy was to coordinate previously independent health agencies, even redrawing agency boundaries to conform to those of the demonstration.

While pursuing these goals Hopkins also tried to harmonize relations at the organizational level. The health demonstration was managed by an executive committee of representatives from the major health and welfare agencies and by a smaller interim committee that provided continuity between meetings. Although the interim committee had been formed to handle a small number of immediate problems, it soon took on the character of a staff, not only addressing immediate issues but also proposing ideas to the executive committee. Soon the larger committee was doing little more than rubber-stamping these proposals, and many members were becoming restive. As a member of both committees, Hopkins proposed a compromise. He would limit the interim committee to its original function of acting only when it was impractical to assemble the full executive group. At the same time he would preserve the small committee's energy and attentiveness to detail by restructuring the executive committee to include only the most active and interested members, "thus making the Executive Committee small and a real working body."[33]

Hopkins had only partial success in implementing these recommendations, since many members favored keeping the familiar structure. These suggestions, however, were minor compared to the more radical view he was developing of the project. It had been formed in part as a partnership between private health agencies and the New York City Department of Health. When he was first defending his position with the AICP, Hopkins had opposed the Health Department's taking over the project. In time, however, his views changed. Private physicians had asked that the project refer clients to them for examinations, but he proposed instead to test how far the private physicians were willing to enter the public health field. Thus, he was prepared to be sympathetic when in 1929 the Health Department, under Commissioner Dr. Shirley Wynne, proposed a major departure.

Wynne wanted to divide the city into thirty health districts supervised by appointees of the Health Department. Under this system local agencies would address their problems independently, approaching the Health Department only with matters requiring a citywide effort. Wynne's goal was to increase local responsibility, which was to be limited only by general guidelines from the Health Department. He proposed to incorporate the project into this system. Most committee members rejected his idea, but Hopkins supported it. He liked having the city Health Department take the initiative. He also anticipated that Wynne's plan would transform the executive committee into an advisory group, and believed that the board of managers should be changed "from a body . . . of persons engaged primarily in city-wide activities to one in which representatives of local interests would predominate."[34]

Hopkins's career in public health work had taught him that administration meant coordinating independent services by providing advice and information. Wynne's plan seemed to put this approach into action. He also saw the advantages of closer cooperation with the Health Department. But if this line of thinking made sense to Hopkins, it did not to the other committee members, who defeated the proposal.

The project had originally been developed as a model for the entire city; its sponsors had thought that out of it would grow a system for delivering health care that the central government could adopt and employ generally. But Hopkins had not seen it this way. He had come to think of the project as simply one part of a larger whole, less a model for the entire city than a particular approach that might work in one neighborhood. As a result Hopkins was able to see the project as only one means of delivering health services and not, as his colleagues seemed to view it, as an end in itself. Wynne's proposal appealed to him primarily because it reflected and supported his own evolving views.[35]

Meanwhile, Hopkins's growing commitment to professionalism in social work was further reinforcing and broadening these views. Since arriving in New York, he had pioneered many innovations in social work, but none was as significant nationally as his role in establishing the American Association of Social Workers (AASW). In June 1921 he had met with other social workers who wanted to establish and maintain professional standards by forming an association. He became a member of the governing body and helped to draft a charter, and in 1923 he became the association's president.

Hopkins started off his presidency in typical style, proposing to limit the association's national council to advisory powers while concentrating authority in the smaller executive committee. As things stood, the council and committee had equal authority and thus could cancel each other out. His proposal, he admitted, would mean that the association would be run by "a small group in the east," but he thought that this would provide effective leadership. He could not overcome the suspicions of the Middle Westerners, however, who defeated his proposal and taught him that regional loyalties often weighed more heavily than rational arguments for efficiency.[36]

Similar problems bedeviled the association's vocational bureau, which provided members with career advice and job-placement services. Although it promoted professionalism by placing association members in the nation's welfare agencies, the bureau drew criticism from its membership because it served mostly New Yorkers and because its budget took up nearly 40 percent of the association's funds.

The bureau was even a source of discord within the association. Hopkins tried to defuse these controversies, agreeing to establish new branches outside New York and urging the council to resolve the employment disputes. In the process, however, he came to realize that the bureau was a liability.[37]

The bureau's job-placement services kept it going until the members discovered that the expense was preventing the association from supporting itself out of members' dues. Many, like Hopkins, believed that as long as the association accepted contributions from charitable institutions, some of whose members might not meet association standards, the AASW could not become a fully professional organization. In 1925 the issue came to a head at the national convention. Hopkins voted with the majority to begin separating from the vocational bureau. "I believe that we should stand on our own feet," he declared from the floor. "We should finance the organization and limit our program to the things that we can finance."[38]

Hopkins's uncompromising stand in favor of self-support and his efforts to preserve the peace within the association revealed the depth of his professional commitment. By the mid-1920s all that remained of his socialist sympathies were those values compatible with the social worker's vocation. In 1924 he presided at a national council meeting that recommended that the association "should not at present aggressively further general social legislation but only insofar as the status effects social workers and their professional standing."[39]

Two years after the AASW adopted this resolution, Hopkins defined its meaning. Public health work, he declared, owed much to nineteenth-century advances in medical science; but it owed its growth primarily to the "humanitarian impulses" of social work. Advances against slum housing, infant mortality, and tuberculosis had succeeded because social workers had first labeled them the products of social injustice and only later warned that they were threats to public health. The solutions—sanitary plumbing, milk feeding stations for infants, health education—were practical expressions of these values. But the most effective expression was the health demonstration project, which experimented with administrative techniques and tested results with statistical objectivity. By developing precise and commonly accepted standards, public health workers had created a model for other welfare agencies to copy. "Why should there not be organized," Hopkins asked rhetorically, " 'social welfare demonstrations,' the purpose of which would be not only to analyze the social work of a community, but to set up adequate experimental machinery to try out on a scientific basis the theories expounded for years by social workers?"[40]

Social progress resulted from social work professionals' combining their humanitarian values and research techniques. There was in this belief more than an echo of the Christian Darwinism of those Grinnell College professors who had proclaimed that service to others was part of the "scientific spirit" of the age.

There was more to Hopkins's personal brand of professionalism. He was constantly in motion, nervously active, intense, his clothes rumpled, his shirts never quite fresh. He darted here and there, snatching only moments of relaxation. His curiosity seemed as limitless as his willingness to help others. When someone expressed concern that workers drilling into rock beneath Forty-second Street were in danger of contracting silicosis, he promised to involve the Tuberculosis and Health Association. His first step was to ask the secretary of the association, "Say, Jack—what *is* silicosis?" John Kingsbury said it best: "Nothing human seemed alien to him."[41]

To his lasting credit with the directors of the Tuberculosis and Health Association, his most regular and responsible trait was sound money management. When he left the association in 1933, the directors publicly thanked him for expanding the organization's income, wisely distributing expenditures, and during the depression years cutting costs so that work could continue "without a deficit."[42]

Hopkins's years in New York developed his native talent for administration. Managing such complex organizations as the New York Tuberculosis and Health Association, the American Association of Social Workers, and the Bellevue-Yorkville Health Demonstration, he came to see that administration was less a matter of establishing lines of authority than of balancing interests. His administrative style was to encourage cooperation for the good of the larger whole. This practice was built on the lessons he had learned with the Red Cross, where he had sought to serve the needs of his chapters and to encourage hesitant volunteers. Thus his was not the attitude of the executive but of the colleague. This was why in later years his administrative behavior so often defied conventional categories. Throughout his career Hopkins preferred to surround himself with people he trusted and to work with them in an atmosphere of joint effort toward a common end.

# Chapter 3

# Escape from Despair

Harry Hopkins needed the satisfactions of his professional achievements to balance the deterioration of his family life. On the surface there were few signs of personal problems. At a time when most Americans made less than $3,000 a year, he was receiving $10,000 from the Tuberculosis and Health Association. He and his family, which in 1925 had grown to three sons with the birth of Stephen Hopkins, lived in prosperous suburban communities, first in Yonkers, then fifteen miles north in Scarborough. They also acquired a summer cottage in the upstate artists' colony of Woodstock on the eastern edge of the Catskill Mountains. These moves coincided with those of their closest friends, the Kingsburys. Harry consulted John about professional and career matters, while John took Harry and his boys on hikes. The children played together, once being discovered in a vacant lot sharing a package of cigarettes. David said that they didn't make him sick as long as he lay on his stomach.

Harry also borrowed heavily from Kingsbury's library. During an illness in 1920 he had begun to read the English romantic poets— Keats, Byron, Shelley—and had moved on to such contemporary poets as Amy Lowell and Carl Sandburg. Their works kindled a flame that never died. (In 1928 Harry reported that a visit to Keats's Walk in London "swelled my imagination and I saw his red head and proud step sauntering thru the green. It was as tho I could reach out and touch him—quite like a dream." Though his interest in poetry remained lively, his expression became more prosaic. An April 1942 journey through the English countryside moved him to remark only that "when you see that country in spring . . . you begin to understand why the English have written the best goddam poetry in the world.") A 1925 letter to his son David showed his taste for literary description when he tried to capture images of rural Ohio from his railroad car. A Ford was "panting alongside the dirt road trying to keep up with the train . . . horses drink thirstily at the farm trough," the country "rolls for miles on either side—corn—oats—pasture land . . ." He even composed a few poems.

> In long straight rows the corn's laid by in hot
> June days.
> Almost tenderly Iowa's corn is nourished
> Its yellow mellowness is soft—its yellowness
> is precious
> Iowa tends its corn like a slick banker watches
> a ticker tape
> Too wet—too dry—early frost—late
> frost
> An Iowa farmer always looks in the dark.

His fondness for rural America was exclusively poetic. Apart from an abiding love for Grinnell College, he had turned away from his small-town past and now denigrated his father's hero William Jennings Bryan as "that stupid ass." Bryan's name had recently been in the news when he appeared in Dayton, Tennessee, to help prosecute a biology teacher who had defied that state's law against teaching the theory of evolution. The eastern press had pilloried Bryan for championing fundamentalist ignorance against scientific truth, and Hopkins probably had that incident in mind when he observed that the town of Bryan, Ohio, "seems to have gone to seed much as the gentleman himself." When a fellow social worker suggested holding the AASW convention in Des Moines, Hopkins was only half-facetious in replying, "It will be quite difficult to induce anyone to have a conference in such a prosaic place."[1]

But behind the new-found success, comfort, and sophistication stirred the turbulence of a failing marriage. Harry and Ethel had grown incapable of satisfying each other's needs. Their problems stemmed from family stress. Ethel's early life had been disrupted by her father's death, the move from Hungary, and then, after their arrival in New York, the suicide of her mother.[2] Ethel had adjusted with courage and resourcefulness, finding work that would make her self-supporting. And she showed her independence by marrying outside her faith and giving up Judaism. She balanced her independence, however, with a need for personal intimacy, for sharing her thoughts and feelings and receiving love and reassurance.

Harry had been attracted to Ethel for many reasons. He admired her independence and executive ability, which reminded him of Adah, the sibling to whom he felt the closest. Her cosmopolitan background appealed to his naive passion for New York's exotic culture. Not surprisingly, her ardent response captured his heart beyond reason. Ethel had raised one danger signal when she had discussed the problem of their different religious backgrounds, although this was not the issue on which their marriage would founder. Harry had come to New York not so much to escape Bible Belt Christianity as to free himself from small-town dullness and a family presided over by a strict, assertive mother and a happy-go-lucky, impecunious father. In marrying, he was contemplating a family life in which he would act as the breadwinner and his wife would support his efforts and yield to his authority. His desire to work hard to provide for his family was appropriate in a culture that assigned males this responsibility. But it was not a sufficient conception of marriage for a wife who had professional experience and executive ability, and who needed his constant loving attention.

Their problems worsened when Harry discovered that although he was able to make money, he was unable to hold on to it. He was incapable of denying his appetites. His literary interests led to expensive purchases at the bookstores. He entertained friends at high-priced restaurants and speakeasies, traveled first class, and stayed at the best hotels. To make up the deficit he borrowed from Ethel's brothers, Edward and Benjamin Gross, but this compromised her desire for independence; and he worked long hours, but at the cost of neglecting her and the children.

Harry's work schedule kept him apart from Ethel, but at a deeper level he was not capable of the intimacy she needed. Ever sympathetic, he could understand her need; but his strength lay in giving others the confidence to stand on their own feet. Maybe he felt that Ethel's persistent demands for attention asked too much of him. In any case he seems to have resisted her entreaties. While he was living in New Orleans organizing the home service, Ethel, still back in New York, wrote a letter almost pleading with him to say that he missed her. He dutifully replied, "I miss you so much and know how much I love you," but added, "You women—damn you—don't need to have men around but my dear I've had to bite my lips hard several times to keep from going astray." This could hardly have been the sort of loving reassurance that Ethel had looked forward to receiving.[3]

For several years they were able to keep their differences in the background. Harry was away from home on Red Cross business as their seventh anniversary approached, and his letter shows his modest but hopeful expectations for their future together:

> My dearest:
>
> I shall think of you every hour on Thursday and wish so much I were at home. Life has really been rather good to us so far—for we have lived seven very perfect years together and I love and care for you more than anyone else on this earth. No one could have been finer than you and we shall work out a useful and complete life together. Thru every crisis you have been perfect—while I am fully convinced we shall never have any money I am equally sure that the finer things in life will be and indeed are ours. I am genuinely and very proud of you—and David has been adorable hasn't he?
>
> And so today if this should come on Thursday—I kiss your warm lips and dream of many more happy years together.
>
> Harry[4]

In the years to come, however, doubts crowded these feelings aside. Harry showed signs of this ambivalence in 1925, when on the way to the AASW convention in Denver he took time for family reunions. In Portland, Oregon, he joined his brothers, Lewis, who had taken up medical practice in Tacoma, Washington, Emery, who was a salesman in a local department store, and Rome, who under the prohibition laws was legally selling alcoholic potions for medical purposes in Minneapolis. Adah, now married to Frank Aime, an electrical engineer, remained in New York. The gathering inspired a description that, although lighthearted, suggests that Harry had a few reservations about the achievements of the Hopkins men:

> If Sinclair Lewis ever gets the complete history of the Hopkins family, he will make "Main Street" look like ten cents. I wouldn't have missed it for the world—Rome engaged to a Follies girl who happens to be Catholic and divorced—the hero selling alcohol a shade or two inside the law. Lewis flat on his back [with a cold] practicing the "honking art" and thoroughly disillusioned—and Emery, the 100% American selling baggage in a department store at $35 per. Rome smiles, plans matrimony and looks for bigger things—Lew smiles a little pathetically—changes the babies [sic] diaper and looks for a better practice from now on— Emery reads of heroes in the American magazine—begets a healthy child,—and plans to make some money soon. All are broke—complain but little—have no alibis—are securely nailed to females who think they could have made a respectable living had they been wearing the trousers.

A family of ineffectual dreamers, disillusioned, pathetic, a burden on their wives: not a very encouraging portrait. One wonders how Harry would have described his own place in the group. His comment about *Main Street,* at the time an enormously popular novel showing how small-town life stultifies personal development and artistic expression, suggests that he wanted to think of himself as the sophisticated New Yorker, risen above his background. But perhaps he was only whistling in the dark. It seems worth noting that he focused on traits—marriage beyond the limits of Methodist approval, financial hopes and disappointments, even ill health—that had troubled his own experience. His observation about the wives' dissatisfactions probably reflected guilty suspicions about his own relationship with Ethel, who complained about having to depend financially upon her brothers.

A visit to his parents did little to increase the Hopkins stock. They had moved from Grinnell to Spokane, Washington, where Al had, inevitably, opened a bowling alley. Harry found his father as optimistic as ever despite being saddled with mortgage payments that took half his monthly income. Harry estimated that his father was about $5,000 poorer than when he had arrived. His mother still ruled at home, which she kept spotless, and longed for visits from her children, "especially Adah."[5]

Ultimately Harry's struggle for financial stability and Ethel's need for loving attention created more stress than their marriage could bear. In the fall of 1927 they decided on a brief separation, with Ethel taking a month's vacation to visit friends in New Orleans. The trip, of course, was no solution. Ethel's problem was that the man she loved had grown away from her, and the separation only heightened her sense of loss and helplessness. Although Harry assured her that the break was "the best move we have made in years," Ethel resented having to live on hospitality. When Harry suggested that she prolong her trip, she despairingly replied that the only way she could stay away from home was to get a job or else take up "a career of mad pleasure," an option which attracted her, she said, because she found that she could still "give pleasure" to men. She thought that she might get "a real kick" out of seeing how long she could make such a relationship last, adding that it would help her "develop a hard-boiled quality that is quite an asset in many ways and that I could never develop with someone I love."[6]

It would have been best for them to recognize that they had lost whatever had balanced their weaknesses and insecurities and to end their marriage as cleanly as possible. But neither was able to do that: Ethel because she loved Harry and continued to hope that he could give her what she needed, and Harry because his sensitivity to her pain and to his own inadequacies had inspired guilt feelings that were further intensified because he had fallen in love with someone else.

Barbara Duncan was a secretary at the Tuberculosis and Health Association. Ten years younger than Harry, she had grown up in Port Huron, Michigan, where her father managed shipping and lumbering businesses. She attended the University of Michigan for two years and then moved to New York, where she trained as a nurse at Bellevue Hospital and then was hired by Hopkins's organization. An attractive young woman with gently rounded features, she had soft good looks and a personality to match. She shared Harry's naive enthusiasm for big-city sophistication and his taste for comfortable living but differed from him in maintaining loving ties to her family, especially to her aunt Myrta Bradley, her mother's sister (her mother having died when she was young), and to her sister Dorothy and her brother Donald, a commander in the navy. In certain ways that undoubtedly attracted Harry, she was unlike Ethel. She did not feel compelled to struggle for a sense of personal freedom. Although capable and efficient, she was an accommodating person who was content to stay in the background. She also possessed a bland optimism that caused her to describe life's incidents as "nice," "perfect," "fine," "wonderful."[7] In short, she would make the kind of wife who would be unlikely to stir in Harry any uneasiness about wearing the pants in the family or about his failings as a provider.

However strong his feelings for Barbara, Harry could not turn his back on Ethel. With their relationship at an impasse, he decided to try psychoanalysis. The eminent New York practitioner Dr. Frankwood E. Williams traced his difficulties to his having felt neglected by his mother because he was a middle child. Williams also encouraged him to mend his marriage and give up his relationship with Barbara. This advice reinforced the morality of the day, which disapproved of divorce, but failed to change Harry's feelings. The treatment in fact only intensified his inner conflicts.

During 1928 Harry tried to commit himself to saving his marriage, and he and Barbara agreed to end their relationship. The Milbank Fund was sending a group of social workers to attend the first International Conference of Social Work in Paris, and Kingsbury suggested that Harry go along to get away from his problems. Harry accepted the offer and expanded the trip to include an investigation of social work practices in Great Britain. On the surface his letters to Ethel suggest that he was trying to honor his commitment. They were all she had said she wanted: frequent, descriptive, and full of his own thoughts and expressions of love. Perhaps she smiled to see that he was the same old Harry, unable to abide the cramped, noisy living quarters and plebeian food of third class and thus paying an extra $100 for first-class privileges by day. "Europe can be done very cheaply," he wrote, "but not by me! It takes the edge off." He thoughtfully sent gifts for her and the children, discussed plans for their schooling, and asked for word of their summer plans. He shared his enthusiasm for Paris ("beyond all expectations—am thrilled with every bit of it"), his admiration for the health work he saw in London's East End ("It was thrilling. We are amateurs indeed!"), his sublime encounter with Keats's Walk, and smaller details from British smoking habits to Paris night life. Most of all he concentrated on their relationship. "Don't worry," he would end his letters, promising to write again soon—"not as a sense of duty but because I want to." He also advised her to enjoy herself and not to spend all her time with the children.[8]

In later years Harry's reassurances would bring hope to desperate people: to the unemployed who were told they would not starve, to the British who were told that America would send them the tools to fight Hitler. His reassurances to Ethel, however, rang hollow; they were born not of hope but of despair.

Harry's venture into psychoanalysis had not reconciled him to his marriage, but it had shown him the possibilities of searching his memory for reasons, even false ones, to justify his estrangement from Ethel. In this frame of mind he sat down with John Kingsbury on the boat to Europe to discuss his marital difficulties. He had, he said, married Ethel for the wrong reasons: because he pitied a poor, struggling Jewish girl, because he admired her devotion to her family, because he wanted to shock the good Methodists back in Iowa. But the differences had been more than he could handle. The litany at a Jewish funeral had repulsed him, and he disliked Ethel's relatives. Responsibility for his sons was burdensome. To be sure that Kingsbury understood that the problems had grown strictly out of his relationship with Ethel, he declared that there was no other woman in his life. (Kingsbury was not inclined to believe this, since some months earlier Ethel had told him her version of their difficulties, but he seems not to have challenged Harry on this point.)[9]

Hopkins's conversation with Kingsbury and his letters to Ethel present such contradictory evidence of his feelings that they defy a definitive analysis. The easiest conclusion is that he was cynically deceiving them both. This was the judgment of many, most notably Adah, who herself became estranged from her brother over these events. But this seems the least plausible explanation. If Harry was determined to divorce Ethel and marry Barbara, he might have felt the need to blame her, but he would not have attempted to deceive Ethel into thinking that he was trying to make their marriage work. Thus it seems more likely that he was only being evasive; he was avoiding confronting the guilt that he felt over loving Barbara and knowing the pain that this would cause Ethel. As Kingsbury remembered their conversation, Harry avoided directly attacking Ethel, blaming the failure of their relationship on her family and her religion, despite the fact that she had sought independence from the former and rejected the latter. Still, to this degree he protected her, just as his reassuring letters were designed to protect her.

Of course his story was built on rationalization and falsehood. The truth was that he had married Ethel because he loved her, naively and immaturely perhaps but nonetheless sincerely. But love had faltered, the marriage had not worked, and he had found someone else. He could no more deny this reality than he could deny his financial extravagances. While he was in Europe, the truth bore in upon him. He wired Ethel to expect him home about August fifteenth. But in fact he was returning earlier, in time for a detour to Saranac Lake in upstate New York, where Barbara had been admitted to a sanatorium with a mild case of tuberculosis. After satisfying himself that she was in no danger, although she needed several weeks, perhaps months, of rest and care, Harry went home, maintaining the pretense that he had just arrived from Europe.[10] Surely his deception involved more than the desire to shield his sensitive wife from a show of harmless concern for a sick employee.

Whatever resolve Harry had made to repair his marriage was obviously bound to fail. Within a year he and Ethel had legally separated. During this period Harry wrote the most despairing letter of his life:

Dear Ethel:

I am returning the enclosed bills because I simply cannot pay them—the rest are paid. It won't do any good to borrow any more money because I couldn't pay it back. As a matter of fact, I am financially bankrupt. On the fifteenth, after I give you $200—I must pay for the auto $65—bank $85—your dentist $50—leaving me $70 until May 1—then on May 1 I will give you $300 more and pay $60 insurance and $50 to the school—leaving me in all $140 to live on for a month. I have only one suit of clothes and am not spending a cent that I don't have to.

I telephoned to Tacoma on Wednesday—father is very low and Lew thinks he will die before another week. He is with Lew.

Harry

P.S. I wrote this last night and it sounds pretty bad—I guess it is.[11]

On May 11, 1931, Ethel obtained a formal divorce. One month later Harry and Barbara were married.

The stress of his failing marriage had not shown Hopkins to his best advantage, but it had revealed some truths about him. It showed that in his interpersonal as well as in his professional relationships his impulses were to be accommodating, to minimize conflict, to reassure the faint-hearted, and to demand much of himself. Professionally these traits had been a source of strength, enabling him to inspire confidence in those under his authority and to work harmoniously with his peers and superiors. The energy that he devoted to his work sprang from a sense of creativity. This he imparted to others, not warning them of the penalties for failure but assuring them that they had the ability to succeed.

To the degree that Hopkins was willing to push himself to his physical limits, even to the point of suffering attacks of the flu and pneumonia, he showed a willingness to sacrifice himself for the good of others. To this extent he carried forward his mother's missionary ethic, and Grinnell College's Social Gospel Christianity. Hard work may have also been a means of escaping the numbing frustration of his marital problems. Seeing Paris had pleased him, he said, because it had shown that "I am not blase and still [am] capable of real enthusiasm."[12]

If Harry saw his career as a chance to be creative and succeed through hard work and sacrifice, he wanted his personal life to be a haven for rest and self-indulgence. He even admitted that he was "a selfish soul."[13] It is hard to say where this selfish streak came from, but it was undeniably a part of his personality. He indulged himself at first in private ways: first-class travel accommodations, expensive restaurants, tennis clubs, cocktails, cigarettes, a vacation cottage. Later he would take his pleasures more publicly, attending horse races with John Hay ("Jock") Whitney and his wealthy friends and dining at fashionable restaurants with movie stars. There was a bit of the small-town boy in the big city about this behavior, the harness maker's son getting a thrill out of seeing how far he had risen in the world. But Harry's enjoyment lacked the element of self-consciousness that usually accompanies that kind of motive. Instead of seeing himself as an outsider who was along to enjoy the view or who had to make a special effort to fit in, he seemed to take the perquisites of success naturally.

Harry's taste for self-indulgence did not create his marital difficulties, but it did exacerbate them. His having to rely financially on Ethel's family had clearly undermined her independence, but on Harry it had had an ambiguous effect. Although he was continually nagged by feelings of inadequacy because of his failings as a provider, he usually gave in to temptation. As a result, his professional and domestic lives diverged. At work he was confident of his abilities; he was willing to take chances, accept new challenges, devise new systems, and he conveyed his confidence to others. Although he usually sought cooperation and agreement, he was able to fight for what he needed and even to resign if he felt that that was his only choice. At home it was a different story. There were too many sources of guilt and inadequacy. He wanted a passive wife who could take pride in his accomplishments, accept his self-indulgences, look after the children, and not nag about money. In this kind of home he could be a happy and loving husband, content to lead a quiet, private existence. After his remarriage Harry successfully subordinated his domestic life to the demands of his career. Although this arrangement never freed him from guilty feelings over his failings as a provider, it did allow him to pursue a distinguished career in public service.

His opportunity for building such a career was almost as much the product of circumstances as of his abilities. High on the list of these circumstances was his being a Democrat in a time of Democratic political ascendancy and a social worker in a time of mass unemployment. Both circumstances resulted from the Great Depression, which began in the fall of 1929 and deepened during the next four years. By this time Hopkins had long since given up socialism for his old Democratic allegiance, which he had combined with his social worker's professional preferences in supporting Al Smith, a New York City politician who worked his way to the governor's office by advocating social welfare reform. Hopkins had supported Smith's presidential bids in 1924, when he lost the nomination, and in 1928, when he won it but was swamped in the election by Herbert Hoover. Thus when the depression hit, Smith was out of office, and his place in Albany was occupied by another Democrat, a wealthy upstate party regular named Franklin D. Roosevelt.

As unemployment worsened in the city, Hopkins responded by giving his free time to help his former AICP colleague Bill Matthews operate an Emergency Work Bureau, which tried to find jobs for the unemployed. At first many social workers, including Hopkins, thought that the depression would be short-lived and that private charities would be able to get people through the crisis. From the beginning, however, local governments supplied 70 percent of the funds for unemployment relief, and as the depression continued through 1930, unemployment reached such dimensions that even these resources faltered. Hopkins joined other social workers in calling on the state government to step in. Governor Roosevelt responded by persuading the state legislature to appropriate $23 million for a Temporary Emergency Relief Administration (TERA) to assist local welfare agencies and to undertake its own employment projects.

Operating the TERA was a three-member board to which Roosevelt appointed Jesse Isadore Straus, the president of the R. H. Macy department stores, John Sullivan, president of the New York State Federation of Labor, and Philip J. Wickser, a prominent Buffalo attorney. These men then turned to the task of selecting an executive director. Roosevelt suggested Edward T. Devine, secretary of New York's Charity Organization Society, and William Matthews of the Emergency Work Bureau. Lieutenant Governor Herbert Lehman recommended William Hodson, head of the New York City Welfare Council. The board offered the job to Hodson, but the council refused to release him.[14] It so happened that Hodson had known Hopkins on the Welfare Council and called to ask if he would like the position.

Hopkins's life was reaching a turning point. He had married Barbara and was sorting out his personal life. At the same time his work at the Emergency Bureau had struck a chord in him—his enthusiasm as an AICP caseworker, the challenge of organizing home service relief, his general eagerness to take on new projects—that was too strong to resist. It was time for a fresh start. He told Hodson that he would take the job. By this time Straus was so desperate to fill the position that he urgently requested the Tuberculosis and Health Association to grant Hopkins a leave of absence. The president and the secretary knew that if they let Hopkins go, they would probably lose him for good. But in view of the unemployment situation and the unwillingness of others to take the job, they agreed to give Hopkins four months' leave of absence. The board acted the same day, and Hopkins prepared to assume his duties the next morning, October 8, 1931.[15]

At TERA Hopkins found much that was familiar. Working with established county welfare agencies and specially created county work bureaus, TERA operated as the central agency of a federal structure that employed regional directors and field supervisors to investigate complaints, audit accounts, and help organize relief procedures. It dealt exclusively with established agencies, county welfare commissions. To encourage professionalism, it required each local agency to have "at least one trained and experienced investigator on its staff." TERA encouraged local responsibility for relief. It pressured districts to increase their relief appropriations and refused to pay claims unless districts made a bona fide effort to raise money locally. Public welfare officials had a "duty" to "seek out persons in need," if necessary with the assistance of local civic leaders.[16]

Hopkins accomplished much in a short time. After only three months, nearly 10 percent of the state's population was receiving TERA relief. Professional standards so improved that within a year well over half the welfare districts were employing trained social workers. At the same time certain problems were apparent. Private agencies were dumping their cases on the public welfare commissions, most of which were staffed by political appointees who did not have the skill to handle such large numbers. Many administrators regarded their allocation of funds as a fixed amount, and in order to stretch it out over the entire period were doling out relief so sparingly that many of the hard-pressed were being denied help.

To conserve money, officials emphasized home relief instead of work relief. Recipients of home relief were given orders for food, clothing, shelter, medical care, and fuel, which they turned in at local retail stores or relief commissaries. Home relief cost less than work relief, which paid cash wages at the locally prevailing rate for projects that required additional expenditures for planning, supervision, and materials. The emphasis on home relief aggravated administrative problems, however, because home relief was handled by public welfare officials while work relief was handled by specially appointed committees.[17]

TERA's fundamental problem was the continuing depression. As the economy continued to falter, it seemed inevitable that more families would fall onto the relief rolls and that contributions to private charity would decline. If TERA ended on June 1, as the law originally provided, thousands would be thrown into extreme distress and the state might face food riots. The board asked Governor Roosevelt to continue TERA with extended powers to apportion home relief and work relief funds according to local conditions and to take over the public welfare commissions and work bureaus when necessary.[18]

In March 1932 Straus and Wickser submitted their resignations from the board. Roosevelt appointed Hopkins to replace Straus, and he took charge on April 25. By then Roosevelt had persuaded the legislature to appropriate $5 million to carry TERA until November, when the voters would decide on a $30 million bond issue to continue it until January 1934. Hopkins joined the campaign, predicting that $150 million would be needed through the following June and pointing out that because of limited funds, half a million eligible people were not receiving relief. "The plain fact . . . is," he warned, "that the crisis is not being met in New York City and New York State." Even the $30 million would not be enough, and he urged increased private giving and local appropriations. Just before election day he reported that the relief appropriation was exhausted. Since local governments could no longer finance both relief and their regular expenses out of property taxes, the bond issue remained the only hope for the unemployed. By that time, however, the issue was no longer in doubt. Both parties had endorsed it, and no significant opposition had arisen. The voters approved it by a four-to-one margin.[19]

All the while Hopkins was enmeshed in emergency administration: endless conferences, memos, and decisions. Welfare departments proposed new uses for TERA funds, and he had to determine if the rules allowed them; conferences with state and local officials called him out of town; reports flooded him with details of projects and activities; cities and counties ran short of funds or needed to be advised how to match their requests for the next month with their balance from the current one; charges of mismanagement, favoritism, or political interference needed to be investigated and the results evaluated.[20] There was nothing unique about such problems individually; they were part of any administrator's job. The difference was their intensity: day after day of meetings, phone calls, memos, letters, telegrams. Hopkins had not been so busy since his days of organizing home service relief in the Gulf states.

Much of the pressure resulted from the emergency character of his work. When everyone was short of money, small problems could not be handled locally, and TERA had to balance emergency appeals against each other. Hopkins also had to attack problems before they spread, for example noting a violation or improper practice in one locality and sending out a general warning against it. This was a job for a top-flight administrator who knew how to make decisions and had the courage to follow through.

He did it all, and with the typical Hopkins touch—reassuring, sympathetic, helpful. John Kingsbury called to tell him that many residents of the artists' colony at Woodstock were near starvation. Hopkins put him in touch with the head of TERA art projects and in the meantime sent out a field representative to start a relief program. Public health workers received a grant to investigate the incidence of tuberculosis in black and Puerto Rican neighborhoods in New York City. Even when Hopkins turned down ideas, he conveyed a reassuring sympathy. One man recalled Hopkins's "humanitarian sympathetic penetrating eyes" as he described his idea to employ cloth cutters in making overcoats for poor children. Hopkins told him, "Not only do I agree that we should make overcoats for the poor kids, but also build houses and give work to bricklayers. But right now our sources are very limited, and every day doctors, lawyers, teachers, and other professionals come to this office, with tears in their eyes, pleading with me to help pay their rent." The next day, however, he figured out a way to allocate $30,000 for such projects. A TERA worker recalled that when he was "struggling, rather helplessly, with the work relief problem in Attica . . . [Hopkins was] the most sympathetic and active member of the state organization."[21]

Hopkins described the relief program in human terms. He told the state conference of mayors that they would be hearing appeals to reduce taxes by cutting relief spending, but that was simply out of the question. "While budgets must be balanced and every unnecessary expenditure eliminated, the desire to cut down expenses cannot be matched against the tragic hunger and distress of citizens of the state who find themselves dependent. There is no question of taxes versus life."[22]

In all of these activities Hopkins drew from his past experience. Even TERA's work relief projects extended his small-scale effort with the AICP. At the same time, however, he was expanding the boundaries of his profession. Traditional methods emphasized the casework approach, which relied on the social worker to visit the relief client in order to establish a friendly and encouraging relationship but also to ascertain that the client actually deserved assistance and to supervise the client's use of that assistance. TERA began with this approach. Applicants for home relief were visited by a caseworker who determined their eligibility and consulted with a staff person to work out a program for their needs. Since home relief clients were paid in kind, the caseworker would, for example, bring clients a grocery order and then accompany them to the store to be sure they got what the order specified. Hopkins did what he could to keep this system functioning, but it gradually became ineffective. As unemployment increased, his job became less to supervise dealing with clients on an individual "retail" basis than to allocate "wholesale" amounts of state aid to ease mass suffering.

Although Hopkins's efforts attracted Governor Roosevelt's support, their relationship remained entirely professional. Between April and December 1932, the two conferred a dozen times, four by telephone. Hopkins's diary entries tell little about the subjects, but most likely they discussed TERA business. Hopkins was not part of Roosevelt's inner circle of policy advisers, later known as his "brain trust." Eleanor Roosevelt, herself a former social worker, also communicated with Hopkins to the extent of recommending recipients for TERA assistance and donating the money she received for radio broadcasts, but she and Hopkins developed no special friendship.[23]

It was solely because of Roosevelt's boldness in providing relief for the unemployed that by 1932 Hopkins was fervently supporting his presidential candidacy. By this time Hopkins was also thoroughly disgusted with President Hoover's unemployment policies. First treating the depression as a fleeting condition and then as a problem to be managed by voluntary local cooperation, Hoover had dismissed proposals for dramatically expanded public works and limited his initiatives to forming a presidential committee to encourage private and

local efforts. Not until the summer of 1932, after almost all private
social work agencies, the governors of industrial states, and other
prominent persons had taken up the call for a federal relief effort, did
he approve a relief bill. The law allowed the Reconstruction Finance
Corporation (RFC), created earlier to make federal loans to businesses,
to lend up to $300 million to the states for unemployment relief.

By this time the Democratic National Convention had nominated
Roosevelt as its candidate for president. Hopkins traveled to Chicago
to observe the proceedings, and when he returned to New York he
wrote his brother Lew that he had "no confidence whatever that the
R.F.C. will help the situation this winter, other than bolster up the
railroads and the banks. He was "very naturally . . . hoping that
Roosevelt will be elected . . . chiefly because he is not afraid of a new
idea, and furthermore, is not identified with big business after the
fashion of 'the great engineer.' " It seemed to him that Roosevelt was
"fearless" and "a very able executive." Rumors of the governor's de-
bilitating health problems were "utter nonsense." (Roosevelt had been
crippled by infantile paralysis in 1921, but some at the time claimed
that he suffered from syphilis.)[24]

New ideas, hard work, courage, suspicion of big business: Roosevelt
was Hopkins's kind of candidate. Millions of others agreed, and
Roosevelt swept into the presidency. His election inspired Hopkins to
predict changes in federal policies. Big business, like Prohibition,
seemed on the way out in Washington, and he found both to be cause
for rejoicing. New taxes would be needed, and as usual Hopkins
favored levies on high incomes, inheritances, and gifts rather than sales
taxes, which were paid by the people "who can least afford it," or high
taxes on alcoholic beverages, which would encourage people to resort
to bathtub gin and other homemade substitutes.[25]

At the moment Hopkins's major concern was to obtain federal assistance for TERA. Expenditures in December had used up $10 million
of the $30 million bond issue, and he anticipated relief needs for 1933
at $100 million. With local governments reaching the limit of their
revenues, only the federal government could fill the gap. Campaign
politics had prevented the state from requesting federal aid, since
Roosevelt had not wanted to run to Hoover's RFC with a confession
that New York was broke.[26]

Fortunately the incoming governor was Herbert Lehman,
Roosevelt's lieutenant governor and a strong supporter of unemploy-

ment relief. Also, Congress was considering ways to amend the RFC relief procedures. During December and January, Hopkins conferred with Lehman to draft an application for an RFC loan, which he followed up by traveling to Washington. As a result, New York received over $13 million during the final weeks of the Hoover administration and another $6.6 million under Roosevelt.

Meanwhile, Hopkins had been conferring in Washington about new relief legislation. He advocated a vast appropriation—$600 million to $1 billion—and grants rather than loans to the states, though with the states still required to contribute their fair share. He wanted the bill passed as soon as possible, even at the risk of a veto from Hoover, so that if Roosevelt called a special session of Congress, the groundwork would have been laid for fast action.[27]

Congress produced no bill for Hoover, but Roosevelt called a special session of Congress to deal with a national banking crisis and then to present a package of depression measures. The new administration had been on the job scarcely a week when Hopkins and Bill Hodson went to Washington to offer their relief plan. Unable to see the president, they called Frances Perkins, a fellow New York social worker who was now serving as secretary of labor. She suggested meeting at the Women's Club, which turned out to be overflowing with people. Finding a cramped spot under a stairway, Hopkins and Hodson warned her that unless the federal government moved quickly to quell unemployment, the country could not hold together. The president would have to create an emergency agency to grant funds to the states for unemployment relief. Because of their recent experience, they proposed that the job of heading the agency should go to one of them; it did not matter which. Perkins agreed to push the plan, but Roosevelt would have to choose the director.[28]

Quick action in an emergency, a new approach to unemployment relief, a chance to serve under a leader he admired: Hopkins ought to have coveted such an opportunity. But in saying that he would be willing to see the job go to Hodson, he was being completely honest. By then he knew that he would be leaving the Tuberculosis and Health Association, but for what he did not know. Governor Lehman had asked him to stay on with TERA, and the legislature had set a salary of $11,500 for the position. But richer prospects were beckoning. Impressed by Hopkins's work, Jesse Straus had offered him $25,000 to join the R. H. Macy department stores, an offer all the more attractive to Hopkins because under his divorce agreement he owed Ethel half his salary for child support. Not until late April did Hopkins decide that if Roosevelt offered him the federal job, he would take it.[29]

Hopkins waited until mid-May before Roosevelt called to invite him to Washington to organize federal unemployment relief. The job, the president said, would be temporary, leaving open the prospect of Hopkins's eventually accepting Straus's offer. Hopkins accepted on Friday, May 19. The next day Roosevelt sent his name to the Senate, which confirmed his appointment without comment. On Sunday, Hopkins took the train to Washington, and the next morning he was at the White House to meet with the president. Congress had created a Federal Emergency Relief Administration (FERA) with $500 million to grant to states for unemployment relief. Hopkins would run it. Roosevelt had two pieces of advice: give the unemployed quick and adequate relief, and ignore the politicians.[30]

Leaving the White House, Hopkins headed for his office in the Walker-Johnson Building, an ancient yellow brick structure on New York Avenue, in a suite previously occupied by the unemployment relief division of the Reconstruction Finance Corporation. He arrived to find the office in chaos; packing boxes and crates littered the hall, files were nonexistent. Hopkins had to act quickly. He got hold of Fred Croxton of the RFC and found out which states' loan applications were on the verge of being approved. Then he set up a desk and began to spend the money. In two hours he disbursed over $5 million. The next morning the *Washington Post* ran his picture on the front page with the headline "Money Flies." That very day Hopkins began firing off telegrams to the state governors, informing them of their opportunities for aid and telling them that they could simply send him a telegram and wait until later to file a formal application.[31] There was work that needed to be done, and done quickly. Harry Hopkins was in his element. He had escaped his private despair and had hit the ground running.

# Chapter 4

# A Changed Man

"I do hope to be able to find time to get together soon," Harry wrote a social worker friend in the summer of 1933. "However the pressure here is terrific at the present time."[1] Indeed it was, for the new federal relief administrator was recruiting a staff, composing rules, and endlessly conferring with governors, mayors, and congressmen. Telegrams, letters, and phone calls ricocheted around his sparsely-furnished office. Often he was off to conferences around the country, explaining the administration's relief program and sizing up his task firsthand.

Chaotic as it might have seemed, all this activity was taking place in a fairly well defined context. Hopkins took office toward the end of the Hundred Days, a period during which the Roosevelt administration was enacting its New Deal program to combat the depression. Basic to its approach were the Agricultural Adjustment Act (AAA) for stabilizing farm prices by reducing production and the National Industrial Recovery Act (NIRA) for stabilizing industry by allowing businesses to make agreements regulating wages and prices. The NIRA also provided immediate stimulation through a $3.3 billion appropriation for construction projects to be administered by a Public Works Administration (PWA) under Secretary of the Interior Harold Ickes. As federal relief administrator, Hopkins was to assist the destitute until the recovery measures could take effect.

That was good enough for Hopkins. Federal relief was only for those no longer able to support themselves. Others worthy of social welfare—the self-supporting unemployed, orphans, widows, the handicapped, chronically ill, or blind—were outside his province.

Nor was his job to run unemployment relief, which still remained under state and local government. The relief act had divided $500 million into two equal parts, the first to be paid to the states as a matching grant, one federal dollar for three state dollars, the second to be granted directly with no strings attached. At Roosevelt's insistence, Hopkins emphasized the matching grants. Distressed to learn that

Hoover's RFC had been picking up over 70 percent of most states' relief bills, Roosevelt was determined to make the states do their part. This meant, as Hopkins saw it, that states should be given wide latitude in offering direct relief and organizations through which to investigate relief clients to assure the public that the money was going only to the needy. In fact he believed that competent investigation would reduce relief rolls by 10 percent.[2]

Hopkins meant business. "Every department of government that has any taxing power left," Hopkins wrote his state administrators, "has a direct responsibility to help those in distress." When states claimed that they were unable to provide relief, he told them to use their imagination. He cut off funds to Kentucky after the state legislature failed to raise revenue for relief and denied Ohio a request for extra funds. When the governor of West Virginia complained that his state could not pay for relief, Hopkins investigated and concluded that the governor "simply does not want to face the music." When New York City warned that it was exhausting its credit, he responded coldly that "the city authorities should think twice before going on record . . . that they could not raise further funds . . . [and] that the bankers [should] think further before allowing the word to be broadcast all over the U.S. that they would not lend to New York City."[3]

Administrative costs were to be held down. Hopkins proposed to run his own temporary operation on a shoestring. He believed that thirty-five to fifty people could staff the Washington office, in addition to a field staff of ten or twelve. He personally supervised hiring at the Washington office, and he instructed the state administrators to recruit their clerical staff from the relief rolls and to make "every effort . . . to secure local persons willing to serve without pay." Any state that misused funds would have the amount deducted from its allotment.[4]

In no instance, however, were the poor to be sacrificed to economy. After looking at conditions around the country, Hopkins concluded that many were hungry, that children needed milk and shoes, that the sick needed treatment. He admonished his field staff that these were "all American citizens and must be treated as such and not as people who have no right to the things they need." Indeed he believed that there were probably thousands who should be on the relief rolls but were not.[5]

In the meantime Hopkins was supporting the New Deal's recovery program. He met with New York's Senator Robert Wagner to suggest ways to encourage states to undertake PWA projects and ordered his staff to help provide workers for them. The NIRA, he said, would rescue the country from "cutthroat competition and racketeering" by stabilizing wages and employment. After a week's tour of eleven southern states he reported to the president that state leaders had faith in him and were enthusiastic about his recovery measures.[6]

The New Deal seemed to be doing as much for Hopkins as Hopkins was doing for the New Deal. Two months after he took office, John Kingsbury reported, "Harry is a changed man already. He is a bigger, better and more serious man—he is an older man. With full power and responsibility for the distribution of $500,000,000, he has something of the air of a member of the Morgan firm! I don't mean that he seems cocky, but he has the air of a man who has great power, who is enjoying it, who is determined to use it wisely, and as a dictator, if necessary." The key to his self-confidence seemed to be Roosevelt's support. The president had backed up his denial of emergency aid to the governor of Ohio and supported his blocking a bid by Roosevelt's political wheel horse Postmaster James A. Farley to get FERA funds for Catholic charities.[7]

Insightful as they were, Kingsbury's observations were not quite on target. What Kingsbury saw was Hopkins enjoying serving in an administration that encouraged creativity and originality. He was far from the Morgan partner willing to act the dictator. Hopkins wanted to have power and to use it not to dominate others but to give them responsibility and opportunity for creative action. "The whole business of experimentation in [FERA] is very broad," he told the National Conference of Social Work. "I am for experimenting with this fund in various parts of the country, trying out schemes which are supported by reasonable people and see if they work." He was willing to listen. "If anybody disagrees with me," he told the U.S. Conference of Mayors, "I have no quarrel with them. As a matter of fact, I don't quarrel with anybody about this whole relief business because I don't think anyone knows too much about it. If you don't agree with me, it is all right. You may be right and I may be wrong."[8]

After four months on the job Hopkins was reaching new conclusions about unemployment relief. As he saw it, his job was to help victims of economic conditions, not to give handouts to lazy or shiftless people. Thus he was moving away from the idea of home relief and toward a preference for work relief for cash wages. Standard home relief procedures, such as sending a social worker out shopping with clients to make sure that they purchased only approved items, may have contributed to administrative efficiency, but they let the clients—and everyone else in the store—know that these were dependent persons not to be trusted to make their own decisions.

Hopkins thought that this was the wrong way to treat the unemployed, who had once been "fine hard-working, upstanding men and women . . . the finest people in America." In a radio address he sympathetically depicted the plight of a typical unemployed worker. He had come to relief reluctantly, Hopkins said, in stages, first losing his job, then using up his savings, then cashing in his insurance policies. The landlords had stopped extending the rent, the grocers had cut off his credit, friends and relatives had become unable to help support his family. Despair pressed in. His children became hungry, then very hungry. One night he and his wife talked it over and decided to apply for relief. But two blocks from the relief office, he turned back. In the end, though, he had no choice. Hopkins believed that relief practices should not further humiliate people like this. Unemployment had not turned such people into paupers, but relief might. They knew how to work, how to handle money. They needed jobs and cash wages to spend.[9]

As the summer of 1933 turned into fall, Hopkins's views remained largely speculative. If he was rethinking the nature of relief, he was not yet proposing to put his new ideas into action. He still intended to hold the states to the matching formula and to keep pressing them to spend more of their own money. In October he instructed his state administrators to prepare for an expected winter rise in unemployment by purging ineligibles from the rolls, although he anticipated that by December, the PWA's construction projects would be lightening the relief load.[10]

Gradually, however, his optimism faded. In July he had estimated that the NIRA might create 6 million jobs by the end of the year, not only solving the relief problem but also reducing the need for new PWA projects. But that did not happen. The number of relief recipients held steady through the summer and fall while relief costs increased as clients stayed on longer, welfare standards were upgraded, and prices rose. At the same time, many states reached the limits of their ability to tax and to borrow. Even more important, the PWA was not taking hold. Secretary Ickes's pinchpenny supervision had limited expenditures to a trickle. As winter approached, when warm weather construction projects would close down and the fall harvests would be in, the relief situation seemed likely to get worse instead of better.

These facts seemed particularly compelling to key members of Hopkins's staff. One was Aubrey Williams, a redheaded Alabamian with rugged features. Williams had had a long career in social work, primarily in Wisconsin. Hopkins first appointed him field representative for the southern states but then brought him to Washington because he admired the way he had fought local political bosses' efforts to convert relief into a patronage machine. Williams had started out as a strong supporter of work relief and direct federal administration. By October he believed that an unemployment crisis was fast approaching.

So did the head of FERA's work relief division, Jacob Baker. A man of tremendously diverse experience (he had been a miner, a cowboy, an industrial engineer, a business consultant, and a book publisher), Baker had organized the Emergency Exchange Association to promote barter among New York City's unemployed. When he joined FERA to head the work relief division, he brought along his associate Arthur ("Tex") Goldschmidt. From the beginning their job was a tough one. FERA regulations limited the kind of projects they could undertake and, even more frustrating, forbade spending money for supervision and materials. As a result many of their projects were meaningless make-work efforts (such as raking leaves in public parks) or small-scale projects that depended on volunteer supervision and donations. That fall Goldschmidt went to Rexford Tugwell, a member of Roosevelt's brain trust and now vice chairman of the PWA, to propose that the PWA provide funds for project supervision and materials. Tugwell liked the idea, and in mid-October Baker proposed asking the PWA for $2 million.[11]

But Hopkins was doubtful. The problem with work relief, he told Aubrey Williams, was that organized labor opposed federal employment programs that competed with union jobs. Williams suggested that they ask John R. Commons, the noted labor economist of the University of Wisconsin, for his advice. Hopkins sent Williams to Madison and in the meantime prepared to leave town himself. He was to give a speech in Kansas City, and he planned to stop on the way to visit President Robert Hutchins of the University of Chicago and to attend a football game on Saturday afternoon.

When Hopkins got off the train Saturday morning in Chicago,

Frank Bane and Louis Brownlow were there to meet him. He was well acquainted with Bane, who was head of the American Public Welfare Association. He had conferred with him during the early days of FERA and had recruited many of Bane's staff, including Aubrey Williams. Brownlow, who headed a clearing house that provided the latest information on public administration, had helped Bane set up state relief organizations. They had been sent to Chicago by Williams, who had urged them to impress on Hopkins the critical nature of the relief situation and to urge him to ask Roosevelt to approve a work program immediately. Their discussions carried through lunch with President Hutchins. Hopkins acknowledged that conditions were serious, but he was hesitant to approach Roosevelt before he had a definite proposal to offer. He imagined that that would take two or three weeks.

But Hopkins was on a faster track than he realized. The next day Williams called to say that Professor Commons had found an old article in which Samuel Gompers, the founder of the American Federation of Labor, had endorsed government employment during times of depression. Elated, Hopkins invited Williams to accompany him to Kansas City, and the two talked things over on the night train from there to Chicago. When they arrived, Hopkins told Williams to draw up a memo for him to take to Roosevelt. Williams went off to a hotel, borrowed a stenographer from Bane, and drew up a plan for federally financed projects for the able-bodied unemployed. Under his plan the federal government would offer jobs to people solely because they were out of work and not because they qualified for relief. Instead of being investigated and supervised like dependents, they would be hired and supervised like employees. Money for the program would come from the Public Works Administration.[12]

It had taken a while to get Hopkins moving, but now he was ready for action. Returning to Washington, he scheduled a luncheon appointment with President Roosevelt for Thursday, November 2. When he explained the plan, Roosevelt approved it and told him to get it under way in thirty days. Hurriedly, Hopkins called Williams, Baker, Bane, Brownlow and others who had promoted the idea to tell them the good news. "You mean the President has approved that project?" Brownlow gasped. "Approved it, hell," Hopkins shot back, "he has just announced it at his press conference."[13]

They plunged into all-night planning sessions, aiming to announce the details at a national conference of governors and mayors on

November 15. Aubrey Williams remembered that the first night they scrawled a code of rules on four sheets of stationery in the Powhatan Hotel in downtown Washington. The next day they huddled in Hopkins's unheated office. So it went, until just before their deadline they produced the details for what Baker named the Civil Works Administration (CWA).

In the meantime Hopkins was rounding up the funds. He had originally proposed to spend $600 million—$350 million from FERA, $250 million from the PWA—to last four and a half months. Subsequently it was decided to have the PWA transfer $400 million to carry the CWA to February 15, 1934.[14]

By mid-November Hopkins was in high gear. He created the CWA's administrative machinery by federalizing all FERA state relief organizations and ordered them to transfer employable relief clients to CWA projects. He assigned them hiring quotas and warned that if they did not fill them by the middle of December, he would reassign the quotas elsewhere. He arranged to use the facilities of the Veterans' Administration to mail out paychecks. He told Baker that as soon as his office worked out a form for states to propose work projects, he wanted an application approved and ready for his signature that same evening.[15]

All this frantic activity produced astonishing results. Hopkins had proposed to employ 4 million people, half from the relief rolls. By November 23, over 800,000 were on CWA jobs; two weeks later 2 million were employed and by mid-January, the high point, 4.25 million. Because most of the CWA's funds came from the PWA, which had been set up as a construction agency, typical projects included street and road repair, sewage and water works, building repair and construction, and recreation projects. Hopkins also found FERA money to fund such white-collar projects as statistical surveys, preservation of public records, artistic decoration of public buildings, manuscript editing, indexing, and translating. In order to avoid projects of the kind that had given FERA a bad name, he forbade such make-work as street sweeping, snow shoveling, and leaf raking.[16]

The CWA experience confirmed the trend in Hopkins's thinking about the significance of the New Deal. The CWA advanced the process of converting relief from a retail to a wholesale operation, broadened its scope, and thus institutionalized Hopkins's belief that the New Deal was being prosecuted for the "average American," and that the unemployed, "the finest people in America," ought to be judged by the standards of their performance rather than the standards of the relief investigator. "Psychologically," Hopkins admonished CWA administrators, "we have got at one stroke, to divorce ourselves from . . . an inquiring point of view . . . in the terms of investigating each man as to whether or not he is in need of relief. This had to be done and I have no apologies to make for it. We have got to divorce ourselves quickly from that point of view and think in terms of affirmative action, in terms of real jobs for these people." He admitted the weakness of FERA. "We feel pretty humble . . . We have had the power [to do this] now for several months . . . and I don't think we have done very much with it."

The CWA had freed him to think in larger terms. The time had come, he declared, when every American citizen should have a right to a job, guaranteed if necessary by the national government. After all, nothing was more important than taking care of peoples' "elemental needs." Quibblers and naysayers gave him "a pain." The needy were citizens and sons and grandsons of citizens.[17]

As Hopkins saw it, the CWA further justified the federal system of relief management. It had been able to get under way rapidly because of the state systems already established under FERA. The more it was run by state and local agencies, the better he liked it. In January, Hopkins lectured Roosevelt's National Emergency Council to beware of centralizing power in Washington. Centralized control carried the risks of great expense, of turning what was intended to be a temporary program into a permanent one, and of inviting charges that the administration was creating a political machine. "No relief committees in the United States have been appointed from Washington," he observed. "They have all been appointed by local people. We join money with them. I would hate to see that become centralized."

If, as his early remarks indicated, Hopkins was thinking that the CWA might become a permanent part of the New Deal, he soon found that Roosevelt had other ideas. Roosevelt steadfastly resisted all efforts to expand federal activities, demanding that the CWA end on schedule. It was an emergency measure. To continue it would be to admit that his recovery program had failed and the depression was permanent. Instead he looked for an economic upturn in the spring.

Hopkins was willing to go along. The key to the success of the CWA, he told the emergency council, was to avoid letting the president down. In this sense relief was "a political matter," though one that still required expert management. He was willing to accept Roosevelt's faith in an economic recovery, but elsewhere in the administration he found widely differing opinions. Sound planning required a consensus, a "meeting of the minds."[18]

His eye for detail and his desire to foster agreement behind a course of action would serve Hopkins well throughout his years in Washington. At the moment, the CWA was also teaching him to have the courage of his convictions. The program had opened to a burst of praise and enthusiasm. From around the country came reports that public officials were relieved to see suffering and discontent subside. The unemployed had gotten a new lease on life and were grateful for it. Shortly, however, complaints began to pour in—that local political bosses were reserving jobs for their supporters, that administrators were using their patronage of the unemployed as a springboard for election to office, that union leaders were getting preferential treatment for their members or were requiring new workers to join their unions and pay half their salaries for "back dues," that blacks were not being hired, that people laid off CWA jobs were being refused relief, that CWA wages were so high that workers were refusing to move on to jobs in private enterprise.[19]

These complaints created a challenge for Hopkins. If work relief was a political issue, one way to keep it from harming the president was to enforce the rules and bolster the able administrators. He instructed all his field employees to send to headquarters for forwarding to the Justice Department any documents and affidavits disclosing "alleged fraudulent activities." He ordered his Wisconsin administrator to remove officials appointed for political considerations; when the man delayed, he replaced him. He responded to evidence of political interference and bad management in Los Angeles by appointing Lieutenant Colonel Donald Connolly of the Army Corps of Engineers to head the CWA there. When the governor of Georgia interpreted an earlier agreement with Hopkins as allowing him to remove an experienced administrator and twelve purchasing agents and replace them with inexperienced political supporters, Hopkins took over Georgia's relief operation and placed it under Gay Shepperson, the former secretary of the state's relief department. When reporters asked him if he intended to wear a sheepskin coat made on a CWA project that had been given him, he said, "That would be graft," and added that he would give it to his public relations administrator so he could be "a walking advertisement for us."[20] In the end his investigations turned up few serious abuses. For an emergency program that had been rushed into operation, the CWA was remarkably well managed.[21]

While Hopkins's administrators were doing their jobs properly, he did everything he could to protect them from political manipulation. His most celebrated tussle occurred in California, where Democratic Senator William G. McAdoo, son-in-law of the late President Wilson and candidate for the Democratic presidential nomination in 1924, accused CWA administrator Ray Branion, a Republican, of inefficiency and political favoritism. Hopkins replaced Branion with one of his own field representatives, but in the end McAdoo succeeded in bringing charges against them both.[22]

These problems were nettling enough. But Hopkins's major difficulty was that the CWA's costs were overrunning its budget. This was largely because Hopkins had decided that, having taken most of his money from the Public Works Administration, he would have to adopt the PWA wage scale. As a result costs rose from $4.25 per week per person under FERA to $15 per person. Early in January, Hopkins confessed to Roosevelt that the CWA could not pay its way past mid-February. Roosevelt "blew up" at the news and forced Hopkins to cut back the program and juggle FERA funds to make up the shortage. By the end of the month the president had relented to the extent of asking Congress for an additional appropriation to carry the CWA through March, but he ordered Hopkins to use the money to liquidate its operations.[23]

Satisfying Roosevelt meant keeping the lid on public protests against closing the CWA so that Congress would not be pressured into keeping it going. Hopkins began by working out a schedule to lay off workers with other financial resources. He responded to protest picketing in New York City by keeping five thousand people employed on white-collar projects. In order to avoid leaving unsightly, partially finished projects, he agreed to pay all bills contracted before the cutoff date and to make supplemental grants to finish those not originally contracted under CWA authority.[24]

Thus the CWA ended. It had not substantially altered either the New Deal or Hopkins's place in it, although it had set the stage for those changes. Most decisively, it had confirmed for Hopkins the value of work relief. He now threw himself into reforming FERA along these lines. With his staff he developed FERA's work division to in-

clude CWA-style projects (in part so that FERA could finish uncom-
pleted CWA efforts) and added substantial categories (15 percent
each) for constructing low-income housing and producing consumer
goods for the unemployed.

Above all, Hopkins was determined to follow the CWA's example by
pursuing "socially useful" projects. Each state staff was instructed to
employ an engineer "experienced in civic or industrial planning or
both" to outline the projects and supervise their development. Nothing bothered him more than comments that his agency produced only
make-work. When a reporter used the phrase in a press conference, he
cut him off and held up a brochure containing pictures of CWA projects. "I am very sensitive about this so-called 'made work.' Now, that is
a building and a park in Texas. It was all done by CWA work, all the
stone was quarried by CWA; it was laid out by CWA, by CWA ar-
chitects. Now, do you call that 'made work'?"

"I was only using that phrase in the popular sense. It is a popular
term."

"I know, but I mean real, genuine jobs of social benefit."[25]

If the CWA redirected Hopkins's thinking about relief, it also
refined his administrative skills. Until the fall of 1933 he had run
FERA cautiously, keeping within Roosevelt's guidelines. The prod-
ding of Williams and Baker and Roosevelt's sudden decisiveness, however, had forced him to subordinate caution to action, to do what he
had said all along was needed. In setting up the CWA, he reapplied the
lessons of his early Red Cross days and established his reputation as a
man who got things done. "You heard what the president said this
morning," he told his staff as the CWA was getting under way, "We
know we can get four million men to work. It is a matter that can be
done, even if we have to cut some corners."[26]

Hopkins was convinced that there was an inverse relation between
accomplishment and formality. Describing FERA's work program, he
told reporters: "The only thing that counts is action, what we actually
do in cities, states and counties . . . This program is going to have
action and we are going to surround it with as few regulations as
possible."[27]

Of course Hopkins could not avoid regulations. Over the years his
agencies' booklets, pamphlets, orders, and letters achieved formidable
proportions. Still, throughout his career Hopkins was one bureaucrat
who consciously avoided chains of command that limited his informa-

tion to what a few subordinates wanted him to hear. He sent unofficial observers into the field and learned as much as he could from informal conversations. Almost anyone with a project to suggest found him attentive. One person remembered that Hopkins once came to lunch to discuss water and land projects in the western states and, after saying that he could spare only fifteen minutes, stayed an hour and a half, "leaning over the table and looking me in the eye with his black shining eyes and alert face, eager to get my viewpoint." "Naturally," he concluded, "you lean to a man who seems so eager to get [a] clear understanding." Another man similarly remembered Hopkins's "immediate comprehension" of his plan to publish a Universal Jewish Encyclopedia and his own joy as Hopkins escorted him out, putting his arm around his shoulders and telling him he wanted to take every rabbi, clergyman, and professor off the relief rolls and put them on the project.[28]

Hopkins ran his own office by group discussion. He encouraged his staff to think less about protecting their individual spheres of influence than about carrying out FERA's general mission. He wanted ideas to flourish, not egos. "I don't want anybody around here to waste his time drawing boxes," he declared. "You'll always find that the person who drew the chart has his name in the middle box." "He did not want charts," one of his administrators later recalled. "We did not have written procedures. We had to manage for our Chief to get the job done."[29]

Among his own staff Hopkins's methods generated a sense of common purpose and cooperation. "He never hesitated to have any subject or problem that affected the activities of the organization discussed freely in his office," recalled John Carmody, who assisted Jake Baker in the works division. Hopkins generated "a great comradery." People arrived at 8:00 A.M. and worked through lunch. Between 8:00 and 10:00 P.M. they went to dinner, small groups meeting to review the day's events. Hopkins would call meetings at any time and take it for granted that everyone would attend. Whenever Carmody tried to visit his family in New York, he was rarely home for more than an hour or two before he got a telephone call asking him to return to Washington. "There were no private problems there," he recalled. "Everybody knew what everybody else's problem was."[30]

In order to succeed, this method of operation required leadership. Hopkins personally approved all hirings, signed all grants and letters of instruction, demanded investigations of wrongdoing, and, most important, advanced one project after another. "I take it for granted," he wrote, "that this whole railroad-transient program is well taken care of." "Please see Mr. Stone about getting women to work in Idaho and Arizona in the light of increased quotas." "Has the South Dakota quota been fixed in light of the drought situation?" In meetings he guided discussion toward a consensus if possible, or at least to the point of clarifying the issues. Then he would make his decision.[30]

Those who worked closely with him rated Hopkins's methods as nothing less than genius. John Carmody recalled: "To me he was a very inspiring personality. He was energetic, resourceful . . . He was, whatever anybody else may think of him, an excellent executive. I can't imagine anyone who could have gotten more done with that program than he got done." Years later Jake Baker summarized his experience. "The thing that breaks frustration and fear," he wrote Hopkins, "is creative effort. I know you believe that, and . . . you have a rare ability for releasing it in other people. You told us year after year that we have to take leadership in meeting tough problems—we have to keep alive to new ideas—and we have to do it fast."[31]

Reporters pictured Hopkins as a superb administrator, a go-getter who arrived at the office early, stayed late, and kept a hectic schedule of nonstop conferences. He was also mild mannered, almost retiring. Feature stories made much of his humble origins, suggesting that the experiences of his youth, along with his training in professional welfare work, especially qualified him to understand the plight of the unemployed. "Few men in the country," one columnist declared, "have the specialized knowledge of relief problems, and the technique of administration, which he has, and President Roosevelt knew that if he could get Hopkins he would get the right man for one of the biggest jobs ever undertaken by the Federal Government."

On Christmas Eve 1933 the *Denver Post* ran a full-page interview with Hopkins, including a flattering pen-and-ink portrait, under the headline

AMERICA WILL NOT STARVE
Says
HARRY L. HOPKINS
Federal Emergency
Relief Administrator

The article quoted Hopkins's desire to upgrade relief standards, to help poor children get the necessary nutrition, to help transients, and to substitute work relief for direct relief. "He believes," the reporter concluded, "that taking care of the millions of Americans who have been plunged by the depression from self-support to relief dependency is one of America's greatest responsibilities."[33]

While he was assuring others, Hopkins was feeling assurances of his own. Of these none was more valuable than his steady confidence in President Roosevelt. He concluded a memorandum on the CWA appropriation with a personal note telling the president "what a great privilege it has been to work under you . . . because of the renewed hope and courage as well as tangible benefits which you have brought to millions of people."[34]

John Kingsbury had described Hopkins as a changed man. What he had seen was the awakening in Hopkins of a great love for government service. Hopkins expressed this feeling in various ways. He wrote his brother Lewis that it was "worth any amount of money to have a ringside seat at this show." In a speech before the Citizens League of Cleveland he called upon Americans to make it a badge of honor to be a public servant. He derided as "insidious . . . propaganda" the charge that people worked for the government only because they were lazy, incompetent, or politically ambitious. "I want to say this," he told the Citizens League: "One of the proudest and finest things that ever happened and ever can happen to me is the opportunity to work for this government of ours and the people who make it up. This is a great country. . . . I wouldn't give this last two years of my life for a life work done in another type of endeavor. I have learned, as I never knew before, what it means to love your country."[35]

# Chapter 5

# Launching the WPA

By the mid-thirties Harry, Barbara, and their baby daughter, Diana, had settled into the life of New Deal Washington. When he first arrived, Harry lived for a month at the Mayflower Hotel. But when Barbara joined him, they moved into a red brick house in the secluded Georgetown area of northwest Washington. By the end of 1933 they had moved into the city, taking rooms at the Kennedy-Warren Apartments on Connecticut Avenue.

In these surroundings they were able to lead a conventional family life. "Leisurely breakfast with Barbara," Harry noted in his diary. "Sunday breakfast is the finest institution in America—will be observed every day when the state is organized properly." Barbara was at first a worshipful wife, blind to his faults, proud of his achievements, and devoted to giving him love and comfort. These things she accomplished with persistent optimism, an unaffected, loving nature, and a kind of naive self-acceptance that she demonstrated by caricaturing her emotions as faces drawn in her letters. Not even Harry's long hours at the office and frequent trips out of town dampened her spirits. "Harry and I are still in love," she wrote her aunt Myrta Bradley, "and if the time ever comes when we can see anything of each other we'll be just as happy as we always have been."

Such patient, loving optimism had its limits, however, and it was soon tested by Harry's chronic financial malady. With half of his $8,000 salary going to Ethel, Harry's new family had to set up housekeeping in difficult circumstances. The Tuberculosis and Health Association had proposed to bolster his government salary by contributing a year's pay in gratitude for his ten years' service, but the association's own financial problems forced it to cancel the arrangement. Barbara, who wanted to provide an attractive and comfortable home, and who felt justly proud of her husband's accomplishments and his opportunity in Washington "to make a name for himself," grew frustrated and angry.[1]

*Barbara Hopkins, c. 1934*

Inevitably, Barbara encouraged Harry to consider other professional possibilities. They had come to Washington expecting to stay no more than a year. As the relief emergency continued, the time came to make choices. A quiet person who shunned publicity and the Washington social scene, Barbara hoped that Harry would accept Jesse Straus's offer to join R. H. Macy. Harry talked the matter over with his staff, who feared that his successor might be less desirable. When FERA's assistant administrator C. M. Bookman alerted John Kingsbury and his fellow social work executive Homer Folks, they approached the Milbank Fund, the Russell Sage Foundation, and the Tuberculosis and Health Association, and raised enough money to supplement Hopkins's salary by $5,000 a year until 1936, when his government pay was increased to $12,000.[2]

It is hard to believe that money alone would have persuaded Hopkins to leave Washington. It would have been out of character for him to abandon an unfinished job. His growing self-confidence and commitment to government service reinforced his determination. Still, his love for Barbara and his insecurities as a provider were a powerful force too. In the end he concluded that sooner or later the uncertainties of government life would cause him to leave the administration.[3] Caught between conflicting values, he would let events decide.

Encouraging him to stay on was his growing intimacy with White House insiders. He became closely attached to Louis Howe, Roosevelt's adviser, mentor, and confidant. During the campaign Howe had urged Roosevelt to appeal to "the little man," the average American who was suffering from the economic collapse. With Roosevelt in office he pursued this theme, discussing FERA policies and political problems and the prospects for establishing a permanent federal relief administration. Hopkins delighted in Howe's support and irreverent wit but probably did not gain much support for his cause. As Howe's biographer Alfred B. Rollins, Jr., has shown, Howe never understood the New Deal as a whole and was more concerned with political strategy than with recovery programs.[4]

Hopkins found a more important champion in Eleanor Roosevelt, who continued to offer suggestions about relief projects. Hopkins did not accept them all, but he and Mrs. Roosevelt conferred frequently and found that they shared common values. Both defined economic distress in human terms, as hungry stomachs, bare feet, strained and shattered families, lost self-esteem, lost hope. Both thought less about the restraints of established procedures and institutional systems than about the need to solve the problem. It was at this point that Harry surpassed Eleanor. She wanted only to do "something"; he was able to examine her ideas critically and to turn the useful ones into reality. Thus he gained her confidence and respect. At her behest, Harry and Barbara were invited to White House social events, cruises, and weekends at Hyde Park and Campobello.[5]

Still, Hopkins's prospects with the New Deal did not depend on Louis Howe or Eleanor Roosevelt. He advanced because unemployment remained a serious national problem and because his resourceful administration gave Roosevelt the kind of results he wanted. As the CWA drew to a close, Roosevelt showed his increased respect for Hopkins by assigning him to investigate ways to help cities with their credit problems, in part so that they could raise money to pay their share of relief costs. He assigned him to help draft a bill establishing a federal housing program. Most important, he appointed him to a Cabinet-level committee to devise an unemployment insurance and pension system. In contrast to other New Deal programs, the initiative to create an insurance fund to aid the unemployed had come from Congress, where New York's Senator Robert Wagner and Maryland representative David J. Lewis had sponsored legislation (the Wagner-

Lewis bill) to require employers to contribute to state insurance funds. In the spring of 1934 Roosevelt endorsed the bill but deferred action until after the fall elections by creating a Committee on Economic Security, composed of Hopkins, Secretary of Labor Frances Perkins, Secretary of the Treasury Henry Morgenthau, Secretary of Agriculture Henry Wallace, and Attorney General Homer Cummings. In late June, Hopkins arranged quarters for the committee's technical staff in the Walker-Johnson Building and then left with Barbara for six weeks in Europe.

Officially Hopkins was going to Europe to gather information on low-income housing and unemployment insurance. Unofficially, Roosevelt had sent him because he was concerned that Hopkins was over-working. Harry and Barbara sailed from New York on July 4 aboard the large and luxurious SS *Washington*. After a voyage on which they were honored as special guests of the captain, they docked in Plymouth. Their itinerary took them from London to Berlin, Vienna, Rome, and Paris. Harry attended a number of conferences and concluded that Americans could profit from studying European housing programs but that they should establish their own insurance system. He did find it instructive, however, that "everywhere" people opposed cash benefits unless the unemployed did some useful work in return.[6]

Overshadowing these issues was the ominous political situation in central Europe. In Germany, Adolf Hitler's Nazi party, not quite a year in power, had been convulsed the previous month by a bloody purge. While Hopkins was in Germany, Nazis in Austria assassinated Premier Engelbert Dollfuss, and tensions ran high as German and Italian troops concentrated along their Austrian borders. These events so occupied Hitler's time that he was unavailable for his interview with Hopkins—an event that Hopkins would later capitalize on by claiming that he had refused to "shake hands with a murderer." However distasteful such a meeting might have proved to Hopkins, one wonders what he would have made of the Führer, especially in light of his graphic observations of his visit with another of Europe's malefactors, Italy's Fascist dictator Benito Mussolini.

Hopkins arrived at the Palazzio Venezia one July evening and was ushered past uniformed guards flashing the Fascist salute. A guard led him up a dark inner stairway to a green-tiled reception room containing "a few old pictures" and Venetian pottery in a display case. He saw a woman dressed in black and carrying a basket of flowers; but before he could ask about her a guard in civilian clothes led him through more rooms until he entered Mussolini's huge office. Here was Il Duce striding toward him, gray suit, light blue tie, soft shirt. At once Mussolini took control with a firm handshake and then marched back to his desk and motioned for Hopkins to sit.

In like fashion Mussolini took charge of the conversation. Hopkins had come to talk about housing and public works, but Il Duce wanted to talk about Germany and Hitler. He pumped Hopkins for information about the purge, the public reaction, the opinion of the foreign colony in Berlin, Hopkins's own reaction to Hitler's speech. Mussolini thought that Hitler had blundered, that he had shown himself to be a weak man whose actions would isolate Germany from the civilized world and bring down his government. Hopkins had heard that Mussolini disliked Hitler, but he was not prepared for such open contempt.

While Mussolini talked, Hopkins sized him up. The Italian was a study in animation, rolling his eyes, gesturing with arms and hands, flashing quick smiles, focusing discussion by planting his elbows on the table, resting his head in his hands, and firing comments "like sharp knives." He was an actor dominating the stage, telegraphing emotions with "great effect." In him Hopkins saw "the face of a strong man and a personality of great power."[7]

Hopkins's observations were revealing in that they showed the importance he attached to force of character, the ability to control a situation. Of course most would now conclude that Il Duce's acting abilities far exceeded any actual force of character, and that misjudging Adolf Hitler was in him—and in a distressingly large number of his contemporaries—a grievous shortcoming. But this was a season for misjudgments. When Hopkins was in London a reporter looked him up and then dashed off a piece characterizing him as quiet and unassuming with neither "push" nor "side" and for good measure confusing his name with that of the American motion picture comedy star Harold Lloyd.[8] Six and a half years later in the midst of the Blitz, Hopkins would return in a way that would pointedly dispel any impression of weakness.

By the time of his return to Washington, the circumstances that would correct such misimpressions were beginning to take shape. Hopkins had already started to assert himself in New Deal politics. He admired politicians as people who took chances and submitted their record to the voters, and this had guided him toward a synthesis of

politics and administration. In the 1920s he had fought for professionalism in social work, in part as a way of taking issues out of the
hands of politicians and giving them to trained experts. Now, however, he was coming to realize that the distinction between administrators and politicans was a false one. FERA had not taken relief out of
politics. Anything that directly touched the lives of millions was a
political issue. If Hopkins proved inept, he would discredit the New
Deal. If he were to succeed, he would need political backing from
elected officeholders who believed in the New Deal and would support
its relief programs.

In any case, attacks by Republicans were putting him in politics
whether he wanted to be there or not. Although a few Republicans
endorsed the New Deal, the core of the party, joined by dissident
Democrats including Al Smith, who formed the American Liberty
League, labeled the New Deal a combination of fuzzy idealism, impractical experimentation, Russian Bolshevism, and corrupt, cynical
manipulation. They predicted that it would either destroy the country
or lock it into dictatorial regimentation. Hopkins's relief programs,
they charged, were expensively mismanaged and politically manipulated, and benefited "chiselers" who were not eligible for relief.

By the fall, however, another line of attack was hitting especially
close to home. Critics were arguing that FERA enticed people away
from private employment and even encouraged them not to accept
jobs when they were available. These charges confronted Hopkins with
a difficult half-truth. Indeed, more and more Americans now believed
that relief was not a sign of failure or disgrace. Some even looked for
status in comparing their relief stipends. But if the critics thought it
wrong to seek security in relief, they overlooked the fact that the
depression had generated a rational distrust of private employment.
Many *felt* more secure on relief because they *were* more secure. To
manage scarce funds properly, Hopkins had to investigate relief applicants and encourage those on relief to take private jobs. These rigorous
investigations, however, caused recipients to fear that if they took
private jobs, they might never get back on relief. And although Hopkins did want to clear the rolls, he did not want to force workers into
the hands of "unscrupulous" employers who paid "starvation" wages.[9]
Thus the relief system created areas of uncertainty and as a result
opened itself to differences of opinion and partisan attack.

Although Hopkins tried to explain these complexities, he took a strong public stand against his critics. He had "never found a private employer yet who was unable to employ a worker on the relief rolls provided he offered him a regular job." He corrected a press release, saying that it was an "allegation" rather than a "fact" that farmers were having trouble hiring workers, and he rewrote a passage stating that men "preferred" relief to "offered" jobs to say that some able-bodied men were "receiving" relief when jobs "were available."[10] Hopkins backed up this rhetoric by requiring states to release relief clients for seasonal labor, and he made sure that this rule was enforced.

"Have you pretty much cut relief in the cotton counties?" he asked Thad Holt, the relief director in Alabama.

"We sent out a bulletin that we will expect cotton pickers to accept jobs offered," Holt responded.

"Are you really making them do it?"

"We made a rule: no work, no relief."

"I think it is very important [that] the people offered work on cotton picking get off the relief rolls . . . I think one way to do it would be to cut down the money given the cotton counties."

"It [has been cut] about twenty-three percent."

"Could you cut it more?"

"I guess we could . . . The only reason we have any cotton pickers on relief today is because landlords have signed affidavits that they could not take care of that family, so we took it on relief."

"Write me a letter on what you are doing on cotton. We are getting a good deal of pressure about that."[11]

Hopkins responded similarly to attacks on FERA's policy of giving relief to workers on strike. The year 1934 witnessed several strikes around the country as unions sought to take advantage of a provision in the National Industrial Recovery Act (NIRA) that encouraged workers to form their own unions to bargain collectively with their employers. In July 1933 Hopkins had ruled that strikers were eligible for relief unless the Department of Labor determined that the strike was "unreasonable and unjustified." No sooner had he returned from Europe than Roosevelt put him in charge of handling a textile workers' strike in Alabama. He told the press, "We are certainly not underwriting any of these strikes," and ordered his staff to limit all public discussion to reciting FERA policy. "This thing is a political issue and the Republicans are using it all over the country," said Hopkins, "and I want to be sure we do nothing that gives them anything to hang on."

He even ordered FERA not to account for its payments to strikers separately but to include them in its general relief accounts. FERA, he declared, did not deal with "strikers as such."[12]

Controlling publicity about controversial issues led to a general supervision of information. Hopkins became convinced that FERA needed "a complete centralization of mail going out." "Our organization here is so complex," he declared, "that there are all kinds of conflicting information going to the States." He was "beginning to understand why Ickes has all mail go over his desk." That fall he instituted a central filing system and procedures to investigate all press charges of wrongdoing as soon as they appeared.[13]

By this time Hopkins was trying to play politics on a larger scale. Roosevelt had staffed the New Deal with a combination of conservative and liberal Democrats, and Hopkins counted himself among the liberals. As professional social workers, he and other members of his FERA staff had long fought for legislation to protect children, to improve living conditions for the poor, and to support the unemployed. Some had taken up other social reforms. Aubrey Williams had fought for tenant farmers in the South, and Jake Baker had worked as a common laborer, had championed the cause of the working man, and had promoted self-help cooperatives for the economically distressed. Lawrence Westbrook, who headed rural relief programs, had helped organize cooperatives and local industries in Texas.

Hopkins entered liberal circles in the fall of 1933, when he and Aubrey Williams began attending informal meetings with a group from the Department of Agriculture, including Paul Appleby (whom Hopkins had known at Grinnell College), Gardner Jackson, Lee Pressman, Jerome Frank, and Rex Tugwell. They discussed various projects to help the poor, from self-help and production for use to ways of increasing the farmer's share in government contracts. The most trenchant ideas came from Tugwell. The New Deal was attempting to increase farm income and to stabilize industry by limiting production to increase prices. Roosevelt had also tried to increase prices by manipulating the price of gold. The NIRA also gave manufacturers certain price-fixing powers. This approach, Tugwell thought, defined recovery solely in terms of higher prices without taking into account the hardships caused by resulting increases in the cost of living. Instead of increasing prices, he thought, the New Deal should encourage a low-price, high-production economy.[14]

Hopkins sympathized with Tugwell's ideas since higher prices complicated his relief job. By mid-1934 FERA was estimating that in the past year relief benefits had increased 12 to 15 percent, while food prices had increased 20 percent. Higher prices also hampered work relief by increasing the cost of materials and supervision.[15]

Tugwell's analysis justified work relief, which expanded production as well as purchasing power. In any case there seemed to be no way to avoid the relief issue. Although employment was picking up, the relief rolls were growing. People on relief had been unemployed for a long time, during which they had exhausted their private resources, and their job skills had deteriorated, while new jobs had gone to those more recently laid off or to young workers just entering the job market. At the same time older workers were postponing retirement to maintain their income, and as prices increased, many retired people who depended on fixed incomes from rents or investments were going on relief.

That fall Hopkins tried to persuade Roosevelt to articulate a New Deal philosophy along Tugwell's lines, but he found the president reluctant. With the fall elections coming up, Roosevelt was looking for the broadest possible endorsement for the New Deal and seemed more inclined to conciliate his conservative critics than to battle them. Twice that fall the president invited Hopkins to represent the liberal side in meetings to present ideas for upcoming speeches. Hopkins's conservative counterpart was Raymond Moley. Formerly the guiding spirit of Roosevelt's brain trust, Moley had resigned as assistant secretary of state for a career in magazine publishing and was working to improve relations between Roosevelt and the business community. On both occasions Hopkins pressed Tugwell's ideas, but each time Roosevelt's speech emphasized Moley's.[16]

Nor did Hopkins fare better trying to advance the liberal cause elsewhere. On August 29 he endorsed the candidacy of Upton Sinclair for governor of California. A former socialist, Sinclair had organized a movement called End Poverty in California (EPIC) and the day before had won the Democratic primary nomination from the McAdoo organization. Hopkins had personal reasons for endorsing Sinclair. McAdoo's Democrats had tried to turn FERA into a patronage giveaway and were prosecuting his FERA administrators Ray Branion and Pierce Williams for fraudulent mismanagement. Also, Sinclair had en-

dorsed the idea of production for use by the unemployed, one of
FERA's favorite work relief programs.

"Would you call him a socialist?" a reporter asked Hopkins about
Sinclair.

"No," Hopkins replied, "he is a good Democrat."[17]

Roosevelt treated Sinclair gingerly, once inviting him to Hyde Park
for a friendly chat but then dropping him. In November, Sinclair lost
the election.

Roosevelt had given Hopkins the first of many lessons in how he
handled his subordinates. The president encouraged and solicited
opinions but on matters of grand strategy made up his own mind. He
valued people like Hopkins for their particular and not their general
skills: their views helped him to see the larger picture, and their special
talents helped him achieve his goals. Thus Roosevelt valued Hopkins
as his minister of relief, and in this role Hopkins exercised his greatest
influence. Hopkins and Roosevelt had reached agreement on the federal approach to relief. They believed that relief given in the traditional
way ultimately degraded and pauperized the recipient. They wanted to
get the federal government out of giving relief and into providing jobs
for the unemployed. That fall, while he was brushing aside Hopkins's
larger arguments to revise New Deal philosophy, Roosevelt was nonetheless defending work relief. "We must make it a national principle,"
he declared, "that we will not tolerate a large army of unemployed . . . I
do not want to think that it is the destiny of any American to remain
permanently on the relief roles."[18]

As Roosevelt spoke, the FERA was planning to expand its work
program by 4 million jobs. To meet the additional cost of $250 mil-
lion, assistant administrator Corrington Gill proposed to tap unal-
located balances from the Emergency Appropriation Act, the lion's
share of which was controlled by the Reconstruction Finance Corporation (RFC). Hopkins approached Roosevelt cautiously, proposing
only to pry loose enough funds to sustain his regular relief program
and saying that he would talk the matter over with Secretary of the
Treasury Henry Morgenthau before proposing ways to raise the extra
$250 million.[19]

Once again he found Roosevelt's response breathtaking. Instead of
approving Hopkins's modest program, the president proposed a wide-
ranging federal commitment to work relief. "The big boss is getting

ready to go places in a big way," he sang out to a PWA administrator in Ohio. As he described the details, his enthusiasm tumbled out:

"Three to five years and going strong by two years. We are talking of five billion a year actually spent."

"If you can get it done," the administrator replied.

"It can be done. We have to prove it. Also there is a throwing over of relief. You can help with this better than anyone in the country. No one could get this set up as [fast as] you with some of the technical people working with you. I think it is in the bag if we can get the right brief."

"Boys," Hopkins said as he and his staff were driving to the race track for an afternoon off, "this is our hour. We've got to get everything we want—a works program, social security, wages and hours, everything—now or never. Get your minds to work on developing a complete ticket to provide security for all the folks of this country up and down and across the board."[20]

To plan the program Roosevelt brought together the men with the greatest responsibilities in relief, public works, and budget: Hopkins, Ickes, and Morgenthau. As their discussions proceeded, Morgenthau played the dynamic role, challenging Ickes and Hopkins to spell out projects and precise costs. Gradually he forced the discussion toward a proposal that, with its sharply defined goals and procedures, would have some credibility with Congress and the public. Hopkins put his staff through hours and hours of preparing detailed charts, tables, and memoranda. In the end, however, Roosevelt simply asked Congress to appropriate $4 billion, and shift an additional $800 million from other agencies, for a works program that would provide useful jobs, pay a high proportion of project costs in salaries, offer a return to the Treasury, spend funds promptly, and employ people from the relief rolls, turning unemployables over to the care of the states.

Roosevelt's message was a turning point for the New Deal and Harry Hopkins. At first a temporary expedient, relief was becoming a recovery measure. By this time various people had suggested that a large works program would help economic recovery by stimulating consumer spending. An intermediate draft by FERA had declared that "the rule of recovery through government expenditures should be that government money automatically goes to the lowest economic strata because it is there that occurs automatically the greatest number of respendings . . . There can never be recovery as long as there are economic strata of people without money to buy security and to spend."[21] Elsewhere in the administration others such as Assistant Secretary of the Treasury Marriner Eccles were arguing along similar lines. By 1937 theirs would be the dominant voices around the president.

Roosevelt's decision would also redirect New Deal politics. The main impact of the works program would be in urban America, where its spending and employment would benefit the big city bosses. By the election of 1936 Hopkins would be the administration's principal liaison with the bosses.

These developments, however, were consequences of Roosevelt's message, not motives behind it. Instead of seeking a dramatic departure, Roosevelt was applying long-standing beliefs in new circumstances. He had always disliked home relief and in any case wanted it administered by state and local governments. He had hoped that relief of any kind would be temporary, but his recovery program had not taken hold sufficiently. He opposed government spending as a recovery measure, but he was not going to stand aside while the unemployed suffered. Hopkins became prominent in the New Deal because circumstances focused attention on the unemployment problem, not because Roosevelt was attracted to his personality or his liberalism.

Despite Hopkins's detailed planning, Roosevelt asked Congress for the $4.8 billion without spelling out a program. The first step toward achieving such a program was to define the relationship of work to the larger issue of worker security. At the same time that Roosevelt was considering the shift to work relief, the Committee on Economic Security was drawing up legislation for a comprehensive social security program. Hopkins and Tugwell had wanted unemployment insurance to take the form of a works program, but Labor Secretary Perkins argued for a cash benefit from a fund contributed to by workers and employers. When they debated the point with Roosevelt, the president, as usual, thought that the two approaches were complementary but that they should be presented separately to Congress. Accepting this decision, Hopkins explained to Congress that unemployment compensation would enable the recently unemployed to spend several weeks looking for a job. If they failed, they would become eligible for the works program, thus transforming the cash benefit into a work benefit.[22]

Hopkins could compromise with Perkins but not with Harold Ickes.

During the discussions for planning the works program, Morgenthau and Tugwell had thought that Hopkins and Ickes were less concerned about the mechanics than about the mechanic. Morgenthau asked Roosevelt to resolve the issue by putting one person in charge, but Roosevelt wanted consensus on the program and refused to do it. This did not stop Ickes from proposing, without success, that Hopkins come to work for him—with responsibilities for Ickes's most troublesome projects and thus with an excellent chance of falling flat on his face.[23]

Certain of Roosevelt's relief proposals—starting quickly, spending most of the money for salaries, and paying weekly wages—favored Hopkins's ideas. But by this time Hopkins realized that Roosevelt was going to do things his own way, so he waited until the president asked his advice about administrative procedures. He then proposed a structure, headed by the president himself and made up of separate agencies, to approve projects, publicize them, and carry them out. He specifically included a department to set up small works projects of the FERA and CWA variety. The size of the appropriation would rule out heavy construction, which required large outlays for materials and would thus not leave enough for wages. Hopkins also argued for a federal structure. The works program was going to stand or fall, he argued, on the strength of the local organizations that carried out the projects. Although these would report to a single authority in Washington, they ought to be given wide latitude.[24]

When Ickes countered with a scheme that emphasized central planning instead of local action, Roosevelt patched together an Advisory Committee on Allotments (under Ickes) to recommend projects for the president's final approval, a Works Progress Administration (under Hopkins) to make sure that the projects employed the largest amount of relief labor and to undertake its own small projects, and a Division of Application and Information (under Frank Walker, a longtime party man of singularly accommodating nature) to process applications for Ickes's committee. This last division was presumably designed to keep the peace between Ickes and Hopkins. Hopkins accepted the arrangement with his usual grace, though he complained that the name of his division was "terrible."[25]

At the first meeting of the allotments committee Roosevelt set the tone by stating that the program should emphasize employment. Hopkins followed up with maps and charts showing how to distribute projects to achieve this end. But Roosevelt's allocations machinery turned on its creator. Various federal agencies had representatives on hand to submit projects, and by the time the committee had accommodated them, it had used up about half the $4.8 billion, much of it for projects that offered insufficient employment. This bothered Roosevelt. When Ickes praised a sewage treatment project proposed for New York City, the president complained that it did not employ many people. Ickes responded that such projects were the only ones that would repay the Treasury under the president's rule that projects should generate funds to pay back their cost. Roosevelt gave way but asked that future proposals be sent to Hopkins for a check of the employment figures.[26]

From Hopkins's standpoint, this division of labor proved a poor bargain. He had expected that the Works Progress Administration (WPA) would employ two-thirds of all relief workers. Anticipating fast action, he had transferred FERA's works division to the WPA, and instructed his administrators to submit as many projects as possible and to approve the best ones on the spot. But Ickes continued to give money to PWA-type projects. As the allocations rolled through June, WPA was left on the sidelines. By the end of August, when the allotments committee completed its work, Hopkins had received only 20 percent of the nearly $3.5 billion allocated.[27]

As he watched the money flow to other agencies, Hopkins's frustration grew. By mid-June he was short-tempered. "I have no money down here," he barked at an inquiring caller from New York. "I have no appropriations. We can't make any commitment about what we can do." A month later he was complaining to Morgenthau that the emergency appropriation was funding projects that should have been paid out of regular appropriations, and that it would take $10 billion to "do the trick of putting people to work."[28]

Just as frustrating were administrative delays. Roosevelt required that state projects be approved through the WPA in Washington, then the allocations committee, then the president, and finally the Bureau of the Budget. If Budget approved, law required that the Comptroller General at the General Accounting Office (GAO) give his final approval.

As they ran this bureaucratic gauntlet, projects bumped up against conflicting definitions and categories. Terms understood at the WPA drew a blank in Budget or General Accounting. Also, the WPA and the GAO allocated funds for projects in a single state, but Budget allocated by regions. Although Budget's approach promised faster action, it often failed to deliver, since an irregularity in a single project could hold up the appropriation for an entire region. The major problem, however, was the lack of a staff to handle the flood of applications. The budget bureau assigned the job to a single assistant, who worked sixteen-hour days in an office stacked high with application forms. The GAO designated one officer and two assistants to review applications. The WPA tried to do better by creating a special applications division and working its staff in three shifts, but it was also overwhelmed. By mid-August it was reviewing $236 million in projects, compared to $197 million in Budget, and only $23 million had trickled through to the comptroller.[29]

Desperately Hopkins looked for a solution. He considered bypassing the comptroller by lending FERA funds to the states so that they could start their projects at once. In the end, however, he had to appoint a liaison to the GAO and to persuade Roosevelt to pressure the comptroller. Not until mid-October was the logjam broken. Another problem was less satisfactorily resolved. In July the comptroller canceled an earlier agreement allowing the WPA to shift funds from one project to another. This meant that unless a project had enough money to be completed, any additional allocation would have to go through the entire approval process. As a result, the WPA had to ask its administrators to propose a fully funded budget, a procedure that tied up funds and introduced a costly financial rigidity.[30]

Gradually, however, warrants squeezed through the bottlenecks and projects got under way. Immediately organized labor objected to the WPA security wage scale. Hopkins had done his best to accommodate labor. He had conferred with Frances Perkins, William Green, the president of the American Federation of Labor, and with other labor leaders and had received "as complete assurance as it is possible to get" that organized labor would agree to the WPA's paying monthly wages at less than the union rate. ("These labor fellows are pretty dumb," Hopkins complained after the meeting, "and Frances talks too much— A tough day in all.") When a union protest broke out in Montana, he advised his state administrator to "take on one or two labor men in your organization." But these efforts did not work. In New York City strikes broke out as the building trades demanded a union wage scale. The city's WPA administration, which was independent of the state's, was headed by General Hugh S. Johnson, an emotionally volatile man not inclined to overlook small irritations. The situation was further complicated by the fact that the AFL was preparing to hold its annual convention in nearby Atlantic City, and it seemed likely that resolutions against the security wage would be offered.[31]

Hopkins was in the Middle West when the crisis broke. He endorsed a plan for the Department of Labor to negotiate with the parties, bypassing General Johnson, who had proposed to go to Atlantic City and work things out with the AFL leadership. At first the outlook was hopeful. Work stoppages became sporadic, and Johnson cooperated by behaving diplomatically. Hopkins supported him when he denounced the strikers for interfering with relief and proposed to reinvestigate the eligibility of workers who walked off the job. Tough talk, he hoped, would induce many to stay at work. When Johnson charged that some of the striking unions were "led by communists," however, Hopkins snapped, "If there is any communistic crowd in the project, I would just close down that project." He considered asking for police protection for nonstrikers, reversing the policy he had established under the FERA.[32]

Then the situation got worse. The AFL Labor Council called a general strike against WPA projects. The United States Employment Service, citing Department of Labor policy, refused to certify new workers to replace those who had walked out. Hopkins asked Secretary Perkins to withdraw the department's sanction. If she refused, he said, he would have the WPA certify its own workers. After hesitating and complaining that she was "in a bad fix on this," she complied. The strikes ended, and work resumed.[33]

Many thought that Hopkins's tough stand had carried the day. But that was only part of the story. Behind the scenes he had told the AFL leadership that he would devise a formula to maintain union wage rates. On September 17, 1935, he conferred with Roosevelt and AFL leaders and two days later issued an order permitting state administrators to set workers' hours below the maximum level. This meant that although workers would still receive their monthly security wage, the shorter hours would bring their per-hour pay up to the prevailing union rate. The compromise also preserved flexibility for state administrators by permitting those not under union pressure to maintain intact the original wage system. When the majority of states did this, some in the WPA thought that Hopkins should get tough with the AFL and cancel the agreement. But Hopkins steadfastly refused, and asserted that whenever the unions sought adjustments for prevailing wages, the WPA would give way. His reasons were largely political. As the works program was getting under way, Sidney Hillman, president of the Amalgamated Clothing Workers, had warned him that Roosevelt was losing labor's support. (Later the Wagner Labor Relations Act committed the administration to support the trade union movement.) Hopkins believed that this adjustment would save President Roosevelt from a rebuff by the AFL convention. With an election year coming up, he was not going to do anything to offend labor.[34]

These compromises had placed the WPA on perilous ground. The allocations procedures had left the agency short of money while still needing to fund all of its projects fully. This shortage tied up funds and put pressure on state administrators to see that their projects proceeded on schedule. But adjusting hours downward in order to ensure prevailing wage rates had meant that less work was being done on the projects. Sooner or later Hopkins was going to be faced with a serious fiscal problem.

At the time, however, these developments were overshadowed by a contest between Hopkins and Ickes for control of the works program. The differences between the two had long since become apparent. Ickes favored centrally planned projects carried out under contract with high outlays for building materials. He had also proved to be a suspicious administrator and a stickler for proper procedure. Hopkins, by contrast, relied on his colleagues, tailored means to ends, and produced small projects operated by "force account" (that is, direct payments for wages and materials) and employing the largest number of workers possible. More than anything else, the two differed over ends. Ickes defined success in institutional terms: an honest and efficient program that helped the economy. Hopkins defined it in human terms: a program that restored people's security and self-confidence.

Not surprisingly, the two had different views of Roosevelt's purposes. Ickes thought that the president would naturally support an administrator who ran a good shop and built substantial projects that returned funds to the Treasury. Hopkins thought that Roosevelt wanted to emphasize works projects with high employment, and to put an end to federal relief. He was also more inclined than Ickes to study the president and tailor his responses accordingly. Thus he bided his time and tried to get along with Ickes, though occasionally he found him impossible to bear. "All day planning the work program," he wrote in a diary he kept infrequently during the first half of 1935, "which would be a great deal easier if Ickes would play ball—but he is stubborn and righteous which is a hard combination—he is the 'great resigner'—anything doesn't go his way, he threatens to quit. He bores me."[35]

Of course playing ball depended on how one understood the game. Hopkins was willing to accommodate Ickes to the extent of agreeing to guidelines that separated their projects. The Public Works Administration (PWA) would have charge of construction projects involving federal loans and costing more than $25,000. Many local officials preferred the WPA's rules, which required no specific contribution on their part, to the PWA's, which required them to put up 45 percent of the cost. But Hopkins held to the bargain. When a state administrator reported that some officials were transferring construction projects from the PWA to the WPA, Hopkins warned him not to "touch [them] with a ten foot pole . . . they shouldn't get away with that kind of stuff."

Still Hopkins would not sacrifice the works program's objectives. If a project fell into a gray area and was being delayed by the PWA, he was willing to redefine it for the WPA. He also encouraged local officials, like Chicago's Mayor Ed Kelly, to submit projects that met WPA specifications. "Ickes wants to get a lot more of this money and by implication take it away from me," he warned Kelly, "which would mean, I think, that the president would be left in a hell of a jam. Ickes is very much opposed to things like [your] road project."

"He wants to do something that would take two or three years," Kelly replied, getting Hopkins's line of thought.

"Yes, he wants that sewage, etc."

"Yes, or the airport."

"Yes, and the result is you never get anybody to work."

"You think," Kelly offered, "a wire [to Roosevelt] about that other thing would work out all right?" There were other projects that he wanted to get started.

"I think it would. It wouldn't tie up directly, but indirectly. Tell him how much money, how many it would put to work."[36]

Moves like this brought Hopkins's relations with Ickes to a flash point. By his quiet methods Hopkins not only took projects from Ickes but also acquired the authority to evaluate PWA projects to determine if they met the president's employment objectives. Using this criterion he turned down some two thousand PWA projects worth $375 million. In the meantime he arranged for grants to be given the WPA in lump sums to provide more flexibility in scheduling projects. This did not actually result in greater efficiency because the budget bureau and the GAO were still reviewing the projects, but to Ickes it seemed to be opening the door to waste and corruption.[37]

Inevitably tensions came to the boil. In the midst of the WPA's wage dispute, the PWA issued a press release congratulating itself on the success of its own wage policy. Hopkins complained to Roosevelt's press secretary Steve Early, "There seems to be a hell of a lot of this kind of stuff coming out of P.W.A. which doesn't help the gayety [*sic*] of the nation any." Before long Hopkins and Ickes were making slighting remarks about each other's programs at their press conferences. By early September, Washington was being flooded with letters—drafted, Hopkins suspected, by the PWA—complaining that Hopkins was undermining the PWA. Ickes was denouncing Hopkins to Roosevelt and preparing another letter of resignation. Under the circumstances, the president decided to invite both men to Hyde Park to settle accounts.[38]

Roosevelt's opening remarks showed that Hopkins had guessed right about the president's goals for work relief. The president emphasized his commitment to transfer 3.5 million people from the relief rolls to works projects during the coming fiscal year. He then estimated that funds that would not have been spent by July 1 plus funds yet to be allocated came to about $940 million. Next Roosevelt asked Hopkins to explain the employment situation. Hopkins estimated that by November nearly 2.1 million persons would be on relief. Roosevelt reduced the number to 1.7 million by assuming that a certain number would be unemployable. Then, taking the WPA's estimated cost of $65 per employee per month, he allotted Hopkins $777 million—80 percent of the $940 million. Ickes wound up with about $200 million, transferred from his agency's own housing program.[39]

Hopkins was entering Roosevelt's inner circle. A few weeks later Hopkins accompanied Roosevelt and others to San Diego, where they boarded the USS *Houston* for a vacation cruise through the Panama Canal to Charleston, South Carolina. This was Hopkins's first extended cruise with the president and, after a couple of days getting his sea legs, he came through in good style, joining in the activities and entertainments—fishing, sightseeing, poker, and movies.

For Hopkins the low point of the trip came on the second day, a Sunday. He was asleep on the deck when church services were announced and he was obliged to join Roosevelt and his party in the front row on the well deck. The hymns included "When the Roll is Called Up Yonder" and "Jesus Savior Pilot Me," gospel standards that probably brought back memories of his youth. Then came "a long-winded sermon from a bright, curly-haired and very obnoxious parson—who went in for home and mother in a big way—his metaphors were pointless—most of his statements weren't true—and when he urged those tough babies to read the New Testament and get their fun at the Navy Y.M.C.A. it was too much." But Roosevelt seemed pleased, so Hopkins "observed a discreet silence."[40]

Roosevelt had invited Ickes along as well, perhaps hoping that the relaxed pace and tropical climate would loosen tensions between the two men. Hopkins was willing to oblige. He and Ickes fished, swam, shopped, and conversed. Hopkins also joined other members of the party in putting out an "extra" edition of the ship's newspaper. A fine example of New Deal humor, it was lighthearted in tone, with mordantly satiric characterizations. One story reported that "signs of genuine activity" had been detected at the PWA, which was confidently predicting that a recently approved sewer project would be completed by 1945. "The only explanation given for this amazing burst of speed," it concluded, "was that the Secretary was at sea." A listing in the "Movie Programme" purported to star Roosevelt's aide Colonel Edwin M. ("Pa") Watson (who was somewhat overweight) in *The Love Life of an Elephant,* Roosevelt (who had been having good luck at the poker table) in *It Is My Pot or The Greedy Fisherman,* and Hopkins (who had suffered an early bout of seasickness) in *The Feeding of the Seas.* "He leaned over the boat," another item elaborated, "looked intently into the blue sea, and was too busy to even give the President a cigarette."

Two items focused on the Hopkins-Ickes rivalry, the first biting ("As we have watched this famous pair we are sure they will both go far and we are quite confident of the place—the ash can!"), the second conciliatory ("The feud between Hopkins and Ickes was given a decent burial today"). But hopes for a complete reconciliation were only wishful thinking. Throughout the rest of their association, Ickes continued to believe that Hopkins was fundamentally an unprincipled schemer.[41]

Schemer or not, Hopkins was now running work relief. He had won.

# Chapter 6

# "In the Interest of the People That Were Broke"

Hopkins returned from his cruise with the president to find his Washington staff in turmoil as they rushed to meet Roosevelt's goal of providing jobs for 3.5 million unemployed workers by the first of December. "dere boss," wrote his friend, the midwest regional director Howard Hunter (adopting the lower-case style of the popular poet Don Marquis), "the mice have been playing some while you and the other cats was away altho the playgrounds these days are not so soft as they once was." Projects were piling up faster than they could be approved, and the staff was growing so quickly that they were all in each other's way. Once projects were finally cleared in Washington, they still faced delays for local certification and worker assignment. "It has been a tough job," Harry wrote his brother Lewis, "loaded down with government red tape of an almost unbelievable variety." Other agencies had "tied pink ribbons on everything but the telephone poles and may have to do that yet!"[1] He had already set hiring quotas for various departments and, perhaps thinking about those telephone poles, put a limit on long-distance calls.

More important, he got to work clipping those ribbons. He pressed his field representatives to move projects along and promised to shift hiring quotas to states that were actually putting people to work. He debated giving jobs to unemployed domestic servants and "derelicts" (or the chronically unemployed), deciding no in each case, offered exemptions to certain projects to start with more than their quota of nonrelief labor, fired off a list of approved projects to Corrington Gill with an order to "PLEASE GET AFTER THESE IMMEDIATELY," and removed a state director who would not give his district administrators authority to start projects. When he heard that it took thirteen forms to transfer a worker from one project to another, he called in a few state administrators "who really know the mechanics" to see what could be done to streamline the process.[2]

He did his job as informally as possible. Lee Pressman recalled that when Hopkins hired him as legal counsel to FERA, he had only one thing to say: "The first time you tell me that I can't do what I want to do, you're fired." Hopkins wanted to be as free as possible to make things work. Formality meant fixed commitments, and in a continuing crisis, commitments could be disastrous. "A lot of water goes over the dam in four months," he observed. Thus he refrained from promising work quotas to governors and mayors, regardless of their pleas.[3]

But heading the WPA demanded more of him than day-to-day administration. As 1935 turned into 1936, he was formulating the New Deal's long-term response to the depression. And because of its visibility and importance, the WPA was likely to become a major issue in Roosevelt's reelection campaign. As a result Hopkins found himself beset by new conflicts. Roosevelt favored small works projects that spent the greatest amount possible on employment. But the president also favored fiscal restraint. Above all he was determined to avoid having to ask Congress for more money in an election year. In this he was supported by Treasury Secretary Henry Morgenthau, who wanted to hold down costs by establishing clearly defined administrative procedures.[4]

Hopkins was also wrestling with a fiscal dilemma. Although Roosevelt had shifted funds to the WPA, Hopkins still had to employ 75 percent of all relief workers with 40 percent of the original appropriation. Also, he had to allocate money to projects in sums large enough to guarantee their completion. But Hopkins had encouraged his administrators to rush through as many projects as possible, so by mid-November 1935 the WPA was running short of money.[5]

Hopkins first approached Morgenthau for more money, moving tentatively and with elaborate explanations. When Morgenthau declared that Hopkins should have more accurate figures on the number of people eligible for relief, he replied that such close checking would require "enormous" administrative machinery while cutting the rolls only 3 to 5 percent. Morgenthau dropped the subject. When Morgenthau said that the program ought to be run by someone who would hold down costs and "do a job for the human beings," Hopkins jumped in to point out, "We have given 85 percent of the money we have received for relief. The people we are handling are the people who don't eat unless we give them relief." Hopkins even accepted Morgenthau's strategy for funding the next relief appropriation by carrying over $1 billion from the current year, shelving a request to reduce the carryover. He even backed up Morgenthau's proposal to fund relief at a level below the president's own estimate. Roosevelt accepted the package.[6]

In this way Hopkins and Morgenthau formed one of the New Deal's most enduring relationships. In later years they would face other major issues together, determining whether deficit spending was necessary for economic recovery, and deciding how to protect American interests against the threat of fascism and global war, how to finance Lend-Lease, how to deal with postwar Germany. It was a relationship that Morgenthau grew to value. "For God's sake get Harry Hopkins back here," he exclaimed once after an argument with Corrington Gill over relief spending. "I at least do business with Harry."[7]

Thus Hopkins maintained control of the works program and emerged as a prominent figure in New Deal politics. He did not seek political prominence, but he could not avoid it. Anyone with $2 billion and a mandate to employ 2.5 million people in an election year was going to be in politics whether he liked it or not. As Republicans sharpened their criticisms of the WPA, Congress stepped in. The emergency appropriation for fiscal 1936 specified that all government appointees who were paid $5,000 or more would have to be confirmed by the Senate.

Hopkins later said that when he heard that, he knew that his career had reached a turning point. "I thought at first I could be completely non-political," he said. "Then they told me I had to be part non-political and part political. I found that was impossible, as least for me. I finally realized there was nothing for it but to be all-political." As Raymond Moley recalled, Hopkins told him that he had decided to turn work relief over to the big-city Democratic bosses, a decision that Moley saw as part of Roosevelt's larger strategy of building a national Democratic majority on the votes of the urban masses.[8]

Exactly how political had Hopkins had to become? More so than made him comfortable, certainly, but less than he claimed. His new awareness signaled not so much a transformation as a synthesis of professional social work and practical politics. Roosevelt shared Hopkins's belief that politics did not include the partisan manipulation of relief. When an FERA investigation turned up evidence that representatives of Ohio's Democratic governor Martin Davey had ordered employees of the relief administration to raise money for his campaign and inaugural ball, Roosevelt authorized Hopkins to take over relief in the state and to accuse Davey publicly of corruption and political chicanery. "The president doesn't take a week to decide things like this," Hopkins wrote admiringly, "nor does he need the advice of the politicians—in fact no one was consulted about an action which will throw into the ash can a Democratic Governor and his political machine. In fact I think the boss liked the idea of their being Democrats." He found himself brushing off complaints from congressmen and governors that the WPA was aiding their political enemies. "Don't lose too much sleep over it," he replied when Howard Hunter reported that a political opponent of the Nebraska administrator had declared that Roosevelt had given him authority to run the WPA. "They say it all over the United States. That doesn't mean a hell of a lot."[9]

However much the WPA might be in politics, it had to stay out of elections. WPA rules forbade any solicitation or organization of WPA workers for political purposes. Hopkins refused to allow his administrators to endorse candidates. He ordered that a Louisiana administrator who was running for office "be thrown out at once," and he rebuked his Maine administrator for public remarks that criticized the Democratic governor, who was running for the Senate. "A federal official working for us can't be in a position where he is attacking somebody else," Hopkins charged. "He may not like [what he sees], but he can't say anything about it . . . The fact that the governor has hired somebody who is a crook is no reason for us to stand up and talk about it." When a Republican senator sent him a report that WPA workers in Pennsylvania had been solicited for political contributions, Hopkins replied, "I am sure you know that I cannot be held responsible for the acts of dumb politicians who take it upon themselves to write letters to our employees."

After awhile, supporting the New Deal's friends at the expense of politicians who cared only for their own power became second nature to Hopkins. His usual style was to avoid open controversy and to act only when he had all the facts and the necessary political support. When the governor of Illinois threatened to cut off state relief after the WPA turned unemployables over to the states, Hopkins quietly checked to make sure that the state actually had sufficient revenues to cover new recipients and then advised the state relief commission to battle the governor instead of involving his administration.[10]

Hopkins was willing to accommodate sympathetic politicians by appointing their political supporters, but not if it meant sacrificing professional standards. Because the WPA depended on congressional appropriations, he knew that he had to conciliate members of Congress. He arranged his office procedures to accommodate visiting congressmen and scheduled priority treatment for projects favored by influential members. Political information he relayed directly to Roosevelt. Still, he believed that he served the president and the New Deal best by delivering competent, efficient administration. To fill a vacancy in Florida he recommended an experienced WPA man who was "really a hard worker, has a fine background, [and whom both senators] could trust to do a good job." When the senators rejected the man, Hopkins agreed to look for a more politically acceptable candidate but insisted, "The first thing I have to decide is whether [he] is satisfactory to *us* or not." In the end he secured the appointment for a man from within his organization.[11]

As the WPA grew in prominence, Hopkins believed that it was coming to represent the New Deal, and that it thus made an inevitable target for anti–New Deal partisans. He warned his field representatives that "the [right-wing] Bourbons . . . are opposed to [the WPA] because it costs too much money. The [left-wing] Radicals . . . are going to oppose it because of the security wage. It is going to become one of the main issues in the whole business of caring for the unemployed in the immediate future." Most of all, he wanted his administrators to stand up for the New Deal. "I don't think the New Deal is over," he told them. "I believe in the New Deal. I don't think it is purely for the emergency."[12] Loyalty to the WPA and to the New Deal became indistinguishable for Hopkins. He was willing to hire Republicans, or indeed anyone with the proper professional credentials. But they had to support the New Deal. Word that a Pennsylvania official had spoken against it sparked a warning from his boss: "I am not going to have people on our payroll who are openly working against us here in Washington."[13]

In fact Hopkins used the WPA to court progressive Republicans. In Wisconsin, Hopkins worked through Governor Philip La Follette to such an extent that Senator Ryan Duffy, a Democrat, complained bitterly of being bypassed. He asked Nebraska's Democratic senator Edward R. Burke to submit nominees for WPA positions, including Progressive allies of Senator George Norris. When Burke named only Democrats, Hopkins ordered his state administrator to make the nominations. He no doubt enjoyed hiring his California appointments through the Progressive Republican Senator Hiram Johnson, since the Democratic Senator William G. McAdoo had so implacably tried to politicize the FERA.

He became skillful at protecting New Deal supporters. The refusal of the governor of Missouri to call the legislature into session to provide for relief put pressure on the pro–New Deal congressman Thomas Hennings of St. Louis. In response Hopkins, after determining that the WPA had exceeded its employment quota in St. Louis, issued a statement holding the governor solely responsible for the city's relief difficulties.[14]

Hopkins followed his own advice in dealing with the New Deal's archenemy, Huey P. Long of Louisiana. Elected governor in 1928 and U.S. Senator in 1932, Long had locked his state in the most forceful one-man rule in modern American history. Posing as a spokesman for the small farmer, the workingman, and the underprivileged, he had undertaken local public works, health, and educational programs and had proposed to fight the depression nationally by confiscating high incomes and dividing the wealth among the poor. "Share Our Wealth" he called his program, and by 1935 polls were showing that it had attracted widespread national support. Some thought that the red-headed bulbous-nosed southerner, who appeared in newsreels singing jingles advertising his political ideas and who generally gloried in a kind of rural buffoonery, might tip the election to the Republicans if he opposed Roosevelt on a third-party ticket.

Hopkins disliked Long and did what he could to work against him. He federalized relief when Louisiana failed to pay its share and brought in a director from outside the state. But nothing he tried weakened Long's control. Then, early in September 1935, Long was shot and fatally wounded at the State House in Baton Rouge. As the senator lay in the hospital, Hopkins received an emergency call from his field representative Malcolm Miller. The National Guard was mobilizing and public order seemed about to break down as people worried about the future. Would Hopkins release $225,000 to maintain relief at its current level to keep the situation from deteriorating further? Hopkins was willing but asked for no publicity. (At the time Long was still expected to recover, and Hopkins may not have wanted to give the impression of supporting his regime.) After Long's death he received a letter from an acquaintance describing in great detail the political arrangements Long's lieutenants were offering the Roosevelt administration in return for its support. Included in the deal was a promise to defeat a bill pending in the state legislature to prohibit the WPA from operating in the state. Hopkins's response is not known, but subsequent negotiations returned much of the Long organization to the Democratic fold, and the WPA stayed in Louisiana.[15]

Meanwhile, Hopkins had stepped into the public spotlight as the scourge of the New Deal's critics. In May he had charged that "a small minority of business interests" were trying to stop President Roosevelt's plans for social security and economic democracy. Later that summer he declared that the country would have to redistribute the national income to provide decently for all its citizens. In the same speech he also denounced President Hoover's welfare policies. "Hoover didn't spend any money on 'em," he said of the needy. "He talked rugged individualism and gave it to 'em for breakfast every day." That fall he weighed in against the Republican governor of Kansas, Alfred M. Landon, who was being touted as a possible presidential nominee. "His way of balancing the state's budget," Hopkins declared, "is by taking it out of the hides of his people." He followed up by calling Frank Knox, owner of the *Chicago Daily News* and another Republican hopeful, "a panting, peripatetic publisher." He attacked the anti–New Deal statements of the National Association of Manufacturers and the Liberty League as "pious resolutions" and called their supporters "suckers." "What they mean to say," he warned his listeners, "is that they don't intend to let this crowd on the bottom of the heap have any part of the national income. They want to divide it up just as it was in 1929." The Republicans' ideas of distributing the wealth, he charged, was "to get the money from the big boys and distribute it around during a campaign year."

Soon the Republicans were returning his fire. He was a dictator, they complained, forcing the states to raise taxes to pay relief; he was an impractical, naive nobody who, in the words of one newspaper headline, allocated "Millions for Expense, But Not One Cent for Efficiency." They invented a catchword to describe what they considered worthless WPA projects, calling them "boondoggles" and the work that went into them "boondoggling." "$280,000,000 is Set Aside for 'Boondoggling' Projects," one headline announced. "A Giant Boondoggle," boomed another. They picked up his incautious remark that "dumb people criticize something they do not understand," made it read "people are too damned dumb to understand" the value of work relief projects, and paraded it as evidence of his arrogance. When he denied that political favoritism influenced work relief, they dug up evidence to the contrary, and Republican columnists like Frank Kent of the Baltimore *Sun* called him a hypocrite for denying it. Polls showed that about 65 percent of the population believed these charges.[16]

One particularly nasty consequence of this criticism struck close to home. Early in 1936 Adah had been appointed a district director for the National Youth Administration, which enrolled people between the ages of sixteen and twenty-five in work relief projects. This upset Mrs. Eugene Meyer, wife of the publisher of the *Washington Post* and formerly recreation commissioner for Westchester County in New York, which was part of Adah's district. In a nationally broadcast radio debate on *America's Town Meeting of the Air,* Mrs. Meyer charged that the WPA had uprooted a successful relief program in her county and replaced competent and knowledgeable workers with political hacks. "And who do you think has now been selected in addition to our numerous Federal missionaries at $3000 a year?" she concluded. "None other than Mr. Hopkins's sister, Mrs. Adah Hopkins Aime." Privately Mrs. Meyer contended that Adah was unqualified for the position, despite evidence of her long and successful career in social work and the fact that her relationship with Harry had actually been a handicap in her being considered for the position. Not wanting to be an election-year liability to her brother and to the WPA, Adah re-signed.[17]

Under the circumstances, Harry's acknowledgment of Adah's sacrifice was colder and more formal than the situation seemed to require, reflecting both the distance that had grown between them since his divorce and his own determination to let nothing interfere with Roosevelt's reelection. He was "terribly sorry," he wrote her, "that the job worked out as it did because I know how embarrassing it was for you," but he was "very sure that it is not wise for me to have any relative working for us."[18]

Democratic regulars, upset by Hopkins's programs and his visibility, were taking their complaints to Roosevelt's political lieutenant, Postmaster General James Farley. When the president invited Hopkins on a trip out West, Farley called Hopkins in, told him that he was the most unpopular man in the administration, and warned him not to make any speeches on his tour. He even asked him to stop giving press conferences. Hopkins gave Farley his candid opinion of that suggestion, and Farley backed off to the extent of advising him to limit his remarks to subjects of local interest in the areas he would be visiting. (Farley believed that people were not disturbed by the idea of relief in their own state or community but were against it elsewhere.) The two parted in anger.[19]

Roosevelt could easily have shared Farley's opinion. A few months earlier he had been worried that the Republicans would campaign against "WPA inefficiency—and there's plenty of it." As the election year progressed, however, he decided to run on his full record. At the same time he wanted to minimize his risks. He and Morgenthau decided that since the WPA was the only federal program that unbalanced the budget, it should be kept only for the duration of the depression. In order to show his commitment to fiscal responsibility, he resisted proposals to increase work relief and forbade Hopkins to draw on the next year's appropriation to finance current work. He even told congressmen that he would rather lose their state than increase the number of WPA projects. In August he had Hopkins review WPA rolls to be sure that all workers were eligible.[20]

Roosevelt may have thought that these measures would help Hopkins defend the WPA. On his western trip he avoided campaign rhetoric and played the role of the concerned chief executive touring drought-stricken areas. Perhaps he thought that Hopkins, visiting WPA sites, would project a similar image to people on relief, although he may have approved Hopkins's uncompromising attacks on his big business critics. (Roosevelt had taken this approach himself in his acceptance speech at the Democratic convention, denouncing the nation's "economic royalists" and promising to overthrow their power.)

Just before he left on his trip, Hopkins, with the help of his staff, had been putting the final touches on *Spending to Save,* a book about federal relief. He had designed the book as a campaign document to the extent that he compared the Hoover and Roosevelt administrations' four years of coping with the depression. The chapters on the Hoover years—revealingly titled "The Rise of Unemployment," "The Decline

of the States," and "The Misery of the Nation"—used public statements, congressional testimony and debate, and federal agency records
to document the nation's decline and Hoover's unwillingness to expand the federal role to stop it. Hopkins contrasted the appeals of state
and local officials and even some members of Hoover's own administration with the president's refusal to act. The chapters on the Roosevelt administration offered a primer on the social and economic
dynamics of the relief problem, described various traditional
approaches, and explained the New Deal's preference for work programs. Hopkins also discussed special programs for transients, and the
problems of farmers and the distribution of surplus commodities.

For the most part the New Deal chapters followed the professional
social worker's system of diagnosis and treatment. Along the way,
however, Hopkins provided comments that were more self-revealing.
Outlining the steps taken to decide the standards of relief, he observed
that "each decision had finally to rest with the judgment of a handful of
men whose opinion might be no better than that of several others who
would have come to a different conclusion." Ending his chapter on
rural rehabilitation, he declared that solving the problems of the rural
poor required three kinds of education: teaching the expert to balance
the needs of America's rural and urban societies, teaching the farmer to
modernize his practices and to cope with changing social and economic realities, and teaching the public that their society was being
harmed by the presence of an underfed, illiterate, and neglected segment of the population. In his final chapter he proposed that a national
commitment to eliminate poverty and illiteracy could be justified simply in terms of economic needs, but that it ought to be justified by the
belief that "the human being should come first, and the serviceability of
the economic system in which he functions should be estimated by the
number of persons who share in its rewards."

Here he was speaking as the professional social worker seeking to
project his values upon society at large. No doubt he expected his book
to help teach America how to deal with poverty. Still, in admitting that
the process of setting relief standards was highly subjective, he was less
the decisive expert than the New Deal administrator who saw problems as the results of political conditions which imposed responsibilities. Everyone knew that there was an unemployment problem
and had a theory about how to handle it. But Hopkins was the one
who actually had to do something about it, and in deciding what to do,

he put himself at the mercy of elected officials and the voters. His final chapter posed a series of choices: between simply rescuing the economy or reorganizing it to serve human needs; between providing cheap unemployment relief or paying the cost of employing people on useful projects that maintained their skills and self-esteem; and finally between deciding that the poor were as valuable to society as the rich or abandoning them. He ended by asking the reader to imagine two children. "Upon one child privilege has only started to take effect. Neglect of the other has scarcely begun." He concluded, "How shall the choice be made between them, and who will dare to be the chooser?"[21]

On his tour he stressed the same themes. Relief was here to stay because unemployment would always exist. Work relief was the most effective if also the most costly form. The United States was rich enough to pay the bill provided the tax laws took money from those best able to pay. He addressed the question of whether undeserving people were on the WPA rolls by asking the crowds who came to hear him to think of friends and relatives who had gone on relief and to decide if they had deserved it. He stood before local projects—stadiums, roads, dams, bridges, schools, water systems—and asked rhetorically if these were boondoggles, wastes of the taxpayers' money built by people who leaned on their shovels. No, he said, they were built by honest, reliable, capable individuals who were being unfairly attacked by people who frequented private clubs and never mingled with the unemployed.

As usual he broke down the barriers between himself and his audience with stories of what it was like to administer federal relief. When he first came to Washington, he said, he had felt personally responsible for people on relief, believed that they depended on him for their food, clothing, and shelter. He was also responsible for making quick decisions: whether a state governor should get all the money he had requested, whether relief clients could stay in their homes, whether their children should have milk to drink. He had decided that those on the spot probably knew what they needed better than he did, and that people on relief needed the best break they could get. If he had made mistakes, he was not going to apologize for them, because he had made them "in the interests of the people that were broke." He had made other mistakes, however, that he did regret very much: "Every night when [I] went home," he explained, "and after [I] got home and remembered there was a telegram [I] didn't answer, the fact that [I] failed to answer the telegram and the telephone call may have resulted in somebody not eating."

He had said this before, at conventions, to relief delegations, and on national radio broadcasts. Now he was saying it directly in Cheyenne, Salt Lake City, Helena, Seattle, Portland, San Francisco, Los Angeles, Denver. He continued to say it, albeit less frequently, throughout the campaign.[22]

In this way Hopkins let his audience in on the great secret of government administration: that there was no secret. Everyone knew what the problems were, and once the country's elected officials had enacted a policy to deal with them it was up to administrators like him to decide how to make the policy work. His simple honesty and conviction touched those who heard him. Letters came in praising his unaffected manner, common sense, and sincerity. Even some who opposed the New Deal and who had skeptically attended his talks left with

*Hopkins at a flood relief camp in Arkansas, 1937*

sympathy for his work. Good reports filtered through to Farley, who concluded that Hopkins's trip had been "very helpful."[23]

Of course some of this favorable comment simply indicated the trend of the campaign. Roosevelt was marching toward one of the most overwhelming electoral triumphs of the century, carrying forty-six of forty-eight states and 58 percent of the popular vote. By these standards or any other, the New Deal was more popular than ever before.

However much Hopkins's speeches may have helped, his real work for the New Deal and for Roosevelt had been carried out in his cluttered office on New York Avenue. He had taken over FERA, CWA, and WPA. He had set up relief organizations that fed and clothed the poor and gave them jobs. He had made mistakes, but none had been fatal. He had shown the voters that the New Deal could take on the emergency of economic collapse. Most of all, he had helped to show them that their votes four years earlier had made a difference, that by changing administrations they could change both policies and results. He had proved to millions of Americans that their institutions worked.

Nothing more forcefully showed him the nature of his achievement than the response to his visit to the WPA Symphony Orchestra and Choir in San Francisco. Members of other WPA arts projects were in the audience, and their applause for him and his party was thunderous. After the orchestra and choir finished their performance, the project director asked Hopkins to say a few words. Although Hopkins was behind schedule and had arrived without intending to speak, he agreed. Visibly touched by their support, he told the audience that it was only "an act of God" that had kept him employed and put them on relief. He had "taken something of a walloping" because of the arts projects, but he was more than willing to take abuse in order to preserve "the precious art life of this country." His critics, he charged, wanted art to be only for the rich and not for all Americans, but since they could not attack all Americans, they attacked him. But the projects belonged to the people, and they had a right to them. "For what I have done," he concluded, "I am terribly proud, and as long as I have anything to do with it, I'LL NEVER LET YOU DOWN."

As he walked from the stage with the orchestra conductor to tumultuous applause, a member of the orchestra stepped forward and led everyone in "The Star-Spangled Banner."[24]

# Chapter 7

# Democracy's Bureaucrat

The 1936 election was as much a victory for Hopkins as for Roosevelt. The WPA had taken its place at the center of the New Deal, and Hopkins was the quintessential New Dealer. He still operated out of his shabby office on the tenth floor of the Walker-Johnson Building, with its whitewashed walls and bare pipes, an uncovered radiator steaming in the corner. He worked at an ancient desk strewn with papers, coatless, in blue-striped shirt and suspenders. He seemed to be talking constantly, on the telephone with field representatives or public officials, in conferences with staff and visitors. He worked through lunch, usually taking fruit, salad, rolls, and coffee at his desk. He was seldom seen without a cigarette, smoking two and three packs a day of Lucky Strikes. Now that he was in his mid-forties, signs of age were appearing: thinning brown hair, glasses (which he never wore in public), and a sagging posture of rounded shoulders and forward-thrust head. At six feet and one hundred seventy pounds he still looked slim, though his weight was beginning to gather around his waistline.

Aside from the plainness and clutter of his office, Hopkins seemed a typical middle-aged executive. But there was nothing ordinary about his face. In solemn or belligerent moods he would stick out his jaw, and his features would become sharply defined, all lines and corners, with a large sharp nose and pointed chin. Relaxed, his features became soft, rounded, almost boyish. Most distinctive were his eyes. Large, round, dark brown, they fixed one's attention. An otherwise unflattering portrait on the cover of *Time* magazine in July 1938 captured their power. Lifting both hands to his face to light a cigarette, Harry looks straight ahead, fixing his gaze on his viewers as if to show his interest and draw them out.[1]

He led a largely sedentary life. His most vigorous activity was an occasional game of golf, usually played on vacation. Otherwise he contented himself with bridge, an occasional game of poker, and visits to the racetrack. Horse racing became his sporting passion. (Once

*Montage of Harry Hopkins delivering a speech in 1936*

when he was preparing to go to Boston to deliver a commencement address, he instructed his state administrator to tell his host that "we have an important engagement and can't stay for lunch. The races start early don't they? . . . Is there any place to eat at the track?")[2]

He was an avid reader, his tastes running to detective stories, political biography (Carl Sandburg's *Lincoln,* Marquis James's *Andrew Jackson,* Lloyd Paul Stryker's *Andrew Johnson*), history (Charles and Mary Beard's *Rise of American Civilization*), historical fiction (Kenneth Roberts's *Northwest Passage*), and fiction (contemporary authors such as Hemingway, Cather, Steinbeck, and Erskine Caldwell, as well as Jane Austen, Tolstoy, and Thomas Mann). He enjoyed movies, and while he was convalescing from a serious illness arranged to have a projector installed in his home and films provided by Paramount Pictures. He also collected etchings and lithographs of American scenes. His favorite song was "Summertime," the contented idyll that opens George Gershwin's *Porgy and Bess.* In a more practical vein, he read books on deep sea fishing (to prepare for a yachting excursion with Roosevelt), silver and silver plate, porcelain, pottery, and china. As his health declined, he also read medical volumes.[3]

In company Hopkins was often entertaining, if occasionally a bit overbearing. He enjoyed telling humorous stories, usually of his recent experiences. A favorite anecdote concerned a Palm Beach millionaire whose children had broken their engagements because they could not decide which one should honeymoon on the larger of their father's two yachts. He had firsthand sources for these stories because he vacationed in such fashionable spots as Palm Beach, Boca Raton, and Saratoga Springs with such wealthy friends as Bernard Baruch and his associate the journalist Herbert Bayard Swope, John Hertz, Joseph P. Kennedy, and John Hay Whitney. Evidently this ex-socialist was no longer so interested in "unhorsing the capitalist class." Still, he avoided paying for these friendships with his New Deal values. "Harry felt that his trip to Palm Beach had been well worthwhile," Secretary of Agriculture Henry Wallace recorded in his diary, "because it indicated where the president could get the money for his big program."[4]

Harry still showed a few rough edges. One time he told a large group that Henry Wallace was planning to reduce pork production by having all male hogs wear roller skates on their hind legs. Similarly inspired, he once stood on a table in a fashionable country club and gave hog calls. A well-wisher who saw him at the theater suggested that he would make a better impression if he would not "walk around chewing gum."[5] He sprinkled his conversation with a certain amount of profanity, enough to attract public attention and to occasion some adverse comment in polite circles. More commonly he settled for period slang. He would ask for "the latest dope," worry about being "kicked in the face" or "getting our fingers burned," hope that his supporters would "sit tight," and warn that a particular project was not "in the wood."

He could also be a bit of a showoff. He would tout his successes with Roosevelt by offering journalists the "inside story" on working with the president, and disparaging the clumsiness of those who lacked his skill. He would boast that personal attacks on him proved that he was joining the ranks of such controversial presidents as Grover Cleveland and Woodrow Wilson. He thought that Rex Tugwell was a little unkind to add Warren G. Harding.[6]

Whatever else the critics might say, none questioned his integrity. He steadfastly opposed using his office for personal gain, despite the fact that during most of his years in Washington he was in financial straits. In November 1937, for example, he told his son David that he had not been able to pay his rent for two months and owed "several hundred dollars worth of bills." In 1940 he spent $650 more than his income. Still, he refused to undertake business ventures while he was in the government. The economist Robert Nathan once wrote an article that was published in a national magazine under Hopkins's name, and Hopkins turned over the entire payment to him. None of Hopkins's children ever received a government job, and he demanded that they receive no special treatment when they entered military service during World War II, even when their commanding officers suggested it. He took just pleasure in an editorial cartoon of a plaque attached to WPA headquarters that read:

To The
Everlasting Honor of
HARRY L. HOPKINS
An American Boy
From Iowa Who
Spent *9 Billions*
Of His Country's
Money *And Not A*
*Dollar Stuck*
*To His Fingers!*[7]

He was acutely embarrassed, both because of the oversight and because he had always advocated paying relief costs out of tax revenues, to discover that while he was living in Washington, he had neglected to pay his New York state taxes.[8]

He continued to offset this kind of scrupulousness with personal indulgences. He enjoyed being driven by a government chauffeur, who would always help him in and out of the car and would carefully smooth a lap robe over his legs once he was seated.[9] When he traveled at government expense, he would pay the extra fare for first-class accommodations. He loved rich foods, silk pajamas, luxurious vacations.

His greatest asset remained his extraordinary sensitivity to others. At times, such as when he was overworked or distracted, he could be brusque, abrasive. But usually he was able to reach out to others and give them the sympathy and understanding they needed. He was able to understand their fears and pain and to offer courage and relief. In 1939 the president's daughter-in-law Betsey Roosevelt thanked Harry for "pull[ing] me through my ordeal" when her husband, James, had been hospitalized with gastric ulcers. "There is always so much to say to you," she wrote. "Please come back soon so I can let my hair down!"[10] He asked that his signature appear on responses to people who had written to inquire or complain about the WPA. They were usually down and out, he said, and would be glad to know that Harry Hopkins was paying attention to them. Dealing directly and sympathetically with people also characterized his approach to administration. He once advised Lawrence Westbrook, who headed rural relief for the WPA, to avoid centralizing control of rural cooperative communities. Westbrook should be less an administrator of the communities than a "consultant" to them, Hopkins said, for "in the last analysis, you will get home only if you can convince them that your ideas are good."[11]

Because he saw management as influence and persuasion, Hopkins looked for administrators who were "loyal," who didn't "talk outside the office." His ideal manager "has a nice personality, nice sense of humor, he doesn't get into fights but at the same time is pretty firm . . . he has good judgment about people." Administrators also had to have courage. Hopkins pressed this upon his Grinnell College classmate and noted drama teacher, scholar, and director, Hallie Flanagan, as they discussed her taking charge of a WPA project to establish a federal theater program:

It takes a lot of nerve to put your signature down on a piece of paper when it means that the government of the United States is going to pay out a million dollars to the unemployed in Chicago. It takes decision, because you'll have to decide whether Chicago needs that money more than New York City or Los Angeles. You can't care very much what people are going to say because when you're handling other people's money whatever you do is always wrong. If you try to hold down wages, you'll be accused of union-busting and of grinding down the poor; if you pay a decent wage, you'll be competing with private industry and pampering a lot of no-accounts; if you scrimp on production costs, they'll say your shows are lousy and if you spend enough to get a good show on, they'll say you're wasting the taxpayers' money. Don't forget that whatever happens you'll be wrong.[12]

Harry never evaded responsibility. He demanded accountability from others ("My God!" he exploded when he learned that a WPA payroll was a month behind schedule. "Whose fault was it? . . . somebody ought to have their head cut off"), and he owned up to his own mistakes, not usually apologizing but rather taking steps to correct them.[13] When Roosevelt gave him an order, even an order he opposed, such as closing down the CWA, he followed through.

He grew to be confident of his abilities and his methods, but he did not become power hungry. He began by administering what he considered a short-term emergency program. He had to be talked into recommending the Civil Works Administration (CWA) to Roosevelt. He was willing to consider leaving Washington for a job in business. If he competed against Ickes to head work relief, he did so because he thought that Ickes's record showed that he would not do the job properly. At first his place in the works program was an inconspicuous one; he did not emerge as its leader until the other agencies had shown that they could not meet Roosevelt's goals—and in the process had used up most of the appropriation. Circumstances accounted significantly for his success in the New Deal.

From time to time he would play up to one person at another's expense. He often disparaged people he disagreed with behind their backs to others who shared his opinion. Although such episodes reveal the smaller side of his character, they do not convict him of sheer pettiness. A good deal of government business involves personal struggles for prominence, and Roosevelt was noted for encouraging such rivalries. In an administration with so many talented, creative, and hard-driving personalities, competition was likely in any case. Thus when Hopkins played people off against each other, he was adapting to the realities of the situation, and was often pursuing a larger objective. He may have denounced his antagonists' attitudes or failings, but never their character.

Hopkins's willingness to play people against each other nonetheless suggests that his self-confidence needed occasional bolstering. He might talk about taking responsibility, but such talk in itself suggests that the weight of those responsibilities was not entirely comfortable. Similarly, his frequent declarations that he would probably not last long in his job were realistic assessments of the risks he was taking but also evidence of a persistent fear that he might not measure up.

But of course he did measure up. His accomplishments, and not his fears and doubts, defined his career in public service. He had his moments of uncertainty and self-pity (he once whined to Morgenthau, "Nobody has the headaches that I have"), but he did not let them get the better of him. Instead he recruited the ablest people he could find and told them to use their imagination and get on with the job. "Damn it," he would bark at a staff member stymied by an overwhelming task, "find a way to do it!" He backed his people up, took the heat, and never let them down.[14]

His greatest inner resource was his ability to keep his eye on his objective and not on himself. He had a leader's faith that he could achieve his goal. When circumstances changed and new problems arose, he worked on, determined to see the job through. Most important, he had faith in the unemployed. He was absolutely convinced that they were good people suffering through no fault of their own, and that their demands for a decent level of assistance were completely just. When he said that the only mistakes he regretted were those that had let down the unemployed, he was being completely honest.

His professionalism gave him the kind of clinical detachment that helped him avoid false loyalties and values. Believing that the unemployed were no different from anyone else, he concluded that society bestowed its favors with little regard to merit. His shabby, cluttered office was his monument to that belief, as was his easy association with dignitaries in and out of Washington. He took people for what they had to offer, whether it was the ability to do a job or to entertain him at their country estate. He judged them by a practical standard and otherwise treated them as equals. He was, to be sure, aware of power, as his position required him to be, and he looked for it in the personalities he encountered and adjusted to it in the political situations he faced. But he dealt with it realistically—as a fact of life, as something to be used to accomplish his objectives, but not for personal reward. Hopkins was many things, but he was not selfish.

His professional experience also helped him define problems and achieve solutions. His most common task involved deciding how to distribute funds to care for the unemployed. Here he was helped by having an ability to digest a series of numbers and to see useful relationships among them. More generally, however, his powers of concentration enabled him to focus the elements necessary to solve a problem. Winston Churchill was to pay tribute to this skill by proposing to dub Hopkins "Lord Root of the Matter." Although this characterization, which became a staple of Hopkins's historical reputation, is an oversimplification, it is true that Hopkins often was able to dissect a complex subject, focus attention on its most important elements, and by the force of reason or expression cause others to see things as he did. But his motives and perceptions were more varied than this suggests. At times he subordinated his objective judgments to the opinion of someone he thought better qualified to decide. At others he defined problems in ways that would help him achieve specific objectives. On many occasions, realizing that the problem facing him was not the issue itself but the fears of those who had to deal with it, he would tailor his remarks to bolster their confidence. And, being human, he occasionally missed the point entirely or failed to persuade others.

Of course one key to Hopkins's success was Franklin D. Roosevelt. The relationship between the two was complex. It seems clear that Hopkins was attracted to Roosevelt during his months with TERA but that Roosevelt did not begin to see special qualities in Hopkins until 1935 or 1936. Even then their relationship was largely professional. Although Hopkins spent an increasing amount of time with Roosevelt on social occasions, there is no evidence that Roosevelt considered him anything more than an enjoyable guest. Above all Roosevelt appreciated Hopkins's ability to put programs into action, his preference for work relief over direct relief, and his willingness to follow orders.

During his years in the Roosevelt administration Hopkins came to be known as the most loyal of FDR's lieutenants, as one who followed his president's orders even when he disagreed with them. This led many of his contemporaries, including Roosevelt himself, to believe that Hopkins lived only to serve the president. But this was not quite the case. Hopkins did not always see Roosevelt and Roosevelt's policies as one and the same. As he grew close enough to the president to become his most trusted adviser, Hopkins made it his job to provide Roosevelt with the best available information in order to serve the greater end of enacting Roosevelt's policies. This larger loyalty made him infinitely more valuable to Roosevelt than if he had been a mere errand boy. But even if Hopkins considered himself an instrument, he never saw that role as an escape from responsibility. His knowledge and Roosevelt's might be imperfect, but they were the men who had to make decisions and bear the consequences. Thus he made the choices that fell to him to make, provided the best advice he could so that others could make theirs, and never hesitated to hold everyone responsible for those choices.

In later years Roosevelt came to see other personal qualities in Hopkins. He enjoyed his irreverence, humor, and straightforwardness. For some reason he associated these traits with Hopkins's middle western background and even imagined him to be a typical Iowa farmer. Also, noting Hopkins's rough edges, he made it a proj ct to tutor him in the social graces. More important, he realized that Hopkins shared his sensitivity to others, his desire to spare people pain and to give them strength and confidence. He even asked Hopkins to act for him in personal matters. For example, when his son James was having marital problems, Roosevelt sent Hopkins to talk to him. Hopkins accepted the assignment with great reluctance and carried it out with even greater embarrassment.

For the most part Hopkins genuinely enjoyed his relationship with Roosevelt, and vice versa. The idea that he studied the president and courted favor with him by getting into his good graces is simply not true. Hopkins was a genuinely likable man. He enjoyed relaxing with cocktails, storytelling, and idle chatter. Part of his sensitivity to other people included an eye for the details of daily life, its touching or humorous moments. He was the sort of person one liked to sit up with, going over the day's events or reminiscing about the past. He was a good listener, apparently able to take pleasure in the pleasure of others. Because he enjoyed relaxation and saw that Roosevelt did too, he was impatient with Cabinet members or others who would interrupt the president's quiet moments with earnest discussions of weighty issues. Roosevelt's irritation with this sort of thing was, he believed, thoroughly justified.[15]

But Hopkins was more than a comfortable old shoe. In addition to being intelligent and incisive, he was also very funny. When Roosevelt sent him and Ickes on a fishing cruise in the spring of 1937, he sent a cable that read:

> Please tell your so called military aide [Pa Watson] that I got my alligator yesterday and when I rode him back to the ship he told me he was a classmate of Pa's and remembers the Colonel unfavorably. When Harold got a strike the other day I yelled [Sen. Millard] Tydings and first the rod and reel and then Harold went overboard and we hoped for a brief moment that we had lost the best fisherman in the cabinet but no luck he came up with a couple of Henry Wallace's bureaus.

For the president's fifty-fifth birthday, he put on a skit that took the form of on-the-scene radio news coverage of a flood, with Hopkins and Roosevelt's press secretary Steve Early playing the roles of various White House staff members. "Since I revived the N.R.A. and carried Massachusetts," Hopkins (as James Roosevelt) declared, "I want it clearly understood that I insist this flood be held in Massachusetts . . . I am sorry that this flood didn't happen before the election. I assure my boys in Massachusetts that I intend to have this flood in their state before nightfall because it is essential I find some way to get jobs for the thousands I promised . . . before the November election."[16]

In his sense of humor and his willingness to maintain friendships with the wealthy, Hopkins proved a better companion for Franklin than for Eleanor Roosevelt. She had originally boosted Hopkins at the White House because they shared the social worker's concern for the unemployed. During Roosevelt's first term she continued their relationship on this level, sending Hopkins inquiries and requests. Unlike Harry and Franklin, however, she believed that devotion to the underprivileged had to be nourished with a certain suspicion of the well-to-do and the self-discipline to restrain one's own appetite for pleasure. The sight of Harry at fashionable vacation resorts and expensive clubs in company with business executives and financiers caused her to doubt his liberalism and to fear that he might influence her husband in the same direction.[17] Although Eleanor remained one of Harry's most enthusiastic supporters, he was already beginning to drift away from her.

*Hopkins delivering a speech at a 1936 charitable conference with Florence Kerr, Eleanor Roosevelt, and Ellen Woodward at the head table*

Hopkins still believed in the good character of the unemployed and their right to a decent standard of living, and he wanted the WPA to help most if not all of them. Here he sustained his most serious defeat. The WPA never employed at any time more than 31 percent of the nation's unemployed. At any given time there were certified for WPA employment between 600,000 and 900,000 people who could not be hired because of budget restrictions. Indeed Hopkins had to stretch his resources to provide for those already on the job. A study of WPA wage payments in thirty cities showed that unskilled workers, who made up about 70 percent of WPA employees, were paid only 60 to 80 percent of what the WPA itself defined as an "emergency budget" for meeting family necessities. Only two-person families were able to meet the emergency standard of living, even though the WPA used a four-person family as its norm.[18]

Many believed that Hopkins manipulated WPA employment to help elect New Deal candidates. But the evidence does not support such charges. The greatest worker enrollments came in the fall of 1936 and 1938, just before the elections. In 1936 a poll indicated that 80 percent of WPA workers, the highest of any category, had voted for Roosevelt. This evidence makes an interesting circumstantial case but not a con-

clusive one. There is no direct proof that Hopkins attempted to manipulate the WPA rolls for political advantage. Conditions at the time—
an increase in drought relief in 1936, the recession of 1937–38—
indicate that the WPA increased its rolls for economic reasons. In 1938
the WPA actually reduced employment in Michigan, where Democratic Governor Frank Murphy, a staunch New Dealer, was fighting a
tough and ultimately losing battle for reelection. The WPA's leading
historian, Searle Charles, has also concluded that the rolls fluctuated
because of economic conditions and congressional appropriations and
that politics played an insignificant part.[19]

Although Hopkins would have preferred to have accomplished
more, what he did achieve shows the extent of his imagination and
energy. The WPA's construction projects built or improved thousands
of miles of roads and thousands of schools, playgrounds, hospitals,
libraries, airports, and sewer and water systems. Today people may
visit the San Antonio zoo, spend a snowy weekend at Timberline
Lodge on Oregon's Mount Hood, or play a round on the Veenker
Golf Course at Iowa State University without realizing that these were
WPA projects. On a smaller scale, the WPA introduced services and
programs that Americans had not known in prosperous times: hot
lunches for the children of poor families, day care for children of
working mothers, literacy and naturalization classes for immigrants.

Hopkins's encouragement of creative thinking yielded especially rich
returns in the innovative and unique arts projects which the WPA
operated under direct federal authority. The Federal Music Project set
up symphony orchestras, bands, choirs, and glee clubs. The Federal
Writers' Project published studies in American ethnic, racial, and regional cultures and produced the American Guide Series to introduce
tourists to America's states and cities. The interviews it conducted with
black Americans still provide historians with a major source for the
study of slavery. The Federal Art Project decorated public buildings
with murals, mosaics, painting, and sculpture, and held classes for
aspiring artists. The Federal Theater Project, administered by Hopkins's Grinnell College classmate Hallie Flanagan, brought drama to
over 30 million Americans, introduced original and experimental
works, and attracted public attention with its "living newspaper," in
which actors dramatized current events.

From time to time Hopkins claimed that in addition to helping the
unemployed, spending money for work relief helped the economy to

recover by stimulating consumer demand. WPA workers with money to spend encouraged businesses to hire more employees and expand production. This was the best case he could make for the WPA, since its light construction projects could not stimulate investment in industry. Ickes's PWA projects and regular federal construction created between one hundred and two hundred jobs in private industry for every hundred workers they employed, while the WPA created only sixteen private jobs for every hundred of its workers.

Because unemployment remained high and the economy sluggish until the United States mobilized for war, the WPA's general effect is difficult to measure, and the question of how to balance stimulation for production and stimulation for consumption remains a subject of de-

*Hopkins with Hallie Flanagan at the opening of a Federal Theater production, c. 1936*

bate among economists and political leaders. We are left with subjective judgments, among which the words of the noted manpower economist Stanley Lebergott carry more authority than most. The WPA, he writes, "was hardly sufficient to end unemployment. But it did provide a positive stimulus to increased private investment and consumption, and thereby to economic recovery . . . More important still, these jobs helped keep the skills and attitudes of the unemployed from total deterioration. They provided money for family needs as well . . . Their contribution was direct, humane."[20]

How "humane" were the WPA's efforts? Ninety-seven percent of WPA workers had been employed before. The existing evidence shows that anywhere between 30 and 70 percent were given jobs similar to the ones they had lost. We might guess from this evidence that a significant number of the others were demoralized by having to take a lesser job with the WPA, but we do not know if any actually suffered from doing so. Many people believed that in hard times one takes whatever work is available. Most WPA workers were no doubt thankful to have any kind of job at all. A WPA poll in 1938 found that 72 percent of the workers claimed to like their job. Of the letters received at WPA headquarters, about half contained requests for employment. Only 3 percent were complaints about job assignments, while between 3.5 and 4 percent were complaints about WPA's management and policies (working conditions, pay delays, work rules, low pay).[21] In a decade when 70 percent of the workers in private industries were fighting to form independent labor unions, the WPA's record of worker satisfaction seems successful indeed.

No one contributed more to this record than Hopkins himself. To achieve it Hopkins had to overcome obstacles uncommon in private enterprise. Unlike a business, the WPA existed in a world of improvisation, without careful analysis, firmly assigned responsibility, or adequate resources. It operated in an atmosphere of on-the-spot decisions, competing with grasping federal agencies for year-by-year funding and presidential allocations. This situation called less for systematic delegation of authority and careful review than for courageous decision making and inspiring leadership.

This Hopkins provided. His leadership was imaginative, expeditious, and humane. He faced limitations and quandaries that would have baffled many business executives and was able to employ the maximum number of workers at a minimum of expense, gaining both their support and the approval of the general public. Polls showed that the majority of Americans favored federal work relief for cash wages, and nearly 60 percent approved the WPA's work in their localities. At the same time, however, they overwhelmingly rejected increasing taxes to give more aid to the unemployed. This distribution of opinion accurately reflects the contradictions that the WPA confronted and testifies to Hopkins's success in dealing with them. Hopkins himself agreed. "Federal relief and the WPA were by no means perfect," he wrote in 1943. The program "had many flaws, but I still think it was pretty good."[22]

In the midst of a crisis, when people were willing to grant unusual power to their executive officials, Hopkins showed himself willing to trust other people's judgment, to distribute responsibility, and to work within the limitations imposed by representative government. Throughout his career as federal relief administrator he defined power as the ability to do a job, not as the ability to dominate. Those who failed in his administration did so simply because in his estimation they could not deliver the goods. Because Hopkins worked this way, he was democracy's bureaucrat.

As the depression years passed, Hopkins grew to believe that the WPA should become a permanent federal agency. In 1939 Congress took a step in that direction by combining various relief programs into a Federal Works Agency, in which the WPA was renamed the Works Projects Administration. Soon afterward, however, the United States entered World War II, and wartime prosperity ended the unemployment crisis. In 1943 Roosevelt terminated the WPA. Although Hopkins's efforts convinced a generation that the federal government should help alleviate economic deprivation and suffering, his methods quickly seemed out of date. Some of his willingness to tailor projects to the special skills of his relief clients survives in the efforts of today's analysts to divide the poor into specific categories, with special attention paid to the "hardcore" unemployed. Still, the WPA's wholesale approach and intuitive methods now belong to another era. Not even the wide-ranging War on Poverty of the 1960s attempted as extensive a public works program. Nor does it seem likely that we will soon see a return to the widespread economic collapse and vast unemployment of the Great Depression. Thus the WPA remains a unique part of our history, and so does its guiding spirit.

# Chapter 8

# Not Born for Happiness

The people's support of Hopkins in the 1936 election campaign suggested to some that the WPA might expand during Roosevelt's second term. Such an expansion seemed possible when Roosevelt announced that he saw "one-third of a nation ill-housed, ill-clad, ill-nourished." But instead of calling for new social legislation or enlarging the WPA, he proposed to add new justices to the Supreme Court. He acted in response to certain decisions in which the Court had declared unconstitutional several New Deal statutes, most notably those creating the National Recovery Administration (NRA) and the Agricultural Adjustment Administration (AAA). Hopkins had consistently supported the president's larger objectives, and this was no exception. He helped Roosevelt write speeches to justify his Court plan and publicly supported it, declaring that its opponents were not afraid "*for* democracy" but "*of* democracy."[1]

Unfortunately for Hopkins the public bought neither his argument nor Roosevelt's plan, and conservatives gained strength by opposing it. During the same session Congress took up the WPA appropriation, and many legislators used the occasion to pay Hopkins back for slighting their patronage claims, supporting their opponents, and other sins, real or imagined. Denouncing him for his arrogance, they undercut his authority by appropriating specific amounts earmarked for various categories of projects. This was a personal affront to Hopkins, who had argued all along for blanket appropriations so that he could allocate funds where they were most needed and plan projects most efficiently. He responded with sarcasm. "We need a fire escape on our building," he remarked to the budget director, Daniel Bell. "Do you think we could get some money to earmark for that?" In turn, before the House submitted the appropriations bill to the Senate, it cut Hopkins's salary from $12,000 to $10,000.

"I don't know what we will get when we get to the Senate," Hopkins sighed. "We will probably get the works." He was right. The Senate added a provision requiring that it confirm the appointment of every employee paid over $5,000 and also considered requiring local sponsors of WPA projects to pay 40 percent of the cost. In the end much of this maneuvering proved a petty exercise in futility as Hopkins rounded up mayors and governors who lobbied successfully to eliminate earmarking and the 40 percent contribution. Congress also restored his salary. Still, it had sent a strong message that many Democrats considered Hopkins a liability to the president and the party.[2]

Roosevelt seemed to be listening. Congress formed a committee to investigate relief, and Vice President John Nance Garner filled it with conservatives. When Hopkins tried to outflank his critics by asking Roosevelt to appoint his own committee, the president did nothing. He also refused Hopkins's request for blanket appropriations, and for good measure ordered Hopkins to increase to at least 30 percent contributions from the state and local authorities that sponsored WPA projects.[3]

In earlier years Hopkins would have accepted these defeats. But now, as conservatives flexed their muscles, he became increasingly determined to advance the liberal cause. His earlier efforts to shape the Democratic party along progressive lines had failed, but his chances of success had improved now that others were thinking along similar lines.

By 1937 New Deal liberals were gathering around a particular theory of depression and recovery. The depression, they believed, had been caused by "oversaving," or overinvestment in capital goods; as a result, industry produced more than the country could consume. Many observers, including some WPA economists, saw evidence that such conditions were reappearing in 1937, accompanied by price increases caused by monopoly price fixing in major industries. The remedy they proposed was a combination of taxes on high incomes to reduce oversaving, spending on work relief to increase consumption, and trust busting to restore competitive pricing.

By the summer of 1937 Hopkins had added historical analysis to the theory. The nineteenth century, he argued, had been a time of saving to build the American industrial plant. The price had been paid in low wages and low welfare standards. In the twentieth century, however, many had come to see that mass production required mass purchasing power. Some businessmen, such as Henry Ford, who paid high wages so that his employees could afford his automobiles, accepted the new reality. But many others preferred the economics of the past. Thus when the depression arrived, the government had stepped in, not to compete with private enterprise in production but to maintain purchasing power by paying wages.

Hopkins believed that such a strategy was needed on a permanent basis. Historically there had always been a reserve of unemployed labor for private industry to draw upon during times of expansion, and this reserve would continue to exist. But in an economy built on mass consumption, even the unemployed demanded a decent standard of living. Politically it was necessary for the government to meet this demand, for once the government began providing benefits, it could not easily turn them off. In any case it was economically desirable to support a high standard of living in order to maintain consumption. Hopkins concluded that by balancing consumption and production, the government could ensure that the national income would grow and produce enough tax revenue to balance the federal budget.[4]

At first he agreed with the liberal economist Leon Henderson that the major obstacle to economic recovery was monopoly pricing. By September 1937 he was denouncing giant corporations and special interest lobbies for opposing aid to the unemployed and the poor. Their price increases, he charged, made them "thieves of our buying power."[5]

To convert his formulations into government policy, Hopkins moved on two fronts. He recommended establishing an executive committee to report to the president, proposing that he chair the committee, with the WPA economist Corrington Gill as executive secretary. Opposition from Treasury Secretary Morgenthau forced him to back down, but Roosevelt did set up an advisory group that included Henderson and other liberals. Hopkins also urged the president to encourage congressional liberals, even to the extent of opposing conservative Democratic incumbents in the 1938 primaries. When Governor Carl Bailey of Arkansas won the Democratic nomination for the Senate, Hopkins congratulated him "not only because you are the Democratic nominee, but also because you represent the liberal forces of a great state."[6]

As the elements of Hopkins's liberal campaign were beginning to move into position, his private life was shattered by tragedy. Early in 1937 Barbara was diagnosed as having cancer. For a time, while she was being treated in New York, she and Harry lived at the St. Regis

Hotel. But when the treatments did not work and the disease spread, the doctors told her that her condition was incurable. That summer Harry and Barbara spent a last vacation at Saratoga Springs. Then in September they moved from their Connecticut Avenue apartment to a small house in Georgetown. Early in October, Barbara entered the hospital. The painkillers she was given induced delirium. She talked of taking another vacation, of buying the clothes she had never been able to afford. Harry humored her, once bringing several sweaters for her to choose from. At length, grief overcame him. He drew inward, seeing her illness as retribution for his sin. Shortly before Barbara died, Aubrey Williams arrived at the hospital to be with Harry. Hopkins wept as he reproached himself bitterly for his failings. His marriage to Barbara, he said, had been pure beauty. Shortly before dawn she died with Harry at her bedside.[7]

Messages of sympathy arrived by the hundreds. Barbara's sister Dorothy came down from New Jersey to manage the household, and Harry's Grinnell classmate Florence Kerr, whom he had hired to help supervise women's projects for the WPA, came to Washington to help look after his daughter, Diana. Even Harold Ickes invited Hopkins to his farm for undisturbed relaxation. But he seemed beyond consolation. His moods swung wildly. He would sit for hours, staring at Barbara's picture, and then would try to lose himself in frivolous entertainment.[8]

In the meantime his own health was failing. His father's death from stomach cancer and Barbara's illness had caused him to suspect that he had the disease as well. In 1935 he had developed a duodenal ulcer for which he was successfully treated. Then during his western trip in September 1936 he had experienced difficulty eating. Throughout that fall he felt ill and worried about his condition. After Barbara's death he took a brief holiday in South Carolina and then went to the Mayo Clinic in Rochester, Minnesota. Examination revealed an adenocarcinoma, which the surgeons removed, along with most of his stomach. The operation, they assured him, had been completely successful, apparently hoping that a good mental attitude would either help his recovery or at least give him a few months of peace, since the cure rate for his kind of cancer was (and remains) only about 2 or 3 percent. Hopkins stayed in Rochester until January and then left for New Orleans and Palm Beach, where he recuperated at the winter home of Joseph P. Kennedy.[9]

His recovery proceeded well. Against all odds, he was cured. By April he had gained nine pounds and could move about with no discomfort. His spirits soared. As Barbara's death had induced self-reproach and guilt, his own escape from death brought him hope. He had gone to Rochester a frightened man, asking the question no healthy person can fathom: am I facing death? But he had escaped. It seemed years since he had had such a sense of well-being. More than ever he treasured his warm, understanding friends and most of all his daughter, Diana.[10]

Soon he was back in the fight for liberalism. Roosevelt had aligned himself in part with the liberals by calling Congress into special session to enact a program that included a bill to establish minimum wages and maximum hours for workers. At the same time he seemed as determined as ever to hold down spending, and showed no concern about inflation or monopoly pricing. Senate liberals were warning Hopkins that the reform movement was losing its leadership and its momentum.[11]

The issues seemed particularly vital because in October the economy had plunged downward, wiping out nearly one-third of the recovery since 1933 and sending unemployment up sharply. If the time had ever been ripe to apply the liberal analysis, it was now.

Hopkins found the chance to make his case when Roosevelt invited him to his vacation retreat at Warm Springs, Georgia. Hopkins sent Leon Henderson off to confer with Aubrey Williams in order to write a memo for the president. Hopkins and Williams then presented the case to Roosevelt, emphasizing the need to support purchasing power through government spending. On the way back to Washington other advisers urged the president to attack monopolies. This time the liberals won. Roosevelt asked Congress for a $3 billion spending program and followed up by recommending an investigation of monopoly practices in industry.[12]

What kind of victory had Hopkins won? Not a bureaucratic one, for Roosevelt subsequently imposed strict spending limits on the WPA.[13] Not an ideological one, for Roosevelt seemed only to be responding to circumstances. With unemployment rising, more spending seemed the most practical course. What Hopkins had won was a personal victory. By this time Roosevelt had decided that Hopkins should succeed him in the White House.

Some time after they returned to Washington that spring, Roosevelt called Hopkins in to discuss his plans for him. The president said that he was disinclined to seek a third term for financial reasons, and because his wife wanted him to retire. He reviewed a number of potential liberal candidates, dismissing each one. Above all Roosevelt wanted to avoid a conservative resurgence in the party. The strongest challenger, or, as he put it, "clearly the most dangerous," because he was not a New Dealer, was James Farley. There was some danger than Farley might run for governor of New York that fall. If elected, he would have a strong chance for the nomination. The man to head him off was Hopkins.

Roosevelt suggested that Hopkins begin his campaign after the fall elections by joining the Cabinet as secretary of commerce. At the same time he would take Farley out of the running by appointing him to another job. Hopkins's two major handicaps, as Roosevelt saw them, were his divorce and his health. No divorced man had ever been elected president, and public prejudice made it a serious liability, but Roosevelt thought that Hopkins's happy but tragically brief marriage to Barbara would compensate. (Roosevelt apparently did not know that Ethel had sued for divorce on grounds of adultery.) Hopkins's health, he felt, should not be a political problem. As far as the public knew he had been operated on successfully for ulcers, and the doctors now said that the chances were two to one against a recurrence of his cancer. For his own sake, however, Hopkins should realize that holding public office could limit his recovery. Roosevelt believed that if he had retired from politics after his attack of infantile paralysis he would have regained the use of his left leg.[14]

An additional consideration was Hopkins's standing in the Democratic party. Although Hopkins had many enemies in the party, he had also acquired some powerful friends, among them the big city bosses, including Ed Kelly of Chicago, Jersey City's Frank Hague, and Kansas City's Tom Pendergast. Other possible supporters included the mayors of San Francisco, Pittsburgh, and St. Louis, and Ed Flynn, boss of the Bronx borough of New York City. On the state level, governors Tom Berry of South Dakota, Frank Murphy of Michigan, Herbert Lehman of New York, Richard Leche of Louisiana, and Burnet Maybank of South Carolina could be counted on, as could a number of New Deal congressmen. If he could get the nomination, such progressive Republicans as Senator George Norris of Nebraska and the La Follettes of Wisconsin would be in his corner.[15]

During the winter and spring of 1938 attention focused on Hopkins's presidential prospects. Earlier, in its October 2, 1937, issue, *Collier's* had listed Hopkins among other presidential possibilities. After his operation, attention naturally shifted to his health, but when he came back to Washington, it returned to his presidential prospects. Some members of the House of Representatives charged that a proposal by Roosevelt to consolidate relief agencies into a permanent Cabinet-level department was part of a plan to promote Hopkins for president. In May the respected Washington columnists Joseph Alsop and Robert Kintner reported that Hopkins was considering a bid for the governorship of New York.[16] Thus Hopkins was firmly in the public eye when he issued a statement saying that if he were voting in the Iowa Democratic primary, he would support Congressman Otha Wearin, who was challenging Iowa's incumbent junior senator Guy Gillette. Both Wearin and Gillette had served in the House and had generally supported the New Deal, but after Gillette entered the Senate to fill two years of an unexpired term, he voted against the Court plan and the wages and hours bill, and supported several amendments weakening an administration proposal to reorganize the executive branch.

Hopkins's statement was part of a strategy by White House liberals, led by the president's adviser Thomas Corcoran, to tie Roosevelt's legislative program to the Democratic primaries. A few weeks earlier, a victory by the liberal Florida senator Claude Pepper against a conservative challenger had helped advance the wages and hours bill. Corcoran believed that a liberal victory in Iowa would keep the ball rolling.[17] Among those supporting the liberal cause, Hopkins, as an Iowa native, seemed the best choice to take on Gillette. Hopkins tried his best to get out of the assignment. He had no political ties in Iowa and was even on poor terms with the state's senior senator, the Democrat Claude Herring, and had almost no chance of influencing the outcome of the election. He also feared that his intervention would inspire charges that he was using the WPA for political purposes. But Roosevelt wanted him to do it, so he went ahead.[18]

Nothing better demonstrates the bungling of the men masterminding the primary strategy. In different circumstances Hopkins was a strong asset to the liberal offensive. That summer, for example, the liberals sought to defeat Representative John O'Connor, an anti–New Deal Democrat from New York City and chairman of the House Rules

Committee. Hopkins scouted possible opponents and settled on James H. Fay, who had run a strong race against O'Connor in 1934 and who was well liked by leaders of the Democratic organization. In addition he had the support of Mayor Fiorello La Guardia and New York's American Labor party. Ed Flynn, the Democratic boss of the Bronx, at length lent his support too. Fay defeated O'Connor, showing how effectively Hopkins could operate when he combined his WPA political connections with the established party machinery.[19]

Hopkins's support of Wearin was his first step on the road to political disaster. With the press predicting that the Iowa contest would be a test of Hopkins's political future, Gillette handily defeated Wearin. Shortly thereafter the journalist Thomas Stokes published a series of articles showing that in Kentucky the WPA was working to renominate Senator Alben Barkley, whom the administration was backing against Governor A. B. ("Happy") Chandler. Hopkins ordered an investigation of Stokes's charges and, discovering little truth to them, ordered mild punishment for the officials involved. Stokes, who had written sympathetically about the New Deal, stood by his story. Hopkins then made things worse with his remark that "there is nothing wrong in supporting the political group that will give you the most," a truism that had long described American politics but which in the circumstances sounded like a confession that he had been using the WPA for partisan advantage. In the meantime Roosevelt had gone on a speaking tour, supporting liberals against conservative Democrats. The press widely reported that this "party purge" was being run out of Hopkins's office.[20]

In the end the "purge" produced mixed results. Several New Deal candidates, including Barkley, won primary races, while a number of conservative southern senators survived liberal challenges. The fall elections, however, proved a more serious setback as Republicans picked up eighty-one House seats, eight Senate seats, and a net of thirteen governorships. Liberal casualties included governors Frank Murphy, Philip La Follette, and Elmer Benson—all potential Hopkins supporters. By mid-November many observers were predicting that Hopkins would be the conservatives' chief target.

The public perception of Hopkins was changing from that of the efficient, energetic, humanitarian idealist to that of the manipulative, partisan zealot. Politics accounted for a certain amount of the change, as Republicans trained their heavy guns on a possible presidential candidate. Hopkins still had his defenders, such as the columnists Heywood Broun and Raymond Clapper. Even Hugh Johnson, who had resigned from the WPA to write a newspaper column attacking the New Deal, believed that Hopkins was "the most able, devoted, sincere, fearless and unselfish" of all the president's intimates. But such voices could not overcome the impression that presidential ambitions had driven Hopkins into partisan politics. When an opinion poll asked in December 1938 if Hopkins should be "kept in mind for higher office," only 9 percent said yes. Another poll, this one specifically for Democrats, found Hopkins more popular, with 60 percent agreeing that he had done a good job of handling relief. Still, even they opposed higher office for him 55 to 45 percent.[21]

In a sense Hopkins had contributed to his own difficulties. He had always felt a need to have strong ideological commitments. He had maintained that the social worker's humanitarian values enabled him not only to promote social welfare but also to persevere against entrenched interests. Such beliefs had strengthened his confidence to act by clarifying his moral objectives; but they had also distorted his perception. In close personal contact and in small groups, Hopkins was able to accept people and to work with them as they were, taking their strengths and weaknesses as he found them. He was also able to present himself as a person who might not know all the answers but did have the responsibility for doing a job. Outside such situations, however, his views became increasingly ideological, and as a result uncompromising and judgmental. He could grant that individually, people had the usual proportion of good and bad traits; but in the mass, he tended to see them as stereotypes. Thus, those on relief were "the finest people in America," while those who opposed helping them were selfish reactionaries, "bastards" who should be "cracked down" upon.

The circumstances of Hopkins's emergence into New Deal politics highlighted these defects. People who could praise him for standing by the unemployed could also ask if power was well placed in the hands of one who appeared willing to purge the New Deal's enemies to satisfy his own desire for higher office. An incident just after the fall elections illustrated his predicament. One day during the summer Hopkins attended the Empire Race Track in New York with a friend. A theatrical producer approached him to ask about New Deal spending and taxation policies. Hopkins replied that the administration felt that it had to keep up spending to support the economy, and that in order to keep up spending, it would have to keep taxes high. He concluded by predicting that those on relief would vote Democratic and the Democrats would carry the fall elections. In late November columnists began commenting that on this occasion Hopkins had declared, "We shall tax and tax, and spend and spend, and elect and elect," a statement that seemed in character with political opportunism. At first Hopkins paid no attention to the matter, then he suddenly issued a categorical denial.

Actually, both Hopkins and his critics were guilty of political exaggeration. The critics had taken his remarks out of context, while Hopkins claimed that he had never made any such statement in the first place. The episode revealed how successfully his opponents had built their case. By the end of 1938 his image as a scheming partisan was so well established that any explanation of the incident would have been taken apart and refashioned against him. Denying the entire charge was his only choice.

Although his candidacy seemed to be on the ropes, neither Hopkins nor Roosevelt was willing to throw in the towel. In December, Hopkins resigned from the WPA and Roosevelt appointed him secretary of commerce. There was much talk that the move was designed to improve his image with the business community. He hired two journalists to feed favorable information to the press. He reestablished his Iowa ties by renting a farm near Grinnell and renewing his membership in the Methodist Church. And with what we may imagine to have been greater sincerity, he accepted an appointment as a trustee of Grinnell College. He delivered his first major address to a businessmen's meeting in Des Moines. Whatever else these maneuvers may have accomplished, politically they failed. When Roosevelt asked that Hopkins be invited to a dinner for administration officials and farm leaders, investigation turned up so much opposition that the president withdrew his suggestion. When Hopkins later asked to be included in the Iowa delegation to the 1940 Democratic convention, he was refused.[22]

Thus ended Hopkins's presidential prospects. The episode had been one of the low points of his career. His intervention in the Iowa primary and his efforts to present himself as a native midwesterner were textbook examples of political ineptitude. Still, his failure was not entirely his own fault. Hopkins had come forward as a candidate when the New Deal was going through its most difficult times because of decisions made by the president. It was not Hopkins but Roosevelt who had decided to pack the Supreme Court, to cut back spending, to encourage Hopkins to endorse Wearin over Gillette, who had pushed forward with the purge. These decisions, which alienated public opinion, aroused the anti–New Deal forces in Congress, contributed to the depression of 1937–38, and exacerbated liberal-conservative tensions in the party, would have handicapped anyone Roosevelt had designated as his heir apparent. By supporting the president's moves, Hopkins confirmed his place in the White House inner circle but at the cost of suffering from Roosevelt's bad judgment.

During these months Hopkins proposed a constructive alternative to the president's disastrous moves. An increase in government spending would both reinforce the welfare policies with which he was closely identified and deal more effectively with the depression. If the administration had followed this course, Hopkins could have campaigned for the presidency from a position of strength. Although he could not use the WPA to pressure voters, he could continue to offer the usual concessions to his political allies, to arrange WPA appointments for people who could influence their state party organizations on his behalf, and to do what he could to sharpen his image as the hard-driving administrator with humanitarian ideals.

About the time his presidential campaign was getting under way, Hopkins had expressed concern about what the effort would do to him personally.[23] The results were not as negative as he had feared. In one respect, however, the campaign did change him. Those who knew him afterward usually commented on his hard-boiled realism. He would say that nations fought out of self-interest, and he would deprecate the shortcomings of world leaders such as Churchill and Roosevelt. There had always been a bit of this cynicism in his outlook, but after 1940 it was more obvious.

His tenure as secretary of commerce was not without result. Hopkins never had much of a chance to reach an accommodation with businessmen in general because most of them would have preferred a Republican administration to a friendly Harry Hopkins. In any case both he and Roosevelt indicated that any rapprochement with business would have to be on New Deal terms, with business accepting collective bargaining, antitrust enforcement, progressive taxation, and welfare spending. In the more limited confines of the department's Business Advisory Council, however, Hopkins was able to win the respect

of council members Averell Harriman, William Batt, and Edward Stettinius. He planned to use the department to institutionalize the New
Deal, establishing a Division of Industrial Economics under the Harvard economist Richard V. Gilbert to develop policy recommendations. He also announced plans to expand trade with Latin America, to
provide credit for small businesses, to expand construction of moder-
ately priced housing, and to remove interstate trade barriers.

But little came of these proposals, for in the spring of 1939 his
health took an ominous turn. Throughout most of 1938 Hopkins had
maintained his health. By Christmas, however, his vitality had begun
to ebb. In March he came down with an illness that hung on so long
that he did not return even to part-time work until May. He remained,
however, in a weakened condition. Because his symptoms included
vomiting and diarrhea, he and his doctor concluded that he had a
touch of the flu. But there were other, more troubling, signs: general
weakness, swelling in his hands and feet, and poor vision. Roosevelt
put him under the care of his personal physician, Dr. Ross McIntire,
who put Hopkins on a strict diet that cut out the rich foods he liked so
much. In mid-June, accompanied by his daughter and his housekeeper,
Hopkins moved to a secluded estate on the Patuxent River in Maryland, fifty miles southeast of Washington. He returned to the capital
occasionally but otherwise spent the time fishing, swimming, and resting. In July his sons Robert and Stephen came for a visit from their
home in Northfield, Massachusetts, where they lived with Ethel. Harry
improved at first, but then his legs began to cramp. He began to spend
more time in bed, his health obviously declining.

At this point David Niles took a hand. A longtime associate of
Hopkins's in Washington and currently a political adviser in the Commerce Department, Niles visited Hopkins and recommended that he
return to the Mayo Clinic. When Hopkins hesitated, Niles got
Roosevelt to recommend the move.[24] By the time Hopkins arrived
again in Rochester, on August 22, 1939, his symptoms were more
defined. His shins were sore, his feet and ankles burned, and his toes
were reddened. Tests showed that his system was not absorbing fats,
vitamins, and minerals. He was starving.

Even in such extreme circumstances he kept up his spirits. Writing to
Mrs. Roosevelt that his tests included "the well-known vaudeville exercise of tube swallowing," he concluded that he had "found a way to
earn my living if and when the New Deal should be thrown out of

Washington." But the doctors' efforts did no good. By early September he was depressed and resigned to dying. This, according to his head physician, Dr. George Eustermann, was the proper outlook. He thought that Hopkins would be dead by Christmas.

Then Aubrey Williams intervened. Visiting Hopkins early in September, he learned that another of the doctors, Andrew Rivers, believed that Hopkins could be saved. Williams asked Hopkins to have Rivers take over his case, but Hopkins told him to mind his own business. Williams then called Roosevelt, who ordered Rivers to go ahead. This resulted in what Hopkins later described as "heroic treatments," including blood transfusions, intravenous feeding, and injections of vitamins and iron. By mid-September he had improved enough to go home. Hopkins was sufficiently dissatisfied with the doctors' diagnosis of "a deficiency disease, cause unknown" to tell Rivers that he was going to make up his own. As for his condition, by November he could report:

> I weigh 140½ pounds, my appetite is excellent, my spirits are "good to very bad." My strength is not so hot but [Dr. Wallace M.] Yater assures me that I am "fine" in spite of being lashed to the bed and doused with innumerable drugs—which I now take every fifteen minutes and am buying by the bushel instead of by the box. I would hate to think of the condition of a patient that Yater would say was only doing "fairly well!"

By the end of the year he had become such an authority on his illness that he was able to compliment Secretary of Agriculture Henry Wallace on his department's *Year Book on Nutrition*.[25]

Neither Hopkins nor his doctors ever fully agreed on the nature of his condition. He clearly had a malabsorption syndrome, the body's inability to absorb nutrients from food. Some doctors thought that he might be suffering from nontropical sprue, a celiac disease characterized by a flattening of the cells of the small intestine so as to inhibit absorption. Nontropical sprue is usually hereditary. Others diagnosed his condition as "largely mechanical," having to do with the reconnecting of his digestive organs during his surgery, one possible consequence of which was the "dumping syndrome." That is, Hopkins's surgery had removed the mechanism by which the contents of his stomach passed into his small intestine. The result was that the contents were "dumped" too rapidly to be adequately mixed with the intestine's digestive secretions. There is some evidence to support both diagnoses, though the dumping syndrome is more likely. Malabsorption results in diarrhea, a decline in the production of stomach acids necessary for digestion, a vitamin B-12 deficiency, pernicious anemia, and liver disease. It was Hopkins's misfortune that vitamin B-12 was unknown at the time of his illness and that his mechanical condition was impossible to correct.[26]

Hopkins emerged from his illness into a changed world. A week after he entered the Mayo Clinic, Adolf Hitler's troops had invaded Poland. Europe was at war. The conflict climaxed a decade during which the Fascist governments of Germany, Japan, and Italy had pursued expansionist policies against their neighbors. Hopkins had advocated taking all necessary steps to check the aggressors. In 1938 an increasing share of WPA funds had gone into projects for national defense. Roosevelt had sent Hopkins on a secret tour of aircraft factories in California, and Hopkins had ordered the Commerce Department to prepare for defending the nation's economy.

In the spring of 1940, as Hitler's troops smashed into Denmark and Norway, then Belgium, Luxembourg, Holland, and France, Hopkins pressed for more U.S. action. All that mattered, he told Morgenthau, was to "take care of the war situation." He immersed himself in defense projects such as stockpiling strategic materials and initiating manpower recruitment, increasing industrial production, and planning for hemispheric defense. On May 24, 1940, Hopkins's Business Advisory Council petitioned the administration to acquire military bases in the Western Hemisphere from the nations fighting Germany, either by leasing them or by taking them in case of a "disastrous" German victory. (Thus he anticipated the arrangement later concluded by Roosevelt whereby the United States traded to the British government several overage destroyers in exchange for strategic territory.) He was "firmly convinced that this fellow Hitler intends to whip us in one fashion or another and I belong to the school that thinks we should not let him do it."[27]

As he concentrated on the defense effort, he revised his New Deal ideology. Mobilizing industry required the cooperation of anti–New Deal businessmen. These businessmen would not work effectively if they thought that the defense effort was a cover for promoting New Deal policies. Thus the government was going to have to determine which New Dealers would be able to shed their antibusiness prejudices and work with business executives to build the nation's defenses.

Hopkins had come a long way. The relief administrator had become a political strategist, policy adviser, presidential hopeful, and defense expert. Not surprisingly, he was also becoming a presidential intimate. On May 10, the day Germany invaded the Low Countries, Hopkins dined at the White House. He was feeling unwell, and Roosevelt persuaded him to stay the night. That night turned into several more, and soon Hopkins was installed as a permanent guest in the Lincoln Room, so called because Abraham Lincoln had used it as an office and there had signed the Emancipation Proclamation. Hopkins became Roosevelt's constant companion, conferring with him several times a day and frequently accompanying him to Hyde Park. He did not much relish his position. He believed that Roosevelt considered him only a companion and that those who thought he could influence the president were overestimating him. Their opinion embarrassed him, and at times he suggested to Roosevelt that he should leave. But Roosevelt wanted him to stay, in order "to have," Hopkins guessed, "someone around he can talk to when he wants to—or not talk to."[28] His perception of Roosevelt as isolated and lonely, needing a companion at his disposal, made him feel that it was his duty to stay on.

But Roosevelt wanted Hopkins around for more than companionship; he wanted him to arrange for the Democratic National Convention in Chicago to nominate him for a third term. Hopkins had long been convinced that Roosevelt would have to seek a third term, and the war emergency left no question. Because tradition had limited previous presidents to two terms, Roosevelt instructed Hopkins to have his nomination appear to be a spontaneous draft by the delegates.

Hopkins had two special advantages in Chicago. His close relationship with Mayor Ed Kelly probably helped him to pin down the details for Roosevelt's nomination. His hotel room was equipped with a direct phone line to the White House. Although the Iowa delegation had not included him as a delegate, the party chairman had arranged for him to get on the convention floor as an assistant sergeant at arms.

His greatest disadvantage was that most people thought that he knew more than he actually did. He had been sent only to arrange for a draft, not to stage-manage the convention. When he first arrived, he announced that he had no authority to speak for Roosevelt—a statement that, although true, was hard to believe once the phone line was installed. To make matters worse, his strategy ran afoul of his old party nemesis, James Farley. Farley had campaigned for the nomination and emerged as Roosevelt's only serious challenger. Hopkins's strategy was to emphasize party unity by persuading Farley to withdraw while staying on as party chairman. But Farley resented Roosevelt's waiting on the sidelines and coming into the game at the last minute to claim victory. In the end he refused to withdraw and resigned as party chairman. Inevitably the press blamed Hopkins, and his old image got a fresh airing as Democratic regulars complained about social workers getting mixed up in politics and muttered sour comments about a "Cabinet clique" of liberal "masterminds" who had taken it on themselves to run the convention.[29]

Thus poisoned by ill will and frustration, the convention lumbered on. On the evening of the third day Kelly arranged a jury-rigged draft. The permanent chairman, Senator Alben Barkley, stunned the delegates by reading a note from Roosevelt declining to run. A voice (belonging to Kelly's superintendent of sewers) boomed over the loudspeaker demanding the president's renomination. A wild demonstration followed, and the next evening Roosevelt was overwhelmingly nominated for a third term. (Since he and Kelly were close, Hopkins had probably agreed to this strategy.)

After the voting Hopkins retired to his secret headquarters at the Ambassador East Hotel. (His daytime quarters were several miles south at the Blackstone Hotel, which was across the street from the convention center.) At 2:30 A.M. Roosevelt called to tell him that he wanted Henry Wallace for vice president. At this point, and for the first time, Hopkins was in charge. Setting up shop at the Blackstone, he sent out orders through Senator James Byrnes of South Carolina and Assistant Secretary of Agriculture Paul Appleby, an old Grinnell classmate, to pass the word and bring the delegates into line. It proved a tough fight. Many delegates were disinclined to accept the former Republican and ultraliberal Wallace, but in the end he succeeded. Wallace responded appropriately, if mistakenly, when he profusely thanked Hopkins for persuading Roosevelt to select him.[30]

The convention was typical of Hopkins's career in government: hard, improvised work that brought him plenty of criticism but ultimately succeeded. It seemed a good note to end on. Hopkins's health remained poor and his recovery slow. The only sensible choice was to leave the government and spend the next few years recuperating. In August 1940 he resigned as secretary of commerce, gave up his Georgetown home, and leased rooms at the Essex House in New York City. From there he would take charge of the library Roosevelt was planning to build on the grounds of his family home at Hyde Park to house his presidential papers.

When Hopkins was recovering from his cancer operation, Florence Kerr had written him that "whatever we were born for, it couldn't be personal happiness."[31] The words seemed to fit a man who had lost his wife, his health, and his vocation. Characteristically, he did his best to take his sorrows in stride. He left Washington with regret but without bitterness. As he thought over his years in government, he could take satisfaction from realizing that the rise of a harness maker's son to the president's Cabinet had proved that democracy worked, and that along the way he had been able to feed the hungry.

Hopkins was out of Washington but not out of the campaign. He conferred with Sam Rosenman, a justice of the New York State Supreme Court who doubled as a presidential speechwriter. One day the playwright Robert Emmet Sherwood dropped by to discuss ideas for an upcoming address, and Hopkins recruited him for the speechwriting team.

The Republicans had nominated an unheralded candidate, Wendell Willkie, a former utilities executive who accepted much of the New Deal and who for several weeks had made almost no impression on the campaign. Then in October Willkie struck a responsive chord by attacking Roosevelt's foreign policy, charging that the steps he had taken to aid Britain were leading the United States into war. Hopkins returned to the White House to help Roosevelt answer the charges. He was on Roosevelt's campaign train as it chugged through New England (in Boston the president declared, "I have said this before but I shall say it again and again and again: your boys are not going to be sent into any foreign wars"), continued to New York, and ended in Cleveland.

On election night Hopkins was with the president and his party at Hyde Park. He and a few others listened to the returns on a small radio in his second-floor bedroom. The early results had Willkie making a strong showing, but before long it was clear that Roosevelt would win by a comfortable margin. Later that evening the townspeople trooped down the front path to salute the president. Hopkins came out and stood in the background while Roosevelt acknowledged his neighbors. It was an exhilarating moment. Hopkins slapped his fist into his palm and turned on his heel. He was going out a winner.

In the crowd someone waved a sign that read, "Safe on Third."

# Chapter 9

# A Little Touch
# of Harry

Roosevelt might be safe on third, but Hopkins seemed destined to ride the bench. After the 1940 election he dropped out of sight. During the last week of November he was away from Washington, attending the funeral of his brother Rome and spending the Thanksgiving weekend with the Averell Harrimans.[1]

During his absence a crisis broke in Roosevelt's foreign policy. The president had been trying to support Great Britain, which under Prime Minister Winston Churchill was preparing for a German invasion and was struggling to defend itself against almost nightly air raids while fighting on the high seas and in the Middle East. Limiting Roosevelt's efforts was American neutrality legislation, passed to satisfy isolationist sentiment, which opposed the United States' being drawn into another European war. The law required countries buying war supplies in the United States to pay for them in cash and to transport them on their own ships. On November 23 the British ambassador to Washington, Lord Lothian, returned from London, announcing to reporters, "Well boys, Britain's broke; it's your money we want."[2] A week later the American ambassador to Great Britain, Joseph P. Kennedy, submitted his resignation. Roosevelt was glad to be rid of Kennedy, who thought little of Britain's chances against Hitler, but the resignation eliminated a potentially useful line of communication at a critical moment. Shortly thereafter, Lord Lothian died suddenly.

Despite these difficulties Roosevelt was determined to get some postelection rest. Telling Morgenthau and others involved with the issue of aid to Britain to "use your imaginations," he left on a Caribbean cruise, accompanied by "Pa" Watson, Dr. Ross McIntire, and Harry Hopkins.

At first the trip went as planned. The party spent endless hours fishing, with uniformly bad luck. They visited fashionable tourist shops, entertained local dignitaries, officiated at shipboard contests, and whiled away the evenings with poker and movies. Then, late on the afternoon of December 9, a Navy seaplane arrived with a long dispatch from Prime Minister Churchill.

The prime minister did not equivocate. Britain would fight on, he declared, relying on sea and air power to defend itself at home and to hold off the Nazis in the Middle East and the eastern Mediterranean. At the moment, however, shipping losses were too high. He hoped that the United States could perform a "decisive act of constructive non-belligerency" by making ships available through "gift, loan, or supply." Mindful of Roosevelt's recent speeches, he assured the president that such a move would not bring the United States into the war. But he warned that if Britain were forced to pay cash for its war supplies, it would be unable to absorb American trade after the war, and the United States would be faced with "widespread unemployment."[3]

Roosevelt had told others to use their imagination; now he had to use his own. For two days he read and reread Churchill's words. On the evening of December 10, Morgenthau telegraphed that the United States could supply the British until Congress met in January. The question was what to do after that. Hopkins favored sending the supplies as a gift, but Roosevelt ruled that out and suggested instead lending Britain the supplies. The United States, he said, was in the position of a man whose neighbor was asking to borrow his garden hose to put out a fire. Common sense and decency recommended lending the hose before his neighbor's house was destroyed, and the fire spread to his own. When the fire was out, the neighbor could either return the hose or replace it.

Roosevelt felt that he needed to look more closely at Anglo-American relations, to size up Churchill firsthand and learn how he stood with Parliament and the British people, to gauge his commitment to his ringing promises to fight Hitler to the end. With the two countries lacking ambassadors at the moment, some sort of personal contact outside the regular diplomatic channels seemed in order. Briefly, Roosevelt considered sending Hopkins to London but changed his mind.[4]

The party docked at Charleston, South Carolina, on Saturday, December 14. Hopkins stayed in town to spend the weekend with Governor Burnet Maybank, a friend from New Deal relief days, and

Roosevelt went to Warm Springs, Georgia, for a brief stop before heading back to Washington. There Hopkins helped him draft speeches presenting his Lend-Lease plan to Congress and the public. He urged the president to make "an optimistic statement" to encourage the British and their allies, so Roosevelt declared, "The Axis powers are not going to win this war." Hopkins cast a cynical eye, however, on Roosevelt's proposal that Americans should work for "four essential human freedoms"—freedom of speech, freedom of worship, freedom from want, and freedom from fear—"everywhere in the world." He thought that most Americans were not much interested in "the people of Java." Roosevelt replied that the world was getting so small that even the people of Java were our neighbors, and the phrase stayed in.[5]

Meanwhile Hopkins was thinking about Roosevelt's earlier proposal that he visit Churchill. He raised the subject during the Christmas week, but Roosevelt said no. Hopkins then sought help behind the scenes from Roosevelt's secretary and longtime friend Missy LeHand and Justice Felix Frankfurter. Still Roosevelt hesitated, fearing that Hopkins might not get along with Churchill.[6]

At last the logic of the situation forced Roosevelt to change his mind. Lend-Lease would put Anglo-American relations on a fundamentally different basis. Some, such as Secretary of War Henry Stimson and Secretary of State Cordell Hull, thought that it would bring the United States into the war, and that in any case the United States would be investing in the British war effort on a scale that would inevitably diminish its own military preparedness. Roosevelt saw that it was essential to sweep aside the ill will and suspicion caused by Ambassador Kennedy and to build a new partnership. Those who agreed were shocked to hear that Churchill might name the appeasement-minded David Lloyd George as the next ambassador to Washington. Nor were they heartened when the prime minister dropped Lloyd George for Edward Lord Halifax, who had also been an architect of prewar appeasement. Sending a spokesman to England with words of American support might, they thought, revitalize Britain's fighting spirit.

Circumstances pointed to that someone's being Harry Hopkins. Morgenthau, who had extensive contacts with the British, was busy supervising the Lend-Lease legislation. A new ambassador could not be confirmed for several weeks. But Hopkins was free to go at once, and his presence in London would nicely complement the domestic campaign for Lend-Lease. Also, it made sense for Roosevelt to send a close associate who was well informed of his plans.

Roosevelt kept Hopkins in the dark about his decision. Then on January 3, Steve Early called.

"Congratulations!" he said to Hopkins.

"On what?"

"Your trip!"

"What trip?"

"Your trip to England," Early replied. "The president just announced it at his press conference."

Hopkins walked over to Roosevelt's office. "Did you say that, Boss?" he asked, relating his conversation with Early. Roosevelt confirmed that he had.

"Well I'm going," Hopkins declared. "I'm going right away. I'm not going to hang around here. I know what you'll want me to do, go over to the State Department for instructions and get the views of a lot of people. I won't learn anything that way; all I need is a long talk with you."[7]

This approach was typical of Hopkins, but for a man with no diplomatic experience, it was not going to be adequate. So he had a forty-five-minute conference with Secretary Hull and a meeting with Jean Monnet, a French banker temporarily attached to the British Purchasing Commission.

Monnet told Hopkins to concentrate on Churchill. "Churchill *is* the British War Cabinet," Monnet declared, "and no one else matters." "I suppose," Hopkins replied, "Churchill is convinced he's the greatest man in the world!" Felix Frankfurter, who had arranged the meeting, immediately cut in: "Harry—if you're going to London with that chip on your shoulder, like a damned little small-town chauvinist, you may as well cancel your passage right now."[8]

In other meetings Hopkins showed himself to better advantage as a prospective diplomat. On January 4 he conferred with Nevile Butler, who was temporarily heading the British Embassy. The president, Hopkins told him, wanted someone with an intimate knowledge of his own mind and his administration to bring back the "over-all picture," including "pretty precise" estimates of Britain's needs for ships, airplanes, and other munitions. With this information he and Roosevelt would be able to override any "departmental attempts to whittle down" British requests. The president's chief desire was that the United States, "in their own interest, should enable Great Britain to beat Hitler."[9]

Hopkins also did a little fence mending, stopping in New York to assure Ambassador Kennedy that Roosevelt was "not sold on the British at all." Roosevelt was anticipating Kennedy's testimony at the Lend-Lease hearings and wanted Hopkins to encourage his support.[10]

On Tuesday morning, January 7, Hopkins arrived at La Guardia airport, accompanied by his children David, Stephen, and Diana. He fended off reporters' questions for an hour, and then, carrying his battered felt hat and two paperback novels, walked to his plane, pausing to give his children a few words of fatherly advice, and was off.

In Lisbon he changed to a British Overseas Airways plane for the flight to Poole on Britain's south coast. When asked if he was going as ambassador, he snapped, "I don't have to fool with that stuff." He arrived about 5:00 P.M. January 9, so exhausted and sick that the welcoming party had to board the plane and help him off.[11]

However ill, Hopkins could not have arrived at a better time to sort matters out. Roosevelt and Churchill had been the victims of a serious misunderstanding. The president had misinterpreted Churchill's choice of ambassador to Washington. The prime minister had intended not to appease Hitler but to get Lloyd George out of the country so that in the event of a Nazi invasion, Hitler could not install him as head of a puppet government (Lloyd George had publicly called Hitler "a born leader of men"). He also wanted to push Halifax out of the Foreign Office and replace him with Anthony Eden. For his part, Churchill had not been able to perceive that Roosevelt was prepared to provide the assistance the prime minister sought. Only the urgent entreaties of the British Embassy had persuaded Churchill to moderate the messages of complaint that he was drafting for Washington.[12]

In London, word of Hopkins's mission sent Churchill's advisers scurrying for information about him. Brendan Bracken, Churchill's minister of information, who had met Hopkins a few years earlier in the United States, was given a place in the welcoming party. Someone (perhaps Churchill's physician, Sir Charles Wilson) suggested that because of his career in social work and unemployment relief, Hopkins was "the old nonconformist conscience of Victorian liberalism arisen in our midst" and that he hoped to discover whether the British leaders shared his aversion to "a world in which some live in the sun and others in the shadow." Someone else found a *New York Times* correspondent whose brother had worked for Hopkins in Washington and who described Hopkins as a practical idealist with great capacities for organization and administration, an engaging personality with a keen sense of humor, and a "decidedly socialistic" outlook.[13] Through the Australian mission Frankfurter had warned Churchill that "there is nothing currently more important than that Hopkins's mission should succeed" and had advised Churchill to court Hopkins by praising Roosevelt. Hopkins, he cautioned, "has such a high regard and affection, amounting to almost reverence for the president that he is liable to react against anyone who does not show evidence of similar regard."[14]

Churchill had arranged first-class accommodations for Hopkins from Poole to London and was prepared to welcome him with dinner at No. 10 Downing Street. Hopkins was too tired to attend the dinner, however, and instead went to Claridge's Hotel, where the American mission, headed by Herschel V. Johnson, was quartered. He dined with Johnson, and afterward the two men met with Brigadier General Raymond E. Lee, the American military attaché, to discuss why the British had relieved certain of their higher-ranking commanders. They talked until 12:45 A.M. Lee, who had heard that Hopkins had arrived at Poole looking "green and ill," reported that by the time he went to bed, "He did not look exhausted at all."[15]

Hopkins began the next day by conferring briefly with the U.S. naval attaché. He then spent an hour at the Foreign Office with Anthony Eden. The two exchanged assurances, Eden predicting that Hitler would "have a go" at England but would fail, and Hopkins declaring that Lend-Lease would pass and that the "bulk of the country" was behind the president. Eden emphasized that any aid the United States could deliver before Hitler's invasion, expected in May, would be twice as valuable as assistance arriving afterward. Hearing this, Hopkins seemed to sag.[16]

After a talk with Halifax, it was time for lunch and a private conversation with Churchill. Brendan Bracken met him at the door of No. 10 Downing Street, showed him around, and at last deposited him in a basement dining room with a glass of sherry. Shortly thereafter Churchill entered, "rotund—smiling—red-faced—clear eye and mushy voice," Hopkins later reported, extending his hand and wishing Hopkins welcome. For the next three hours Churchill did his best to advance the British cause. When Hopkins told him that Roosevelt was eager to meet him in April, he replied, "The sooner the better," and suggested arrangements. When Hopkins pointedly stated that "in some quarters" people thought that Churchill disliked America, Americans, and Roosevelt, the prime minister bitterly attacked Ambassador Kennedy for creating such a false impression and produced a copy of a telegram he had sent to Roosevelt expressing "warm delight" at his reelection. He also promised to provide Hopkins with full information about Britain's war needs.

Churchill assessed the strategic situation with confidence, realism, and a measure of self-congratulation. After the fall of France he had not known whether England could stand alone. But it had and would continue to do so. He now doubted that Hitler would invade, but if he did, his armies would be driven back into the sea. Elsewhere in the world, he saw Germany overrunning Spain in the spring and invading Greece, which he declared "lost." Losing Greece would damage British prestige and would have "a profound and disappointing effect in America as well." He thought that Turkey would stay out of the war until Hilter moved through Bulgaria. In response to Hitler's moves, he promised that Britain would hold the Mediterranean and would win in North Africa, relying on air power for its final victory. "This war," Churchill declared, "will never see great forces massed against one another." Britain soon would be able to "hold their own in the air," and with U.S. help they would achieve "mastery." Then "Germany with all her armies will be finished."[17]

Churchill had reviewed the British strategy with confidence, determination, openness, and above all optimism that, with substantial American aid, England would win the war. Gone were the sense of doom, the complaints about U.S. isolationism, the haggling over details. Stressing air power reflected his hopes while requiring relatively little American aid. But if Churchill had expected promises of help in exchange for his optimistic prediction of victory, he must have been disappointed. Hopkins did not pledge U.S. support in defeating Hitler, nor did he predict the passage of Lend-Lease. He did not even assure Churchill that the Americans were firmly behind the president. Perhaps he had offered these assurances to others and assumed that Churchill had been told; perhaps the prime minister left him no time to reply; or perhaps he simply wanted to see how Churchill responded to pressure. Whatever the reason, he left Churchill unsure of the depth of the U.S. commitment.

Still, Churchill had cleared one important hurdle. He had personally impressed Hopkins. Hopkins was always impressed by strength and boldness in political leaders, and Churchill had left no doubt that he possessed these qualities. "I have never had such an enjoyable time as I had with Mr. Churchill," Hopkins told General Lee after leaving No. 10 Downing Street, "but God, what a force that man has!"[18]

The next day, Saturday, January 11, Hopkins was off with Churchill for a weekend at Dytchley, a seventeenth-century country house north of Oxford. In this setting Churchill planned to woo Hopkins with his best skills. His major effort came that evening after dinner, when the women had left the table and he had the floor to himself. He began a sweeping historical discussion of the origins and course of the war, leaving no doubt that all present were participating in events that were shaping human destiny. At the end of his monologue he outlined Britain's war aims in a way that his informants had suggested would especially appeal to his American visitor:

> We seek no treasure, we seek no territorial gains, we seek only the right of man to be free; we seek his right to worship his God, to lead his life in his own way, secure from persecution. As the humble laborer returns from his work when day is done, and sees the smoke curling upwards from his cottage home in the serene evening sky, we wish him to know that no rat-a-tat-tat [here he rapped on the table] of the secret police upon his door will disturb his leisure or interrupt his rest. We seek government with the consent of the people, man's freedom to say what he will, and when he thinks himself injured, to find himself equal in the eyes of the law. But war aims other than these we have none.

Here he paused and, perhaps thinking that he had done a fair job of restating Roosevelt's Four Freedoms, announced about a week earlier, looked at Hopkins and asked, "What will the president say to all this?"

Hopkins paused while his audience waited anxiously for his reply. "Well, Mr. Prime Minister," he began slowly and softly, "I don't think the president will give a damn for all that." He sat there, readying himself for his next sentence, while his listeners' stomachs knotted at the thought that somehow Churchill had missed his chance.

"You see," he continued, "we're only interested in seeing that that goddam sonofabitch, Hitler, gets licked."

Loud laughter erupted, dissolving the tension and dispelling any further thoughts of "the old nonconformist conscience of Victorian liberalism."[19]

The weekend at Dytchley gave Churchill additional opportunities to impress Hopkins with his personal force. Consuming prodigious quantities of weak whiskey, he read communiqués, issued orders, conferred with Cabinet ministers, and kept up a running commentary on the historical significance of events present and past. He retired late and rose early, napping only briefly after lunch, and was forever pressing weary aides to get on with one project or another.[20]

Churchill also gave Hopkins his first look at wartime leadership in action. Hopkins was amazed by the calm with which Churchill received the news that German dive bombers had sunk or severely damaged two cruisers and a new aircraft carrier in the Mediterranean. The news arrived at 2:00 A.M., and Churchill, never faltering or despairing, kept Hopkins up until 4:00 A.M. outlining his response.

In these ways Churchill made his case. The day after he returned from Dytchley, Hopkins scribbled a few paragraphs on hotel stationery and handed them to General Lee for delivery to Roosevelt. "The people here," he wrote, "are amazing from Churchill on down and if courage alone can win—the result will be inevitable." By now he knew that "*Churchill* is the gov't in every sense of the word." He could not "emphasize too strongly that he is the one and only person" for Roosevelt to meet. Churchill, he assured the president, liked Americans and wanted a meeting. He cabled separately that he was doing his part by "urging the British Government not to advertise or accentuate any differences that may exist between us pending passage of the Lend-Lease Bill."

By this time Hopkins had been infected with the British spirit of determination. "This is no time to be out of London," he wrote, "so I am staying here—the bombs aren't nice and seem to be quite impersonal. I have been offered a so called bomb proof apartment by Churchill—a tin hat and gas mask have been delivered—the best I can say for the hat is that it looks worse than my own and doesn't fit—the gas mask I can't get on—so I am alright." If the British could be undaunted in the face of crisis, so could Harry Hopkins.[21]

Hopkins finished his notes just before leaving to accompany Churchill, Halifax, and others to Scapa Flow in Scotland, where Churchill was to tour naval facilities and see Halifax off as ambassador to Washington. It was an overnight journey, which gave Churchill a chance to keep Hopkins up late again, this time talking military strategy. The next morning Hopkins enthusiastically reported to General Lee that Churchill was sure that Hitler would not invade Britain but would mount an offensive in the Balkans. Churchill called Hitler's end "certain." (Lee wondered a bit sourly how much of Churchill's optimism was for Hopkins's benefit.)

In order to get to Scapa Flow in the Orkney Islands, the party had to board a destroyer at the tiny Scottish port of Scrapster. Hopkins almost fell into the sea when he missed his step onto the rolling deck. Thoroughly miserable in howling January weather (the sheep, Lee grumbled, either grew Harris tweed or froze to death), he crept to a sheltered spot on deck and huddled there until an officer politely told him that he was sitting on a depth charge.[22]

Churchill's tour lasted nearly a week. Hopkins tried to keep up but usually trailed behind the prime minister, coat buttoned to his neck and hat pulled down over his ears. He was stunned by Churchill's energy and strength. One night after another 2:00 A.M. session he found a warm spot in front of a fire in the bedroom of Oliver Lyttleton, the president of the Board of Trade, and sat there muttering, "Jesus Christ! What a man!"[23]

Actually the pace was taking its toll on Churchill, who had developed a bad cold and was refusing entreaties to rest. The prime minister was determined not to miss any chance to use his new friend to advertise American support. Thus the two tired men ended their Scottish tour with a dinner at the Station Hotel in Glasgow for a final show of friendship. In his after-dinner remarks Churchill drew out Hopkins with praise for Roosevelt and a reference to "the Democracy of the great American Republic." When Churchill finished, attention fell on Hopkins's thin, unkempt figure. He sat there a long moment, then rose and turned to the prime minister. "I suppose you wish to know what I am going to say to President Roosevelt on my return," he began in a soft, measured voice. "Well, I'm going to quote you one verse from the Book of Books in the truth of which Mr. Johnson [Tom Johnson, the secretary of state for Scotland and a member of the party] and my own Scottish mother were brought up: 'Whither thou goest, I will go; and where thou lodgest, I will lodge; thy people shall be my people, and thy God my God.' " Then, dropping his voice, he added, "Even to the end." No one could have said it better. Churchill sat with tears in his eyes.[24]

Hopkins returned to London hopeful of drawing Anglo-American relations even closer. The opportunity arose when Hull suggested to Roosevelt that Hopkins stay on until the arrival of the newly confirmed American ambassador, John G. Winant. Hopkins's trip, which had originally been planned for no more than two weeks, would thus last about six.

Hopkins used the extra time to broaden his contacts with anti-Axis governments. London had become the center for exiled European heads of state, and Hopkins easily gained access to them. He met with the king of Norway, the queen and foreign minister of the Netherlands, and the prime minister of Poland. Most of these were courtesy calls, for Hopkins was not authorized to offer these leaders the kind of aid he and Roosevelt had in mind for Great Britain. With their countries already under Nazi occupation, most were in no position to use it in any case. To the Polish prime minister, for example, Hopkins declared that the United States wanted to see the independence and integrity of his country restored. The Foreign Office noted with some concern that the word *integrity* had encouraged the Poles to believe that the Americans were supporting their territorial objectives beyond the promises of the British.[25] Given Hopkins's inexperience in diplomacy, however, he probably intended only to stress the United States' determination to free Poland from the Nazis.

Hopkins also met briefly with Wendell Willkie, Roosevelt's Republican opponent in 1940, whom the president had sent with a message of encouragement for Churchill (with the ulterior motive of building bipartisan support for Lend-Lease in the United States). Roosevelt's letter encouraged Churchill with a quotation from Longfellow:

> Sail on, O ship of State!
> Sail on, O Union, strong and great!
> Humanity with all its fears,
> With all the hopes of future years,
> Is hanging breathless on thy fate!

Declaring himself "deeply moved" by Roosevelt's sentiments, Churchill ordered first-class treatment for Willkie. Ever the loyal partisan, Hopkins was less enthusiastic about Willkie's visit and hoped to avoid him. But Herschel Johnson thought that courtesy demanded a meeting, so Hopkins spent an hour at Willkie's hotel. They discussed strategies for passing the Lend-Lease bill, Willkie warning Hopkins that former President Hoover would be "the real brains" behind the opposition. Hopkins passed along Willkie's information to Roosevelt, but he put it to personal use ten days later in a conversation with Anthony

Eden. Halifax had cabled that Hoover had asked Britain to lift its blockade of Continental Europe to allow U.S. ships to carry relief supplies to Belgian civilians. Halifax had opposed the request on the grounds that the relief would indirectly help Hitler while the blockade would hasten more substantial relief in the form of a British victory. Perhaps recalling that at their first meeting Churchill had warned that aiding occupied countries would relieve Hitler of being surrounded by "dejected and despairing people," Hopkins "entirely agreed" that Hoover's "agitation" was helping the Germans and suggested that Secretary Hull respond in a press conference. He expressed "the strongest views" against putting any further pressure on Britain or other allied governments on this matter.[26]

Meanwhile, Hopkins was gaining the trust and confidence of the British people. General Lee observed Hopkins's style at his first conference with British reporters. Hopkins asked for questions, and after an embarrassed silence one reporter asked what he had done that day. It was a weak question, betraying the general British ignorance of Hopkins and his mission, but Hopkins turned it to just the right effect. "I got up this morning about eight o'clock," he began, "and I took a look out of the window for the weather. Then I went into the bathroom and turned on my bath and when the tub was full I got into it." He went on this way, describing his preparations for the day. Lee noted that the reporters were at first surprised, then amused, and in the end they relaxed as Hopkins established informal rapport with them all. Hopkins used a similarly informal approach with individuals. When he first met Churchill's private secretary, John ("Jock") Colville, he told him that he had been anti-British until the king and queen had visited Washington in the spring of 1939. He and his daughter were guests in the White House at the time, and little Diana, he said, had so hoped to see the queen dressed in the finery that her fairy tales described. But on the night of the state banquet she had a high temperature and could not leave her room. When Mrs. Roosevelt heard that Diana was in tears, she asked Her Majesty for a favor, and the queen visited Diana's sickroom wearing all her jewels and emblems. "And that," said Hopkins, "is how I first came to think you people must have some good in you after all."[27]

Hopkins's quiet, self-effacing charm added strength to his words of assurance. On January 22 he spoke informally to London's most prominent newspaper editors and publishers at a gathering organized by the publishing magnate Lord Beaverbrook. Looking "lean, shy and untidy, grasping the back of his chair," as Beaverbrook recalled, Hopkins delivered his standard message. He spoke of the fine spirit of the British people, the "astonishing vigor" of the prime minister, President Roosevelt's determination to "whip Hitler," and his own role in portraying the British to the president. After his talk he walked around the dinner table, stopping to pull up a chair and talk individually to the guests. All were astonished at how well he understood their papers' policies and problems. One guest reported that Hopkins's speech had "impressed [him] very deeply," and all commented favorably on his charm and "dynamic personality." Two weeks later, after a similar dinner, another guest wrote to Hopkins: "You got right under all our skins. You made us feel you were with us materially—yes, but in ideals and spirit just as much."

Hopkins had said what needed to be said on those freezing nights when death screamed out of the sky. His soft, unassuming words reassured England that help would come. Churchill shrewdly kept Hopkins in tow, setting him up with leading questions in the knowledge that the answers would hearten and inspire his countrymen in ways that his own polished oratory could not. It was a measure of Churchill's own need for reassurance that Hopkins's quotation from the Book of Ruth moved him to tears. "We were happy men all," recalled one of the guests at the Beaverbrook dinner, "our confidence and our courage had been stimulated by a contact for which Shakespeare, in 'Henry V,' had a phrase: 'A little touch of Harry in the night.' "[28]

Although Hopkins established many personal relationships in Britain, he always kept his own role in perspective. He consistently expressed only general support and neither undertook negotiations nor offered suggestions on policies. Even before he left the United States, he knew that his job would be to establish a link between Roosevelt and Churchill, not to put himself forward. "I suppose you could say," he observed after his first meeting with Churchill, "that I've come here to try to find a way to be a catalytic agent between two prima donnas."[29]

In this spirit Hopkins's discussions of American attitudes and policies centered on Roosevelt. One Sunday evening at Chequers, Churchill's private residence, he asked Hopkins about American objectives. Hopkins replied that the president was less interested in the distant future than in the next few months, and except for a few "liberal intellectuals," who were with Roosevelt anyway, the American people felt the same way. Hopkins then divided the American public into four groups: a small number of Nazis and communists who sheltered themselves behind Charles Lindbergh and called for a negotiated peace; those who, like former Ambassador Kennedy, wanted to help Britain while avoiding war; the majority, who supported Roosevelt's determination to send all possible aid to Britain regardless of the risk; and a small group of about 10 to 15 percent, including Knox, Stimson, and most of the military, who favored entering the war immediately. "The important element in the situation," he declared was "the boldness of the president." Roosevelt would "use his powers . . . make people gasp with surprise." The president did not want war, but, Hopkins assured Churchill, "he would not shrink" from it.[30]

The most important use to which Hopkins put his extra days was to acquaint himself with British supply problems. Hopkins met with a full range of British experts in finance, production, and shipping. With his usual interest in detail, he requested and received information on food imports and aircraft, including the number of planes in operation and the volume of production, losses, repairs, and imports. He investigated the effects of the Blitz, asking for figures on the number of raids and alerts, on casualties and services for the injured and homeless, and on the amount of damage.

By the end of January, Hopkins was sending specific requisitions to Roosevelt and Hull: for B-17 bombers, ready for immediate operation, with spare parts, engines, bombs, and ammunition, as well as experienced American reserve officers and men to deliver them and put them into service; for more training aircraft, personnel for flying schools, and help in ferrying the planes across the Atlantic; and an urgent call—"now (repeat now)"—for rifles and ammunition. In a February 3 cable he reviewed the British shipping situation, emphasizing the seriousness of British losses and urging that even at the risk of "sacrificing important economic advantages to our own economy and shipping throughout the world," the United States should "try to find additional shipping in substantial amounts at once." He also recommended selling the British some usable but obsolete destroyers.[31] In the end Hopkins's hours of conversation and requests for specifics produced a list of fourteen items (labeled by the American military "Hopkins 14 Points") that identified Britain's most urgent supply needs.

On January 30 Chancellor of the Exchequer Kingsley Wood brought Hopkins a public relations problem. Morgenthau had announced that Britain did not have the funds to pay for additional planes. Since the British were going to order the planes anyway, Wood was worried that news would leak out and jeopardize the Lend-Lease bill. Hopkins recommended that either Halifax or Sir Arthur Purvis of the British Purchasing Commission confer with Morgenthau and work out a joint statement.[32]

As his support for the British cause grew, Hopkins felt the frustrations of American neutrality. Eden asked him what the United States could do to restrain Japan from attacking British possessions in Asia. He replied, "I am pretty certain what the president would do if Hong Kong were attacked, but I guess I cannot tell you about it." He thought that Roosevelt should call in the Japanese ambassador for a talk "in words of one syllable," and he left Eden with the impression that he would urge Roosevelt to employ the Pacific Fleet more menacingly.[33] In the end, however, Hopkins realized that he had overstepped his authority and would have to content himself with reporting the conversation and letting Roosevelt draw his own conclusions.

The best he could do was to urge Roosevelt to rush all possible aid to Britain. The United States should act "on the assumption that an invasion will come before May 1st . . . If Germany fails to win this invasion . . . I believe her sun is set." All of this echoed Churchill, as did his declaration that bold and prompt action "on a few major fronts" would give Britain enough strength to defeat the enemy. "Your decisive action now," he told the president, "can mean the difference between defeat and victory in this country."[34]

Hopkins wound up his trip by conferring with Churchill about a radio address the prime minister proposed to give on the need for U.S. aid. The speech they worked out followed familiar lines, emphasizing Britain's steadfastness, eschewing the need for American troops, and calling for "an immense and continuous supply" of war materiel. Striking just the right bipartisan note, Churchill mentioned Willkie's visit and read the quotation from Longfellow that Roosevelt had sent. He concluded with a typically ringing declaration: "Give us the tools and we will finish the job."

*Hopkins and Winston Churchill, January 1941*

Hopkins heard Churchill's speech at Bournemouth the night before he was to leave for home. He had left behind a note scrawled on Chequers stationery:

My dear Mr. Prime Minister:
   I shall never forget these days with you—your supreme confidence and will to victory—Britain I have ever liked—I like it the more. As I leave for America tonight I wish you great and good luck—confusion to your enemies and victory for Britain.

Ever so cordially,
Harry Hopkins[35]

He arrived in New York on Saturday, February 15, and reached Washington two days later. Hopkins's mission had been an altogether remarkable achievement. He had succeeded beyond all reasonable expectations in obtaining the "overall picture." He had interviewed all of Britain's top civilian and military leaders, including Lord Halifax, the new ambassador to Washington. He had visited defense installations from northern Scotland to Dover. He had read British newspapers and spoken with their publishers. He had been thoroughly briefed on Britain's economic, political, and military situation and had been entrusted with a bundle of top secret documents to take on his return trip. No one could have been better prepared to advise the president on how to build the Lend-Lease partnership.

Hopkins had also succeeded in establishing a relationship of trust with Churchill and other British leaders. This was the most unexpected benefit of his mission, for he had shown an intuitive gift for personal diplomacy. Direct, low key, unaffected, Hopkins was the perfect emissary to a nation in crisis. His rapport with Churchill was especially valuable, forging as he had a bond of friendship with Britain's most dominant figure.[36]

Of course Churchill valued Hopkins for other than his personal qualities. Harold Ickes put it accurately, if a bit too cynically, when he remarked that if Roosevelt had sent someone with the bubonic plague, Churchill would have taken him in tow.[37] Still, Churchill seems to have valued Hopkins as more than just a channel to the president; he felt Hopkins's sympathies for Britain and realized that he was a man worth cultivating in his own right. This estimation, and not Churchill's desperation alone, explains why the prime minister was so candid with Hopkins, and why he avoided the temptation, indulged in by Eden and others, to try to manipulate Hopkins for his own ends. Hopkins's simple directness and unaffected friendship encouraged Churchill to be frank and thus made a vital contribution to building a workable and lasting Lend-Lease partnership.

It may be argued that Churchill was indeed trying to maneuver the United States into the war, and that in this respect his assurances that Britain intended to fight on alone were designed to deceive. It is also true that the records of the Hopkins-Churchill conversations do not show whether the issue of U.S. entry into the war was raised. Still, Hopkins was aware that the question existed. R. A. Butler, parliamentary undersecretary at the Foreign Office, recalled years later that during his discussion with Eden about the threat of Japanese expansion, Hopkins asked "anxiously" whether Britain really wanted the United States in the war. Butler said yes, adding that great democracies only got to work when they were "up against it." Hopkins was evasive, saying only that everyone should wait to see how Lend-Lease turned out.[38]

Hopkins had gone to London to see if the British were tough enough to keep on fighting. Churchill had passed this test with flying colors; indeed the prime minister's toughness had almost run Hopkins into the ground. Eden and Halifax too had measured up, in unexpected ways. If Hopkins had studied their records, he would probably have thought well of Eden, who had resigned from the Chamberlain government to protest its appeasement policies, and would have disliked Halifax, who had been an architect of those policies. But Hopkins came away from his meeting with Eden convinced that the foreign secretary was "suave, impeccable, unimportant." "I am sure the man has no deeply rooted moral stamina," he went on. "A goodly number of soft Britishers must like him . . . and I fancy Churchill gives him high office because he neither thinks [nor] acts—much less says anything of importance." Halifax he found to be a "different and somewhat tougher breed," and recommended him to Roosevelt. He was suspicious of the new ambassador's Tory social views and hoped that he would not have a say in the postwar peacemaking, but he thought that his faults were unimportant as long as "we can get on with our business of licking Hitler."[39]

Hopkins was certainly mistaken about Eden, and as the war went on he modified his opinion of him. Still, for the most part Eden found himself, like Secretary Hull, cut off from the highest levels of policy making. From the standpoint of the Anglo-American alliance this may have been for the best, since Churchill was consistently more inclined than Eden to compromise with the United States.[40] Hopkins's good opinion of Halifax meanwhile enabled the ambassador to play a constructive part in the war effort, largely because of the cordial relations he enjoyed with Hopkins in Washington.

Hopkins's concern for toughness shaped his admiration of Churchill, and indeed of the British people as a whole. It also showed in his thinking about war aims. On one occasion Churchill, still probing for the "nonconformist conscience of Victorian liberalism," declared that peace should be established on the principles of the Sermon on the Mount. Hopkins replied that the problems of reconstruction would be greater than the prime minister had implied and that he "would have to send men to the conference table who were tough and not sentimental."[41]

In the end Hopkins concluded that the British were worth supporting because they were "about as tough a crowd as there is."[42] This was probably all one could have expected from someone with Hopkins's lack of experience in diplomacy and military science. But for Hopkins himself the mission to Britain was invaluable. It had jolted him off the track toward listless retirement onto which his failing health had seemed to shunt him. The question now was how far this new opportunity would take him.

*Chapter 10*

# Delivering the Goods

Hopkins returned from England just as the Senate was beginning floor debate on the Lend-Lease bill. Outside administration circles no one realized that he was carrying the key to the Anglo-American partnership. Aside from helping to defeat a limiting amendment to the bill, Hopkins stayed out of sight. On March 8 the Senate approved Lend-Lease by a vote of sixty to thirty-one. The House then approved the Senate version and sent the bill to Roosevelt on the evening of March 11. He signed it at once. Now he had authority to aid any nation whose defense he deemed essential to U.S. security by transferring up to $1.3 billion in weapons and other war materiel from American stocks or by paying for their manufacture from a special appropriation (which was later set at $7 billion). He could "sell, transfer title to, exchange, lease, lend, or otherwise dispose of" the materiel. Congress had removed the dollar sign.

During Congress's final consideration of the bill Hopkins kept in touch with Churchill. The prime minister was grateful but cautious. Britain needed help immediately. Lend-Lease would work only if the supplies arrived rapidly.[1]

By this time Hopkins was seeking the power to be sure that they did. The day he returned from England Morgenthau privately told him that he and Stimson had proposed to administer Lend-Lease through a Cabinet committee composed of the secretaries of state, war, the Navy, and the Treasury. Hopkins told Morgenthau that he wanted to spend the next two or three months expediting aid to Britain. Next he persuaded Roosevelt to appoint him the committee's executive secretary. In the meantime he practiced for the job by personally moving along a shipment of rifles and ammunition.[2]

He was back on his familiar track of emergency management. Rapidly he pulled together a staff. From the Treasury Department he obtained Philip Young, who had previously consulted with the War Department on Britain's supply needs, and assigned him to organize files, keep records, and maintain communication with other agencies. For legal advice he acquired another Treasury assistant, Oscar Cox, who had helped draft the Lend-Lease bill. He soon learned that Cox was far more able than he had imagined. Creative and deft, Cox not only invented ingenious ways to unsnarl legal tangles but also anticipated problems and fine-tuned policies and procedures. His memoranda flowed like water from a mountain spring. He became a key member of Hopkins's staff and one of his most loyal coworkers.[3]

Even more valuable than Cox was General James H. Burns. A career army officer and former head of the Army Ordnance Department, Burns was well respected in the War Department and in Congress. A strong advocate of the U.S. defense buildup and of aid to Britain, he had served on committees to expedite sending supplies through the British Purchasing Commission and to assist the Office of Production Management, which Roosevelt had created to stimulate defense production. Burns had the breadth of view necessary to keep Lend-Lease independent of established, self-interested agencies. He had been the only army officer to insist that the president rather than the War Department should control the Lend-Lease appropriation. Perhaps less imaginative than Cox, he was nonetheless better equipped to map out large-scale objectives and to suggest strategies for attaining them.[4]

With his staff in place, Hopkins was poised for his customary running start. By the time Lend-Lease became law, Cox had drawn up a form to transfer defense materiel. Hopkins proposed to test the procedures by immediately transferring ten Coast Guard cutters to convoy Lend-Lease supplies from Nova Scotia. In the meantime Burns worked up a budget and a production program that minimized War Department interference. Hopkins had already sent the War Department his list of Britain's fourteen top-priority requests and had in hand from Arthur Purvis, head of the recently created British Supply Council in North America (which had replaced the British Purchasing Commission), a complete statement of British requirements to June 30, 1942.[5] Hopkins had also arranged with Roosevelt to send Averell Harriman to London to keep track of British needs.

Immediately Hopkins ran into snags. When the army examined his Fourteen Points, they found that they could fulfill some. But they were either unable or only partially able to meet requests for .50 caliber machine guns, bombers, and engines and parts for other combat aircraft. Particularly troublesome was the Army Air Corps, which was undertaking its own large buildup. General Henry H. ("Hap") Arnold, deputy chief of staff for the Air Corps, derided Hopkins's "piecemeal reinforcement" and warned that siphoning off supplies would leave the United States unable to defend the Western Hemisphere.[6]

Hopkins had a scare when one of his optimistic assurances to the British also came back to haunt him. In London he had encouraged the chancellor of the exchequer, Kingsley Wood, to place war orders in the United States on the assumption that Roosevelt would take care of any financial difficulties. Wood thought that this meant that the United States would take over British contracts entered into before Lend-Lease became law. Hopkins did not know that Roosevelt, fearing that such a deal might jeopardize the Lend-Lease bill, had ordered Morgenthau to eliminate this aspect of the arrangement.[7]

When Hopkins returned, the British continued to place orders on the assumption that Lend-Lease would pay off their previous contracts. Then Budget Director Harold Smith informed Congress that none of the appropriation would be used for this purpose. To keep this from stalling work on all current British contracts, Burns and Cox recommended that the two governments sign letters of intent so that U.S. manufacturers could go ahead with production, with contract details to be worked out when the Lend-Lease appropriation passed.[8]

To some, the need for this kind of improvisation suggested that Hopkins was not doing his job. As late as May 17, Morgenthau, who had been in almost constant contact with Hopkins over Lend-Lease administration and finance, commented to Philip Young, "I get the feeling that Harry is still sort of fishing around and really doesn't know what he wants." Purvis complained of difficulty working with Hopkins, who did not always know what he wanted.[9]

Those who blamed Hopkins, however, were blaming him for a communication problem not entirely of his own making. Halifax described the situation accurately when he wrote to Churchill: "I do not think the president ties up awfully well; I am quite sure Harry Hopkins doesn't, and as for the Government Departments they might almost as well be the administrations of different countries. The result is, I suspect, that individuals like Hopkins try to do too much and have no means of following up their activities, and that a great deal of what we try to do from the outside seems like hitting wads of cotton wool."[10]

Halifax's assessment would have been even more accurate if he had said that Hopkins did not "tie up" largely because Roosevelt did not.

As he had with the WPA appropriation, the president was handling Lend-Lease piecemeal, without attending to the program's interrelationships. It made good political sense, for example, for Harold Smith, whom Congress respected in fiscal matters, to present the administration's case for the Lend-Lease appropriation. Allowing Smith to work independently of Hopkins and Morgenthau, however, resulted in his undercutting their financial arrangements with the British. Roosevelt certainly kept Hopkins and Morgenthau in the dark about the Lend-Lease appropriation and perhaps even kept Smith uninformed about important aspects of the subject.

Hopkins had done his best to prevent this from happening. The day Roosevelt signed the Lend-Lease bill Hopkins told him: "You've just got to get a-straddle of this now; you can't act the way you're acting about this, you've got to have this [advisory] committee together once a week. Otherwise, we're going to get all balled up here and I'm working like hell on these things and it's got to be done one of two ways. Either I've got to go each week and spend a great deal of time with each member of the committee, which I think is very unsatisfactory, or you've got to have them together so they're in the room with you during these early weeks of this thing." The president appreciated the problem, but he allowed things to continue to slide. "He's not easy to handle, Henry, you know," was all Hopkins could tell Morgenthau when he reported the conversation.[11]

By the end of March, Hopkins was beginning to free himself from these administrative difficulties. The advisory committee sputtered and gradually died. Authority then gravitated to the president, who controlled the $7 billion appropriation and approved all transfers. Once his authority had been confirmed, Roosevelt declared that he would approve each Lend-Lease item individually rather than allocating money in lump sums to executive departments. At the same time, he officially designated Hopkins "to advise and assist me in carrying out the responsibilities placed upon me" by the Lend-Lease Act. He set Hopkins's salary (Hopkins had not been on the federal payroll since he resigned as secretary of commerce) at $10,000 a year.[12]

Before he could get on with his job, Hopkins had to settle a dispute within his own organization. He had let it be known that he intended to appoint General Burns his second in command, but Treasury objected, arguing that no army man would allow sufficient transfers of military equipment to Britain. Morgenthau wanted his associate Philip Young to have the job. But Hopkins insisted on Burns.

Actually Hopkins was playing a more complicated game than Morgenthau and Young realized. Of course he knew that Burns's ties to the army would not compromise his loyalty to Lend-Lease and that Burns's years of military experience well qualified him to evaluate Britain's requests. But the real issue was Hopkins's own administrative objectives. Young advocated setting up an independent, centralized Lend-Lease administration with the power to force U.S. agencies to comply with its aid program. But Hopkins saw his organization instead as a channel through which all interested parties could work toward agreement.[13] This reflected the advisory, persuasive approach he had employed throughout his career and which now was promising its greatest results. Over the years Roosevelt's style had been to bring competitors together to achieve a common purpose. (A classic example was his organization of work relief.) More often than not the result had been inefficient wrangling. In Hopkins, however, he now had someone who could make this approach work. To be effective, Hopkins had to remain close to Roosevelt and wear a badge of presidential authority. Setting up an independent agency would have reduced his power by making him only one self-interested party in the general competition for the president's favor.

Hopkins's approach also suited his fragile health. As a presidential adviser he could continue to live in the White House and to work out of his living quarters. Soon Morgenthau was calling Cox and Young the "Harry Hopkins Bedroom Boys." They and many others transacted their business while Hopkins sat in a bed littered with memoranda, cables, production charts, and other documents. Working at the White House also shielded Hopkins from the routine of a regular bureau chief, enabling him to see only those people he wanted to see, maintained his ready access to the president, and made it easier for him to arrange ad hoc meetings to work out problems. The drawback, of course, was that everyone knew who was to blame if things went wrong. Hopkins was, he admitted, "in about as hot a spot as any man can be in."[14]

Hopkins began by courting both the British and the U.S. Army. He first told the British that he expected the army to oppose many of their supply requests. To help Roosevelt overcome such opposition, he suggested that Churchill arrange for the British military chiefs to examine all proposals so that the prime minister could assure the president that the supplies were absolutely necessary. Warning them that the United States might not be able to meet all requests, he suggested that the

British draw up a list of priorities, and he arranged with the British vice air marshal, J. C. Slessor, to form a small committee of military and production representatives. Hopkins then dropped in for lunch with Army Chief of Staff George C. Marshall and in a "purely casual" discussion expressed concern that the British had asked for too much and that it might be a good idea to discover their "actual necessities." He suggested that Marshall, General Arnold, and the navy chief Harold Stark visit London to confer with the British. When Arnold left for Britain, Hopkins warned Churchill that the general wanted to build up the American army "at all costs" and had "a tendency to resist efforts to give adequate aid to England." Still, he recommended him as "an excellent officer," who should be given an "intimate" view of the British situation.[15]

If Hopkins's methods lacked candor and tended toward telling people what they wanted to hear, they were at least realistic. The truth was that the hard-pressed British were bound to ask for more than the United States could supply, and American officials were bound to object. Under the circumstances the best that he could hope for was to bring the parties together to begin resolving their differences. And if Hopkins was going to make himself a channel for this kind of communication, it was essential that the parties trust him. Among the British he had better success with Churchill, Eden, and other high-ranking officials than with Purvis and Halifax, who were bewildered by his methods and unsure of his aims. Still, as Hopkins confirmed his authority, he gained their confidence by expediting their requests.[16]

Hopkins succeeded spectacularly with the Americans. Morgenthau had feared that Hopkins was not healthy enough to take on the job, but Young assured him that Hopkins could handle the work and was seeking advice in the right places. Cox was even more enthusiastic, praising Hopkins's "genius" for personal relations, his stamina, and his ability to get results. At first Stimson feared that Hopkins had absorbed too much of the British point of view. A subsequent talk with Hopkins, however, convinced him that "it is a Godsend that he [Hopkins] should be at the White House and that the president should have sent him to Great Britain where he has gotten on such intimate terms with the people there." He had come to appreciate and respect Hopkins "more and more the more I see him."[17]

No one appreciated Hopkins more than George Marshall. In many ways the friendship with Marshall was the most unusual one Hopkins formed during these years. Hopkins had much in common with the bright, energetic Cox and Young, the genial Morgenthau, and the blunt, no-nonsense Stimson. But Marshall was a different case altogether. Self-contained and almost totally humorless, he acted with a stiff, cold formality that was singularly forbidding. If anyone should have had a hard time warming up to Harry Hopkins, it was Marshall. But the two cooperated splendidly. Perhaps Marshall felt indebted to Hopkins. Many years later he said that he had always believed that Hopkins had been responsible for his appointment as chief of staff. Still, it seems more likely that it was Hopkins who broke through to Marshall. Hopkins admired Marshall's steadiness, self-control, and devotion to duty. Throughout the war he praised the general without reservation and constantly spoke well of him to President Roosevelt. Marshall especially appreciated Hopkins's support because he felt that the president, an old navy man, all but ignored the army. Eventually Marshall also came to see in Hopkins the same kind of self-sacrificing devotion that he valued in himself. Hopkins's willingness to risk his fragile health touched and alarmed him. When in 1942 Hopkins became engaged, Marshall wrote to Hopkins's fiancée:

> To be very frank, I am intensely interested in Harry's health and happiness, and therefore, in your approaching marriage. He has been gallant and self-sacrificing to an extreme, little of which is realized by any but his most intimate friends. He is of great importance to our national interests at the present time, and he is one of the most imprudent people regarding his health that I have ever known. Therefore, and possibly inexcusable as it may seem to you, I express the hope that you will find it possible to curb his indiscretions and see that he takes the necessary rest.[18]

Hopkins's success with the War Department paid important dividends to Lend-Lease. Stimson called in his leading civilian and military advisers and gave them a fighting talk in support of aid to Britain. At once the department went to work establishing informal committees to work out expenditure programs with the British. That was just the spirit that Hopkins had hoped to inspire.

Hopkins's informal methods could not overcome the need for some organization. Lend-Lease needed a filing system to keep track of orders, and Congress wanted a regular accounting system. To satisfy these needs, Roosevelt created the Division of Defense Aid Reports under General Burns. In so doing the president left Hopkins free to handle the special problems that kept cropping up. At times Hopkins must have thought that he had been transported back to his most hectic days as relief administrator. He arranged to build trawlers and mine sweepers in Canada and dispatched tugs and lighters to the Suez Canal. He blocked an attempt by the navy to appropriate Lend-Lease funds to repair its own ships but compensated them by arranging to take the money from the Reconstruction Finance Corporation (RFC). He hurried along a contract for a hydraulic press to satisfy Robert A. Taft, the Republican senator from Ohio, who complained that red tape was holding up the Ohio manufacturer.[19]

All the while Hopkins kept a lookout for top-flight administrators. He praised one U.S. Maritime Commission official who rounded up fifteen ships to transport extra tanks that the British had ordered at the last minute. "This fellow . . . is a honey," Hopkins reported to Harriman. "He moves rapidly and cuts through all red tape and I am sure that if the ships are here he will get them."[20]

Hopkins thought that Lend-Lease would work most effectively if it avoided financial matters. He consistently advised the British to think only about the quantities of supplies they needed and to let the United States worry about paying the bill. As a result the British Supply Council officially catalogued only the items they ordered and made no financial accounting of their Lend-Lease transactions.

But some financial issues were easier to eliminate than others. The Lend-Lease Act provided that the United States could transfer up to $1.3 billion of its own war supplies. It did not require the president to fix the terms of repayment before approving transfers, and Roosevelt himself assured Halifax that the only stipulation was that the British "go on fighting." Roosevelt had no sooner signed the bill, however, than he began to tell Hopkins about his ideas for a British "quid pro quo." Hopkins still thought that the United States should give the supplies without expecting anything in return; but since Roosevelt would not see it that way, he proposed to set up accounts under a few large headings such as shipping or ordnance. Ideally, Hopkins felt, repayment could be handled in "one big over-all deal." But he never got beyond these vague speculations as Roosevelt turned the matter over to Morgenthau, who initiated complex and wearying discussions that took months to complete.[21]

The biggest financial headache arose over the contracts predating Lend-Lease. Harold Smith had assured Congress that Lend-Lease would not pay off these contracts, which amounted to about $400 million, although this contradicted promises Hopkins and Morgenthau had given the British. But since the administration was going to have to ask Congress for more money, no one wanted to renege on Smith's commitment.

In May the British forced the issue by sending the noted economist John Maynard Keynes to Washington. He arrived with a proposal that complicated matters even further. In addition to asking the Americans to pay off the previous contracts, he also asked them to allocate an additional $650 million to buy items that would be politically difficult to acquire under Lend-Lease. This was bad enough, but Hopkins found Keynes's attitude particularly annoying. "He sort of assumes that we don't give a damn," Hopkins complained to Morgenthau, "and it just—it irritates me." Hopkins was afraid that "if he hangs around here until we get mixed up in a new Lend-Lease bill, he's apt to pull some real boners with some of the people on the Hill or something and he'll be telling us how to write a Lend-Lease bill and people will get madder than hell around here about it." Worst of all, Keynes was using him to outflank the Treasury Department. "You see what he's going to do," Hopkins observed to Morgenthau. "He's going to move on any front he thinks he can move on."[22]

If Keynes was moving on several different fronts, it was partly because of the peculiarities of Lend-Lease administration. Morgenthau might have promised the money in March, but by May, Hopkins had it. On another front Roosevelt had assigned the State Department responsibility for negotiating the terms of Britain's repayments of Lend-Lease. After a few weeks Keynes was convinced that "everything is done, so to speak, backstairs, and unless one spends three quarters of the day seeing people on one pretext or another, one knows nothing and can effect little."

The illogic of the situation caused Hopkins to realize that he had to take matters in hand. He began diverting British contracts into Lend-Lease categories, telling Morgenthau that his "main interest" was to relieve the Treasury of this commitment.[23] By these means he whittled down the British obligation to $100 million. Oscar Cox then proposed to have Lend-Lease take over this amount, with Britain promising to repay after the war. At a meeting with Treasury officials, Hopkins responded cautiously to Cox's plan.

"You are pretty sure this doesn't violate Smith's testimony?" he asked.

"No," Cox replied.

"You have no doubt about that?"

"No."

Hopkins explored another line. "Are you sure the British will agree to this? After all, this is a fancy deal here, Oscar. As far as I can see, [they are] coming back at you and saying, 'Well, my God, you aren't relieving me of anything. All you are doing is postponing the evil day when I have got to pay dollars.' "

"If [they are] smart, [they] won't say that," chimed in Ed Foley, who had helped Cox draft the Lend-Lease bill.

"If [they are] smart, [they] would," Hopkins replied.

Foley and Cox felt that since the British were complaining about their immediate cash problems, they would probably accept a plan to defer payment. Cox suggested that if Britain won the war, a debt of $50 to $100 million would not be much to worry about. At last Hopkins was satisfied and ready to go to work.[24]

Morgenthau followed up by suggesting that British representatives meet daily with Lend-Lease and Treasury representatives to examine all British contracts so as to get as many orders as possible under Lend-Lease and to keep abreast of Britain's financial condition. Seeing a chance to rid himself of the issue, Hopkins jumped at the suggestion. "That's a damn good idea," he told Morgenthau, when the secretary told him that he was planning to have the first meeting that afternoon. Morgenthau invited him to attend, but he begged off and promised to send Cox.[25]

In the end Keynes was properly grateful. "If there is a hitch," he reported, "it will not be the fault of either Morgenthau or the Treasury officials or of Hopkins and his lend lease [sic] boys. They are stretching their ingenuity and using their time in trying to find ways to replenish our dollars."[26]

Thus Hopkins put Lend-Lease into operation. Indeed he performed remarkably. He kept his independence of established departments while winning the trust and confidence of their high-ranking officials. He recruited an active, resourceful staff. Although he made mistakes by promising the British more financial aid than the United States could conveniently offer and then hampered Morgenthau's efforts to resolve the matter, he made up for these faults by helping Morgenthau settle his problems with Keynes.

The key to Hopkins's power was his relationship with Roosevelt.

The president's decision to send him to Britain had given him his chance, and Roosevelt's decision to supervise Lend-Lease gave him the means to follow through. In performing his duties Hopkins evoked presidential authority more effectively than he conveyed it. That is, it was much easier for him to take charge of a situation, to open new lines of communication, or to provide information than to issue presidential orders. Sometimes this was so because he disagreed with Roosevelt's policy, as in the case of requiring the British to repay Lend-Lease aid; at other times it was because the president's caution in dealing with Congress or his habit of vaguely considering various alternatives left Hopkins without the direction he needed to get fast action. On these occasions Hopkins could only advise the president or ask others to state their case. During the early days of organizing Lend-Lease he lacked both the will and the means to force the president's hand.

Hopkins's greatest disappointment was caused by the slow pace of the Lend-Lease program. By May 20 only $17 million in aid had actually been shipped. This was, he admitted, "discouraging news," but he was not going to apologize. When the time came for the president to make his first quarterly report to Congress, Hopkins rejected a speech draft by General Burns, which put too much emphasis on explaining why the program was taking so long to develop, and approved one by Oscar Cox which outlined the positive accomplishments of American aid, noted that more needed to be done, and promised that it would be. "These facts of Lend-Lease's accomplishments," Cox wrote, ". . . do not present the most important fact of all—the strong will of our people to see to it that these forces of aggression are stamped out."[27]

These were fighting words, but for Harry Hopkins, who believed in doing rather than talking, they raised a most serious prospect. Since his mission to London, Hopkins had done far more than anyone would have expected of him. But despite all his meetings, memos, and phone calls, despite all his last-minute adjustments, explanations, assurances, and decisions, he had come to believe that one more thing needed to be done. So it was that during the course of a luncheon with Admiral Richmond K. Turner, director of the navy's War Plans Division, he asked what steps the army and navy ought to take on the assumption that by August 1 the United States would be at war.[28]

# *Chapter 11*

# Supplies and Strategy

Hopkins's decision that the United States would have to enter the war was based on his fear that Hitler might be able to defeat or at least isolate Britain before Lend-Lease could become effective. Even as Hopkins was flying home from London in March, German submarine "wolf packs" were prowling the North Atlantic. By the end of the month British ships were going to the bottom faster than they could be replaced. The Luftwaffe shifted its major bombing runs from London to Britain's port cities. On March 25 Hitler extended his war zone to the east coast of Greenland. Churchill cabled Hopkins, "The strain at sea on our naval resources is too great for us . . . We simply have not got enough escorts to go round and fight at the same time."[1]

Throughout April, Britain faced one setback after another. Hitler's armies overran Yugoslavia and Greece. When Churchill shifted troops from the Middle East to meet the Greek invasion, the Germans bottled up the Tobruk garrison. Desperate, Churchill asked Roosevelt to extend the American neutrality zone, through which the U.S. Navy would escort merchant ships, eastward. He hoped that the United States would ship supplies directly to Egypt, which the British were defending and using as their base in the Middle East.

Churchill's appeal evoked a divided response. Morgenthau feared that shipping directly to the Middle East would violate the Neutrality Act, which forbade American ships from sailing into combat zones. Hopkins thought that the issue was essentially military. Many American generals doubted that the British could hold the Middle East and feared that Lend-Lease supplies would be wasted. To settle the issue Hopkins wanted the British to bring their Middle East commander, General Archibald Wavell, to Washington for consultations.

In seeing the connection between supplies and strategy Hopkins had uncovered the central issue in Lend-Lease. At that moment, however, with Lend-Lease not yet firmly established, with lines of authority unclear, and with his reputation for insight into fundamental issues as

162

yet unrecognized, he was unable to convince others of the connection. Morgenthau actually persuaded Arthur Purvis of the British Supply Council to divert attention from Hopkins's suggestion to bring Wavell to Washington, and Roosevelt concentrated on building up U.S. naval strength in the North Atlantic.[2] On April 3 the president extended the neutrality zone, east to include Iceland. For the moment Hopkins sank into a morass of detail, finding ways to implement Roosevelt's decision.

As he lurched from one issue to another, Hopkins became convinced that the time had come to organize Roosevelt's sources of strategic military information more systematically and to improve coordination between the Americans and the British. Indeed, Anglo-American military discussions had broken down. By early April the American generals thought that the British should pull back and concentrate on protecting their home islands and the Atlantic sea lanes. But because they feared that such advice would damage British morale and strengthen Churchill's appeasement-minded opponents, they kept quiet. Thus when Roosevelt asked General Marshall what would happen if the British had to withdraw from Greece, the chief of staff could not answer because he did not know what forces the British had in the area. He was so sure that the British were caught in a "tragic" situation that he had thought it would be cruel to ask for the information.[3] Nor did the Cabinet see a connection between Lend-Lease supplies and military strategy. Morgenthau was uninterested in strategic questions, Hull was overcautious, and Stimson and Knox were inclined to go along with their military chiefs. The Lend-Lease apparatus seemed inappropriate, especially since Morgenthau had talked Purvis out of having General Wavell sent to Washington. If Hopkins wanted to move strategic planning off dead center, he would have to do it himself.

Between April 11 and April 15 he tried to put together a committee consisting of General Stanley Embick, a top army planner, Admiral George C. Reeves of the navy's planning staff, General Sir Frederick Beaumont-Nesbitt, the newly-arrived army attaché at the British embassy, and Admiral Victor Danckwerts, Britain's chief naval planner. He wanted these four to meet informally with President Roosevelt to keep him up to date on British and American strategic thinking. He also recommended a regular air shuttle between Washington and London so that officers could carry messages too sensitive for wireless transmission.

In his first meeting with Beaumont-Nesbitt, Hopkins candidly described the U.S. military's pessimistic attitude toward the situation in the Middle East and asked the general to be prepared to give his views to the president. Roosevelt was determined to help Britain, he said, but he still had to guide public opinion. To open communications with Marshall, Hopkins suggested that Beaumont-Nesbitt ask the general if the Americans were getting enough information. He then told the British ambassador, Lord Halifax, to have military representatives ready to confer with Roosevelt on April 14.[4]

In the meantime Hopkins also primed the American side. He interrupted a discussion among Stimson, Knox, and Marshall about the Middle East to declare that the time had come for Roosevelt to decide whether the United States should go to war, and if so, when. The president was not getting the necessary information, he complained; the State Department was wasting time with "trivial" diplomatic moves, and as a result the United States was "frittering away" its supplies without tangible results. He announced to the three men that Roosevelt was planning to meet the next day with Marshall, Embick, Chief of Naval Operations Harold Stark, and other military advisers. Hopkins's efforts broke the impasse. Marshall and the British reopened discussions. At the White House meeting Roosevelt announced that the United States would support the British in defending the Middle East.[5]

This was just what Hopkins wanted. All along he had encouraged a strong stand against Hitler. Now he proposed to maintain the momentum. In late April he acquired a summary of a tentative plan worked out earlier that year by American and British representatives. If the United States entered the war, according to the plan, the allies would blockade and bomb Germany and Italy while preparing for a land offensive. If Japan entered the war, Germany would remain the primary enemy. Though neither Stimson, Knox, nor Roosevelt had approved the plan, Hopkins wanted the United States to prepare as if they had. This was why he had asked Admiral Turner how the navy could be ready to enter the war by August 1.

Turner recommended a number of steps, and Hopkins assured him that if these recommendations went to the president, Roosevelt would have them carried out.[6] But almost immediately problems arose. Turner found that the army lacked the necessary antiaircraft weapons and wanted no American troops sent to Britain before September. Roosevelt heeded cautionary advice from Hull and Stark and delayed transferring ships to patrol the Atlantic neutral zones.[7]

At the same time Hopkins was fighting for more ships to carry Lend-Lease supplies. As the wolf packs' attacks climbed to disastrous levels, Averell Harriman, Hopkins's Lend-Lease representative in London, reported that Britain's shipping needs ranked ahead of its needs for tanks, bombers, and food. Roosevelt had ordered merchant ship construction increased, but his orders had come up against an obstacle in the person of retired Vice Admiral Emory S. ("Jerry") Land, the chairman of the U.S. Maritime Commission, the nation's shipbuilding authority. "If you want fast ships, fast shipbuilding, fast women, or fast horses," Land liked to say, "you pay through the nose." This tough-talking sailor disliked paying through the nose, especially for Britain. "If we do not watch our step," he warned Roosevelt and Hopkins, "we shall find the White House en route to England with the Washington Monument as a steering oar." Building more ships, Land argued, would be like trying to douse a fire with gasoline. Instead he recommended that Great Britain concentrate on bombing German construction sites and providing better protection for ships at sea. Although in the end he worked hard to accomplish Roosevelt's expansion program, in the tense atmosphere of that spring he seemed an obstructionist. By the end of April, Hopkins was describing the shipping situation as "the most God awful mess."[8]

Whenever there was a mess to clean up, Hopkins found himself holding the mop. During March and April, Hopkins kept in touch with Vice Admiral Land, with Commander (later Vice Admiral) Howard L. Vickery, who had charge of ship construction, and with Sir Arthur Salter of the British Shipbuilding Mission. He helped Vickery recruit executives from the shipbuilding industry and channeled ideas between him and Salter. Steel shortages led him to look into a rumor, which proved unfounded, about lax security on the Soo Canal, through which passed practically all iron ore shipments to eastern mills. Then the British ("God damn them," exclaimed Hopkins, hearing of this new demand) put in an exceedingly large order for steel, and Hopkins had to figure out how to oversee their requests.[9]

Most important, Hopkins persuaded Land to gear up the Maritime Commission for emergency production. He drafted a letter from the president urging Land to concentrate on completing ships already under construction, even if that meant rewriting the contracts. By the end of the year construction was running ahead of schedule.[10]

Still, Hopkins's many efforts were not enough. In mid-April, Churchill urged Hopkins to return to London. "All was not well," Hopkins recorded, "and our help was needed." Roosevelt caused dismay when he carelessly remarked that further British withdrawals in the eastern Mediterranean would not cause "any great debacle or surrender." Losing the Middle East, Churchill shot back, would "increase the hazards of the Atlantic and Pacific and could hardly fail to prolong the war." Indeed, he felt that the time had come for the United States to enter the fighting.[11]

Although nothing would have pleased Hopkins more than to accept Churchill's invitation, he knew that as a practical matter, U.S. entry into the war would do little to improve Britain's chances. The United States was not yet prepared, psychologically, politically, or materially, for such a step. That meant searching for more avenues to aid Britain short of joining the war. But his proposals for action got nowhere. When Morgenthau argued that the United States should enter the war immediately, Hopkins put him off. But Morgenthau then proposed that Roosevelt do "something internally" by declaring a national emergency and asking Congress to establish Cabinet positions for supply and home defense. Roosevelt could announce these moves in a speech he was planning to give on May 27 in honor of Pan-American Day. Hopkins sold the idea to Roosevelt. Just to head off any second thoughts, he told FDR's speechwriters Robert Sherwood and Samuel Rosenman to include the announcement in the president's address. As Roosevelt was reviewing the first draft, he broke off: "I hereby proclaim that an unlimited national emergency exists . . . what's *this?* Hasn't somebody been taking some liberties?" Since Hopkins had slipped out of the room, Sherwood was left to explain that Hopkins had told them to put it in. Roosevelt said nothing more, and the passage, differently worded, stayed in.[12]

Roosevelt's message declared that the Nazis were seeking world domination. He proposed to deny them control of the seas and to aid Great Britain. Warning that "our Bunker Hill of tomorrow may be several thousand miles from Boston," he concluded by proclaiming a national emergency.

To Hopkins it seemed that U.S. policy was at last on the right track. Public response supported Roosevelt's speech, and administration officials once again talked of taking tough measures against Germany in the Atlantic. But suddenly the air went out of the balloon: plans for new moves were set aside, and Roosevelt began to qualify his remarks to mollify the isolationists.

Then at 6:00 A.M. on May 21 the American merchant ship SS *Robin Moor,* carrying nonmilitary goods from New York to Cape Town and flying an American flag with an American ensign and U.S.A. painted on her sides, was ordered to stop by a blinking signal from a submarine with the name *Lorricke* or *Lorickke* (observers were later unsure) and a picture of a laughing cow on its conning tower. The ship was just above the equator and, at 25° 40′ west longitude, just outside the American neutrality zone, although under international law the location had no bearing on the legality of the submarine's action, since the *Robin Moor* was not carrying military cargo. The *Robin Moor*'s chief officer was summoned to the submarine and given half an hour to abandon ship. After the thirty-eight crewmen and eight passengers, including one child, had cleared the ship in four lifeboats, the submarine fired one torpedo and some thirty-odd shells, sinking the vessel in about twenty-three minutes. The submarine commander informed the passengers that he would radio their position. He left them some food and sailed off on the surface. None of the passengers or crew doubted that the commander and his craft were German. After waiting twenty-four hours with no sign of rescue vessels, the lifeboats headed west toward Brazil. On May 26 they separated, and on June 4 a British ship picked up one lifeboat and carried the occupants to Cape Town; four days later a Brazilian ship located another boat and took its passengers to Fortaleza. American vessels found the other boats and returned the passengers to the United States. All arrived in good health.[13]

Three days after word of the incident arrived in Washington, British officials huddled to take advantage of it. Because the submarine had not searched the *Robin Moor* for munitions, it had violated international law. This, they concluded, would justify the United States's upgrading its observation patrols to security patrols ordered to defend the freedom of the Atlantic, by force if necessary. Not only would this move the United States closer to war; it would also relieve the hard-pressed British navy, enabling it to concentrate on the Mediterranean.

Informed of the British strategy, Hopkins approved of having Churchill present the plan to Roosevelt but at the last minute changed his mind and told the British to wait while he tried a tactic of his own.[14] Hopkins decided to approach Roosevelt himself, stating the British argument as though it were his own. On June 14 he sent Roosevelt a memorandum:

The sinking of the *Robin Moor* violated international law at sea; it violates our policy of freedom of the seas.

The present observation patrol of the Navy for observing and reporting the movement of ships that are potential aggressors could be changed into a security patrol charged with the duty of providing security for all American flagships traveling on the seas outside of the danger zone.

It occurred to me that your instructions to the Navy Deparment could be that the United States Atlantic patrol forces, to be specific are to, in effect, establish the freedom of the seas, leaving it to the judgment of the Navy as to what measures of security are required to achieve the objective.[15]

Hopkins probably adopted the British plan because its advice seemed well in tune with Roosevelt's inclinations. By mid-June he believed that Roosevelt wanted the United States to enter the war but felt that nothing less than a German attack would stir public opinion to permit it. Since Roosevelt seemingly preferred to set the stage for such an incident one step at a time, Hopkins framed his advice along similar lines. But the implications of his memo were undoubtedly as clear to him as they were to the British and would be to Roosevelt. If the United States began to escort its merchant ships, even outside the danger zone, before long American destroyers would be shooting at German submarines on the prowl for other *Robin Moors*.

More revealing, his methods were those of a desperate man. As the president's most highly placed and trusted adviser, Hopkins certainly ought to have informed Roosevelt that he was passing along a recommendation from the British. Instead, he tried to manipulate Roosevelt on their behalf. Still, this episode offers little ammunition to those who believe that Hopkins always operated this way. After all, Hopkins was not proposing anything that Stimson and Knox had not been advocating for over a month. Nor was he proposing a policy that in any way conflicted with Roosevelt's sense of U.S. national interest. If, as most historians believe, Roosevelt favored U.S. entry into the war, any difference with the British was only over the best methods of bringing it about. At a time when many proposals for American action were under consideration, it made good sense for Hopkins to back one that took into account both the facts of the German attack on the *Robin Moor* and Roosevelt's preferred methods of measured response. Whatever the case for or against Hopkins as manipulator, as it turned out, Roosevelt did not take his advice.

Indeed the episode says less about Hopkins's relations with Roosevelt than about his relations with the British. Throughout the spring Hopkins had been administering Lend-Lease and arranging strategy conferences so that the British and the Americans could be made fully aware of each others' needs and purposes. Hopkins had gone a long way toward winning the confidence and good will of such officials as Morgenthau, Stimson, and Marshall. Now he had taken the tremendous chance of acting as an advocate for British strategy in order to win their confidence. It was a risky step, but in those frustrating, anxious days, perhaps a necessary one, toward his great wartime achievement of building the Anglo-American alliance.

Only a few days later Hopkins saw another chance for action. The German invasion of the Soviet Union on June 22 seemed, for the moment at least, to take the pressure off the British Isles and the North Atlantic. Wanting to capitalize on the situation, Hopkins urged Secretary Stimson to "push the president for action during this precious time." Spurred by Hopkins, Stimson recommended throwing American naval strength into winning the battle of the North Atlantic. This time the president reponded, ordering the navy to escort merchant ships as far as Iceland and to transfer additional ships from the Pacific Fleet. Hopkins also persuaded Roosevelt to declare that he was acting to protect the North Atlantic shipping lanes.[16] (Although renewed fear of a Japanese attack canceled the transfer, the escorting policy remained in place.)

Hitler's invasion of Russia reopened the debate over sending supplies to the Middle East. In mid-May another round of strategy conferences had resulted in more aid to that theater. Now Churchill thought that the Russian campaign would allow Britain to take the offensive. The U.S. military demurred. The Germans had captured Crete and had recently smashed an attempt by General Wavell to link up with the garrison based in Tobruk in northern Libya. When Harriman visited British forces in North Africa, he sent back gloomy reports of inefficiency, poor facilities, divided command, and self-indulgent living among British forces. In these circumstances the Americans were inclined to recommend building up their own forces instead of helping the British.[17]

Hopkins soon had the chance to address these problems. Roosevelt assigned him to visit London in order to invite Churchill to a conference in August. Laying down some ground rules for the talks,

Roosevelt instructed Hopkins to tell the prime minister that the United States would not discuss economic or territorial deals. He also wanted Hopkins to explain how he planned to escort merchant ships to Iceland. Tearing a map from a copy of *National Geographic,* the president drew a broken line at about 10° west longitude to just south of Iceland, where he curved it over to 26° and sent it south with a firm, solid stroke. That put Iceland in the American zone of responsibility. Ships other than American or Icelandic vessels could join the escorted convoys, but, Roosevelt said, the United States would consider going to war only if the Nazis attacked an American ship.

In his notes of this conversation Hopkins wrote, "No talk about war." In his book *Roosevelt and Hopkins,* Robert Sherwood interprets this to mean that Roosevelt wanted to avoid the subject at his meeting with Churchill, but it seems more likely that he was instructing Hopkins not to discuss it in London.[18] The prime minister had made no secret of wanting the Americans to join the war, and he would certainly not have let Roosevelt avoid the matter at the conference.

If Hopkins was not going to be able to talk about U.S. participation in the war, he was determined to settle the Middle East problem. With the Russians now asking for Lend-Lease aid, American supplies were in danger of being stretched too thin. Roosevelt seemed inclined to supply the British in Egypt simply because that was their only active front against the Germans. But he wondered if it might make better sense to ship the supplies instead to Russia, where they would be used to kill more German soldiers.

As he prepared to present these issues in London, Hopkins was mulling over all the debates and decisions of the previous six and one half months. He was beginning to realize that Lend-Lease aid and military strategy had to be coordinated. Otherwise things would lurch along on a "day-to-day hit-or-miss basis."[19] Harriman had suggested that the United States take over supplying the Middle East so that Britain could devote its production to home defense. But before the United States could commit itself to any plan, it would have to know how the British proposed to hold the Middle East.

Hopkins left Washington on Sunday morning, July 13, and flew to Montreal, where bad weather held him up. He then flew to the U.S. air base at Gander, Newfoundland, where the president's son Elliott, stationed there as a captain in the Air Force, took him off for a day of trout fishing. Elliott thought that Hopkins looked in fine health, but by the time his B-24 landed in Scotland, the flight had taken its toll. Neither he nor Churchill could wait to renew their acquaintance, however, and as soon as he landed, he was off to London.

His first stop was a War Cabinet meeting. Whatever Roosevelt had meant by his instruction "no talk about war," Hopkins disregarded it. The American people were not eager to enter the war, he told the Cabinet, but if the president decided that the time had come, the vast majority of both parties would support him. The Americans, he assured them, had "warmly supported" the president's decision to send troops to Iceland.[20]

After the meeting Hopkins and Churchill retired for a private chat in the enclosed garden behind No. 10 Downing Street. Hopkins alerted Churchill that plans for sending aid Russia would cut into Britain's share and warned him that some U.S. officials thought that Britain was attempting to do too much by preparing to defend against an invasion while trying to hold the Middle East. Last of all, Hopkins told Churchill that Roosevelt wanted to meet him "in some lonely bay or other." The prime minister jumped at the invitation, and a few days later the arrangements were completed for what was to become known as the Atlantic Conference.[21]

Churchill reciprocated by extending an invitation to Hopkins to visit Hitler's aide Rudolph Hess, who on May 10 had parachuted into Scotland with a bizarre suggestion for working out a peace settlement between Britain and Germany. Although the offer to see Hess probably attracted Hopkins, who loved intrigue and could have milked the event for many hours of lively conversation back home, he turned it down, fearing that if the news got out, people would speculate about a U.S. accommodation with the Nazis.[22]

For the next few days Hopkins played the dutiful representative. But his mind was on the larger matter of coordinating supplies and strategy. He now wanted to organize Lend-Lease into an efficient machine so that he and Roosevelt could attend to other issues. That meant bringing Roosevelt and George Marshall together. "The only thing I really want to do as my contribution to the success of this war," Hopkins told General Raymond Lee, "is to arrange for General Marshall to establish and maintain complete free access to the president." Hopkins was worried because he was making decisions without the necessary military knowledge, and "great events" might turn on what he decided.[23]

Of course Hopkins was being overly modest. At the moment he was the only highly placed American who was pressing this line of cooperation and the only one who saw the need for this perspective. This became apparent as Hopkins discussed British supply needs. As he followed the details of British aircraft and tank requests, his eye for the larger picture caused him again and again to focus on the Middle East. American reports satisfied him that the British could use the equipment being sent there but left open the question of whether their strategic situation made the aid worth the effort.

At a late-evening meeting on July 24 Hopkins, Churchill, Harriman, and representatives of the American and British military addressed this question. Churchill invited the Americans to state their case, and Hopkins led off by observing that an all-out U.S. commitment to supply the Middle East would require more than one hundred ships in constant use. But the problems of the Middle East, the interests of the Muslim world, and the interrelationship of Egypt and India were not well understood in the United States. (Most Americans, he said, were not sure whether the Nile flowed north or south.) The British had never given Roosevelt a broad statement of their Middle Eastern strategy but had only asked for help with individual campaigns. Now was the time for such a statement so that the Americans could have full confidence in the enterprise. The head of the American military mission in London followed by emphasizing U.S. fears that resources were inadequate for both British home defense and holding the Middle East. Admiral R. L. Ghormley made a similar point, saying that the navy could not protect both the North Atlantic convoys and a sizable supply line to the Middle East.

Churchill replied by painting a rosy picture of the war situation. The battle of the Atlantic was turning in Britain's favor, especially since the American patrol had released many ships from duty in home waters. Home defense was stronger than it had been the previous fall. The Japanese posed a serious threat in the Far East, but they would probably not enter the war until they were sure of Britain's defeat. Things looked similarly bright to Churchill in the Middle East, where Britain had committed 600,000 men. Britain could not withdraw from the Middle East even if it wished. Further reinforcements there would not weaken home defense and "might produce great results."

The British chiefs backed Churchill, declaring that the war in the Middle East was needed to tie up German troops and supplies, to bolster the spirit of the Muslim peoples, to protect vital petroleum supplies, and to hold the Mediterranean. Churchill concluded by taking up one of his highest priorities: bringing the United States into the war. Britain could maintain its present commitments, but it was necessary for the United States to defend other areas, such as Gibraltar, Dakar, North Africa, and Norway.[24]

From the British standpoint the meeting had come off exceedingly well. But for whose benefit had it been held? Not for Hopkins, who had probably already heard the British justifications for their Middle East strategy. More likely the meeting was designed for the benefit of the American military representatives, upon whom the War Department relied for appraisals of British strategy, and for the purpose of setting up Hopkins to stage-manage the upcoming Atlantic Conference. The next day Hopkins alerted Roosevelt that the British had given "very convincing" reasons for holding the Middle East. After conferring with Churchill, he advised Roosevelt to bring Marshall and Arnold to the conference and dispatched Harriman to Washington to report on the discussions.[25]

He wound up his visit by delivering a radio talk, in which he assured the British people that American war production was gearing up to help them and their allies as well. In order to avoid breaching American neutrality (he had promised the State Department, "I . . . will not upset the diplomatic apple-cart"), he had to resort to platitudes in his speech, rejecting a rousing version drafted by the American correspondent Quentin Reynolds ("Hell, Quent," he exclaimed, "you've got me declaring war on Germany"). But he did conclude, "People of England, people of the British Commonwealth of Nations—you are not fighting alone."[26]

While in London, Hopkins had an inspired thought: why not take a short side trip to Moscow to learn what he could at firsthand about the situation in Russia? He cabled Roosevelt, who at length agreed. On July 27, after conferring with Churchill about British plans to aid Russia, Hopkins boarded a special train for Scotland, and then flew on to Moscow. He planned to be back in time to accompany Churchill to the Atlantic Conference. (See Chapter 12 for a detailed discussion of Hopkins's mission to Moscow.)

He landed again at Scapa Flow on August 2, ill and exhausted but bringing from Russia information that would transform the Anglo-American partnership. A waiting British naval launch delivered him to the HMS *Prince of Wales,* which would carry Churchill and his party to Placentia Bay in Newfoundland, where it would rendezvous with a U.S. cruiser bringing Roosevelt to the historic meeting. Hopkins's worn appearance horrified the others on board, but considerate of Ambassador Winant, who had flown up from London for a report, Hopkins persevered through dinner. By then it was obvious that he was exhausted, and the commanding admiral ordered him to bed in his own cabin. Asking Winant to wait "until I've had a little rest," he dropped into the bunk and slept for eighteen hours. The next day he was on deck, standing in the shadow of a gun turret while biting winds snapped his loose tweed overcoat, waiting for Churchill to come aboard.

"Ah, my dear friend," Churchill piped up, "how are you? And how did you find Stalin?"

"I must tell you all about it," was Hopkins's slow, weary reply. They linked arms and went below. A bugle sounded, a bell rang, and the *Prince of Wales* was under way.[27]

If anyone needed an invigorating sea voyage it was Harry Hopkins, and Churchill saw that he got it. Although the prime minister conferred with his chiefs, read the daily dispatches, and drafted the necessary orders, he treated the voyage as something of a vacation, exercising on deck, playing backgammon, watching movies, and reading the sea novel *Captain Horatio Hornblower.* Throughout he kept up his familiar incessant, wide-ranging chatter. Hopkins conferred with Churchill on his Moscow visit and discussed the upcoming conference. He also took part in the strolls on deck and other amusements (the British joked about the unkind view of his new Russian friends in the spy film *Citizen X*) and found time to catch up on his correspondence, including making arrangements to pay his London hotel bill, which he had overlooked in his hurried departure for Russia. He offered Churchill and his party a gift of caviar from Stalin. Churchill observed that it was good to have such a treat even if it meant fighting on the side of the Russians to get it. When Hopkins refused a second brandy after dinner, Churchill said that he hoped that his friend was not going to become more temperate as he got closer to home. Churchill challenged Hopkins to backgammon, and Hopkins duly took him for seven guineas.

High winds on the first day caused the *Prince of Wales* to lose its destroyer escort for a time, and the second day out the ship changed course to avoid a U-boat disguised as a sailing ketch. Thick fog near

Iceland gave way to clear weather the rest of the way. No enemy ships, planes, or submarines were sighted. The most upsetting event occurred when, after seven days, the party reached the rendezvous point at Placentia Bay in Newfoundland and discovered that because the U.S. Navy was keeping different time, the *Prince of Wales* had arrived an hour and a half early. The ship had to wheel back out to sea to pass the time, and Churchill, who was on deck, keyed up for his historic meeting, was furious. In due course the great battleship sailed smoothly into the bay and at 9:06 A.M. August 9 drew alongside the heavy cruiser USS *Augusta*.

For Hopkins this meeting was the fruit of eight months' labor. He knew, however, that once the conference was under way, he would have to take a subordinate role. Neither Roosevelt nor Churchill was likely to seek his guidance. His health also precluded his taking a leading role at the conference. The few days of rest aboard the *Prince of Wales* had restored him to a degree, but he still remained weak and tired.

Still, Hopkins wanted to be sure that the conference started well. "Bringing together Roosevelt and the prime minister on a ship," he once predicted, "would cause the biggest explosion ever seen." However much he chuckled at that statement when he made it, he knew that an explosion was the one thing he had to prevent. He had put too much into orchestrating this meeting to see personality conflicts blow it up. As soon as he saw the *Augusta* with Roosevelt sitting patiently in his wheelchair on the quarter-deck, he rushed to his cabin, threw his clothes and papers into his suitcases, and hurried back to be one of the first to see the president. "How are you Harry?" Roosevelt asked as he came on board. "Are you all right? You look a little tired." "The Russians are confident," Hopkins blurted out, brimming with eagerness to tell Roosevelt about his meeting with Stalin. Then, reassuring Roosevelt that he was all right, he urged him to spend as much time as possible with Churchill. This was a puzzling and inept performance to say the least. Roosevelt was waiting to meet Churchill; he was in no mood for a report on Russia, and he certainly didn't need anyone to tell him to spend a lot of time with the prime minister. But Hopkins soon relaxed and was back in form, acting as Roosevelt's go-between by inviting Churchill aboard to present his views on the war. "The president, of course," he told the prime minister, "does not want anything formal about it."[28]

For the rest of the conference Hopkins served a subordinate role,

*Hopkins (behind FDR) watches Roosevelt and Churchill confer at the Atlantic
Conference, 1941. Admiral Ernest King, General George Marshall, and Sir
John Dill look on*

sending an occasional message and regaling fascinated listeners with
stories of his mission to Moscow, all the while watching to see how the
two leaders were getting along. To keep the tone light, he would pass
along an occasional joke.[29]

Still, if his presence seemed as slim as his emaciated figure, his impact
was substantial. Near the end of the conference the two sides were at
loggerheads over an American proposal that their joint declaration—
to be known as the Atlantic Charter—should affirm that all peoples be
allowed access to world markets "without discrimination and on equal
terms." To this implied criticism of Britain's imperial trading preferences Churchill cunningly replied that he would have to consult the
Cabinet before responding. This meant that if the Americans persisted,
the joint declaration could not be issued until many days after the

conference had broken up and the world learned that it had occurred. That, of course, would ruin the declaration's impact. Hopkins suggested redrafting the section to prevent delay. He found it "inconceivable that the issues of the joint declaration should be held up by a matter of this kind."[30] This was one of those moments that Churchill had in mind years later when he wrote: "Harry Hopkins always went to the root of the matter. I have been present at several great conferences, where twenty or more of the most executive personages were gathered together. When the discussion flagged and all seemed baffled, it was on these occasions he would rap out the deadly question, 'Surely, Mr. President, here is the point we have got to settle. Are we going to face it or not?' Faced it always was, and, being faced, was conquered."[31]

Hopkins's suggestion completely gave away the U.S. negotiating position by showing that the Americans cared less that the declaration was perfect than that it was timely. Infuriated, Sumner Welles, undersecretary of state, argued against any modifications. But he was overruled. Roosevelt invited Churchill to submit a statement, which proved sufficiently qualified for the British and broad enough for the president. Roosevelt "will not like this very much," Churchill cabled the Cabinet, "but he attaches so much importance to the Joint Declaration, which he believes will affect the whole movement of the United States' opinion, that I think he will agree."[32]

Nothing definite came from the military discussions, in which the British chiefs repeated their case for aid in the Middle East and asked for supplies in what the Americans considered fantastic amounts. But Hopkins was pleased by the personal relationships that were established, especially the success of General Marshall, who emerged, Hopkins said, as "the dominating figure" at the meeting. The British recognized Marshall's strength of character and his leadership. He particularly impressed Sir John Dill, the Chief of the Imperial General Staff, who would later distinguish himself as the head of the British Joint Staff Mission in Washington.[33]

Hopkins's persistent efforts resulted in an American proposal to set up machinery to coordinate supplies and strategy. General "Hap" Arnold later wrote that the conference "certainly brought home to Stark–Marshall–Turner and I believe to Hopkins and Harriman the necessity for setting up a board to determine . . . policies re-allocating war supplies." In Hopkins's case it would probably be fairer to say that it brought home to others an idea that had been in his mind since April, when he realized the need to tailor American aid to British strategic objectives.

The conference showed up certain differences between the British and the American points of view. General Marshall criticized the British argument that naval power and strategic bombing would defeat the Axis without the need for a mass invasion of the Continent. He also doubted the wisdom of supplying British forces in the Middle East. And Roosevelt disappointed Churchill by rejecting his proposal to send Japan a strong warning against further expansion.

On most topics, however, the gains that came out of the conference far outweighed the losses. When word arrived that the House of Representatives had agreed to extend national conscription for one year by a vote of 203 to 202, the British better understood Roosevelt's hesitation to enter the war. Still, Churchill returned to Britain encouraged that the president intended to "wage war but not declare it," employing provocative action to force an incident that would justify hostilities. The warning to Japan, British Foreign Service officer Alexander Cadogan wrote, was less than Britain wanted, "but we must remember that it must be read in conjunction with the Joint Declaration, which will give the Japanese a jar." In the discussions on grand strategy, the British chiefs undoubtedly noted that although Marshall strongly criticized their views, the navy representatives and General Arnold seemed sympathetic. And if Arnold spoke for most of the Americans when he declared that after hearing the British supply requests, he felt lucky to have gotten away with his pants, the British left with a more realistic appreciation of how limited U.S. resources actually were.[34]

The conference produced other positive results which strengthened the Anglo-American partnership. Roosevelt finally broke through the weeks of contradiction and backsliding by ordering the escorting of ships in the western Atlantic and agreeing to occupy the Azores once the British arranged an invitation from Portugal.

When Hopkins returned to Washington, he found that it had been easier to plan the conference's objectives than it would be to implement them. He pressed for a plan to occupy the Azores and to attack German submarines, but Stimson held back. He and Lord Beaverbrook discussed the possibility of Britain's opening a second front to divert Nazi troops from Russia by landing troops in northern France at about the time of an upcoming supply conference in Moscow.[35] Beaverbrook presented the idea at home, but without success.

Once again Hopkins seemed to be taking one step forward and two steps back. Churchill's optimism turned to gloom, and he cabled Hopkins predicting disaster by 1942.[36] Hopkins showed the message to Roosevelt, arguing that the United States should enter the war before the appeasers took charge in Britain. Roosevelt assigned extra ships to the Middle East and seized upon an incident in the North Atlantic to announce a firmer stand against German U-boats. In the waters southwest of Iceland in the American neutrality zone the American destroyer *Greer,* carrying mail to Iceland, had been warned by a British plane of a German U-boat ten miles ahead. The *Greer* caught up to the submarine and hung on its tail while the plane attacked with depth charges. Two hours later, with the *Greer* still shadowing it, the U-boat suddenly fired two or three torpedoes at the destroyer, which dodged them and laid down a depth charge attack. After another two hours it found the submarine again and dropped more depth charges. Then it turned over the chase to the British destroyers and planes.

Hopkins wanted Roosevelt to order American destroyers to sink all German ships in the neutrality zone. Roosevelt refused, but he did refer to the U-boats as the "rattlesnakes of the Atlantic" and charged that their very presence in American defensive waters constituted an attack.[37] Two days later Roosevelt ordered the navy to protect both U.S. and foreign ships in American convoys to Iceland. If they encountered Axis vessels, they were to shoot on sight.

Although Roosevelt's policy was less than Hopkins had wanted, he was pleased that it nevertheless went beyond the caution urged by Secretary Hull. "He has in recent months," Hopkins concluded, "given me the impression that he isn't prepared for the implications of a tough row with Hitler."[38] The *Greer* incident helped broaden the distance between Hopkins and the secretary of state. It had seemed to Hopkins that whenever a situation required aggressive action, Hull had tried to talk Roosevelt out of it. The recent example of Welles and Cadogan apparently willing to stall the Atlantic Conference by squabbling over foreign trade issues seemed a perfect example of State's obstructionism. Hopkins had returned from Moscow convinced that the United States could not work effectively through its embassy there. The lesson seemed clear: no one got anywhere by sticking to diplomatic niceties. And for the moment, Hopkins thought, Roosevelt seemed ready to bypass diplomacy and act, not only for Britain but also for the United States' new partner against the Axis, Soviet Russia.

# Chapter 12

# Ever So Confident

In the early morning of June 22, 1941, Germany attacked Russia. Hopkins originally considered Hitler's invasion a mixed blessing. He realized that the invasion temporarily took the pressure off Britain, but he feared that this very fact might enable Hitler to seek support in the United States, capitalizing on American anticommunism and encouraging the isolationists, who would argue that since Britain was in no immediate danger, the United States should turn to strengthening its own defenses. Hopkins was especially worried about the Irish Catholics, who were traditionally pro-Democratic but were also unsympathetic to Britain and fiercely anti-Soviet. He could only muster the vague hope that the American public would not stand for a compromise with Hitler and that Roosevelt would be able to direct opinion into safe channels.[1]

Other circumstances clouded the Russian picture. Many congressmen who had opposed Lend-Lease had proposed amendments to cut out Russia. Opinion polls showed that although most Americans wanted Russia to defeat Germany, a majority opposed aiding that country on the same basis as Britain. Military opinion also argued for restraint, as both American and British military chiefs predicted that the Soviet Union would fall in a matter of weeks.

Hopkins and many others around him preferred to avoid the question of what to do about Russia. Some favored increasing aid to Britain while Hitler's attention was diverted elsewhere. Churchill encouraged this view, and Hopkins supported Stimson's plan to throw all America's strength into the battle of the Atlantic.[2]

But Roosevelt would not ignore the Russian front. He began by offering limited aid, hoping that the Russians could tie up the Germans until the winter weather kept them from invading Britain. At first he assigned the job to the State Department, but when State faltered, he turned it over to Hopkins, who set up an aid program just before he left for London in July.

By this time Hopkins was reconsidering the Russian situation. A few days earlier he had conferred with Joseph Davies, a middle western businessman who had served as U.S. ambassador to the Soviet Union in the late 1930s. A strong partisan of aid to Russia and of friendly relations with the Russians generally, Davies had argued that the United States should go all out to support the Soviet war effort.[3]

In London, Hopkins found opinion mixed, though most believed that Britain had been granted "only a temporary breather."[4] The British military chiefs realized that a German victory in Russia would open another line to the Middle East and jeopardize their position there. American aid was organized but was moving so slowly that Hopkins could not plan any action with the British. In the meantime Josef Stalin was pressuring Churchill to open a second front in Europe. By late July the Russian situation was still unresolved. Hopkins grasped the opportunity to act. "I am wondering," he cabled Roosevelt, "whether you would think it important and useful for me to go to Moscow?"[5]

The story of Hopkins's request is buried in contradiction. The journalists Forrest Davis and Ernest K. Lindley wrote that Churchill suggested the trip to Hopkins in order to find out the truth about the Russian military situation. The Soviet ambassador to Great Britain, Ivan Maisky, claimed that he suggested that Hopkins visit Moscow when he was unable to answer Hopkins's request for information about Russian supply requirements. The American ambassador, John G. Winant, recalled that he had planned to make the trip himself but Hopkins had asked, "How would it be for me to go?" In his doctoral dissertation John Daniel Langer suggested that Hopkins had had the idea before he left Washington but proposed it in London in order to put pressure on Roosevelt. Robert Sherwood believes that Hopkins conceived of the idea himself and contradicts Davis and Lindley by stating that Churchill tried to discourage him from going.[6]

The only direct evidence about Hopkins's motives comes from the dispatch that, according to Sherwood, Hopkins sent Roosevelt on Friday evening, July 25: "I have a feeling that everything possible should be done to make certain the Russians maintain a permanent front even though they be defeated in this immediate battle. If Stalin could in any way be influenced at a critical time I think it would be worth doing by a direct communication from you through a personal envoy. I think the stakes are so great that we mean business on a long term supply job."[7] Thus Hopkins emphasized bolstering the Russians' will to fight by cultivating their friendship. This detracts from Maisky's explanation, since it shows that Hopkins's motive was to support the Russians, not to get information from them.

The timing of Hopkins's trip further helps explain its rationale. Hopkins had originally planned to discuss Middle East strategy with the British commander General Claude Auchinleck and then to accompany Churchill to the Atlantic Conference. Since Churchill was scheduled to sail on August 2, and Auchinleck was not due to arrive until July 29, a trip to Moscow would cancel the meeting on the Middle East and might even delay the Atlantic crossing. Thus Hopkins drafted another cable asking Roosevelt to decide which was more important. Although he never sent the message, it nonetheless suggests that both Churchill and Hopkins were willing to forego the Russian trip and thus weakens the view that either was urging it. Most likely, as Sherwood surmised, Hopkins proposed the trip on the spur of the moment.[8]

Hopkins found Roosevelt enthusiastic. The president replied that he and Undersecretary of State Sumner Welles "highly approve Moscow trip, and assume you would go in a few days." Roosevelt's cable set off a flurry of activity. Hopkins showed it to Churchill, who grabbed the telephone. Late that afternoon a circling plane flashed a message to the crew of a PBY Catalina to break up their picnic by Loch Lomond. They were to fly to Invergordon on Scotland's east coast to pick up passengers for Archangel, the Russian port on the White Sea. Meanwhile Hopkins was arranging to take along an American pilot who could teach the Russians to fly the American P-40s that Churchill had recently promised. As it turned out, Ambassador Winant had already called General Marshall, who nominated General James T. McNarney and fighter pilot Lieutenant John K. Alison to go. In the last-minute rush Winant could not locate a Soviet official to stamp Hopkins's passport, so Maisky had to write a diplomatic visa by hand. Winant reached Euston Station just in time to hand the papers to Hopkins as his train began to pull out.[9]

Hopkins left London carrying a more important document in the form of a letter from Roosevelt to Stalin spelling out the purposes of his mission. He had originally proposed the trip to bolster the Soviets' fighting spirit, but Roosevelt's letter said that his purpose was to learn the Russians' most urgent requirements in order to speed up the shipment of American supplies. The United States was planning a long-term commitment but wanted to concentrate on materiel that could reach Russia in the next three months. "I ask you to treat Mr. Hopkins with the identical confidence you would feel if you were talking directly to me," Roosevelt declared.[10]

If Roosevelt could have seen the man in whom he was placing such trust, he might have reconsidered. Hopkins had not yet recovered from his Atlantic flight. Those who saw him in England were shocked by his appearance, describing him as frail and "a physical wreck," and noting that he seemed exhausted and at times unable to concentrate. He tried to pass off his illness as "a touch of the grippe," but Mrs. Churchill was especially alarmed by his appearance and insisted on looking after him while he was staying with them at Chequers. He was in no condition for twenty-four hours of rough Arctic flying.

The air field at Invergordon was socked in by bad weather. During the delay Hopkins drove around the moors, had tea, attended a cocktail party, and was on his way to dinner when word came that the plane was going to take off despite the weather. Conditions aboard were crowded, with extra fuel tanks taking up space as well as a large stove in the center of the aircraft to protect against the subzero temperatures. Hastily procured flight suits fit poorly. On takeoff the plane's anchor hatch blew open, and the pilot had to land to close it. Some of the passengers complained that the craft was overloaded.

The plane was crowded but not overloaded, and apart from its length (twenty-one and one-half hours), the trip was uneventful. Hopkins sat toward the rear in a Plexiglas blister and imagined using its machine gun against German planes. He tried his hand at cooking, since the crew was one man short, and tried to get a little sleep on a canvas stretcher, but he suffered too much from the Arctic cold. Arriving on the north Russian coast, the plane wandered a bit over fog until it picked up a radio signal from Archangel which guided it in. Thanking the crew for a pleasant flight—a statement which told them more about his selflessness that about the actual conditions on board—Hopkins emerged to warm Russian hospitality, featuring a four-hour banquet of fresh vegetables, butter, cream, and greens, and a crash course in vodka toasting, which he finally mastered by spreading a chunk of bread with caviar and swallowing it and the vodka at the same time. ("Don't play with that stuff," he wrote later of his reaction to vodka. "Eat while you're drinking it—something that will act as a shock absorber for it."[11]) He had time for only two hours' sleep before flying to Moscow, where he arrived on Wednesday morning, July 30.

After another hearty welcome Hopkins retired to the American embassy. The ambassador, Laurence Steinhardt, assured him that the Russians would fight fiercely to defend their homeland but emphasized how little information he or any other foreigner had been able to get about the gravity of the military situation.

That evening Hopkins, Steinhardt, and their interpreter arrived at the Kremlin to meet with Stalin. After being led down seemingly endless corridors, they arrived at an office numbered 1 and entered. There sat Stalin, a short, square figure with a wiry mustache and full head of hair combed straight back. He was dressed simply in khaki, his uniform blouse unbuttoned at the neck and his trousers tucked into shiny black boots.

The conversation opened with Stalin and Hopkins expressing their shared hatred of Hitler's regime. After reading Roosevelt's message to Stalin, Hopkins asked him to name Russia's needs, both immediate and long term. Stalin was ready with detailed specifications. He also said that he would welcome American technicians, and he requested that supplies be shipped through Archangel. He painted an optimistic picture of the military situation, claiming that the Germans were going on the defensive; he did not expect them to advance more than a hundred kilometers. But he also predicted that the present battle would not end until October. He wound up by appealing for the United States to enter the war. He even invited American troops to fight on the Russian front under their own commanders. Hopkins put him off, saying that his mission was only to discuss supplies. He did add, though, that he doubted that the United States would want to station an army in Russia.[12]

If Hopkins carried out Roosevelt's instructions, he also carried out Churchill's. In London he had discussed the possibility of holding a three-way supply conference, and Churchill had encouraged him to take up the subject with Stalin. This he did, proposing that the conference be held in early October, after the major fighting had ended. Stalin preferred early September, but after conferring subsequently with Churchill on the way to the Atlantic Conference, Hopkins dispatched a proposal that the meeting be held no earlier than the end of September.[13]

Hopkins also took the opportunity to make his own on-the-spot observations. Conversations with other Russian officials convinced him that only Stalin could supply the information that the Americans and the British needed. Indeed he found that the most frustrating thing about dealing with the Russians was their secretiveness. American and British military attachés did not even know where the battlefront was, let alone how the fighting was proceeding. Hopkins had learned the connection between supplies and strategy and believed in putting one's cards on the table, so he attempted to press Stalin to be more forthcoming. Neither the United States nor Britain, he warned the dictator, would be willing to send long-term supplies until he agreed to a conference at which "the relative strategic interests of each front, as well as the interests of our several countries, was fully and jointly explored." Stalin readily approved, stipulating only that it be held in Moscow.

Although meetings took up most of his time, Hopkins found a free afternoon for shopping and sightseeing. Ever the enthusiastic tourist, he visited one gift shop after another, inspecting dozens of items and firing off questions. En route he chatted with Steinhardt and the photographer Margaret Bourke-White about the Russian people, their facial expressions, their behavior, and their living standards. Margaret Bourke-White helped him select two dresses: a peasant-embroidered frock for Diana and white linen lined with a pattern of roses for Betsey Roosevelt. By the time they arrived at an antique store that dealt in silver, Hopkins seemed to be running low on energy and simply told Steinhardt, "I don't understand this stuff." So the ambassador rummaged in a barrel behind the counter and came up with a teapot engraved with a picture of the Kremlin and presented it to Hopkins as a memento of his trip.[14]

Hopkins left his final meeting with Stalin convinced that Russia would hold out against the Germans. "I feel ever so confident about this front," he cabled Roosevelt, Hull, and Welles the next day. "The morale of the population is good. There is unbounded determination to win."[15] Hopkins had based his conclusions, presumably, on his observations during his brief stop in Archangel, his shopping tour of Moscow, his conversations with Stalin and other Russian leaders, and briefings from Steinhardt, although he might have been more skeptical of Stalin's optimistic picture of the battle front. Certainly the dictator's astonishing invitation to the United States to send its own troops to the Russian front entirely under American command indicated that he was desperate.

But Hopkins drew no such inferences from Stalin and probably did not look for any. Roosevelt and Churchill had asked him to arrange to expedite aid to Russia, and only overwhelming evidence that the country was about to collapse would have convinced him that it was not worth the effort. Even if he had sensed Stalin's desperation, he would probably have recommended as he did. After all, neither Churchill's tears nor his entreaties that America enter the war had shaken his resolve to aid Britain.

In Stalin, Hopkins saw not desperation but realism and command. Stalin paid tribute to the officers and men of the German army, admitted that the invasion had caught him unawares, and vowed not to make the mistake (which he believed the British had made) of underestimating them. He thought that Hitler had attacked Russia less to destroy communism than simply to protect his eastern flank before attacking again in the west. Stalin's administrative skills impressed Hopkins. The Soviet dictator spoke in simple, brief sentences with an extraordinary grasp of detail. On the few occasions when he needed information, he touched a button and got what he wanted from a secretary who appeared and then left again in an instant. Hopkins thought that he saw Stalin's detailed and systematic intelligence reflected in the streets of Moscow, where each night supply trains moved through on their orderly way to the front, where the government distributed food to people with certification cards, and where the citizens went calmly about their work.

The image of Stalin as administrator influenced Hopkins's estimation of him. Stalin's sense of realism, his intimate control over the war effort, and his informal, unpretentious manner conveyed confidence and determination. Thus, although Margaret Bourke-White, who photographed Hopkins and Stalin after their second meeting, thought that Stalin looked gray and tired, Hopkins remembered him as a strong man with large, hard hands and the small, rugged stature of "a football coach's dream of a tackle." Bourke-White captured something of this impression when she photographed the two men standing side by side. In her picture Stalin looks relaxed, his arms hanging naturally, elbows slightly bent, stomach protruding against his blouse, his face turned toward the camera with a softness, a suggestion of a smile, about his lips and eyes. Hopkins, by contrast, stands in an almost military posture, shoulders square, arms straight, eyes wide and staring straight ahead, chin firm, mouth pinched and grim. Nothing here suggests the sharp wit, the easy laugh, and the get-tough attitude of Roosevelt's adviser or the irreverence, good nature, and warm sentimentality of

*Hopkins poses with Josef Stalin, August 1941*

Churchill's confidant. In the presence of a steely, hard-boiled fighter, Hopkins was determined to show that the United States was just as firm, just as determined.[16]

As it turned out, Hopkins needed plenty of determination on his own account to return to Britain alive. Sumptuous meals and safe, comfortable shelter had helped him build up his strength, but they could not make up for the effort expended in hours of conferences and the hardships of the flight from Scotland. Those who saw Hopkins could see the vitality in his large, bright eyes and the expressiveness of his features, but they could also see how his collar hung loosely around his neck and how when he crossed his legs his full-cut trouser legs revealed shockingly thin thighs. They also noticed the dark circles under his eyes and how he mumbled his words, his soft voice carrying scarcely five feet.[17] His strength was still low when he packed to leave Moscow on August 1, accidentally leaving his medicines behind. He looked very tired and ill when he arrived at Archangel. Flight Lieutenant McKinley asked if he would like to rest awhile before taking off, but Hopkins replied, "Whatever the next twenty-four hours may bring it cannot be as trying as the last three days."

The Catalina took off in a gathering storm and was severely buffeted as it made its way across the White Sea. Along the Murmansk coast unidentified destroyers fired on them. Hopkins offered to man a gun turret, but he was so obviously ill that the crew told him to rest. In the end he slept for seven of the flight's twenty-four hours. The plane arrived at Scapa Flow in more bad weather and heavy seas, and with no particular idea where it was supposed to drop off its passenger. After one false landing McKinley found the right spot, but he had to try several approaches before bringing the plane down in a crowded harbor on tossing waves. It pitched so wildly that the launch assigned to pick Hopkins up could not come alongside. He finally had to jump on board from the port blister. McKinley and the crew hurled his luggage after him, across several yards of open water. Then they took off, marveling at Hopkins's "unbelievable courage, determination and appreciation for the services of others." "His was a noteworthy example," McKinley wrote, "of unparalleled devotion to duty."

Hopkins returned the crew's admiration. While he was aboard the *Prince of Wales,* Hopkins wrote to Air Marshal Sir Charles Portal, "I want particularly to thank you for the arrangements for my flight to Archangel. It could not have been better. If you get a chance, will you tell Captain McKinley and his crew how fine and patient I thought they were. There wasn't a hitch in the whole performance."[18]

Now aboard Churchill's ship, Hopkins found the prime minister ready to get on with aiding Russia. He instructed Lord Beaverbrook, an enthusiastic supporter of aid to Russia who had recently been appointed minister of supply, to meet him in Argentia to work out preliminary arrangements for a Russian aid program. After the Atlantic Conference, Beaverbrook would be off to Washington to plan for the Moscow supply conference.

The decision to send an Anglo-American mission to the conference drew Hopkins into the center of the Russian supply question. Indeed it seemed logical for Roosevelt to appoint Hopkins to lead the American delegation, and Churchill hoped that he would do so. But Hopkins, realizing that he needed time to regain his strength, and with his recent flight still fresh in his memory, suggested that Averell Harriman go instead.[19]

The American delegation to Moscow was a Hopkins creation. General James H. Burns represented both Lend-Lease and the army; General Sidney P. Spalding, who had been assigned to Lend-Lease since March, handled communications in Washington; William L. Batt, a member of Hopkins's Business Advisory Council, represented the Office of Production Management; and Colonel Philip R. Faymonville served as executive secretary. Faymonville was a new addition and a unique kind of army officer. He had served in Russia during the American intervention of 1918–19, had learned the language, and had served as military attaché in Moscow from 1933 through 1938, winning the confidence of the Russian authorities and, inevitably, arousing suspicions in the army that he was procommunist. On Burns's suggestion, Hopkins arranged for Faymonville to remain in Russia to expedite American aid. When army intelligence objected, Hopkins stood his ground: "You might as well get his papers ready, because he's going over."[20] Perhaps because Hopkins had observed that Stalin had spoken more freely when Ambassador Steinhardt was absent, he recommended that Harriman outrank the ambassador. Hopkins also arranged to monitor all communications with Moscow.[21]

Once Harriman's team had been selected, Hopkins argued that the United States should establish a production program to ensure that the Russians received the necessary supplies. He and Burns had been promoting such a program for several months, and now he had the chance to propose it to Roosevelt. After a discussion at Hyde Park, the president ordered the army and navy to draw up schedules for supplying Britain and Russia. The services complied by September 11, and three days later Harriman left for London and Moscow.[22]

The course of the conference diverged from Hopkins's intentions. Inspired by his conversations with Stalin, Hopkins had hoped that the conference would be a planning session with the participants sharing information about their needs and production capabilities. But Harriman found the British unwilling to press this line of discussion. Churchill feared that unless the allies showed faith and good will, the Russians would sign a separate peace with Germany. Beaverbrook supported this view, telling Harriman that the mission was "not going to Moscow to bargain but to give." Thus when they arrived to find the Russians secretive and evasive, they simply accepted their requests at face value. Even in their conversations with Stalin, Beaverbrook and Harriman told him that their only objective was to give him the supplies he needed. When Stalin responded warmly, Harriman praised Beaverbrook's "genius."[23] The conference ended with the parties signing a protocol committing the Americans and the British to supply a list of specific items.

In Washington, Hopkins labored to begin aid shipments to Russia. Because domestic opposition to communism kept Roosevelt from putting the country under Lend-Lease, he had to unsnarl a tangle over financing the first shipments. He also relayed Russian complaints, prodded the Russian aid section not to allow "lesser lights" to hold up progress, and kept a wary eye on the army to be sure that it was cooperating.[24]

Hopkins's methods got supply shipments under way and bought time while Congress considered a request for an additional $6 billion appropriation for Lend-Lease. By late September, Hopkins knew that Roosevelt had decided to make Russia eligible for Lend-Lease but wanted to minimize any discussion of the subject. Even as late as October 30 Hopkins warned the War Department that the names Russia and Lend-Lease should not be used in the same communication by "anybody, anywhere at any time." In the meantime the president waged a publicity campaign, going so far as to persuade Pope Pius XI to declare that Roman Catholics could approve of aid to Russia without endorsing communism. Administration officials, including Secretary of War Stimson, General Marshall, and the recently appointed head of Lend-Lease, Edward Stettinius, testified on behalf of Russian aid. In the end these tactics paid off, as Congress soundly defeated anti-Russian amendments and passed the $6 billion appropriation on October 24. Roosevelt signed the bill four days later.[25]

By the fall of 1941 Hopkins was a key figure in U.S.-Soviet relations. The pattern begun in January in London had repeated itself in Moscow. Even the diplomatic outcomes were similar. Hopkins had gone to London to fill in for an American ambassador who had been discredited in the eyes of both Roosevelt and Churchill. His Lend-Lease mission had succeeded so well that it threatened to upstage the efforts of Ambassador Winant. That fall in Moscow, Stalin denounced Ambassador Steinhardt as a "defeatist." Shortly after Harriman returned, Hopkins concluded that Steinhardt's usefulness was over and he and Roosevelt decided to replace him with General Burns.[26]

In handling aid to Russia, Hopkins found that he had less of a free hand than in aid to Britain because President Roosevelt was personally supervising the program. Roosevelt was determined to keep the Russians in the war by showing them that they could count on American support. Roosevelt's approach, which was to supply the Russians with no questions asked, moved Hopkins away from his role in coordinating supplies and strategy and toward bringing U.S. agencies into line with the president's purposes. Early in November, Douglas Brown, who had attended the Moscow conference with Harriman and had remained behind to head the American supply mission, complained that he and the other American experts had been prevented from doing anything to help the Russians. He had spent less than an hour on "direct work" and many hours playing poker. He thought that he might as well come home. Brown discussed his complaints with Colonel Faymonville, who disagreed with his conclusions. The Russians had ordered large quantities of materiel, Faymonville responded, on account of their desperate military situation. They preferred to handle it themselves because they believed that they could "master complicated mechanisms without outside assistance," and because they feared that "over-meticulousness" from foreign experts might delay the equipment's getting into battle. Faymonville thought that the United States should continue to send advisers and experts, provided that they were single-minded, patient, sober, and able to work under hard conditions. Such people, he thought, would be able to help the Russians even though the Russians had never directly appealed for their assistance.[27]

When Hopkins compared the two evaluations of Russian attitudes, he decided that Brown ought to come home. "I don't quite see what he can do over there," he wrote, "and it seems to me the test of whether our experts are going to be used depends entirely on what happens after the tanks, airplanes and trucks arrive and whether they will let our personnel help them get going on it." There was no point, he later wrote, in encouraging "a lot of conversations . . . that will only irritate the Russians over something that is not really important to us."[28]

Hopkins considered the frustrations of American diplomats and technicians a small price to pay for the larger dividends of Russian aid. The largest of all was the 280 divisions the Russians were keeping in the field against the Nazi invaders. Next to this, other considerations seemed insignificant. "There is still an amazing number of people here," Hopkins wrote Churchill, "who do not want to help Russia and who don't seem to be able to pound into their thick heads the strategic importance of that front."[29] But there were other hopeful signs coming from the Kremlin. Stalin seemed willing to conciliate Americans diplomatically. After Harriman complained about the Soviet ambassador's habit of speaking to various American officials instead of working through Hopkins, Stalin replaced him with Maxim Litvinov, who had been popular with the Americans when he had served as the first Soviet ambassador to Washington in the 1930s.

Since it was Hopkins's job to deliver aid to Russia, his morale paralleled theirs. Delays and foul-ups not only angered him, they also depressed him. He would become deeply discouraged when things went wrong. Placing the burden on his own country led him inevitably to find the causes of his discouragement at home. If he was "ever so confident" about the Russians, he was decidedly less so about his fellow Americans. As the weight of his responsibilities bore down on him, as the criticisms from Roosevelt's detractors seemed as unending as they were irresponsible, as he recalled talking with Londoners sleeping in subways and cheering their prime minister as they stood before their bombed-out homes, of seeing Muscovites, living at a standard he judged to be well below that of the average American, apparently oblivious to the peril of war as they went about their daily routine, he came to conclude that Americans were not doing enough. His next job was to get them to do more.

# Chapter 13

# The Long-Term–
# Short-Term Balance

A week before Lend-Lease became law, General Burns wrote to Hopkins: "The time has arrived when this country must plan on a balanced maximum industrial effort objective for munitions . . . and for transportation. However, long-range production should not be allowed to interfere with early production."[1] Burns had not just defined an objective; he had defined a dilemma. Long-range planning and immediate production made sense in a nation mobilized for war, with military objectives clearly defined, raw materials stockpiled or programmed for delivery, and plants, equipment, and labor ready to swing into full operation. But the United States was not mobilized. It had few military priorities, idle plants, unemployed workers, a complacent industrial leadership, a deeply divided citizenry, and an Atlantic partner in acute crisis. Burns's recommendation failed to note that this long-term–short-term balance had to be achieved with too few resources.

Many of the production problems resulted from overconfident assumptions made a year earlier by civilian and military planners. At that time it had seemed that the United States could produce for its defense needs simply by taking up the slack in its depression economy. Production for defense, in this view, would not seriously interfere with production for civilian use. It also seemed that the most urgently needed materials could be manufactured on time simply by assigning them a preference or priority rating so that industries would schedule them ahead of others. But things had not turned out this way. Lend-Lease aid and expanding U.S. commitments had swamped industry. Almost overnight the volume of high-priority programs increased so much that they threatened to use up all available industrial material. By April serious shortages existed in machine tools, aluminum, nickel, copper, magnesium, semifinished steel, and other materials vital to defense.

Since production for defense meant production for Lend-Lease, Hopkins was inevitably drawn to the problem. Not surprisingly, he encountered difficulties similar to those he was already facing: conflicting interests that needed to be reconciled and loose ends that needed to be tied, as well as President Roosevelt's administrative peculiarities and consequent spells of action and passivity. He had to solve the overall problem by increasing production and simultaneously sharing out the shortages. No one could have been expected to perform such tasks faultlessly or to solve all the inherent problems. Indeed this did not even seem an objective in an administration that carried out its main purposes through negotiation. As a result Hopkins's efforts fell into the usual rhythm of administrative adjustment followed by frantic, frustrating attempts to make the system work, followed by other administrative adjustments.

Despite these obstacles Hopkins quickly defined the United States' production objectives. The same day that Burns sent his memorandum, Oscar Cox argued forcefully to Hopkins that America's "master objective" should be to outproduce the Axis powers. Richard V. Gilbert, the former head of the Division of Industrial Economics in Hopkins's Department of Commerce and now an analyst for the president's National Defense Advisory Commission, followed by denouncing the "poverty of imagination and lack of drive" of officials in charge of production who were not even aiming at parity with the Axis. Gilbert noted, for example, that the army's $7 billion ordnance program for 1941 and 1942 was $2 billion short of requirements for a force of 2 million men, and this at a time when Germany had a fully equipped army of 8 million. The planned rate of construction of merchant ships would not outpace the rate at which submarines were sinking them. And yet Undersecretary of War Robert Patterson had reported that the current program represented the country's "maximum production" rate for the next two years and that peak production was still three to four years off. Gilbert urged that all programs be expanded and speeded up, and he asked Hopkins to help see that this was done.[2]

Hopkins and Burns moved on various fronts. Burns recommended that the army expand to 4 million men. Hopkins worked through the journalists Joseph Alsop and Robert Kintner to criticize existing production programs and drafted a memo from Roosevelt to his defense chiefs calling for a survey of production needs to "exceed by an appropriate amount that available to our potential enemies."[3] Although

Roosevelt was willing to concede this much to long-term objectives, he preferred to increase the production of those items specifically ordered by Britain.

Hopkins soon learned that increasing production meant increasing the supply of machine tools. From Isadore Lubin of the Bureau of Labor Statistics he learned that only one-fifth of the machine tool industry was working second or third shifts, and that employers were planning to hire far fewer workers than the industry could absorb. Lubin also charged that American businessmen did not realize the critical state of the U.S. defense program and were operating on too many conventional and overconfident assumptions.[4]

Lubin's analysis underplayed the government's own role in encouraging this complacency. In February the president's Office of Production Management (OPM) had reported that steel production would be more than adequate for defense needs well into 1942. Within a few weeks it had become clear that this forecast was wildly inaccurate and that steel supplies were critically short. At the same time, manufacturers hesitated to gear up for full production, fearing that they would fill all their orders and be left with excess capacity. It became the government's responsibility to pressure business by putting the entire defense program under contract.[5]

As usual Hopkins looked for the quickest results. Throughout May he pressed OPM to divert machine tools from nondefense industries. He wanted to know, for example, "whether or not these factories making small arms ammunition are continuing to make just as much sporting ammunition as before." Perhaps it would be possible "to discontinue the manufacture of all small arms ammunition other than that needed for our arms programs and the law enforcement of the country." If the tools could not be transferred to defense, the workers could be. By the end of May he had arranged for the army and navy to give OPM a list of "the machine tools they need at once."[6]

More important, Hopkins worked with Roosevelt to pressure defense contractors. When the president instructed Secretaries Stimson and Knox to place all of their contracts by the first of July, Hopkins again pushed for a comprehensive production program. When John D. Biggers of OPM's production division sent him a memorandum asking the president to order a comprehensive production statement "at the earliest date," Hopkins personally read it to Roosevelt.[7]

On July 9 the president finally took the kind of action that Hopkins had been waiting for. He ordered the army and navy to design an overall production program, and he informed OPM that "a large part" of consumer goods production would have to be cut back. Hopkins followed up by discussing new cutbacks in automobile production and by soliciting nominations for a director of priorities for transportation, shipping, and raw materials.[8]

As Hopkins wrestled with these and other production problems, he grew increasingly to resent what he perceived to be the indifference of the American people to the defense effort. He bristled when the owner of a Lockheed Lodestar transport plane refused to release it to OPM for transfer to Britain. He thought about turning over the correspondence on the matter to the Senate committee that was considering a bill to permit the government to requisition private property for defense. "Frankly I think the Administration should have fairly broad powers," he wrote in a draft of the letter supporting the legislation. "For example who would have thought a few weeks ago that any American citizen who owned a needed transport plane [would] set up his personal private judgment against that of his own government as to the uses or needs for such a plane[?]" In the end he decided against sending the offender's name to the committee for fear that people would think that Roosevelt was "persecuting" the man. His name "will leak out fast enough," Hopkins concluded.[9]

His trips to Britain and Russia in that summer of 1941 only intensified his feelings. "Hopkins was very bitter as to [the] attitude of [the] American public with regard to all-out industrial production," Hap Arnold reported at the Atlantic Conference. "[He] calls attention to 600,000 autos [produced] last month when we need airplanes—engines—tanks so badly."[10]

Hopkins was even more than bitter toward those who actively opposed the defense effort. He routinely forwarded to the Justice Department and the Federal Bureau of Investigation all evidence of opposition and disloyalty to the cause. This included a telegram opposing convoy escorts and declaring, "We are in no danger . . . if our equipment is not given away. Your masters Jews and British radio and movie propaganda are selling Americans fear psychology"—this from "another fellow who indicates very clearly that he is a Nazi-minded person," Hopkins observed. A report on an American businessman's close connections with the Germans through his association with the conservative American financier Harris Forbes caused Hopkins to advise, "I should think the F.B.I. would have a fellow like this under the closest surveillance."[11]

Hopkins wanted actual troublemakers prosecuted to the limits of the law. A few days before the German invasion of Russia he had suggested action to block "communist efforts not only to organize but to sabotage our whole defense program . . . From my point of view they are just as much a potential enemy as the Germans." Germany's attack on Russia in no way lessened Hopkins's desire to crack down on subversives. When the FBI arrested a number of people for violating the Espionage Act of 1917, he suggested that the law's applications be expanded and that Americans who refused to serve on British ships be prosecuted under the Conspiracy Act. "My own feeling," he wrote, "is that we should use every legal weapon at hand to hit [subversives] and I am sure the country is delighted at the recent action of the FBI."[12]

Hopkins also wanted to tighten government security. He responded sympathetically when the British complained that published OPM reports revealed too much about shipping losses, exports, and war production. He especially wanted to discourage leaks to the press. When the *New York Times* quoted "an OPM source" in a story about U.S. tank production, he recommended that Roosevelt's press secretary Steve Early or the FBI "find out who in the government is giving out this information and make an example of him." "I realize that under ordinary circumstances it is supposed to be bad form to find out how a newspaper man gets stories but when vital defense information like this is given out to newspaper men I think the person who gave out this information should be fired." If secret information "falls into the hands of the Germans," he pointed out, "it may well result in men being killed."[13]

One secret no one seemed able to keep was that by the time Hopkins returned from the Atlantic Conference, defense production was slower than ever. On August 28 the president's special assistant for defense, Wayne Coy, whom Roosevelt had ordered to speed up aid to Russia, reported that production of aircraft and antiaircraft guns had fallen far behind schedule and that tank production was unlikely to meet the growing need. The United States had produced only two heavy bombers in July and by August 1 had in stock only enough 37 mm. ammunition to fire a single gun for half an hour.[14]

Up to this time Hopkins had believed that presidential leadership and a comprehensive program would solve the production problem.

*The Supplies, Priorities, and Allocations Board (front row: Hopkins, William Knudsen, Henry Wallace, Donald Nelson; back row: James Forrestal, Robert Patterson, Leon Henderson, and Sidney Hillman), September 1941*

By August he saw a need for firmer administrative guidance. At the Atlantic Conference he had learned that the U.S. military had been planning to have its own joint board coordinate production, allocation, and strategy. He recommended the idea to Roosevelt, but the president sidestepped and created a Supplies, Priorities, and Allocations Board (SPAB), under a neutral chairman, Vice President Wallace. The board would include representatives from OPM and the military and, for good measure, Hopkins.[15]

In fact Roosevelt seemed inclined to reduce the military's influence. At the same time that he established SPAB, he appointed a civilian administrator to replace General Burns as head of Lend-Lease. The man was Edward R. Stettinius. He had come to OPM from the United States Steel Corporation, where, at age thirty-eight, he had become chairman of the board. Handsome, square-jawed, silver-haired, impeccably well groomed, he exuded the cooperative spirit and friendliness of a YMCA secretary, which in fact he once had been. Stettinius had also been one of Hopkins's "tame millionaires" on the Business Advisory Council. Roosevelt soon gave Stettinius a firmer administrative position by creating the Office of Lend-Lease Administration (OLLA).

Hopkins monitored the results of these moves. On September 11 the military joint board produced its victory program, calling for an American army of 8.8 million men, doubled merchant shipping capacity, and $143 to $150 billion in supplies by June 30, 1943. A few days later Stacy May of OPM's Bureau of Research and Statistics returned from London with a report on Britain's industrial capacity, which showed that despite its vastly greater resources, the United States would not outproduce Great Britain and Canada until the second half of 1942. In order to help defeat the Axis, the United States would have to double its production. The report shocked many but confirmed Hopkins's belief in the need for an all-out effort.[16]

Behind the production estimates lay the assumption that the United States would have to enter the war. The joint board concluded that Hitler would not be overthrown until Germany was near military defeat, and there was no assurance that a new government would be willing to agree to acceptable peace terms. Nor could Britain, Russia, and their allies defeat Germany, even with increased American aid. The United States would not only have to fight; it would have to stay in the war even if Britain and Russia collapsed. In a letter to his Grinnell College friend James Norman Hall, Hopkins went right to the point: "I . . . don't believe we can ever lick Hitler with a Lend-Lease program. It, unfortunately, is going to take . . . much more than that."[17]

Unable to get the United States into the war, Hopkins threw himself into the production effort. He asked Lubin to prepare studies of critical materials, assuming that "defense needs are all *under* stated." He worked to restrict machine tool exports, obtaining a list of tools scheduled for shipment to Britain and Canada, and informing Undersecretary of War Robert Patterson, "We could get some of these immediately for you if there are some that you need badly." As a result machine tool exports declined, and U.S. officials began urging the British to use their tools more effectively.[18]

Still, shortages persisted, and by mid-November Hopkins was declaring, "Almost every shortage we have finally comes down to machine tools." But rather than gear up, the industry seemed willing to congratulate itself on its past performance, and OPM seemed just as self-satisfied. Lubin informed Hopkins that William Knudsen, the head of OPM, "has little desire to move machine tools from non-defense plans to defense plants." He added, "OPM has little or no control over the machine tool data and . . . the folks in the machine tool division do not seem to know much about their job." When he heard this, Hopkins advised Roosevelt to have Knudsen hire "some hard-hitting fellow with a national reputation for achievement and quick action to take charge of a national campaign under the OPM to increase the production of machine tools," and he suggested that Stettinius use funds from the new Lend-Lease appropriation to place blanket orders for machine tools "so that we can give the industry some very real production goals to shoot at" and can "put the heat on them for not delivering." When Knudsen replied rather complacently that OPM was bringing the problem under control, Hopkins urged Patterson to organize a machine tool committee within SPAB. "I believe," he declared, "that until the Army and Navy really get inside that machine tool allocation it will never be done properly."[19]

To balance allocations with production Hopkins sought to strengthen Lend-Lease. He advised Stettinius to place representatives in OPM's three major commodity divisions "to fight for our interests" and "to be sure that in the allocation of commodities we are getting a fair break." He also made sure that OPM representatives sent to Britain to discuss steel allocations would be attached to Averell Harriman's Lend-Lease office.

He warned Stettinius especially to beware of the military. The services were so afraid of shipping to Britain more equipment than they could spare that they were preventing Roosevelt's plans from being implemented. They preferred to prepare to defend the United States rather than take a chance on the British.[20] Stettinius needed Hopkins's support, because the military was pressing to cancel Lend-Lease's authority to transfer items from its stocks and to force it to allocate money to build new defense plants. Hopkins opposed the army on both counts and persuaded Roosevelt to back up Lend-Lease.[21]

The more controversies Hopkins refereed, and the more requests and complaints he received, the more he realized the need to increase production. But all that increased were his problems. When the British reported alarming shortages of high octane aviation fuel, he investigated and, as usual, proposed to "get [somebody] behind this high octane gas business and give it a real push." But when he pushed, nothing moved. He asked Burns if gasoline could be stored in anticipation of increased demand. Burns replied that demand was already outrunning supply, so the problem was production, not storage. He asked the economist Leon Henderson if it would be "a good thing to prohibit all private airplanes from using high octane gas" only to learn that "there is really no civilian use of high octane gas." The only solution was to produce more; until then the shortages would have to be shared. That, of course, meant more emergency arrangements and more raised tempers. Late in September, over Marshall's strenuous objections, Roosevelt gave Lend-Lease aid priority over efforts to build up U.S. forces. In October, Hopkins overrode Stimson's opposition to sending heavy bombers to Britain. The next month Sir John Dill, the chief of Britain's general staff, persuaded Marshall to assign all U.S. medium tanks for the next three months to the Middle East. At the same time Hopkins fought to send more fighter planes, and OLLA went through financial gymnastics to balance its commitments to Britain and Russia.[22]

The Russian situation was particularly critical. Hopkins did everything he could to speed supplies. He arranged for equipment ordered for October to be loaded by the last of September. He labeled a request for trucks "extremely urgent" and told Stettinius "to do everything possible" to expedite it. At a time when his orders usually took weeks to get action, arrangements were completed in four days. He asked Burns to check on fighter plane production "in the hope that we might get an additional number of P-40E's off to Russia at an early date." He put Stettinius to work with Jerry Land of the Maritime Commission "to be sure that no stone was left unturned . . . to supply the required number of ships to deliver the materials . . . that had been agreed upon at the Moscow Conference." "Above everything else now," he wrote Oscar Cox, "we have got to keep the stuff rolling to Russia and the Middle East. I am sure we have got to get far more stuff than we have so far agreed to send."[23]

Hopkins also confessed, "I am worried about shipping." He would continue to worry for the next three years. That fall, however, the problem was desperately serious. In September the military joint board estimated that its victory program would require a 60 percent increase in shipping tonnage. Although the Maritime Commission had cooperated splendidly, increasing construction by 25 percent between May and September, the extra ships would not be coming out of the yards until early 1942, and the program would not hit its stride until the second quarter of that year. In the meantime, more ships were being sunk than were being launched.[24] For the moment, better use had to be made of available shipping. Hopkins pushed to increase cargo capacities, and Roosevelt persuaded Congress to permit U.S. ships to sail into belligerent ports. The British improved their cargo handling so that ships would spend less time in port.[25]

The most awkward problem was shipping to Russia. The Russians had asked that most cargoes pass through Archangel, the port that was closest to the fighting front. But it was soon evident that ice and other difficulties would restrict the port's capacity far below expectations. For a time Hopkins considered transferring cargoes to the Persian Gulf, but its capacity proved too limited, and the Russians continued to demand the northern route.

That meant pressing U.S. shipping to the limit. Hopkins enlisted Roosevelt to find ships to carry Russian aid. Land did his best, but in the end he was stymied. When the Russians asked him to send ninety-eight ships in six weeks, he was able to round up only half that number.[26]

But Hopkins would not give up. Responding to reports of delays and Russian complaints, he grabbed the phone and asked General Sidney Spalding for a list of the supplies that would be left behind when the forty-nine ships sailed for Russia. When he learned that one hundred tanks and nearly two hundred planes were being left on the loading docks, he gave the general a typical Hopkins grilling. Why not, he asked, leave other supplies behind to make room for the tanks and planes? Why not send the planes on the ships scheduled for the Persian Gulf? The answer was that all the planes were carried on deck, and the tanks could be unloaded only from certain holds. Still, the army had given "firm orders" to load the maximum number of planes and tanks and were trying to break down the planes into smaller crates that could be carried below deck.

That might be good enough for the army but not for Hopkins. Blaming the British for overemphasizing Archangel's limitations, he rounded up more ships for both Archangel and the Persian Gulf. When the British warned that port facilities at Basra were too limited for his proposed shipments, he rushed construction equipment to the area and recommended sending the ships anyway, since no one could tell him exactly how many ships could be accommodated, and "under any circumstances it is better to have the material there than sitting on the docks here."[27]

Alliance politics also motivated Hopkins's efforts. At the time of these shipping difficulties Churchill was preparing to send Anthony Eden to Moscow to discuss war aims with Stalin. When Secretary of State Hull and Roosevelt learned of the mission, they hastened to warn against making any secret treaties or understandings. Hull cabled Ambassador Winant in London that U.S. aims had been expressed in the Atlantic Charter, and he emphasized that "the test of our good faith with . . . the Soviet Union is the measure to which we fulfill the commitments" of the aid program. Hopkins followed the next day with a cable to Harriman declaring that "all airplanes, spare parts and ammunition, all tanks, spare parts and ammunition and all other items including TNT in the Russian protocol for which we made a firm commitment prior to January first will be shipped before January first . . . Show this cable to Winant, Churchill and Beaverbrook," he went on, "because it is extremely important that they understand that this country is meeting its Russian commitments."[28]

All of Hopkins's efforts clearly revealed the fundamental problem of the American defense program, which remained, as General Burns had originally defined it, the balancing of long-term and short-term needs. Hopkins had done what he could to strike this balance, favoring control over long-term planning by the joint board and later by trying to strengthen SPAB while keeping Lend-Lease independent and personally working to meet the short-term needs of Britain and Russia. The trouble was that the weak U.S. production effort always left him unable to satisfy either alternative. He was trying to balance a seesaw all by himself; when he sat on one end, he threw the other off kilter. He simply had to choose which end to take, and he usually chose to support the short-term requests of Britain and Russia.

Roosevelt also emphasized short-term objectives, and given the realities of the time, this was the wiser approach. Since the United States did not have a military program that could tip the balance of the war decisively, it made sense to supply the immediate needs of the fighting Allies. This was where Hopkins became especially useful. His ability to deal with issues in detail enabled him to define the shipping problem in terms of the number of tanks and planes on board or the production problem in terms of the number of machine tools properly allocated. For example, in October he sent General Burns a memo asking for "a list which would include the major munitions items, showing in column 1 the amounts which will be produced in this country by months for the next six months and secondly, the present plan for distribution of these. Include what you consider the important munitions of war."[29] In this way, Hopkins could operate a system of priorities that better served the needs of the war effort than the so-called balanced program of the long-term planners. By concentrating on a few major items, he could contribute to defeating the Axis while building a partnership of mutual confidence and cooperation.

Hopkins did not concentrate on such short-term adjustments merely because they suited his administrative style. As in his New Deal days he continued to look for ways to bring order and regularity to his job. Establishing the Office of Lend-Lease Administration was a step toward efficiency in handling short-term problems, and long-term planning would have moved in the same direction if SPAB had taken hold. But it did not. SPAB started out in a spirited fashion but bogged down in tangled administrative relations with OPM, since it had to rely on OPM's creaking administration to execute its policies. Thus it was unable to make its efforts felt in that fall's hectic deliver-the-goods atmosphere.

SPAB's decline inspired Hopkins to look for new ways to organize long-range production. He did this in part to satisfy his own inclinations, but also because Marshall, Morgenthau, and Undersecretary of the Navy James Forrestal were calling for more comprehensive planning. Morgenthau and Forrestal offered Hopkins a clear choice. Morgenthau criticized the military for failing to deliver supplies. He wanted a Ministry of Supply set up, to be run by civilians, while Forrestal recommended a joint committee of military and Lend-Lease personnel. Hopkins gave Morgenthau his usual sympathetic hearing but endorsed Forrestal's plan.[30]

Hopkins's decision took on larger implications when Harriman returned from Britain to advocate organizing boards in London and Washington to allocate supplies in accordance with military strategy. Harriman sold his idea first to General Burns and then to General Marshall. Harriman and Burns then turned to Hopkins. They proposed to establish a Strategic Munitions Board, including Hopkins,

Burns, and Marshall, and a Strategic Shipping Board of these three plus Admiral Land. Hopkins agreed to the proposal and approached Roosevelt, who put off acting on it.[31]

In these autumn months of 1941 Hopkins's frenetic activity came at a high cost to his health. On the last day of October he accompanied Roosevelt to Hyde Park, where, after an intense survey of production problems, he wrote a series of letters on machine tools, bomber and shell production, and internal security. Then he started to experience difficulty in walking. On November 5 he returned to Washington and at once entered the naval hospital, where he remained for the rest of the month. Since the hospital was only a few blocks from the White House, he was able to spend an occasional evening with the president, but he wrote all of his memos and held his conferences in his hospital room. He tried to pass off his illness with joking remarks about being "bounced around by these Navy doctors," but he realized that he was in a seriously debilitated state. While his doctors gave him blood transfusions, he read novels and listened to the radio, which he concluded was "as bad as the motion pictures and worse than the average detective story." He improved noticeably after the first week, and while the doctors ran tests to prescribe a treatment, he advised them how to run their hospital. By December 3 he had decided that he had had all the rest he could stand and told the doctors to send him home.[32]

In the meantime, as November passed into December, U.S. defense efforts appeared to have sunk into a hopeless muddle. The Lend-Lease people were squabbling with the army, SPAB was comatose, and Hopkins had struggled unsuccessfully to set up a new plan of organization. As it turned out, though, he had achieved more than he realized. Months of informal arrangements had placed Hopkins at the center of every major branch of the American defense effort. His singular ability to gain people's confidence and to bring them together for creative work had given that effort a focus and an energy that were absolutely vital to its progress.

He had also provided coherence by gathering around him a group of associates that others were calling the Hopkins Shop. There was nothing unique about the name, since many administrators referred to their circle of advisers as their shop. The uniqueness of the Hopkins Shop came from its close connection to the president and its far-reaching interdepartmental character. Lend-Lease provided its main base, with Burns, Cox, Harriman, and later Stettinius occupying the principal places. From Lend-Lease the shop reached into the Treasury Department via Cox and into the army via Burns and the head of the Defense Aid Division, Colonel Henry S. Aurand, a creative administrator who, with the skill of a typical New Deal bureaucrat, built his ad hoc agency into a key element of the army's supply section. The Hopkins Shop also cooperated closely with the British Supply Council, and at one time Hopkins suggested employing commodity specialists from the council to represent Lend-Lease's interests in SPAB. Although the Maritime Commission had no direct representation in the shop, Hopkins worked closely with Commander H. L. Vickery and later with Lewis Douglas of the War Shipping Administration.[33]

One of the strengths of the Hopkins Shop was its informality. Its top members could bring to Hopkins's attention any topic of sufficient importance. Hopkins realized, however, the need to work through specific channels so that his people would not compete with each other or unnecessarily complicate the work of other departments. Thus he warned the Harriman mission in London against trespassing on Ambassador Winant's responsibilities and tried to refocus Harriman's attention on Britain's supply problems after his return from Russia. "Mr. Hopkins feels it is important to somehow get across to Harriman," Stettinius noted, "that his job is London and not Russia or the Middle East, although he is happy to have Harriman continue to be informed on the latter two. However, he feels Russia and the Middle East will have to be run by Burns from here."[34]

The Hopkins Shop cohered and accomplished as much as it did because of Hopkins himself. Wise in the strategy and tactics of government administration, he nurtured Lend-Lease by protecting it here, extending its influence there, husbanding its resources, focusing its energies. Roosevelt's support and authority helped, but the president did not involve himself in the details of building Lend-Lease. That was Hopkins's job, and he did it splendidly. Still, those in the Hopkins Shop were attracted less to the organization than to the man himself. Hopkins invited opinions and information, knew what needed to be done, and never lost his nerve, despite setbacks and illness. Stettinius almost glowed as he reported to a group of top production officials in November, "Harry is better—lots better. He'll be able to leave the hospital soon, and he'll be back with us before long." "I can see what a personal hold you have taken over some of us youngsters," Oscar Cox wrote him in the hospital. "When I get a tug across the middle I darn well know it. It doesn't happen often. But by getting laid up you've done it. That's one of your minor rewards for spending yourself for a goal other than yourself." Years later Averell Harriman simply referred to Hopkins as "one of the truly great men of my generation."[35]

If Hopkins had failed to fulfill Roosevelt's purpose of making the United States the "arsenal of democracy," he did succeed in making Lend-Lease the key element in the country's anti-Axis partnerships. However inadequate, Lend-Lease aid was the tangible evidence of U.S support for Britain and Russia. Not surprisingly, as the war continued, members of the Hopkins Shop rose through that alliance system. General Burns was considered for the post of ambassador to the Soviet Union, and after the unsuccessful tenure of Admiral William Standley, Averell Harriman took the job. Stettinius entered the State Department as undersecretary and became Secretary of State in late 1944. Hopkins himself might have become an ambassador at large or U.S. high commissioner in Germany if his own poor health and Roosevelt's death had not prevented it.

Hopkins returned from the hospital in early December to find the White House filled with talk of war—not with Germany but with Japan. Earlier that fall Roosevelt had decided to take a strong stand against any further Japanese expansion in the Far East. Hopkins had encouraged Roosevelt to take a tough stance. The president had hoped to stall the Japanese through diplomatic means but was prepared to ask for a declaration of war if they moved against Singapore, Malaya, or the Dutch East Indies. He would counter the isolationists by claiming that Japan had fired the first shot.

On the evening of Saturday, December 6, a navy commander delivered to the White House an intercepted message, decoded by the intelligence unit that had broken the Japanese code. He found the president with Hopkins in the study. Hopkins paced the floor as Roosevelt read the message, a memorandum from Japan's Foreign Minister Shigenori Togo reviewing the course of negotiations with the United States. The document contrasted Japan's "fairness and moderation" with America's indifference to Japanese interests. Charging that the United States was trying to neutralize Japan in order to enter the war against Germany and Italy, it rejected the most recent American proposal to settle the countries' differences. After he finished reading Roosevelt handed the message to Hopkins, waited for him to read it, and then commented, "This means war." Hopkins agreed. The two men discussed the deployment of Japanese forces, expecting that they would strike from their bases in Indochina. Eager to get into the fighting, Hopkins observed that it was too bad that the United States could not strike the first blow and prevent a surprise attack. Roosevelt replied that the United States, a democracy and a peaceful people, could not do that. But, he declared, "we have a good record." That record of seeking peace while opposing aggression, the president seemed to believe, would in the near future justify a declaration of war against Japan.[36]

But not that night, or even the next day. Sunday morning, after a late breakfast, Hopkins, dressed in slacks and a sweater, strolled into the Oval Office to find the president looking forward to spending that Sunday with his stamp collection. Hopkins was lounging on a sofa when the telephone rang. Roosevelt picked it up, listened, and then told Hopkins that Japanese planes were attacking the U.S. Pacific Fleet at Pearl Harbor in Hawaii. Stunned, Hopkins blurted out that there must be a mistake; surely Japan would not attack Honolulu. The president countered that this was just the kind of unexpected thing the Japanese would do. Once the shock had worn off, Roosevelt wanted to believe the news, for the attack meant an end to the maneuvering, to watching the opinion polls and checking the votes in Congress, reaching again and again into the hat for some new trick and never knowing what he would find. Now he was free to act. Calmed by this realization, the president went to work, instructing Hull how to handle his meeting that afternoon with the Japanese ambassador and special envoy, dictating a press release to Steve Early, and calling a conference with Stimson, Knox, Marshall, and Chief of Naval Operations Harold Stark. They arrived similarly calm but aware that a hard struggle lay ahead.

While the meeting was in progress, Churchill called from Chequers. Harriman and Winant were with him. They had picked up the story from a BBC newscast on a flip-top radio Hopkins had given the prime minister.

"Mr. President," Churchill asked, "what's this about Japan?"

"It's quite true," Roosevelt replied. "They have attacked us at Pearl Harbor. We are all in the same boat now."[37]

Churchill put Winant on the phone and set to work calling Parliament into session and having the Foreign Office prepare a declaration of war. A few days earlier he had promised that if the United States went to war with Japan, Britain would follow "within the minute." As he did so, he reflected on his own feelings of relief, his sense that Britain's narrow escapes were over and the war was finally about to be won. The Americans, he knew, would fight ferociously, and their enemies would be crushed. The next day he and Harriman cabled Hopkins, "Thinking of you much at this historic moment."[38]

In the White House the lights burned on into the night. Hopkins saw Roosevelt grow tense and angry as messages arrived revealing the full scale of the disaster in the Pacific. The Japanese raid had been a complete surprise and nearly as total a success. The Pacific Fleet was crippled; the aircraft at Hickam and Wheeler fields had been destroyed on the ground. Casualty figures were incomplete but were expected to be high. Still, Roosevelt kept his nerve. There was no point in laying blame, he said; everyone had to get on with the job of winning the war.

After reviewing the situation with Cabinet members and congressmen, Roosevelt settled down for a talk with Hopkins and the newsman Edward R. Murrow, with whom the president had made an appointment days earlier. It was after midnight before he felt ready to sleep. Hopkins invited Murrow to his room to talk over the day's events while Hopkins got ready for bed. He called the Japanese attack a godsend, for no other event could have brought the country unified into the war.

It had been quite a year for Hopkins. He had built up the Anglo-American alliance, established personal contact with Stalin, helped organize war production and shipping, and was in the process of coordinating them with military strategy. In the meantime he had moved heaven and earth to make up for the weaknesses of the defense effort, sacrificing his health in the process. Now, as he sat on the edge of his bed in the White House, his pajamas sagging about his frail, wasted body, he suddenly thought of all that lay ahead. In a low tone, as if speaking to himself, he whispered, "Oh God—if I only had the strength."[39]

---

*Chapter 14*

# Laying the Groundwork

On Monday, December 8, President Roosevelt went before Congress to ask for a declaration of war against Japan. The outcome was never in doubt. In London, Churchill had acted so swiftly that Parliament had already declared war on Japan several hours earlier. Three days later Hitler declared war on the United States. Italy followed suit the same day, and so did Japan, which for some reason had not yet made the state of belligerency official.

Hopkins was optimistic and eager to get to work. On the trans-Atlantic telephone he promised Beaverbrook and Harriman, "We will undoubtedly increase our [Lend-Lease] amounts." "Don't worry . . . don't worry," he repeated as Harriman tried unsuccessfully to tell him that no one was worrying. "You can count on it; we are not going to let [the British] down." When the military asked Congress for an extra $8 billion, Hopkins ordered Stetinnius to list the "urgent items . . . not now ordered in adequate quantity." He suggested that the War Department "make examples" of defense contractors who did not make an effort to shift to a round-the-clock, seven-days-a-week schedule.[1]

Of course the country needed more than Hopkins's reassuring words to mobilize. Without adequate supervision, war mobilization would simply create a grab-bag in which all interested parties would try to acquire scarce resources for themselves. At the moment the most successful grabbers worked for the War Department. The day after Pearl Harbor the department stopped all Lend-Lease shipments, even recalling ships at sea. At the same time Stimson persuaded Roosevelt and SPAB to divert all Lend-Lease appropriations to the army.

Not surprisingly, others failed to see things Stimson's way. Stettinius called for "a tough, hard-hitting strategy outfit" with a "high caliber staff of military, naval, and civilian experts" to advise the president on military strategy and Lend-Lease allocations. SPAB resolved that the United States and Britain should decide how to divide up strategic raw materials, and Hopkins went to work organizing an American committee and inviting British representatives to Washington. The Maritime Commission opposed efforts by the army and navy to set shipping priorities and charged that the army had "stolen" one of its new buildings. "The Maritime Commission," Hopkins noted, "cannot work under the present scheme."[2]

For the moment Hopkins felt inclined to conciliate the army. By December 10 the War Department had relaxed its grip on Lend-Lease supplies to the extent of releasing tanks and airplanes that had already been loaded for shipment. Hopkins advised Stettinius "not [to] ask the Army for anything" but instead to work closely with Assistant Secretary John J. McCloy, who was handling Lend-Lease matters for the War Department. He also assured the army that he was "eminently satisfied" and the British were "more than pleased" that Lend-Lease transfers had been unfrozen.[3] He also persuaded Roosevelt to create boards composed of himself and the military chiefs to allocate supplies and shipping.

Actually Hopkins was playing a more complicated game than the army realized. He had asked Roosevelt to establish the boards not to confirm the army's authority but to place supplies and shipping under the president's "*immediate supervision.*" Hopkins also agreed to combine the Lend-Lease and War Department appropriations because he knew that Roosevelt was planning to ask Congress to appropriate all war funds directly to himself. The president would then allocate dollars to the War Department to produce "common items" for both American and British forces while retaining "sole authority" to transfer them as he saw fit. Hopkins wanted Roosevelt to have this authority, but he also hoped that the arrangement would keep the president close to George Marshall. Many meetings that fall had convinced him that the general was a great strategic thinker who would give Roosevelt the advice he needed to coordinate supplies and strategy.[4]

As things turned out, Hopkins's strategy went awry. The munitions board never met, the shipping board proved ineffective, and Roosevelt gave up his plan to control all war appropriations. On December 26 Congress passed a supplemental defense appropriation which placed Lend-Lease funds under the War Department. But none of these setbacks deflected Hopkins from his determination to bring Marshall forward. When Roosevelt complained about a navy statement that there might not be enough ships to transport troops to northwest Africa, Hopkins summoned Colonel Charles P. Gross, chief of the

Army Transportation Corps, for a lecture on initiative. In no uncertain terms Hopkins told Gross that the army should take the lead in shipping allocations. Hopkins felt that instead of working through the army and navy joint board, Marshall should make recommendations to President Roosevelt through Secretary Stimson. Hopkins would support Marshall and try to persuade the president to give the army all the ships it needed.[5]

Hopkins's efforts to encourage a Roosevelt-Marshall partnership indicate his belief that military strategy should set priorities for Lend-Lease aid, shipping, and production. To the extent that he followed this line, he had to scale down his own responsibilities. He was no military strategist, and he knew it. A single memorandum, listing such strategic questions as "How many planes to reinforce Panama and when will they be there?" constituted the sum of his independent thinking about the subject.[6] Instead of offering advice, he kept himself informed in conferences and informal chats with military officers.

At the time Hopkins was placing his plans for a Roosevelt-Marshall partnership in the larger context of an Anglo-American partnership. Two days after Pearl Harbor, Churchill suggested that he and Roosevelt meet. Because the president had to be in Washington to supervise American mobilization, Churchill once again boarded a battleship, this time for a full-dress council of war, code named Arcadia. The prime minister and his party arrived on the evening of December 22 at Hampton Roads, Virginia, and flew to Washington in time for a late dinner.

The Americans were ready with strategic plans. Roosevelt had already approved an overall defensive strategy, but he was particularly interested in offensive opportunities, and that left him open to Churchill's plan for an Anglo-American invasion of French North Africa (Operation Gymnast). That evening Hopkins listened as Churchill argued for the operation and Roosevelt agreed to begin planning for it. Churchill left the meeting so exhilarated at his success that he had to take two sleeping pills to drop off.[7]

We have no record of how well Hopkins slept that night, but the evening's events probably troubled him. Hopkins had hoped that the discussions would proceed along lines more suitable to Roosevelt's free-wheeling, speculative, good-natured ways. He had even gone so far as to warn Churchill not to show up in Washington with cut-and-dried plans since the American chiefs were so concerned with the

Pacific that they would probably react negatively to suggestions touching other fronts. But now Churchill had persuaded Roosevelt to endorse a strategy without even consulting the War Department. That would doubtless alienate General Marshall. The next day Hopkins tried to dampen the president's enthusiasm for Gymnast by arguing that the pro-Nazi puppet government in France would tip off the Germans.[8]

Hopkins's advice may have done some good. At the first formal session that afternoon Roosevelt returned to the War Department's priorities. In the end Roosevelt and Churchill instructed their military advisers to study ways to carry out Gymnast in 1942, with or without the cooperation of the French. The president ordered the navy to keep on hand enough troop transports to carry out the operation. When the navy representatives responded doubtfully, Hopkins lectured Colonel Gross on Marshall's responsibilities to provide the shipping. (Marshall would make his influence felt in other matters, and new arrangements would transform the character of the shipping problem. The North African operation survived the conference, however, and, as Churchill had hoped, became the centerpiece of Anglo-American strategy.)

On Christmas Day, Hopkins was contemplating these matters when Stimson phoned. The War Department had recently assigned troops to reinforce the beleaguered Americans fighting in the Philippines. Stimson had just heard that Roosevelt had agreed to divert them to support the British. No one had consulted the War Department about this; indeed it was improper even to discuss such a thing while the battle for the Philippines was still raging. If Roosevelt planned to do business this way, the agitated secretary announced, he was going to resign. Shocked, Hopkins calmed Stimson as best he could and promised to look into the matter. At once he went to Roosevelt, who was talking with Churchill. Both denied having made such an agreement. Hopkins reported this to Stimson, but the secretary read him a British memorandum backing up his charge. That was enough for Hopkins. Roosevelt had again let the British take advantage of his loose talk. Hopkins assured Stimson that he now saw things his way. He marched back down the hall to lecture Roosevelt about the trouble he was creating at the War Department and to admonish him to be properly formal with Churchill. A few hours later Roosevelt called in Hopkins, among others, and airily dismissed the British memo as nonsense.[9]

As Hopkins looked for a way to put the Anglo-American partnership on a sounder footing, some much-needed help arrived. Marshall proposed to form unified theater commands with one person responsible for directing operations in a given area. Roosevelt and Churchill would still decide grand strategy but would be less likely to blunder into details like providing reinforcements for the Philippines.[10] Any plan of Marshall's was good enough for Hopkins. He had no trouble convincing Roosevelt, who endorsed the plan at once.

Hopkins had to maneuver to win Churchill's support. When Roosevelt presented Marshall's proposal, the prime minister backed away, arguing that unified command was impractical in theaters separated by thousands of miles. As Churchill was concluding his remarks, Beaverbrook passed Hopkins a note saying that the prime minister was only following advice and was open to discussion. Hopkins jumped at Beaverbrook's invitation. "Don't be in a hurry to turn down the proposal," he told the prime minister, "before you know who is the man we have in mind." To play up to the British, the Americans had decided to nominate General Archibald Wavell to command Anglo-American forces in the American, British, Dutch, and Australian (ABDA Command) Pacific territories. Hopkins knew that he was playing a weak card. Everyone believed that the ABDA area would soon be overrun by the Japanese, so Wavell was being nominated to take the first Anglo-American loss. Churchill graciously played down this aspect of the suggestion but put Hopkins off with arguments about the wisdom of placing land, sea, and air forces under a single command.[11]

Hopkins responded brilliantly. He had entered the conference eager to promote General Marshall, and now was the perfect time to do so. He arranged for Marshall to present his plan to Churchill. Marshall justified all of Hopkins's expectations, answering Churchill's practical questions and brushing aside his speculative objections.[12] Hopkins then made sure to rush the agreement in principle into an agreement on paper. He helped the prime minister draft a telegram to the War Cabinet endorsing Marshall's system. The next morning he took the message to a meeting of the president and the American chiefs, where it was put into final form.[13]

At this point one of Hopkins's suggestions came back to haunt him. In discussing the wording of the prime minister's telegram, Roosevelt and Churchill reached an impasse over describing how Wavell was to receive his orders. The conference had not as yet set up any machinery for combined operations, and given the variety of national interests in the ABDA area, resolving the issue promised to be time consuming. Bent on pushing Marshall's plan, Hopkins suggested that Churchill simply say that Wavell would receive his orders from "an appropriate joint body." In the War Cabinet sharp eyes picked up the vague phrase, and the return message asked for a clarification. Within a few days the words had, according to Hopkins, "kicked up a hell of a row."[14]

One problem was that "everybody and his grandmother"—New Zealand, Australia, Holland—wanted to be represented on the appropriate joint body. A more serious question was how to coordinate the command system between Washington and London. The British and American chiefs proposed to consult the other nations in London, but Roosevelt wanted them represented in Washington as well. At first Hopkins supported the president, but when the chiefs held their ground, he tried to dispose of the issue by arguing that wherever the joint body met, the British and the Americans would run it. Roosevelt gave in, and on January 1, 1942, he and Churchill approved the chiefs' recommendation. At the same time Wavell's orders went out, and on January 15 he assumed his new command.[15]

Organizing the ABDA area also raised the question of China's status in the alliance. At the moment Generalissimo Chiang Kai-shek and the British were arguing over who should have authority in Burma. For Chiang, Burma was the source of the supplies that wound and bumped their way along the Burma Road to Chungking; for the British it was their front line for the defense of India. By now the Chinese had become particularly irate because British troops in Rangoon were seizing their Lend-Lease supplies.

Hopkins had shown little interest in Far Eastern affairs and might normally have stayed out of the China squabble. But Roosevelt was hoping to build China into a major power and thus wanted Chiang included in all important war decisions. On December 29 Hopkins invited himself to an afternoon conference at which Stimson and Marshall were drafting a letter offering Chiang a Far Eastern theater command. He pressed Roosevelt's proposal to include Chiang in all strategic decisions and sympathized with the American officers who argued vigorously to include Burma in the Chinese theater. Harmony with the British took precedence, however, and the British argued so strongly against any Chinese command in Burma that Chiang was offered only Thailand and Indochina, where the Japanese were already entrenched. Hopkins grumbled that Chiang was not "getting much of a command out of this," but he could only advise Roosevelt to send Chiang a conciliatory telegram.[16]

Hopkins found the British determined to move on various fronts to secure their interests. At the beginning of the Arcadia conference they had asked the United States to scale down its aid to Russia. The War Department had already delayed Russian shipments and could be expected to ask to divert supplies from Russia. But Lend-Lease was determined to stand against such claims. On December 26 Stettinius sent Hopkins memos recommending that Russian aid be reestablished "as promptly as possible" and deficits made up "as soon as practicable."[17]

Such vague language fitted the uncertainty of expanding commitments. But to Hopkins, who was pressing the army to take charge of shipping, promoting unity of command with Churchill, and correcting Roosevelt's strategic fluffs, it would not do. Roosevelt had made Russia a top priority, and Hopkins intended to leave no doubt that it should remain one. Throwing out most of Stettinius's draft, he composed a letter ordering the War Department to resume Russian aid on schedule on January 1, with all deficits to be made up by April. "The whole Russian program is so vital to our interests," he wrote, "that I know that only the gravest consideration will lead you to recommending our withholding longer the munitions our government had promised the U.S.S.R."[18] Roosevelt approved Hopkins's draft with only a few minor changes.

At the same time Hopkins balanced Russian needs against the army's. Marshall proposed sending abut 22,000 troops to the southwest Pacific, remarking that the operation would reduce Russian aid by 30 percent for four months. When Roosevelt and Churchill expressed dismay and seemed ready to reject the suggestion, Hopkins consulted the shipping tables in his head and announced that 30 percent of Russian shipping amounted to only seven ships out of some 1,200 available, with another forty due for launching. If shipping to Russia were not affected, he asked, would Marshall's plan be approved? When all agreed that it would, he suggested that Roosevelt and Churchill take the responsibility of finding the ships. The meeting then approved Marshall's proposal, and Roosevelt asked Hopkins and Beaverbrook to follow up.[19]

These moves on behalf of Russia came at a time when Roosevelt and Churchill were discussing with Ambassador Litvinov the text of a proposed declaration of the United Nations, the official title of the Allies. Although Hopkins wanted the declaration to highlight the partnership among the United States, Britain, China, and Russia, he especially wanted the document to express American war aims. Recalling that many Americans had opposed aid to Russia on religious grounds and had criticized the Atlantic Charter for not mentioning the goal of religious freedom, he advised Roosevelt to "make every effort to get religious freedom in this document." He recommended other language from the Atlantic Charter but had to settle for only a dry reference. He had better luck promoting the charter's principle of national self-determination when he persuaded the British to allow India to sign the declaration. Anticipating that Russia might balk at a clause that defined the enemy as "the Government or Governments which signed the Tripartite Pact" (thus including Japan, with which Russia was not at war), he suggested a revision to "those Axis forces of conquest with which each government is at war." Finally, he suggested that the four major partners be listed first in the declaration.[20]

With these and other details out of the way, Hopkins attended the signing ceremony in the Oval Office on the evening of January 1. He had all the more reason to be somber on this occasion, since more than anyone else he knew the gritty, niggling work that the war effort would demand. But Roosevelt was in high spirits, brimming with a sense of the occasion's historic significance. The president reminded Churchill to sign on behalf of Great Britain and Ireland and wondered out loud if he should have signed as commander in chief. "President ought to do," Hopkins commented drily.[21]

Then, just as the conference seemed to be proceeding smoothly, it crashed into a controversy over allocating war materiel. As usual, various individuals had been acting independently along lines that converged at a collision point. Yet again in the history of the Anglo-American partnership, at that point stood the frail figure of Harry Hopkins. The trouble began when SPAB proposed to form a joint committee to control raw materials. Hopkins mentioned this idea to Beaverbrook, claiming that it was "of the greatest importance." But Beaverbrook did not want to waste his time on details. He had come to Washington to reorganize the whole U.S. production effort. Flatly declaring that "the production of weapons in the United States, Britain, and Canada is entirely inadequate," he had predicted enormous deficits in tanks, planes, and artillery unless there was "an immense increase in production here and in Great Britain." To accomplish this he proposed to scrap the Americans' convoluted committee system and create a "Supreme Command in supplies as well as in strategy," coordinated by Hopkins.[22]

Beaverbrook was talking Hopkins's language. By the time of Arcadia, American production had almost broken down. Private industry seemed disinclined to convert to full-time war production, and Hopkins was concluding that "the selfish interests of big business" were the greatest obstacle to an all-out mobilization effort. When the attorney for a Swedish arms manufacturer complained that the United States was violating its contract by Lend-Leasing its guns to foreign countries, Hopkins snapped, "If I had a client who asked me to do what you are asking your Government to do I would tell him to jump in the lake." He may also have favored Beaverbrook's proposal for a supreme command. For the moment, however, he had to back away from the idea because Roosevelt preferred to readjust the existing system.[23]

Next, the British chiefs developed their own allocations plan. They did not believe that Lend-Lease could appropriately coordinate supplies with military strategy, and were alarmed to learn that Holland had been placing large orders in both Britain and the United States, playing each country off against the other and justifying the requests to neither. In order to avoid more such situations, the chiefs proposed to establish a joint allocation committee in Washington. The committee would allocate American war production to the United States and Great Britain, which in turn would assign their shares to designated "protégé" nations according to the agreed-upon military strategy.[24] Obviously the plan served British interests, giving Britain a claim on American production but reserving Britain's production for its own uses. More important, the protégé scheme assigned to Britain all the European countries other than Russia, which was a joint Anglo-American responsibility, and left the United States with the less industrialized nations—China, Latin America, and Iceland. Since the chiefs had long since agreed that defeating Germany was the first priority, the American chiefs predictably opposed the plan. After further discussion turned up too much disagreement and uncertainty, the chiefs approved only a general recommendation to establish boards in Washington and London. They agreed that Hopkins should head the Washington board.[25]

While the American and British chiefs were revising their plan,

Lend-Lease was trying to scuttle the whole idea on the grounds that it would be easier for the United States to get other nations to cooperate with its war needs if they had gotten their supplies directly from the United States. What the country needed was not an Anglo-American board but its own supreme committee—chaired, of course, by Hopkins, who had "the originality, imagination, and astuteness to see the over-all picture and be aware of the reactions of the leaders and people of the countries in a way no military or naval expert could."[26]

Thus all the plans, however diverse and conflicting, had a place for Hopkins. This certainly showed how many friends he had acquired in the past year. Of course, one might well ask: with friends like these, who needed enemies? For a time he was saved by blissful ignorance. Although he was kept informed of these developments, he was not following them closely enough to worry about becoming the point at which they would collide. At the moment he wanted only to protect Lend-Lease from the War Department. On January 13 Hopkins, Supreme Court Justice James Byrnes, and Budget Director Harold Smith agreed that future war appropriations should set aside 25 percent to the president for Lend-Lease transfers. That afternoon Hopkins had lunch with Roosevelt and obtained his agreement.[27] He had no idea that the next day would be the most critical of the entire conference.

January 14 was the last day of the Arcadia conference. By that time all mechanisms for confirming Anglo-American cooperation seemed to be in place. The military leaders had created a Combined Chiefs of Staff (CCS) and Roosevelt needed only to announce a U.S. Joint Chiefs of Staff (JCS) to give American participation the necessary formality. Discussions about allocating raw materials and shipping had led to the creation of a Combined Raw Materials Board and an Anglo-American Shipping Adjustment Board. A proposal to establish Munitions Assignments Boards adopted Beaverbrook's idea of having the chairmen report directly to Roosevelt and Churchill. But already the storm clouds were gathering. Two days before the British chiefs had warned Churchill that this kind of arrangement conflicted with their desire to have the CCS supervise allocations. Roosevelt had not heard from the American military, however, so just before the final session was to meet in the White House, he and Hopkins summoned General Marshall and asked for his response.

Marshall had been having a bad twenty-four hours. His sacred principle of unity of command seemed in jeopardy. Only the day before he

had warned the Combined Chiefs against creating independent allocation boards in Washington and London. There could be only one
Combined Chiefs of Staff, he had declared, and the boards would have
to operate under its control. Then that morning he had heard that the
new military appropriations bill would allow Congress the allocation
of American aircraft. At once he fired off a memo to Hopkins complaining that the proposal "in effect . . . upsets our whole conception of
unity of control and strategical direction of this war." Now, in the
presence of Roosevelt and Hopkins, he heard the president explain
that the two munitions boards would report to their heads of government. That was the last straw. Angrily he denounced the proposal for
violating the unity of command and for granting the British the authority to allocate American production. If it was adopted, he declared,
he would resign as chief of staff.

Hopkins quickly stepped in. To Roosevelt's surprise, he vigorously
supported Marshall, agreeing that the boards should be subcommittees
of the CCS and declaring that unless this was done, he would not
participate in them either. It is possible that Hopkins had received
Marshall's earlier complaint about congressional allocation of aircraft
and anticipated his reaction. Indeed the fact that only Marshall was
called to respond to the allocations arrangements suggests that Hopkins may have staged the meeting so that Marshall could air his views.
Whether this was the case or not, his response was inevitable. He had
spent too much time building Marshall up and had put too much effort
into establishing unity of command to see everything lost on this issue.
Supporting Marshall was his only choice.[28]

While Hopkins was saying his piece, Churchill, Beaverbrook, and
the British chiefs were filing into the room. Roosevelt had to decide on
the spot whether to support the original proposal or to support Marshall and Hopkins. But Marshall and Hopkins had forced his hand.
The threat of losing his chief of staff was bad enough, but to lose the
services of Hopkins, whose participation in the allocations machinery
was virtually the only thing that all the interested parties had consistently agreed on, would be too much. When the session's agenda
reached the question of munitions allocation, the president proposed
to establish the Washington and London boards as subcommittees of
the CCS. Astonished and upset, Churchill and Beaverbrook argued for
the original system, but Roosevelt and Marshall held their ground.
Hopkins tried to help but made the mistake of saying that the Wash-

ington board would report to the Joint Chiefs of Staff, the name that was being used to describe only the American chiefs, and Marshall had to correct him. In the end Churchill grudgingly agreed to try out the system for a month, and Beaverbrook added that he foresaw many difficulties in London.[29] On this sour note the conferees agreed to establish Munitions Assignment Boards in Washington and London, with Hopkins in charge of the Washington board. Hopkins chose General Burns as his executive officer.

It was particularly fitting that Hopkins should have wound up with this responsibility. For over nine months he had been working to coordinate Lend-Lease aid with military strategy. His friendly relations with the War Department and his support of British strategy in the Middle East had won him the kind of support he needed if both nations were to favor his appointment. For once the furtive logic of history followed the script.

It also seems clear that the logic of history was not always the logic of Harry Hopkins. Hopkins had not understood the relationship between munitions allocation and unity of command. Perhaps his loyalty to Lend-Lease had led him astray, encouraging him to keep allocations out of the hands of the military. Only his decision to discuss the allocations proposals with Marshall before the final meeting prevented what would have been an even more explosive and embarrassing scene. On this occasion Lord Root of the Matter had a narrow escape.

As it turned out, Hopkins came away from the Arcadia conference having played the key role in setting up the most successful collaboration in military history. He had soothed Stimson and Marshall, cautioned Roosevelt, prodded the War Department, helped frame the Anglo-American command system, and gained a central place in the allocations machinery. And he had brought forward General Marshall. Midway through the conference Churchill's physician, Charles Wilson, noted, "Marshall remains the key to the situation. The P.M. has a feeling that in his quiet, unprovocative way he means business, and that if we are too obstinate he might take a strong line. Neither the P.M. nor the president can contemplate going forward without Marshall." When Churchill left Washington early in January for a brief vacation in Florida, he took Marshall along to get better acquainted.[30]

Hopkins succeeded less well in persuading Roosevelt to rely on Marshall. The president insisted on closely supervising the American war effort himself. Not only did he intend to be his own grand strategist; he even told Marshall that he considered himself the chairman of the Joint Chiefs of Staff. Personal differences also separated the two men; Roosevelt could never feel comfortable with a man of Marshall's stiff, humorless temperament. Marshall also felt the distance between himself and his commander in chief, and although he admired Roosevelt, he thought it wise to save his contacts for the most important matters, even if that meant accepting defeat on a number of smaller ones. So he rejected Hopkins's advice to develop a personal relationship with Roosevelt and chose the wiser course of working through Hopkins. Years later Marshall recalled that Hopkins "made the technique . . . of the military position . . . plainer to the president than I could possibly have done myself."[31]

The Arcadia conference had gone a long way toward sorting out the Anglo-American war effort. Russian aid was given a privileged position that both nations had to support. Britain's interests in Burma took precedence over China's. American and British generals were going to run the ABDA command regardless of what "everybody and his grandmother" thought about it. The Americans hoped that India would sign the United Nations Declaration, but the decision was up to the British. And the British were not going to be allowed a voice in allocating American war production unless they gave Americans a voice in allocating British production.

To Hopkins the significance of these decisions was not that they enacted some grand design but that they showed that the Americans and the British were able to adjust their policies in order to cooperate with each other. The participants at the conference could easily foresee that ahead lay many opportunities for controversy. The day after the conference adjourned, Marshall sent Hopkins a memo outlining some of the problems he anticipated in munitions allocations and emphasizing the need for "diplomacy and sound judgment." Hopkins realized this, but at the moment he was thinking more of what had already been accomplished. Permitting himself a bit of ceremonial rhetoric, he wrote the same day: "There are great and heroic days ahead. I think we have laid the groundwork for final victory."[32]

# Chapter 15

# No Front Stairs
# in Washington

A man in Hopkins's position was entitled to a few heroic thoughts—indeed to almost anything to lift his spirits and stiffen his courage in the days that followed the Arcadia conference. As soon as the conference ended, an exhausted Hopkins went back into the naval hospital. Meanwhile the war was going badly. In the Pacific, Japanese advances threatened Australia and India. In the Middle East, Field Marshal Erwin Rommel pushed back the British forces. In the Atlantic, shipping losses reached record levels by the end of January, with worse still to come.

While the Allied military chiefs wrangled over strategy to meet these emergencies, Hopkins returned to gear up the administrative machinery. He soon learned that, far from being easy to implement, some of the Arcadia decisions required a great deal of further planning. Instead of managing routine operations, Hopkins again found himself having to improvise ad hoc arrangements.

One urgent job was to support the Arcadia machinery with an American agency for war production. Although Lord Beaverbrook had not been able to persuade Roosevelt to create a supreme command for production, he did manage to spur the president to increase production objectives. On January 3 Roosevelt announced goals far above all previous estimates. Production of aircraft would increase from 28,600 to 45,000, of tanks from 20,400 to 45,000, of antiaircraft guns from 6,300 to 20,000. Even Hopkins, who usually yielded to no one in demanding all-out production, wondered if the president was expecting too much. But Roosevelt waved aside his doubts, responding, "Oh—the production people can do it if they really try." That was assurance enough for Hopkins, and he immediately adopted the president's goals as his own.[1] But how were they to be met? By the time of the Arcadia conference American industry had failed to meet the more important ones in almost every vital munitions category, and Hopkins had convinced Roosevelt that SPAB had broken down. Hopkins still hoped that the army and navy would take on more responsibility.[2] Thinking in the military ran along the same lines, and Stimson and Knox proposed placing the responsibility for production with the Army and Navy Munitions Board (ANMB).

Roosevelt, however, wanted to set up another civilian agency under multiple leadership. He first proposed a triumvirate of Morgenthau, Supreme Court Justice William O. Douglas, and Wendell Willkie. Morgenthau was dropped because of his other responsibilities and replaced by Donald Nelson, a Sears-Roebuck executive and executive secretary of SPAB.

Hopkins had never known multiple leadership to work (memories of Roosevelt's first work relief apparatus still rankled), but instead of arguing against the principle, he narrowed the list of candidates. Douglas, he said, knew nothing about production and seemed uninterested in the job. Willkie too was uninformed and might use the office to promote himself politically at Roosevelt's expense. That left Nelson. Hopkins had reservations about Nelson, who was more the calm, self-possessed compromiser than the two-fisted executive he usually looked for. Still, Nelson's relations with the president were cordial, he had a "good record under severe conditions," and he was determined to increase production. In the end Roosevelt accepted Hopkins's arguments and appointed Nelson to head a new agency called the War Production Board (WPB).

Hopkins had anticipated that the production shuffle would bruise some feelings, and he was right. That evening Jesse Jones, the chairman of the Reconstruction Finance Corporation, called to say that the OPM head, William Knudsen, was threatening to quit. Although Hopkins considered Knudsen a weak link in the production chain, he realized that the public had come to accept him as the nation's production expert. Hoping to head off a politically embarrassing defection, he, Justice James Byrnes, and Budget Director Harold Smith had proposed to offer Knudsen a commission in the army and an assignment to work under Robert Patterson in the War Department. Working rapidly, Hopkins told Jones to calm Knudsen, called Patterson to get his consent, and persuaded Roosevelt to offer the commission. He then had Jones pass the word to Knudsen so that when Roosevelt made the offer, Knudsen was ready to accept on the spot.[3]

As Hopkins carried out Roosevelt's orders, he revised his views of recent events. Now it seemed clear that the president had been right all along, that the cries in the press for a production czar had been "in reality an attack on the president" by "enemies [who] wanted him to really give up being president and let somebody exercise the power to which the people had elected him." Big business had been selfish, the army and navy "short-sighted," and Congress blind to the need for maximum production. "As far as I know," Hopkins declared, "the president is the only person in the whole crowd who . . . was pushing . . . for all-out production."[4] Thus Hopkins dismissed such key elements in the development of production policy as Roosevelt's responsibility for the failures of SPAB, his own campaign for more military authority, and even his own influence in shaping the WPB's leadership.

Hopkins's rewriting of history reveals much about himself and his relations with Roosevelt. Of course it shows the depth of his loyalty to his chief, the extent to which he was willing to subordinate his own views to Roosevelt's. This was the quality that made him so trustworthy in carrying out Roosevelt's decisions. Hopkins could put himself in Roosevelt's place, see things through his eyes. This explains why Roosevelt once told Willkie that he could use a man like Hopkins, who "asks for nothing except to serve you."[5]

Of course when he said this Roosevelt was misjudging his relationship with Hopkins. His remark shows how much he felt the need of someone who fitted this image. But the truth was that Hopkins was valuable to Roosevelt as far more than a willing servant. Hopkins's skill lay in his ability to see things from various perspectives. Thus he could convince the military that he was protecting their equipment from transfer to the British while assuring the British that he would get equipment for them from the military. He did not play the chameleon for the sake of peace and quiet. Rather, he gained people's confidence so that he could accomplish larger objectives. In this manner he had begun the process of coordinating Lend-Lease with military strategy, recommended an overall victory program in production, brought forward George Marshall, and fought successfully for unity of command. He had even tried to maneuver Roosevelt to respond aggressively to the *Robin Moor* incident. None of this compromised his loyalty to Roosevelt; indeed his loyalty was of a higher sort than Roosevelt imagined. By acting independently and creatively, Hopkins used his persuasive powers to implement Roosevelt's decisions. He was not the president's servant; he was his junior partner.

Once Nelson was in place, Hopkins tried to make sure that he got the authority he needed. On his advice Roosevelt disapproved a move by the military to control weapons production. The WPB, Hopkins insisted, should set priorities for all production.[6] He even shielded the board from suggestions by the British about forming an Anglo-American production board.

A few months later, however, circumstances were changing his mind. The Combined Chiefs had fallen into disputes with various production agencies, and pressure tactics by British purchasing agents had created an impression that the British were blind to America's production problems. A combined board would convince Americans otherwise by providing for Anglo-American cooperation. On a visit to

*Hopkins and Roosevelt in the president's study, 1942*

London that spring, Hopkins was impressed to see how well the combined American and British weapons committees were functioning. He even went so far as to say that he would resign from the Munitions Assignments Board to head the Washington wing of a combined production authority.

Above all, Hopkins hoped that a combined board would help Donald Nelson, who by that time had lost control of important priorities to the military. Thus in order to save both Nelson and the British from interference by the American military, Hopkins persuaded Roosevelt to agree to a Combined Production and Resources Board (CPRB), which was established in June.[7]

Whatever this says about Hopkins's enthusiasm for Anglo-American cooperation, it shows him at his worst as an administrative thinker. Trying to compensate for the weaknesses of the WPB by creating a higher agency was like papering over a crumbling wall. The CPRB wound up having to rely on the WPB to carry out its policies and proved largely ineffective.

In fact, although the decisions that came out of the Arcadia conference pointed in the other direction, the trend in American war administration was toward national agencies that coordinated domestic interests and, often through Hopkins, negotiated a combined policy with the British. In other words, the Americans continued to administer the alliance from the bottom up.

Shipping was a case in point. Shortages in every category had caused a predictable scramble among the army, Lend-Lease, and the British. (Learning that the United States had diverted one-third of the shipping from Britain's civilian supply needs, Churchill exclaimed to Hopkins that such losses were "catastrophic.") Roosevelt had ordered massive increases in construction, but the Maritime Commission was pessimistic, and with German submarine wolf packs prowling with deadly effect, some observers were predicting actual shrinkages in shipping by the end of the year.[8]

Part of Hopkins's purpose in promoting Marshall had been to give the army control over shipping. But by the end of the Arcadia conference he had learned that there were too many interests involved to make this plan practical. The conference had established a combined shipping board but had left control in the hands of national agencies. It seemed to Hopkins that the military was too self-interested to be allowed the final authority, and he recommended that the responsibility go to Admiral Land of the Maritime Commission, who would give everyone a hearing with the right to appeal to Roosevelt. The president approved this approach, and on February 7 established a War Shipping Administration (WSA) under Land.[9]

Having put the military in its place, Hopkins now performed the same service for Admiral Land. Land intended to set up the WSA "inside the Maritime Commission circle" by appointing commission administrators to head its major departments. But Hopkins wanted his own man on the inside, and in Lewis W. Douglas he had just the one. A personal friend of Roosevelt, Douglas had served as budget director but had resigned when the president refused to balance the budget. "This is the end of western civilization," he had declared, a remark that established his credentials as a conservative and a poor prophet. Although neither quality stood high with Hopkins, he had sent Douglas to London as Harriman's assistant. Douglas had scarcely settled in before Hopkins brought him back to Washington to spend a few weeks getting acquainted with shipping tables before Roosevelt appointed him to the top job in ship allocations.[10]

As soon as Douglas was on board, Hopkins recruited him for the Hopkins Shop. "H.L.H. thinks all makes sense," Douglas noted after an early conference. Hopkins gave Douglas "his complete endorsement," called his ideas "excellent," and encouraged him "to stay with it and to persevere until the [WSA's] point was achieved." The WSA, Hopkins declared, "knew more about shipping than anyone else in the Government." Hoping that Douglas was made of stronger stuff than Nelson, Hopkins warned him against being taken in by the military and advised him to settle any problems that arose before they could cause trouble at the White House.[11]

Douglas was all that Hopkins had hoped he would be. Gracious and good-natured when he held the upper hand, Douglas was a sarcastic, plain-speaking combatant in an administrative tussle. He was also wise enough to stay near the source of his power, and he cooperated with Hopkins and his network throughout his tenure with the WSA.

As Hopkins and Douglas looked for a key to sorting out the shipping tangle, they found it in the Russian aid program. In response to Russian complaints Roosevelt had ordered top priority for Russian shipping and had appointed Hopkins to oversee preparations for a second supply conference. When it turned out that General Burns could not be spared to replace Laurence Steinhardt as ambassador to the Soviet Union, Hopkins arranged to upgrade Philip Faymonville temporarily to major general to strengthen the Lend-Lease mission. Hopkins had hoped to hold a full-dress supply conference in which the Americans, British, and Russians would discuss strategy as well as supplies. But Faymonville talked him out of it, arguing that supplies would make the Russians better friends and allies.[12]

Faymonville also raised the issue of Anglo-American competition, declaring that accepting Russian requests at face value would overcome ill-will that was being generated by the British. It so happened that at the time, in order to pry loose more Lend-Lease supplies for themselves, the British were proposing that the Russians be forced to justify their requests. When Hopkins visited London that spring, he persuaded the British to cancel plans for a conference but came away suspecting that their military leaders were not "too anxious to get supplies to Russia and that we have got to overcome a good deal of resistance."[13]

Thus by mid-April, Hopkins had decided that all hope for assuaging Russia lay in expediting supplies. Just at that time a major shipping crisis arose. With waterways iced in on the northern Russian route, most of the ships in a recent convoy had had to return to Iceland. But other ships were already loading, and Roosevelt's orders had sent more on the way, so the area had become a enormous shipping logjam. To make matters worse, WSA schedules were inaccurate, so no one knew the real dimensions of the problem. With each new report the situation grew worse.

Frantically the Americans worked out new schedules and routes. Hopkins tried to control the problem by slowing the flow of cargo to Russian ports, rescheduling the berthing of ships and sailings for Iceland, and increasing the number of ships bound for the Persian Gulf. In the end, however, he had to inform the Russians that shipments would fall behind schedule, and that vessels would have to be reloaded with high priority items. The Russians protested but got no results. When Foreign Minister Vyacheslav Molotov visited Washington in late May, Roosevelt asked him to reduce requests by 35 percent and promised only "to move the maximum amount of supplies."[14]

The only gain was administrative. Throughout the crisis Lend-Lease and the WSA worked closely together. Burns organized shipping conferences and contributed ideas. Harriman reported on the shipping situation from London. As a result the WSA was further incorporated into the Hopkins Shop.

No sooner had the schedules been worked out than a new difficulty arose. Perpetual daylight along the northern route was making the ships easy prey for German submarines. In July convoy PQ 17 was torn to pieces in the Barents Sea, losing twenty-three of its thirty-four ships and delivering only 70,000 of its 200,000 tons of cargo. For a time Hopkins, Burns, and Roosevelt remained determined to push through more convoys by arranging better protection. But Churchill pressed to suspend shipping, and they had to agree. Hopkins followed up the decision by ordering new shipping schedules to send as many supplies as possible through the Persian Gulf and to release the extra ships to other duties. He also arranged to divert the ships to Operation Bolero, the Anglo-American buildup for invading Europe in order to establish a second front against Germany.[15]

The Russians were not impressed. They were facing a "black summer," Stalin proclaimed, with the Germans driving toward the Caucasus in the south and threatening Moscow and Leningrad. Now more than ever before Stalin wanted Anglo-American supplies. Soviet naval experts, he told Churchill, were convinced that "with good will and readiness to fulfill" the protocol that committed the Western allies to supply the Soviet Union with specific amounts of materiel, the convoys could continue and even inflict heavy losses on the enemy. Shifting supplies to the Persian Gulf "could in no way compensate for the cessation of convoys to the northern ports." In the United States, Ambassador Litvinov complained bitterly that while the Russians were fighting, the British and the Americans were only planning.[16]

Russian complaints produced a black summer in Washington too. During his visit Molotov had warned that the German offensive might force the Russians to withdraw to the Volga River line, leaving Germany in possession of food crops and raw materials of the Ukraine and the oil fields of the Caucasus. In that event, he said, the "whole brunt" of the war would fall on the United States and Britain. In response Roosevelt had promised to establish a second front in 1942. But shortly afterward the plan was changed to an invasion of North Africa. Roosevelt feared that Stalin would see this as another incidence of bad faith and might even resort to signing a separate peace with Hitler. This caused him to redouble the effort to get the Lend-Lease supplies through. By the end of August he and Churchill had agreed to send three convoys to northern Russia during September and October.[17]

Hopkins expedited the plan with his usual determination. When others warned that new Russian convoys would hurt other programs, he replied that the convoys would have to go regardless. But a new obstacle had arisen. During the summer critical shortages of aluminum had developed. The WSA and the WPB had decided that the United States had to import at least 300,000 tons of bauxite per month from Dutch Guiana. German submarine strikes in the Caribbean, however, had sunk half of the original bauxite fleet, and the WSA had to arrange special escort protection in order to keep up deliveries. Looking over the shipping tables, Douglas concluded that there were too few escorts and too few merchant ships to provide for planned military maneuvers, keep up the bauxite trade, and make up the three Russian convoys as well. Hopkins was sympathetic but undaunted: "It seems to me," he wrote, "that you should press as vigorously as you can [for] internal production of bauxite . . . I gained the impression at the meeting today [of the WPB] that there could be some increase in U.S. production of bauxite if we put our shoulder to the wheel."[18] In the end, however, Hopkins's tough talk yielded to Douglas's tougher realities, and between September and December only one convoy went to Russia.

One way out of these difficulties was to build more ships. Roosevelt had ordered an ambitious construction program, and by June the Maritime Commission reported that it had the capacity to build even more ships than the president had requested. By that time, however, even the existing program was in danger because of a mad scramble for steel. Unclear lines of authority complicated matters even more. The Army and Navy Munitions Board (ANMB) set priorities for war production, the WPB allocated materials, and the CPRB tried to coordinate not only with the British but also with the CCS, both of which went their separate ways.

At first Hopkins gave the steel crisis only fitful attention. He learned of the problem just as he was preparing to receive another visit from Churchill to discuss military strategy. During the conference the issue arose as a debate over whether it was wiser to have the Maritime Commission build more merchant ships or to give the steel to the navy to build escorts. Land and Douglas came away believing that Roosevelt had given them priority, and they drew up an expanded program which they took to Hopkins on the morning of July 9. Hopkins said that he would try to have Roosevelt approve it that day. Later that morning Hopkins learned that Land and Douglas had arrived a day late. The day before, Donald Nelson had persuaded Roosevelt to freeze the Maritime Commission's program and to accelerate building escorts.

By coming into the matter late, Hopkins had found himself outmaneuvered by the military. But no one outmaneuvered Hopkins for long. That fall the services overplayed their hand, calling for control over all the Maritime Commission's construction and at the same time trying to claim its steel allocations. Since these cuts in steel would reduce production, the services were actually proving their own worst enemy. At once Hopkins began conferring with Douglas to restore the commission's construction program. Hopkins recommended that the commission tie its case for more shipbuilding to increased escort construction, which Roosevelt had consistently supported. Douglas then drafted a memorandum declaring that solving the shipping shortage required steel for both merchant ships and escorts. The extra steel, Douglas observed, would amount to less than 1.5 percent of annual steel production. Hopkins took the memo to Roosevelt and, when the president asked how to proceed, pulled out a memorandum to the JCS calling for another review of steel allocations. Douglas, however, wanted to give the military no chance to bury the memo. He requested a conference to settle the matter once and for all. Hopkins rounded up the parties and Roosevelt gave orders to cut back on public works and civilian construction to make the necessary steel available.[19]

Hopkins's offensive on behalf of shipping came at a particularly propitious time in Anglo-American relations. A few weeks later Britain's minister of supply, Oliver Lyttelton, arrived in Washington to argue for more merchant shipping. With the way already cleared for more construction, Hopkins was able to persuade Douglas to allocate ships to Britain if in return the British reduced their orders for steel in the United States.[20]

As 1942 drew to a close, Hopkins had expanded ship construction but had not solved the shipping dilemma. That problem would simply assume other forms throughout the rest of the war. Hopkins's accomplishment lay elsewhere, especially in establishing the War Shipping Administration, an achievement which suggests that Hopkins's perceptions were often as keen and pertinent in large matters as in small. If Hopkins could see in a moment's discussion that Marshall's demand for unity of command required military control of munitions allocations or that reinforcing the southwest Pacific meant deploying half a dozen ships to Russia, he could also see that shipping construction and allocation held the key to American strategy. So he encouraged the WSA to find ships for Russia when the British were ready to cut back, recommended transferring those ships to Operation Bolero when the logjam in Iceland held up some convoys and the German raiders devastated others, and maneuvered for an increase in construction when he realized that the military services were allocating steel against their own best interests. As he brought Douglas into his shop, Hopkins was able to use the WSA as he had used home service, the WPA, and Lend-Lease: as a flexible instrument for meeting a widespread emergency.

Ironically Hopkins had less success with his own agency, the Munitions Assignments Board (MAB). In his desire to support Marshall, Hopkins had arranged for the military to direct the war effort by determining grand strategy. He had assumed that the CCS would produce a truly Anglo-American strategy that would guide the combined war effort. In his idealized view, MAB would function automatically, assigning weapons according to strategic principles. As chairman, he would keep the members' attention on those principles. His plans for MAB illustrated his assumptions. He played down the board's importance, kept its staff to a minimum, and relied on the services to carry out the board's decisions. The board met in a sparsely furnished room in the Federal Reserve Building, its members seated at a plain wooden table with staff members and invited officials arranged in rows before them. Its meetings were secret, and little effort was made to publicize its activities. Throughout the war it went largely unnoticed.

Hopkins further reduced MAB's decision making by assigning most of its work to committees. Called munition assignment committees, they met to consider allocations for ground, air, and navy, and were thus designated MAC(G), MAC(A), and MAC(N). When they made their allocations, the committees reported to the weekly meetings of the board, which routinely approved their decisions unless the American and British committee members had disagreed on particular items. Then MAB acted as a court of appeals. Each member had one vote, with the Americans outnumbering the British on the committees and each having three service members on the board. The tendency to vote along national lines usually meant that disagreements in the committees produced a deadlock in the general meeting. When that happened, Hopkins would appoint an ad hoc committee of one American, one Briton, and himself to decide the dispute. Occasionally Hopkins unilaterally decided an assignment, claiming "reasons of state."

As the war years passed, Hopkins gradually lost touch with MAB. He presided whenever he could during 1942 and 1943, but a long

illness in 1944 took him away from the board's routine, and after he
returned to work, he appeared for only two sessions. After September
1944 he attended no more. During the last months of his absence the
board members, especially the British, recalled his leadership with a
kind of nostalgic warmth. "The smooth working of the machinery in
the past," the British observed, "has been largely due to the presence of
the Chairman Mr. Harry Hopkins." Sentiments such as these support
Robert Sherwood's judgment that "whenever Hopkins was well
enough to give it his personal attention [MAB] worked harmoniously;
when he was too ill . . . or too preoccupied with other matters . . . there
was apt to be strife aplenty."[21]

Hopkins hoped that his methods would encourage agreement.
MAB's structure recognized the independence of the military services
at the lowest level but subordinated that independence to combined
judgments higher up. This reflected his hope that MAB would merely
translate the Combined Chiefs' grand strategy into munitions allocations. To avoid disturbing the CCS, Hopkins tried to contain MAB
disagreements within the board. He succeeded so spectacularly that
during the war only five appeals went from the board to the CCS.[22]

Hopkins also found that MAB quieted the squabble between the
military and Lend-Lease. The Lend-Lease staff had feared that the
military would deprive other nations of their legitimate needs, but
MAB prevented that from happening. Since MAB did not begin with a
strategic directive, it kept existing transfer programs in force and exercised the power to review requests to change them. Hopkins also
recommended that MAB committees contain representatives from
combined British-American committees and the services' defense aid
sections. He further conciliated Lend-Lease by appointing General
Burns as the board's executive officer.[23]

Of course there was no way to avoid British-American conflict on
the board. Because the British had been fighting for a longer time, they
wanted first priority given to forces in active combat, while the Americans favored a high priority for forces about to become active. Because
the British had major interests in Europe, the Middle East, and the
Indian subcontinent, they favored a protégé system for allocating munitions, while the Americans preferred to deal with all the nations
individually. Although Hopkins hoped to achieve Anglo-American
harmony, he made sure that the Americans stayed united. Early on he
called the Americans together and instructed them to agree on their
assignments and vote as a unit.[24]

One consequence of this was to negate the protégé system. Because at the Arcadia conference the British had assigned themselves the most important protégés, they needed American production to supply them. But Hopkins refused to cooperate. When he determined that "the top people [presumably Roosevelt and the Joint Chiefs] are not going along with" the protégé system, he asked Burns to tell the American military representatives that any nation could request assignments from the American board. From then on he defined the protégé question as a political issue, outside the purely military scope of the MAB.[25] In the end the British were left with only the hope that their protégé nations would apply to them for aid first.

However disappointed the British might have been over losing the protégé system, some early allocations left them enraged at the way the Americans treated them. On one occasion the War Department promised them a number of bombers, only to reallocate them later to Russia and the United States, all without reference to MAB. This and lesser incidents caused the British to draw sinister inferences from Hopkins's handling of the board. Those ad hoc committees by which he had intended to charm the dissenters into agreement now seemed to them devices for making "unilateral decisions" in favor of the Americans. Since these committees never kept records, some doubted that they ever met. Others may have noted that when the British complained about Hopkins's announcing a decision without first discussing it with them, he replied that he had worked it out informally with Marshal Dill, who was heading the British Joint Staff Mission in Washington. The workings were unpredictable and mysterious, if not actually contrived. It helped, though not much, when the British appealed a bomber assignment and Hopkins chaired an ad hoc committee, at which he said that he sympathized with the British but that the need to reinforce Russia was so important that only the president and the prime minister could change the decision. On that basis he advised against appealing the decision to the CCS. No appeal was made.[26]

As the weeks passed, MAB's authority further eroded. In May, Roosevelt decided to allocate American aircraft on the principle that no American pilot should be without a plane. Hopkins did what he could to conciliate the British. The Americans were eager for combat, he said, and in any case they would probably fly American planes more skillfully than British pilots. Also the Americans owed the British some relief from the losses they had been suffering for so long. Hopkins emphasized that the president's plan called only for substituting American fliers for British fliers and would in no way weaken combat strength in any theater or change the war's overall strategy. The truth was, however, that "it was going to be impossible for the United States to give away to other nations aircraft and equipment which could be used in theaters of war by American pilots and troops . . . United States equipment was likely to be only available to other United Nations in so far as trained American troops cannot be shipped and brought face to face with the enemy."[27]

Such adjustments were a necessary part of the United States' gearing up to take a major role in the war. What put an end to Hopkins's Arcadia conference plans, however, was the failure of the CCS to provide strategic direction to MAB. The problem was twofold: the United States and Great Britain disagreed on the major area of attack, and the army and navy disagreed with each other whether to emphasize the European or the Pacific front. As the argument dragged into March 1942, Hopkins tried to force a decision by holding a conference of MAB members and the Anglo-American military planners. At the meeting he declared that assignments should be made for strictly military reasons, without political considerations. Lacking a strategic directive, MAB itself was deciding assignments. This was "clearly wrong." A strategic policy "MUST, repeat MUST" be produced to guide allocations and future production programs. His efforts helped, but not enough. The CCS approved a strategic directive, but with enough loopholes to permit any number of special arrangements. By mid-May the British were complaining that strategic considerations were taking a back seat to predetermined formulas "ruthlessly subjected to political considerations." Without clear strategic guidance their only course of action seemed to be to cultivate influential Americans, since, as one newly-arrived Briton observed, "There are no front stairs in Washington."[28]

During the summer and fall a showdown struggle between the military and the WPB engraved these words as an epitaph for Hopkins's Arcadia hopes. As he had with MAB, Hopkins had tried to persuade the military to provide strategic guidance to the WPB, and on August 28 he met with Donald Nelson and the Joint Chiefs to work out a system. But nothing came of it, and by September WPB officials and Hopkins's representative on the board, Isadore Lubin, were calling for a high-level strategy board to do the job. The military opposed the suggestion and proposed to set its own production priorities. They would permit advice from MAB because of its close ties to the CCS and "the sympathetic chairmanship of Mr. Hopkins."[29]

This time, however, the WPB was not backing down. Early in October the board rejected a military production program. At the meeting board member Leon Henderson argued that if the military could not adjust its demands to economic reality, the country should get a new Joint Chiefs.

While the chiefs reduced their requests, Hopkins upset the British by warning them that the United States was scaling down its aircraft program. Churchill invited Hopkins to London to discuss the subject, but Hopkins suggested that Minister of Supply Oliver Lyttelton come to Washington instead. By this time it seemed clear that the allocations machinery was in ruins. Instead of relying on item-by-item assignments guided by strategic plans, the British had decided to follow the Russian example and get an American commitment to a fully detailed supply program. "I do not propose to ask for a protocol," Lyttelton declared, "but I aim to secure its equivalent."[30]

It so happened that before Lyttelton arrived, Hopkins was able to resolve the aircraft and shipping issues. Still, Hopkins urged Lyttelton to come to Washington as early as possible. He was especially pleased when Lyttelton arrived with a British memorandum on grand strategy. Although he had been instructed to show the paper only to the Joint Staff Mission, since it had not been approved by the War Cabinet, Lyttelton discussed it with Hopkins and found him enthusiastic. Declaring that the Joint Chiefs "had no long range strategic plans," Hopkins encouraged Lyttelton to prepare a summary for Roosevelt and to present it to the CCS. Here was the chance to get the overall direction the production boards and MAB had been calling for.[31]

Then the plan fell apart. Churchill disapproved the strategy paper and ordered it withdrawn. Dill protested but got nowhere. In the end Lyttelton's mission resolved itself into a series of ad hoc agreements. Hopkins's previous arrangements on merchant shipping and aircraft production guided the agreements in those categories. Ground equipment was provided for in a special agreement between the American and British supply services. In all these the British accepted less than they had previously expected but were compensated by American promises to make good on the new assignments.[32]

The Lyttelton mission sealed the fate of the Munitions Assignments Board. By the end of 1942 it was clear that whenever major decisions had to be made about assigning war materials, others would make them. MAB continued to perform usefully in making routine assignments and in keeping a record of the flow of materiel in order to recommend refinements in production schedules, but it never became an effective instrument for requirements planning. Given the circumstances, this was probably as much as could have been expected. For all its achievements the Arcadia conference had not fully integrated the British and American war systems, mainly because the American war effort, in the New Deal tradition, remained amorphous. The War Production Board, War Shipping Administration, and Joint Chiefs of Staff might fit into the Anglo-American effort at one point or another, but they did not effectively connect with each other. From time to time they all collided with each other, and in these collisions the British were apt to become not arbiters so much as tools used by such domestic American arbiters as Hopkins.

If in the end the question of the American war effort proved too contentious for the machinery of the combined boards, it still needed to be answered. Harry Hopkins found a way. During these months of trial, dissension, and frustration, Land and Douglas found him an effective advocate for their construction program; General Brehon Somervell, head of the army's supply service, praised his "sympathetic chairmanship" of MAB; and even British Air Vice Marshal MacNeece Foster reported that he was "more alive than most people in this country to the vital nature and obligation of U.S. commitments to England." When Lyttelton's mission produced an agreement on aircraft allocations dangerously close to Britain's minimum requirements and so vaguely worded that it left room for the Americans to cut it even further, the British put off signing until Hopkins promised them, "You can count on us to make a fair division."[33]

Part of Hopkins's success came from his ability to give interested parties what they wanted: ships for the Maritime Commission, control of MAB to the JCS. Just as important, however, he succeeded because his talent for making ad hoc arrangements, however much they might confuse and alarm the British at first, was suited to the realities of the situation. If there were no front stairs in Washington, people found that the backstairs led directly to Hopkins's bedroom. Although, as in the case of the Maritime Commission's construction program, Hopkins often used the backstairs himself for the sake of pushing a particular program, he also used them to bring people together.

Hopkins's willingness to make these adjustments kept him from becoming trapped by abstract loyalties and thus allowed him to appraise realistically the development of the Anglo-American alliance. Thus while Lyttelton was declaring the Arcadia theory of production assignments out of date, Hopkins was raising the same point with Stettinius. At first Stettinius had wanted to stop distinguishing American from British contributions to the war effort, but he had come to see that Lend-Lease was popular with the public and that it reflected well on Roosevelt's leadership. Also, the Lend-Lease office had arranged with the other U.S. agencies to calculate the value of reciprocal Lend-Lease that came to the United States from other countries. For these reasons he thought that the prewar Lend-Lease pattern whereby Americans allocated their own resources should continue and be broadened to include postwar relief and rehabilitation. Hopkins agreed with Stettinius, especially his idea of using Lend-Lease for postwar reconstruction. After the conversation Stettinius reported, "I am clear there has been a swing on the part of the Administration away from the pooling idea and there is a desire to have the United Nations feel an obligation to the United States from the standpoint of value—that it was an economic leverage."[34]

If Hopkins was thinking twice about the Arcadia proposals, he was holding on to the larger principle of combined strategy. His efforts during the Lyttelton mission to have the JCS accept the British strategy paper showed that his main goal remained Anglo-American unity and overall strategic direction of the war. Indeed he had learned from firsthand experience that combined decisions on strategy were even less easily achieved than agreement on munitions assignments.

# Chapter 16

# The Man in the Middle

When it came to military strategy, Hopkins knew his limitations. He was no strategist, and so he was willing to let others take the lead, a direction in which his close association with the War Department and his desire to boost General Marshall naturally inclined him. But Roosevelt had complicated the picture by showing at the Arcadia conference that he was determined to have the final say in all military matters. The president also seemed distressingly open to Churchill's strategic ideas. This put Hopkins in a particularly uncomfortable position. As Marshall's strongest supporter and Roosevelt's closest adviser, he was bound to be the man in the middle.

In the six weeks following the conference what Hopkins seemed most to be in the middle of was mounting chaos. Japanese troops were sweeping through Southeast Asia and the western Pacific. The ABDA command was wiped out almost before it could get under way. In North Africa, British troops retreated before Rommel's thrusts. Reports from Russia described the battle there as a stalemate and warned of "a Russo-German accommodation." In Moscow, Stalin pressed the British to recognize his territorial claims in Eastern Europe, and Churchill was inclined to go along. In London, Churchill returned to face probing questions about his conduct of the war and responded to criticism by reorganizing his Cabinet. The prime minister seemed worn out and on the defensive. Averell Harriman wrote that the military defeats and parliamentary wrangles had taken much out of him and that it was impossible to predict whether he would regain his popularity. Still, he felt confident that "we will see the rebirth of greater determination." Ambassador Winant supported Harriman, interpreting the Cabinet shakeup as a response to the British people's insistence on offensive action.[1]

Talk of offensive action was what Hopkins wanted to hear. He agreed with Roosevelt that such thrusts would marshall public support for the war effort. One way to start was to appoint some fighting generals. Roosevelt, he thought, faced a liability in the form of generals and admirals whose records looked good but who were thinking "of retiring to farms somewhere" and were unwilling to take bold risks. He believed that Roosevelt should speedily replace them, and he felt fortunate that "he has got in [Admiral Ernest] King, Marshall, and Arnold three people who really like to fight." In this state of mind he told Harriman that "most people here are expecting a shake-up [in Churchill's Cabinet] with more aggressive and dynamic personalities in the government." Opposition to Churchill in the United States, Hopkins reported, came only from the *Chicago Tribune* and "similar pro-Fascist interests."[2]

Hopkins found the army ready to take the offensive—not only against the Axis but also against the British and the navy. The War Department planners had opposed Operation Gymnast as much because it would give the British the advantage in determining Allied strategy as because of its military shortcomings, and they were critical of the navy's plan to divert supplies to the Pacific.[3]

Hopkins backed the army, especially in its differences with the navy. He supported the army's efforts to keep equipment from being diverted to the Pacific and criticized the navy for failing to promote its younger officers. He especially favored an army plan to appoint a single chief of staff for both services, a move that the army hoped would diminish the navy's influence on the president. In order to sell the proposal to the navy, Hopkins and Stimson recommended that Roosevelt name as chief of staff his friend Admiral William D. Leahy, who was currently serving as American ambassador to Vichy France.[4]

Thus Hopkins had enlisted in the army's service as it put together its own strategic plan. In its early version the plan called for concentrating a large land force in Britain and gaining control of the skies over northern France. This scheme followed through on the principle of making Germany the primary enemy and opposed the suggestions of the British and of the U.S. Navy to disperse forces in the Middle East and the Pacific. At this point nonstrategic considerations came into play. When the British criticized the plan, General Arnold revised it on the spot to include it as part of an invasion across the English Channel to establish a beachhead in northern France.[5]

In this form the army's plan tied together some high-priority objectives. The preinvasion build-up in Britain would clear the Atlantic sea lanes; the troop concentration would guard Britain from German attacks and bolster British morale; and the invasion itself would take pressure off the Russian front. Helping the Russians was particularly appealing as a means of strengthening Roosevelt's policy of offering Stalin substitutes for his territorial objectives in Poland and the Baltic States. Sending Lend-Lease aid while establishing a second front in Europe would meet the Russians' needs directly and would tangibly demonstrate American good will. When Roosevelt heard of the army's plan, he responded favorably.

Hopkins wanted to ensure that Roosevelt would stay in this frame of mind. On March 14, 1942, a week after the army offered its plan, he urged Roosevelt to accept it. "Arnold's plan," he advised, "should be pressed home." He doubted that "any single thing is as important as getting some sort of front this summer against Germany," and "if we are going to do it plans need to be made at once." He followed up by pressuring the Combined Chiefs of Staff to work out a strategic plan to guide the Munitions Assignments Board.[6]

By March 25 the time had come to decide. Accompanied by Stimson and Marshall, Hopkins met with Roosevelt and the other U.S. chiefs well prepared to keep up the pressure. Cutting off rambling introductory remarks by the president, Marshall presented the plans for the cross-Channel attack in detail. When Roosevelt suggested referring the plan to the Combined Chiefs, Hopkins declared that "someone" should present it directly to Churchill and the British chiefs. Roosevelt ordered Marshall to put the plan in final shape over the weekend.[7]

On April 1, the day scheduled for the final meeting to approve the invasion, Hopkins met Arnold for one last strategy session. They concluded that because British public opinion favored "an 'all-out' offensive," Churchill would not dare to oppose the operation, and that because Marshall "carried more prestige with the British Chiefs," he and not Arnold should travel to London.

With the president in line and the British provided for, Hopkins set his sights on the last possible obstacle: the U.S. Navy. When Roosevelt approved the plan, Hopkins turned to Admiral King and asked, "Do you see any reason why this cannot be carried out?"

"No," King replied, "I do not."

"Assuming that commitments in the Far East stand as they are, will this program interfere with your operations and will you have sufficient airplanes?"

"I will not have as many as I should like, but I am willing to make the sacrifice in numbers because I think I can get along."

"You are pretty well satisfied then on carrying out this program and your operation in the Far East?"

"Yes, I am."

The meeting then decided that Hopkins and Marshall should fly to London. For the next two days Hopkins conferred with Roosevelt and Marshall while Arnold arranged transportation. On Saturday, April 4, the party flew out of Baltimore. "See you soon," Hopkins cabled Churchill. "Please start the fire."[8]

The American plan called for invading Western Europe with a combined Anglo-American force of forty-eight divisions and 5,800 combat aircraft. The time required to assemble the force in Britain (Operation Bolero) would put off the attack (Operation Roundup) until at least April 1, 1943. While the build-up was taking place, the Allies would carry out continuous raids along the French coast to gain information, to confuse the Germans about their intentions, and perhaps to cause them to divert substantial troops from the east. They would launch an emergency attack (Operation Sledgehammer) in case either the Russians or the Germans showed signs of immediate collapse.[9]

For Hopkins the plan achieved several goals he had been working toward since the Arcadia conference: it confirmed the primary role of General Marshall and the War Department, offered MAB the strategic guidance it needed, and promised to revitalize sagging British spirits and to kindle Russian good will.

Relaxing in the comfortable accommodations of a Pan American flying boat, the party flew from Baltimore to Bermuda. Engine trouble caused a layover, during which Hopkins caught enough fish for dinner, attended a children's party, and arranged for crates of fresh vegetables to be loaded on the plane as gifts for Churchill and the Chief of the Imperial General Staff, Field Marshal Alan Brooke.

Although the clipper had comfortable sleeping beths, Hopkins woke early, and at 6:00 A.M. awakened Colonel Albert Wedemeyer of Marshall's staff to point out that they were approaching the Irish coast. After arriving in London they checked into Claridge's. Marshall gave the American officers the rest of the day off, and he and Hopkins went to No. 10 Downing Street for a 4:00 conference with Churchill.

Hopkins found his British partners wrestling with internal conflicts.

Their military chiefs had been considering initiating operations in northwest Europe to back up the Russian front, but they were more wary than the Americans about the risks of the operation, which loomed large in the mind of Churchill. Brooding over recent defeats and doubting the abilities of his generals, he was disinclined to approve any operation freighted with such uncertainty. At the same time he feared that unless he cooperated, the Americans might shift their efforts to the Pacific.[10]

At the meeting that afternoon Churchill acted like a man who had not resolved these conflicts and wished the whole issue would disappear. When Hopkins and Marshall presented their plan, he assured them that Britain was prepared to go ahead. Hopkins thought that Churchill's tone suggested that the British were ready to go ahead even without the Americans. This sensitive reading of the conversation was probably right. Just a few weeks earlier, on March 27 and 28, British commandos had raided the French coast, and Churchill probably thought that Operation Sledgehammer would involve a series of similar raids.

But when he learned that the Americans wanted to establish a permanent beachhead in France, the prime minister temporized. He spoke favorably, but Hopkins thought that he did not take the operation seriously. Also his general views seemed "none too optimistic." That evening at dinner Churchill maintained his detachment, offering observations about the American Civil War and World War I. By this time Hopkins was sure that he was trying to evade the issue.

Of course Hopkins was not going to let him do that. The next day, when the prime minister tried to steer the conversation to Asia and the Middle East, Hopkins brought up the cross-Channel operation and declared that Roosevelt and Marshall expected to carry it out. The United States, he said, was simply not going to immobilize large numbers of troops indefinitely and was prepared to take great risks to relieve the Russian front.[11]

Hopkins thought that his remarks had convinced Churchill that the Americans meant business. And so they had, although they had only deepened the prime minister's pessimism. Now he could only hope that his chiefs could dissuade the Americans. But in their discussions with the British chiefs, Marshall and Wedemeyer supported the plan by arguing from premises that the British had already accepted, blunting their objections. Since Germany was the number-one enemy, they said, and since Germany's main objective in 1942 was to defeat the Russians, Anglo-American strategy should aim to establish a second front in Europe. Thus they dismissed the Middle East and the Indian Ocean as secondary theaters and argued that dispersing resources to these areas would cripple efforts to help the Russians.

The British chiefs accepted Operation Roundup for 1943, by which time the United States would be able to carry its share. The real difficulty arose in connection with land operations in 1942. Marshall thought that the Allies might have to launch Operation Sledgehammer in the next three to four months to save the Russians, but he admitted that the Americans could not get many troops to Britain before mid-September. This, of course, raised in Field Marshal Brooke's mind the prospect of having to send thousands of his own troops on a suicide mission. But the British were also determined to help the Russians, so Brooke proposed that the two sides agree to the 1943 operation (Roundup) and let conditions on the Russian front determine the need for Sledgehammer.[12]

Meanwhile, Hopkins was conciliating the prime minister on the matter of India. Roosevelt had upset Churchill by urging him to move India toward independence. Churchill was furious when he received a report that Roosevelt's emissary, Louis Johnson, had reached a military agreement with the Indian nationalist movement, the Congress party. Hopkins saw at once that the prime minister was not going to stand for any American interference. Roosevelt, he assured Churchill, would take a role in India only if Britain and the Congress party asked for his help and agreed to accept his advice. That was just what Churchill wanted to hear. He snatched up a pen and dashed off a cable to the viceroy saying that he was sure that Johnson was not speaking for Roosevelt. As far as Hopkins was concerned, that settled the issue. On April 11 he cabled Roosevelt that although the American party was disappointed by the turn of events in India, he was satisfied that the British had made a fair offer and that further discussion would be "futile."

Two days later Hopkins and Churchill were having one of their talks in the small hours of the morning when a cable arrived from Roosevelt asking Churchill to continue negotiations with India. The American people, he warned, held the British responsible for the deadlock in the talks, and if Japan conquered India, the "prejudicial reaction on American public opinion [could] hardly be overestimated." When it came to estimating Churchill's reaction, Roosevelt had been dead wrong. Forming a nationalist government in India, the angry prime minister argued, would simply hand India to the Japanese. If the Americans were upset by conditions in India, he would gladly resign, but he thought that the Cabinet and Parliament would still oppose negotiations.

Churchill was really addressing Hopkins instead of Roosevelt. Hopkins had made it plain that he wanted to protect Roosevelt from a rebuff over India. Now Churchill was forcing his hand. In the end the two decided that Hopkins would advise Roosevelt to support Churchill's position, and Churchill would send a milder though unmistakably firm reply to the president.[13] When Roosevelt saw that pressing the subject would do real damage to Anglo-American relations, he dropped his efforts. Hopkins's mediation may have encouraged Churchill to accept the idea of a cross-Channel attack. In the same message in which he replied to Roosevelt on India, Churchill expressed "full agreement in principle" to the American strategic plan.[14]

Thus by the session on Tuesday, April 14, the stage was set for formal agreement. With minor reservations, the British endorsed the American plan. Marshall assured the British that establishing a single plan of attack would streamline the U.S. production program, and he promised that all theaters could be adequately supplied during preparations for "the main project."

Then Hopkins arose to deliver strangely emphatic remarks. Although American public opinion, he began, favored the United States' concentrating its fighting against Japan, the president and his military advisers had decided to focus on Germany. They had decided this because they wished to fight on land and in the air as well as at sea, because they wanted to fight in the most useful place, and above all because they wanted to be able to fight alongside the British. The United States was determined to make the greatest possible contribution to the operation. Even the American navy "would join with the British to the full in bringing the enemy into action." He concluded by repeating that the Americans wanted to fight alongside the British and assuring everyone that the United States would contribute its best effort to the joint project. This was a momentous decision upon which rested the fate "of all that democracy held dear," and once it had been made, it could not be reversed.[15]

The record of the meeting suggests that Hopkins spoke persuasively,

emphasizing the reasons for the cross-Channel attack, America's determination to see it through, and the impossibility of backing out once
the decision had been made. Why had he spoken thus, when everyone
seemed so well agreed? The occasion probably accounted for part of
the explanation: Hopkins had a taste for dramatic statement whenever
he addressed a group, large or small. He probably also wanted to get
the discussion back to the main issue. Just before he gained the floor,
Churchill and Marshall had been discussing steps to reinforce troops in
the Indian Ocean. Lord Root of the Matter was not one to let others
stray from the point. He also recognized that unless the two sides fully
committed themselves to the cross-Channel attack, the preferences of
the U.S. Navy, American public opinion, and all the other interests
that favored concentrating on the Pacific could easily have their way.
He may also have sensed that, as other sources and subsequent events
revealed, the British weighed their reservations to the cross-Channel
attack more heavily than their support of it.

Still, the notes he scribbled while waiting to speak suggest that he
was more concerned about a reservation that the British had not expressed but that nevertheless seemed to lie heavily on the Allied war
effort: the fear that the job they faced was too much for them. For that
reason he assured the meeting that the Americans were committed to
the operation ("This is what we WANT to do," his notes read) and were
determined to do their share of the fighting. "Fight with you," he
wrote, "first for our country"—or, as he expressed it in his remarks, for
our own national interests—"second our freedom," between which
notations he inserted, "Must not bring men here to rest."

In other public forums Hopkins emphasized the same point: that the
Americans would fight. "This war," he announced to the press on his
arrival, "is not going to be won by production, but by tough fighting
men of the United Nations . . . You can be sure that our contribution is
not going to be confined to the production of guns." Production was
not the problem; morale was not the problem. "The problem is battles
by sea, air, and land, and it is going to be a tough business."

In the case of at least one important Briton, Hopkins had direct
evidence that such an encouraging approach was needed. "Oh how
glad I am you are back with us all once more, to encourage, to cheer,
and to charm us," Clementine Churchill wrote him. "You can't think
what a difference it makes to Winston. He is carrying a very heavy load
and I can't bear his dear round face not to look cheerful and cherubic in

the mornings, as up to now it has always done. What with Singapore and India . . . we are indeed walking through the Valley of Humiliation."[16]

Hopkins had less luck trying to persuade the British to substitute military operations and supply shipments for territorial deals with the Russians. He emphasized Roosevelt's displeasure at any territorial deals and "impressed on Eden as strongly as I could the president's belief that our main proposal here [for the second front in Europe] should take the heat off Russia's diplomatic demands upon England." But his assurances made no impression on Eden, who left the conversation determined to go ahead with the Russian treaty.[17]

For the moment, however, it seemed that all was working according to the American plan. Churchill and Roosevelt exchanged messages confirming the cross-Channel strategy. Roosevelt declared that he now felt better about the war than at any other time in the past two years. Churchill's spirits also seemed to revive. Eden found the prime minister "in better form than I have known him for ages," and credited Hopkins with the change.[18]

Hopkins's success largely compensated for several small miscalculations. Churchill and his British guests at Chequers managed a wry laugh when Hopkins's gift crate of fresh vegetables turned out to contain Brussels sprouts, about the only vegetable that still abounded in Britain. During a visit to the U.S. Army base in Northern Ireland, Marshall tried to safeguard Hopkins's health by arranging for a stay in a country house, but the house turned out to be freezing and the cupboards bare. ("That night at dinner," Hopkins wrote, "I surely learned what rationing means!") Just before the Americans were to fly home from Scotland, Roosevelt sent a telegram reporting a rumor that the Nazi collaborator Pierre Laval would take over the Vichy government and that French North Africa might not take orders from him. Roosevelt suggested that Hopkins and Marshall return to London to talk over this new development with Churchill. Hopkins and Marshall tried to call Roosevelt from a small village, where the authorities suspected them of being enemy agents, in part because they used their code names, A. H. Hones and G. C. Mell. They escaped arrest only because the local authorities routed the call to No. 10 Downing Street, where they were identified before Scotland Yard closed in. In the end Hopkins and Marshall learned that there was nothing to the rumor about Laval and decided to take off for home. They left on the evening of April 18, and after a restful night arrived in New York the next morning. "I returned from England greatly encouraged about everything," Hopkins wrote his former FERA colleague Jake Baker, "but I think the whole business is going to take a lot of doing. I wish I were 25 years younger."[19]

Well might Hopkins wish it, since the events of the following weeks were enough to add a few years to anyone's age. While the Americans and British went about constructing the machinery to carry out the cross-Channel operation, pressures arose to transform the plan. The British reassessed Sledgehammer and concluded that it could work only if the Russians held fast in the east; that rather than offering help to the Russians, the operation called for Russian help. In the United States a serious delay developed in the production of landing craft, originally a low priority but now suddenly crucial to the year's major operation. Stalin disregarded Roosevelt's appeals to defer territorial deals and refused to meet with him. Stalin even praised the "speed and efficacy" of British supply efforts and charged that the United States had "lamentably failed to keep its pledges with respect to the supply of war material." The failure of the north Russian convoys gave the Americans no chance to disprove his charges.[20] Under the circumstances only Sledgehammer seemed to offer Roosevelt a viable approach to Stalin. On May 6 the president called for "active operations to be conducted in 1942."[21]

The effects of Roosevelt's decision rippled throughout the war effort. Ships from the north Russian convoys were diverted to Operation Bolero (the supply build-up in Britain). Shipping and landing craft shortages caused the Joint Chiefs to minimize the role of ground troops and to emphasize the Air Corps's contribution and in turn to assign more aircraft to the United States so that Americans would have planes to fly.

In London, Hopkins had tried to bolster British morale by insisting that the Americans would do their part. Back in Washington he pressed the same theme. Britain would have to reassess its supply requests in light of the United States' determination to expand its role in the war. This would benefit American troops by giving them combat experience and would get the American people behind the war effort by showing them that their production was not simply underwriting British strategy.[22]

Hopkins's advice illustrates the process by which he and his American colleagues were increasing their investment in Sledgehammer. Indeed they had begun to see the operation as a kind of cure-all that would reassure the Russians, encourage the British, and inspire the Americans. This was one of the less fruitful consequences of Hopkins's efforts. By promoting General Marshall, Hopkins had become a partner in selling the cross-Channel operation to Roosevelt and Churchill. Having accomplished this, he was now inclined to look at the Anglo-American partnership through the lens of his loyalty to Marshall's operation. This in turn put him in a position that contrasted starkly with the role he was playing in the shipping and supply programs. Instead of balancing interests and flexibly responding to changing realities, he was supporting a military strategy for its own sake. This caused him to overlook the influence of such nonstrategic imperatives as national pride, interservice rivalry, and politics, which had shaped the decision. As a result he failed to appreciate the danger of selling Sledgehammer as a panacea for more ills than it reasonably could cure.

Soviet Foreign Minister Molotov's visit to Washington at the end of May made this painfully apparent. By this time the British had expressed their reservations, and Marshall had scaled down the objective of the operation to achieving air superiority without an actual invasion. Hopkins supported Marshall's modifications, but in doing so he was arguing against the logic of a situation he had helped to create. With the convoys faltering, Roosevelt had only Sledgehammer to offer the Russians as a substitute for territorial deals with Britain. When Molotov persisted in demanding a second front and a firm date for the operation, Roosevelt had no choice but to promise an operation for later that year.[23]

As usual Hopkins looked on the bright side. Molotov and Roosevelt had gotten along "famously," and he was "sure that we at least bridged one more gap between ourselves and Russia." The immediate task was to carry out Roosevelt's commitment. In the middle of Molotov's visit Hopkins and Roosevelt drafted a cable to Churchill emphasizing the need for the Allies to invade Western Europe before the end of the year. Thus Sledgehammer, which had gone through several definitions since its conception, finally received a definite form. Hoping to strengthen British resolve, Hopkins stressed American "confidence in the ability of our joint air forces to gain complete control of the channel [and the] bridgeheads to be covered."[24]

But his confidence did not prove particularly infectious. On his return trip through London, Molotov found Churchill unwilling to back up Roosevelt's promise of establishing a second front that year. In fact the prime minister was planning another visit to Washington to knock the props from under Sledgehammer and to promote his original idea of Operation Gymnast in North Africa, despite opposition from his own military chiefs, who wanted to focus all efforts on readying Operation Roundup for 1943.

In Washington strategic thinking was similarly divided. The Joint Chiefs still favored Sledgehammer and opposed Gymnast. But word from Britain that landing craft shortages would make Sledgehammer impracticable, and a growing crisis in the Mediterranean, where Axis troops were battering the British garrison on Malta, and in the Middle East, where Rommel had cut off Tobruk, had caused Roosevelt to give serious consideration to Gymnast. Hopkins passed this information along to Churchill, so the prime minister knew that he had an opening bid for Gymnast when he and his chiefs arrived in Washington on June 18.[25]

The circumstances of the conference prevented Churchill from gaining any advantage. Upon arriving he had to travel to Hyde Park to see Roosevelt and Hopkins, leaving the American and British chiefs in Washington to build a case against Gymnast. Hopkins and Roosevelt listened to his arguments and arranged for a full-scale discussion when they all returned to the capital. At the meeting word arrived that the British garrison at Tobruk had surrendered to Rommel. The news hit Churchill like a body blow. No one had anticipated such a disaster; enemy action did not seem to have forced it. The surrender was a disgrace to British arms. Shattered by the news, Churchill lost the initiative. While the Americans promised additional aid to the Middle East, they gained the upper hand on the large issue. When the meeting adjourned, Sledgehammer had become the main operation, and Gymnast had been reduced to a planning project.[26]

But all the Americans had achieved was a delay. When Churchill and his chiefs returned to London, they concluded that Sledgehammer would not work, and they agreed to press the Americans to support Gymnast. When the proposal arrived in Washington, Marshall played his last card, threatening to scrap the Germany-first strategy and concentrate American power in the Pacific. Marshall's ploy naturally enlisted the support of Admiral King, who was eager to get more men and supplies for the Pacific war, and it also picked up support from

Dill, who favored Sledgehammer in order to support the Russian front and to preserve Anglo-American unity. But Churchill refused to take the American threat seriously.[27]

Thus within a month a second crisis had arisen over strategy. It was time for someone on the American side to take hold of the situation and press for an agreement. Events had shown that this time someone other than Hopkins would have to take charge. Roosevelt stepped in. Realizing that Marshall had overplayed his hand by threatening to forsake Europe for the Pacific, the president ordered Marshall, King, and Hopkins to return to London under his personal instructions. He told Hopkins that he wanted Bolero and Roundup to proceed. He still favored Sledgehammer, but if that operation was out, the best alternative theaters for 1942 were the Middle East, where the British and the Russians were "sorely pressed," and North Africa, where Operation Gymnast had the advantage of being purely an American initiative. More important, however, Roosevelt made it plain that he was committed not so much to one particular strategic plan as to Allied cooperation and to establishing "definite plans for the balance of 1942."[28]

Roosevelt seemed not to realize the tactical risk he was taking in sending Hopkins to London. By this time Hopkins had invested a good deal in Sledgehammer. His continuing close association with Marshall and Stimson and his own interest in pinning down an overall strategic plan to guide MAB had caused him to look on Sledgehammer as the essential ingredient in Allied cooperation. His enthusiasm for the operation and the circumstances under which it had been proposed tended to blind him to the true nature of Britain's reservations, encouraging him to ascribe them to defeatism or failing will instead of to the military realities that seemed so unpromising to them. Sledgehammer seemed an opportunity for the fresh, vigorous, hard-fighting Americans to take the initiative and turn the course of the war around. Just a few hours before he met with Roosevelt, he had used Marshall's Pacific-front threat to intimidate Dill into supporting Sledgehammer.[29]

Indeed Hopkins arrived in Britain so committed to Sledgehammer that not even a gruff reception from Churchill could alter his perceptions. His party arrived at Prestwick, Scotland, on July 18, and proceeded by train to London, where instead of calling on Churchill, they huddled with General Dwight Eisenhower to plan their approach to the British. This enraged Churchill. He invited Hopkins for a weekend at Chequers, where he lectured him, marching back and forth across the room, on the Americans' violation of protocol. He illustrated his point by reading from a volume of British war regulations, tearing out each page as he finished it and throwing it on the floor. Unruffled, Hopkins failed to apprehend Churchill's belligerent spirit. "The prime minister threw the British Constitution at me with some vehemence," he reported to Roosevelt. "As you know, it is an unwritten document so no serious damage was done."[30]

Nor did Hopkins see anything to worry about in the prime minister's remarks during his first formal session with the Americans. Churchill was willing to say that he supported Roundup for 1943, but anyone who listened carefully had to conclude that he had almost defined the operation out of existence. Rhetorically he asked if Roundup ought not to be thought of more broadly than as an attack on western France. What he actually had in mind, although at the moment was keeping from American view, was to define Roundup broadly enough to include Gymnast as part of the second front. To the Americans, however, he only proposed Gymnast as an alternative in case Sledgehammer was ruled out. These subtleties slipped by Hopkins, who passed the word that the British were going along with the idea of establishing a second front within the year and that his mission would be a success.[31]

In the end, however, the British military chiefs and the prime minister put up a united and unyielding front against Sledgehammer. On the afternoon of July 22 a meeting was held at No. 10 Downing Street to decide what steps to take next. Churchill speculated on various possibilities and concluded that the time had come to report the disagreement to President Roosevelt and the War Cabinet. The defeat of Sledgehammer hit Hopkins hard. He picked up a card on the table and scribbled, "I feel damn depressed." Still, his quick, penetrating intelligence enabled him to size up the situation accurately, and he immediately grasped Churchill's train of thought. The American and British chiefs should not discuss alternative strategy, he declared, until the Americans had received instructions from the president, and "no breath of this disagreement should get noised abroad." Neither ally could win the war alone; the effort had to be a joint one. Marshall agreed with Hopkins, and the meeting adjourned.[32]

The other Americans took the British intransigence hard, and none harder than Marshall. In his view the debate had brought the Anglo-

American alliance to a crisis. With Sledgehammer stopped and Gymnast becoming the most likely alternative, his worst fears seemed to be coming true. He was determined to use Churchill's wish for unity as a device to hold diversions to a minimum and keep all eyes focused on readying Operation Roundup for 1943. This ruled out diverting forces to Gymnast. Stalling for a way to outflank the British, he asked them to defer making a final decision on operations until mid-September, by which time the Russian situation would have clarified.[33]

With Marshall so disposed, the way was open for Hopkins once again to disregard Roosevelt's instructions and put on the pressure for Roundup against Gymnast. But he did not. Hopkins had been hurt by the destruction of his and Roosevelt's hopes for Sledgehammer, but unlike Marshall, he realized that the president placed his highest priority on unity with Britain and on getting American troops into action in 1942. Thus he saw Churchill's call for unity not so much as an opportunity to bid for Bolero and Roundup as an invitation to agree on Gymnast.

As a result Hopkins did everything he could to undermine Marshall's strategy of delay and to focus on Churchill's preference for Gymnast. When Roosevelt replied to news of the impasse on Sledgehammer by suggesting four alternative strategies, Hopkins prodded him to support the prime minister instead. "I believe," he wrote, "that our people will finally turn to an expanded Gymnast, first because of the difficulty of mixing our troops with the British in Egypt, and secondly because if we go to Syria we may not do any fighting there." When Roosevelt replied that he would rather abandon Roundup than forego putting American troops into "useful action" in 1942 and that Gymnast was his preference, the issue seemed settled. But because the president did not order his chiefs to adopt Gymnast, Marshall felt that he could still ask the British to postpone a final decision until mid-September. When the Combined Chiefs acceded to Marshall's request, Hopkins sent an urgent message to Roosevelt declaring that "the decision should now be made to launch" Gymnast no later than October 30. Without such a decision he feared that there would be "procrastination and delay." Although he blamed the delays on "secondary personnel," he had seen enough to realize that the main obstacle was George Marshall.[34]

Hopkins's failure to single out Marshall in his message to Roosevelt left his achievement incomplete. Seeing no need to whip his chiefs into line, Roosevelt replied only that it was his "opinion" that the Gymnast landings ought to get under way no later than October 30.[35] Eager to return home, and busy darting around the American mission's hotel suite entertaining guests and waiting for a trans-Atlantic call from Roosevelt with orders to return, Hopkins overlooked this loophole. But Marshall and King did not. Thus they arrived back in Washington thinking that they still had room to maneuver in favor of Bolero and Roundup and to oppose the North African operation, which had been renamed Operation Torch. After his return Hopkins played no part in the decisions that eventually confirmed Torch as the Anglo-American offensive for 1942.

His reasons for this, and for wanting to hurry back from England, were personal. Early in the year he had met Louise Macy, who had come to Washington looking for a wartime job. Harry had asked her to marry him, and she had accepted, setting their wedding day for July 30. Immediately after his arrival from England they were married and left on a honeymoon that kept them out of Washington until August 10.

On July 30, the day of Hopkins's wedding, the Joint Chiefs assembled under a new head, Admiral William Leahy, who favored the North Africa operation. When Marshall and King pressed for a delay, Leahy declared that the matter would have to go to Roosevelt to be resolved. The president firmly committed the United States to the operation.

Although Hopkins had by no means shaped strategy during 1942, his participation had illustrated the peculiar circumstances under which the strategy had been shaped. His desire for aggressive action, his efforts to support General Marshall's Germany-first strategy against the navy's Pacific operation, his and Roosevelt's wish to bolster Churchill in the face of dispiriting military reverses, their hopes of building good will with the Russians and inhibiting territorial arrangements between the Russians and the British, and his campaign to get strategic guidance for MAB had all converged in support first of Sledgehammer and then Bolero and Roundup.

Of course Hopkins was not the only one who had allowed Sledgehammer to cloud his perceptions. Marshall, Stimson, and Roosevelt had also pinned their hopes on the operation to the extent that it became a panacea for all of the United States' military and diplomatic problems. This state of mind had encouraged the Americans to consider loyalty to Sledgehammer a test of the Anglo-American partnership and to resist any British objections to American leadership. Certainly Marshall had fallen victim to this way of thinking when he declared that if the British refused to go along with Sledgehammer, the United States should focus its strength on the Pacific. In the end, however, Roosevelt and Hopkins provided the necessary corrective to this attitude. Roosevelt deserves the greater credit for anticipating the British objections and ordering Hopkins and Marshall above all to obtain British agreement for operations that year. Hopkins played his part by carrying out Roosevelt's orders so that as soon as he realized that the Allies could not agree on Sledgehammer, he pushed for agreement on another operation and tried to keep Marshall and King from stalling the decision.

Hopkins's involvement in strategy showed the limitations of his contribution to the war effort. As long as he left strategy up to the military, he focused on implementing decisions made by Marshall and Stimson. This meant that, unlike his role in supervising supplies, which required him to balance the various interests of the War Shipping Administration, Lend-Lease, his British contacts, and the military, he had only one source from which to provide the president with the information for deciding major policies. But by undertaking to boost General Marshall and to subordinate supply questions to military strategy, his only source of alternative views became the president himself. By advocating only Marshall's strategy, he accomplished his only successful manipulation of Franklin Roosevelt. But in the end, in order for American strategy to retain its focus on cooperation with the British, the president had to seize the initiative. Here, Hopkins's ability to shift his perspective to see things through Roosevelt's eyes became especially valuable. The president's order gave Hopkins the vision he needed to accept defeat on Sledgehammer, to bring Roosevelt immediately into the decision making, and to counsel against further delays. Churchill's insight was perfect when he cabled Roosevelt, "I doubt if success would have been achieved without Harry's invaluable aid."[36] Hopkins's performance in London showed him at his best as Roosevelt's representative.

For Hopkins the London conference had been both an opportunity to serve the president and something of a warning against allowing himself to act as the advocate of the military. Earlier in the year he had revised history to declare that Roosevelt's formula for organizing war production had been correct all along, when he himself had consistently tried to involve the military more directly in production matters. Eight months after his midsummer visit to London he ran across the notes he had made when he and Roosevelt had discussed the purpose of the trip. Before tucking them back into the files, he revised history again by appending the note: "It was perfectly clear to me that we were not going to cross the Channel in 1942 and the Army and Navy had no plans to fight anywhere else."[37] If the note speaks ill of Hopkins's skills as a historian, it at least indicates that he was trying to teach himself a lesson.

# Chapter 17

# The Third Card

Although Hopkins had played an important role in the decision to undertake Operation Torch, the leadership had come from Roosevelt. By the fall of 1942 the president had swept to the forefront of the Western alliance. His programs of Lend-Lease aid and combined strategy were at the center of the Anglo-American partnership. He had played these cards to prevent the alliance from making separate territorial and political arrangements. Roosevelt especially hoped to cement relations with the Russians, helping them militarily and cultivating enough good will to keep them from signing a peace treaty with Hitler. With Torch in the works, he reached up his sleeve for his third card: demanding the enemy's unconditional surrender. Hopkins's role in this decision was uncertain.

Hopkins also faced an uncertain situation on the Russian front. The decision to launch Torch had resolved a number of problems, but not all. The British and the Americans agreed that the operation would take the place of Sledgehammer and thus would qualify as the second front promised the Russians. It would not take place until November, however, and with the Russians in the meantime taking ferocious attacks on their southern front, where the Germans were driving toward the city of Stalingrad, the Western Allies wanted to do what they could to bolster Russian morale and fighting strength. At the same meeting at which he committed the United States to Torch, Roosevelt told the Joint Chiefs that he wanted the northern convoys to Russia resumed. Early in September convoy PQ 18 sailed with twenty-seven ships, only fourteen of which arrived at their destination. Roosevelt also discussed offering Stalin aircraft and crews to reinforce his troops in the Caucasus. But the Joint Chiefs objected, and before anything could be decided, the president left Washington on a secret tour of war production plants.

With decisions left to be made, Hopkins sank into bewilderment and doubt. Morgenthau found him confident that the Russians would hold

Moscow but fearful that they would lose Stalingrad and allow the Germans to break through to the Caspian Sea. When Morgenthau offered the hope that Allied bombing would help the situation, Hopkins replied, "We haven't taken on any of the tough cities like Hamburg or Brest," and added that the Americans' pet project of daylight precision bombing had not proven itself. To make matters worse, he was also expecting a strong Japanese attack on Guadalcanal and the Solomon Islands.[1]

With Roosevelt out of town and Hopkins stumped, the way was open for Churchill to force a decision. On September 22 the prime minister proposed to suspend the north Russian convoys in order to have enough ships for Torch. He also recommended Operation Jupiter, his own plan for the invasion of northern Norway.[2]

The proposal stung Hopkins into action. He was willing to suspend the convoys, but he realized that neither Roosevelt nor the Joint Chiefs favored Jupiter. Thus he pushed the plan to put British and American air forces into the Caucasus. Without even waiting for the Joint Chiefs to respond to Churchill's proposal, he wired Roosevelt to "give full consideration" to the Caucasus project. In so doing he outflanked both the chiefs, who wanted the British to undertake the operation alone, and the British, who wanted to go ahead only if developments in the Middle East permitted it. "The only thing that will do the trick," he advised, "is a firm commitment to put a token force on this winter and a real force on ready to make the fight next spring."

Hopkins backed up his proposal with some creative strategic thinking. Without consulting the Joint Chiefs he reversed his earlier pessimistic views of the Russian situation and told the president, "We must assume that Germany cannot break through the Caucasus this winter." Suspending the convoys, he thought, made it "almost imperative" that the Allies send their armed forces to fight alongside the Russians. Adopting Churchill's proposal would be "a terrible wet blanket at this particular time."[3]

Hopkins's initiative paid off. Roosevelt agreed to suspend the convoys but advised Churchill not to inform Stalin until the Caucasus project had been worked out. When Churchill accepted this strategy, Hopkins pressed Britain's military representative, John Dill, for a "definite promise" to carry it out by the following spring and for promises of other aid, however small, for "the psychological value of a positive undertaking . . . to encourage Russian resistance through this critical month." As a result Churchill agreed to run merchant ships to northern Russia individually in the hope that they could evade German detection. Stalin labeled the Caucasus project a "first priority" and authorized an American military mission in Russia to survey facilities in the area. He also sent an urgent request for more aircraft.[4]

Hopkins moved quickly to put the new arrangements into play. He rounded up ships for Russian aid and assigned General S. P. Spalding to make sure that Stalin's special requests got top priority. He had less luck finding aircraft, but Marshall proposed to organize a heavy bombardment group for the Caucasus.[5]

Along with these efforts went a great deal of whistling in the dark. Would the Russians collapse? Did they trust their Western allies? Would they sign a separate peace? Everyone strained to spot clues and usually inferred too much from the ones they found. When Churchill visited Moscow to tell Stalin about Torch, he received the dictator's typical treatment of warm friendship alternating with bitter, sarcastic reproaches. By the end of his trip the dispirited prime minister was declaring that he ought not to have come. Then, just before he left, Stalin invited him to a late-night dinner where he offered good food and good fellowship. Churchill was ecstatic. "I was taken into the family," he announced. "We ended friends." But when Churchill subsequently informed Stalin about suspending the convoys, he received only a curt "Thank you." "I am frankly perplexed," the worried prime minister wrote Roosevelt, "and would be grateful for your thoughts at the earliest possible moment."[6]

Churchill was asking the blind to lead the blind. Roosevelt had been haunted all fall by his own phantoms of Russian ill will. News that Admiral William Standley, the ambassador to Moscow, was returning to Washington with a special message from Stalin left the president fearful and uncertain.

At the same time the American military was bedeviled by the Russian aid program. Some predicted that the supplies would fall into the hands of the victorious German armies; others charged that the Russians were dividing their Pacific shipments with the Japanese. Many also warned that the Russians would sign a separate peace with Germany and that sometime in the future the United States would have to fight them both. For Hopkins's benefit many claimed that if any of these things happened, it would be his fault. Hearing the criticism, Hopkins confessed to Joseph Davies, a former U.S. ambassador to

Moscow and his confidant on Russian policy, that he would be "on one hell of a spot if things went wrong."[7]

But he refused to give in to events. Others might be fearful, baffled, or stymied; he swung into action. During October, while he worked to straighten out the shipbuilding program, to put new energy into aircraft production, and to prepare to discuss supply arrangements with the British representative Oliver Lyttelton, he seized the initiative to reorganize America's Russian policy. Every decision, he told himself, had its risks, and all one could do was to decide on the basis of the best available advice and information.[8] Since the military had so often been wrong about the Russians, he dismissed their fears as "bunk" and conferred with General Burns and Davies about new possibilities in American-Russian relations.

Both Burns and Davies thought that the United States should increase its cooperation with the Russians. Burns emphasized the military advantages of this policy, both in the European war and potentially in the war against Japan. He also stressed the postwar economic advantages of Russian friendship, pointing out that Russia's reconstruction needs would make the nation an excellent market for U.S. production. Davies advocated a more comprehensive diplomatic understanding between the United States and Russia, especially with regard to postwar planning, feeling that the United States should realize that Russian territorial claims in Eastern Europe represented legitimate security interests and a desire to reclaim lands wrongfully taken earlier.

Burns and Davies proposed to encourage Russian trust and good will by holding high-level meetings: Marshall and King should travel to Moscow, and Roosevelt should meet with Stalin. The president would have "a great influence on Stalin," Davies predicted, "because he could convince him that we had no Empire or other ambitions; no hostile ulterior purpose or interest; and all we sought was our own safety to stop aggression and to establish law and order in the world." Burns and Davies also recommended encouraging a more cooperative attitude in various U.S. agencies, and Burns suggested that the United States send a new ambassador to Moscow.[9]

Burns's suggestion was pointed directly at the incumbent ambassador, Admiral Standley. By this time it was clear that Standley had soured on his job. Months of dealing with the obstructionist, secretive Russian bureaucracy while listening to their unending complaints about American aid had repelled this proud, patriotic, and assertive man. The only way to secure Russian cooperation, he concluded, was to attach conditions to Lend-Lease aid. This conclusion had also soured him on General Faymonville, a solid supporter of unconditional aid.

As a result the whole Lend-Lease operation seemed arranged to bypass Standley. Faymonville ignored him, and Harriman superceded him during Churchill's visit that fall. The last straw was a visit from Wendell Willkie, who proposed to take his place in sensitive negotiations with the Russians. Shortly after Willkie left, Standley asked to return to Washington, where he planned to demand full authority and expected to resign. At his first meeting with Hopkins and Roosevelt he declared that the United States should "stop acting like a Santa Claus" to the Russians. Specifically he criticized Faymonville and declared that he would not return unless the administration gave him authority over Lend-Lease.[10]

Standley's criticisms were the last thing that Hopkins wanted to hear. He sympathized with the ambassador's complaints about Willkie and other "visiting firemen," but he otherwise thought that Standley was getting upset over small incidents and was missing the larger objective of building cooperation with the Russians. On balance it seemed that, as Burns had suggested, Standley would have to go. A week after the meeting Hopkins told Lord Halifax that Standley might not return to Russia. He then asked Davies if he would take Standley's place. Davies declined on account of his health and urged Hopkins to take the job, but Hopkins's own health and his many responsibilities in Washington made that impossible. He failed to produce a suitable substitute, and when Standley persisted in his demands, Hopkins had Burns draft a cable giving the ambassador general authority over Faymonville in matters "political in character" or affecting "established policies." As a result Standley went back to Russia, for the time being.[11]

Hopkins supplemented his attempts to revise Russian diplomacy with an effort to reorganize Russian aid. Eight agencies were involved in the protocol deliveries, and by mid-October growing complaints about the divided and often conflicting machinery had caused Stettinius to ask Burns to coordinate the program out of Lend-Lease. Hopkins approved the idea but Burns opposed it, claiming that it would identify him too closely with Lend-Lease and thus would diminish his influence as Hopkins's personal representative. In the end Hopkins and Roosevelt decided to create a Soviet Protocol Committee, representing the eight agencies, with Hopkins as chairman.[12]

Whatever else the committee accomplished, Hopkins wanted to be sure that it would neutralize reservations like Standley's about unconditional aid. At the first meeting Hopkins admitted that the Russians were difficult to deal with and to understand and that the United States was doing for them things that it would not do for other nations. But although the "decision to act without full information was made with some misgivings," it had been made "after due deliberation," and "no further consideration" should be given to requests to reopen the subject. Nor should anyone ask if the Russians had a deal with the Japanese to divide Lend-Lease supplies. The Americans simply had to assume that all supplies were arriving in Russia. The committee's only job was to get the supplies there as expeditiously as possible.[13]

This strategy provided the context in which Roosevelt had developed the idea of demanding the enemy's unconditional surrender. Roosevelt accepted those aspects of the Russian strategy that suited the conduct of the war effort: Lend-Lease aid, combined military planning, and top-level diplomacy. He also noted that the Russians had responded favorably when he proposed that after the war the three major Allies act as world policemen to guarantee peace and order. Molotov had reported Roosevelt's idea to Moscow and announced that it had been approved. Hopkins also approved. "We simply cannot organize the world between the British and ourselves," he observed, "without bringing the Russians in as equal partners." Hopkins also favored a major postwar role for China. "The days of . . . 'the white man's burden' are over," he wrote. "Vast masses of people simply are not going to tolerate it and for the life of me I can't see why they should. We have left little in our trail except misery and poverty for the people whom we have exploited."

This note of anti-imperialism suited one of Roosevelt's more subtle purposes in his world policemen proposal. Roosevelt had first mentioned the idea to Molotov as an alternative to Churchill's notion of reviving the old League of Nations. Perhaps Roosevelt thought that his suggestion would not only appeal to Molotov's political instincts, since his plan, he admitted, amounted to "peace by dictation," but would also emphasize that neither the United States nor the Soviet Union had belonged to the League. Roosevelt's effort to distinguish the U.S. approach to the postwar world from that of the British fit in with Hopkins's reservations about Churchill's leadership. Hopkins told the columnist Raymond Clapper that Churchill was a superior war leader who towered head and shoulders above all other Britons, but that he was interested only in war problems and thus recognized Roosevelt's leadership in such areas as economic policy. "Churchill will get out as soon as the war ends," Hopkins predicted, "after taking a bow at the first peace conference and in the victory parade, etc., and then [will] retire to write a book." Thus at this early stage in the war Hopkins was looking forward to a postwar world free from Churchill's dynamic leadership and stout defense of British imperialism.[14]

Roosevelt further believed that acting as world policemen would enable the Allies to carry out the Atlantic Charter's promise to "disarm nations which threaten, or may threaten, aggression outside of their frontiers." A necessary step in this direction, he thought, would be for the Allies to define as one of their war aims the unconditional surren-der' of the enemy. Like the idea of world policemen, the idea of uncon-ditional surrender had emerged in the spring of 1942, when a subcom-mittee on security problems had recommended that the Allies avoid the precedent of World War I, when military hostilities had been ended with an armistice that left the door open to negotiations with the enemy. Unconditional surrender would not permit the Axis to strike a bargain for territorial or political guarantees. In Germany, for example, the Allies would simply march into Berlin, disband the Wehr-macht, and take any other steps—such as breaking Germany up into several states—to keep it from again threatening the peace.

Defined in this way, unconditional surrender would admirably serve a number of purposes. By ruling out territorial deals with the Axis, it would presumably rule them out among the Allies as well and would remove any suspicions about signing a separate peace. By committing the United States to maintaining the peace, it would guard against a resurgence of isolationism at home. Roosevelt also thought that the time had come to renew his attack on European colonialism, which he believed would bring on another war. He seized on an anti-imperialist speech by Willkie to propose converting colonies into trusteeships, which an international organization would prepare for independence. He also proposed to readjust European boundaries along ethnic lines and suggested dismembering Germany.[15]

Roosevelt's ideas were projected on the rays of a growing optimism.

The Torch landings had gone well, Morocco was under Allied control, and with the British pressing Rommel from the east, it seemed possible that victory in North Africa might come in a matter of weeks. At the same time the Russians had broken the German offensive at Stalingrad and were readying for a counterattack. Hopkins thought that the war might be over by the fall of 1943. Further sweetening the atmosphere were the words of Josef Stalin. Those who had winced at the brevity of his October replies were now reading of his "heartfelt regards" and "best wishes." More substantially, Stalin promised to cooperate with his allies and on November 27 agreed to hold a joint military conference.[16]

Hopkins hoped that Stalin's offer would build a Russian-American partnership through combined military planning. He also hoped that Turkey could be brought into the war to make possible combined planning in the eastern Mediterranean. To coordinate such planning, he felt that the United States should appoint as ambassador to Moscow a highly qualified man of military rank who sympathized with the Russian war effort.[17]

Hopkins also wanted to arrange a meeting between Roosevelt and Stalin. The ony way to get anywhere with the Russians was to talk directly to Stalin. Since Churchill was also calling for a meeting with Stalin, Roosevelt invited the Russian leader to join them to discuss "vital strategic decisions," including—and here he prepared the way for the idea of demanding unconditional surrender—what steps to take in the event of a German collapse.

By early December Hopkins's strategy had assumed a definite form. The Russian supply program had been reorganized. Closer cooperation was being promoted through the reinforcement of troops in the Caucasus, a top-level military conference, and the proposed meeting between Roosevelt, Churchill, and Stalin. Admiral Standley was going back to Moscow with assurances that his prerogatives would be respected. The president had proposed the demand for unconditional surrender as a first step toward Allied postwar cooperation. He also hoped to disarm the smaller nations and to unravel the system of colonial exploitation that had set the big powers at each other's throats. These objectives, which he believed fit within the principles of the Atlantic Charter, would guarantee the Allies sufficient security to keep them from seeking territorial or colonial prizes after the war.

Roosevelt hoped to raise some of these issues with Churchill and

Stalin. Just how far he intended to go or what strategy he intended to use is not known, because almost as soon as he and Hopkins had worked out their strategy, it began to come apart. In late November, Churchill advised against a conference among the military chiefs, predicting that the Russians would only tie up the agenda with demands for a second front. Then Stalin declined Roosevelt's invitation, declaring that he could not take time away from the Stalingrad campaign. Roosevelt suggested postponing the meeting until March, but Stalin still refused. Next the Caucasus reinforcement plan fell through as the Russians, no longer feeling pressure from the German offensive, said that they had plenty of pilots and wanted only Allied planes for them to fly. That left nothing but the prospect of another meeting between Roosevelt and Churchill. Since the Americans and the British needed to decide how to follow up Torch, and since Roosevelt was eager to get out of Washington, he and Churchill arranged to confer in Casablanca.

In Hopkins's opinion Stalin's absence meant that postwar planning ought to be set aside. On the evening of December 18 he made this point with particular force at a dinner to which Felix Frankfurter had invited Hopkins, Wallace, Morgenthau, Halifax, Stimson, and Byrnes to discuss postwar planning and Anglo-American relations. In a voice breaking with emotion, Frankfurter began by appealing for postwar unity between the United States and Britain. When Wallace observed that Willkie's visit to Russia and China had uncovered distrust toward the Allies, Hopkins sensed that the conversation was moving in an unfortunate direction and decided to speak his piece. Willkie had been taken in by Chiang Kai-shek and Stalin, he charged. Relations with China and Russia would be determined by mutual self-interest. As for Anglo-American relations, Churchill would serve as prime minister only during the war, after which the British would undoubtedly choose someone else. Having thus disposed of postwar planning by disposing of Churchill, he went on to say that people ought not to be so concerned about the subject. If they had real faith in democracy, he declared, they would believe that people would find the right answers to peace when the time came. For his part, he had faith in democracy.

It was a typical Hopkins performance, full of practical idealism and based on inside knowledge. Dismissing Willkie was second nature to him. In any case, by this time the Republican standard bearer's star was waning. His call for internationalism in the fall congressional campaign had failed when Republican isolationists survived primary challenges and gained enough seats in the off-year elections to form a powerful coalition with conservative Democrats. Since May, Hopkins had been predicting that Churchill would leave office after the war, and Roosevelt's anticolonial campaign made the prime minister's retirement all the more desirable. Even Hopkins's reference to democracy was rooted in Allied politics, specifically policy toward France. Britain had long since broken relations with the Vichy regime and was supporting the Free French under General Charles de Gaulle, while the United States had maintained diplomatic relations with Vichy. The different policies had freed Britain for military raids on strategic French targets, while the United States put pressure on Vichy not to cooperate too closely with the Axis. Roosevelt believed that good relations with Vichy would help Torch by undermining France's will to resist the invasion. Thus he proposed to recognize no political leader of France until the French people chose a government after the war.

But because Hopkins did not explain any of these thoughts running through his mind, his impassioned expression of faith in democracy was less than convincing. Halifax, perhaps a bit stunned by Hopkins's outburst against Churchill, backed him up to the extent of saying that the atmosphere would change rapidly once the war ended. But Wallace and Frankfurter insisted on their views, and Wallace left believing that Hopkins "has no faith in anyone and believes everyone moves in response to self-interest." A perplexed Morgenthau could only say that Hopkins was "a funny fellow" and that he could not understand him.[18]

Even as Hopkins was speaking, new problems were filling the Casablanca agenda. High on the list was a diplomatic complication in North Africa. The Torch invasion had forced the Americans and the British to face the consequences of their opposing French policies. Hoping to take advantage of his relations with the Vichy regime, Roosevelt had persuaded Churchill to let the Americans lead the operation and had brought along with the invasion General Henri Giraud, an anti-Nazi with loose connections to Vichy, a respected military leader who might persuade the French army not to resist the invasion. A temporary complication arose when General Eisenhower and his adviser Robert Murphy offered political control in North Africa to the Vichyite admiral Jean Darlan in exchange for Darlan's ordering the Vichyite troops to lay down their arms. Opinion in Britain and America sharply opposed the "Darlan Deal" because it appeared that the Allies were compromising with Nazi collaborators. Darlan ceased to be a problem when he was shot and killed on Christmas Eve, but Roosevelt read the episode as further evidence that the United States should stay out of French politics. Still, the United States was committed to Giraud, while the British continued to back De Gaulle.[19]

Added to these complications was a sudden crisis in shipping. By the fall of 1942 British civilian imports had hit rock bottom. The British calculated that they had to increase their import program from 23 million tons per year to 27 million tons for 1943. Of this the United States would have to supply 7 million tons. Hopkins thought that supporting the British in this aim would help justify the War Shipping Administration's construction program. At the same time that he was sponsoring the WSA's request for a larger steel allocation, he was advising Lyttelton to make the 27 million ton figure an absolute minimum. Finding the WSA agreeable, Hopkins drafted a letter from Roosevelt to Churchill promising that the United States would meet "the minimum needs of the [British] civilian population." On the same day Roosevelt instructed Admiral Land to consider British merchant shipping "one of the top military necessities of the war."[20]

Then problems arose. Production schedules revealed that no help could be offered Britain until the last half of 1943. At the same time ships suddenly became available for a massive increase in Russian aid, including 150,000 to 200,000 tons a month to the northern ports for the first half of the year. The United States had scheduled no sailings to northern Russia for all of 1943. Since Russian aid deliveries were running 50 percent behind schedule, Hopkins wanted to take advantage of this opportunity. Still, he realized that he was sitting on a logistical time bomb. The North African campaign, the Bolero build-up in Great Britain, the British merchant shipping commitment, and pending decisions on strategy for the coming year would probably overtax the Allies' shipping resources. Hopkins had seen this kind of situation often enough to realize that if things drifted along, sooner or later one powerful, self-interested party would force a decision that could destroy the whole shipping program. Once again the time had come for a high-level discussion at which all the cards were put on the table and a broad policy agreed on.

Hopkins's handling of the shipping crisis revealed how the Anglo-American alliance had organized itself by the end of its first year. Instead of working through the combined agencies, he went first to the

WSA, where Lewis Douglas was criticizing the military for not providing him with useful information about their shipping needs and plans. To get that information Hopkins approached the army and suggested they ask the Combined Military Transport Committee to prepare a report for the CCS. The committee's study, he suggested, should include figures on the British import program. At the same time he warned Dill and Admiral Noble of the Joint Staff Mission that they should be ready to protect their interests, including the import program. Then, having set the stage for a discussion, he unilaterally decided to give Russian aid top priority and had Roosevelt issue an order to that effect. This meant that the issue would surface again at Casablanca.[21]

Of course at the time no one knew just how the decision to increase shipping to Russia would affect military strategy because no one knew the strategy for 1943. Hopkins had been working all year to develop an overall plan for guiding the combined supply and production programs. This and his desire to boost General Marshall had made him a partisan of Operation Roundup. Once the decision had been made in favor of Torch, however, he turned away from Marshall and toward the strategic plan that Lyttelton had recommended in November but which Churchill had withdrawn because he wanted to carry out Operation Roundup in France. After this reversal strategic thinking languished. When Hopkins surveyed the Joint Chiefs, he found them confident that the Allies would soon drive the Germans out of North Africa but uncertain about their next move. Some, including Marshall, still favored invading France, but Hopkins found that whenever he asked for a definite plan, the military responded with irritation.[22]

In the following weeks the Americans did not fully resolve their indecision, but they did gravitate toward Marshall's preference for Roundup. Marshall argued that further operations in the Mediterranean would overtax the Allies' shipping resources. Although Marshall was unable to convince others in the American military, he was able to sway Hopkins, who was probably persuaded by the shipping considerations.[23] If the Americans leaned in one direction, however, the British inevitably leaned in the other. After weeks of debate the British chiefs converted Churchill to the idea of following up Torch with offensives in the Mediterranean. This set the stage for a full-dress strategy debate.

By this time the Casablanca conference was at hand. On January 9 Hopkins and Roosevelt took a train to Miami, where they boarded a

Pan American clipper. The flight to Africa, with stops in Trinidad and Belem, Brazil, took many hours, which they spent sleeping, chatting, and reading. An experienced world traveler, Hopkins taught Roosevelt's physician, Dr. Ross McIntire, to play gin rummy to pass the time and enjoyed the president's childlike enthusiasm for the journey. ("I sat with him, strapped in, as the plane rose from the water," Hopkins observed, "and he acted like a sixteen-year-old.") In a more serious vein, he noted that the president occasionally looked pale, and Dr. McIntire was concerned that the altitude might be bad for his heart. He also sensed that the trip indicated a change in his own status. Although he felt that Roosevelt was going to Africa primarily for the fun of the trip itself, he also felt that the president "was tired of having other people, particularly myself, speak for him around the world." It was natural enough for Hopkins to suspect that his influence with Roosevelt was waning. He had recently come under heavy criticism in the press and in Congress for having accepted an expensive wedding gift from Beaverbrook and for having attended a lavish dinner given for him and his wife by Bernard Baruch. Indeed, as the trip to Casablanca began, he was fighting to save his reputation and to avoid becoming a political liability to the president.[24]

After awhile these worries dissolved as he busied himself with sightseeing and thinking ahead to the conference. On January 14 the clipper landed at the mouth of the Gambia River, and the passengers changed planes for the overland flight to Casablanca. Just before the plane took off, the Secret Service announced that confusion had arisen over the president's exact destination, and Hopkins indulged his democratic sensibilities with a laugh at the thought of so powerful and important a man in such a situation. The trip went smoothly, however, and at 6:20 P.M. the plane landed fifteen miles outside Casablanca. The party drove to the Anfa Hotel just south of the city and moved into luxurious villas in a compound surrounded by barbed wire and protected by elaborate army security. Learning that Churchill was already there at a villa about fifty yards away, Hopkins brought him to see the president. Less than an hour after they arrived, the Casablanca conference was under way.

Hopkins followed his custom of staying out of the military chiefs' strategy discussions. He attended an initial briefing by the Joint Chiefs, who had arrived a day earlier and were already in conference with the British. The small amount of evidence about his strategic views suggests that he kept in mind Roosevelt's belief that agreement with the British was more important than promoting any particular strategy. Thus, though he favored Marshall's plan to undertake Roundup in 1943, he kept his eye on the primary objective. As the discussions wore on, he grew worried. Late in the proceedings he complained to Churchill that the conference was turning out to be "a pretty feeble effort," but the next day he brightened considerably when Dill told him about the fruits of the chiefs' deliberations. Although their plan centered on a Mediterranean offensive to capture Sicily (Operation Husky), and thus eliminated Roundup, Hopkins was enthusiastic: "I think this is a VERY good paper and damn good plan—so I am feeling much better."[25]

When attention turned to finding ships to implement this strategy, Hopkins was ready for action. In their discussion the American and British chiefs had squabbled over Russian shipping. The United States proposed cutbacks that the British said were too severe. Still, the chiefs agreed that they should offer the Russians only a tentative commitment. At this point Hopkins made a startling suggestion: that the Allies stop the north Russian convoys entirely and instead offer the Russians extra shipments of airplanes. Just to make sure that his suggestion was heard, he repeated it, emphasizing ways in which the shipping and cargo could be used for other operations. The CCS, he observed, had been inclined to consider Russian aid a political expedient when they should have been considering it "from the standpoint of military necessity."

Why Hopkins proposed to scrap the commitment he had energetically supported only a few weeks before is a question that calls for a precise answer. Unfortunately the documents provide no such certainty. Hopkins knew of the American military's reservations about Russian shipping and Marshall's concern that Operation Husky would overtax Allied shipping. Perhaps he wanted to reassure Marshall that Husky would have adequate support. He and Marshall may have discussed this before the meeting, for when Marshall spoke again, he specifically referred to Hopkins's remarks to make the point that the previous year's shipping losses on the north Russian route had interfered with Bolero.[26]

Here was another case, as Churchill was later to phrase it, of Hopkins's "rapping out the deadly question." Neither the prime minister nor the president, however, was willing to go as far as he was suggesting. Churchill proposed to stop the convoys only during Husky, and

Roosevelt opposed even that. When Admiral King backed up the president, Churchill agreed to run the convoys during Husky if conditions allowed it. The result was to undercut Hopkins's suggestion and to leave the shipping picture as tentative as ever. The incident raised Hopkins's stock with the army and clarified the differences between Roosevelt and the military but failed to settle the issue.[27] No one discussed the British import program because the CCS had earlier approved Roosevelt's commitment to replace Britain's merchant shipping losses.[28]

Hopkins found plenty of time in Casablanca for unofficial activities. His son Robert, a sergeant in the Signal Corps, was plucked from his front-line assignment and ordered to Casablanca for a family reunion. Hopkins spent an afternoon of sightseeing and souvenir hunting with General George S. Patton, who was commanding the American troops in Morocco, and attended a state dinner given by Roosevelt for the sultan of Morocco. He accompanied Roosevelt on an all-day inspection of U.S. troops, eating a lunch of ham and sweet potatoes while an army band played "Deep in the Heart of Texas" and "Alexander's Ragtime Band." They all finished the trip by accompanying Churchill to Marrakesh, which the prime minister had recommended as "the Paris of the Sahara."

Hopkins's reactions were perfectly in character. Always an avid sightseer, he relished poking around Casablanca, though he found the shopping "pretty fruitless except for some rugs." He also looked for signs of military action and observed with a note of satisfaction "how the [Royal] Navy had knocked the hell out of the [French cruiser] Jean Bart." He weathered the formalities and ceremonies with his usual irreverence. He put on his best squint or blank stare for the picture-taking sessions, and at the dinner for the sultan gave up entirely on the proprieties and chatted out of the side of his mouth with General Patton and Robert Murphy. His record of the occasion itself shows what he thought about official protocol:

> The Sultan arrived at 7:40, which caused me to put on my black tie for the first time on this trip. He had expressed a desire to see the president alone prior to Churchill's arrival at eight, and he came loaded with presents—a gold dagger for the president, and some gold bracelets for Mrs. Roosevelt and a gold tiara which looked to me like the kind the gals wear in the circus, riding on white horses. I can just see Mrs. Roosevelt when she takes a look at this. The Sultan proved to be a [sic] undersized,

inconsequential looking man, in white silk robes, age 32. He said little or nothing before dinner, during dinner, or after dinner. He put on a pretty sickly smile and occasionally agreed with the Grand Protocol Officer, who was an old gent with white whiskers and bad teeth, who talked incessantly and said nothing. The old man spent his life agreeing with the Sultan. There was a tough-looking old bastard who was known as the Grand Vizier, who didn't say a word, and who I learned, later from General Patton, runs the show. Apparently the etiquette prevents the drinking of liquor publicly, so we had nothing alcoholic either before, during or after dinner. I fortified myself an hour earlier, however . . . At dinner I sat next to General Nogues, the Governor, who is the bird that de Gaulle wants pitched out of here. He has been the Resident Governor here for many years. He obviously likes it, because he lives in a big palace and is the big shot in this part of the world. I wouldn't trust him as far as I could spit . . . Churchill was glum at dinner and seemed to be real bored. A smart British Marine walked in about the middle of the dinner with a dispatch, but I have a feeling Churchill cooked up that beforehand, because I saw the dispatch later and it certainly wasn't one that required the Prime Minister's attention at dinner.[29]

Hopkins's comments about General Nogues and General de Gaulle point up a serious problem that had arisen at the conference. He and Roosevelt had come to Casablanca carrying a plan by Jean Monnet to settle the question of French leadership. Monnet proposed to form a governing body composed of Free French and Vichy elements but under Allied supervision and strictly limited to local administration. The main effort was to go into creating a French national army, entirely equipped by the United States. This army would serve as a symbol of both French liberation and American Allied leadership. General Giraud would command the army. Monnet also volunteered to go to Algiers to report on political developments for Hopkins.[30]

When Roosevelt and Hopkins arrived in Casablanca they found a situation tailor-made for Monnet's plan. De Gaulle was popular with the French settlers, and Giraud was popular with the French army. Since the British press was still criticizing Allied cooperation with the Vichyites in North Africa, Hopkins suggested that Giraud and De Gaulle join forces and that Monnet be brought in to keep them happily united. When Roosevelt asked Hull's opinion, however, the secretary of state objected that Monnet was too closely identified with De Gaulle and the British. Though this objection temporarily sidetracked Hopkins's proposal, it left intact the rest of Monnet's strategy, especially his idea of having the Americans concentrate on creating a French army. This seems to have been on Hopkins's mind when he and Roosevelt first met Giraud on January 19. "I gained a very favorable impression of Giraud," Hopkins wrote shortly afterward. "I know he is a Royalist, and is probably a right-winger in all his economic views, but I have a feeling that he is willing to fight." Also in Giraud's favor, Hopkins felt, was that he had made up his mind to do whatever Roosevelt wanted.[31]

But Hopkins soon discovered that French affairs could not be so easily managed. Giraud readily agreed to their suggestions, but, offended at not having been consulted about the Torch invasion, De Gaulle bristled when Churchill invited him to Casablanca for discussions with Giraud. He was perfectly willing to talk, he said, but not at the beck and call of a foreign power. As a result De Gaulle remained in London while Roosevelt twitted Churchill that he had produced the bridegroom and it was the prime minister's job to produce the bride. Embarrassed and enraged, Churchill fired off a message ordering De Gaulle to show up or risk losing his support. This persuaded De Gaulle to attend the conference, but on his arrival he demanded that Giraud join his Free French organization and help depose all Vichy officials. In return he was willing to give Giraud command of the French army. Giraud refused.

This controversy arose at a particularly inopportune time. Roosevelt had hoped to wind up the conference on Friday, January 22, and leave the next morning. As the days passed with no decision from De Gaulle, tempers flared. When the general finally arrived on the morning of January 22 no one was in a mood to accommodate him. This was particularly true of Churchill, but also of Roosevelt, who after spending twenty-four hours trying to charm De Gaulle into an cooperative state of mind decided to announce publicly that he was an obstacle to prosecuting the war and that the United States would therefore work only with Giraud. Robert Murphy agreed with the president.[32]

Hopkins refused to give up. He enlisted the aid of the British political adviser, Harold Macmillan, to win concessions from De Gaulle. On the evening of January 23, with the conference now scheduled to end the next day, Murphy and Macmillan told Hopkins that De Gaulle had given in to the extent of agreeing either to alternate with Giraud as head of a single French committee or to have their two organizations proceed along parallel lines. Seeing an opening, Hopkins asked the two diplomats to draw up a joint statement for the French leaders. The morning found Giraud agreeing in principle to the new text but De Gaulle unwilling to commit himself. When Hopkins got this news, he urged Roosevelt to be conciliatory toward De Gaulle and let Churchill talk tough, since it was the British who were paying De Gaulle's bills. Believing that the two Frenchmen genuinely wanted to work together, Hopkins told Roosevelt to expect "an agreement on a joint statement . . . and a picture of the two of them" at the concluding press conference, which by this time was only an hour or so away. When De Gaulle arrived at the president's villa, however, he announced that he would agree in principle to the Anglo-American proposal but would not sign a joint statement. Roosevelt was attempting to change his mind when Churchill walked in, having said good-bye to Giraud outside. What happened next is obscured by conflicting testimony. Hopkins recalled that when he saw Churchill enter he decided to adopt one of Roosevelt's favorite devices of bringing everyone together in the same room in order to reach an agreement and went out to get Giraud.[33] His manuever worked. De Gaulle and Giraud agreed to issue a statement that they were willing to cooperate. They also agreed to appear together at the press conference, where Roosevelt talked them into shaking hands for the newsreel cameras.

Hopkins's intervention fundamentally changed the outcome of the conference. A few minutes before De Gaulle visited Roosevelt, Giraud and Murphy presented the president with two documents cementing a partnership between the United States and Giraud. The first one reviewed American estimates for equipping the French army and set the exchange rate between the dollar and the franc. The second one recognized Giraud as the man "to safe-guard France's past, her present, and her future" and conferred on him "the right and duty of preserving all French interests under the military, economic, financial, and moral plan." Roosevelt looked over the first memo carefully enough to make marginal notes approving its points and also approved the second, probably without giving it close attention. The memos were based on the assumption that no agreement could be reached with De Gaulle. Thus they directly contradicted Hopkins's efforts to bring the two Frenchmen together as equals. Indeed, Hopkins had seen the memos the night before and had advised Roosevelt not to sign them.[34]

In light of Hopkins's intervention the memos had the potential for considerable mischief. Not only did they undercut the last-minute agreement between Giraud and De Gaulle, but because Roosevelt had signed them without consulting the British, they also threatened Allied unity. Roosevelt was willing to make amends. When Churchill learned of the memos, he revised the texts to give De Gaulle equal standing with Giraud. Roosevelt gladly accepted the changes, and the incident ended without further disruption.

The episode reveals a fundamental difference between Hopkins and Roosevelt in their approach to alliance politics. Both had arrived in Casablanca hoping to resolve the French problem along the lines suggested by Monnet. But when discussions bogged down, Roosevelt gave up while Hopkins persevered. Roosevelt was willing to pursue a unilateral American policy—siding with Giraud and leaving the British to deal with De Gaulle—while Hopkins placed a higher priority on Allied unity. Hopkins's views would prevail and would influence the decisions at the Yalta conference two years later.

Roosevelt's anticolonialism showed in his willingness to pursue American objectives at British expense. He left little doubt about his plans for the European empires. He had been appalled at the sight of the African laborers in Bathurst, the Gambian capital. Ragged, dirty, disease ridden, sullen, the Africans worked for meager rations and wages of fifty cents a day. To a man who had spent twelve years as governor and president trying to improve opportunities and living standards for his own countrymen, such conditions were an outrageous indictment of imperial exploitation. At the conference he went out of his way to advertise his feelings. He met privately with the sultan of Morocco before their dinner, the first time the sultan had met with any major head of state other than a Frenchman. For the benefit of Churchill and General Nogues he spent much of the dinner discussing with the sultan how to improve living conditions for the native population and promote postwar economic cooperation with the United States. Neither Churchill nor Nogues missed the point, and neither appreciated it very much.

During the dinner Hopkins seemed oblivious to Roosevelt's anticolonial thrusts. As we have seen, he thought that Churchill seemed "real bored," and he interpreted Nogues's discomfort as the fear of losing his comfortable job. When Murphy suggested that the general was upset because Roosevelt was giving the impression that the Americans had designs on the French empire, he dismissed the subject with a shrug.

The next day, however, he met with the sultan's grand vizier to follow up the president's initiative. The grand vizier asked what America's postwar policy toward Morocco would be and declared that when it came time to write the peace treaty, the sultan intended to "throw himself in the arms of Mr. Roosevelt." Hopkins avoided giving specific assurances but promised that the United States would not leave occupation forces in Morocco after the war and had no intention of changing the sultan's government or of imposing any other changes on the Moroccan people. He also declared that "powerful countries have exploited smaller countries; wealth and resources have been siphoned out for the benefit of the powerful countries." The United States did not intend to treat Morocco this way. Instead the United States only wanted closer economic relations.[35]

Hopkins also assured the grand vizier that "the war will be pursued until Germany, Italy, and Japan agree to unconditional surrender." This doctrine, when announced by Roosevelt the next day, became the centerpiece of the conference. (Roosevelt even suggested that Casablanca be called the "unconditional surrender conference.") The president firmly believed that an unconditional Axis surrender was the necessary first step of his plan for establishing peace on the basis of disarmament and peacekeeping by the major powers.

In the context of the conference Roosevelt's remarks suggest that unconditional surrender had a different meaning for him than for Hopkins. The president saw the doctrine as an American initiative, aimed at postwar cooperation with Russia. This becomes clear in light of Roosevelt's anticolonialism. If Roosevelt hoped that unconditional surrender would serve as a bridge to the major powers' policing the world, he was anticipating that the Western European powers would be without their colonial empires and that the United States would have strong ties to the former colonies. In this situation the United States would be the leading Western power. His efforts to meet privately with Stalin suggest that he wanted to build a special relationship between the United States and the Soviet Union by distinguishing himself from Churchill. In December, when plans were being discussed for a tripartite conference, Hopkins drafted a cable to Churchill that expressed Roosevelt's desire to avoid giving Stalin "the impression that we are settling everything between ourselves before we meet him" but went on to stress "the importance of you and me going into that conference only after the fullest exchange of views and a complete understanding." Roosevelt accepted the first statement but crossed out the second and specifically rejected any prior conference with the prime minister.[36]

At Casablanca, Hopkins still pursued cooperation with the British. He worked mightily to accommodate all parties on the French issue and suggested halting the north Russian convoys to help the Anglo-American campaign in the Mediterranean. Of course he mentioned the hopes for unconditional surrender to the grand vizier of Morocco, but only in a brief and unrevealing way. To the extent that he understood the doctrine more fully than that, it was probably in the context of his discussions with Churchill about whether or not to mention it in the official communiqué. In the end they decided to omit it because Churchill did not want it to apply to Italy, which he thought would only be frightened into fighting harder. They considered only the question of whether unconditional surrender would help or hinder the Allied war effort and did not discuss its usefulness as a bridge to postwar peacekeeping. It seems likely that Hopkins realized that Roosevelt would publicize the doctrine at the conference but did not realize the danger inherent in that procedure.

As soon as the agreement between Giraud and De Gaulle had been wrapped up, Roosevelt and Churchill met the press on the lawn outside Roosevelt's villa. Roosevelt took advantage of Hopkins's work to orchestrate a handshake between Giraud and De Gaulle as he announced their agreement to cooperate with each other. He also announced that he and Churchill were determined to achieve the unconditional surrender of the Axis nations in order to eliminate their war power, discredit their philosophies, and thereby gain "a reasonable assurance of future world peace." His words repeated those he had spoken earlier in his State of the Union address and linked the doctrine to postwar peacekeeping.[37]

Since that time much attention has been given to the question of whether Churchill knew that Roosevelt was going to issue his demand for unconditional surrender.[38] Interesting and useful theories have been offered on this topic, but they have missed the main point. The record conclusively shows that Roosevelt was determined to make the announcement regardless of Churchill's opinion. Roosevelt wanted to use the doctrine as an approach to Stalin. He had made this clear in a meeting with the Joint Chiefs a week before leaving for Casablanca, where, he had said, he "was going to speak to Mr. Churchill about the advisability of informing Mr. Stalin that the United Nations were to continue on until they reach Berlin, and that their only terms would be unconditional surrender. He also proposed to discuss with Mr. Churchill some political questions particularly with regard to disarmament after the war."[30] Thus Roosevelt saw unconditional surrender as a device—along with Lend-Lease aid and the promise of a second front—for convincing Stalin of his good will.

If this was Roosevelt's purpose, both his formulation and presentation were seriously flawed. The brevity of his presentation and the lack of any previous exploration of the subject with the Russians meant that his larger purposes were almost sure to be lost. Not surprisingly, Stalin, who was less concerned about brave formulas for fighting through to the end than about getting the Western Allies to invade Western Europe, attached little importance to the idea, except perhaps to suspect that it was only another dodge to avoid establishing a second front.

This points to a larger failure in Roosevelt's step-by-step approach to postwar planning. With Stalin absent, Roosevelt would have been well advised to defer discussions of postwar policy. Here, however, Roosevelt's sense of dramatic timing probably encouraged him in the opposite direction. Although he often stalled, backtracked, and sidestepped on important issues, he had just as often moved forward with rapid bursts of activity. In the midst of enthusiasm for Operation Torch and growing confidence that Germany's days were numbered, Roosevelt may have thought that the conference provided his best chance to preempt the subject of postwar planning. He was determined, he told Harriman, to avoid Wilson's mistake of announcing his Fourteen Points before the German surrender. He wanted to rule out any hope on the part of the Nazis, or suspicion on the part of the Russians, that the United States was going to offer their enemies any opportunity to negotiate.[40] But this meant rushing ahead with his announcement before any discussions to clarify the doctrine and delivering it in an offhand, general way that was bound to cloud its meaning. This made the demand for unconditional surrender the weakest card in his hand. In the end all that Roosevelt gained from his surprise performance was the appearance of bringing along the British in his wake, as Churchill, for the sake of Allied unity, backed him up in general terms.

If Roosevelt erred in this way, he needed someone to step in and correct him. Of course the logical candidate was Hopkins, who had already shown his willingness to part company with the president on northern Russian shipping and French politics. The circumstances of Roosevelt's announcement, however, make it difficult to evaluate Hopkins's inaction. On the one hand, he clearly agreed with the doctrine of unconditional surrender and was willing to raise it in diplomatic conversation with the grand vizier of Morocco. On the other hand, he may have thought that Roosevelt and Churchill had agreed to defer the subject to later conferences and been as surprised as the prime minister when the president made his announcement. Thus it is hard to say whether he found himself trapped by his own confidence in Roosevelt's judgment or caught unawares, as so often in the past, by the president's sense of timing.

Once the press conference had ended, everyone decided to put aside these unresolved matters and enjoy some sightseeing. Hopkins and Roosevelt piled into an olive drab Daimler limousine and, along with the prime minister and his party, headed for Marrakesh. They stopped along the way for a picnic lunch and arrived in time to visit a fair in the central city, complete with snake charmers, storytellers, and dancers. Their quarters for the night were in the luxurious home of a wealthy American, which was occupied by the American consul, Kenneth Pendar. At sunset the president and the prime minister made their way to a tower to see a spectacular sight: pink light upon the snow of the Atlas Mountains. Everyone was in the mood to relax. Hopkins joked with Roosevelt and Churchill, saying that Murphy had done all the work at the conference, and Churchill replied that Hopkins would have been "a great strategical general."[41]

The next day Hopkins was up early for the return flight. Churchill, who had decided at the last minute to see the Americans off at the airport, drove up dressed in red bathrobe and bedroom slippers, smoking his "inevitable" cigar. In a last brief chat he told Hopkins how pleased he was with the conference and how confident he was of victory but that a hard road still lay ahead.[42] Soon after, the plane took off. Skirting the Atlas Mountains, it arrived at Bathurst eight hours later. Roosevelt had developed a fever and a cough and looked worn out. The party went to bed early on board the U.S. cruiser *Memphis*, and Hopkins fell asleep reading a history of the Gambia River. On January 30 he arrived in Miami and the next day returned to Washington to begin implementing the new design for the war effort.

# Chapter 18

# Lord Root
# of the Matter

Hopkins returned from Casablanca in an optimistic frame of mind. As he saw it, the conference had created an agenda for both winning the war and increasing the American role. Top priority went to the military effort, which now seemed likely to drive the Germans out of North Africa by April 1. When Roosevelt was preparing to report to the nation on the conference, Hopkins advised him to "dramatize the impending battle" in North Africa, emphasizing the confidence of the American soldiers and the determination of the Allies to keep the pressure on Germany with "even more *dangerous* and *costly*" campaigns in Europe and the Mediterranean. He matched his confidence in the war effort with confidence in the U.S. military leadership, which he described as "far above" that of the British.

American military prominence pointed to American political prominence. Hopkins thought Churchill a "hopeless" imperialist, but he believed that the British people were sympathetic to Roosevelt's anti-colonialism and that Anthony Eden, who was scheduled to visit Washington in March, would be sympathetic to their views. Hopkins saw Eden's visit as a chance to bring him into the fold. In the meantime he felt that the United States should protect its interests. At the upcoming United Nations Food Conference, he advised Roosevelt, the United States should resist any British efforts to seat independent delegations from Canada and Australia in order to avoid being "constantly out-voted." "We should put our foot down in the very beginning," he said, to demand equal representation for the United States, Britain, Russia, and China. Furthermore, he anticipated that "our control of shipping would be a powerful weapon at the Peace Table and that we should not hesitate to use it."

Hopkins realized that problems still remained. Stalin's failure to attend the Casablanca conference meant that the United States would still have to rely on unconditional aid and other good will gestures to prepare for postwar cooperation. He advised Roosevelt to reaffirm that the Americans would not compromise with the Fascists and to emphasize "that we can come to an understanding with Russia after the war." China also remained a problem, because the Allies did not have enough resources to devote to that theater and because Generalissimo Chiang Kai-shek's regime seemed in a "precarious position." Something needed to be done to "hearten" the Chinese people.[1]

At the moment Hopkins did not realize that the entire Casablanca agenda was in danger because of a mounting crisis in shipping. Poor communication among the Allies at Casablanca had led them to miscalculate their shipping resources. More serious, the British and Americans had fundamentally misunderstood each other about the U.S. commitment to the British import program. When the Joint Chiefs had agreed to abide by Roosevelt's promise to maintain British imports, General Somervell thought that they were promising only to make up British shipping losses and in any case to provide no more than 300,000 tons each month, an amount which came to just about 2.5 million tons for the year. The British, however, read the agreement as a commitment to supply enough shipping to maintain their program, which would require over 7 million tons a year. The War Shipping Administration (WSA) which agreed with the British interpretation, could have cleared up this misunderstanding, but it did not have a representative at the conference. Roosevelt further complicated matters by promising Giraud to rearm the French forces in North Africa without telling either Churchill or General Marshall. By the end of February, Dwight Eisenhower, the Allied commander in North Africa, was calling for supplies for Giraud, and the WSA was warning that it could not provide the shipping without depleting other operations.[2]

Thus, many clouds were on the horizon when Eden arrived in Washington for what Hopkins and Roosevelt were hoping would be an important step in realigning the Anglo-American partnership. Roosevelt set the tone, stressing the value of personal diplomacy and declaring that he preferred private meetings, like the Argentia and Casablanca conferences. He and Hopkins assured Eden that the United States would not withdraw into isolation after the war, and Roosevelt gave qualified support to a Senate resolution that the United Nations create a police force for postwar peacekeekping.[3] Roosevelt also proposed a three-way meeting with Stalin, suggesting

July as the best time. These encouraging approaches, as well as the president's chatty good nature and charm, made Eden's visit pleasant enough.

The tone of the meetings changed, however, when it came time to discuss Roosevelt's postwar plans, which included making territorial adjustments to separate hostile ethnic groups in Europe and elevating China to the status of a great power. Eden was opposed to creating new small states, and he believed that China was on the verge of revolution. Roosevelt's knowledge of world affairs, Eden concluded, was too shallow to be useful but broad enough to be dangerous. When he tried to account for Roosevelt's ideas, he could only suppose condescendingly that the president's hobby of stamp collecting had encouraged him to think that he knew more about Europe than he actually did.[4]

As a result Hopkins found himself in somewhat the same position he had occupied at Arcadia, mediating between the president and the British. As usual Hopkins dwelt on the details of the issues, so that even if he highlighted points of disagreement, he at least appealed to Eden's taste for order and precision in a way that contrasted with Roosevelt's facile monologues. The first item on Hopkins's agenda was postwar Germany. All agreed that Germany should be divided, but Roosevelt hoped to encourage natural, internal separatist movements instead of stimulating German nationalism by arbitrarily dividing the country by force. This was not a strong enough approach for Hopkins, and he pushed Roosevelt and Eden to agree that Germany should be divided by any means necessary.

Next came the American role in postwar Europe. Eden thought that Russia would want the United States to participate in the occupation of Germany, since Stalin would not want to do the job alone. This, he thought, also figured into Stalin's call for a second front. Hopkins agreed, declaring that unless the United States, Britain, and Russia agreed on a plan for postwar occupation, Germany would fall either to communism or anarchy. The same could happen in any of the other European countries. Dividing Germany would be simpler, he advised, if the Americans and British were fighting in Europe at the time of its collapse, but they should be prepared to move if Germany fell before the invasion.[5] Hopkins was less interested in stopping communism in Europe than in reaching an occupation agreement that would promote Allied cooperation. As a result of his prompting Roosevelt issued a statement that after the war U.S. armed forces would occupy Germany and Italy.

The mention of Russia also raised the issue of Soviet postwar territorial claims. Eden expected Stalin's demands to be modest, and Hopkins agreed. When Roosevelt expressed concern about Russia's taking over the Baltic States, Hopkins was unmoved, feeling that Britain and the United States should accept Russian expansion as inevitable. He especially objected to a charge by William Bullitt, Roosevelt's friend and former ambassador to the Soviet Union, that Russia's taking over the Baltic States would violate the Atlantic Charter. The charter, Hopkins declared to the journalist Raymond Clapper, could not be used as a stick to beat the Russians. The United States was going to have to be realistic if there were to be any peace at all. When he learned that the Finns were dragging their feet on negotiations with Russia, he snapped that he was "fed up" with their stalling.[6]

Conciliating Eden had its limits. Hopkins backed up the president and the State Department in opposing Eden's idea of creating regional confederations or councils of smaller European states. Roosevelt believed that the formula would undercut his plan to create a United Nations organization, with peacekeeping controlled by the great powers. Hopkins also warned Eden that the isolationists would respond to a European confederation by proposing a confederation in the Western Hemisphere. He so strongly criticized Churchill for raising the idea in a recent speech that Eden was forced to claim that Churchill's remarks had been misunderstood.[7]

Hopkins got an unexpected chance to show Eden his talent for crisis management when a shipping emergency erupted. The British had handed the Americans a statement of their shipping needs, placing the import program off limits for discussion and suggesting that the United States might be asked to contribute as much as 9 million tons of shipping. The Americans heatedly replied that the British schedule would cut troop deployments by nearly 50 percent just when the North African campaign and preparations for Operation Husky were nearing completion.[8]

The British had timed their requests so that Eden could state their case. Their strategy was a better one than they had realized. If Roosevelt and Hopkins wanted to establish friendly relations with Eden, they were going to have to make sure that he was satisfied on this matter. Hopkins first proposed to set up a special Anglo-American committee, with himself in the chair; then, perhaps realizing that the British and the Americans had already spent enough time arguing with each other, he decided instead to approach the parties individually. Drawing on the good will he had cultivated at Casablanca, he told the army that he wanted to prepare "the American position" on the overall shipping problem and then get President Roosevelt to approve it. He would tell the president, he said, that the army would not be able to carry out its planned operations unless it could have ships previously assigned to north Russia and the British import program.[9]

But Hopkins neglected to tell the army that they would not be making the final decision. For that responsibility he turned to Lewis Douglas and the WSA. Douglas fundamentally differed with the army, seeing the British import program as a presidential commitment and "as important to the military success of our armies as is, for example, the bauxite movement to the United States." Douglas had recently come through a bitter controversy with the army over ship loadings and was inclined to see the army's attack on the British import program as another effort to usurp the WSA's responsibilities.[10]

With the army neutralized and Douglas and the British in his pocket, Hopkins was ready to do business. He briefed Roosevelt and on March 29 staged a meeting to impress Eden with America's good will. Prompted by Hopkins, Douglas blasted the army and supported the British import program as "a very essential and strategic movement." Hopkins then offered his own criticisms of the army's shipping methods, and Roosevelt promised Eden that the United States would meet its commitment to the import program. Later calculations fixed that at 7 million tons.[11]

At once Hopkins moved to conciliate the army. When it appeared that the U.S. contribution would bring the total import program to only 25 million tons instead of the 27 million they had hoped for, Hopkins suggested that the British "spontaneously" announce that they were reducing their program to accommodate the Americans. Such a move would bring credit "in quarters where it would be useful" and would prove helpful in discussions of "other matters." The day after Roosevelt decided to support the British import program, Hopkins told a meeting of the Joint Chiefs and heads of the civilian war agencies that nothing should interfere with shipping for military operations and that the "necessity for decision was immediate."[12]

It was a typically successful Harry Hopkins juggling act, but the star performer had decided to bring down the curtain. Preparing for the next Anglo-American conference (Trident), scheduled for Washington in late May, Hopkins urged Douglas to work out a statement on shipping with the Joint Chiefs and then consult the British. He encouraged cooperation between the army and the WSA by assuring them that they could bring all their problems to Roosevelt. Douglas then took the U.S. statement to the Trident conference and worked out a combined shipping budget that became part of Anglo-American strategy. As a result, for the first time operations proceeded without being waylaid by another shipping crisis.[13]

Thus Hopkins at last broke through the tangled web that had enveloped the Arcadia agreements. As the war effort turned from combined cooperation to negotiation, he had been forced to build up national negotiating agencies like the WSA. But, like his own WPA earlier, the WSA had depended upon support from the top to make its influence felt, and when Hopkins's attention was elsewhere—as at Casablanca—the results could be awkward for all. It was the embarrassment of the shipping crisis that convinced Hopkins of the need for a new approach. Ironically that crisis was resolved by random circumstances, as the army made the mistake of challenging Anthony Eden, whom Roosevelt and Hopkins wanted to court as Churchill's heir apparent.

Hopkins deserves great credit for resolving the March shipping crisis, but he deserves even more for learning the lesson of the crisis and applying it to the Trident conference. Aside from Roosevelt only Hopkins had the standing to command the attention of the interested parties. Though his handling of shipping between the Arcadia and Trident conferences was occasionally shortsighted and insufficiently informed, it nevertheless stands high on the list of Lord Root of the Matter's achievements.

Eden's visit also inspired Hopkins to strengthen Anglo-American collaboration on developing atomic energy and the atomic bomb. This collaboration had been born in the harried, brink-of-disaster atmosphere of 1941 and had received a somewhat sentimental but heartfelt baptism in June 1942, when Roosevelt had promised Churchill that the United States would work with Britain as a full and equal partner, sharing all information. By the end of the year, however, the Americans in the Office of Scientific Research and Development (OSRD) were recommending that the United States restrict information be-

cause the British wanted much of it for postwar industrial and commercial development. On January 13 the United States informed the
British that they would receive information only if it could be used for
the war effort. The British objected, and at Casablanca, Churchill mentioned the issue to Roosevelt and Hopkins. Hopkins promised that
when he got home, he would put everything right.[14]

A few weeks' investigation convinced Hopkins that Anglo-American
cooperation on this front should continue into the postwar period. On
both sides those who wanted to withhold information were identified
with big business, and Hopkins suspected them of putting selfish private interests above those of their countries.[15] Hopkins kept his opinions to himself, however, so the issue carried over to the Trident
conference, where it assumed an entirely different form. On the last
day of the conference Hopkins invited Vannevar Bush of the OSRD to
a meeting at the White House with Churchill's science adviser, Lord
Cherwell. With Hopkins's support Cherwell pressed the case for sharing. The British wanted to build their own atomic bombs after the war,
but their aims were strategic and not commercial or industrial. When
Bush replied that the OSRD needed to study this point, Hopkins
rapidly ended the meeting, saying that he understood the subject for
the first time and that Bush should take no further steps.[16]

Once again Hopkins seemed ready to jump into the nearest telephone booth and emerge as Lord Root of the Matter, ready to leap tall
issues. But this time he did not—with embarrassing consequences. A
few hours later Roosevelt and Churchill agreed to resume sharing
information on the assumption that a bomb would be completed before the end of the war. Neither mentioned postwar uses of atomic
energy.[17]

Shortly after the conference ended, Hopkins learned about the
Roosevelt-Churchill agreement and decided that the matter had finally
been settled. The fact that it had been settled on terms different from
those he had developed with Cherwell and Bush did not concern him,
since Bush had promised to wait until he heard from Hopkins. Apparently Hopkins thought that he would wait forever. Then the situation
blew up. Roosevelt learned of Hopkins's meeting and declared that the
United States would not share information so that Britain could build
bombs after the war. Bush suggested that the president hear Hopkins's
version of the meeting, and Roosevelt may have done so, for when
Churchill cabled to express his dismay that no progress was being

made, Roosevelt asked Hopkins what he should reply. This was Hopkins's chance to make up for his mistake, and he took advantage of it. He simply told Roosevelt that he had made a "firm commitment" to Churchill and there was "nothing to do but go through with it." At the same time he drafted a letter instructing Bush to resume full sharing with the British, without giving him any reason for the decision. Churchill later disavowed any interest in postwar atomic energy.[18]

The next month at the Sextant conference in Quebec, Roosevelt and Churchill signed an agreement to resume collaboration.[19] Churchill concluded, properly if a bit too confidently, that Hopkins had been largely responsible for so satisfactory a result and made sure that future high-level correspondence on atomic energy was routed through him.

None of these difficulties seemed as intractable as the problem of China. By the time of the Casablanca conference Hopkins was caught in the middle of a Chinese offensive, directed at the Americans instead of the Japanese. Generalissimo Chiang Kai-shek supported a military strategy advised by Major General Claire Chennault, a tough-talking air corps officer who had moved to China in the 1930s and in 1941 had organized American volunteer pilots into an arm of the Chinese air force called the Flying Tigers. Chennault proposed to strike the Japanese by air, disrupting their shipping and later directly attacking their industrial centers. Opposing Chennault's strategy was the equally salty Major General Joseph W. ("Vinegar Joe") Stilwell, U.S. commander in China, who favored a ground campaign in Burma to open supply lines from India and to keep the Japanese at a safe distance.

Chennault was a favorite with Chiang, in contrast to Stilwell, who called the generalissimo "the Peanut" and delcared that the war would be won in spite of him. Chiang recommended that Chennault be given an independent command, and he put off approving any campaign against the Japanese until he received substantially more Lend-Lease aid.[20]

Those with by far the strongest influence on Hopkins favored Chennault. In addition to Madame Chiang herself, who had come to the United States to be treated for health problems, Hopkins heard from Joseph Alsop, a journalist who had served as Chennault's public relations officer before Hopkins appointed him Lend-Lease representative in China, and General Arnold, who wanted to fight the war by bombing Japan.[21]

Despite these pressures Hopkins kept his perspective. After the

Combined Chiefs agreed at Casablanca to undertake Stilwell's Burma campaign (Operation Anakim), he told Raymond Clapper that the Chinese would never be satisfied with Anglo-American aid; the plans, he feared, "would be nothing like [the] Chinese want." "Nor do I think," he later assured Anthony Eden, "that the Australians or the beautiful Mme. Chiang can change our strategic policy," though he did warn Eden that if she visited England, "you had better look out!"[22]

The one who succeeded in turning Hopkins in favor of Chennault was Roosevelt. He was hoping to build China into a major postwar power to balance Russia in the Far East. This meant bolstering Chiang by helping him win victories over the Japanese. Short resources and an occasional warning from Chiang that he might make a separate peace with Japan turned the president's strategic thinking toward Chennault's plan, which promised immediate returns at little cost. Hopkins showed that he was thinking along similar lines when he told Clapper that it was "important to keep China in the war although they [are] not fighting now . . . [It is] necessary to do everything possible to bolster the Generalissimo." At Casablanca, Roosevelt and Churchill had ordered reinforcements for Chennault, and Roosevelt later gave Chennault an independent command.[23]

During the first half of 1943, however, Hopkins's main efforts favored Marshall and Stilwell. He rejected warnings that there might be too few ships for Operation Anakim. Only when Churchill and the British chiefs soured on the operation did he back down. Then during Trident, Roosevelt rashly promised the Chinese ambassador, T.V. Soong, a "firm commitment" to Anakim. Hopkins grabbed Roosevelt's memo and rushed it to Marshall with a note: "Could you rewrite or amend this to conform to our policy[?] This is a hot potato . . . I can stall Soong till this afternoon."[24] Marshall translated Roosevelt's commitment into vague generalities, emphasizing the American desire to undertake the operation. When the CCS scaled down the operation, Hopkins presented the package to Soong as a victory for the president, declaring that Roosevelt had worked day and night on Anakim and had done his best to strengthen the operation. He also assured Soong that General Stilwell would be made aware of the president's great respect for the generalissimo, and that if Stilwell overstepped himself, one message would be enough to have him transferred.[25]

Still, Hopkins shared Stilwell's worries about Chiang's weakness, evidence of which was reaching his desk from Lauchlin Currie, whom he had recruited to supervise Lend-Lease aid to China. Currie ascribed widespread malnutrition among Chinese soldiers at Ichang to "corruption and neglect" by Chiang's government. He also sent Hopkins an uncensored story of famine conditions in Honan province written by the *Time* magazine correspondent Theodore H. White, which blamed the situation on the corruption and greed of Chiang's officials and supporters. "Tremendously interested," Hopkins suggested sending the story to Soong. Currie feared, however, that informing the Chinese might ruin White's "effectiveness" in China.[26] Later events were to show that China's difficulties were too complex and deep-seated to be cured by American tinkering.

Apart from the problems in China, the war seemed to be moving according to American plans. Eden had been courted; shipping was in hand. Still, there remained one major American project yet to be achieved: forging close and lasting ties with the Russians. On that score, things were not yet going the Americans' way.

# Chapter 19

# Lining Up with the Russians

Relations with the Russians had never been worse as the war moved on into 1943. Shipping difficulties had forced the Allies to halt the northern Russian convoys. General Burns and Lewis Douglas of the WSA had protested, but Hopkins took a tolerant view, arguing that with shipping so short, it was better to ship only those items that would go directly into battle. His problems were less logistical than political. From army intelligence Hopkins learned that the Russians were negotiating with the Nazis about the possibilities of making a separate peace. In the meantime Ambassador Standley had renewed his request to put Lend-Lease on a bargaining basis and had publicly declared that the Russian leaders were jeopardizing Lend-Lease by not telling their own people about it. Standley was probably trying to outflank Philip Faymonville, with whom he was still wrestling for authority, and to please Washington, which wanted some favorable comment from the Russians to help with the upcoming Lend-Lease appropriations.[1]

Although Standley's remarks did little harm and actually raised morale among many who had experienced years of frustration dealing with the Russians, Hopkins was alarmed. It seemed to him that Standley had undercut all progress in Russian relations since the previous October. This seemed particularly unfortunate because at the moment the British seemed closer to the Russians than the Americans were. Hopkins thought that this situation was "haywire," because after the war Britain would be bankrupt and the United States and Russia would have the main responsibility for keeping the peace. For some reason, however, Britain seemed determined to "run the show" after the war. In any case it seemed clear to him that Standley had lost Stalin's confidence and would have to be replaced. Once again Hopkins and Roosevelt turned to Joseph Davies for advice. Davies thought that Russian-American relations had deteriorated because the United States had failed to sign the twenty-year treaty that Britain and Russia had signed in 1941 and had not approved Russia's territorial claims in Poland. Stalin also feared that the United States intended to support British interests in the eastern Mediterranean. Once again Hopkins offered Davies the ambassadorship, but he still felt that his health was too poor and, as earlier, urged Hopkins to take the job.[2]

In October failure to find a replacement had led to Standley's going back to Moscow. But now, nearly six months later, Hopkins felt that something had to be done. In April, Burns visited Moscow, where he conferred with Faymonville and Stalin, by-passing Standley. Meanwhile Hopkins briefed Davies with a list of questions about Stalin's postwar plans and sent him off carrying a personal invitation from Roosevelt to a private meeting in Alaska and a copy of a pro-Soviet film based on Davies's memoir *Mission to Moscow*. Davies's job, Hopkins emphasized, was like Eden's in December 1941, when the foreign secretary had gone to Moscow to conclude a treaty of friendship. Although Davies negotiated no treaty, he followed Burns's example of offering kind words to Stalin and a cold shoulder to Standley.

Hopkins also sent Burns and Davies to report on the attitudes of U.S. officials toward the Russians. He was concerned that many in the diplomatic corps opposed America's Russian policy. Davies found no evidence of extreme disloyalty but reported that Standley and his staff were trying to undermine Faymonville and Lend-Lease. On this basis Hopkins decided that the time had come to clean house. Standley helped by sending in his resignation, and Hopkins recommended that Roosevelt replace him with Averell Harriman. Although Harriman had come to favor hard bargaining with the Russians over Lend-Lease, he assured Hopkins that he favored postwar cooperation. In order to relieve his fears that he would become nothing more than "a glorified communications officer," he was given leave to reorganize the U.S. mission in Moscow. The former secretary of the Joint Chiefs, General John R. Deane, was placed in charge of a reorganized military mission, purged of anti-Soviet officers, and including a Lend-Lease division under Sidney Spalding. The shuffle gave Marshall leverage to recall Faymonville, whom he considered pro-Russian to the point of disloyalty.

Hopkins coordinated these moves in Moscow with similar ones in Washington. Following the advice of Burns and Davies, who feared that unsympathetic officials might "sabotage" Russian aid, he persuaded Roosevelt to remove from the State Department the two strongest critics of unconditional aid and to move in Charles ("Chip") Bohlen, a junior-grade Foreign Service officer who had served in Russia and who was close to Harriman. Another change came accidentally, when Sumner Welles resigned as Undersecretary of State in the wake of a personal scandal. Roosevelt replaced Welles with Stettinius, indicating to State that he wanted to conduct Russian policy through Hopkins.[3]

Hopkins's urge to get the United States back on the inside track with the Russians colored his response to a flare-up in Polish-Russian relations. In March the Germans announced that they had discovered the graves of some ten thousand Polish army officers in the Katyn Forest in Byelorussia. The Russians, they charged, had killed them after they had marched into eastern Poland in 1940. When the anticommunist Polish government in exile in London called for a Red Cross investigation, the Russians broke off relations. Angered by this complication, Hopkins dismissed the Poles as troublemakers influenced by "large Polish landlords" who wanted to make sure that their estates were not lost to the Russians.[4]

Hopkins also distanced himself from British policy toward Russia. In April the British proposed to recast the coming year's supply agreement, or protocol, as a treaty and to require the Russians to let them establish bases in Russian territory to protect their supply lines. They also wanted to combine all foreign aid into a single list without identifying the supplying country. When he first saw the draft of the British proposals, Hopkins objected to the combined list but accepted the other provisions. Lend-Lease, however, opposed the whole plan, pointing out that a treaty might be delayed in the Senate ratification process and that a combined list would obscure the fact that the United States was providing 95 percent of the supplies and 85 percent of the shipping. Hopkins endorsed Lend-Lease's position, which the Americans then forced the British to accept.[5]

In courting the Russians, Hopkins renewed his skepticism of British grand strategy. Though the campaign in Sicily seemed to rule out Operation Roundup for 1943, the Joint Chiefs were so determined to carry out the invasion of France in 1944 that they had even revived their scheme of threatening to withdraw to the Pacific unless they got their way. Once again their determination infected Hopkins. On the eve of the Trident conference he told Douglas that if the British made trouble over the shipping estimates, "We will just pick up our toys and leave the British alone and fight the war in the Southwest Pacific."[6]

Not surprisingly, Hopkins and the Joint Chiefs were worried about Roosevelt, who previously had seemed to go out of his way to accommodate Churchill. This time, however, they found that their fears were groundless. When the Trident conference opened, Roosevelt announced that invading France had to be the top priority. Hopkins was delighted. To Churchill's physician, Sir Charles Wilson, he sardonically imitated Churchill's appeal to follow up victory in Sicily by conquering Italy. Roosevelt, he said, had stood fast for the cross-Channel attack. The president could now safely be left alone with the prime minister. In the end the Joint Chiefs accommodated the British only to the extent of accepting a general plan to invade Italy, with the reservation that the CCS approve all specific operations. When Churchill later tried to get Roosevelt to agree to a specific operation, Hopkins told him that he was wasting his time.[7]

Events immediately following the Trident conference further encouraged the Americans to stand their ground. Throughout May the Russians had been praising their Western partners. Stalin had even accepted Roosevelt's invitation to a meeting. But the news that establishing a second front would again be postponed abruptly changed the atmosphere. Angrily accusing Roosevelt and Churchill of again breaking their promises, Stalin recalled his ambassadors from Washington and London. Soon U.S. intelligence was reporting new negotiations between the Russians and the Germans.[8]

Hopkins had anticipated Stalin's reaction. Now he feared that Stalin would further suspect Churchill's motives and doubt Roosevelt's influence. He would probably call off plans for the meeting. As Hopkins saw it, "Things were bad and had been breaking fast."[9]

The result of the new impasse with Russia was seen in heightened American suspicions that Churchill intended to block Operation Roundup. We now know that Churchill was committed to carrying through the operation. At the time, however, he was so intent on supporting his chiefs' argument for an operation against Italy that he failed to anticipate the Americans' concern. When Stimson visited London in July, Churchill made the mistake of warning him about the risks of Roundup. When Hopkins heard this, he concluded that Churchill was trying to shelve Roundup so that Britain could attack in Greece and the Balkans.[10]

Stimson conveyed Churchill's warning as Hopkins was preparing to accompany Roosevelt to his August conference with the prime minister in Montreal. As a result Hopkins arrived at the conference determined to secure Churchill's commitment to the cross-Channel attack. So determined was he that at the beginning of the first session he broke in to ask if plans for the strategic bombing of Germany included air operations from Italy. He probably meant to move directly to the subject of the cross-Channel operation, which had been renamed Overlord, but Churchill beat him to it. Confirming Hopkins's suspicions, the prime minister remarked that if Germany proved stronger than estimated, the Overlord plan should be revised.

Hopkins was not going to let Churchill argue for that. The Allies, he declared, interrupting the prime minister, ought not to take a rigid view. Germany might have thirteen divisions or fifteen at two-thirds strength. Also, it would be hard to determine their fighting strength. He thought that the plans which the British had drawn up were too inelastic. Perhaps the tone of his remarks suggested that there was more at stake than just flexibility, for Churchill responded by deliberately misinterpreting Hopkins's statement to mean that there should be elasticity in deciding whether or not to undertake the operation. He immediately followed, however, by declaring that he strongly favored Overlord and offered practical suggestions for strengthening it.

This response satisfied Hopkins. The next day he told Sir Charles Wilson that Churchill "came clean," "threw in his hand," and accepted the second front. Hopkins's tone was strident and his voice edged with bitterness. Churchill's obstinacy, he believed, had prolonged the war. Nor was he entirely sure that Churchill was "really converted" and would not change his mind, as he had over Sledgehammer in 1942.[11] For the moment, however, he was satisfied that he had gotten as much from Churchill as the prime minister was willing to give, and for the rest of the conference he held his peace.

Hopkins returned to Washington exhausted and went directly from the train to the naval hospital for another series of blood transfusions. Although he later joked that Quebec and Churchill had been too much for him, he admitted that he was "in pretty bad shape." The doctors released him on September 13, but he remained weak and spent several mornings in bed before resuming his schedule. He may have allowed himself a little extra rest because he felt that the conference had turned out so well. Now, he told Raymond Clapper, the Allies had a step-by-step plan to knock out Germany.[12]

Even as Hopkins spoke, however, the plan was coming apart at the seams. The design of limiting the Italian operation to establishing airfields north of Rome had begun to unravel when, in July, dissident Italian officials had overthrown Mussolini and initiated negotiations to surrender to the Allies and even to join them in fighting Germany. Heading the new government were King Victor Emmanuel and General Pietro Badoglio, both of whom had previously cooperated with Mussolini's Fascists. Roosevelt and Hopkins had hoped to treat this regime as an instrument of military convenience, obtaining Italy's unconditional surrender, declaring that its future would be decided by democratic means after the war, and in the meantime permitting Eisenhower, the Allied commander, to respond to situations as they arose. At the Quebec conference in August, however, Churchill argued that without a strong government on the scene, Italy would either go communist or disintegrate into anarchy. He persuaded Roosevelt to approve surrender terms that implied recognition of the Badoglio government. Before these "long terms" could be presented, Badoglio accepted "short terms" of a simple military surrender. Then Hilter occupied northern Italy, installed Mussolini as his puppet ruler, and mobilized to drive out the Allied occupation force. This was the situation that faced Hopkins shortly after he returned from the hospital.[13]

Hopkins saw a chance to apply to Italy lessons he had recently learned from dealing with the French. Following the Casablanca conference General De Gaulle had moved to take control of the French Committee of National Liberation. Jean Monnet, whom Hopkins had sent to Algiers to keep peace between De Gaulle and General Giraud, warned Hopkins that De Gaulle was selfish, authoritarian, and, more seriously, completely dependent on the British. To make matters worse, Giraud, he said, was "lost" when it came to politics and was clearly no match for De Gaulle. A visit by Giraud to the United States convinced Hopkins that Monnet was right, and that under the circumstances the United States should avoid political commitments to either side and should concentrate on forming a French army under Eisenhower's command. Neither pressure from Robert Murphy, who wanted the United States to recognize the French committee in order to keep De Gaulle from taking it over, nor urging from Churchill, who generally favored political commitments, could shake Hopkins. As he saw it, the committee's authority should not extend beyond the requirements of military necessity, and should be exercised only on the condition that its members achieve "real unity." (At the Quebec conference the Americans and the British had debated their differences on this score without resolving them.)[14]

If the French situation convinced Hopkins that the French people and not the Allies should choose their leaders, the Italian situation was even more convincing. The surrender of Italy should give the Allies a chance to eliminate "the entire Fascist Party membership from the highest to the lowest" and to restore religious and civil liberties. Hopkins wanted to prepare the way for organizing postwar Europe along democratic lines. He had "grave misgivings" about both the king and Badoglio, neither of whom, "by any stretch of the imagination, can be considered to represent a democratic government." He feared that "it is very easy to recognize these people, but it is awfully hard to throw them overboard later." Nor did he like the idea that "these former enemies can change their minds when they know that they are going to get licked and come over to our side and get help in maintaining political power." At any rate he had heard that the king was "ga ga" and Badoglio merely "an old man [who] means well." At the very least he thought that Roosevelt should wait a week before deciding about recognition.[15]

Hopkins succeeded to the extent that Roosevelt advised Eisenhower to withhold the "long terms," but he decided to treat Italy as a cobelligerent and to help the country "to wage war" against Germany. A few days later Churchill rounded up Stalin's support for the "long terms" and urged Roosevelt to go along in order to avoid future haggling over the issue. Roosevelt approved the "long terms," and the signing took place on September 29. In the end, then, the combined pressure from Churchill, who wanted to stop the advance of communism, Stalin, who was willing to ally with anyone who might help fight the Germans, and Eisenhower, who wanted to avoid shouldering political responsibilities, proved more than Hopkins could contend with.

During September, Hopkins's attention was on another subject. Just after the Quebec meetings Roosevelt and Churchill had agreed that Marshall would command Operation Overlord. The press picked up rumors of the arrangement, and anti-Roosevelt columnists claimed that Marshall was being "kicked upstairs" against his will. Army officers who opposed a proposal by General Somervell to reorganize the Army Service Forces charged that Marshall was being moved out so that Somervell could become chief of staff. Since Somervell had once headed the WPA in New York City, some also inferred that Hopkins was the evil genius behind the plot, and that the ultimate objective was to create a global WPA.

The only gleam of truth in this cloud of nonsense was that Hopkins indeed thought that Marshall should command Overlord. Of course Hopkins wanted neither to kick Marshall upstairs nor to diminish his influence in the war effort in any way; his reasoning pointed entirely in the opposite direction. Because he regarded Marshall as the war's premier general, Hopkins wanted to be sure that he commanded the premier Allied operation. As he saw it, the Quebec conference had completed the planning phase of the war effort, clearing the way for an active phase in which the commander of operations would inevitably outweigh the chief of staff. Giving Marshall the Overlord command would thus expand his influence.

Indeed Hopkins wanted Marshall to command not just Overlord but all Anglo-American forces in Europe. He argued for this on military grounds, claiming that Marshall's authority would be needed to keep theater commanders in North Africa and Italy from holding on to resources that would be vital to the invasion. "Above everything else," he declared, "we want liquidity in our offensive . . . against Germany and, whether we want it or not, the march of events . . . will undoubtedly require it." He was even prepared to turn over the command of Overlord to the British "in order to get our main objective of Marshall's command of the whole business."[16]

As with most ideas that appealed to him, Hopkins thought that the British could be persuaded to cooperate. He was even willing to offer them the Mediterranean command in order to get them to cooperate in putting Marshall in overall charge. Churchill's willingness to appoint Marshall the chief U.S. military representative in London—a position like Dill's in Washington—and his desire to announce the command arrangements "at an early date" also encouraged Hopkins to believe that he could be persuaded. He was, however, thoroughly mistaken. Churchill opposed appointing a supreme commander, who, he believed, would outrank the Combined Chiefs and, in the case of Marshall or any other American, would be directly responsible to President Roosevelt, by-passing Churchill and the War Cabinet. When Dill informed Hopkins of the prime minister's opinion, Hopkins seemed to him to abandon the idea.[17]

Now it was Dill's turn to be mistaken. To Hopkins and the other

Americans, Marshall's command meant more than guaranteeing that Operation Overlord would run smoothly; it meant guaranteeing that Overlord would in fact take place. Although he might declare that the Quebec conference had produced the final plan for winning the war, Hopkins could not escape the feeling that the British were not to be trusted and that Churchill would come up with some last-minute ploy to scuttle the operation. As he had with Sledgehammer, he now made Overlord the single standard for judging all other strategic proposals. Anything that even suggested a diversion from the main objective was unacceptable.[18]

An episode later that fall convinced Hopkins that such resolution was needed. When Italy had surrendered in late September, Churchill had pressed to capture the Italian garrisons on key islands in the Aegean Sea before the Germans could move in. The CCS approved the operations as a British undertaking, but the Germans beat them to the punch. Churchill responded by requesting troops for an assault on the island of Rhodes before the Germans could dig in. On October 7 he cabled Roosevelt and followed with a phone call. Roosevelt was out of town, so Hopkins, who had read the cable, tried to let Churchill know gently that his request would most certainly be rejected, as indeed it was.[19]

Once again Hopkins's support of Marshall and Overlord had led him to misread Churchill. If he had kept his usual balance, he would have seen the prospects for accommodation in Churchill's willingness to accept Marshall as both commander of Overlord and the principal day-to-day contact between the American and British chiefs of staff. Of course, given past experiences and the uncertainties of the moment, it is hard to place too much blame on his shoulders. Grand strategy had never been his area of expertise. Still, in an alliance that depended so much on personal sensitivities—and at a time when the president and his chief of staff seemed more in tune than in the previous year—he ought to have looked for opportunities to relieve American suspicions on the one hand and British frustrations on the other. As things turned out, Churchill's entreaties on behalf of the Aegean operation only strenthened American suspicisions, and with them Hopkins's determination to install Marshall as the supreme commander.

Growing frustration with the British made it all the more important to cultivate the Russians. The opportunity arose when Stalin agreed to meet with Roosevelt and Churchill in Tehran. Looking toward the meeting, Hopkins asked Davies to assess Allied relations. Davies replied that the British still had the inside track with the Russians. When Hopkins asked if Stalin would sign a separate peace, Davies said that he would only if he thought that the Western Allies were ganging up to deny him fair treatment at the peace table.[20]

That put extra pressure on the Americans' main instrument in Russian relations: Lend-Lease. At the September meeting of the Soviet Protocol Committee, Hopkins departed from his usual role as cheerleader to fire sharp questions about various aspects of the program. He particularly emphasized that he wanted the British fully informed that the Persian Gulf supply route was open to them. He did not want the British telling the Russians that the Americans were obstructing their use of the route.[21]

Nor was Hopkins going to let the British restrict American aid to Russia. By the fall of 1943 some British military leaders were suggesting that Germany was on the verge of collapse and that the Western Allies could best advance the process by keeping up the pressure on their forces in the Mediterranean. At the same time, some Americans opposed supplying the Russians with certain equipment that they could not put into use until after the war. In the spring, when the United States and Britain were gathering materiel for the summer offensive, Hopkins had agreed to limit Russian aid to items that could be used within two years. But then, when the Tehran conference was only weeks away, Burns recommended dropping the two-year rule in order to persuade the Russians to enter the war against Japan and to cooperate at the peace table. Agreeing that the end of the war was not yet in sight, Hopkins endorsed the idea and took it a step further by asking the Russians about their plans for ordering equipment after the war. He may even have suggested forming a committee to study the subject.[22]

Hopkins also wanted to reach an agreement with the Russians on the postwar treatment of Germany. He was thinking primarily of how to deal with Germany when it collapsed. Unless the British and Americans were willing to discuss this topic, the October meeting of the Big Three foreign ministers in Moscow would do more harm than good.[23]

Despite various problems Hopkins believed that the meeting could succeed. He felt that the Russians appreciated the American contribution to the war and were friendly enough to justify hope that relations could be improved. Events bore out his optimism. Stalin and Molotov were cordial and accommodating. Stalin promised that after Germany's defeat Russia would join in the war against Japan. The Russians also signed a Four-Power Declaration (including China) committing the Allies to remaining united in war and peace. This convinced Hopkins not that the Russians were reliable allies but that the way was open for "continuous discussions" among the Big Three. The way to make progress with the Russians, he believed, was to talk to them face to face. Failure to make them equal partners in winning the war and making the peace would only lead to another war.[24] Hopkins had handled a number of problems in the preceding few months, but none as important as this.

It was with a sense that much could be gained that Hopkins, Roosevelt, chairman of the Joint Chiefs Admiral Leahy, and "Pa" Watson left the White House on the evening of November 11. They drove to the Marine base at Quantico, Virginia, where they boarded the presidential yacht *Potomac* for Chesapeake Bay. Five miles in the distance loomed the battleship *Iowa*. The cream of American battleships, and with its sister ship *New Jersey* the largest man-of-war afloat, the *Iowa* offered spacious and comfortable accommodations as well as almost perfect security against enemy submarines. The party boarded the next morning, and since Roosevelt shared the old navy superstition against beginning a voyage on Friday, spent the day relaxing. Just after midnight on Saturday, November 13, they sailed toward the Atlantic and by 2:00 A.M. were on the open sea.

This was the first of Hopkins's wartime trips to include Pa Watson, and he wasted no time making the most of the opportunity. For years he had loved to tease the genial, warm-hearted aide, who always took the ribbing in good humor but never seemed able to give as good as he got. The first night on the *Iowa,* Hopkins bet Watson five dollars that he could catch a fish from the deck. Watson took him up on it, and in the middle of the evening movie Hopkins walked in with four fish and a Marine and a mess boy to back up his story. Watson protested "ice box" but in the end had to pay up.[25]

Two days later all thoughts of joking were suddenly put aside. During a lull in an antiaircraft drill an officer two decks above began shouting: "It's the real thing! It's the real thing!" The ship started to zigzag; whistles sounded, flags went up, commands came from everywhere. A torpedo wake had been sighted on the opposite side of the ship. Hopkins passed the word to Roosevelt, who had cotton in his ears to dull the sound of the guns during the antiaircraft drill, and had not heard the alarm. Roosevelt asked where the torpedo was, and Hopkins made his way across the ship, arriving just as the *Iowa* cut loose at a wake some six hundred yards away. The fire missed, but so did the torpedo, which passed about twelve hundred yards astern. Fears of a German attack soon changed to anger and shock when an escorting destroyer reported that it had accidentally fired the torpedo when moisture from the rough seas grounded a firing circuit. Admiral King and the *Iowa*'s captain were not going to accept that story in the presence of their commander in chief, and they ordered an investigation. Hopkins passed off the incident with a bit of graveyard humor: "Can you imagine our own escort torpedoing an American battleship —the newest and biggest—with the President of the United States aboard—along with the Chief of Staff of the Army and the Chief of Naval Operations[?] In view of the fact that there were twenty Army officers aboard, I doubt if the Navy will ever hear the last of it." He concluded that the perpetrator "must have been some damned Republican."[26]

The rest of the voyage passed quietly, with the passengers free to enjoy themselves over gin rummy, movies, conversation, and books from the ship's library. The voyage took a week, giving Hopkins and the others time to confer about the upcoming conferences, which now included a meeting with the Chinese in Cairo. Hopkins stuck to his previously expressed values. In the Italian campaign the question had arisen whether to declare Rome an open city in order to save it from a destructive battle. Hopkins thought that military considerations should be decisive. If the Germans were pulling out, it would be better to allow Eisenhower to take advantage of Rome's communication and transportation facilities and move in with Allied troops. If not, he saw "political advantage"—a reference to the Italian-American vote—in asking the Germans to declare Rome an open city. The Italian vote and his desire to uproot fascism figured into Roosevelt's effort to reform the Badoglio government by including Count Carlo Sforza, a leading anti-Fascist and a popular figure among Italian-Americans. An outspoken opponent of the Italian monarchy, Sforza had refused to serve unless the king abdicated, but Churchill had objected. Hopkins saw this as another example of Churchill's "old tactics" of aligning himself with the reactionary forces of monarchy, imperialism, and the status quo. Hopkins suspected him of wanting to blame the United States if things went badly.[27]

Hopkins also contributed briefly to a discussion of what to do if Germany should suddenly collapse. Most of the talk dealt with positioning American troops for the occupation, but at one point Roosevelt remarked that there would be an Allied race for Berlin. Sources do not show why he believed this, although the most likely reason is that he thought that capturing the enemy capital would add to the prestige of the nation that accomplished it. Hopkins suggested preparing an airborne division to drop into the city "two hours after the collapse of Germany."[28]

On the evening of November 19 the *Iowa* passed through the Straits of Gibraltar and at about sunup arrived at Oran, Algeria, where the party disembarked and flew on to Tunis. There they were joined by Robert Hopkins, who had been at the Italian front as a signal corps photographer. After a couple of days' sightseeing they flew first to Cairo to meet with Churchill and Chiang Kai-shek. They left at night, Roosevelt and Hopkins taking sleeping berths and passing the trip asleep.

In order to affirm U.S. independence from the British and to strengthen the status of China as a major power, Roosevelt had instructed the Joint Chiefs to meet separately with the Chinese in Cairo. He and Hopkins did their part by dining privately with Chiang and his wife on the second night of their stay. Unable to offer Chiang much military aid, they discussed territorial arrangements. Chiang's requests were modest: the return of Manchuria, Formosa, and the Pescadores Islands. Hopkins drafted a press release that promised to return to China "such territory as Manchuria and Formosa" and also declared that "all of the conquered territory taken by violence and greed by the Japanese will be freed from their clutches." He then showed the draft to the British diplomat Alexander Cadogan, who noted that it said nothing about returning British possessions. As a result Hopkins, Cadogan, and Chung-hui Wang of Chiang's staff spent what Cadogan called "a silly afternoon" going over the document. Whenever Cadogan suggested a change, Wang replied that he preferred the original, to which Cadogan would respond: "I'm sure you do, Dr. Wang. My point is that I definitely don't." Hopkins sat back, apparently willing to let this go on indefinitely. At last Churchill sent a draft that deleted the phrase "freed from their clutches" and inserted, "Japan will also be expelled from all other territories." By changing "freed" to "expelled," Churchill avoided any ambiguities about whether British possessions might gain their independence. Wang was satisfied, and Churchill's draft became the basis of the formal communiqué.[29]

That evening Hopkins held a private meeting with Chiang. His cryptic notes on the conversation suggest that Chiang was worried about Russian interest in the warm-water port of Dairen, a traditional object of Russia's Asian diplomacy. He checked on this with Harriman, who told him that Russia desired peace with a strong China under Chiang's leadership, had no designs on Chinese territory, and had not raised the issue of a warm-water port.[30]

Hopkins's main concern was Overlord. His October exchange with Churchill had aroused his suspicions that the British were coming to the conference with a torpedo deadlier than the one the *Iowa* had evaded—a torpedo aimed at the cross-Channel attack. The situation had become even more muddied when word arrived in Washington that the Russians wanted to see a more vigorous effort in Italy and might even be willing to accept a postponement of Overlord to ensure it.[31]

These possibilities set the wheels spinning in Hopkins's head. At Oran he asked the U.S. Air Corps commander, General Carl Spaatz, whether strategic bombing could defeat Germany without Overlord. Spaatz assured him that it could and predicted that Germany would surrender three months after spring weather permitted the bombing to resume in full force. Spaatz's opinions, in addition to the threat of British and Russian opposition to Overlord, changed Hopkins's thinking about the command situation. Carrying out Overlord called for Marshall's leadership, but operations in the Mediterranean could be maintained with Eisenhower in charge.

In the past Hopkins had followed Marshall's lead. This time, however, there was another force that seemed to outweigh the general. Time and again at Oran, Hopkins described the Russian military effort in superlatives: "amazing," "astounding," "miraculous." Indeed the Russians seemed on the way to winning the war in Europe. Hopkins thought that this put them in a position to demand that the Western Allies do whatever was needed to support their efforts, even if it meant giving up Overlord. He carefully quizzed Spaatz about air operations that would most help the Russians.[32]

As a result Hopkins arrived in Cairo inclined to see British strategic opinions as irrelevant. Of course if the British could be persuaded to agree, so much the better; Hopkins had not lost sight of the goal of promoting cooperation among the Allies. Still, the frustrations of past encounters with Churchill had worn his good nature thin. Now, instead of encouragement and reassurance, he could offer only sharp words of impatience. Sitting through a CCS session at which Churchill dominated the discussion with pessimistic observations about declining Allied fortunes in Italy and the Balkans, missed opportunities in the Aegean, and the need to balance Overlord against operations in the Mediterranean, Hopkins lost all patience. Sir Charles Wilson found him "full of sneers and jibes" as he dismissed Churchill's reservations and charged that the prime minister had gotten "cold feet" about Overlord. "Some of us," he snarled, "are beginning to wonder whether the invasion will ever come off." Then he delivered a warning: "Sure, we are preparing for a battle at Tehran. You will find us lining up with the Russians."[33]

Hopkins's remarks and the manner in which he delivered them went a long way toward accomplishing U.S. purposes for the Tehran meetings. Emphasizing disagreements on strategy helped frustrate British efforts to achieve a united front. Going to the conference intending to respond to Russian requests, Hopkins interjected a note of indeterminacy that suited his and Roosevelt's taste for improvisation, personal diplomacy, and on-the-spot deals. This freewheeling approach knocked out whatever advantage the British might have expected to gain from their methods of careful, systematic staff work and formal discussion. Quite possibly Hopkins's comments to Wilson were his way of inviting the British to follow the American lead at Tehran, but he succeeded only in dimming their hopes for a fruitful outcome.

On the morning of November 27 Hopkins flew to Iran. When he arrived in Tehran the Secret Service carried off a successful charade by which the president and his party drove unescorted to the American embassy along back streets and byways while a formal procession followed the public route. Soon after they arrived, the Russians announced that they had uncovered a plot to kill one or more of the Allied leaders. Since the U.S. embassy was half a mile from the Russian and British embassies, which were separated by only a narrow alley, the Russians invited the Americans to move in with them and thus minimize the risks. The British had earlier offered to take in the Americans but had been refused because Roosevelt wanted to avoid appearances of Anglo-American collaboration. Now, however, the assassination story provided a handy excuse to dodge the British invitation while obtaining more convenient quarters for the conference, and the invitation was accepted.[34]

No sooner had the Americans settled into their new quarters than Roosevelt began to side with the Russians. At a private meeting with Stalin the president offered military assistance to the Russian campaign and postwar economic aid, attacked De Gaulle and the French political leadership generally, and agreed "one hundred per cent" with Stalin in opposing Western colonialism, making an exception only with regard to India for tactical leverage in dealing with Churchill.[35]

This meeting set the pattern for the conference. Roosevelt twice again met alone with Stalin and even went so far as to refuse an invitation from Churchill for a private talk. At dinner Roosevelt and Stalin would mercilessly tease the prime minister, once enraging him with light banter about how many high-ranking German officers they would shoot after the war.

In the meantime Hopkins tried to persuade the British to align with the United States. As soon as Roosevelt finished his conversation with Stalin, Hopkins reported it to the British to assure them that no plots were being hatched against their interests. Even his own teasing of the prime minister was filled with such good humor and affection that none could take offense. At one of the dinners he toasted Churchill by declaring that after a thorough study of the British Constitution he had learned that its provisions and powers were "whatever Winston Churchill wants them to be at any given moment." Churchill heartily joined in the laughter.[36]

Hopkins also tried to bring the British along on grand strategy. Although Roosevelt offered Stalin his choice of Western operations, Stalin favored Overlord. Immediately the Joint Chiefs adopted him as an ally against the British. As far as Hopkins was concerned, that settled the matter; there was "no God damned alternative left." When Churchill seemed bent on obstruction by refusing to set a date for Overlord to begin, Hopkins bluntly told that he had no choice but to yield as gracefully as possible. The next afternoon Churchill acknowledged that the decision had been made and spoke only of means to ensure Overlord's success.[37]

The conference produced accommodation on other issues. Stalin promised to enter the war against Japan as soon as Germany was defeated. On political issues he seemed willing to negotiate. He preferred Roosevelt's idea of breaking Germany into several small states to Churchill's more modest division that would incorporate southern Germany into a "Danubian confederation." He parried but did not rule out Roosevelt's proposal to hold elections in the Baltic States in order to satisfy American public opinion. He deferred comment on Russia's other territorial claims and expressed polite interest in Roosevelt's plan for a postwar peacekeeping organization. Much of the conversation was general and rambling, and did little more than introduce the subjects; but given the way Roosevelt and Hopkins had orchestrated the conference, this was beside the point. They had gone to Tehran not to settle issues but to learn if Stalin was open to discussion—if he was, in Roosevelt's phrase, "get-atable." They had found him not only that but supportive as well.

On one occasion Stalin took advantage of the conference's informality to put Roosevelt on the spot. At the second plenary session he asked who would command Overlord, declaring that until a leader was named, the Russians could not be fully confident of the operation. This demand caught Roosevelt off guard since the British had blocked plans to name Marshall to the post. In the end Roosevelt promised to decide within three or four days after the conference.

Robert Sherwood thought that the Tehran conference represented the peak of Hopkins's wartime service. Certainly it represented a peak in the recognition of that service. Harriman noted that Stalin, who usually waited for others to come to him whenever he entered a room, walked directly up to greet Hopkins when he first saw him. At one of the dinners Churchill proposed a toast to Hopkins, and after it had been drunk, Roosevelt leaned across the table and said, "Dear Harry, what would we do without you?"[38]

It was also a high point of Hopkins's service as a diplomat. Stalin and Churchill arrived in Tehran with their foreign ministers, but Roosevelt had left Hull behind and instead assigned Hopkins the job of representing the United States at the meeting of the Big Three diplomats.

The discussion got off to a peculiar start. Hopkins wanted to talk about how to establish postwar peacekeeping bases in Europe, while Molotov wanted assurances that France would be punished for its collapse and subsequent collaboration with the Germans. For several minutes Hopkins and Molotov pursued their topics in parallel, with Eden merely responding to each in turn. But even Eden's approach failed when he turned to Hopkins and in a friendly way said that Britain had leased bases in the West Indies to the United States not so much because it wanted U.S. destroyers in return as because it liked having the United States there. This, he ventured, might serve as an example for postwar arrangements. Probably wanting to demonstrate America's independence in Molotov's presence, Hopkins at once rejected Eden's views. Eden kept trying, and finally steered the discussion onto common ground.

At this point Hopkins drew the entire discussion into sharp focus. The president, he said, wanted postwar security arrangements worked out to ensure that the United States, Britain, and Russia would not arm against each other. This statement, which Hopkins ought to have made at the outset, got the others' attention and allowed him to proceed by specifying the problems likely to arise in establishing bases. How would the big powers set up such bases while still respecting the sovereignty of the host nations? The United States, he said, intended to keep bases in the Philippines. Perhaps other bases in the Far East could be placed under China or the United Nations. Establishing bases to protect against Germany would be a problem for the British and the Russians since Germany did not directly threaten the United States. He thought that this would be one of the most important postwar problems and that it would be worthwhile if the heads of state discussed it further.

They next turned to Turkey's role in the war. Roosevelt and Stalin doubted that Turkey would enter the war, for its leaders feared that Germany would overrun their country. But Churchill wanted to encourage Turkey, perhaps because he saw this as the last hope for his campaigns in the eastern Mediterranean. Hopkins, Eden, and Molotov all agreed that it would be desirable to have Turkey enter the war, but no one was able to respond to Eden's question of how this could be achieved without further discussions with the Turks. As the conversation faltered and drifted toward banalities, Hopkins offered a new perspective. Turkey's entry, he said, might lead to operations that would interfere with Overlord. Molotov at once declared that Stalin would oppose this. That was the response that Hopkins wanted. A week earlier, when he had thought that Russia might request U.S. help in the eastern Mediterranean, he had favored Turkey's entering the war and had minimized the possibility of its interfering with other operations. Now that Overlord had been confirmed, however, he moved rapidly to confirm the operation and its supporting landing in southern France.[39] Throughout the rest of the conference he cautioned against making too great an effort to entice the Turks. When the next plenary session agreed to invite the president of Turkey to Cairo for discussions aimed at encouraging him to enter the war, Hopkins broke in to declare that the Allies had to agree beforehand precisely what military assistance they could offer. The U.S. chiefs, he emphasized, had not considered detailed plans for the eastern Mediterranean and believed that no landing craft would be available for Churchill's operation against Rhodes. The Turkish president could not be told or even led to infer that such an operation was contemplated. All agreed to this, Churchill and Eden declaring that they would offer only aircraft, mostly fighter squadrons, and a few antiaircraft regiments.[40]

That night the conference ended in an effusion of good will. Churchill toasted the proletarian masses, and Stalin drank to the Conservative party and declared that without American aid Russia would have lost the war. Roosevelt ended the evening by observing that the different customs, philosophies, and ways of life represented at the conference had, like separate colors, come together to form "that traditional symbol of hope, the rainbow."[41]

Elated by the outcome, Hopkins flew on to Cairo to tie up the loose ends with the British and the Turks. With Overlord now beyond debate, he was in a mood to conciliate the British. His first chance arose when Churchill moved to cancel Operation Buccaneer, an amphibious landing in the Andaman Islands designed to complement the offensive in Burma. The operations in France, he declared, would leave too few landing craft. Roosevelt objected, calling the operation a moral commitment to Chiang Kai-shek and claiming that its cancellation would undercut all operations in Asia. As the talk moved back and forth, Hopkins took up the British argument and declared that everyone ought to decide whether the operations in France were so important that they should be augmented by landing craft from Buccaneer. When no one responded, he tried another tack, suggesting sending a wire to Admiral Louis Mountbatten, the British commander in Southeast Asia, to ask if he could complete the operation with the landing craft he had on hand. When Churchill grumbled that the operation's troop requirements were overblown, Hopkins brushed his objections aside, arguing that the issue was landing craft, not manpower. This temporarily turned the conversation back to his original point about augmenting the landings in France. The meeting adopted both of his suggestions—to study ways to support the operations in France and to wire Admiral Mountbatten. Before the results were in, however, Roosevelt agreed to cancel Buccaneer.

As the United States was giving up Buccaneer, the British were struggling to bring Turkey into the war. President Ismet Inönü was friendly but hopelessly afraid of Germany. After two sessions it was clear that Turkey would not declare war without adequate preparation, and opposed such preparations lest they lead to a German invasion. Hoping to get off this treadmill, the meeting resolved to give Eden and Hopkins the chance to try their luck with the Turkish foreign minister, Numan Menemencioğlu.

At the meeting Hopkins grilled Menemencioğlu in his best Lord Root of the Matter style: What were Turkey's minimum requirements? When Menemencioğlu evaded his question by complaining that Britain had not met its supply commitments, he rephrased to ask how far short the Turks were from having their minimum requirements. When Menemencioğlu gave a muddled and contradictory response, he persisted. "Was he to understand that the Turkish President considered he should have twice the air force suggested? Was he to understand that the anti-tank preparation was not enough? Were the Turkish railways a limiting factor? He asked because if Turkey was not coming into the war she must understand that these munitions, so vitally required elsewhere, would not come into Turkey at all."[42]

Faced with this prospect, Menemencioğlu backed off, declaring that Turkey intended to enter the war. He then batted figures back and forth with the British representatives until Hopkins cut in to drive home his point:

> In the last analysis [he declared] a country went to war in its own interests. [The Allies] wanted Turkey in the war even if she could not have all she wanted. Great Britain, Russia, and the United States had not all they wanted when they entered the war. At this critical period in the war the entry of Turkey might save the lives of hundreds of thousands of allied nationals. January 1st was not a set date but Turkish participation might not be useful very long after that date. [The Allies] wanted Turkey to enter the war about February even though [they] knew that in doing so Turkey might suffer. [They] hoped Turkey would enter because all allied

military and political opinion considered that her entry would shorten the war. Only the Turks themselves could speak for Turkish self-interest. If however discussions were prolonged about the adequacy of material etc. Turkey's entry would be futile. Turkey could be sure that if she came in [the Allies] would do everything [they] could—all possible military and air support would be offered her. He knew he was correctly interpreting President Roosevelt when he said that he hoped that Turkey would in her own interests come in willingly and wholeheartedly.[43]

Menemencioğlu again responded evasively, and Hopkins had to content himself with having stated the Allied case as clearly as possible. His efforts may have had some effect. At the last plenary session the heads of state agreed that after February 15 Turkey would begin to support the Allies while officially remaining neutral. This prompted Hopkins to scribble a note to Roosevelt: "Couldn't you see the President [of Turkey] *alone* for five minutes to say good bye—and *ask him to be ready to go to war Feb. 15?* Too many people here."[44] Roosevelt did take President Inönü aside for a final chat, but no evidence exists to indicate whether he followed Hopkins's advice.

Whatever the effect on Roosevelt, Hopkins's efforts encouraged Churchill. The prime minister left Cairo still hoping to bring Turkey into the war and to mount attacks on the Aegean islands. In both projects he was to be disappointed.

The final decision at Cairo also went Churchill's way, but in spite of and not because of Hopkins. In naming a supreme commander for Overlord the British now held the high cards. Roosevelt's promise to Stalin to name a commander within three or four days meant that the British had only to hold out a short time to block the American demand for one supreme commander for all of Europe. And in light of Stalin's uncompromising support, which guaranteed that Overlord would be carried out, Marshall seemed less essential to the success of the operation. Still, Hopkins believed that Marshall deserved the command to ensure his rightful place in history. Roosevelt preferred to keep Marshall in Washington, but to satisfy Hopkins, he let him ask the general about his own wishes. Marshall declined the opportunity to state a preference and told Hopkins that he would wholeheartedly support whatever the president decided. When Hopkins repeated this to Roosevelt the next day, the president decided to appoint Eisenhower to command Overlord.[45]

Hopkins returned to Washington from the conferences with his usual optimism. He believed that the war would be won within four months after the Allies landed in France. Stalin's territorial claims seemed modest, and he appeared willing to cooperate in keeping the peace. Churchill was still a stumbling block when it came to foreign policy, but Eden should be a helpful ally. Still, it looked as though the United States would wind up aligning itself with Russia and China against Britain and the other colonial powers. Hopkins's concerns show that military matters were fading from his thinking while diplomacy was assuming a larger role. Perhaps he thought, as he had every right to do, that the Cairo and Tehran conferences had turned not only the war effort but also his own career in new and promising directions.

His high spirits were short-lived, however. During a New Year's Day celebration with several friends, his vitality seemed to drain away. Saying that he felt a cold coming on, he excused himself and went to bed.[46]

# Chapter 20

# Where the Going
# Was Rough

Hopkins's cold turned out to be influenza. He stayed in bed for a few days and on January 5, 1944, checked into the Bethesda Naval Hospital. Tests revealed that his intestinal problems had recurred; his weight was down to 126 pounds, and other indications showed that his condition was poor. Initially he responded well to treatment, but then failed to progress. A consulting physician recommended an operation to enable more of his small intestine to absorb nutrients. He advised Hopkins to spend a few weeks in a warm climate to build up his strength and then to return to the Mayo Clinic, where his first surgery had been performed. Hopkins took the advice and in mid-February traveled to Miami, packing "an ungodly amount of medicine" and accompanied by a nurse to give him two injections a day.[1]

Some of the doctors, including a few at the Mayo Clinic, advised against the operation, fearing that they would find cancer. But Hopkins was determined to settle his condition once and for all and pressured them into going ahead. After he had spent three weeks building up his strength, the doctors operated on March 29.

"O.K., boys," Hopkins sang out as he was wheeled into the operating room, "open me up. Maybe you'll find the answer to the Fourth Term, or maybe not!"[2] The operation produced no news bulletins about Roosevelt's political plans, but the doctors found no cancer and were able to refashion Hopkins's intestine as planned.

Apart from Hopkins's wife and family, no one was more concerned about his illness than George Marshall. "My prayers are for your early and complete recovery," he telegraphed on the day of Hopkins's surgery. "I know you have one great reserve in your favor and that is cold nerve and great courage."[3] Marshall arranged for Hopkins to use the army hospital and rest cottages at White Sulphur Springs, Virginia, and when Hopkins was well enough to leave Rochester, Marshall flew there to accompany him. Friends who visited Hopkins in Virginia thought that he was recovering quite well, but in May he had a setback and could not return to Washington until July 4. After his return he gradually took on more work, husbanding his strength so that by mid-November he was feeling his old self and looking forward to getting off his medication.

While he was away, those who had worked closely with him felt his absence in ways difficult to express. "We miss you a lot down here," Bill Somervell wrote, "both your counsel and—well, just having you around."[4]

What had it meant to have him around? One thing his associates missed was his versatility. Hopkins once said that people who wanted to get ahead in Washington should not waste time with the big shots but should cultivate the "office boys" who knew how to get things done.[5] During the war he had come to know everyone in authority and at one time or another had had a hand in their business. He had become the supreme office boy of the war effort and probably of all American history. He had refused to let his WPA staff draw organizational charts, scoffing that they only wanted to put their own names in the middle box. By keeping to that principle, he had wound up with his name in the middle box on everyone else's chart. This led one observer to suggest that "perhaps a beginning point in understanding how our war effort operates is to get a true picture of how Harry Hopkins operates."

His associates also missed his warm sympathy and support. In a crisis he always seemed to understand what they were driving at, believed that it was the right thing to do, and enthusiastically did what he could to help. They appreciated how he always told them that the president thought that they were doing a great job and wanted to hear their ideas. When they challenged him on a point, he would put them at ease by responding with a smile or a soft laugh and admitting that he did not know all the answers. They knew that he could be short-tempered—snapping at a weak suggestion, cursing an unfortunate development—and impatient with or indifferent to subjects that did not interest him. But this was not the Harry Hopkins of their common experience. On countless occasions they had seen him lighten the atmosphere of a tense, argumentive session with a laugh, a grin, or a joke. That was what made meeting with him a refreshing experience.

Another key to his success was his ability to master detail, to examine columns of figures or a series of cables and to draw useful generalizations or spot particular problems. Like all successful executives he could see both the forest and the trees. In the same way he had developed a sense of personnel, of how individuals fit into an overall scheme. He had brought exceptionally able men—Harriman, Burns, Lubin, Cox—into the Hopkins Shop to solve problems before they reached him or the president. His detailed knowledge of the war effort enabled him to get action by calling the right people. His knowledge of people allowed him to offer sound advice about personnel changes and to smooth ruffled feathers. Most important, he worked as well as he did because he understood President Roosevelt's objectives and his conception of his office. Thus he could act on the president's behalf, settle disputes for him, and, when the president needed to be involved, lay out the alternatives and an appropriate course of action. Once he even ordered the Map Room, the White House communications center, not to send a message from Roosevelt to Stalin and afterwards persuaded the president to approve his action.[6]

Many appreciated his thoughtfulness. Any act of kindness or hospitality brought a personal note of thanks and often a small gift. He once arranged for Churchill to autograph a photo for the father of the pilot on one of his missions to London. He returned from Casablanca with a letter from a G.I. to his parents in Indianola, Iowa. He also sent the soldier a fountain pen to replace one he had borrowed and then misplaced.

Of course friends and relatives asked him for favors. He handled their requests by checking into the procedures and criteria while carefully avoiding using his influence, although he once broke his own rule to help the nephew of his former brother-in-law get an appointment at Annapolis, where he was made a first alternate in a selection process saturated with favoritism and political influence. And he arranged for his wife's brother-in-law, Commander Nicholas Ludington, to interview Churchill in connection with an assignment to study naval aircraft, although Ludington had to leave London before the arrangements for the interview could be completed. He firmly refused to help anyone get a deferment from military service.

His friends also missed his sociability during his long absence from Washington. Hopkins was an entertaining conversationalist, an eager and vivid storyteller always ready with an enjoyable quip or comment, and his meetings with Churchill and his dramatic flight to Moscow had given him some good stories to tell. Like most of his contemporaries in the White House he also liked to gossip about prominent figures on the Washington scene. Backgammon, poker, gin rummy, bridge, and sporting interests (he had the racing form specially delivered to his room) rounded out his social skills.

People also missed his sense of humor. It came through in the stories he told and in the one-line quips inspired by specific situations. As long as the United States continues to have a problem with agricultural surpluses, people will be able to laugh at his crack about reducing pork production by having boars wear roller skates on their hind legs. Or at a line that was much more original in 1942: "Mrs. Hopkins and I know that two can't live cheaper than one but it is much more fun."[7]

Upon hearing that his son David had bet his father's hat to columnist Leonard Lyons and had lost the bet, Hopkins, himself an inveterate gambler, remarked: "What is this nonsense about a father being responsible for the gambling of his children? Nothing doing. I doubt very much if they made the bet. I can't imagine a child of mine gambling!"[8]

Few escaped his good-natured jibes. When his race-track buddy Howard Hunter sent him someone's system for playing the horses, Hopkins acknowledged: "Whatever system this fellow has is surely better than anything you have!"[9]

Not even the Churchills escaped. Anticipating the contemporary birthday greeting card, he cabled the prime minister: "Dear Winston happy birthday. How old are you anyway?" Looking on the personal side of Anglo-American relations he commented: "All your British officers seem to be marrying American gals but this time the gals haven't any money."[10]

This kind of irreverence carried over to other things British. Lord Halifax spent a few trying weeks adjusting to Hopkins's addressing him as "Ed." During one of his visits to London, Hopkins contributed to a discussion of how the British might repay Lend-Lease by suggesting that they ship over some of their statues.[11]

He was equally irreverent about himself. He finished a letter commenting on charges from Republican Senator Charles Tobey, "I think somebody should hit Tobey right between the eyes," and adding, "That is a figure of speech." Thanking Leonard Lyons for showing his son Stephen around New York City one summer, he observed: "I trust that New York night life doesn't take hold on him in a big way. However I suppose there are things in life worse than that. He might become a columnist or a special assistant to the president!"[12]

His humor helped him keep his balance in otherwise grim situations: "David has been here for a while but has just been ordered to duty in the Pacific again. It is just as well because he is drinking up all my Scotch." Two days before his operation at the Mayo Clinic he reported: "Louie [his wife, Louise] is here and already knows everyone from the garbage collector to the Mother Superior. I am being prayed over no end."[13]

Hopkins's humor expressed the man: irreverent, direct, self-aware, entertaining. His relentless kidding was his way of trying to break through to others, to open them up and establish bonds of intimacy. At the same time his humor showed an assertiveness and self-confidence that belied his oft-expressed wonderment over his rise from humble origins. It demonstrated in a way his faith in democratic principles, his sense that people could tease each other and make fun of their titles and claims to distinction because, inside, they had so much in common.

There is evidence that others responded in kind. When Hopkins was convalescing from his illness, Roosevelt reported on a holiday at Bernard Baruch's estate in South Carolina. "I slept twelve hours of the twenty-four," he wrote, "sat in the sun, never lost my temper, and decided to let the world go hang. The interesting thing is the world didn't hang." Hopkins even inspired George Marshall to a witticism. Marshall reported on a weekend of gardening at his home in Leesburg, Virginia: "In effect, it is global war for me here in Washington and manure for me down at Leesburg. I prefer the manure problem to those of war."[14] Both remarks show the influence of Hopkins's trick of balancing one's personal feelings and official duties. Marshall's joke is all the more remarkable because it is almost the only evidence that he even had a sense of humor. Anyone who could inspire Marshall to joke about the relative attractions of manure and global warfare had accomplished a good deal.

There were some things, however, that Hopkins could not laugh off. Near the top of the list was criticism from the press. Hopkins was no stranger to press attacks and usually tried to ignore them. Still they hurt, and often with good reason. Before the war the press had helped thwart his presidential ambitions. Roosevelt's own mistrust of the press, which for a short period in 1940 caused him to conceal listening devices in his office to check how accurately the papers were reporting his press conferences, fed Hopkins's suspicions. Louise Hopkins, who was new to public life and politically unsophisticated, was hurt and upset by public criticism of her husband.

Of course many of the charges were nonsensical enough to convince any reasonable person that they had been contrived purely out of malice. The story about Hopkins's moving General Marshall into the Overlord command so that he could bring in Somervell and set up a global WPA is one example. Others charged that Hopkins arranged the promotion of his wife's brother-in-law and then sent him on sight-seeing trips in Britain. In fact Ludington's study of naval aviation won praise from Undersecretary of the Navy James Forrestal. One story, allegedly based on information from a "federal interdepartmental war bond committee," charged that Hopkins and other White House officials were not buying their share of war bonds. When Hopkins calculated his purchases, they came to 18 percent of his income, comfortably above the recommended 15 percent. A radio commentator claimed that Louise had taken an army plane to visit Hopkins at White Sulphur Springs, when the evidence indicates that she took the train. A particularly outrageous fabrication charged that Hopkins and Louise had commandeered a private yacht for their honeymoon. One version had it that they forced the Coast Guard to seize the vessel at sea with the owner and his wife on board. Actually the Hopkinses had spent their honeymoon on dry land, at a farm in Connecticut.[15]

Taking the cake was the *Chicago Tribune,* bastion of isolationism and diehard Republican reaction. During the Quebec conference in August 1943 that paper published a feature article comparing Hopkins to the Russian monk Grigori Rasputin, who had held sway over an easily hypnotized Czar Nicholas and Czarina Alexandra during World War I. It was a hatchet job if there was ever one. Astonishingly incompetent as comparative biography, the article could only have been intended to undermine Hopkins as a presidential adviser. The story appeared at a critical psychological moment for Hopkins. All that month he had been upset about unfair press comments. The *Tribune* piece, complete with a cartoon picturing Hopkins with Rasputin at his shoulder, was the last straw. In the past he had considered suing his detractors for libel, but Roosevelt and Hopkins's Lend-Lease associate Oscar Cox had talked him out of it, saying that public figures simply had to take this kind of abuse in stride. This time he would not be deterred, however. He asked Joseph Davies if he could "dig up some bright young men in your office who will tell me that these bastards can be sued for libel." Davies thought that Hopkins could put up a "formidable" case but warned that a suit would only give the story wider circulation. In the end Hopkins calmed down and decided not to sue.[16]

He was protesting a little too much. His public image was not as negative as he seemed to think. In 1941 *Life,* one of the nation's most popular magazines, ran a feature article that presented him favorably. The story referred to him as Washington's "other president," observed that he "loves children," emphasized how uncomplainingly he endured his physical ailments, and highlighted his "unique ability to get things done and his outstanding success where others have failed." Two years later Geoffrey Hellman wrote a similarly favorable profile for the *New Yorker.* Nor did he lack for allies in the battle for public opinion. He was friendly with the radio commentators Walter Winchell and Raymond Gram Swing and the columnists Raymond Clapper, Quentin Reynolds, and Leonard Lyons. At one time Lyons specifically offered Hopkins the use of his column to rebut press attacks. In addition Oscar Cox personally looked after Hopkins's public image and fed stories to the press to build him up.[17]

While none of the arrows shot in his direction hit the bull's eye, at least a few landed on the target. One such criticism concerned a lavish party Bernard Baruch gave in mid-December 1942 as a wedding present to the Hopkinses. Word of the affair leaked out, and since Hopkins had recently published an article calling upon Americans to sacrifice for the war effort, the anti-Roosevelt press was unsparing in running down the menu of delicacies and contrasting it with the spare offerings Hopkins had recommended for the average American. Although the occasion certainly reflected as badly on Baruch, revealing how he used his wealth to ingratiate himself with men of power, it also revealed in Hopkins an uncharacteristic loss of balance. In the past he had separated his public responsibilities and private entertainments. Vacations at fashionable resorts, he liked to say, showed him where the money for the WPA was coming from. Now, when he was helping to direct the war effort—and was devoting all his public energies to its success—he did himself no good by defending the occasion as just another party.[18]

Nor did he do himself much credit in reacting to another shot that landed closer to the bull's eye. Lord Beaverbrook sent Louise a wedding present of an eighteenth-century diamond spray brooch, consisting of eleven graduated leaves and nine clustered flowers on a diamond stalk. The gift cost Beaverbrook £1,260. Louise felt that there were no words to describe its beauty, and Harry called it "quite too much."[19] For once Hopkins and his critics agreed. News reports, however, exaggerated the gift, describing it as emeralds worth $500,000. Republicans in the House seized on the story and suggested that the gift was a pay-off for Lend-Lease. It so happened that the Lend-Lease appropriation was about to come up, and it seemed that the opposition might use the story to try to whittle it down. While the British embassy frantically tracked down the facts, Hopkins took advantage of the story's inaccuracies to issue an angry denial, but he failed to set the record straight.[20] In the end Congress decided not to investigate, and the Lend-Lease appropriation passed without difficulty.

Hopkins had found himself in the position of a public figure whose personal life had impinged on a public issue, and he had taken the usual way out by shading the truth. He had also acted to protect Louise, who was new to politics and whose associations with the wealthy inclined her to accept their extravagances as tributes to her husband.

Still, such conventional explanations do not satisfactorily exonerate a man of Hopkins's unconventional character. His ability to persevere in difficult situations, to find ways to surmount obstacles and take command by employing an uncompromising realism and candor, contrasts surprisingly with these sour and defeatist evasions. The best explanation seems to be that for one of the few times in his public career he was in an essentially helpless position. Holding no office other than chairman of the insignificant Munitions Assignments Board, he had to leave it to Roosevelt to speak on the central issues of the war. His knowledge of the highest military secrets and his tendency when speaking publicly to let his tongue run away with him caused him to avoid newsmen. During the war he held no press conferences. These constraints made it all but impossible for the public to gain a clear picture of his achievements. The resulting frustration encouraged him to see press criticism as unfair and politically motivated.

Beyond this, Hopkins's commitment to the war effort led him to think that attacks on its leaders aided the enemy. As a result he concerned himself excessively with internal security. Although the

Roosevelt administration's record in handling internal security showed more restraint than that of the Wilson administration in World War I, it was still marked by notable excesses, especially the internment of Japanese residents and Japanese-Americans. Historians have explained this action by citing military reverses in 1942, ethnic and racial prejudices, and the lack of a strong commitment in the Roosevelt administration to civil liberties.

These are valid and useful criticisms. But it may help to fill out the picture to note that the administration had entered the war after five years of almost unrelieved political frustration. Roosevelt's second term had recorded one major defeat after another, prompting one suggestion that between Dr. New Deal and Dr. Win-the-War there was Dr. Stalemate.[21] These failures had encouraged in the Roosevelt White House a kind of garrison atmosphere in which everyone expected to have to fight the war at home as well as abroad. Early in February 1942 Lubin sent Hopkins a memo purporting to describe the strategy of "The Disloyal Opposition." These "anti-democrats" including appeasers, profascists, Nazis, and many prewar isolationists, were suspected of planning to sabotage the administration by calling for an Asia-first military strategy and harping on the menace of Russian communism. The memo identified the movement's leaders as "the very senators, congressmen, and public figures who opposed the defense program and Roosevelt's foreign poicy . . . Hating Roosevelt more than they hate Hitler, they are apparently willing to see the country defeated rather than have a victory secured by a democratically-elected president with whose opinions they disagree."[22]

The memo told Hopkins what he was prepared to hear. A month earlier he had arrived at similar conclusions while reading over congressional comment on a special commission's report on the Pearl Harbor attack. He found it "ironical" that those who had opposed preparedness were now blaming the administration for the disaster. Included among the critics were a bipartisan trio of senators—David I. Walsh (Democrat of Massachusetts), who "hates the British more than he cares about his own country," C. Wayland Brooks (Republican of Illinois), who "is a Nazi-minded person," and Bob La Follette (Progressive Republican of Wisconsin), who, according to Hopkins, was a "pacifist" and whose brother Philip was "undoubtedly a Nazi."[23]

As usual he wanted to respond by—to use a favorite figure of speech—hitting them right between the eyes. He proposed tracking down favorable prewar comments about Hitler made by leading isolationists. He was sure that "we still have in this country many fascist-minded people, to say nothing of a flock of outright Nazis."[24]

Thus a suspicious Hopkins looked for threats to the war effort. Some of this suspicion arose from the perfectly proper need to keep sensitive war information out of the press. "Where in God's world," Hopkins wanted to know, "did [Arthur] Krock get that story" about Lend-Lease aid to Russia running behind schedule? He also fretted about the press getting information about shipping losses and production. He was probably wise to keep tabs on enemy aliens working on the docks. Inevitably, however, Hopkins's concern shaded into questionable areas. At one meeting he complained that it was "highly detrimental" to civilian morale and the war effort for the Rubber Director to complain that priority ratings for gasoline would make it impossible to accomplish the rubber program.[25] As a rule no one knew better than Hopkins the importance of morale in meeting challenges; but neither did anyone better appreciate the value of candor and realism.

Within the inner circles of the war effort Hopkins was able to keep these values in balance. The farther his view extended, however, the more one dimensional and uncompromising it became. He agreed entirely with a Democratic congressman who said that the war meant killing Germans and Japanese regardless of their character. "The whole kit and kaboodle of them are our enemies," he wrote, "and no nice talk about good Japs goes with me." For him that included American citizens of Japanese ancestry. Early in 1942 Roosevelt ordered the internment of all Japanese, both aliens and American citizens. Hopkins's role in the decision is unclear, but given his belligerent posture he probably said nothing against it. He consulted Assistant Secretary of War John J. McCloy about providing federal supervision for the sale of the internees' property in order to persuade them to move along more rapidly to the concentration camps. He also passed along a suggestion from a college friend who was a Congregational minister in Berkeley that Roosevelt publicly thank the Japanese for their patriotic cooperation in order to encourage them to go voluntarily and at the same time discourage white vigilantes. Steve Early thought the suggestion too controversial, and nothing came of it.[26]

In dealing with supporters of the European enemies, Hopkins was more selective but no more restrained. He asked for a list of all Americans who had received decorations from Nazi Germany and had not returned them. He read an antifascist publication, *The Hour,* sponsored by the Jewish Anti-Defamation League of New York City, and followed up their warnings about the domestic activities of Axis sympathizers. He proposed to Attorney General Francis Biddle to take away the citizenship of every naturalized member of the German-American Bund, the major prewar organization of Nazi sympathizers. And he passed along information about suspicious persons and publications to FBI Director J. Edgar Hoover.[27]

Such evidence shows more about Hopkins's state of mind than it does about the Roosevelt administration's official policies. Although Hopkins wanted the administration to take stern measures, he recommended neither new legislation nor any changes in the nation's internal security apparatus. And his response to press attacks on him contained no aspersions against the loyalty of his critics. Tempted though he might have been, he worried more about attacks on the administration's war policies than upon its policy makers.

By the time Hopkins was expressing these feelings, he was becoming more broadly involved in the domestic war effort. In December 1942 he began conferring with Roosevelt about manpower policy, and after the Casablanca conference the president appointed him to a special committee to study the subject. At issue was how to balance the army's request for a force of 11 million men against the nation's production needs. The committee approved the army's program and called for forceful management, especially by the Department of Agriculture, to staff the civilian economy. It stopped short, however, of recommending national service legislation that would have given the government the power to assign people to necessary jobs. Still, it concluded that "no person should be able to decide for himself whether or not he is to take part in the war effort and at what time or in what manner."[28]

No committee member favored this conclusion more strongly than Hopkins. Throughout the war his watchwords were military necessity. No civilian mail should take up air cargo space that the military might need. The army, he said, should run "this whole transportation business." Companies that tried to carry on business as usual or refused to "go all out" should be "taken over promptly." A protest over the closing of the Santa Anita race track in Los Angeles got nowhere with him: "Somebody must run this war and make decisions and those decisions can't possibly suit all of us . . . I would not presume to know what the military situation is that would require this action, but I would not be disposed to question the wisdom of it."[29]

Hopkins had just as little patience with striking labor unions as with laggard industrialists. When the United Mine Workers struck in the spring of 1943, he counseled the president to take a tough line, arguing that the War Labor Board should set the miners' wages. He and Cox wanted to threaten the miners by having Selective Service reclassify all those of military age for the draft. When the government took over the mines, he also proposed to penalize union officials who led a strike against any government-operated industry. "I am hoping," Hopkins declared, "that we are going to lick [United Mine Workers president John L.] Lewis this time. He is either bigger than the United States Government or he is not and it is high time we found out."[30] Over Roosevelt's veto Congress passed the Smith-Connally Act, which went beyond anything either he or Hopkins had contemplated in curbing wartime strikes. Lewis responded with undaunted defiance, though his men went back to work, and disputes in the coal industry continued into 1944.

Difficulties with Congress also drew Hopkins's attention. In early October 1943 five senators returned from a tour of the war fronts and chastised the administration for allowing Britain to run the war at American expense, and especially for sending U.S. troops to restore the British Empire in the Pacific. Hopkins advised getting British troops to the Pacific as soon as possible, preferably sending them across the United States to draw the maximum amount of publicity. He met with others in the administration to plan strategy for handling the incident in Congress and personally advised Churchill on how to respond to the senators' charges.[31] As usual he favored a belligerent response to the critics, but it was finally decided to offer calm rebuttals, supplemented with some behind-the-scenes politicking in Congress to end the dispute as soon as possible.

Hopkins preferred these trouble-shooting assignments to any permanent role in the domestic war effort. When Isadore Lubin suggested that he head a war cabinet to coordinate civilian and military production, he rejected the idea. In 1942 he coordinated the administration's anti-inflation strategy, but when Roosevelt decided to create an Office of War Mobilization to oversee the domestic war effort, he rushed to recommend someone else—James Byrnes—for the job. Hopkins recognized Byrnes's political assets—his long career in the Senate and his support of New Deal legislation—but to Roosevelt he emphasized Byrnes's personal qualities, his "loyalty, knowledge, judgment, and political sense," as well as his usefulness in advising Roosevelt "on other matters," traits that qualified him to take on broad responsibilities.[32] Byrnes agreed to accept the job, and the day after Roosevelt created the office, he announced the appointment.

Hopkins's recommendation showed that he expected Byrnes to be his counterpart in domestic matters and hoped that they would cooperate as Roosevelt's major advisers. Shortly after Byrnes had taken up his duties, however, Hopkins strolled over to his office to pay his respects, and got a surprise. "There's just one suggestion I want to make to you, Harry," Byrnes told him, "and that is to keep the hell out of my business." He said it with a smile, but Hopkins knew that he meant it. "I'm going to keep the hell out," he said to Robert Sherwood.[33]

And he did—almost. A few weeks later Hopkins offered Byrnes some advice on how to manipulate the Department of Agriculture, the War Production Board (WPB) and the Office of Price Administration to control food prices.[34] Byrnes knew good advice when he heard it and followed up. After that Hopkins held his peace, though he and Byrnes conferred on various topics.

If Hopkins wanted to stay on the fringes of domestic mobilization, many others wanted to be on the inside. Indeed by the end of 1942 they were falling over each other. Particularly ardent for a place of prominence was Bernard Baruch. A wealthy financier with a taste for high-level administration and political influence, Baruch was typical of the conservative businessmen with whom Hopkins had socialized in his New Deal days and with whom he was working closely in the war. The two had a cordial relationship—they were on a "Harry" and "Bernie" basis—and shared several friends in common, most notably Baruch's public relations manager Herbert Bayard Swope. It was even rumored that Baruch had lent Hopkins money so that he could stay in Washington after resigning as secretary of commerce.

Most of Hopkins's wealthy friends knew that they would be wasting their time trying to use his friendship for personal advantage, but Baruch hoped that Hopkins would help him take charge of war production. He had headed the War Industries Board during World War I, and now wanted to run the War Production Board. But Hopkins thought that it was better to promote someone from the ranks, and his choice was Donald Nelson. Baruch took the defeat with outward grace but began to talk against Hopkins behind his back.[35]

By the time Hopkins returned from Casablanca, things appeared to be going Baruch's way. Beset by conflicts with the military over priorities and challenged by pro-Baruch administrators on his staff, Donald Nelson seemed to have lost control. Hopkins was not surprised; he had been hearing of Nelson's inadequacies from Lubin, his representative at WPB meetings. Baruch had also worked his way into Byrnes's good graces, and about a week after Hopkins returned, Byrnes suggested that Baruch replace Nelson. Hopkins agreed.[36] Roosevelt took Hopkins's advice and offered the job to Baruch. But Baruch put off accepting long enough for Nelson to fire Baruch's main supporter on the WPB and to persuade Roosevelt to keep him on. Although Baruch had muffed his opportunity, he blamed Hopkins for the outcome.[37]

Nelson had survived Baruch's maneuver but he could not survive others. By the middle of 1944 he was being pressed by military opposition to his production plans and by a dissident faction led by Charles E. Wilson. Seeing the handwriting on the wall, Hopkins and Roosevelt decided to send Nelson to China to get him out of the way for a while. The arrangements were just being completed when the Nelson-Wilson feud blew up: Nelson denounced Wilson, Wilson threatened to resign, and eighty of his administrators said that they would go too.

To a team player like Hopkins, Nelson's behavior was incomprehensible. "What's the matter with Don?" he exclaimed when he heard the news. Nelson could never go to China if it became public knowledge that WPB wrangling was driving him out. With Byrnes's help Hopkins kept the lid on long enough for Roosevelt to announce Nelson's China trip and to say that he would return to the WPB. But this proved too much for Wilson, who then announced his resignation. Hopkins thought that Nelson ought to resign in order to pass off the incident as a "friendly disagreement" instead of a power struggle.[38] But Nelson would not go along, so Roosevelt named an acting chairman in his absence.

But Hopkins had not heard the last of Nelson. When Nelson returned from China, he agreed to resign only if the president would appoint him ambassador at large with an office in the State Department and a seat at Cabinet meetings. Hopkins sneered at Nelson's desire for "a fancy title" and feared, correctly, that State would object. But with election day only weeks away, he had to work out a compromise that would satisfy State and keep Nelson from resigning. It proved a tricky business—Nelson once blurted out that he was "going to drop the whole damn thing"—but Hopkins was finally able to use his ally at State, Stettinius, to complete a satisfactory deal and to make Nelson see that he had to give up something for the sake of the election.[39]

If Hopkins had trouble with businessmen like Baruch and Nelson, he had just as much difficulty with the administration's highest ranking liberal, Vice President Wallace. The two men were cordial but not close; Hopkins was the insider, Wallace the outsider. Thus while Hopkins worked to achieve balance and harmony among various interests and played the role of power broker, Wallace strove to keep liberal ideals alive. In a widely heralded speech, "The Century of the Common Man," Wallace called upon the United States to improve living standards in less developed countries, to oppose European colonialism, and to establish a world organization to maintain world peace. He also advocated postwar cooperation with Russia, both to preserve the peace and to prevent reactionaries at home from using anticommunism as a weapon against domestic reform.

Although there was nothing in Wallace's formulation that Hopkins could disagree with, their contrasting positions in the administration led to misunderstandings. A gathering one December evening in 1942 at Justice Frankfurter's was a case in point. Hopkins spoke against various of Wallace's statements, not because he opposed the principles behind them but because he believed that Wallace's formulations would cause trouble at the upcoming Casablanca conference. By failing to explain his reasons, however, he left Wallace thinking that Hopkins was a cynic who believed that everyone was motivated by self-interest.[40]

Bureaucratic rivalries disposed Wallace all the more to see Hopkins as a cynical manipulator. Shortly after Pearl Harbor, Roosevelt had appointed Wallace to head the Board of Economic Warfare (BEW), which had been established to acquire strategic raw materials and to keep American goods out of the hands of the Axis. When Roosevelt refused to allow the BEW to supervise Lend-Lease, Wallace chalked up the defeat to Hopkins.[41]

Other disappointments further alienated Wallace from Hopkins. In 1943 Roosevelt disbanded the BEW in the wake of a public feud between Wallace and Jesse Jones, the head of the Reconstruction Finance Corporation. Because Jones and Hopkins were bridge-playing friends, Wallace concluded that Hopkins had supported Jones against him and believed a (probably false) rumor that Hopkins had drafted the order that dissolved the BEW. The next year Wallace again thought that he saw Hopkins's hand at work when the Democratic National Convention dropped him as vice president and named Senator Harry Truman of Missouri. Since Wallace saw himself as the administration's outstanding liberal, he blamed his defeat on Hopkins's conservatism and warned Roosevelt against his influence.[42]

Wallace was misreading the signs. His difficulties resulted not from anyone's working against him so much as from his own failings. By letting his disputes with Jones make headlines and by failing to build a broad-based constituency in the party, he had made himself expendable. No one recognized this more clearly than Roosevelt, who long before the national convention had told his staff that he would not keep Wallace on the ticket. If Hopkins spoke against Wallace, it was because Roosevelt had given him his cue. Of course Roosevelt covered his tracks by telling Wallace that he wanted him as his running mate, and Wallace accepted his words too uncritically.

Wallace's doubts about Hopkins's liberalism were also uncritically formulated, though here the evidence was more substantial. While Wallace wanted the war effort to raise the living standards of the common man, Hopkins was trying to mobilize the common men and women of America to sacrifice for the war effort. While Wallace supported liberalism in the tradition of Jefferson by calling upon government to educate the public about policy objectives, Hopkins was acting as a power broker, shaping policies and ideas to balance the claims of self-interested parties. While Wallace was using the BEW to contract for raw materials from South America on terms that would improve conditions for workers on rubber plantations, Hopkins was writing to the BEW's executive director, "I have a feeling we can write the ticket pretty much in Liberia provided we do not do a lot of high grade exploiting of the natives."[43]

All that these contrasts really suggest is that Hopkins's liberalism was shaped by a different perspective. While Wallace, the outsider who was at home in a world of ideas, hoped to encourage public values to promote liberalism at home and abroad, Hopkins, the insider who moved easily among men, interests, and affairs, looked on liberalism in the context of power and practical accomplishment. In this sense Hopkins represented the New Deal's institutional legacy, which sought to keep liberalism alive by establishing a power base for it.

Hopkins intended to keep the New Deal afloat during the war by keeping power in the hands of New Dealers. Whenever the chance arose, he recommended people on the grounds that they had been New Dealers and were loyal to Roosevelt. Many of these were former associates in the WPA. When Hopkins and Oscar Cox once discussed a possible replacement for Stettinius in Lend-Lease, Hopkins emphasized that the person "ought preferably to be a New Dealer." "Don't get too downhearted," Hopkins assured someone who was concerned that labor was not being well represented in the administration, "because the president is still running this show and he is still surrounded by people who believe in the New Deal."[44]

Nor did Hopkins's definition of the New Deal change significantly. He had always maintained that prosperity depended on business expansion and that the social insurance and public works machinery should be kept active for help in hard times. Seeing full employment in wartime convinced him that there should also be full employment in peacetime. He did not abandon his New Deal faith that government had a responsibility to make up for the shortcomings of private enterprise. When Baruch recommended that reconversion to a peacetime economy should aim at "taking the government out of business" and curbing public works spending, Hopkins attacked him for ignoring "all the human aspects for whose benefit our great industrial system should be organized." After the 1944 election Hopkins joined Mrs. Roosevelt to lecture the president on the need to organize "our economic life in such a way as to give everybody a job."[45]

Thus Hopkins's wartime association with conservatism was largely a marriage of convenience. The war had confirmed his faith in the New Deal. Postwar prosperity would depend not on returning to laissez-faire free enterprise but on applying the goals of the New Deal: antimonopoly policies, a minimum wage, expanded social security, and public works. Tax policy should encourage capital expenditures, and the government should sell its wartime assets to broaden the investment base and discourage monopoly. The United States could profit from postwar reconstruction by making loans to foreign countries on the condition that they buy American goods. It could also expand its trade by selling industrial equipment to undeveloped countries. "Surely," Hopkins declared, "a new world is in the making and our whole concept of exploiting the under-privileged countries of the world simply will not do. It is going to be a pretty difficult pill to swallow for the die-hards here and in other countries, but I am convinced that the great mass of people in both the United States and England fully understand the necessity of genuine cooperation."

If Hopkins had been allotted a greater life span, he would have raised his voice against those revisionist historians who by the late 1950s and early 1960s were claiming that during the war the United States had sought to expand its influence by dominating world markets, that breaking down trade barriers and opening up colonial markets constituted an Open Door imperialism. He would have done so because he looked on America's role from a New Deal perspective that combined his social worker's desire to improve living standards with a Wilsonian belief that political freedom and democracy were a necessary part of a healthy world order. If the United States remained true to these values, it would not simply shoulder aside the European colonial powers and take their place; it would develop relations that benefited all concerned.

The key here was international cooperation. Managing the war emergency had required the Allies to pool their resources and through negotiation to discover that they shared the same values—the four freedoms. Thus Hopkins had hope for the future. No chart of organization or method of assigning authority could guarantee peace and friendship; only values in "the hearts and minds" of Americans could do that.

This vision, which Wallace could easily have endorsed, shows that Hopkins had not strayed from liberalism. Of course his behind-the-scenes experiences proved that the war effort was a good deal less idyllic than the harmonious affair he pictured. Indeed he often achieved harmony by playing special interests off against each other. Still, his public views were not merely liberal pap for the masses. Hopkins honestly believed that the United States could achieve a cooperative, universally beneficial world order. He bristled at suggestions that his country was fighting for its own imperialistic advantage.[46]

Hopkins's relations with Eleanor Roosevelt also revealed his connection with wartime liberalism. As he moved into the president's inner circle and devoted his energies to managing the war, he drew away from Eleanor, not because of any differences on their part but because Eleanor and Franklin had long since taken up separate lives. Anyone who entered the White House faced two strong personalities who demanded undivided loyalty. Hopkins, who worked easily with women and who shared Eleanor's social worker values, would probably have preferred to move in both circles. While living in the White House, however, he learned that he could not do this, and so by necessity he gravitated into the president's orbit. This encouraged Eleanor to see Hopkins as others on the fringe of the president's circle saw him. Feeling rejected, Eleanor concluded that he had only used her friendship to get closer to her husband.

As she reassessed Hopkins's motives, Eleanor also reassessed his principles. Instead of the liberal idealist, he now seemed a frivolous opportunist, less the socialist than the socialite who sought the favor of the wealthy and encouraged the irresponsible playboy streak in her husband's character. Like many other New Deal liberals who found themselves outside the Roosevelt and Hopkins circle, she concluded that he had allowed the war effort to crowd out New Deal reform.

At the time of his third marriage Hopkins was still living in the White House, and Louise's arrival brought another uncomfortable adjustment. With a stepmother on hand, Eleanor's relationship to Hopkins's daughter, Diana, became ambiguous, and a few awkward moments over Louise's placing guests at dinner and accompanying the president to official receptions further dimmed Eleanor's enthusiasm for the living arrangement. As a result she assigned to Louise the same traits of fun-loving shallowness she had attributed to Harry and began to tell people that she feared that being raised at the White House was bad for Diana.[47]

Hopkins might have shut out Eleanor completely (some of Eleanor's partisans thought that he did just that), but, despite the strains on their personal relationship, he tried to make a place for her in the war effort. He encouraged her to take a post in the Office of Civilian Defense and suggested that she visit England in the fall of 1942, even helping with the arrangements. Just after he returned from Casablanca to discuss postwar planning with Eden, he invited her in for a talk about food and education policy. A few weeks later he got a shock when Eleanor told him that army counterintelligence had been keeping her under surveillance and had placed microphones in the room she had occupied in the Blackstone Hotel in Chicago. She did not like it and wanted it stopped. What followed is unclear, but Hopkins seems to have had the counterintelligence operation dismantled. The following year he and Eleanor collaborated to encourage the president to revive the New Deal after the war. Such overtures overcame Eleanor's bitterness. On

April 1, 1944, she replied to an angry, abusive attack on Harry from his brother Rome's widow by declaring, "He has never gone back on a friend."[48]

Actually, if Hopkins's relations were wearing thin with anyone in the White House, it was with FDR. This friction in no way devalued the importance of their partnership: Hopkins remained Roosevelt's most trusted lieutenant and most congenial companion, and as the war continued, Roosevelt's regard for Hopkins grew. His sentimental toast to Hopkins at the Tehran conference was one indication of this. Early in 1944, after Hopkins had been ill for nearly a month, Roosevelt and Harold Smith discussed increasing Hopkins's salary from $10,000 to $15,000 a year. Roosevelt had suggested the increase earlier, but Hopkins had blocked it, arguing that it would only bring criticism of the president. Now Roosevelt brought up the subject again, proposing to reduce the amount to $12,000 and to delay putting it into effect until Hopkins returned to work. As Roosevelt discussed Hopkins, Smith noted that there was "a certain amount of emphasis in his voice when he said that 'Harry is very ill.'" Smith also thought that Roosevelt felt "deeply" about the financial sacrifices Hopkins had made to serve him.[49]

It was in the nature of their relationship, however, that Roosevelt could never be too solicitous of Hopkins's well-being. As the president's most trusted and effective subordinate with wide-ranging and critical contacts, Hopkins had become an instrument of state and thus had to be at the president's disposal. In this regard it may be worth noting that Hopkins visited London only at Roosevelt's request, never at Churchill's. The only time Churchill successfully used his friendship with Hopkins to outmaneuver Roosevelt was on the subject of sharing information about the atomic bomb. If some of his other efforts appeared to succeed, it was only because Roosevelt independently came around to Churchill's position.

Inevitably Hopkins came to believe that Roosevelt was manipulating him. "The president has never given me a job because he thought I could do it," he told Morgenthau. "That has never influenced him. He has only given me a job when he wants me to do it." This feeling of being at the president's beck and call was particularly evident in his family life. He and Louise were afraid to make so much as a dinner engagement lest Roosevelt should suddenly decide that he wanted their company.[50]

Thus for Hopkins living in the White House was not everything that outsiders imagined it was. Ministering to wounded egos, drawing the fire of the anti-Roosevelt press and the suspicions of frustrated bureaucrats, juggling the president's problems, trying to head a family with an uncertain domestic status, and going broke in the process all pushed him into a dark corner of his room at the top. By the middle of 1943 he knew he had to get out. Hopkins asked Roosevelt's permission to move. "Louise and I are hoping to get a house before the first of November," he wrote Donald Duncan, "which will suit me no end." Actually the Tehran conference delayed the move until December, but at last he, Louise, and Diana rented a house in quiet, residential Georgetown. Still, not even this came easily; Republicans falsely charged that he had used his influence to obtain a new refrigerator.[51]

Hopkins hoped that having a home of his own would allow him more time with his family. He also wanted to continue the process begun at Tehran, where he had represented the president at the foreign ministers' meetings. With the war effort moving toward victory, the crises he had previously managed seemed under control, and he needed to go on to new and less familiar territory. Shortly after Hopkins recovered from his illness, he suggested that the president appoint him high commissioner in Germany to supervise the military occupation. Roosevelt did appoint him to a special committee to consider policy toward Germany but suggested that for the longer term he consider replacing Winant as ambassador to Britain. Hopkins doubted that the Senate would confirm him, but Roosevelt thought that it would in order to get him out of the country. The conversation was general, however, and nothing was decided while Roosevelt and Hopkins were preparing for the upcoming Big Three conference at Yalta. As his hopes for an assignment faded, Hopkins began to think about serving as a roving ambassador without portfolio, representing the president somewhat as Colonel Edward House had represented President Wilson.[52] Ironically, his chance for such a role came only after Roosevelt's death.

As things turned out, Hopkins gained an independence that he could not have sought. His strength had not fully returned, and he could work only briefly each day. Roosevelt, who had always worried about Hopkins's health, knew that the doctors feared that in his weakened state, another major setback would kill him. So the president kept him out of principal decisions and sought advice from others, most notably Morgenthau.

Perhaps Roosevelt also wanted to keep Hopkins in the background for political reasons. By the end of 1943 Hopkins was convinced that bad publicity had turned him into a political liability for the president.[53] Since the war would continue beyond the election, there was no doubt that Roosevelt would run for a fourth term. By the time Hopkins returned to Washington, the Republicans had nominated Governor Thomas E. Dewey of New York for president and Senator John Bricker of Ohio for vice president. A couple of weeks later the Democrats endorsed the Roosevelt-Truman ticket. Throughout the year Hopkins had been developing a case of campaign jitters, fearing that the election would be close and that only the continuation of the war would give Roosevelt a chance.[54] This view dictated that he keep a low profile. Still, he remained active behind the scenes, advising on campaign strategy and drafting speeches. He and Louise contributed $100 to the campaign. As election day approached, he relaxed a bit and confidently predicted a Roosevelt landslide.[55]

In the end the election proved not to be the landslide Hopkins had predicted but was still a comfortable victory for Roosevelt by a margin similar to that of 1940. Hopkins thought that the outcome showed that the American people had confidence in Roosevelt's handling of the war, though many opposed the fourth term and, Hopkins said, "our past domestic policies." At home Americans accepted the New Deal but opposed more economic experimentation.[56] Thus the election confirmed the wisdom of Hopkins's growing involvement in foreign affairs, since opportunities for creative work on the domestic front seemed to be coming to an end.

Hopkins's heavy government duties took their toll on his family relationships. During the war Hopkins had drifted apart from most of his family. Although he and Adah had resolved their differences over his divorce, they were in touch only occasionally. His contact with Lewis primarily concerned health matters, his own and those of Emery, who had developed multiple sclerosis. His communication with Rome's widow ceased altogether, causing her to complain bitterly that he had turned his back on his family. He heard from his mother's relatives, and enjoyed visits from Barbara's brother Donald Duncan and Louise's brother-in-law Nicholas Ludington, both of whom were naval officers.

His relations with Diana, who was in grade school, were difficult. He spent what time he could with her, but his crowded, unpredictable schedule and preoccupation with the war severely limited his capacity

*Harry, Louise, and Diana in their Georgetown home, 1945*

for involved fatherhood. At times being a parent seemed a burden. Eleanor Roosevelt had tried to rear Diana but could not give her the affection a young child needs. Louise's arrival promised some hope, but the tensions of White House domestic life moved her to take a volunteer nursing job in a nearby hospital, which meant that she was away most of the day. Diana made the best of it. Bright and resourceful, she hung around with the servants, rode the dumbwaiter, listened to radio serials, and devised other entertainments. Still, nothing quite compensated for the lack of a close and ready source of affection.[57]

For himself, Hopkins did find love in his marriage to Louise Macy. She had grown up in a fashionable society in Pasadena, California, attended private schools in the East, and became Paris fashion editor of *Harper's Bazaar*. When the war came she returned to the United States, where she tried unsuccessfully to establish a dress shop in New York City. She then took a job as a nurse's aide and began looking for other war work. She and Harry met early in 1942, when a friend recommended her for a job. Louise was then a sweet, poised woman of thirty-five with plain good looks, a bright, ready smile, and a tactful good nature. They saw each other as often as they could. Early in July 1942 he asked her to marry him and she agreed. They scheduled the wedding for July 30. Then Hopkins flew off to London to discuss the second front with Churchill. "You better keep that date," Louise admonished him from Washington.[58]

It would be tempting to speculate that Louise gave Hopkins quiet comfort amid the grim burdens of war mobilization and strategy. She probably did, but more to the point she awakened his boyish spirit. From London, Hopkins wrote to General Hap Arnold: "Will you please let Louise Macy . . . know from time to time about this trip of mine? And will you tell your secretary if she calls to let her talk to you? It wouldn't hurt you at all to talk to a good looking gal once in a while!"[59]

But not even Louise could take him away from the war. Inevitably Hopkins's immersion in the war effort fostered a moral commitment. When a conscientious objector asked about obtaining a job in a postwar planning agency, Hopkins discouraged him from applying. Modern war, he told the young man, involves "the whole civilian population." All civilian jobs were related to the war, and a conscientious objector should accept the jobs provided by Congress.[60]

In this spirit Hopkins published a series of magazine articles that encouraged the American people to accept home-front mobilization. All Americans—men and women—would be assigned useful work. Taxes and rationing would regulate their standard of living. The wealthy would be less well off and the poor would live better. All, however, would live better than their allies. The average Russian, he pointed out, subsisted on 1,500 calories a day and the average Briton on 2,900; the average American would have 3,000 calories and a balanced diet. The changes would take some getting used to, he admitted, but there was no alternative if the United States were to win the war. In the end Americans would learn through sacrifice. As "the casualty lists begin to come in," he predicted, "the public and private conscience will be aroused. Men and women won't want to do less than their duty. And when your neighbors and your conscience are aroused you'll get in there and do your part."[61]

The response to Hopkins's articles was not what he expected. Congress failed to pass comprehensive manpower legislation, and the vast majority of Americans felt the government's hand, if at all, much more lightly than he had predicted. Still, his appeal to the American people struck a responsive chord. A few complained that he was advocating regimentation or quibbled about specific recommendations, but most who responded to his articles wanted to help the war effort. A large number were in their fifties and sixties, people who considered themselves able-bodied but who had been turned away from war work because of their age. One fifty-seven-year-old man who had offered his services to the army, navy, and FBI and been rejected wondered why women should be accepted for war work before men like himself had been placed. A few, young and old, saw the war as a chance to realize personal ambitions and asked for help in landing specific jobs. Others seemed genuinely inspired by the chance to sacrifice for their country, such as the beauty-shop operator and gift-store owner who were willing to sell their businesses to do war work. One woman asked if she should continue preparing to teach; she decided to go ahead when Hopkins advised her that "the education of young persons is a job which cannot be allowed to lapse even in war time." One mother of three small children felt that she had to explain to Hopkins that she was not looking for war work because her husband was away in the service and her children "felt better" with her at home. A woman in her fifties reported that she had withdrawn $1,200 from her retirement fund and traveled from Long Beach, California, to Washington, where she went from office to office until, with only one dollar left, she wound up in Caracas, where she worked for the Venezuelan government for two months before finding a secretarial job at the U.S. embassy.

None of these letters touched Hopkins more deeply than one from a black man in Selma, Alabama, who wanted to leave his job as a typist in a mattress factory for a drill-press or punch-press job in a war plant. He had heard of such jobs in Baltimore and Richmond and had also heard that excellent work was being done there by persons who, like himself, were blind. "I want to answer this," Hopkins wrote Lubin. "Can you tell me to whom I can refer it?" Lubin passed it and the others to the War Manpower Commission, where the Industry Program Division drafted a reply.[62]

When one correspondent said that it was too bad that more Americans did not think as Hopkins did, Hopkins replied that his mail had convinced him that "the American people have become well aware of the meaning of total war, and are determined that everything necessary to insure a victorious conclusion must be done."[63] As he looked over these letters, he may have heard echoes of those New Deal experiences that had been captured by Lorena Hickock's reports on relief conditions for his WPA, his own observations, and his social worker's conscience, which led him to assume that, as Labor Secretary Frances Perkins put it so well, "The People Mattered." Hopkins had become a power broker and had come to expect that government initiative would be needed to mobilize Americans for war. The responses he received showed that a large number seemed capable of mobilizing themselves.

Still, for him no job counted as much as being a soldier. He believed that all young men who were physically fit should be trained to fight, without exception. He did not believe that "Clark Gable or Jimmie [sic] Stewart are more important as movie actors in building up morale than they are as soldiers."[64]

Not surprisingly, Hopkins warmed to the military conception of "blooding," an inelegant but descriptive term meaning that soldiers best learn their trade in combat. "I have long believed in the thesis," he wrote one of the American combat generals, "that the only way an army gets morale is by fighting. And certainly all the outfits I saw in Africa have acquired it. The only thing they want to do is fight some more and when they do, I am sure they are going to do it extremely well." He even studied the faces of American soldiers, surprising Gen-

*Hopkins inspects troops in North Africa in January 1943 while General George Patton looks on*

eral George Patton by commenting on "the similarity of the set of the
mouth" among men who had been wounded or decorated.[65]

Hopkins's attitude toward suffering and death matched the experience of combat soldiers. Many, perhaps most, came away from war
ascribing their survival to good luck. That was the way with most of
life's events, or so it seemed to Hopkins. By the time of the war many
of his friends had experienced the death of loved ones, and he himself
had been hurt beyond consolation. Characteristically he saw such
losses as "a terrible bit of luck," "a very bad break." Even the war itself
was a tough break that people would have to accept. "After all," he
observed, "we are all in the same boat and if it is worth fighting for
someone has got to do it."[66] There was nothing to do but pick up the
pieces and get on with living. He admired Churchill because he had
taken the shock of Tobruk and, though shaken, was soon thinking of
new ways to win the war. Similarly he admired the way Roosevelt
guided the war effort with grace and balance amid the sniping of his
critics. He set a standard for himself to see the conflict through with
humor, courage, and a sense of adventure.

Thus he was proud that his sons were taking their share of the risks,
Robert as a photographer in the Signal Corps in North Africa and Italy
and David as a naval officer in the Pacific. They had entered the service
the Hopkins way, without special favor, and had come up through the
ranks. He expected no less of them than of any other soldier. "I had a
letter from Robert the other day," he wrote his friend Harry Butcher
of Eisenhower's staff, "and he seemed to be a little unhappy because he
is not seeing any action. I assume that is true of all the boys over there
that are not in it. However, anything that you could properly do to get
him near whatever fighting takes place I know would please him very
much." When Butcher informed him that Robert would take part in
the invasion of Italy, Hopkins was "very pleased that he is going in the
hard way . . . It will be a great adventure for him to look back on years
from now."[67]

Stephen also fit the Hopkins pattern. As soon as he graduated from
high school in 1943 he enlisted in the Marines. He passed up an
opportunity for officer's training so that he could follow his drill in-
structor into action. He was assigned to a machine gun company and
sent on the invasion of Namur in the Marshall Islands. His job was to
carry ammunition, but in relieving a battered company he got into
action chasing some retreating Japanese soldiers from their front-line

pillbox. As he and his company ran past fallen enemy soldiers, one suddenly rose up to throw a grenade. Stephen shot him down. During the next few hours he carried ammunition through heavy fire. He had moved to his position on the flank and was digging a foxhole when a sniper's bullet struck him in the head. His buddies, many of whose lives he had saved, carried him to the medical area, and from there he was taken to the hospital ship. He died without regaining consciousness and was buried in a lagoon at one end of the island.[68]

Words of sympathy poured in to Hopkins from those high and low. Churchill sent a card engraved with brave words from *Macbeth*. Even Hopkins's critics joined in mourning his loss, noting that he had not used his political influence to protect his sons.

Stephen's death affected him deeply but did not change him. When George Marshall offered to pull Robert out of Italy, he turned him down. At their meeting in Tunis he and Robert had agreed to meet in Berlin, and he wanted to keep that date. In any case, as he told Marshall, he was sure that Robert would "now have a personal reason to stay for Robert and Stephen were very close and devoted. It would break his heart to be sent home now."[69]

Several weeks later, as the troops were poised for the Normandy invasion, he wrote Eisenhower: "I hope you will let Robert go on the invasion whenever it comes off. I am fearful—and I am sure Robert is too—that because one of my other boys had some bad luck in the Pacific that Robert's C.O. may be a little hesitant about putting him in. The war is 'for keeps' and I want so much to have all of my boys where the going is rough."[70]

# Chapter 21

# Comeback

Hopkins was well enough to return to work in July 1944 to face a summer and fall filled with familiar difficulties. The war effort seemed to have slipped into a formless muddle. Crises kept cropping up, demanding on-the-spot resolution. To make matters worse, his own status with Roosevelt was uncertain. Even the British were considering abandoning him as a useful ally. But Harry Hopkins had made astonishing comebacks before, and he had another one in him. By the end of the year not only had he been reinstated as Roosevelt's chief adviser but also because of him the war effort was operating more systematically than ever before.

Achieving this, however, was an uphill struggle. He had no sooner returned to work than the British tossed him a tough Lend-Lease problem. As usual the culprit was the War Department, which had proposed to curtail Lend-Lease severely during the interval between the anticipated defeat of Germany and the eventual fall of Japan. (In their persistent efforts to maintain a language barrier the Americans called this Phase Two of Lend-Lease and the British Stage Two.) Specifically the War Department objected to any aid for the British civilian economy or any military aid that would permit the British to convert their war industry to civilian production. When Isadore Lubin warned Hopkins that this policy would lead to a trade war and deteriorating relations between the two nations, Hopkins went to work on Britain's behalf, suggesting that the chancellor of the exchequer attend the next Roosevelt-Churchill conference in Quebec and that the British plead their case to Morgenthau, who was to visit London shortly. Most important, he proposed that Roosevelt simply declare that Lend-Lease would continue as usual during Phase Two. He then arranged for Halifax to visit Roosevelt to settle the matter.[1]

When Halifax arrived at the White House, however, Roosevelt evaded the issue of Phase Two and instead seemed preoccupied with his campaign for reelection. When Halifax mentioned his conversation with Hopkins, the president "did not seem particularly interested." The reason soon was clear: Hopkins had become irrelevant. Within a week Halifax was advising London that Hopkins's opinions "should not (repeat not) be decisive in determining our action in this matter."[2] From that time forward Phase Two discussions centered on Morgenthau. Hopkins did not attend the Quebec conference.

What had happened? The common explanation is that during Hopkins's long illness Roosevelt had come to rely on other advisers and in any case wanted to spare Hopkins the physical strain of his previous duties. Some evidence supports the first explanation. Shortly before Halifax had his conversation with Roosevelt, Morgenthau had briefed the president on his trip to London. The secretary's obvious concern for helping the British during Phase Two inspired the president to turn the matter over to him. Thus Roosevelt was indifferent when Halifax brought up his conversation with Hopkins. Hopkins also believed that he had fallen from Roosevelt's favor and made a point of mentioning it to Churchill.[3]

Morgenthau's replacing Hopkins in the president's good graces was a personal blow for Hopkins, but at least it caused no disruption of Phase Two policy; at the second Quebec conference in September, Roosevelt and Morgenthau stayed on the course Hopkins had set and offered an agreement that Churchill accepted with tears of gratitude. When it came time to discuss the postwar treatment of Germany, however, matters were entirely different.

Morgenthau had returned from London convinced not only that Britain needed generous Lend-Lease aid during Phase Two but also that the Allies' agreement at Tehran to dismember Germany, as he understood it, was being undermined by the State and War departments. Believing that world peace required a weak Germany, he set about conferring with Roosevelt and Hull and then setting up a committee in Treasury to work out a specific policy. This took the initiative away from Hopkins, who had been conferring with Stettinius at State and Assistant Secretary of War John J. McCloy about the U.S. occupation of Germany. As soon as he heard that Morgenthau believed that State and War were opposing his efforts, Hopkins advised Stimson and McCloy to meet with Morgenthau. He also told Morgenthau that McCloy wanted to be "tough" on Germany. A few days later Roosevelt brought the interested parties together by appointing a special committee that included Hopkins.[4]

The Treasury (or Morgenthau) Plan, as it came to be known, proposed to deindustrialize Germany by internationalizing major manufacturing areas such as the Ruhr Valley and removing plants and equipment as reparations to the Allies. It also proposed to divide Germany into northern and southern states. Morgenthau argued that limiting German industry would also help Britain's economic recovery by creating a European market for its own industrial production.

At first Hopkins was skeptical of Morgenthau's plan. As he remembered it, at Tehran the Allies had agreed only to partition Germany and had reserved the right to discuss the subject further. He himself was inclined to seal the German borders and let the Germans deal with their Nazi masters themselves. The trouble with the Americans and the British, he thought, was that when they saw someone about to be hanged, they rushed in to stop it regardless of who the miscreant might be. The more he thought about Morgenthau's approach, however, the better he liked it. With the Allies sweeping into Paris after breaking out of the Normandy beachhead, the war might end at any time, and the Morgenthau Plan promised a simple, direct solution to the German problem. Also, Morgenthau seemed to have Roosevelt's support. So Hopkins went into the committee on Morgenthau's side.[5]

At the first meeting all seemed agreed except Secretary Stimson, who argued that Western Europe's economy depended on German industry. Seeing a chance to settle things quickly, Hopkins approached Morgenthau after the meeting and proposed that they meet with Roosevelt and allow Stimson to discredit himself before the president. Stimson's views were "terrible," Hopkins declared. The Secretary had "grown up in that school [where] property, God, becomes so sacred." Hopkins assured Morgenthau that he would prime Roosevelt for the meeting.[6]

Yet again, however, Hopkins and Roosevelt moved in different directions. At the meeting Hopkins tried to focus the discussion with a strong argument against Germany's being allowed any steel mills or war plants. But the president diverted him and Morgenthau with irrelevant remarks and hustled them out of his office.[7]

Once he saw that Roosevelt was not going to provide leadership on this issue, Hopkins threw himself into reconciling the parties. The next day he helped the War and Treasury departments draft a directive to Allied troops to maintain order behind their lines when they entered Germany. Hopkins pressed for a simple policy that would not hamper the fighting. "Until this damn German outfit gives up," he declared, "Eisenhower isn't going to be brought in on this thing. I think he will do all he can to implement that directive but God Almighty there will be fighting like hell and Eisenhower isn't going to waste much time thinking about this in terms of the battle." He did object to a proposal to have German officials remain in their jobs. The War Department argued that this would make it easier to arrest them, but, recalling the controversies generated by deals with the Fascists Darlan and Badoglio, Hopkins feared that it would only produce an embarrassing "publicity kickback."

While he developed a common ground between Treasury and War, he also pushed State's recommendation to appoint a high commissioner to supervise the occupation after the fighting ended. He first recommended James Byrnes, who had wanted the vice presidency and who, Hopkins thought, should have a consolation prize. When Byrnes turned down the offer, Hopkins discussed other choices with Morgenthau. The secretary rejected Harriman and McCloy, so Hopkins turned to Assistant Secretary of War Robert Patterson, who had made a good record in war production. Morgenthau thought that Patterson would be "perfectly swell," and from then on, Hopkins boosted Patterson's candidacy whenever he got the chance.[8]

This came at a high cost to his own ambition. As Morgenthau suspected, he would have liked the job himself. But his health seemed to rule it out. When Hull openly recommended him at a White House meeting, Roosevelt dismissed the idea out of hand. "Harry needs a lot more pipes on his insides," he said, "and I don't know whether we can get any pipes over there." His hopes thwarted, Hopkins looked for a way to use the issue to soothe the antagonism between War and Treasury. He still hoped for the post, however, and recommended Patterson for the job to everyone but Patterson.[9]

But if Hopkins was still the administration's peacemaker, he was also Lord Root of the Matter, determined to settle major issues. When he realized that he would not be attending the Quebec conference, he used the last White House meeting to try to nail down American policy toward Germany. He started off in fine form, by leading Roosevelt through the partition question. Though he followed a Treasury Department outline, he stated the issues so objectively that Morgenthau could not tell where he stood. All the while he monitored Roosevelt's comments until he asked the president directly, "Would it

be correct to define your position saying you agreed to partition?"
Roosevelt said yes.

Hopkins then lost control of the meeting. Stimson and Morgenthau
debated deindustrialization and the treatment of Nazi war criminals,
while Roosevelt thumbed through Treasury memoranda interjecting
appreciative commments. When the meeting adjourned, the president's only definite commitment had been the one Hopkins had ex-
tracted from him.[10]

In a short time the whole subject became a major fiasco. Morgenthau
attended the Quebec conference, where Roosevelt and Churchill
signed a memorandum agreeing to dismantle German industry after
the war. Then the press picked up the story, emphasizing the War
Department's objections to deindustrialization. The influential commentator Arthur Krock argued that the Morgenthau Plan would cause
the Germans to fight harder, and the Republicans charged that
Roosevelt was mishandling the war. Although Hopkins had been one
of the plan's strongest supporters, his name did not arise. In this sense
his not attending the conference proved a blessing.

But in late September, with the election campaign in full swing,
Hopkins was thinking less about personal escape than about damage
control. Realizing that the Morgenthau Plan was dead, he turned to
the modest directive he had worked out earlier with War and Treasury.
Approved by all departments and filed as JCS 1067, it was the best
device he had for demonstrating the Cabinet's unity. Everyone agreed
to release it—Treasury called the move a "master stroke"—and Hopkins got Roosevelt's approval.

Hopkins also knew that this was the end of the line for Morgenthau.
When the secretary asked to continue the special committee, Hopkins
recommended disbanding it. Roosevelt agreed with Hopkins and refused even to discuss the subject with Morgenthau. Hopkins was willing to extend Morgenthau his sympathy—he blamed the whole mess
on Stimson—but was otherwise of no practical help.[11]

Morgenthau's embarrassment marked the turning point in Hopkins's comeback. The incident discredited his major competitor for
influence with Roosevelt, gave him the chance to tidy up the damage,
and allowed him to build a key alliance with the State Department.
Hopkins had placed Stettinius in State the previous year, and now he
moved to take advantage. He told Stettinius that "Quebec had been a
great blunder" because Hull had not attended the conference. Hull, he

said, with an eye on the election, was popular with the voters; he had millions of votes, while Morgenthau had none. Hopkins asked Roosevelt to assign postwar planning to State.[12] This Roosevelt did in part, dividing the job between State and the Foreign Economic Administration.

In the meantime Hopkins was running into trouble releasing JCS 1067. Eager to get the document before the public, he had hoped to release it without consulting the Allies. But Morgenthau thought that the British should be informed, so Hopkins took it to Halifax and Cadogan, emphasizing its usefulness in the presidential campaign, and asking them to let Roosevelt publish it unilaterally. Halifax suggested that the British and Americans do so jointly, provided agreement could be reached speedily. Hopkins rushed off the document to the British with a warning to have Churchill's "nit pickers" lay off, and adding that "it would be very much to the President's interest" to release it.[13]

Hopkins's efforts failed. Churchill objected that an Anglo-American directive would violate the principle of agreement among all three Allies. Hopkins then proposed that Russia also adopt the directive. He drew support from War and State but got nowhere with the British. Eventually JCS 1067 disappeared into the mills of committee discussion and did not emerge until the end of the war.[14]

For the moment, then, Hopkins's comeback remained fixed in Washington. There it blossomed in alliance with the State Department. Early in October, Hull fell ill, and at the end of November he resigned. Many in Congress recommended their old friend James Byrnes for the job, but Roosevelt rejected him as "too independent" and instead chose Stettinius. This was a bolder challenge to Congress than Hopkins would have made. Hopkins's unpopularity on Capitol Hill, which stemmed from New Deal days, when he had offended many congressmen by interfering with their patronage schemes, had made him leery of affronting legislative leaders. Thus he was cautious when Stettinius called him in to discuss the appointment of several new assistant secretaries. Fearing that there would be trouble on the Hill if his name were linked to any of the nominees, he insisted on elaborate precautions to keep his involvement secret.[15]

Stettinius's choices also sent Hopkins a danger signal. Dean Acheson would remain in the department taking on new responsibilities as assistant secretary for international conferences and congressional relations. Hopkins had no objection to that. But Stettinius's other recom-

mendations were a different story: Nelson Rockefeller as assistant secretary for Latin American affairs, William L. Clayton as assistant
secretary for economic affairs, James C. Dunn as assistant secretary for
political affairs, and Joseph C. Grew as undersecretary and second in
command. New Deal liberals were bound to oppose both Rockefeller,
because of his family ties to Standard Oil, and Clayton, a wealthy Texas
cotton trader who was suspected of favoring international cartels.
Dunn was a career foreign service officer, who had accompanied Secretary Hull to the Moscow conference in 1943 and was currently helping
with the negotiations to frame a charter for a postwar United Nations
organization. He was suspect because in 1937 he had supported an
arms embargo to the Spanish government in its civil war with General
Francisco Franco's Fascists. Grew, who had served as ambassador to
Japan in the 1930s, was under a cloud because he had said publicly that
the Japanese emperor might have to stay in power after the war in
order to maintain stability.

Hopkins suggested steps to placate the opposition. Dunn should
make a liberal speech. Stettinius should appoint the New Dealer Benjamin Cohen as his counsellor instead of assistant counsellor. Clayton's
confirmation testimony should emphasize his opposition to international cartels. By December 6 the nominations were ready to go to the
Senate. "It will be a three day wonder," Hopkins predicted.[16]

But the confirmation process was anything but that. Hopkins's strategy failed to mollify the liberals, who gave him "unshirted hell" over
the nominees. Even the conservative Senator A. B. ("Happy") Chandler of Kentucky was wondering "who won the election." "Instead of
poor folks obtaining jobs," he declared, "the Wall Street boys are
obtaining jobs, and we are clearing everything with Harry Hopkins."
Chandler's remarks may have sent a chill through Hopkins, but this
was the only time his name was mentioned. In the meantime, however,
liberals were threatening a filibuster to make Roosevelt withdraw the
nominations. Then, conservatives on the Foreign Relations Committee tried to block the one bona fide liberal nominee, the poet and U.S.
publicity officer Archibald MacLeish, and Hopkins had to join in a
frantic effort to round up enough votes to send his name to the floor.[17]

Looking for a way to compromise with the liberals, Hopkins suggested that they be allowed to block confirmation while Stettinius put
in his men as interim appointees.[18] But Stettinius, determined to push
the nominations through, appealed to Roosevelt to intervene. The

president warned the liberals that he would resubmit the nominations
to the next Congress but assured them that he would replace any
nominee who did not support his policies. On this basis the liberals
gave way, and all were confirmed.

While these proceedings were under way, Roosevelt and Stettinius
were formalizing their partnership by appointing a liaison between the
White House and State. Stettinius suggested Charles ("Chip") Bohlen,
who had accompanied Roosevelt and Hopkins to Cairo and Tehran as
adviser and interpreter and who was currently chief of the State Department's division of Eastern European affairs. Roosevelt had
thought that Bohlen would be reporting to his secretary, Grace Tully,
and to Admiral Leahy of the Joint Chiefs, but the final arrangement
routed him to Hopkins. Hopkins admired Bohlen and had already
sought his advice on several matters. He was pleased that instead of
having to grab the phone and bark, "Chip, get the hell over here," he
would now be able to meet with him regularly.[19]

Hopkins was finally back at the top of Roosevelt's diplomatic structure and was determined to take advantage of the possibilities. Closer
relations with State would give Roosevelt expert advice that might
temper his eccentricities. Perhaps a better informed president would be
less likely to promote a formula such as unconditional surrender in
unpromising circumstances, or to baffle the British foreign secretary
with speculations about creating a state of Walloonia in northwest
Europe. Hopkins was particularly concerned because Roosevelt kept
no record of his high-level discussions. He had tried to rectify this
omission at the earlier conferences and had been pleased to see Bohlen
taking notes at Cairo and Tehran.

Hopkins had told the British that the new men at State would be
sympathetic to them, and almost immediately he showed them how. A
new shipping crisis had arisen, this time because too many ships were
clogging European ports. As usual the military proposed to solve the
problem by cutting everyone else's allocation. Also figuring in the crisis
was the problem of providing civilian relief behind Allied lines. In late
1943 the army had taken over this task and, not surprisingly, had
subordinated it to military necessity, limiting relief to the minimum
necessary to curb "disease and unrest." By the fall of 1944, however,
the Allies had occupied so much territory and uncovered suffering of
such horrifying proportions that they decided to turn the job over to
Jean Monnet, who was still operating in the role of mediator between

the Allies and the French. Monnet went to work to reconcile the various interests.[20]

Hopkins became involved in the civilian relief issue. In an effort to court the Italian-American vote, Roosevelt decided to increase the bread ration in southern Italy. When the military raised various objections, he assigned Hopkins to see that his wishes were carried out. Hopkins conferred with the parties and drew up a program that incorporated everyone's recommendations.[21]

At this point, however, the problem assumed an entirely different form. In London the Foreign Office decided that the military's "disease and unrest" standard was too low, and that unless it was raised, "disruptive elements within the communist and resistance groups" might undermine the exiled governments the British were supporting. The Foreign Office approached the Joint Chiefs, who replied that European civilians were no worse off than they had been under the Germans and that it was better to have a hungry Italy than a delayed victory.[22]

The British did not waste time despairing over the Joint Chiefs' decision. After all, they knew that there were no front stairs in Washington. In fact French and Belgian representatives were already asking the War Shipping Administration to increase their imports beyond those allowed by the military. Eager to keep its independence, the WSA recommended that the Europeans be allowed to bid for shipping without seeking military approval, and that "some civilian body or individual" be authorized to decide. When the British learned of the WSA's position, they decided to send over their minister of state, Richard Law, who had recently negotiated with the Americans about Phase Two of Lend-Lease. Because Law represented the Foreign Office, contacts with the State Department seemed in order; but at the time State was being reorganized. Because of this, and because Law's mission seemed to cut cut across department lines, attention centered on Hopkins, who had recently supported additional civilian relief for Italy.[23]

Since Hopkins had just worked out a shipping formula, he was reluctant to unravel his own knitting. At his first meeting with Law he painted a gloomy picture of Anglo-American relations and suggested that after the war the United States might again retreat into isolationism. He also doubted that the Joint Chiefs could be persuaded to change their position on shipping allocations. He would agree only to help Law set up another shipping survey. He changed his mind, however, when Law sent him a long letter arguing that the success of military operations depended on political stability in Europe. This provided Hopkins with the kind of insight he needed. At their next meeting he was in top form. The immediate objective, he declared, should be to scrape up enough ships for a two- or three-month emergency program for Belgium, Italy, Greece, and Yugoslavia. France should be considered separately because it was a war zone. He thought that the shipping survey should proceed, although he had not decided whether to involve the military. During the meeting he called up the WSA to get its support and arranged an appointment with Stettinius and Halifax. He ended by promising to try to persuade General Somervell to accept the British recommendations. He hoped to wrap everything up by the end of the week.[24]

Having seized the issue, Hopkins refused to let go. After a few hours of checking, he decided to have the Combined Shipping Assignments Board prepare an overall shipping survey while the British embassy and the State Department studied the political considerations. The next day he took Law and his party to the State Department. All agreed that political stability in Europe was essential for military victory. Indeed if victory produced only chaos and suffering, Europe might again fall under some form of "political absolutism" that would leave the victors disillusioned. Hopkins added that the newly established United Nations Relief and Rehabilitation Administration would have to achieve some results or be seen as an international fraud. He thought that the military commanders were learning the value of civilian relief, but in any case the European nations were only asking to use their own shipping, which until now had been under Allied control. Unless the Allies heeded their requests, relations with these countries were bound to worsen.

Once all had agreed on the principles, Hopkins proposed that Law meet with Roosevelt. He advised Law to be cautious and not try to force a decision. The Germans had recently launched a major counterattack against the Allies in France, and Hopkins thought that this would weaken the case for cutting back military shipping. He suggested that Law might even want to return to Britain while the shipping survey was being prepared.[25]

In the meantime Hopkins went to work on the military. He persuaded Somervell to acknowledge the importance of civilian relief and to endorse the shipping survey. Next he convened a meeting between the departments of War and State. Summarizing the principles he had previously worked out with State and the British, he declared that the key consideration for the Allies was to support democracy. When democratic nations waged war, they expected an orderly government to spring up in the wake of battle. If civil war and unrest broke out, as it had in Greece, democratic peoples were inclined to question the wisdom of having gone to war. Those present generally agreed with this analysis, but the military still refused to loosen its hold on shipping. Winning the war as quickly as possible, they argued, would best help Europe's civilian population. To this Hopkins replied that it was hard to tell the Belgians that their ships were taking supplies to Russia when their own people were starving. He changed no minds, however, neither then nor on the next day, when he brought the British in to discuss the matter. For one of the few times during the war, his conciliatory methods had failed to produce agreement.[26]

Hopkins might have been out of ideas, but he was not out of luck. It so happened that several weeks earlier Jean Monnet had worked out a civilian import program for France. Declaring that the import program had to be considered independently of military control, he warned that any further discussions would have to include General de Gaulle, who had recently taken charge of a provisional government in Paris.[27] Monnet's ploy worked beautifully. By threatening to turn civilian relief into a political issue, he forced the military to guarantee ships for France—and, for good measure, Belgium too—for the first quarter of 1945.

Monnet's success revitalized Hopkins's efforts. On January 14 he and Law signed an agreement ratifying the French and Belgian shipping schedules and including an allocation of relief ships for Italy. Except for the schedules, the document was a collection of vague phrases which the parties could interpret to their own satisfaction.[28] Thus it accomplished nothing beyond the first quarter of 1945. In this sense it was a typically ad hoc arrangement of the kind Hopkins had been negotiating throughout the war. He realized its limitations and considered it only a basis for discussion at the Big Three conference in Yalta scheduled for February.

Still, the agreement showed the degree to which Hopkins retained his personal standing. As so often in the past, the parties' confidence in the agreement reflected their confidence in him. The WSA declared that it was "vital" that the agreement contain a clause making Hopkins the final judge of shipping allocations. When Hopkins tried to pass off that responsibility, John J. McCloy, representing the War Department, declared, "If the military felt that they could bring a case to Mr. Hopkins they would have less objection to the procedure than they were likely to have if they felt they were precluded from stating their case."[29]

Hopkins had retained the confidence of the war establishment. But the episode showed more than that. It revealed a shift in his method of operation. In the past he had operated as President Roosevelt's representative, using the president's office as his badge of authority. In his negotiations with Law he had laid the groundwork with the State Department. It was a natural course for him to take, since his longtime friend Stettinius was now secretary of state. But as later events were to show, Hopkins's association with State was part of a process of involving that department more systematically in policy making, to set up regular channels for making decisions that he had previously arranged ad hoc. In this regard his relations with State represented a step in the development of the American war machine similar to the development of the New Deal. During his second term Roosevelt had tried to set up a permanent administrative structure for the emergency agencies of the New Deal, and Hopkins himself had looked forward to trading the daily administrative headaches of running the WPA for the settled policy-making position of secretary of commerce. Now Hopkins was finding a stable institutional home for making wartime decisions.

The time was fast approaching when he would be able to put these new arrangements to the test.

# Chapter 22

# Dawn of a New Day

Chip Bohlen's appointment as White House liaison was important not only because it put Hopkins directly in the foreign policy system but also because it focused attention on Russian affairs. Bohlen was an experienced hand at Russian diplomacy and a supporter of Roosevelt's policy. He had accompanied Hopkins and Roosevelt to Tehran. His appointment nicely balanced Hopkins's widely recognized ties with the British.

In addition to his other activities that fall, Hopkins had monitored discussions in Washington among the Big Three about forming a postwar United Nations peacekeeping organization. Hopkins considered the United Nations a top priority and counseled the U.S. negotiator, Stettinius, on handling the subject. Not surprisingly, he believed that cooperation began with agreement on general principles and not with drawing boxes and allocating authority. The negotiations should not get bogged down, he advised, in attempts to set up a detailed, complex structure or in debating national boundaries and spheres of influence.

Hopkins thought the issue important enough for Roosevelt to raise in the presidential campaign. Although he usually sought to avoid confrontations with Congress, he wanted the president to ask Congress for authority to commit American armed forces to United Nations peacekeeping operations. Having to go to Congress each time a crisis arose would cause delays, and "the fat would be in the fire" by the time the United States could act. If Roosevelt campaigned on the issue, his reelection would give him a mandate to settle it on his own terms. Roosevelt followed Hopkins's advice in a speech before the Foreign Policy Association in New York City.[1]

By the time Roosevelt spoke, however, the Washington talks had stalled as the Russians demanded representation in the United Nations General Assembly for each of their sixteen republics and rejected a Western proposal to prohibit the great powers from vetoing peacekeeping actions against themselves. The conferees had agreed to give charge of peacekeeping to a United Nations Security Council, on which the major powers would serve as permanent members and smaller nations as temporary members on a rotating basis. When the British and Americans proposed that the Security Council be empowered to condemn the conduct of the permanent members, the Russians objected. The Russians also wanted power to block discussion of disputes that concerned the permanent members. The issues of Soviet representation in the General Assembly and of the extent of the Security Council's powers had arisen in an atmosphere of national competition, as Britain and the United States sponsored membership for nations they expected to be friendly to themselves. The British and the Americans also posed as the protectors of the smaller nations, claiming that these countries would be concerned if the United Nations charter did not limit the big powers. They further argued that the smaller nations would object to a Russian proposal to require them to furnish bases for peacekeeping forces.[2]

Hopkins thought that the Western Allies were taking the wrong approach. He told Stettinius that it was dangerous for the United States and Britain to build themselves up as the protectors of the small nations against the Soviet Union. He wanted Stettinius to devise an alternative and write the president a memo about it. Stettinius demurred, saying that the next step should be another Big Three conference. To this Hopkins agreed, but in the meantime he arranged for Roosevelt to discuss the issue with the Russian representative, Andrei Gromyko. When the meeting failed to produce agreement, Hopkins helped draft a direct appeal to Stalin. But Stalin remained firm, and the talks adjourned with the issues unresolved.[3]

Meanwhile in Moscow a familiar pattern was reappearing in Russian-American relations as Harriman and General Deane were recommending that the United States encourage a more cooperative Russian attitude by carefully reviewing their supply requests. Harriman was particularly distressed by the Russian response to the Warsaw uprising of the Polish underground army against the Germans. The Poles had struck early in August, shortly after the Red Army had reached the outskirts of the city. Believing that the Russians had encouraged the uprising, Harriman was shocked when the Red Army halted its advance and the Soviet government denounced the Poles as ill-advised adventurers and "criminals" who were only seeking political power for themselves. Not only did the Russians refuse to aid the Poles, but they also blocked British and American requests to land at Russian bases after dropping supplies to them.[4]

It was easy to conclude that Stalin was motivated by political considerations. Only days before the uprising the Russians had recognized a communist-dominated Polish Committee established to administer affairs behind Russian lines. Now they seemed determined to set that body up as the recognized government of Poland, replacing the exiled government, with which they had earlier broken relations over the Katyn Forest incident. The Warsaw uprising was led by Poles affiliated with that government, which was operating out of London. In assessing Russian motives Harriman was not prepared to go quite this far, but he did believe that the Soviets had become "bloated with power" and were determined to force their will on others regardless of their objections. For these reasons he asked the United States to change its policy and demand more cooperation, including support for the Poles. Churchill also strongly supported aid to those behind the Warsaw uprising.[5]

Hopkins found little support for the Polish underground in Washington. Roosevelt was inclined to conciliate Stalin. The State Department advised against pressing the matter, and the military was unenthusiastic. The Joint Chiefs were seeking a closer liaison with the Red Army, hoping to expand its basing agreements and to get Russia into the Pacific war. The attitude of the military was driven home to Hopkins by Major General Fred Anderson, aide to General Carl Spaatz, the commander of strategic air forces in Europe. On a visit to the White House, Anderson told Hopkins directly that the British were using the Warsaw issue to manipulate the United States and in the process were needlessly jeopardizing relations with the Russians. Only 5 percent of the supplies that could be dropped into Warsaw, he declared, could be expected to reach the underground. Hopkins responded by assuring him that he personally would screen cables from Britain to be sure that the president did not hastily commit the United States to the project.[6]

With the war establishment so firmly in agreement, not even the threat of a political backlash could change Hopkins's mind. To a report that influential members of the Roman Catholic clergy intended to oppose Roosevelt's reelection unless the United States aided Warsaw, he responded sarcastically that he had always felt that the Vatican was more interested in the defeat of Russia than of Germany and that its policies had given the enemy "great comfort." In any case, no leader of the church had ever been able to make Catholics vote as he directed.[7]

Only Stalin could change Hopkins's mind. When the Russian leader suddenly decided to allow Allied relief planes to land in Russia, Hopkins conferred with the State Department and Marshall to arrange the aid. The assistance helped the Poles hold out a few extra days but came too late to avert their crushing and savage defeat. Afterward, Hopkins treated Poland as a public relations problem, advising Roosevelt to meet with a Polish delegation from Chicago and expediting news releases that emphasized Lend-Lease aid to the Polish army.[8]

Nor was Hopkins sympathetic to the idea of tougher bargaining with the Russians. He convinced Roosevelt that Harriman should stay in Moscow instead of coming home to argue for a stronger line. He also shelved a request from Arnold to negotiate a fourth supply protocol to give the United States more leverage with the Russians.[9]

While Hopkins was thus helping to keep U.S.-Soviet relations in their usual channels, he was warily eyeing British-Russian relations. From time to time Hopkins had feared that Britain would get on the "inside track" with the Russians, and in October his concern arose again. Churchill proposed to visit Moscow to discuss Russia's entry into the Pacific war and the postwar future of Eastern Europe. Before leaving he asked Roosevelt to cable Stalin that he approved the mission. It so happened that Hopkins dropped by the White House Map Room and read Roosevelt's reply, which wished the prime minister "every success" and even expressed the hope that Churchill would be able to solve the problems that had arisen at the United Nations talks. Realizing that this gave Churchill broad authority to speak for Roosevelt, Hopkins ordered the transmitting officer to cancel the message and called Bohlen in for a conference. Bohlen agreed that Churchill should not be allowed to speak for Roosevelt. Indeed he feared that a Churchill-Stalin meeting would either result in "a first class row" about European politics or lead to "the division of Europe into spheres of influence."

From Hopkins's point of view either of these outcomes was likely to destroy the great goal of Allied peacetime cooperation. Dividing the world into power blocs would undermine the U.S. design for global security just as surely as would squabbling over the spoils. Thus he had

Bohlen draft a series of messages dissociating Roosevelt from any of Churchill's proposals and asking Harriman to sit in on the major discussions.[10]

Hopkins's intervention proved wise. Churchill indeed negotiated with Stalin about spheres of influence, arriving at percentages that apportioned Russian and British influence in Greece and the Balkans. As part of the arrangement Stalin agreed to discourage the Greek communists, who were trying to seize control in their country. This in turn produced disruptive consequences in December, when Britain sent troops into Greece to put down the communist forces. Typical American comment came from the widely read columnist Drew Pearson. He published an order from Churchill to shoot all armed men who opposed the British army, accused the prime minister of blocking a coalition government that would have settled the matter peacefully, and hinted that the prime minister was actually intervening to protect loans to the Greek government made by bankers who had helped him out of personal financial difficulties in 1912.[11]

Hopkins was in no mood to preach sermons to the British. A few days before the 1944 presidential election he had warned them that for domestic political reasons U.S. policy toward occupied countries might conflict with Britain's. In asserting that Italy, for example, should be spared a harsh occupation, Hopkins was obviously concerned about the Italian-American vote; but the principle of opposing harsh measures could easily have applied to Greece. His efforts at conciliation were complicated, however, because Stettinius had issued a statement criticizing the British intervention, and Roosevelt, who was at Warm Springs, was routing his messages through Admiral Leahy and the State Department. But Hopkins was as resourceful as ever. He not only offered Churchill his personal support but intervened on his behalf. One morning he wandered into the Map Room and learned that Admiral King had ordered the navy not to deliver supplies to Greece. Since the U.S. fleet was supposedly under the control of the British commander in the Mediterranean theater, King seemed to be acting for political reasons. Believing that following King's order would be like "walking out on a member of your family who is in trouble," he asked Leahy to have King withdraw the order. He then persuaded Churchill to abandon a sizzling protest he was ready to send.[12]

But Hopkins could not fully assuage Churchill's bitterness, which had been deepened by further disagreements over reorganizing the Italian government. That November a broadly based regime headed by Ivanoe Bonomi had experienced a Cabinet crisis when the American protégé Count Sforza had demanded to be made foreign minister. When the British vetoed the move, Bonomi refused Sforza's claim, and the State Department responded by officially regretting the British action. In a press statement Stettinius declared, "We expect the Italians to work out their problems of government along democratic lines without influence from the outside. This policy would apply to an even more pronounced degree with regard to governments of the United Nations in their liberated territories."[13] It was this statement, with its implied criticism of British intervention in Greece, that had so angered Churchill.

These episodes left Hopkins on edge. The British, manipulating Italian politics and struggling to save a sphere of influence in Greece, were setting a precedent that might undermine the peace. In the meantime Churchill was making things worse by declaring in the House of Commons that the United States was delaying agreement on the future of Poland and jeopardizing the prospects for establishing a United Nations peacekeeping organization. Particularly disturbing was Churchill's statement that the Allies could make their own territorial arrangements before holding a peace conference. As he surveyed the London scene, Hopkins concluded that there was enough blame to go around. The British had "messed the whole thing up pretty thoroughly," while the American embassy in London had shown "rank incompetency" for not anticipating the crisis. He thought that the time had come to replace Ambassador Winant.[14]

Hopkins wanted above all to prevent these difficulties from influencing American public opinion before the heads of state could address them at a Big Three conference. Fortunately, prospects for the conference seemed bright. Churchill's trip to Moscow had been a huge success. Stalin's hospitality had surpassed its usually superhuman standard. Stalin even appeared publicly with Churchill, attending a ballet, where the audience greeted the two leaders with thunderous applause. He also praised the United States and wound up his conference by cabling Roosevelt, "We can, without great difficulties, adjust our policies on all questions standing before us."[15]

Hopkins interpreted Stalin's message as an expression of faith in the United States' sincere desire for Allied cooperation. Thus he was furious when his chief adviser on Russia, Joseph Davies, brought him news that the United States had tried to recruit as a spy a member of the Soviet Purchasing Commission and that Secretary Hull had been informed of the recruiting effort. The man, Victor Kravchenko, had defected from the Soviet Union in April 1944 and had sought asylum in the United States. The Russians had then attempted to extradite him as a deserter from the Red Army. "My God," Hopkins exploded, "what if Stalin knew that a member of the President's family had been a party to this desertion!" To him it made "just plain sense" to return a deserter to an ally who was helping to fight Hitler. Public opinion, he believed, would back him up. When he took up the subject with Roosevelt, the president suggested that it might be easier to return the man if the Russians promised not to shoot him. Hopkins was willing to accept this, but drily observed that once he was in Russian hands, no one would know whether he had been shot or not. In the end Kravchenko remained in the United States and wrote a book condemning the Soviet system.[16]

Hopkins was willing to placate the Russians on such matters as the Kravchenko affair because he wanted nothing to interfere with the upcoming conference, at which the Allies would take their first steps toward establishing a postwar peace. The location of the conference owed much to Hopkins. In October he and Ambassador Gromyko had discussed the subject and agreed on the Crimea, a section of the southern Ukraine located on the Black Sea. Believing that Stalin would want to be close to his military front, Hopkins advised Roosevelt to settle on the site to avoid "a lot of long-winded, irritating cables back and forth getting exactly nowhere." His advice proved out in all respects, as Roosevelt and Churchill tossed about alternative sites for the next couple of months and Stalin vetoed them all. By the end of December the location was fixed at the Crimean city of Yalta.[17]

Preparations for the conference also benefited from Hopkins's influence. His close contact with the State Department made Yalta, in contrast to Tehran, one of the best prepared and best staffed of the wartime meetings. The State Department provided Roosevelt with detailed memoranda, compiled in briefing books, for his guidance on key issues. Roosevelt advised State on preparing these materials and studied them aboard ship on his way to the conference. Stettinius assembled a team to represent the United States in conferences with the foreign ministers. Thus the conference represented the maturing of the Hopkins Shop in the conduct of American diplomacy.

Hopkins aided in the preparations by flying to London, Paris, and Rome ahead of the president's party. It was the first time anyone had undertaken this kind of advance consultation. He was hoping to clear up as many problems as possible, but he was not going to sacrifice American objectives to do it. When Churchill continued to complain about U.S. criticism of his Italian policy, Hopkins concluded that the State Department should be brought into closer cooperation with the army to counter the British Foreign Office, which regularly advised British military officers. Also, he decided, Roosevelt should insist that an American head the Allied Control Commission for Italy, and that the Italians take more responsibility for running their own affairs. During his visit to Rome he avoided British officials and held an impromptu news conference at which he criticized British interference in Italy. He had once believed that the Allies should put off discussing political issues until after the victory, but the situation in Italy and Greece had convinced him that these problems should be dealt with immediately.[18]

Hopkins also saw that there would be difficulty over the question of voting in the United Nations. The State Department had wanted to keep permanent members from vetoing Security Council recommendations on disputes to which they were a party. Churchill had recommended a veto on all decisions involving the use of force. In Britain the Foreign Office agreed with the Americans, but the Cabinet was divided, and Eden claimed that Roosevelt did not support the State Department.

Hopkins saw other danger signals over the treatment of Germany. Especially disturbing was the failure of Britain and the United States to agree on postwar zones of occupation. Winant worried about what would happen if the Russians passed the western border of their proposed zone before the agreement had been ratified. Hopkins thought that before the conference Roosevelt and Churchill ought to agree on the British and American zones.[19]

When he arrived in Paris, Hopkins expected to be welcomed as the bearer of good news. He had long supported giving France a substantial role in postwar affairs, and he could now report that the British favored giving France a permanent seat on the Security Council and an occupation zone in Germany. But he found the atmosphere chilly. General de Gaulle received Hopkins with a haughty show of wounded dignity at the tardiness of American aid and the refusal of the Allies to invite him to Yalta. Surprised but not daunted, Hopkins suggested that De Gaulle might come to Yalta to discuss political questions but not military ones, and he invited De Gaulle to meet with Roosevelt after the conference. The general turned down the first suggestion but accepted the second.[20]

While in France, Hopkins also discussed military strategy with General Eisenhower. Hopkins feared that the old conflict among the Joint Chiefs over Europe versus the Pacific—that is, between Marshall and King—would arise again at Yalta, with King predicting that Russia would not enter the Pacific war and therefore urging that all extra troops should be assigned there. Not surprisingly, Hopkins sided with Marshall, and he assured Eisenhower that he would have all the troops he needed for the final drive against Germany.

Hopkins also discussed the question of how to handle Germany after the war. He thought that the military would do a good job of establishing order—"getting the water turned on"—but he feared that the officers, some of whom had connections with large American corporations, might want to revive the German economy too rapidly. To guard against this he thought that German affairs should be directed by someone "of the liberal school." He was thinking of himself. A high commissioner had not yet been chosen, and he had recommended himself to Stettinius.[21]

But Hopkins's hopes for the post were fading. His health had seemed to improve in November, but a month later it had begun to decline again. By the time he completed his European swing and joined Stettinius in Naples, he was weak and suffering from diarrhea. Stettinius sent him to bed during the flight to Malta, where the Americans were to confer with the British before traveling on to the Crimea.[22] He did not improve significantly, however, and spent much of the Yalta conference in his room. When he returned home, he went back into the hospital.

But his sacrifice was not in vain. He had laid the groundwork for a successful Anglo-American conference. Alerted to the importance of fixing the occupation zones, the Americans and the British worked out their differences and signed the protocols before Roosevelt arrived. Eden and Stettinius also agreed to give France a seat on the United Nations Security Council and an occupation zone in Germany. They decided that the United States would have to take the lead in opposing Russia's request for sixteen votes in the United Nations, since the British were sponsoring a seat for India. Hopkins won recognition of his shipping agreement with Richard Law when the Combined Chiefs included its allocations in their shipping budget. The British and the Americans also agreed to press for a coalition of communist and nationalist forces in China and in Poland, hoping later to establish a permanent Polish government based on free elections.

Notes of discord still lingered. Churchill arrived still angry at the Americans over their disagreements about Greece and Italy. Eden also mentioned Greece to Hopkins, defending the British action. Both Eden and Churchill seemed depressed about world affairs in general. At an evening meeting aboard his ship, Churchill wept as he mourned the misery of the world's people. The future, he declared, depended on Anglo-American unity.[23]

Roosevelt's arrival brought a new worry. The president had traveled by sea in order to rest, but many thought that his health had deteriorated markedly. He appeared aged, drawn, and worn. He seemed unable to grip the point of a discussion and follow it through. Churchill's physician, Sir Charles Wilson, guessed that the president was suffering from advanced hardening of the arteries and suspected that he had only months to live. Roosevelt's poor health and the failure to settle differences over Italy and Greece caused the British to fear the outcome of the Yalta conference. Just before they left for Russia, Eden warned Hopkins that both countries "were going into a decisive conference and had so far neither agreed what we would discuss nor how to handle matters with a Bear who would certainly know his mind." This alarmed Hopkins so much that when he arrived in Yalta he urged the president's daughter, Anna Boettiger, to have her father settle things with Churchill. The president, he ranted, had asked for this job and was going to have to take the responsibility of seeing it through. Anna calmed him down by reminding him that her father always preferred to dissociate himself from the British to reassure the Russians that their allies were not ganging up on them.[24]

Hopkins's improved mood did not match his physical condition. To Sir Charles Wilson he seemed "only half in this world . . . his skin was a yellow-white membrane stretched tight over the bones." At one point Roosevelt's physician Ross McIntire wanted to hospitalize him on the communications ship. Hopkins would not hear of that, but still he spent most of the time in his room, which as a result became a site for American strategy sessions. He missed most of the formal dinners, saving his strength for the plenary sessions, where he sat behind Roosevelt and Stettinius, passing notes of advice.[25]

Each nation came to Yalta with certain fundamental objectives. The

British were determined to protect their empire and to limit Soviet influence in Europe. The Russians were determined to protect themselves from another German attack by dividing up German territory, taking large reparations, and establishing a sphere of influence in Eastern Europe. The Americans wanted to establish the United Nations as an effective peacekeeping organization. To this, however, Roosevelt added an overriding objective. The president had gone to Yalta to promote Allied cooperation. This meant that he was less interested in accomplishing specific goals than in reaching an agreement, a goal that led him in turn to play the role that Hopkins and Davies had long advocated for the United States: the "honest broker" between the British and the Russians.

From Hopkins's point of view, working for agreement did not conflict with American objectives. Regarding the United Nations issue as "more important than anything else," he focused on the veto issue. Because Roosevelt would be presiding at the plenary sessions, Hopkins feared that it might be awkward for him to present the American proposal, so Roosevelt decided that Stettinius should do the job.

Stettinius offered the American proposal on the afternoon of February 6. It allowed the permanent members to veto action on an issue to which they were party but forbade them from vetoing discussion. The meeting with the Russians proved tense. They were wary that the Americans might try to slip something past them. When the Russians asked for time for further study, Churchill declared that he now supported the Americans and believed that their proposal adequately protected the interests of the major powers. The session then put off further consideration until the next day.

The fruits of preparation were becoming evident. With the British now in line behind the American proposal, Hopkins moved to get the most from the State Department team. The next morning he made sure that Stettinius was prepared for the foreign ministers' meeting. But Molotov blocked the discussion and referred the issue to the afternoon's plenary session, where the Russians accepted the American proposal but immediately asked for two or three additional votes in the General Assembly. At Malta, Hopkins had said that the United States would take the lead in opposing such a request so that the British could avoid embarrassment over the seating of India. Now Roosevelt launched into a rambling monologue which clearly suggested that he wanted to avoid the issue. From his seat in the rear Hopkins sensed that the president was getting nowhere and sent up a note: "I think you should try to get this referred to the Foreign Ministers before there is trouble." Roosevelt took his advice and recommended that the foreign ministers study both the time and place to hold a United Nations conference and decide which nations to invite. He then suggested that the conference open sometime in March. Churchill jumped in to say that he would not agree to this until he had consulted the War Cabinet. Surprised, Hopkins dashed off another note suggesting that they drop the subject until they had had a chance to discuss it with Churchill. Roosevelt replied that Churchill was only concerned about "local politics" (that is, not allowing the United Nations conference to interfere with parliamentary elections scheduled for that summer). Stalin agreed to refer the subject to the foreign ministers, and the session ended calmly.[26]

Churchill's intervention had deferred the subject. But during his remarks he had also supported the Russian request for extra votes. Hoping to avoid an Anglo-American split on this issue too, Hopkins discussed it with Roosevelt and told Sir Charles Wilson that Churchill's strong stand had persuaded the president to support the Russian request. He also pushed Stettinius to get on with planning the conference, suggesting that it be held in the isolationist heartland of the United States: Minneapolis, Cincinnati, Kansas City, or St. Louis. He also ran down a list of possible U.S. delegates, including the leaders of the Senate Foreign Relations Committee and the newly elected governor of Ohio, Frank Lausche, a New Deal loyalist. He thought that it would be a nice gesture to ask Cordell Hull to preside over the conference but not to be a member of the U.S. delegation, although he believed that Hull's health was too bad to allow him to attend in any case.[27] In the end the foreign ministers agreed to open the conference on April 25 in the United States. The same day, Roosevelt told Stalin that he supported the Russian request for extra seats.

This left only one more point. At the plenary session Stalin asked about the status of ten nations that did not recognize the Soviet Union and of certain Latin American nations that had broken diplomatic relations with Germany but had not declared war. Hopkins advised Roosevelt that Sumner Welles had recommended against these nations' declaring war because they were not strong enough to defend their coastlines against the Japanese. Roosevelt made no use of this information but instead asked that these countries be invited to join the United Nations, for they had been friendly to the United States and had supplied vital raw materials for its war effort. He thought that the issue could be resolved if the nations in question declared war and signed the United Nations declaration. When Stalin asked if this offer applied to nations like Turkey, which had wavered from one side to the other, Hopkins saw a chance to settle the matter and passed Roosevelt a note: "But they *must* declare war in order to be invited."[28] Roosevelt took up this point, and Stalin agreed.

Hopkins made his major contribution to the conference in these United Nations discussions. Still, he participated in other meetings, including those on the future of Poland. The Russians wanted to set up a government based on the communist puppet regime they had installed in Warsaw. The British and Americans wanted to expand this regime to include representatives from noncommunist, anti-Nazi parties. These elements would form a provisional government that would rule until free elections could be held. Along the twisting, tortuous path that the discussions followed, Hopkins used his State Department assets to work toward consensus and decision. He and Bohlen drafted a response to the first Russian proposal. He advised Roosevelt to refer their second proposal to the foreign ministers, but the president discussed it privately with Stettinius. The secretary recommended Hopkins's approach of reaching an agreement on general principles and working out the details through the ambassadors in Moscow, and Hopkins urged him to fly directly to Moscow after the conference and settle the details "even though we have to give two or three days to it."[29]

Toward the end of the discussions Hopkins intervened again. The conference had agreed to recognize the Warsaw government as the basis of a provisional Polish government that would also include noncommunist members and would hold free elections in one to two months. At this point Churchill noted that the formula did not mention Poland's boundaries. The conference had agreed that Poland's eastern boundary would be adjusted in favor of Russia, but Churchill had objected to a proposal to compensate Poland in the west by giving it most of Prussia. He wanted to be sure that the conference settled the issue and published a statement of agreement.

Hopkins saw that Churchill's position would create a dilemma for Roosevelt. Under the U.S. Constitution the president could not approve boundary changes, but any attempt to dodge the issue might alarm Stalin. Thus in two notes he warned Roosevelt about his constitutional difficulties and recommended that he privately assure Stalin that while he favored the eastern boundary, he thought that the official communiqué should discuss boundary changes only in general terms. Roosevelt took Hopkins's advice but, in order to conciliate Churchill, asked the British to draft the statement. The draft confirmed the eastern boundary and spoke generally of the west. Although this was not exactly what he wanted, Roosevelt said that he would accept the statement, provided that Churchill and Stalin help him out of his constitutional difficulty by agreeing to sign as "heads of government" and not as "powers."[30]

Hopkins also conciliated Britain on the subject of France. Both Roosevelt and Stalin favored giving France an occupation zone in Germany but opposed giving it a seat on the Allied Control Council. As the discussion developed into a debate between Churchill and Stalin, Hopkins saw a chance to put Roosevelt in the mediator's role. He proposed that the session agree to a French zone and ask the foreign ministers to discuss France's presence on the council. He had to offer this suggestion twice, but Roosevelt finally accepted it. For the next few days he and Bohlen argued the French case to the president, who at the last session declared that he now thought that Churchill was right and that the French should be on the council. Stalin then threw up his hands and, declaring, "I surrender," made it unanimous.[31]

But Hopkins had not come to Yalta just to support the British. When it came to the treatment of Germany he supported the Russians. So did Roosevelt, who was inclined to treat Germany harshly. On this issue they differed from Churchill, who wanted to rebuild Germany to strengthen the Western European economy and to serve as a counterweight to Russian influence in Central Europe. Thus when the subject of dismembering Germany arose, Churchill and Stalin sparred with each other, and the prime minister objected when Roosevelt proposed a compromise that would include dismemberment in the surrender terms. At this point Hopkins and Stettinius resorted to their usual device of referring the question to the foreign ministers. Hopkins urged Roosevelt to conciliate Stalin by declaring the subject "an important and urgent matter" that the ministers should resolve "at an early date." Stalin refused to refer the issue, however, and at last Churchill agreed to accept Roosevelt's proposal.

In later meetings the issue of Germany reappeared in a debate over reparations. Stalin had come to Yalta with a plan specifying the kind, amount, schedule, and claimants for reparations from Hitler's Reich. As with other German issues, Churchill proved his major antagonist, putting the Americans once again in the mediator's role. At first the Americans tried to steer the debate onto the subject of manpower. Hopkins believed that it would be easier to get agreement to transport "Gestapo-Storm Troopers and other Nazi criminals" to Russia. But Stalin brushed aside this recommendation.

As the conference entered its final days, the Russians and the Americans agreed to create a reparations commission in Moscow. The Russians wanted to instruct the commission to consider the sum of $20 billion for total reparations to the Allies or $10 billion as reparations to Russia alone. The British objected, and Roosevelt seemed to side with the British by objecting to including a money figure in the formula. Actually his reasons were unrelated to Churchill's. Roosevelt was concerned that mentioning a figure would conjure up in the United States memories of the 1920s, when the United States had lent billions to Germany so that it could make its reparations payments. To Stalin this seemed a distinction without a difference, and he felt that Roosevelt was running out on their agreement.[32]

Stalin chose to express his suspicions privately, and Gromyko passed the word to Hopkins. Stalin hoped that this would prompt Roosevelt to make a public statement of the American position, but Hopkins only recommended that Roosevelt explain his position to Stalin "privately later."[33] That was not good enough for Stalin. When Roosevelt did not respond to the behind-the-scenes prompting, he asked him publicly if he was backing out of their agreement.

Stalin prefaced his challenge to Roosevelt with an uncharacteristic show of emotion. Rising, he gripped the back of his chair so that his knuckles showed white against his brown hands. To Hopkins he seemed to spit out his words as though they burned his mouth. No one moved. Great areas of his country had been laid waste, he declared; peasants had been murdered. Nothing could ever make up for Russia's loss. Hopkins understood. If war meant sacrifice, none of the Allies had given more than the Russians. Quickly he reviewed the conference: the Russians had accepted the American plan to organize the United Nations, they had allowed France to join the Control Council, had agreed to reorganize their puppet government in Poland and to allow free elections, had supported a coalition government in China headed by Chiang Kai-shek, and had agreed to enter the war against Japan. While Churchill and Stalin debated the reparations figure, he scrawled another note to Roosevelt: "The Russians have given in so much at this conference that I don't think we should let them down. Let the British disagree if they want to—and continue their disagreement in Moscow. Simply say it is all referred to the Reparations Commission with the minutes to show the British disagree about any mention of the 10 billions."[34]

If ever Hopkins deserved to be called Lord Root of the Matter, it was then. He not only saw the importance of the issue to the Russians, but he also realized that the British were not going to back down. This made it practical to refer the subject to the commission with a statement that the United States was supporting the Russians. But Roosevelt followed only part of his advice and proposed to refer the subject without expressing American support. As a result the discussion dragged on through dinner until it was finally decided that the conference protocol include the formula Hopkins had suggested.

It seems clear that at Yalta, Hopkins did not enjoy the personal triumph of Tehran. Ill health and the presence of the State Department team limited his independence. Nor does he seem to have conferred privately with Roosevelt, though the record is not complete enough to confirm this conclusively. He did not discuss the full range of issues, being uninvolved in the sessions on China and the Far East. His suggestions were not always followed: Stettinius did not go to Moscow to pursue the reorganization of the Polish government; the United Nations conference was scheduled for San Francisco and not the Middle West; and Roosevelt slighted his advice during the reparations debate.

Still, he performed credibly. He helped guide the United Nations issue to a successful resolution, especially by satisfying Stalin's requirement that the Latin American nations declare war before being admitted to membership. He mollified the British by arranging a luncheon between Roosevelt and Churchill to make up for their lack of personal discussion at Malta. He also credited Churchill with persuading Roosevelt to support additional General Assembly votes for Russia. He consulted the British on drafting a policy letter on Poland and helped them obtain a seat for France on the Control Council. He suggested the compromise on the reparations issue.

Hopkins's contributions supported the overall American role of acting as a broker between the British and the Russians. As Diane Shaver

Clemens has shown, on four of five major issues at Yalta the United States took the middle position and moved the discussion toward a final agreement.[35] Only on United Nations issues did the United States stand its ground. Hopkins was as actively partisan as any on behalf of the American position, but even here he played a broker's role, helping to persuade Roosevelt to permit extra Russian votes and then telling the British that Churchill had changed the president's mind.

Hopkins must have taken satisfaction from the State Department's role in the conference. Stettinius's team of Bohlen, H. Freeman Matthews, and Alger Hiss had effectively represented the American positions and provided helpful background information and on-the-spot advice. At long last it seemed that the promise of the Arcadia conference was being fulfilled. In 1942 Hopkins had helped to devise a structure for the Anglo-American partnership. Within a few months, however, that structure had been overwhelmed by crises and had been subordinated to ad hoc arrangements, many of them thrown together with his own last-minute assistance. At Yalta it seemed that in various commissions and arrangements for consultation the Allies had fashioned a three-way structure for postwar cooperation. Roosevelt recognized this aspect of the conference and at one plenary session recommended turning an issue over to the foreign ministers because they were proving to be "very effective."[36] Hopkins especially wanted to breathe life into these institutions. His pep talks and advice to Stettinius were designed to give the new secretary the kind of self-confidence he needed to negotiate effectively. His frequent suggestions to refer issues to the foreign ministers or to a special commission were not stalling tactics to put off difficult decisions or to allow tempers to cool; they were honest efforts to make the negotiating process work.

Hopkins could have confidence in the State Department because its negotiating style was so similar to his own. He always studied the parties to the negotiation, gained their confidence, defined the issues, and aimed for an agreement that respected the parties' vital interests. That was Stettinius's method of operation: open, friendly, positive, tirelessly helpful. If the secretary was an inexperienced and superficial diplomat, he nevertheless faithfully pursued American objectives. Considering his performance, it was unfortunate that he did not follow Hopkins's advice and pursue the Polish question in Moscow immediately after the conference ended.

The Yalta conference formally adjourned at 3:45 P.M., February 11. Roosevelt drove to Sevastapol to view battle damage and to spend the night on the communications ship *Catoctin*. A little earlier Hopkins had left Yalta with his son Robert and a few military personnel for Simferopol. They arrived at the railroad station without a translator and spent hours walking up and down before finding someone who told them which train to take. As it turned out, the train had previously belonged to the royal family of Romania, and Hopkins immediately claimed the bedroom car. The next morning he told Stettinius that from then on he was going to befriend all foreigners he met in American railroad stations by offering them a drink and showing them the way to the toilet.[37]

The train chugged into Saki, where Hopkins and his party joined Roosevelt to fly to Egypt, where his ship the *Quincy* was waiting at the Great Bitter Lake. Roosevelt had announced that he would meet with King Ibn Saud of Arabia, an arrangement which Hopkins dismissed as the president's whim of ending his trip with a flourish. Actually Roosevelt wanted to help Eastern European Jews to relocate in their ancient homeland of Palestine. At the meeting he directly asked Ibn Saud to increase Jewish immigration. With austere and stony conviction the king refused, confirming Hopkins's prediction that the meeting would be a waste of time.[38]

Roosevelt had not told Churchill that he intended to meet with Ibn Saud. Alarmed when he heard the news, the prime minister cabled Hopkins to arrange a meeting with the president so that he could make sure that the United States would not jeopardize British interests in the Middle East. The meeting turned out to be a brief, uneventful luncheon aboard the *Quincy*. When Churchill left for his own conference with Ibn Saud, he said good-bye to Roosevelt. It was to be the last time.

This was a time, too, for other, more painful farewells. Aboard the *Quincy*, Pa Watson suffered a stroke. He did not live out the return voyage. Hopkins also lay ill in his cabin. He was able to muster enough strength to persuade Roosevelt not to retaliate when General de Gaulle cancelled their scheduled meeting, but soon he realized that he needed time alone to rest. He arranged to leave the *Quincy* at Algiers so that he could spend a few days at the villa where he, Roosevelt, and Churchill had wound up the Casablanca conference. His decision upset

Roosevelt, who had counted on his help in drafting his report to the nation on the Yalta conference. There was a chill in the air when the two parted, also for the last time.[39]

Hopkins rested for three days before flying to Washington by way of the Azores and Bermuda. He was still pale and weak, but his spirit was strong in the belief that Yalta had opened the way to a lasting peace. "We really believed in our hearts," he said to Robert Sherwood, "that this was the dawn of the new day we had all been praying for and talking about for so many years. We were absolutely certain that we had won the first great victory of the peace—and by 'we' I mean *all* of us, the whole civilized human race. The Russians had proved that they could be reasonable and farseeing and there wasn't any doubt in the minds of the president or any of us that we could live with them and get along with them peacefully for as far into the future as any of us could imagine." He had only one reservation to add. The Americans felt that they could cooperate with Stalin but could not be sure what would happen if he passed from the scene.[40]

Hopkins carefully qualified his enthusiasm. Yalta had ushered in a new day, but it was still only dawn. "I am sure we are off on the right foot," he wrote Russell Davenport, "but the Communique will need a lot of implementing."[41] From one who had seen so many cooperative arrangements collapse, it was an appropriately cautious statement.

# Chapter 23

# On His Own Feet

By the time he returned to Washington, Hopkins was in no condition to help implement anything. He spent a few days at home, but when his health failed to improve, he flew to the Mayo Clinic. By March 1 he had lost seventeen pounds in two months and had little appetite. The doctors diagnosed pneumonia and a low blood count but found no recurrence of his digestive problem. Medication and transfusions improved his condition briefly, but he soon suffered another setback and, though still cheerful, was clearly losing strength. On April 12 his health had just taken another upward swing when Chip Bohlen telephoned to say that earlier that afternoon President Roosevelt had died. Stunned, he sat silently for a long moment and then said simply, "I guess I better be going to Washington."[1]

As he prepared for the trip, he marshaled his emotions. Instead of collapsing into sorrow and self-pity, he strengthened himself with memories. Roosevelt had become a historic figure to him, "the world's most outstanding champion of human freedom and justice," a friend of "the oppressed people of the earth," champion of "a just and enduring peace," the nation's "noblest leader since Abraham Lincoln."[2] These thoughts restored him. When he phoned Robert Sherwood the next day, he had his feelings well in hand.

> You and I have got something great that we can take with us all the rest of our lives. It's a great realization. Because we know it's true what so many people believed about him and what made them love him. The president never let them down. That's what you and I can remember. Oh, we all know he could be exasperating, and he could seem to be temporizing and delaying, and he'd get us all worked up when we thought he was making too many concessions to expediency. But all of that was in the little things, the unimportant things—and he knew exactly how little and how unimportant they really were. But in the big things—all of the things that were of real, permanent importance—he never let the people down.[3]

The new president also bolstered Hopkins's spirits. The evening Hopkins arrived in Washington, Harry S Truman called to convey his good wishes and to arrange an appointment for the next day. When Hopkins arrived, he found Truman eager to learn about Roosevelt's policies. Truman had suffered the typical vice-president's fate of having been kept almost totally uninformed. He admitted as much, and although he felt equipped to handle domestic issues, he knew that he was completely ignorant of foreign policy. Hopkins was pale, thin, and shaken, but he knew his duty. For two hours he answered Truman's questions, employing the eye for detail and insight into personality that had always made his service so valuable. Stalin, Hopkins said, was a "forthright, rough, tough Russian . . . a Russian partisan through and through, thinking always first of Russia." But he could be talked to frankly. When he came to Churchill, Hopkins stressed the good relations between Roosevelt and the prime minister and encouraged Truman to work closely with the British. Above all he encouraged Truman to carry on Roosevelt's policies. Toward the end of the conversation he informed the new president that he intended to resign from the government. Truman urged him to stay on if his health permitted, and Hopkins promised to think it over.

The next day Hopkins conferred with Eden and Halifax to help them adjust to the new situation. He told them that he had not been surprised by Roosevelt's death. He had seen the president fail to the point where he had been unable to do much work. He doubted that Roosevelt had heard half of what had been said at the Yalta sessions. He was only glad that the end had come quickly and that Roosevelt had not lingered, impaired like Woodrow Wilson.

Hopkins characterized Truman as honest, capable, and methodical. The new president's background tied him to the Senate, and Hopkins expected him to work closely with that body. He also expected that Byrnes would replace Stettinius as secretary of state. He could not say whether Truman would have the necessary courage or skill to choose able people. He only knew that, despite Truman's invitation to stay on, there would be no place for him in the new administration.[4]

Still, Hopkins considered his future with conflicting emotions. He yearned to be of service and felt obliged to a president who had sought his advice. He and the new president had cooperated well during the WPA days. But that was not much to count on. They had gone their separate ways and had lost touch. Truman would undoubtedly feel more comfortable with familiar friends and advisers. Hopkins was still wrestling with these ambiguities when, after the funeral service, Robert Sherwood dropped by his Georgetown house for a talk. As Hopkins spoke, sparks seemed to shoot from his eyes:

> God damn it [he said] now we've got to get to work on our own. This is where we've really got to begin. We've had it too easy all this time, because we knew he was there, and we had the privilege of being able to get to him. Whatever we thought was the matter with the world, whatever we felt ought to be done about it, we could take our ideas to him, and if he thought there was any merit in them, or if anything that we said got him started on a train of thought of his own, then we'd see him go ahead and do it, and no matter how tremendous it might be or how idealistic he wasn't scared of it. Well—he isn't there now, and we've got to find a way to do things by ourselves.

Thus spoke the hopeful Hopkins, ready to get back into harness. But there were other considerations. His closeness to Roosevelt had made him enemies. Wallace, Byrnes, and Ickes had all coveted the vice presidential nomination in 1944, and each probably blamed Hopkins for keeping him from becoming president. This was not true of course; others had advocated Truman's nomination, and in any case Roosevelt had had his eye on the Missouri senator. Still, under the circumstances Hopkins concluded that he had better turn in his resignation. "Truman has got to have his own people around him," he concluded, "not Roosevelt's. If we were around, we'd always be looking at him and he'd know we were thinking 'the president wouldn't do it that way!' " It was time to regain his health and then look for work outside the government. His doctors felt that he had progressed enough to stay in Washington. So he settled down in his Georgetown house, diverted by visits from friends and an occasional official caller. But for the moment he was adrift.[5]

At the White House, Harry Truman was, in a different way, also adrift. Despite Hopkins's briefing he faced an uncertain future. Of the many trials he anticipated none seemed less attractive than negotiating with Churchill and Stalin. (Hopkins had realized this and advised against Churchill's visiting the United States because "Truman would have felt ill at ease from the consciousness of how completely unprepared he was to discuss wide issues at present.") Indeed, thoughts of filling Roosevelt's shoes at a Big Three conference caused Truman to wish that he had never been nominated for vice-president. He countered these feelings as best he could. Following Hopkins's advice to continue Roosevelt's policies, he read through the record of wartime diplomacy, focusing on the Yalta agreements. These he came to consider a benchmark for Allied cooperation.

The problem was that the Yalta accords seemed to be slipping away, largely because of Soviet policy in Eastern Europe. The Russians had blocked progress toward reorganizing their Warsaw regime and were trying to install it as the legitimate government of Poland. In Bulgaria and Romania they were also setting up communist-controlled governments and shutting out Allied influence. No one viewed these developments with greater alarm than Ambassador Harriman. In mid-April he returned to Washington determined to have the new president take a tough stand against the Russians. When Truman heard that the Russians were undermining the Yalta accords, he took Harriman's advice and spoke sharply to Molotov when the Soviet foreign minister stopped in Washington on his way to the San Francisco conference to establish the United Nations. Truman's performance pleased not only Harriman but also others in the State Department who had long suffered from the Russians' uncooperative behavior and who believed that only American firmness would prevent them from expanding their influence westward.

If, as some may have thought, Truman was applying a lesson of history—that firmness could halt aggression—events quickly suggested that he had applied the wrong one. When Molotov arrived in San Francisco, he demanded that the conference admit Poland as a charter member—under its Warsaw government. On May 4 he stunned Stettinius by casually announcing that the Russians had arrested sixteen Polish underground leaders who had been promised safe conduct to Moscow to discuss reorganizing the Polish government. By this time Molotov was in full stride. He also objected to admitting Argentina on the grounds that it had supported the Axis. Next the United States and the Soviet Union fell into arguing over whether the permanent members of the Security Council could veto bringing items to the floor for discussion. The United States claimed that under the Yalta accords the permanent members could veto only those procedures leading to action by the Security Council. As April turned into May, it seemed that the conference was on the verge of collapse.

Though responsibility for these squabbles was not always easy to assign, the United States was clearly at fault in another matter that strained relations with the Russians. Everyone realized that when Germany surrendered, Lend-Lease aid to Russia would have to be revised. Harriman had advised Truman to end unconditional aid and convert Lend-Lease into a tool for diplomatic bargaining. At the same time, however, he wanted the United States to take no provocative action while negotiations over Poland were proceeding. Through a series of misunderstandings and literal readings of procedures, however, Harriman's cautious plan was translated into a full-scale halting of Lend-Lease, even to the extent of recalling ships at sea. Truman countermanded the order, but not before the Russians had officially complained.[6]

In these circumstances another Big Three meeting seemed inevitable. When Churchill raised the point, Truman stalled, claiming that Stalin should propose the next meeting. By mid-May, however, he had come to agree that "an early . . . meeting is necessary to come to an understanding with Russia." Churchill said that he would take the initiative and approach Stalin, but as things turned out, he did not follow through, and Truman wound up making the first move.[7]

When Truman decided to act, he was in effect facing up to the failure of his tough-guy approach to Molotov. Instead of making the Russians more accommodating, it had made them more intransigent. Even Admiral Leahy thought that a meeting with Stalin was the only hope for containing Russian influence in Eastern Europe. At the same time others were arguing against the policy itself. Stimson thought that it could not lead to positive results, and Marshall feared that it would jeopardize Russia's entry into the war against Japan. On May 13 Joseph Davies offered Truman a broader critique by reviewing Soviet-American wartime relations in a way that justified Russian suspicions of American good will. Davies called on Truman to continue Roosevelt's policy of acting as the "good broker" between Russia and Britain. It was his feeling that Molotov had come to the United States to size up the new president and to see if he intended to continue Roosevelt's policies.

Davies's analysis put Soviet-American relations in a new light. Briefed by Harriman and others, Truman had been led to believe that Roosevelt had grounded his policies in the Atlantic Charter and the Yalta accords. Now Davies was telling him that Roosevelt had been concerned less with principles than with maintaining a particular negotiating stance: as the mediator between Britain and Russia.

Davies's account of Roosevelt's efforts to overcome Russian suspicions suggested that Truman's get-tough talk with Molotov had been needlessly provocative. Truman could see Davies's point with added clarity since the shutting-off of Lend-Lease a few days before had shown how easily the United States could blunder into upsetting Russian sensibilities. Truman listened sympathetically and asked Davies to take over as ambassador to Moscow. For reasons of health, Davies declined.[8]

If Truman was having second thoughts about the Russians, so was Harriman. The troubles at San Francisco had convinced him of the need for a personal approach to Stalin. He first thought of taking on the job himself, but on the flight back to Washington on May 9 Bohlen suggested offering the assignment to Hopkins. Harriman quickly accepted the suggestion, and soon after they arrived in Washington, they paid Hopkins a visit to see how he felt about it.

Hopkins was ready to hear what his friends had to say. About a week earlier he had discussed such a mission with President Truman but had heard nothing since. He was still in precarious health, but as the conversation progressed, he seemed to gain strength just from considering the idea. As far as he was concerned, if the president wanted him to go to Moscow, he was willing and able.[9] Hoping for the best, he put off his retirement plans.

Then his previous doubts returned. Truman would want to rely on his own people. And indeed when Harriman first proposed Hopkins's name, Truman turned him down, suggesting that Harriman approach Stalin himself. But Harriman persisted, and in the end Truman had to yield to the logic of circumstances. Truman did not want to undertake the job himself, preferring instead to attend a Big Three conference after his current duties of preparing the budget had been completed and after the test of the atomic bomb, scheduled for that summer, had been carried out. Most important, he did not want to attend a conference without adequately understanding Soviet motives and intentions, something the contradictory advice of Harriman and Davies had left unclear. Stettinius was tied up in San Francisco, fighting to save the United Nations conference, and in any case Truman intended to replace him with James Byrnes. If Truman wanted to undertake a personal initiative with Stalin—and to show that he wanted to carry on Roosevelt's policies—Hopkins was his only choice.

In 1941 this kind of logic had persuaded Roosevelt to send Hopkins to London; but Truman was a different president in different circumstances. He sought further advice, bypassing both Stettinius and Byrnes and checking with the lower echelons of the State Department, which recommended against the mission on the grounds that Hopkins would concede too much to the Russians. Counterbalancing State's advice, and ultimately tipping the balance in favor of the mission, was Secretary Hull. The strong endorsement from a man who had stood high in the opinion of Congress and who might have been expected to be critical of Hopkins, who had so often neglected his department and had even taken his place at wartime conferences, deeply impressed the new president. When Byrnes dropped in the next day to make his case against Hopkins, Truman responded that he probably would send him anyway. Stalin's rapid and positive response to a telegram proposing a Hopkins mission satisfied Truman that he had made the right choice.[10]

Truman cabled Stalin on May 19, and on the same day he called Hopkins in to discuss the mission. He wanted Hopkins to arrange a Big Three meeting, if possible by persuading Stalin to take the initiative. He also hoped that Hopkins would encourage the Soviets to compromise with the United States on reorganizing the Polish government. He told Hopkins that he wanted "a fair understanding" with the Russians, but he interpreted those words with a distinctive flavor. Hopkins should tell Stalin "just exactly what we intended to have in the way of carrying out the agreements purported to have been made at Yalta . . . that we never made commitments which we did not expect to carry out to the letter and we intended to see that he did." Hopkins, he said, could use diplomatic language, a baseball bat, or anything else he thought appropriate to convey this message.[11]

Such instructions indicated that Truman was thinking of the Hopkins mission as a way of pursuing fixed objectives by other means. He still wanted the Russians to live up to the letter of the Yalta accords as he understood them. But now he wanted someone to convey a sense of American good will and cooperation. Truman probably saw this approach as a new diplomatic posture that would dispel Soviet fears of his unfriendliness. Just as important, a successful trip by Hopkins would make it easier for him to carry out the difficult task of negotiating with Stalin and Churchill. Thus it seems clear that in sending Hopkins to Moscow he was not trying to reopen negotiations in the style of the Yalta conference. Nor was he, as some historians have suggested, using Hopkins to stall for time, holding off a showdown with the Soviets until the United States had tested the atomic bomb. Truman simply hoped that Hopkins would be able to clear up the difficulties in U.S.-Soviet relations so that by the next Big Three conference "most of our troubles would be out of the way."[12] That is, he hoped that Hopkins could persuade Stalin to see things his way.

Truman took a similarly distinctive view of Joseph Davies's idea that the United States should serve as an honest broker between Britain and Russia. After talking with Hopkins, Truman called Davies in and asked him to visit Churchill. The president thought that it would balance things nicely if he sent Davies, a friend of Stalin's, to London and Hopkins, a friend of Churchill's, to Moscow. When Davies suggested having Hopkins report to Churchill, Truman vetoed the idea, not wanting to appear to be ganging up with the British against the Russians.

To anyone familiar with Roosevelt's approach to the Allies, it was clear that Truman was getting things backwards. Roosevelt had not hesitated to use Hopkins as a go-between with both Churchill and Stalin. Indeed the whole idea of the honest broker presupposed the confidence of both parties. But Truman's logic, as he explained it to Davies, was to negotiate through men who had the confidence of each other's opposite number. This was an approach better designed to indicate U.S. independence from both parties. Truman's comment about not ganging up on the Russians further suggests a strategy of independence. It was true that Roosevelt had employed the strategy in his own approach to Stalin, but only insofar as he would not meet with Churchill before meeting with Stalin. But Davies had proposed that Hopkins report to Churchill after meeting with Stalin, an approach that Roosevelt had often employed. Truman's response was so unlike what Davies had expected to hear from a president who claimed that he wanted to carry on Roosevelt's policies that Davies came away thinking that he was being sent to London to tell Churchill that Truman intended to meet privately with Stalin before the next Big Three conference. As a result his visit to London proved to be a major fiasco.[13]

Like Davies, Hopkins also left the White House with a modified understanding of his instructions. He had advised Truman to continue Roosevelt's policies, and now he had a chance to follow his own advice. As he packed his bags for Moscow, he took with him the experience of four years of U.S.-Soviet diplomacy. That experience had taught him that American policy should challenge the Russians as little as possible, that relations worked best when the Americans tried to see things from the Russians' point of view. It had also impressed him with the Russian contribution to the war effort. The Russians had taken everything the Germans could throw at them, had sustained enormous losses, and had still fought to victory. Most important, the Russians were willing to cooperate. At Yalta, Stalin had proved less a hard bargainer than an accommodating ally, willing to trade, able to appreciate others' views. True, he had wanted Germany treated roughly; but who could blame him for that? After all, the war had shown that Germany was a continuing threat to world peace. That was a major reason why the Allies had to cooperate and why the Russians especially deserved to have friendly states on their borders.

Also important was the nature of Allied diplomacy. Yalta had not produced a formula for settling postwar problems so much as it had initiated a negotiating process by which the major powers could remain united by understanding each other's objectives. The conference had further shown that within the alliance Russia's main antagonist was Great Britain, and that it suited the United States in its broker's role for Churchill to be suspicious of Russian motives and purposes. Hopkins was wary of the British, fearing that Churchill was trying to maneuver the United States into supporting his policy in Europe against the Russians. Thus Hopkins balanced Truman's instructions to confront the Russians with his own desire to understand their views. He also balanced Truman's strategy of taking a stance independent of both allies with his own willingness to counter the negative influence of the British. As at Tehran, so Hopkins believed, it was time once again to line up with the Russians.[14]

It was with this reinterpreted view of his purposes that Hopkins flew out of Washington's National Airport on the morning of May 23, accompanied by Louise to look after his health and Chip Bohlen to advise and translate. They changed planes in Newfoundland and flew overnight to Paris, where they spent the next day and night before flying on to Moscow. This time, in contrast to Hopkins's first flight four years earlier across the Arctic Circle, they flew directly across Germany—or what was left of it. "It's another Carthage," Hopkins exclaimed as he looked down on the ruins of Berlin. They arrived in

Moscow on the evening of May 25, and twenty-four hours later Hopkins found himself again in the Kremlin facing Stalin and Molotov across a green-covered table in a sparsely furnished conference room.

Hopkins quickly cast the mantle of Franklin D. Roosevelt over the discussions. He described the circumstances of Roosevelt's death, his support for the Russian war effort, and his hopes for continued cooperation after the war. He then recalled his own flight to Moscow in 1941 and his advice to Roosevelt to help the Russians. He even remarked that he had risen from a sickbed to undertake his present mission. Stalin fell into the nostalgic mood, remarking that, like Roosevelt, Lenin had died of a stroke. Several times he acknowledged the value of Lend-Lease to the Russian victory.

In this atmosphere of good will several issues were rapidly disposed of. Showing the independence he had occasionally displayed as Roosevelt's emissary, Hopkins suggested a Big Three meeting near Berlin only to learn that Stalin had already made such a proposal to Truman. (Later it was learned that the proposal had actually come from Molotov in a cable to Joseph Davies.) When he suggested that the Russians appoint a representative to the Allied Control Council for Germany so that body's efforts could get under way, Stalin replied that he would shortly announce the appointment of Marshal Georgi Zhukov. Although Stalin was not then prepared to discuss Russia's entry into the Pacific war, he consulted his advisers and a few days later promised to honor this commitment and to support the Chiang Kai-shek government in China. Hopkins lightly complimented Molotov for having quoted Roosevelt and Hull in his argument against seating Argentina in the United Nations. When Molotov and Stalin laughed, Hopkins offered the friendly warning that in the future he might have occasion to quote Stalin's own words to him.

The accommodating atmosphere and ready agreements went a long way toward dispelling Hopkins's warning that U.S.-Soviet relations had seriously deteriorated since the Yalta conference. The next evening it seemed that everyone was ready to take up where Yalta had left off. Both Hopkins and Stalin were willing to concede issues that lay in the other's area of special interest. At Yalta the United States had set a priority on organizing the United Nations. Thus, after Molotov and Harriman briefly debated seating Argentina, Stalin cut them off by saying that the question was settled and nothing could be done about it. Similarly, the Russians had pressed for reparations from Germany,

so when Stalin objected to including France on the Reparations Commission (presumably because he feared that France would oppose large
reparations), Hopkins declared that the United States was not inflexi-
bly committed to French membership. When Hopkins explained that a
technical misunderstanding had caused the abrupt suspension of Lend-
Lease, Stalin played down the incident by allowing that the United
States had a right to curtail shipments after Germany's surrender. He
wished only that Russia could have been informed in advance. In
return Hopkins assured Stalin that the United States would never use
Lend-Lease to pressure the Russians. When Hopkins remarked at a
later meeting that Stalin had changed from his posture of supporting
the dismemberment of Germany, Stalin said that he had done so because he thought that the British and Americans had also decided
against it. Hopkins hastened to correct this impression, saying that
Truman had not decided and would want to discuss the issue at their
meeting. Stalin replied that he would keep an open mind. Hopkins
eased Stalin's suspicions that the Western Allies were reneging on their
agreement to divide the German naval fleet with Russia by initiating
action to form a commission to settle the issue. In these various matters
Hopkins felt that he had allayed Russian fears that the Truman administration was changing Roosevelt's policies.[15]

As these issues fell away, the problem of Poland gained an ominous
definition. At the first meeting Hopkins declared that Russia's failure
to reorganize the Polish government had caused American public
opinion to turn against the Soviet Union. Nevertheless, he assured
Stalin that the events had been unimportant in themselves, that the
United States wanted Poland to be friendly to the Soviet Union, and
indeed wanted the Soviet Union to have friendly states all along its
borders. When he heard this, Stalin declared that they should be able
to settle the issue easily.

At their second meeting Hopkins further defined the Polish issue in
a conciliatory way. The United States, he said, considered Poland a
symbol of the United States' ability to work out problems with the
Soviet Union. This meant establishing a Polish government that was
both popularly elected and friendly to the Soviet Union. Stalin's reply
was also conciliatory. Russia wanted Poland to be strong and friendly.
He welcomed the participation of the United States and proposed that
the present Warsaw government be made the basis for a new regime
that would include no more than four noncommunists among the

eighteen or twenty ministers. Stalin was ready to nominate some non-communist ministers, but Hopkins put him off by asking for time to study his suggestions. That evening he cabled Truman that "the implications of [Stalin's] reaction to the Polish matter are complex and . . . under any circumstances I am sure that the . . . matter cannot be settled while I am here."[16]

Actually Stalin's position was not as complex as it was disturbing. Hopkins had said that the United States wanted to guarantee Soviet security and to establish a representative government in Poland. In reply Stalin had addressed only the first point. When the question of Poland next arose, Hopkins went directly to the second matter, declaring that in order for the United States to be sure that the Soviet Union was not going to dominate Poland, the Poles should be granted a parliamentary government with guaranteed freedom of speech, assembly, movement, religious worship, and political party membership, and fair and equal treatment under the law. To this Stalin replied equivocally, stating that such freedoms could be offered only in peacetime and then would have to be regulated according to the security needs of the Soviet Union. Instead of pressing the issue of Polish freedom, Hopkins immediately moved to reassure Stalin on the security issue. The Yalta accords had not specified whether the new Polish government was to be a reorganized version of the Warsaw regime or an entirely new creation. Now Stalin complained that the British were maneuvering to include in the provisional government members of the exiled Polish regime with which the Soviets had had such stormy and hostile relations. Hopkins denied that either the United States or Britain had any interest in including them. Furthermore, he said, "President Roosevelt and now President Truman had always anticipated that the members of the present Warsaw regime would constitute a majority of the new Polish Provisional Government." He wished to state that "without equivocation."[17]

The Yalta accords had also provided for a consultation in Moscow between communist and noncommunist Poles to begin the process of establishing a provisional government. In order to show good faith Hopkins offered to remove from the list any Pole whom Stalin considered hostile to the Soviet Union. This turned everyone's attention toward working out a suitable list. It was a brilliant stroke on Hopkins's part, since it focused attention on practical steps to settle the question. It also worked. By the next evening he and Stalin had agreed on a list. Eager to maintain the momentum, Hopkins urged Truman to accept it and to press Churchill to agree and to use his influence to gain the approval of the exiled Poles in London. "I believe, in recommending this to you," he declared, "that it carries out the Yalta Agreement in all its essential respects."[18]

The breakthrough caused Hopkins to reconsider his earlier opinion that he could not settle the Polish question before leaving Moscow. He decided to stay on. He and Harriman now moved to the case of the arrested Polish underground leaders. Believing that Stalin wanted to form a new Polish government because he had been assured that pro-communist elements would dominate it, Hopkins planned to say that unless the majority of the prisoners were released before he left Moscow, the negotiations would probably not advance.[19] On June 1 he discussed the subject in a private meeting with Stalin. The Polish issue, he said, was dominating U.S.-Soviet relations. Most Americans, himself included, thought that the Poles had been arrested for political reasons. Stalin's response was conciliatory. He acknowledged that the situation was having a bad effect in the United States and, he assumed, in Britain also. Thus, although he had additional information that the Poles had engaged in "diversionist activities"—presumably hampering the Red Army's advance through Poland—he would see that they were treated leniently. They would have to stand trial, however. Along the way he made a few sour references to Britain's conniving with the exiled Poles in London, eliciting from Hopkins further assurances that the United States did not support the London group.

Hopkins considered Stalin's response satisfactory, and he urged both Truman and Churchill not to demand that Stalin release the prisoners before going ahead to form the new Polish government. "Though I have made some impression on Stalin," he wrote Truman, "I simply do not know what he is going to do about these prisoners." "I am doing everything under heaven to get these people out of the jug," he cabled Churchill, "but the most important thing is to get these Poles together in Moscow right away."[20]

Hopkins's advice fell on suspicious British and Polish ears. In London the Polish prime minister, Stanislaus Mikolajczyk, warned the Foreign Office that the Russians would manipulate the talks to delay establishing a new government. It was essential, he argued, that the Polish prisoners be released before the talks started. He also objected to Hopkins's proposal that Stalin grant the Poles "amnesty," which in

Russia allowed the government to continue to hold an accused person. Churchill agreed with Mikolajczyk and warned Truman that Stalin's offer was not really an advance over what he had offered at Yalta. He also bemoaned the United States' decision to withdraw its troops to their assigned zone of occupation, "thus bringing Soviet power into the heart of Western Europe and [the] descent of an iron curtain between us and everything in the East." Still, if Hopkins could arrange to send a Polish delegation to Moscow, he was willing to go along.[21]

For the moment Churchill carried the day. Truman instructed Hopkins to demand the release of the Poles. The president feared that unless Stalin freed the prisoners, the American public would overlook the progress being made to form a new Polish government. His message crossed one from Hopkins asking for instructions, and when he replied again, he merely advised Hopkins to "do what you can" to obtain agreement based on the points raised by Mikolajczyk and Churchill.[22]

Although Truman and Churchill recommended the same negotiating strategy, they conveyed a different emotional tone. Truman treated the arrested Poles as an inconvenience to negotiation, while Churchill dramatized the situation as a diplomatic crisis in its own right. When Hopkins met the next day with Stalin, he adopted the president's line. After a lengthy discussion of the list of Poles to be invited to Moscow, Hopkins made a mild effort on behalf of the prisoners, emphasizing the importance of the issue to American public opinion but leaving Stalin to deal with the matter "in his own way." Stalin promised to consider it and thanked Hopkins for helping to move along the Polish question.[23] With that Hopkins allowed the subject to drop.

At once he took up an entirely new issue. He had just received a message from President Truman reporting on the impasse between the United States and the Soviet Union on Security Council voting procedures: the question of whether members could veto the discussion of an issue. Hopkins hoped that Stalin would change the Soviet position and permit discussion. Stalin conferred briefly with Molotov, who stood by the veto. Then he swung the Soviet Union behind the American position.

Although different explanations for Stalin's decision suggest themselves, the one most solidly based in historical evidence is that he was repeating the pattern of the Yalta negotiations. At Yalta, Stalin had supported the American position on United Nations voting on the same day the United States had supported his formula for reorganizing the Polish government. Now he was again giving the United States its way in organizing the United Nations in return for a free hand in Poland. He accompanied his concession by observing that the great powers ought not to commit themselves to the interests of the small nations lest they wind up being manipulated by them. He did not believe, he remarked, that "a country is virtuous because it is small." Indeed he thought that the small countries had done a good deal of mischief in the world. He clearly seemed to be implying that great power unity often required sacrificing the interests of the smaller nations. Hopkins evaded Stalin's point and tried to divert the conversation to the question of how the smaller nations could present their grievances to the United Nations Security Council. The argument between the United States and the Soviet Union over this subject, he said, had arisen because of misunderstandings and not real differences. It was a clever attempt to reduce the issue to manageable terms, but Stalin did not accept it and emphasized his point a second time. Hopkins failed to respond, and the discussion turned elsewhere. A short time later the meeting ended with Hopkins and Stalin agreeing that since the two nations had so much in common, they should be able to find a way to work out their problems.[24]

Certainly Hopkins was entitled to such an observation. His conversations with Stalin had breathed new life into the spirit of Yalta. Indeed in a year of deteriorating relations with the Soviets his performance was the only sign of cooperation. Hopkins's accomplishment showed the possibilities of pursuing that cooperation. Like Roosevelt at Yalta he had pressed the American case with an eye to achieving agreement instead of winning a total victory. He had taken advantage of Stalin's remarks about British support for the exiled Poles in London to make it clear that the United States was taking a moderate position. In order to advance the discussion on the reorganization of the Polish government he had conceded to Stalin the major influence in forming the Polish delegation and the treatment of the Polish underground leaders and, most important, had assured him that the Warsaw regime would be the basis of the new government. In response Stalin had broken the deadlock over voting in the United Nations Security Council. The result was a bargain in which each side conceded points that seemed near to the interest of the other.

Still, the negotiations over Poland revealed an important difference between Hopkins's approach and Stalin's. Hopkins treated Poland as an important issue in itself, declaring that it was a symbol of U.S.-Soviet cooperation and stressing that the worldwide character of American interests justified the United States' involvement. This formulation contained a strong hint of the kind of unilateralism Truman had expressed when he had challenged the Soviets to live up to their agreements. Of course Hopkins had not negotiated from such a premise, and to this degree he had deflected the course of Truman's earlier diplomacy. Still, he had not responded to Stalin's suggestion that the fate of the small nations ought to be manipulated to suit the interests of the big powers, indicating that he could not accept such an approach.

Of course Harry Hopkins was no sentimentalist ready to shed tears over others' misfortunes. He had long since realized that war meant sacrifice, and he believed that the major fighting powers had made the largest sacrifices, and none greater than the Russians. Thus he fully approved of the Russians' having friendly states on their borders. At the same time, he sincerely believed in Roosevelt's Four Freedoms and felt that America should promote them "everywhere in the world." Hopkins also hoped to counter isolationism at home by giving Americans noble values to promulgate abroad. His conversations with Stalin showed him how Soviet security interests could conflict with the Four Freedoms, and although he was willing to conciliate the Russians in Poland, he realized that a conflict would arise between the two powers if the Soviets attempted to promote communism worldwide.[25]

At the moment of his departure from Moscow, Hopkins was not thinking of long-run objectives or implications. He had asked Stalin to let him visit Berlin on his return trip, and Stalin had readily agreed. On June 7 Hopkins, Louise, and Bohlen flew to Tempelhof Airport. Three years later this was to be the site of one of the great dramas of the Cold War, as American pilots flew supplies to West Berliners cut off by a Soviet blockade of ground transportation. That afternoon, however, no one could have foreseen such a grim future. Hopkins and his party were warmly received by a contingent of Red Army brass. Everyone fell into the spirit of friendship. As they walked from the airport, Louise took the arm of a Soviet general, and they arrived in a nearby square smiling and light-hearted, a camera catching Hopkins as he was about to burst into laughter. Later the Russians gave Hopkins some books from Hitler's library as a souvenir of victory. At lunch Hopkins reviewed his Moscow discussions with Marshall Zhukov and

*Louise, Harry, and Charles Bohlen (behind Hopkins) with Soviet generals in Berlin, June 1945*

Andrei Vyshinsky, who was directing political affairs in Berlin. He was pleased with what he had accomplished but thought that hard discussions lay ahead. When Vyshinsky offered a hopeful remark about the ability of the Allies to work together, Hopkins sat a moment, sipping his coffee, and then said with a sigh: "It's a pity President Roosevelt didn't live to see these days. It was easier with him." They all stayed for dinner and then flew to Frankfort to visit General Eisenhower's headquarters.

At Frankfort, Eisenhower invited the Hopkinses to be his personal guests. Hopkins was eager to discuss Soviet relations with Eisenhower and Robert Murphy, his political adviser. He told them that it was possible to do business with Stalin, and he dismissed Churchill's warnings about the Russians as overwrought and insubstantial. He told Eisenhower, however, that both the Russians and the British intended to have their political and not their military experts determine their policy for the German occupation, and he supposed that several departments in Washington had similar thoughts about American policy. He gave Eisenhower an invitation from Stalin to visit Moscow, and Eisenhower readily accepted, commenting that the War Department had, he thought, unwisely denied him permission to accept an earlier one. Eisenhower also recommended inviting Marshal Zhukov to Washington. They agreed that the United States should withdraw its troops to its assigned occupation zones in order to put the Allied Control Council into operation as quickly as possible and to move ahead the arrangements for the occupation of Austria. Hopkins cabled these recommendations to Truman, describing the issue as "of major import to our future relations with Russia" and recommending prompt action before the Big Three conference in order to avoid the impression that the withdrawal had been caused by Russian pressure. Truman approved the recommendations and forced a reluctant Churchill to go along. Churchill had hoped to deny the Soviets some territory in Central Europe by keeping Western troops in the Soviet occupation zone. When Murphy insisted that the withdrawals include guarantees of Western access to Berlin, which lay well inside the Soviet zone, Hopkins promised to take it up with Truman and Marshall. He did so, and both Truman and Churchill raised the issue with Stalin; but the final agreement said nothing about access rights.[26]

Hopkins also used his conversations to size up Eisenhower as a person. The general seemed well placed in his unpretentious, rural surroundings. He told Hopkins that many people had suggested that he run for president but that he wanted to stay out of politics. He had voted Republican until the last election, in which he had supported Roosevelt. He seemed satisfied with his wartime record and was not looking forward to serving on the Control Council, where he would be only an agent of the politicians. Such remarks coming from a man who gave Hopkins "no impression of . . . having any side," and who was a Republican to boot, might have suggested that the Control Council was just the place for Eisenhower. But Hopkins saw Eisenhower's apprehension as more than thwarted egotism. There was something in the man that impressed Hopkins, and when he reported to President Truman, he recommended that Eisenhower be spared from routine administrative duties so that he could be of greater service to the country. It was the same sort of recommendation he had made four years earlier on behalf of George Marshall.[27]

Hopkins hoped that he would be able to wind up his mission by reporting to Churchill in London. Throughout the war he had sought close collaboration with the British. Yalta seemed to have borne out the wisdom of his approach; prior consultations with the British had ironed out issues between their two nations without committing the United States to an Anglo-American front against the Russians. During his conversations with Stalin he had felt hampered by not having discussed the issues first with Churchill. This had caused him to spend much time dissociating the United States from Stalin's characterizations of British policy. He had done what he could to compensate for the difficulty by conferring with the British ambassador, Archibald Clark Kerr, but he found that an unsatisfactory substitute. Still, he remained loyal to President Truman's instructions. When Churchill invited him to London, he put him off. Churchill then appealed directly to Truman, who flatly turned him down. Hopkins tried to change the president's mind when he returned, urging Truman publicly to speak favorably about Anglo-American cooperation. But Truman declared that he did not want to be "in cahoots with" either Britain or the Soviet Union.[28]

Hopkins had better luck advising Truman on other matters. Although Polish affairs were "in the works" again, he cautioned the president against optimistic predictions of success. He thought that the best way to proceed would be to confront Stalin directly and frankly with American objectives. Stalin's giving way on Security Council voting had shown that he was adopting a realistic attitude. Thus, instead of reacting to Soviet initiatives, the United States ought to state its own policy. Hopkins thought that Stalin would welcome such an approach.[29]

Others agreed. Harriman continued to have reservations about future dealings with the Russians but thought that Hopkins's mission had accomplished more than he had hoped for and had created a much better atmosphere for the upcoming Big Three conference. Stettinius was elated at Hopkins's achievements, and the conservative Undersecretary of State Joseph Grew welcomed heartily the news of progress on the questions of Poland and Security Council voting. In Britain, Hopkins received favorable mention in the House of Commons, and *The Times* pronounced his mission "a conspicuous service to the United Nations."[30]

Hopkins's friend, the broadcaster and columnist Raymond Gram Swing, saw the larger significance of his achievement. "Those who knew intimately the nature of his counsel and services," he declared, "regard him as one of the strongest war leaders in the Administration. But he came to be thought of as being only a friend of President Roosevelt. His mission to Moscow he made on his own feet and the success he achieved there came from him and his own stature. [It] is dawning on the public that he was a friend of President Roosevelt because he had great abilities to contribute, as well as devotion and affection."[31]

Hopkins's own evaluation was characteristically offhand. "The business went, I think, very well," he wrote Beaverbrook, "and I am sure those Polish prisoners got off easier than they otherwise would have."[32]

By this time Hopkins knew that his government service was over. Truman invited him to attend the Big Three conference at Potsdam, but he declined. The president intended to take along Byrnes as his new secretary of state, and Hopkins did not want to risk upstaging him. He was even more concerned about his health. He had come through his trip in good shape, but he was underweight and was aware that he had a long way to go to build himself up. Potsdam, he knew, would be followed by other assignments. "If I keep that kind of merry-go-round going I have no chance in the world of regaining my health," he wrote to Beaverbrook. He was also worried about his financial situation. He had saved almost nothing from his years in government and knew that he had to face the responsibility of providing for his family. On July 2 he sent Truman his resignation.[33]

Truman accepted it with words of appreciation for Hopkins's past services and hoped that after Hopkins regained his health he would once again provide "the benefit of [his] counsel." The public announcement brought the inevitable flood of good wishes from friends and associates. Those who had worked with him commented on how much they had admired his selflessness and how his support had given them comfort and courage. Particularly pleasing was a letter from his Grinnell College history professor, Charles Payne, who said that Hopkins, Chester Davis, and Norman Hall were "my Grinnell boys who have done the kind of thing I am most interested in." "Well, you measured up," Payne concluded, "and now you can take a well-earned rest." Hopkins knew that he had to rest, but he had not quite accepted the thought of retiring. He realized that leaving government was "the end of a great phase of my life" but felt that there were "many things still to be done and I surely intend to have a part in their doing."[34]

Still wanting to be involved in shaping the world's future, he was shaken by the British general elections, which overwhelmingly turned Churchill out in favor of a Labour government. He had anticipated that Churchill would leave office after the war, but his friendship for him was too deep and his political instincts too strong to accept the fact without anguish. The effect on Churchill, he supposed, must have been dreadful. "He has been so gallant throughout this war," Hopkins wrote Beaverbrook, "that I find I am greatly dejected that this should happen to him at this time in his life."[35]

But his dejection passed. Hopkins was soon busy reorganizing his life. In August he and Louise moved to an apartment on Fifth Avenue in New York City. He had been appointed impartial chairman of the coat and suit industry, assigned to mediate labor-management disputes for $25,000 a year. He expected that his duties would require no more than one day a week, leaving him time to recuperate and to apply himself to the writing projects through which he hoped to add substantially to his income. Several publishers had expressed interest, and he was entertaining grandiose plans—perhaps two volumes on the war years and another volume on the relations among Roosevelt, Churchill, Stalin, and Chiang Kai-shek. He hired a literary agent and hoped to negotiate a large advance which could be paid over several years. To sort through his massive collection of papers he engaged the services of Sidney Hyman, a Middle Westerner with a distinguished war record and a background in liberal politics. He also hoped that Raymond Gram Swing would help with the actual writing.[36]

Honors came his way. Oxford University offered him an honorary degree, and he happily accepted, expecting to spend part of his time in England visiting Churchill. Then Truman invited him back to Washington, where on September 4 he awarded him a Distinguished Service Medal. The citation spoke of the "outstanding value" of his services; his "piercing understanding of the tremendous problems incident to the vast military operations throughout the world"; and his "selfless, courageous, and objective contribution to the war effort." Those who had worked with him knew that these words were the truth and not the inflated rhetoric typical of awards ceremonies. He was thrilled by the sincere words and was further complimented by their source. "I know perfectly well," he wrote George Marshall, "you instigated the Distinguished Service Medal for me and I want to hasten to tell you how greatly I appreciate it. Anyone would be less than human not to be altogether flattered."[37]

Experiences like this revived his spirits. By mid-September he was joking with Beaverbrook that "the only effect of the Labor victory here has been a rise in the stock market."[38]

Of course things could never be the same. Roosevelt was dead, Churchill was out of office, the depression was over, the war had been won, and for the first time in twelve years he was out of government and out of Washington. At last the world seemed to have gained a chance for a fresh start. His era had ended as neatly as possible. It was time for him to reflect on his part in it by writing his memoirs.

He tried to face up to these changes, writing to remind President Truman to disband the Soviet Protocol Committee and declining to sign a memorandum of citation for General John York of the Munitions Assignments Board because "now that I am out of the government and have nothing to do with the MAB it would be inappropriate." When reporters asked him to appraise the Potsdam conference, he declined, saying that one needed to have been on the scene to know how the conversations had progressed. But he was still too close to events to adopt a reflective frame of mind. News reports about wartime issues sent him rummaging through his files to check the story, but he never formed any systematic overview of the materials. He made it clear to Hyman, however, that his interest was in setting the record straight. "The whole story of Roosevelt—and my story is part of it," he declared, "is going to come out anyway in the next fifty years. I feel we will both come out with credit. And I don't see any point in trying to edit my past by destroying papers which showed precisely what I did and how I did it. I want people to know that I played politics; I also want them to know why I played politics."[39]

His interest in contemporary affairs also crowded out any inclinations toward writing history. Learning and doing were still his objectives. He thought that mediating labor disputes would put him in a position to restructure the garment industry. Strikes by elevator operators and coal barge operators temporarily inspired him to think that he could broaden his role as a mediator. And a visit from an art auctioneer, whom he had called to consult about selling some of the etchings he and Barbara had collected, gave him the chance to learn about the art business. He also studied up on modern painting and department store retailing.

Only financial pressures forced him to consider writing his memoirs. After some investigation he signed a contract with Harper and Brothers for a 20 percent royalty to be paid over fifteen years and a substantial advance. He also acquired the services of Cass Canfield, editor of *Harper's*, to help with the writing. He asked Beaverbrook to arrange for publication in Britain. When Beaverbrook let the matter slide, Hopkins spurred him on. "I am going to discuss chapter and verse and tell this story properly," he wrote. "I do not intend to rehash material that is known. I do not intend to try to write an objective history of the war but only a history of the war as I knew it and saw it. While there will be no scandal in the book, I intend to freely express my opinion of the personalities, including the Generals, and describe exactly how and why things happened as I saw them." Then, almost pleadingly, he added, "You well know my financial situation and I quite frankly hope, from this book, that I can set up some kind of competence for my family."[40]

In the end he produced a few pages that summarized the lessons of his years in government service: the need for government to supplement private enterprise to maintain prosperity, the need for the Allies to cooperate and for the United States to promote the Four Freedoms around the world.[41] There was nothing surprising in his formulations, though his abstract and general language was disappointing. Hopkins had succeeded in government by managing problems and persons in detail. The real value of his memoirs lay in his day-by-day observations and his assessments of mighty figures. He was, of course, fully capable of this kind of writing, and his editors would have steered him toward it. At the moment, however, he was not content to retreat into the past but instead wanted to teach its lessons to the present.

Through the summer and fall of 1945 Hopkins sensed that postwar negotiations were not turning out as he had hoped. He and Louise were spending a few weeks in Maine with her sister's family when Chip Bohlen arrived from the Potsdam conference. Bohlen was apprehensive about Soviet intentions because of the refusal of the Russians to countenance any interference with their sphere of influence in the Balkans. He was also inclined to think that ideological differences between the United States and the Soviet Union further limited the chances for cooperation. Hopkins was more hopeful. His own experience with Stalin caused him to think that the Russians could be brought along with care and patience. He was inclined to dismiss ideology, believing that nations largely pursued self-interest. But the situation did not improve, and by mid-November he was writing Eleanor Roosevelt: "I cannot say I am too happy about the way the atom bomb is being handled. In fact, I think we are doing everything we can to break with Russia which seems so unnecessary to me."[42]

But he was not in a position to confront the ambiguities that were emerging from the victory. Since his collapse in 1944 his health had been especially precarious. Periods of vitality and strength would be followed by spells of vomiting and diarrhea, signs that his digestive illness was recurring. In some ways he had hampered his own recovery. Although he drank in moderation, usually less than his friends, he did not curb his appetite for rich foods. Even worse, he smoked constantly—four packs a day starting as soon as he got out of bed. Often, even in the middle of the night, he would call for a snack of something bland to settle his stomach. When his strength was particularly low, he would take a transfusion of a pint of blood plasma. Mount Vernon Lewis, his butler, rigged up a stand from which to hang the container, and Hopkins would insert the needle himself. He had persevered in this condition to see the war fought to victory, but now his time had run out. In October his health took another bad turn; his food would not stay down, and he frequently soiled his bed with diarrhea. In November he entered the hospital for another round of tests— "putting me through the hoops in a big way," as he put it.[43]

He was his usual optimistic self, saying that the worst he feared was boredom. But worse than that was to come. His doctors diagnosed a recurrence of his nutritional problem, but they had run out of ideas for treating it. His previous operation had accomplished all that could have been hoped for, and in any case his weakened condition argued against another one. None of the doctors considered the possibility that, as a recent study has suggested, he might actually have been suffering from hepatitis, contracted from his many injections and transfusions.[44]

As he continued to decline, his friends looked for ways to pull him back to health. Halifax encouraged Churchill to pay a visit. "There could be no better tonic for him," he wrote, "than seeing you." After visiting the hospital in January his son Robert called President Truman to ask him to send his father on another mission to revitalize him. It was an excellent idea, but it came too late. When Truman consulted the doctors, they refused to let Hopkins leave the hospital.[45]

On January 22, 1946, Hopkins wrote his last letter. It was to Churchill, who was vacationing in Miami Beach. Full of his old vitality and wit, he joked about having developed cirrhosis of the liver "not due, I regret to say, from taking too much alcohol." He especially regretted the bad reputation of cirrhosis, since he neither deserved it nor had he enjoyed its pleasures. He told Churchill that he was looking forward to talking over the world situation, "to say nothing of our private lives."[46]

It was not to be. He continued to fail, his body wasting to skin and bones. He lost his appetite. He began to stare blankly into space. As he felt death approach, he could have complained that at fifty-five years of age he was getting a bad break. But no one knew better that bad breaks were part of life. Often in the past he had sunk low enough to graze the line separating life from death, and now he realized that he was not going to turn back. "You can't beat destiny," he said to Mount Vernon Lewis.[47] The next day he slipped into unconsciousness. On the morning of January 29 he failed rapidly. Louise, who was with him, left his side long enough to telegraph the news to his closest friends. Then she returned to his bedside. At 11:30 in the morning Harry Hopkins died.

# Abbreviations

| | |
|---|---|
| AASW | American Association of Social Workers |
| ARC | American Red Cross |
| Arnold Papers | Henry Arnold Papers, Library of Congress, Washington, D.C. |
| Aurand Papers | Colonel Henry Aurand Papers, Dwight D. Eisenhower Library, Abilene, Kansas |
| AVIA | Ministry of Aviation Records, Public Records Office, London |
| BCW | Board of Child Welfare |
| CAB | Cabinet Office Records, Public Records Office, London |
| CCS | Combined Chiefs of Staff |
| Clapper Papers | Raymond Clapper Papers, Library of Congress, Washington, D.C. |
| COHC | Columbia University Oral History Collection, Butler Library, Columbia University, New York City |
| COS | Chief of Staff (Great Britain) |
| Cox Papers | Oscar Cox Papers, Franklin D. Roosevelt Library, Hyde Park, N.Y. |
| C/S | Chief of Staff (United States) |
| CSS Archives | Community Service Society Archives, New York City |
| CSS Collection | Community Service Society Collection, Butler Library, Columbia University, New York City |
| CWA | Civil Works Administration |
| Davies, diary | Joseph Davies, diary, Joseph Davies Papers, Library of Congress, Washington, D.C. |
| EGH | Ethel (Gross) Hopkins |
| ER | Eleanor Roosevelt |
| ERS | Edward R. Stettinius |
| FDR | Franklin D. Roosevelt |
| FDRL | Franklin D. Roosevelt Library, Hyde Park, N.Y. |
| FERA | Federal Emergency Relief Administration |
| FO | Foreign Office (Great Britain) |

| | |
|---|---|
| *FRUS* | *Foreign Relations of the United States* (Washington, D.C.: Government Printing Office, 1958–1969) |
| GCML | George C. Marshall Library, Lexington, Virginia |
| HHP | Harry Hopkins Papers, Franklin D. Roosevelt Library, Hyde Park, N.Y. |
| HLH | Harry L. Hopkins |
| HLH, Speeches and Press Conferences | Speeches and Press Conferences of Harry L. Hopkins, Division of Information, Records of the Works Progress Administration, RG 69, National Archives, Washington, D.C. |
| HMJr | Henry Morgenthau, Jr. |
| HMJr, diary | Henry Morgenthau, Jr., diary, Henry Morgenthau Papers, Franklin D. Roosevelt Library, Hyde Park, N.Y. |
| HMJr, presidential diary | Henry Morgenthau, Jr., presidential diary, Henry Morgenthau papers, Franklin D. Roosevelt Library, Hyde Park, N.Y. |
| HST | Harry S Truman |
| JAK | John A. Kingsbury |
| JCS | Joint Chiefs of Staff |
| JSM | British Joint Staff Mission, Washington, D.C. |
| Kingsbury Papers | John A. Kingsbury Papers, Library of Congress, Washington, D.C. |
| LC | Library of Congress, Washington, D.C. |
| LWD | Lewis W. Douglas |
| MAB | Munitions Assignments Board |
| Marshall Papers | George C. Marshall Papers, George C. Marshall Library, Lexington, Virginia |
| NASW | National Association of Social Workers |
| OF | Official File, Franklin D. Roosevelt Library, Hyde Park, N.Y. |
| PPF | President's Personal File, Franklin D. Roosevelt Library, Hyde Park, N.Y. |
| PREM | Prime Minister's Office Records, Public Records Office, London |
| PSF | President's Secretary's File, Franklin D. Roosevelt Library, Hyde Park, N.Y. |
| RG | Record Group, National Archives and Records Service, Washington, D.C. |
| ROGNY | Records of the Governor of New York, Franklin D. Roosevelt Library, Hyde Park, N.Y. |

| | |
|---|---|
| Sherwood Papers | Robert Sherwood Papers, Houghton Library, Harvard University, Cambridge, Mass. |
| Sherwood, *Roosevelt and Hopkins* | Robert E. Sherwood, *Roosevelt and Hopkins: An Intimate History* (New York: Harper and Brothers, 1948) |
| Stettinius Papers | Edward R. Stettinius Papers, University of Virginia Library, Charlottesville, Virginia |
| Stimson, diary | Henry L. Stimson, diary, Henry L. Stimson Papers, Yale University Library, New Haven, Conn. |
| SWHA | Social Work History Archives, Minneapolis, Minn. |
| TC | Telephone conversation |
| WAH | W. Averell Harriman |
| *War Telegrams* | *Great Britain, Cabinet Office, Principal War Telegrams and Memoranda, 1940–1943, Washington* (Nendeln, Liechtenstein: KTO Press, 1976) |
| WPA | Works Progress Administration |
| WSC | Winston S. Churchill |

# Notes

## Prologue

1. Edward Lord Halifax to WSC, Feb. 1, 1946, Halifax Papers, Churchill College, Cambridge, microfilm reel 1.

2. Conversations with Grinnell College athletic director John A. Pfitsch, January 1978, June 1983.

## 1. Harness Maker's Son

1. Sherwood, *Roosevelt and Hopkins,* pp. 14–15; Rome Miller to HLH, Aug. 29, 1937, Hopkins microfilm, reel 19, HHP; Lewis Hopkins to HLH, May 7, 1915, letter in possession of Dr. James A. Halsted, hereafter cited as Halsted Papers (Dr. Halsted died in March of 1984, and the location of the collection is now uncertain); *Sioux City Journal,* Oct. 13, 1889, Hopkins microfilm, reel 3.

2. HLH to Wilder Hobson, May 28, 1935, Publicity folder, FERA New Subject File, Box 129, RG 69.

3. Lewis Hopkins to HLH, May 15, 1915, Halsted Collection.

4. C. B. Viggers to HLH, June 11, 1939, Hopkins microfilm, reel 3; Sherwood, *Roosevelt and Hopkins,* p. 15; Mrs. R. J. Peterson to HLH, Jan. 3, 1941, Hopkins microfilm, reel 19.

5. Sherwood, *Roosevelt and Hopkins,* pp. 15, 17; Charles K. Needham to HLH, June 24, 1933, FERA Old Subject File, RG 69; Stella Willis to HLH, June 15, 1939, Hopkins microfilm, reel 10; Peter Norbeck to HLH, July 16, 1935, Hopkins microfilm, reel 19; Robert Sherwood, interview with Robert Kerr, Oct. 12, 1947, Sherwood Papers.

6. Grinnell College, *Scarlet and Black,* Jan. 27, April 9, 13, 20, June 1, 15, Oct. 5, 12, 15, 19, 1904, March 1, 25, April 12, May 27, June 14, 1905.

7. *Grinnell Herald,* April 22, July 1, Dec. 12, 1913, Feb. 20, 1914; Adah Hopkins, "City Funds in a Small Community," *Fifteenth Iowa State Conference of Charities and Corrections, 1913,* Parks Library, Iowa State University, pp. 85–87.

8. Adah Hopkins, "City Funds," p. 87; *Grinnell Herald,* Jan. 14, 21, Feb. 11, 18, April 12, 25, May 20, 23, June 27, July 18, Sept. 30, Oct. 14, 28,

Nov. 21, Dec. 12, 1913, Jan. 16, 20, March 3, 10, 13, 24, April 3, 7, 24, 1914.

9. Robert Sherwood, interview with Adah Aime, Nov. 13, 1947, Sherwood Papers, Box 411.

10. *Grinnell Herald,* May 17, 1912, May 8, 1914; Kenneth Sills to HLH, Aug. 26, 1936, Hopkins microfilm, reel 7; Jasper Robinson to HLH, January 8, 1934, ibid., reel 9.

11. *Grinnell Herald,* Sept. 3, Nov. 19, 1909, Sept. 9, 1910, June 23, Aug. 1, 1911, April 5, 29, 1910, March 7, 1911.

12. *Grinnell Herald,* Sept. 14, 1909, Dec. 22, 1911; Anna Tiede to HLH, Jan. 11, 1939, HHP, Box 113; Frank Harding to HLH, April 6, 1939, Hopkins microfilm, reel 8; Dwight Bradley to HLH, Dec. 24, 1938, ibid., reel 13; Gladys Ferguson Mossman to HLH, May 9, 1934, HHP, Box 93; *Montana Standard,* Sept. 11, 1936, ibid., Box 54; LaMar G. Orndorff to HLH, Jan. 12, 1939, ibid., Box 299.

13. Sherwood, *Roosevelt and Hopkins,* p. 16; Newton Olson to HLH, Aug. 16, 1934, Hopkins microfilm, reel 9; Floy Manny to HLH, Jan. 27, 1939, ibid., reel 7.

14. Sherwood, *Roosevelt and Hopkins,* pp. 16, 939; Dwight Bradley to HLH, Dec. 24, 1938, Hopkins microfilm, reel 13; B. M. Bemon to HLH, March 1, 1939, ibid., reel 7.

15. HLH, speech at Grinnell College, Feb. 22, 1939, HHP, Box 12.

16. Herron's writings include *Social Meanings of Religious Experience* (New York: Crowell, 1896); *The Christian Society* (Chicago: Fleming H. Revell, 1894); and *The Christian State* (New York: Crowell, 1895). Gates's ideas are presented in Jesse Macy, "George Augustus Gates: A Tribute," in Isabel Smith Gates, *The Life of George Augustus Gates* (Boston: Pilgrim Press, 1915); Gates, "Municipal Ownership a Corollary of Democracy," 1899, talk to Iowa League of Municipalities; "High Standards of Honor in the Business World," and "Scales of Values," n.d., chapel talks at Grinnell College, Gates Collection, Grinnell College Archives, Grinnell, Iowa.

17. Jesse Macy, "The Scientific Spirit in Politics," *American Political Science Review,* 9 (1916), 6–7; *Scarlet and Black,* Jan. 15, 1910; J. H. T. Main, *Baccalaureate Addresses* (Cedar Rapids, Iowa: N. W. Wehran, 1931), p. 41; G. P. Wyckoff, "The Study of Society," *The Faculty Corner* (papers contributed to *The Unit* by members of the faculty of Iowa College, 1901), p. 170.

18. John S. Nollen, *Grinnell College* (Iowa City: State Historical Society of Iowa Press, 1953), p. 96; Florence Kerr, oral history interview, April 1, 1967, Grinnell College Archives.

19. *Scarlet and Black,* April 16, May 7, 1910; Main, *Baccalaureate Addresses,* pp. 25–26; Jesse Macy, "Twentieth Century Democracy," *Political Science*

*Quarterly,* 13 (1898), 516–517; Edward A. Steiner, *From Alien to Citizen* (New York: Fleming H. Revell, 1914), p. 321.

20. Jesse Macy, *Our Government* (New York: Ginn and Co., 1886), pp. 136–137.

21. Edward A. Steiner to Robert Sherwood, Nov. 11, 1947; Lewis Hopkins to Sherwood, Nov. 5, 1947; Robert Sherwood, interview with Adah Aime, November 13, 1947, Sherwood Papers, Box 411; Paul Appleby, oral history interview, COHC, p. 5; Florence Kerr, oral history interview, p. 3; HLH, chapel address at Grinnell, Feb. 22, 1939, HHP, Box 12; Jesse Macy bibliography, Nov. 1937, RG 69.

22. *Scarlet and Black,* Dec. 2, 1908, Nov. 25, Dec. 8, 1911, June 8, 1910.

23. Chester Davis, oral history interview, COHC, p. 70; Florence Kerr, oral history interview, p. 5.

24. *Scarlet and Black,* Nov. 3, 1909, Feb. 9, 1910, Jan. 17, 1912.

25. Ibid., March 25, 30, 1911; Roscoe Macy to HLH, Dec. 10, 1937, Hopkins microfilm, reel 16.

26. *Scarlet and Black,* Feb. 23, 1911.

27. HLH, academic record, Grinnell College Archives; Florence Kerr, oral history interview, p. 3.

28. Sherwood, *Roosevelt and Hopkins,* p. 14.

29. Ida Hinkle to HLH, Sept. 18, 1936, HHP, Box 89.

30. Transcript of radio broadcast by Robert St. John, "Who's Who in the News," Jan. 5, 1943, ellipsis in original, Hopkins microfilm, reel 11.

31. *Scarlet and Black,* May 4, 11, 1912.

## 2. Innovative Social Worker

1. Louis D. Hartson to Earl D. Strong, July 12, 1956, Hopkins Collection, Grinnell College Archives, Grinnell, Iowa.

2. Florence Kerr, oral history interview, April 1, 1967, Grinnell College Archives, Grinnell, Iowa, p. 5; Sherwood, *Roosevelt and Hopkins,* p. 23.

3. EGH to John Dickson, Sept. 30, 1941; EGH, undated resumé of work experience; HLH to EGH, Feb. 24, 1913, Halsted Collection.

4. HLH to EGH, Feb. 24, 1913; EGH to HLH, March 14, 1913, ibid.

5. HLH to EGH, Feb. 23, 24, 1913, ibid.

6. EGH to HLH, March 5, 1913; HLH to EGH, March 7, 1913, ibid.

7. JAK, notes on HLH employment record, Box B84, Kingsbury Papers; *Seattle Star,* Sept. 11, 1936, clipping in Hopkins Papers, Box 54.

8. Arnold S. Rosenberg, "John Adams Kingsbury and the Struggle for Social Justice in New York, 1906–1918" (Ph.D. diss., New York University, 1968), pp. 139–140, 307–319.

9. HLH to Claude Kitchin, April 10, 1917; HLH to the Class of 1912, April 23, 1917, Halsted Collection.

10. "Study of Methods Employed by the A.I.C.P. to Secure Work for Unemployed Applicants," n.d., CSS Collection, Box 16. It is hard to tell if Hopkins wrote this report, but it seems likely that if he did not, he had access to its findings since they are in line with his recommendations. See Hopkins's remarks, recorded in "Meeting of the Religious Citizenship League to Consider the Question of Unemployment," Feb. 6, 1914, ibid., Box 181; HLH, "A Detailed Plan of Organization and Administration of State Employment Offices, as provided for by Chapter 184 of the Laws of 1914," n.d., Halsted Collection. Some suggestion that Hopkins may have written the report can be found in Superintendent of the Bureau of Public Health and Hygiene to Paul Kennady, Jan. 16, 1914, CSS Collection, Box 16.

11. William H. Matthews to HLH, Dec. 24, 1938, HHP, Box 14; *New York World-Telegram,* Dec. 24, 1938, clipping in General Records of the Department of Commerce, file 101880, RG 40; Hopkins's remarks in "Meeting of the Religious Citizenship League"; *New York Times,* Feb. 3, 1914.

12. HLH to JAK, Dec. 31, 1914, Kingsbury Papers, Box A4.

13. P. C. Wilson of the mayor's office to H. Bruere, Nov. 17, 1916; HLH to Wilson, Nov. 23, 24, 1916, Mayor's Papers, Child Welfare Board, Mitchel, 1916, Municipal Archives, New York City; BCW, *Annual Report,* Oct. 1917, p. 12, Municipal Library, New York, N.Y.; HLH to H. Bruere, n.d. (July–Aug., 1917), Hopkins microfilm, reel 24-4, HHP; HLH, "Office Report for November of 1917," Dec. 17, 1917, BCW minutes, Municipal Archives, New York City; HLH, "Office Report for November of 1916," Dec. 20, 1916, BCW minutes. Hopkins instructed investigators to be respectful and friendly toward their clients. BCW staff to HLH, March 2, 1917, Halsted Collection.

14. Memorandum, Nov. 16, 1916; HLH to Miss H. M. Patterson, March 30, 1916; HLH to Joanna Colcord, Nov. 24, 1916, May 12, 1917; Colcord to Director, Feb. 18, 1916; Colcord to HLH, Dec. 26, 1917, CSS Collection, Box 97; HLH to JAK, April 20, 1917, Kingsbury Papers, Box A37.

15. W. Frank Persons to HLH, Dec. 20, 24, 1917, Hopkins microfilm, reel 24-4.

16. Ruth Walrad, "The History of the Home Service, 1916–1924," typescript, vol. 9 in "The History of the American National Red Cross" (Washington, D.C.: American National Red Cross, 1950), pp. 72–73; HLH, "Monthly Report," June 1918, ARC file 149.01, RG 2. Items on Hopkins's draft status are in Hopkins microfilm, reel 24-4. Sherwood, *Roosevelt and Hopkins,* p. 26.

17. HLH, "Monthly Report of the Bureau of Civilian Relief for September 1918," ARC file 149.18, RG 2; HLH, remarks at Conference on Rural Home Service, April 12, 1919, ARC file 149.01, ibid.; HLH to James L. Feiser, April 5, 1920, file 149.01, ibid.; Walrad, "History of Home Service," p. 80.

18. HLH, "Monthly Report," September, November, December 1918; HLH, "Monthly Reports," February, March, July 1919, ARC file 149.18, RG

2; "Conference on Rural Home Service, Gulf Division Headquarters, April 12, 1919," ARC file 149.01, ibid.

19. Clipping attached to Kate Markham Power to HLH, June 19, 1937, HHP, Box 95.

20. Sarah M. Jennings to HLH, Aug. 2, 1938, ibid., Box 91; Laurence P. Moomau to HLH, Jan. 12, 1938, Hopkins microfilm, reel 14; Homer Borst to Everett A. Golway, Dec. 16, 1951, Jan. 7, 1952, ARC Archives, Washington, D.C., hereafter cited as ARC Archives.

21. "Conference on Rural Home Service, Gulf Division Headquarters, April 12, 1919"; W. H. Matthews to HLH, Dec. 24, 1938, Hopkins microfilm, reel 14; Helene Ingram to Edwin P. Maynard, Nov. 6, 1915, Halsted Collection.

22. R. J. Colbert, "Report of the Activities and Accomplishments of Educational Service in the Gulf Division of the Red Cross from January 10, 1920, to March, 1921," ARC file 149.18, RG 2.

23. Leigh Carroll to J. Byron Deacon, April 18, 1919; Deacon to Carroll, April 21, 1919; Carroll to F. C. Munroe, May 21, 1919; Munroe to Carroll, July 11, 1919, Hopkins microfilm, reel 24-4; W. Frank Persons to Livingston Farrand, Sept. 27, 1919; Farrand to Persons, Oct. 8, 1919; Sir David Henderson to Farrand, Oct. 14, 1919; Persons to Deacon, Oct. 15, 1919, Halsted Collection; HLH to Curtis E. Lakeman, Nov. 7, 1919; Lakeman to HLH, Nov. 10, 1919; John Melpolder to HLH, Nov. 17, 1919; HLH to Henderson, n.d.; HLH to Farrand, Nov. 12, 1919; Farrand to HLH, Nov. 18, 24, 1919; Henderson to HLH, n.d., Hopkins microfilm, reel 24-4.

24. HLH to Leigh Carroll, n.d. (spring, 1920); F. C. Munroe to Carroll, May 20, 1920, ARC Archives. Hopkins's role in his promotion to division manager is suggested by statements in his own handwriting on the back of Red Cross stationery outlining the main points of Munroe's letter; see Hopkins microfilm, reel 24-4.

25. On the progress of social workers in their careers, see William Walling Bremer, "New York City's Family of Social Servants and the Politics of Welfare: A Prelude to the New Deal" (Ph.D. diss., Stanford University, 1972), pp. 26–27; Florence Kerr, oral history interview, COHC, p. 5; HLH to EGH, Feb. 24, 1913, Halsted Collection; W. H. Matthews to HLH, June 16, 1933, Hopkins microfilm, reel 9.

26. HLH on back of American Red Cross stationery, n.d., ibid., reel 24-4. Comparing Hopkins's notes with F. C. Munroe to Leigh Carroll, May 20, 1920, ARC Archives, suggests that Hopkins was composing a draft for Munroe.

27. F. C. Munroe to Leigh Carroll, May 20, 1920, ARC Archives.

28. See the quantitative compilation of division activities in folder entitled "Chapter Activity Reports, 1920–1945," ARC file 150.08, RG 2; HLH to

James L. Feiser, Sept. 12, 1922, ARC Archives. Hopkins suffered from ill health during this time, which also caused him to consider leaving the Red Cross. EGH to Robert Sherwood, Sept. 13, 1947, Sherwood Papers, Box 411; W. Frank Persons to HLH, April 15, 1922, Hopkins microfilm, reel 24-4.

29. HLH to B. B. Burritt, Nov. 6, 1919, file 321, CSS Archives; Robert Sherwood, interview with JAK, Oct. 29, 1947, Sherwood Papers, Box 411; JAK to Linsly R. Williams, Nov. 1, Dec. 7, 1921, Kingsbury Papers, Box B23; JAK, notes on HLH, ibid., Box B84.

30. ? to B. B. Burritt, July 6, 1922, file 321, CSS Archives; JAK, notes on HLH, Kingsbury Papers, Box B84. EGH indicated her support for the move by signing the letter of resignation in Harry's absence; HLH to James L. Feiser, Sept. 12, 1922, ARC Archives; Sherwood, *Roosevelt and Hopkins,* p. 27.

31. HLH to B. B. Burritt, Feb. 24, March 26, 1923; HLH, "An A.I.C.P. Health Program," April 1, 1923, file 321, CSS Archives; HLH to Burritt, May 4, 1923; [Secretary to HLH] to Elsie M. Bond, June 26, 1923; HLH to Burritt, July 20, 1923, file 321, ibid.

32. C.-E. A. Winslow and H. I. Harris, *Public Health Bulletin No. 136* (Washington, D.C.: U.S. Public Health Service, 1923); HLH to B. B. Burritt, July 20, Aug. 2, 31, 1923, file 321, CSS Archives. C.-E. A. Winslow, "The First 50 Years of the New York Tuberculosis and Health Association," n.d., pamphlet printed by New York Lung Association, New York City; HLH, "The Consolidation of Private Health Work," *Proceedings of the National Conference of Social Work* (Chicago: University of Chicago Press, 1927), pp. 202–204; Sherwood, *Roosevelt and Hopkins,* pp. 27–28.

33. HLH to B. B. Burritt, Jan. 4, 1926, CSS Collection, Box 17.

34. Minutes of the Executive Committee, Oct. 22, 1929, March 27, 1930, CSS Collection, Box 64.

35. Hopkins knew that his opinions would be controversial. A year earlier, when he had investigated social health work practices in London, he observed that "the same row between local and centralized authority seems to go on the world over"; HLH to EGH, July 24, 1928, Hopkins microfilm, reel 24-4.

36. Minutes of the National Council Meeting, June 29, 1924; Minutes of the Annual Meeting, June 30, 1924, folder 19, NASW: AASW, SWHA.

37. Minutes of the National Council Meeting of the AASW, April 12, June 29, July 1, 1924, folder 19, NASW: AASW, SWHA.

38. Minutes of the Annual Meeting of the AASW, June 15, 1925, folder 2, ibid.

39. Minutes of AASW National Council Meeting, April 12, 1924, folder 19, ibid.

40. HLH, "The Place of Social Work in Public Health," *Proceedings of the*

*National Conference of Social Work* (Chicago: University of Chicago Press, 1926), pp. 222–227.

41. Sherwood, *Roosevelt and Hopkins,* pp. 28–29; JAK to Donald S. Howard, April 16, 1956, Kingsbury Papers, Box B11.

42. Linsly R. Williams to HLH, June 19, 1930; resolution enclosed in Williams to HLH, June 30, 1933, HHP, Box 7. Sherwood quotes from this resolution but omits the parts referring to the association's finances, in Sherwood, *Roosevelt and Hopkins,* pp. 27–28.

## 3. Escape from Despair

1. Kingsbury Milbank Fund Diary, Feb. 29, April 10, 1923, Kingsbury Papers, Box B39; HLH to B. B. Burritt, Aug. 2, 1923, file 321, CSS Archives; HLH to David Hopkins, [May or June 1925], Halsted Collection; Sherwood, *Roosevelt and Hopkins,* pp. 27, 35, 37, 529; EGH to Sherwood, Sept. 13, 1947, Sherwood Papers, Box 411; HLH to Ralph J. Reed, June 5, 1924, file 321, CSS Archives; Robert Sherwood, interview with Adah Aime, Nov. 13, 1947; Robert Sherwood, interview with Robert Kerr, Oct. 12, 1947, Sherwood Papers, Box 411.

2. J. Halsted, interview with Mrs. Cherry Bandler and Mrs. June Giffen, Dec. 31, 1977, Halsted Collection.

3. EGH to HLH, Aug. 26, 1918; HLH to EGH, [Sept. 6, 1918], Halsted Collection. Other letters that bear on their relationship during this period are HLH to EGH, [July 19], Aug. 21, 26, Sept. 21, 1918; EGH to HLH, Aug. 7, Sept. 15, 1918, ibid.

4. HLH to EGH, [Oct. 1920], Hopkins microfilm, reel 24-4, HHP.

5. HLH to EGH, June 2, 1925; HLH to EGH [June 4, 7, 1925], ibid.

6. HLH to EGH, [Nov. 1, 1927]; EGH to HLH, Nov. 8, 1927, Halsted Collection.

7. Barbara Duncan to Myrta Bradley, Aug. 3, 1927; Barbara Hopkins to Myrta Bradley, June 21, 23, 1931, June 13, 1933, Feb. 20, 21, 1934; Barbara Hopkins to Dorothy Stephenson, July 29, 1936, Halsted Collection. Although the traits revealed by Barbara's letters suggest that Harry was attracted to her because, unlike Ethel, she accepted life uncomplainingly and was content to remain quietly on the sidelines, there is not enough evidence to conclude that this was the most important basis of their relationship. In his courtship of Ethel, Harry had shown himself to be a passionate suitor, and he probably found qualities in Barbara that went beyond mere compatibility.

8. HLH to EGH, n.d. [aboard ship], July 6, [8], 18, 19, 22, 24, 26, 1928, Hopkins microfilm, reel 24-4.

9. JAK, notes, n.d., Kingsbury Papers, Box B84.

10. HLH to EGH, cable, n.d., Halsted Collection. Harry discussed his

arrival plans giving a similar late date in a letter to EGH, July 24, 1928, Hopkins microfilm, reel 24-4. HLH to Myrta Bradley, Aug. 2, 1928, Halsted Collection.

11. HLH to EGH, [April 1929], Halsted Collection.

12. HLH to EGH, [July 8, 1928]; HLH to EGH, July 18, 19, 26, 1928, Hopkins microfilm, reel 24-4.

13. HLH to EGH, July 22, 1928, ibid.

14. FDR, memo for Unemployment Relief Administration, Sept. 29, 1931; Jesse Straus to Herbert Lehman, Oct. 7, 1931, Franklin D. Roosevelt papers, ROGNY microfilm reel 173. Sherwood reports that Hodson himself decided against taking the job out of fear that his reputation would be damaged if things went wrong; Sherwood, *Roosevelt and Hopkins,* p. 32. John Kingsbury recalled that Homer Folks of the Tuberculosis and Health Association asked him if he would like the position. Kingsbury replied that he preferred to be at the Milbank Fund; JAK, notes, Kingsbury Papers, Box B84.

15. Linsly Williams to HLH, June 7, 1933, HHP, Box 7; Williams to Kendall Emerson, Oct. 19, 1931, New York Lung Association Archives, New York City; Jesse Straus to Herbert Lehman, Oct. 7, 1931, ROGNY, microfilm reel 173.

16. Emma Octavia Lundberg, "The New York State Temporary Emergency Relief Administration," *The Social Service Review,* 6 (1932), 545–566; TERA rules, enclosed in Jesse Straus to FDR, Nov. 5, 1931, ROGNY, microfilm reel 173; *New York Times,* Sept. 21, 1932.

17. The dilemma was intensified because the unemployed preferred work relief to home relief. As the work relief rolls filled up, TERA actually had to encourage people to sign up for home relief. Jesse Straus to FDR, Jan. 5, 1932, ROGNY, microfilm reel 173.

18. "Statement of Jesse Isador Straus, Chairman," "Statement of Philip J. Wickser," in *Report of the Temporary Emergency Relief Administration,* Feb. 23, 1932; Douglas P. Falconer to FDR, Jan. 28, 1932, ROGNY, microfilm reel 173; Susan Dyckman Johnston, memo, Nov. 3, 1931, ARC file DR 419.02, RG 2.

19. *New York Times,* June 8, Aug. 24, Oct. 15, 21, 31, Nov. 7, 1932.

20. HLH, appointment diaries, 1932–1933, Hopkins microfilm, reel 4.

21. JAK, notes on Hopkins, Kingsbury Papers, Box B84; JAK to HLH, Feb. 14, 1933; Victor S. Woodward to HLH, Feb. 23, 1933, ibid., Box B11; Dr. Shirley W. Wynne, "A Valuable Tuberculosis Project," *Better Times: The Welfare Magazine,* 14 (1933), 5–6, copy in HHP, Box 7; Hopkins also discussed making a statewide survey to discover whether relief recipients were receiving adequate medical care. HLH, appointment diary, Nov. 17, 1932, Hopkins microfilm, reel 4; Abraham Appleberg to HLH, n.d. (Dec. 1939),

ibid., reel 13; HLH, appointment diary, Sept. 22, 1932, ibid., reel 4; Charles A. Miller to HLH, Dec. 23, 1938, ibid., reel 14.

22. *New York Times,* June 8, 1932.

23. HLH, appointment diary, April 5, 29, May 12, 13, 26, 31, June 10, 24, Oct. 11, 27, Dec. 8–9, 1932, Hopkins microfilm, reel 4; FDR to Jesse Straus, April 30, 1932, ROGNY, microfilm reel 173; ER to HLH, June 3, Oct. 26, Dec. 19, 1932; ER to Margaret Brown, July 27, Oct. 29, 1932, HHP, Box 7.

24. HLH to Lewis Hopkins, Sept. 8, 1932, in Sherwood, *Roosevelt and Hopkins,* p. 33.

25. HLH to Lewis Hopkins, [Dec. 1932], ibid., pp. 34–35.

26. Robert Bondy to James Feiser, Dec. 3, 1932, ARC file DR 419.02, RG 2.

27. Senator E. P. Costigan to HLH, March 13, 1933, HHP, Box 7; HLH, appointment diaries, Dec. 1932–April 1933, Hopkins microfilm, reel 4; HLH to Herbert Lehman, Dec. 15, 1932, Office of the Governor, Correspondence, microfilm reel 45, New York State Library, Albany, N.Y.

28. HLH, appointment diaries, March 14–15, 1933, Hopkins microfilm, reel 4; Frances Perkins, interview, COHC, bk. 4, pp. 471–473.

29. HLH, appointment diary, Dec. 27, 1932, Jan. 5, 1933, Hopkins microfilm, reel 4; JAK, notes, n.d., Kingsbury Papers, Box B84; Donald Duncan, oral history interview, COHC, pp. 525–526. On Hopkins's concern over money, see JAK, notes on Hopkins, n.d., Kingsbury Papers, Box B84, and Allen T. Burns to HMJr, April 27, 1933, Henry Morgenthau Correspondence Files, Box 123, FDRL. Letters from Burns and Joanna C. Colcord of the Russell Sage Foundation suggest that Hopkins may have been actively seeking the position; Colcord to FDR, April 28, 1933, ibid.

30. HLH, appointment diary, May 19, 20, 21, 1933, Hopkins microfilm, reel 4; "Biographical Sketch of Harry L. Hopkins," June 1, 1938, Works Progress Administration Division of Information, RG 69.

31. *Washington Post,* May 23, 1933; HLH to Governor Floyd Olson (Minnesota), May 23, 1933, HHP Box 94.

## 4. A Changed Man

1. HLH to Elwood Street, June 23, 1933, HHP, Box 98.

2. "Conference on Public Works Features of National Industrial Recovery Act," May 27, 1933, Office of the Governor, Correspondence, microfilm reel 95, New York State Library, Albany, New York; "Record of Conference Held in the Office of the Federal Relief Administrator, Harry L. Hopkins," June 26, 1933, file 179, FERA Old Subject File, Box 7, RG 69; HLH, speech to the Conference of Governors and State Relief Administrators, June 14, 1933,

HHP, Box 9; HLH, radio address on station WRC, Washington, D.C., June 24, 1933; and HLH, address to the annual meeting of the U.S. Conference of Mayors, Sept. 23, 1933, ibid.; HLH to FDR, Sept. 14, 1933, ibid., Box 95; HLH, report to the National Executive Council, July 18, 1933, ibid., Box 43.

3. Quoted in Searle Charles, *Minister of Relief: Harry Hopkins and the Depression* (Syracuse, N.Y.: Syracuse University Press, 1963), p. 37. See also HLH, address to Conference of State Relief Administrators, June 11, 1933, HHP, Box 9; HLH, conversation memorandum, July 6, 1933, ibid., Box 40; HLH, address to the General Assembly of Kentucky, Aug. 22, 1933, ibid., Box 9; *Monthly Report of the Federal Emergency Relief Administration, May 22– June 30, 1933* (Washington, D.C.: Government Printing Office, 1933), pp. 4–5, and *July 1–31, 1933,* pp. 4–6, hereafter cited as FERA, *Monthly Report;* HLH to FDR, Aug. 14, 15, HHP, Box 38.

4. HLH, "The Developing National Program of Relief," in *Proceedings of the National Council of Social Work* (Chicago: University of Chicago Press, 1933), p. 66; HLH to State Emergency Relief Administrators, n.d., HHP, Box 22; HLH to Field Representatives, Sept. 15, 1933; HLH memos to staff, Aug. 2, Oct. 10, 1933, FERA Old Subject File, RG 69.

5. Report of remarks by HLH to conference of FERA staff, field representatives, and field statisticians, Sept. 5, 1933, HHP, Box 24.

6. "Conference on Public Works Features of National Industrial Recovery Act," May 27, 1933, Office of the Governor, Correspondence, microfilm reel 95, New York State Library, Albany, N.Y.; HLH to Governors and State Relief Administrators, June 10, 1933; HLH to State Emergency Relief Administrators, n.d., HHP, Box 22; HLH to FDR, June 12, 1933, ibid., Box 40; HLH, address to the Kentucky State Legislature, Aug. 22, 1933, ibid., Box 9; HLH to FDR, Aug. 29, 1933, ibid., Box 40.

7. JAK to Homer Folks, July 22, 1933, Kingsbury Papers, Box B10.

8. HLH, "The Developing National Program of Relief," p. 69; HLH, untitled address, Sept. 23, 1933, HHP, Box 9.

9. HLH, radio address on the *National Radio Forum,* Oct. 11, 1933, ibid., Box 9.

10. HLH to State Emergency Relief Administrators, Oct. 20, 1933, ibid., Box 22.

11. John A. Salmond, *A Southern Rebel: The Life and Times of Aubrey Willis Williams, 1890–1965* (Chapel Hill: University of North Carolina Press, 1983), pp. 51–52; "Jacob Baker," Biographies of WPA Officials, Box 561, RG 69; Jacob Baker to Rexford Tugwell, Oct. 16, 1933, Work Relief, General Correspondence, FERA Old Subject File, Box 17, RG 69.

12. This account has been reconstructed from the following sources, which individually confuse the sequence of events: Forrest A. Walker, *The Civil Works Administration: An Experiment in Federal Work Relief, 1933–1934*

(New York: Garland Publishing Company, 1979), pp. 29–33; Katie Louch-heim, ed., *The Making of the New Deal: The Insiders Speak* (Cambridge, Mass.: Harvard University Press, 1983), pp. 187–188; Louis Brownlow, *A Passion for Anonymity* (Chicago: University of Chicago Press, 1958), pp. 286–287; Salmond, *A Southern Rebel,* pp. 54–55. Some help in straightening out the sequence, but not as much as one might hope, was provided by HLH, appointment diary, October 1933, Hopkins microfilm, reel 4, HHP.

13. Robert Sherwood, interview with Louis Brownlow, Feb. 13, 1947, Sherwood Papers, Box 411.

14. Robert Sherwood, interview with Aubrey Williams, March 18, 1947, ibid.; Walker, *Civil Works Administration,* p. 36; HLH to Harold Ickes, Nov. 6, 1933, Administration folder, Nov. 8 to Feb. 1, CWA Administrative Correspondence, General, Box 53, RG 69.

15. Jacob Baker to Donald Stone, Nov. 17, 1933, Memoranda folder A-B, CWA Administrative Correspondence, General, Box 53, ibid.; HLH, report to the National Executive Council, Nov. 28, 1933, HHP, Box 44.

16. Edward A. Williams, *Federal Aid for Relief* (New York: Columbia University Press, 1939), p. 113; Charles, *Minister of Relief,* p. 52; FERA, *Monthly Report, December 1–31, 1933,* pp. 30–36; Alfred Baruch to Perry Fellows, "Review of Civil Works Projects, an Estimate of their Utility and Social Value, and Suggestions for the Future," March 1, 1934, Policy folder, CWA Administrative Correspondence, General, Box 99, RG 69; "Testimony of Mr. Harry L. Hopkins . . . Before the Bureau of the Budget," Jan. 22, 1934, HHP, Box 80.

17. HLH, speech to general meeting of CWA, Nov. 15, 1933, ibid., Box 9; HLH, remarks to FERA Conference on the Emergency Needs of Women, Nov. 20, 1933, ibid., Box 24.

18. HLH, remarks to the National Emergency Council, Jan. 9, 1934, in Lester G. Seligman and Elmer E. Cornwell, Jr., eds., *New Deal Mosaic: Roosevelt Confers with His National Emergency Council* (Eugene: University of Oregon Press, 1965), pp. 37–39, 76, 125–130.

19. Walker, *Civil Works Administration,* chap. 6; "Hearing of Delegation from the National Council of the Unemployed, Convening in Washington, D.C.," Feb. 5, 1934, in HLH, Speeches and Press Conferences.

20. Walker, *Civil Works Administration,* pp. 58, 137, 152–153.

21. Mrs. Kathryn Godwin [secretary to HLH] to Bruce McClure, Dec. 18, 1933, CWA Administrative Correspondence, General, G-I, Box 53, RG 69; HLH press conference, Feb. 9, 1934, in HLH, Speeches and Press Conferences. Evidence that Governor William Langer of North Dakota was collecting political contributions from CWA employees led Hopkins to federalize the North Dakota operation and to fire the administrator in charge of the collecting. The Justice Department later indicted and convicted Langer but lost the

case on appeal. See "Summary of events and evidence re FERA problems in North Dak.," n.d., HHP, Box 39.

22. Of 750 serious charges, 240 were proved, 77 involved criminal violations, and 17 of these resulted in convictions; see Charles, *Minister of Relief,* p. 59. Even one of the reporters at a press conference remarked, "The thing that has surprised me so far [is] that the cases have been so petty—none of them big"; HLH, press conference, Jan. 27, 1934, in HLH, Speeches and Press Conferences.

23. Governor Eugene Talmadge to FDR, Jan. 10, 1934; Alan Johnstone to HLH, Jan. 19, 1934, HHP, Box 40; Walker, *Civil Works Administration,* pp. 110–123; "Hearing of Delegation from the National Council of the Unemployed, Convening in Washington, D.C.," Feb. 5, 1934, in HLH, Speeches and Press Conferences.

24. HLH to All State Civil Works Administrators and State Emergency Relief Administrators, March 6, 1934, HHP, Box 23; HLH TC Fred Daniels, April 7, 1934, ibid., Box 76; T. J. Edmonds to HLH, April 8, 1934; M. Milford TC Edmonds and Floyd B. Olson, April 7, 1934, ibid, Box 94; HLH press conference, April 9, 1934, in HLH, Speeches and Press Conferences; HLH TC Jos. L. Carney, April 13, 1934, HHP, Box 36; HLH TC Gay Shepperson, May 8, 1934, ibid., Box 37; HLH TC Floyd B. Olson, April 19, 1934, ibid., Box 75.

25. Draft "Outline of Suggested Projects for Work Divisions," March 1934, with corrections and suggestions by HLH, Daily Record folder, FERA, Office of Jacob Baker, Box 1, RG 69; HLH to State Emergency Relief Administrators, March 20, 1934, HHP, Box 23; HLH to State Emergency Relief Administrators, March 20, 1934, ibid.; HLH, press conference, Feb. 19, 1934, in HLH, Speeches and Press Conferences.

26. FERA staff meeting, notes, Dec. 6, 1933, HHP, Box 49.

27. HLH, press conference, March 2, 1934, in HLH, Speeches and Press Conferences.

28. For example, see HLH to W. J. Ellis et al., Dec. 11, 1933, Conferences folder, FERA Old Subject File, Box 7, RG 69, and H. L. Lurie to S. P. Breckinridge, Aug. 8, 1933, folder 26, Lurie Papers, SWHA; J. V. Cardon, oral history interview, COHC, pp. 396–397; Isaac Landman to HLH, Jan. 5, 1940, Hopkins microfilm, reel 8.

29. Sherwood, *Roosevelt and Hopkins,* p. 49; Ellen Woodward, interview with Robert Sherwood, Oct. 11, 1947, Sherwood Papers, Box 411. Hopkins's informality has posed a certain amount of difficulty for historians and biographers. Because of his casual attitude toward office procedures, he did not compile an office file from which his activities can easily be reconstructed. The closest thing to such a record was kept by Jacob Baker, but it records only his necessarily partial view.

30. John Carmody, oral history interview, COHC, pp. 303–305.

31. HLH, memos to staff, various dates in 1933 and 1934, HLH memos to staff folder, FERA Old Subject File, RG 69; Brownlow, *Passion for Anonymity,* p. 288; staff meeting notes, Dec. 1, 1933, HHP, Box 49.

32. Carmody, oral history interview; Jacob Baker to HLH, Aug. 29, 1942, HHP, Box 314.

33. Various clippings, June–August 1933, and *Denver Post,* Dec. 24, 1933, in scrapbooks, ibid., Box 272.

34. HLH to FDR, Dec. 29, 1933, ibid., Box 95.

35. Sherwood, *Roosevelt and Hopkins,* pp. 63, 84; HLH, speech to the Citizens League of Cleveland, May 24, 1935, HHP, Box 9.

## 5. Launching the WPA

1. HLH, appointment diary, March 10, 1935, HHP, Box 6; Barbara Hopkins to Myrta Bradley, June 13, 14, 1933, Feb. 20, 21, 1934, Halsted Collection; HLH to Lewis Hopkins, June 29, 1934, Hopkins microfilm, reel 3, HHP.

2. JAK, notes (n.d.), Kingsbury Papers, Box B84. Kingsbury's notes are unclear as to the date when Hopkins proposed to resign, placing it in the winter of 1933–34 or 1934–35. The earlier date seems more likely. Hopkins had thought of staying on the job only a year; Bookman, who conveyed the message to Kingsbury and Folks, left FERA in January 1934; and by the winter of 1934–35 Hopkins was deeply involved in planning the works program that produced the Works Progress Administration. Marquis Childs, "The President's Best Friend," *Saturday Evening Post,* April 19, 1941, p. 128.

3. HLH to Lewis Hopkins, June 29, 1934, Hopkins microfilm, reel 3.

4. Alfred B. Rollins, Jr., *Roosevelt and Howe* (New York: Knopf, 1962), pp. 394–395, 453–454; Louis Howe to HLH, [June–Sept., 1933], Hopkins microfilm, reel 3; Howe to HLH, Oct. 20, 1933, Feb. 17, 1934, HHP, Box 37; HLH to Howe, Sept. 14, 1933, ibid., Box 38; HLH to Howe, Dec. 22, 27, 1933, Louis Howe Papers, Box 82, FDRL.

5. Joseph P. Lash, *Eleanor and Franklin* (New York: Norton, 1971), pp. 345, 384, 386, 388–389; Eleanor Roosevelt, *This I Remember* (New York: Harper and Brothers, 1949), p. 128; HLH to William Hodson, March 17, 1934, Hopkins microfilm, reel 8; ER to Barbara Hopkins, Aug. 30, 1933, Aug. 13, 1934; Edith Holm to Barbara Hopkins, Dec. 8, 1933, ibid., reel 3; Barbara Hopkins to Myrta Bradley, Feb. 21, 1934, Halsted Collection.

6. HLH to FDR, July 25, 1934, Hopkins microfilm, reel 6.

7. HLH, memorandum, July 25, 1934; HLH notes, n.d., on the stationery of the American Embassy, Rome, ibid.

8. Unidentified clipping, ibid.

9. Summary of "The State of the Nation" as presented by State Relief Administrators, April 1, 1934, HHP, Box 67. See also reports from special investigators to HLH, various dates, Nov.–Dec. 1934, ibid., Boxes 65 and 66. HLH, interview with Henry Pringle, *American Magazine,* Sept. 12, 1934, ibid., Box 8.

10. HLH, interview with Henry Pringle, ibid.; Lawrence Westbrook to HLH, Sept. 19, 1934, enclosing statement with corrections in Hopkins's handwriting, FERA Old Subject File, Memoranda folder T-Z, Box 27, RG 69.

11. HLH TC Thad Holt, Sept. 11, 1934, HHP, Box 36.

12. FERA, *Monthly Report, July 1–31, 1933,* p. 7; Rexford Tugwell, diary, June 3, 1934, Rexford Tugwell Papers, Box 20, FDRL; HLH to FDR, Aug. 29, 1934, HHP, Box 95; HLH, interview with Henry Pringle, ibid., Box 8; HLH, press conference, Aug. 29, 1934, in HLH, Speeches and Press Conferences; HLH TC Aubrey Williams, Aug. 30, 1934, Labor Relations W.D. folder, July–Dec. 1934, FERA, Office of Jacob Baker, Box 4, RG 69; HLH to Gertrude Springer, Sept. 12, 1934, folder 623, Survey: Editorial, SWHA; HLH TC Thad Holt, Sept. 11, 1934, HHP, Box 36.

13. HLH to Aubrey Williams, Sept. 17, 1934; K. Godwin [secretary to HLH] to M. Milford, Williams, and Dallas Dort, Nov. 15, 1934; HLH to Williams, Jacob Baker, Corrington Gill, Lawrence Westbrook, and Bruce McClure, Oct. 26, 1934, Memoranda folder G-H, FERA Old Subject File, Box 27, RG 69.

14. Bernard Sternsher, *Rexford Tugwell and the New Deal* (New Brunswick, N.J.: Rutgers University Press, 1964), pp. 163, 165, 166, 168, 194–196; Arthur Schlesinger, Jr., *The Coming of the New Deal* (Boston: Houghton Mifflin, 1959), pp. 123–124, 126–127, 234–246; Gardner Jackson, oral history interview, COHC, pp. 478–479.

15. HLH, reports to the National Executive Council, July 18, Aug. 21, Sept. 12, Nov. 21, 1933, April 24, 1934, HHP, Box 43. On the cost of the work program, see FERA, *Monthly Report, May–Aug. 1934,* p. 4; Corrington Gill, "Relief Needs This Winter," Aug. 30, 1934, HHP, Box 49; Rexford Tugwell, diary, Nov. 22, 1934, Box 20, Rexford Tugwell Papers, FDRL.

16. HLH, remarks at FERA conference, Aug. 27, 1934, HHP, Box 25; Tugwell, diary, Nov. 22, 1934, Box 20, Tugwell Papers; HLH, memorandum, n.d., Hopkins microfilm, reel 9, HHP.

17. HLH, press conference, Aug. 29, 1934, in HLH, Speeches and Press Conferences.

18. FDR, fireside chat, Sept. 30, 1934, in Samuel I. Rosenman, ed., *Public Papers and Addresses of Franklin D. Roosevelt,* 13 vols. (New York: Random House, 1938), III, 420.

19. Corrington Gill to HLH, Sept. 6, 1934, HHP, Box 49; Jacob Baker to

Thomas Hibben, Sept. 7, 1934, Daily Record folder, FERA, Office of Jacob Baker, Box 4, RG 69; HLH to FDR, Sept. 20, 1934, HHP, Box 95.

20. HLH TC Colonel Henry M. Waite, Oct. 18, 1934, HHP, Box 78; Sherwood, *Roosevelt and Hopkins,* pp. 64–65.

21. "A National Program of Economic Recovery," Nov. 13, 1934, Daily Record folder, 1934, FERA, Office of Jacob Baker, Box 2, RG 69.

22. Frances Perkins, *The Roosevelt I Knew* (New York: Viking Press, 1946), pp. 188–189, 284–285; *Economic Security Act, Hearings Before the Committee on Ways and Means,* 74th Cong., 1st Sess., 1934, pp. 213–214.

23. Entry for Dec. 5, 1934, Tugwell, diary, Box 20, Tugwell Papers; John M. Blum, *From the Morgenthau Diaries: Years of Crisis, 1928–1938* (Boston: Houghton Mifflin, 1959), p. 237; entry for Nov. 19, 1934, in Harold Ickes, *The Secret Diary of Harold Ickes: The First Thousand Days* (New York: Simon and Schuster, 1953), p. 228.

24. HLH to FDR, April 17, 1935, HHP, Box 95.

25. Searle Charles, *Minister of Relief: Harry Hopkins and the Depression* (Syracuse, N.Y.: Syracuse University Press, 1963), pp. 109–111; Arthur W. MacMahon, John D. Millett, and Gladys Ogden, *The Administration of Federal Work Relief* (Chicago: Public Administration Service, 1941), p. 72; HLH to Harold Ickes, April 8, 1935, HHP, Box 91; HLH TC General Noname Key, May 31, 1935, ibid., Box 77.

26. "Proceedings of the Advisory Committee on Allotments," May 7, 1935, ibid., Box 47.

27. HLH TC Thad Holt, May 11, 1935, ibid., Box 73; HLH TC Hugh Johnson, July 2, 1935, ibid., Box 76; HLH TC Smith, Aug. 8, 1935, ibid., Box 78; A. Williams TC Malcolm Miller, May 15, 1935, daily record, FERA, Office of Jacob Baker, Box 3, RG 69; HLH TC Fiorello La Guardia, May 17, 1935, HHP, Box 76; HLH TC E. J. Griffith, May 18, 1935, ibid., Box 77; memorandum, "Conference Held at Hyde Park, New York, on September 12, 1935," ibid., Box 90; "Memorandum of Conference on Status of Emergency Funds Held at the President's House At Hyde Park September 12, 1935," Sept. 14, 1935, in HMJr, diary, vol. 10.

28. HLH TC Alfred Schoellkopf, June 13, 1935, HHP, Box 76; entry for July 17, 1935, HMJr, diary, vol. 8.

29. "Project Procedure," *WPA Bulletin,* no. 6, June 28, 1935, HHP, Box 15; Lawrence Westbrook to HLH, Aug. 11, 1935, Lawrence Westbrook folder, WPA Central File 105, Box 102, RG 69; Lee Pressman to HLH, Aug. 20, 1935, Lee Pressman folder, Box 100, ibid; MacMahon, Millett, and Ogden, *Administration of Federal Work Relief,* pp. 114–115.

30. HLH TC Robert Dunham, Sept. 10, 1935, HHP, Box 73; MacMahon, Millett, and Ogden, *Administration of Federal Work Relief,* p. 119; Lee Pressman to HLH, July 22, 1935, Lee Pressman folder, WPA Central File 105, Box 100, RG 69.

31. HLH, appointment diary, May 14, 1935, HHP, Box 6; HLH to FDR, May 18, 1935, ibid., Box 95; HLH TC Hugh Johnson, July 2, 1935, ibid., box 76; HLH TC Hart, July 19, 1935, ibid., Box 75; Fred Daniels to Jacob Baker, Aug. 2, 1935, Labor Relations folder, WPA, Aug. 8–Oct. 31, 1935, FERA, Office of Jacob Baker, Box 4, RG 69.

32. HLH TC Jacob Baker, Aug. 3, 1935, Labor Relations folder, WPA, Aug. 8–Oct. 31, 1935, FERA, Office of Jacob Baker, Box 4, RG 69; HLH TC Fiorello La Guardia, Aug. 7, 1935; HLH TC Hugh Johnson, Aug. 7, 1935, HHP, Box 76; HLH to Jacob Baker, Aug. 22, 1935, WPA Proposed Bulletins folder, FERA, Office of Jacob Baker, Box 5, RG 69.

33. Jacob Baker TC Anna Rosenberg, Aug. 8, 1935, Labor Relations folder, WPA, Aug. 8–Oct. 31, 1935, FERA, Office of Jacob Baker, Box 4, RG 69; HLH TC Hugh Johnson, Aug. 9, 1935; HLH TC Fiorello La Guardia, Aug. 9, 1935, HHP, Box 76; Frances Perkins TC Jacob Baker, Aug. 9, 1935; Baker TC Johnson, Aug. 10, 1935, Labor Relations folder, WPA, Aug. 8–Oct. 31, 1935, FERA, Office of Jacob Baker, Box 4, RG 69.

34. Barbara Blumberg, *The New Deal and the Unemployed: A View From New York City* (Lewisburg, Pa.: Bucknell University Press, 1979), pp. 52–57; WPA Administrative Order no. 24, Sept. 19, 1935, HHP, Box 17; Nels Anderson to Jacob Baker, Sept. 18, Oct. 1, Nov. 6, Dec. 2, 1935; John J. Leary to Mort Milford, Oct. 20, 1935; Baker TC Ray Branion, Jan. 11, 13, 1936, Labor Relations folder, WPA, 1936, FERA, Office of Jacob Baker, Box 4, RG 69; Malcolm Miller TC Baker, Oct. 9, 1935; Baker TC Gay Shepperson, Oct. 14, 1935, Labor Relations folder, WPA, Aug. 8–Oct. 31, 1935, ibid; HLH TC Ray Branion, Jan. 11, 1936, HHP, Box 76.

35. HLH, appointment diary, May 13, 1935, ibid., Box 6.

36. WPA Bulletin no. 14, July 3, 1935, Policy folder, WPA, July–Dec. 1935, FERA, Office of Jacob Baker, Box 5, RG 69; HLH TC Frank Dryden, Aug. 15, 1935, HHP, Box 74; HLH TC Thad Holt, July 19, 1935; HLH TC Mayor Ed Kelly, Sept. 10, 1935, ibid., Box 73.

37. *Baltimore Sun,* Sept. 11, 1935, ibid., Box 282; HLH to FDR, July 25, 1935; ibid., Box 95; Harold Ickes, diary, Aug. 27, 1935, in *Thousand Days,* p. 427.

38. HLH to Steve Early, Aug. 16, 1935, Harry Hopkins folder, WPA Central File 105, Box 96, RG 69; PWA-Congressional folder, FERA New Subject File 352, Box 146, ibid; HLH TC Speaker of the House William Bankhead, Sept. 11, 1935; HLH TC Mayor Ed Kelly, Sept. 10, 1935, HHP, Box 73.

39. D. W. Bell, "Memorandum of Conference on Status of Emergency Funds Held at the President's House at Hyde Park September 12, 1935, at 11:30 A.M. to 5 P.M.," HMJr, diary, vol. 10.

40. HLH, memo, Oct. 6, 1935, HHP, Box 51.

41. "Presidential Cruise, 1935—U.S.S. Houston," ibid., Box 51. The ex-

tent of Hopkins's role in the "extra" edition is suggested by a notation in this log of the cruise: "During dinner this evening [October 16], Mr. Harry Hopkins startled the Presidential party by his issue of an extra of the ship's paper." The edition itself is attached as an appendix to the log. Ibid.

## 6. "In the Interest of the People That Were Broke"

1. Howard Hunter to HLH, Oct. 21, 1935, HHP, Box 90; HLH to Lewis Hopkins, Oct. 30, 1935, Hopkins microfilm, reel 3, HHP.

2. HLH TC Malcolm Miller, Nov. 7, 1935, HHP, Box 73; HLH TC F. Dryden, Nov. 8, 1935; HLH TC Howard Hunter, Nov. 9, 1935, ibid., Box 74; WPA Administrative Order no. 33, Nov. 9, 1935, ibid., Box 17; HLH to Corrington Gill, Nov. 7, 1935, Harry Hopkins folder, WPA Central File 105, Box 96, RG 69; HLH TC David Niles, Nov. 8, 1935, HHP, Box 74; HLH to Smith, Dec. 17, 1935, ibid., Box 78.

3. Lee Pressman, oral history interview, COHC, p. 20; HLH TC Fiorello La Guardia, Nov. 7, 1935, HHP, Box 76.

4. HMJr, memo, Nov. 11, 1935, in HMJr, diary, vol. 11; HMJr, memo, Feb. 6, 1936, ibid., vol. 17.

5. Corrington Gill to FDR, Dec. 4, 1935, Hearings-Appropriations Bill folder, WPA, Office of the Commissioner, RG 69; HLH to FDR, Nov. 20, 1935, HHP, Box 40; D. W. Bell, "Conference at the White House . . . February 6, 1936, Regarding Additional Funds for Work Relief," HMJr, diary, vol. 17.

6. HLH to FDR, Nov. 20, 1935, HHP, Box 40; HMJr, memo, Nov. 16, 1935, HMJr, diary, vol. 12; memos, March 4, 6, 1936, ibid., vol. 19; John M. Blum, *From the Morgenthau Diaries: Years of Crisis, 1928–1938* (Boston: Houghton Mifflin, 1959), pp. 266–267.

7. Ibid, p. 272.

8. Sherwood, *Roosevelt and Hopkins,* p. 68; Raymond Moley, *The First New Deal* (New York: Harcourt, Brace and World, 1966), p. 532.

9. HLH to State District Attorney, Lucas County, Ohio, March 18, 1935, HHP, Box 39; Hopkins, appointment diary, March 16, 1935, ibid., Box 6; HLH TC Howard Hunter, Nov. 9, 1935, ibid., Box 73; HLH TC Hunter, Jan. 31, 1936, ibid., Box 75.

10. HLH TC Malcolm Miller, Jan. 2, 1936; HLH to Senator Arthur Vandenburg, Feb. 28, 1936, ibid., Box 52; HLH TC Wilfred Reynolds, Jan. 2, 1936; HLH TC Robert Dunham, Jan. 2, 1936, ibid., Box 73; HLH TC Arthur Abrahamson, May 21, 1936, ibid., Box 74.

11. HLH to FDR, Aug. 23, 1935 (two memos), HHP, Box 95; HLH to FDR, Sept. 11, 1935, ibid., Box 92; HLH to Aubrey Williams, Lawrence Westbrook et al., Nov. 20, 1935, Memoranda Harry L. Hopkins folder, FERA New Subject File, Box 127, RG 69; HLH TC Thad Holt, July 19,

1935; HLH TC Speaker of the House William Bankhead, Sept. 11, 1935, HHP, Box 73; HLH TC [?] Goodman, Sept. 7, 1935, ibid., Box 74; HLH, speech at Columbus, Ohio, Nov. 12, 1937; HLH, confidential speech to state WPA administrators, Oct. 22, 1937, ibid., Box 10; HLH TCs C. O. Andrews, Nov. 19, 1936; George Hill, Dec. 10, 1936; Malcolm Miller, Dec. 11 (two calls), 14, 15, 1936, ibid., Box 73. See also Ronald E. Marcello, "The Selection of North Carolina's WPA Chief," *North Carolina Historical Review,* 52 (1975), 59–76.

12. HLH, address to WPA field representatives, Dec. 28, 1935, HHP, Box 9.

13. HLH TC Robert Hinckley, Jan. 14, 1936, ibid., Box 73; HLH TC Jones, July 15, 1935, ibid., Box 77; HLH TC Howard Hunter, Jan 20, 1936, ibid., Box 76.

14. HLH, appointment diary, July 19, 1935, ibid., Box 6; Senator F. Ryan Duffy to James Farley, Aug. 20, 1936, ibid., Box 96; HLH TC Howard Hunter, Nov. 9, 1935, ibid., Box 73; D. F. Felton to Hunter, Sept. 9, 1935, ibid., Box 90; HLH to FDR, Sept. 11, 1935; Hunter to Henry C. Luckey, Oct. 5, 1935; Hunter to D. F. Felton, Oct. 6, 1935; Felton to Hunter, Oct. 8, 1935, ibid., Box 92; HLH TC Hinckley, Dec. 29, 1935, ibid., Box 36; HLH TC Tom K. Smith, April 30, 1936, ibid., Box 75.

15. John Robert Moore, "The New Deal in Louisiana," in John Braeman et al., eds., *The New Deal: The State and Local Levels* (Columbus: Ohio State University Press, 1975), pp. 145–148; HLH TC Malcolm Miller, Sept. 9, 1935, HHP, Box 74; anonymous memo to HLH, n.d. (September 1935), ibid., Box 92.

16. *New York Times,* May 5, 1935; *Des Moines Register,* July 27, 1935; *Washington Herald,* Nov. 1, 1935; *St. Louis Post Dispatch,* Dec. 4, 1935; *Memphis Press-Scimitar,* Jan. 17, 1936; *Washington Post,* Nov. 9, 1935, April 26, Sept. 21, 1936; *Charleston (S.C.) News and Courier,* March 13, 1936; *New York Sun,* March 14, 1936; *Chicago Daily News,* Dec. 6, 1935; *Baltimore Sun,* May 31, Aug. 30, 1936; clippings in HHP, Box 283; HLH, press conference, April 4, 1935, in Sherwood, *Roosevelt and Hopkins,* pp. 60–61.

17. *New York Sun,* Feb. 28, 1936; *New York Herald Tribune,* March 13, 1936; clippings in HHP, Box 283.

18. HLH to Adah Aime, March 6, 1936, ibid., Box 1.

19. Entry for Aug. 24, 1936, HMJr, diaries, vol. 30; HLH to Emery Hopkins, Aug. 25, 1936, Hopkins microfilm, reel 3; James Farley to ER, Sept. 3, 1936, James A. Farley Papers, Box 4, LC.

20. Arthur Schlesinger, Jr., *The Politics of Upheaval* (Boston: Houghton Mifflin, 1960), p. 603; memo, March 4, 1936, HMJr, diaries, vol. 19; C. J. Peoples to HMJr, Aug. 11, 1936, ibid., vol. 29.

21. Harry L. Hopkins, *Spending to Save: The Complete Story of Relief* (New York: W.W. Norton & Co., 1936).

22. *Wyoming State Tribune,* Sept. 9, 1936; *Butte Standard,* Sept. 11, 1936;

*Seattle Guild,* Sept. 14, 1936; *Portland News Telegram,* Sept. 14, 1936; *Phoenix Republic,* Sept. 22, 1936; *Topeka Capital,* Oct. 6, 1936; *Philadelphia Record,* Oct. 13, 1936; clippings in HHP, Box 285; Sherwood, *Roosevelt and Hopkins,* pp. 83–85.

23. Robert Hinckley to Aubrey Williams, Oct. 11, 1936, enclosing several letters on Hopkins's speaking tour, Hopkins microfilm, reel 8; Lieutenant Donald Connolly to HLH, Sept. 30, 1936, HHP, Box 9; Jean Hard, Jr., to James Farley, n.d., enclosed in Farley to HLH, Sept. 23, 1936, ibid., Box 37; Isadore Dockweiler to Farley, Sept. 22, 1936, enclosed in Farley to HLH, Sept. 30, 1936, ibid., Box 53.

24. Robert Hinckley to Barbara Hopkins, Oct. 10, 1936, ibid., Box 89; Ida Hinkle to HLH, Sept. 18, 1936, ibid., Box 53.

## 7. Democracy's Bureaucrat

1. *Time,* July 18, 1938; J. V. Cardon, oral history interview, COHC, pp. 394–395.

2. HLH TC John McDonough, June 9, 1937, HHP, Box 74.

3. List of books checked out of the Library of Congress, in Hopkins microfilm, reel 8, HHP; John Hertz to HLH, Nov. 20, 1939, ibid., reel 8; Ann Craton to Arthur ("Tex") Goldschmidt, May 14, 1935, C-E file, FERA New Subject File, Box 127, RG 69; HLH to John Taylor Arms, March 9, 1937, HHP, Box 40; V. Sholis to Jimmy Wharton, April 17, 1940, file 101880, Office of the Secretary, General Records of the Department of Commerce, RG 40.

4. Henry Wallace, diary, entry for Jan. 30, 1935, in Henry Wallace, oral history interview, COHC.

5. Wallace, oral history interview, COHC, pp. 263–264; Henry B. Hawes to HLH, Jan. 27, 1940, Hopkins microfilm, reel 8; "A well-wisher" to HLH, postcard, n.d., HHP, Box 85.

6. Raymond Clapper, notes, Feb. 7, 1939, Clapper Papers, Box 18, LC; Clapper notes, May 3, [1937], ibid., Box 8; Wallace, diary, Jan. 30, 1935.

7. HLH to David Hopkins, Nov. 28, 1937, Halsted Collection; HLH TC Governor Richard Leche (Louisiana), March 11, 1937, Hopkins microfilm, reel 8.

8. HLH to Mark Graves, Commissioner of the New York Department of Taxation, Nov. 4, 1939, Hopkins microfilm, reel 16.

9. Aubrey Williams to Robert Sherwood, n.d. (1947 or 1948), Sherwood Papers, Box 411.

10. Betsey Roosevelt to HLH, Sept. 5, 1939, Hopkins microfilm, reel 18.

11. HLH to Lawrence Westbrook, Aug. 26, 1936, HHP, Box 99.

12. HLH TC William Hodson, June 22, 1937, ibid., Box 78; Hallie Flanagan, *Arena* (New York: Duell, Sloan, and Pearce, 1940), p. 26.

13. HLH TC Ray Branion, May 18, 1936, HHP, Box 76.

14. HMJr, memo of meeting, Feb. 16, 1937, HMJr, diary, vol. 55; Ellen Woodward, interview with Robert Sherwood, Oct. 11, 1947, Sherwood Papers, Box 411.

15. Sherwood, *Roosevelt and Hopkins,* pp. 114–115, 181–182; HLH, interview with Raymond Clapper, May 3, [1937], Clapper Papers, Box 8, LC.

16. HLH to FDR, April 18, 1937, PSF, Subject File: Hopkins, Box 152; "Skit by Messrs. Early and Hopkins at the President's Stag Birthday Party. White House 1/30/37," enclosed in K. Godwin to M. LeHand, March 29, 1937, HHP, Box 92.

17. James R. Kearney, *Anna Eleanor Roosevelt: The Evolution of a Reformer* (Boston: Houghton Mifflin, 1968), pp. 172, 176, 178, 265.

18. Searle Charles, *Minister of Relief: Harry Hopkins and the Depression* (Syracuse, N.Y.: Syracuse University Press, 1963), p. 172; *Security, Work, and Relief Policies: Report of the Committee on Long Range Work and Relief Policies to the National Resources Planning Board* (Washington, D.C.: Government Printing Office, 1943), pp. 177–181.

19. "Summary of Public Opinion Relating to the WPA and Relief," attached to Emerson Ross to HLH, Feb. 21, 1939, HHP, Box 55; Donald Howard, *The WPA and Federal Relief* (New York: Russell Sage Foundation, 1943), pp. 590–591; Charles, *Minister of Relief,* p. 173.

20. John Kenneth Galbraith, assisted by G. G. Johnson, Jr., *The Economic Effects of the Federal Public Works Expenditures, 1933–1938* (Washington, D.C.: Government Printing Office, 1940), p. 51; Stanley Lebergott, *The Americans: An Economic Record* (New York: W. W. Norton and Co., 1985), p. 463.

21. "Summary of Public Opinion Relating to the WPA and Relief," HHP, Box 55; "Analysis of Letters Regarding Labor Relations Acknowledged by Corresponding Division," Nov. 1, 1936 to Oct. 31, 1937, Mail Analysis folder, file 101.4, Boxes 85 and 86, RG 69.

22. "Summary of Public Opinion Relating to the WPA and Relief," HHP, Box 55; HLH to Shelby M. Harrison, Oct. 6, 1943, ibid., Box 299.

## 8. Not Born for Happiness

1. HLH TC Jerome Frank, March 1, 1937, HHP, Box 78; Sherwood, *Roosevelt and Hopkins,* p. 89.

2. HLH TC Daniel Bell, May 25, 1937, HHP, Box 78; Sherwood, *Roosevelt and Hopkins,* p. 90; Searle Charles, *Minister of Relief: Harry Hopkins and the Depression* (Syracuse, N.Y.: Syracuse University Press, 1963), pp. 164–165.

3. FDR to HLH, July 9, 27, 1937, HHP, Box 96.

4. "Outlook for Employment, Unemployment, and Relief," enclosed in

Arthur F. Burns to HLH, Feb. 25, 1937, Bp-Bz folder, WPA Central File 105, Box 92, RG 69; Mordecai Ezekiel and Louis Bean, "How to Prevent Another 1929 in 1940," [Feb. 1937], Roosevelt Papers, PSF, Box 30; Leon Henderson, interview with Joseph Alsop, Aug. 19, 1938, Alsop Papers, Box 37, LC; "Meeting at 2201 R Street on Selective Federal Expenditures," April 1, 1937, HMJr, diary, vol. 62; HLH, commencement address at Babson Institute, Boston, June 12, 1937, HHP, Box 10; HLH to FDR, July 1, 1937, ibid., Box 95; HLH, interview with Raymond Clapper, May 3, [1937], Clapper Papers, Box 8, LC.

5. HLH, speech at Wahpeton, N.D., Sept. 12, 1937, HHP, Box 10.

6. HMJr, memo, April 1, 1937, HMJr, diary, vol. 62; HMJr, memo of conference, April 13, 1937, ibid., vol. 64; HLH TC Rexford Tugwell, June 22, 1937, HHP, Box 98; HLH to Governor Carl Bailey, Sept. 13, 1937, Hopkins microfilm, reel 7, HHP.

7. Aubrey Williams, interview with Robert Sherwood, March 18, 1947, Sherwood Papers, Box 411.

8. Donald Duncan, oral history interview, COHC, p. 538; Florence Kerr, COHC, pp. 33–34; ER to Anna Boetigger, Feb. 13, 1938, in Bernard Asbell, ed., *Mother and Daughter: The Letters of Eleanor and Anna Roosevelt* (New York: Coward, McGann, and Geohegan, 1982), p. 98.

9. James A. Halsted, "Severe Malnutrition in a Public Servant of the World War II Era: The Medical History of Harry Hopkins," *Transactions of the American Clinical and Climatological Association,* 86 (1974), 24.

10. HLH to M. C. Harrison, April 6, 1938, HHP, Box 89.

11. Claude Pepper to HLH, Dec. 15, 1937; Robert La Follette to HLH, Jan. 8, 1938, Hopkins microfilm, reel 1; Pierce Williams to HLH, Jan. 8, 1938, ibid., reel 16.

12. Leon Henderson to HLH, March 23, 1938, HHP, Box 54; Henderson to HLH, Nov. 9, 1942; Benjamin Cohen to HLH, Nov. 10, 1942, ibid., Box 96; John M. Blum, *From the Morgenthau Diaries: Years of Crisis, 1928–1938* (Boston: Houghton Mifflin, 1959), pp. 417–425.

13. FDR to HLH, April 26, 1938, HHP, Box 96; HLH to FDR, April 28, 1938, Hopkins microfilm, reel 9.

14. HLH, handwritten notes, n.d., HHP, Box 298.

15. Howard Hunter to HLH, Nov. 21, 1938, ibid., Box 90; HLH to James Roosevelt, Nov. 15, 1937, Hopkins microfilm, reel 9.

16. *Washington Star,* May 21, 1938, clipping in HHP, Box 286.

17. Thomas Corcoran, interview with Joseph Alsop, Sept. 10, 1938, Alsop Papers, Box 37, LC.

18. Robert Kerr, interview with Robert Sherwood, Oct. 12, 1947, Sherwood Papers, Box 411.

19. HLH to FDR, Aug. 3, 1938, HHP, Box 95. O'Connor was vulnerable

because of demographic changes in his district and because of the decline of the Democratic machine. Still, Hopkins's connection to Mayor La Guardia, who managed Fay's campaign, was a key element in the outcome. Richard Polenberg, "Franklin D. Roosevelt and the Purge of John O'Connor: The Impact of Urban Change on Political Parties," *New York History,* 49 (1968), 306–326.

20. Clippings, June–September 1938, HHP, Boxes 287–288.

21. Joseph Alsop and Robert Kintner, *Washington Star,* Nov. 14, 1938; Ernest K. Lindley, *Washington Post,* Nov. 18, 1938; Jay G. Hayden, *Detroit News,* Nov. 22, 1938; *New York World Telegram,* April 11, 1938; Gallup Poll, *Washington Post,* Dec. 23, 1938, in HHP, Box 288; Sherwood, *Roosevelt and Hopkins,* p. 105. The poll also reported that the largest proportion (32 percent) agreed that Hopkins "has made mistakes but on the whole has handled his job well."

22. Henry Wallace, diary, Feb. 13, April 4, 8, 1940, in Wallace interview, COHC, pp. 862, 868–869, 1003, 1052–1053; Claude Wickard, oral history interview, COHC, pp. 1392–1393.

23. Paul de Kruif to HLH, March 2, 1938, Hopkins microfilm, reel 7.

24. David Niles to Robert Sherwood, March 4, 1947, Sherwood Papers, Box 411.

25. HLH to ER, Aug. 31, 1939, Hopkins microfilm, reel 9; Ross McIntire, interview with Robert Sherwood, March 14, 1947; Aubrey Williams, notes, n.d., Sherwood Papers, Box 411; HLH to Dr. Andrew Rivers, Nov. 25, 1939, Hopkins microfilm, reel 16; Henry Wallace, diary, Dec. 21, 1939, in Wallace interview, COHC, p. 635.

26. Dr. John Harper to Lewis Hopkins, Feb. 21, 1942, Lewis Hopkins Collection, Grinnell College Archives, Grinnell, Iowa. Dr. James Halsted, who carefully studied Hopkins's medical history, leaned toward the diagnosis of nontropical sprue, though he admitted that his evidence was inconclusive and was contradicted by the autopsy of Hopkins's small bowel; Halsted, "Severe Malnutrition," pp. 27–30. After looking over the evidence, Dr. George Hegstrom of the McFarland Clinic, Ames, Iowa, concluded that the "dumping syndrome" was more likely; conversation with Dr. Hegstrom, July 6, 1985. For a clinical discussion of nontropical sprue and the dumping syndrome, see Marvin H. Sleisenger and John S. Fordtran, *Gastrointestinal Disease,* 2 vols., 2d ed. (Philadelphia: W. B. Saunders, 1978), I, 285, 291, 932–938. Hopkins's condition is discussed, with a free-hand diagram, in Frank H. Leahy to Lewis Hopkins, March 13, 1944, Lewis Hopkins Collection Grinnell College.

27. HMJr, conversation with HLH, May 3, 1940, HMJr, presidential diary, vol. 2; HLH to Dr. Andrew Rivers, July 1, 1940, Hopkins microfilm, reel 16; Business Advisory Council resolution, May 24, 1940, HHP, Box 10.

28. Entries of May 28 and July 11, 1940, in *The Journals of David E. Lilienthal: The TVA Years, 1939–1945* (New York: Harper and Row, 1964), I, 169–170, 192.

29. Hopkins carried a message from Roosevelt to the convention declaring that he did not wish to continue in office. The reading of this message was the signal for a prearranged demonstration in favor of Roosevelt's nomination. A few days before he left for the convention, Hopkins wrote that Roosevelt would have to be the nominee: "I am certain he should be drafted." HLH to Albert Pfander, July 1, 1940, Hopkins microfilm, reel 9; Henry Wallace, oral history interview, COHC, pp. 1212–1216; Alsop and Kintner, *Washington Star,* July 15, 1940.

30. Paul Appleby, "Roosevelt's Third-Term Decision," *American Political Science Review,* 46 (1952), 758–759; Henry Wallace to HLH, Aug. 1, 1940, HHP, Box 124.

31. Florence Kerr to HLH, Feb. 4, 1938, Hopkins microfilm, reel 18.

## 9. A Little Touch of Harry

1. Marie Harriman and WAH to HLH, Nov. 26, 1940, Hopkins microfilm, reel 8, HHP; *Grinnell Herald-Register,* Nov. 25, 1940.

2. Warren F. Kimball, *The Most Unsordid Act: Lend-Lease, 1939–1941* (Baltimore: Johns Hopkins University Press, 1969), p. 96.

3. WSC, *Their Finest Hour* (Boston: Houghton Mifflin, 1949), pp. 558–567.

4. Forrest Davis and Ernest K. Lindley, *How War Came* (New York: Simon and Schuster, 1942), pp. 116–117.

5. Sherwood, *Roosevelt and Hopkins,* pp. 227–228; Samuel I. Rosenman, *Working with Roosevelt* (New York: Harper and Brothers, 1952), pp. 263–264.

6. Sherwood, *Roosevelt and Hopkins,* p. 230; Robert Sherwood, interview with Felix Frankfurter, May 25, 1946, Sherwood Papers, Box 411.

7. Sherwood, *Roosevelt and Hopkins,* p. 231; Davis and Lindley, *How War Came,* pp. 173–174.

8. Sherwood, *Roosevelt and Hopkins,* p. 232; Sherwood, interview with Frankfurter, May 25, 1946, Sherwood Papers, Box 411.

9. Nevile Butler to FO, Jan. 4, 1941, FO 371/26179.

10. Michael Beschloss, *Kennedy and Roosevelt: An Uneasy Alliance* (New York: Norton, 1980), p. 24.

11. *New York Times,* Jan. 8, 1941; Sherwood, *Roosevelt and Hopkins,* p. 234; James E. Brown, Jr., "List of Mr. Harry Hopkins' Appointments," HHP, Box 304.

12. Joseph Lash, *Roosevelt and Churchill, 1939–1941: The Partnership that*

*Saved the West* (New York: Norton, 1976), pp. 271–273; Kenneth Young, *Churchill and Beaverbrook* (New York: James H. Heineman, 1966), pp. 172–175.

13. Handwritten memo, n.d., with notation "Sir Charles Wilson?" PREM 4 25/3; J. Delforn, Jan. 7, 1941, FO 371/26179.

14. Lash, *Roosevelt and Churchill*, p. 274.

15. James Leutze, ed., *The London Journal of General Raymond E. Lee, 1940–1941* (Boston: Little, Brown, 1971), pp. 216–217.

16. Sherwood, *Roosevelt and Hopkins*, p. 237; Anthony Eden, *The Reckoning* (Boston: Houghton Mifflin, 1965), p. 294.

17. Sherwood, *Roosevelt and Hopkins*, pp. 238–239.

18. Leutze, *Lee*, p. 220.

19. Oliver Lyttelton, *Lord Chandos: An Unexpected View from the Summit* (New York: New American Library, 1963), pp. 157–158.

20. John Colville, *Footprints in Time* (London: Collins, 1976), pp. 75–78.

21. Sherwood, *Roosevelt and Hopkins*, pp. 240–246.

22. Ibid., p. 246; Leutze, *Lee*, p. 226.

23. Alexander Cadogan, note, Jan. 29, 1941, FO 371/26179.

24. Lord Moran, *Churchill: Taken from the Diaries of Lord Moran* (Boston: Houghton Mifflin, 1966), pp. 5–6; Gerald Pawle, *The War and Colonel Warden* (New York: Knopf, 1963), p. 80; Sherwood, *Roosevelt and Hopkins*, p. 247.

25. FO, minute (comment), on report of Hopkins's conversation, Jan. 30, 1941, FO 371/26740.

26. Sherwood, *Roosevelt and Hopkins*, pp. 254, 239; Anthony Eden to Lord Halifax, Feb. 5, 1941, FO 371/26177. Halifax and the Roosevelt administration publicly criticized Hoover's proposal, which attracted public attention for a few weeks and then faded away. See *New York Times*, Feb. 17, 18, 26, 1941.

27. Leutze, *Lee*, pp. 218–220; Colville, *Footprints*, p. 146. Hopkins was rewriting history a bit, since at the time of this event he had spoken not of the queen's graciousness but of Mrs. Roosevelt's. Katherine Lenroot, oral history interview, COHC.

28. Sherwood, *Roosevelt and Hopkins*, pp. 248–250; note, Jan. 29, 1941, FO 371/26179; Sherwood, account of the dinner, July 27, 1946, Beaverbrook Papers, Box C/175, House of Lords Record Office, London; Harold Balfour to HLH, Feb. 5, 1941, Hopkins microfilm, reel 19.

29. Sherwood, *Roosevelt and Hopkins*, pp. 236; Sherwood, interview with Frankfurter, May 25, 1946.

30. Colville, *Footprints*, pp. 148–150.

31. HLH to FDR and Cordell Hull, Jan. 30, 31, Feb, 1, 3, 1941, HHP, Box 304. Sherwood, *Roosevelt and Hopkins*, pp. 257–258.

32. HLH to Cordell Hull and HMJr, Jan. 31, 1941, HHP, Box 304.

33. Eden, *The Reckoning*, p. 358; Sherwood, *Roosevelt and Hopkins*, pp. 258–259; David Dilks, ed., *The Diaries of Alexander Cadogan* (London: Cassell, 1971), p. 354.

34. Sherwood, *Roosevelt and Hopkins*, pp. 257, 260.

35. HLH to WSC, n.d., PREM 4 25/3.

36. In his memoirs Churchill describes Hopkins as "that extraordinary man . . . a true leader of men, and alike in ardour and wisdom in times of crisis . . . rarely . . . excelled." WSC, *The Grand Alliance* (Boston: Houghton Mifflin, 1950), pp. 23–24.

37. Harold Ickes, diary, Feb. 8, 1941, Ickes Papers, Box 25, LC.

38. R. A. Butler, *The Art of the Possible* (London: Hamish Hamilton, 1971), p. 86.

39. HLH to FDR, Jan. 10, 1941, Hopkins microfilm, reel 19.

40. Elisabeth Barker, *Churchill and Eden at War* (London: Macmillan, 1978), pp. 125–126.

41. Colville, *Footprints*, pp. 149–150.

42. *London Daily Express*, Feb. 17, 1941.

## 10. Delivering the Goods

1. Lord Halifax to HLH, March 9, 1941; HLH, memo, March 11, 1941, HHP, Box 305; Sherwood, *Roosevelt and Hopkins*, p. 265; WSC to HLH, March 28, 1941, PREM 3 224/1.

2. Richard M. Leighton and Robert W. Coakley, *Global Logistics and Strategy*, 2 vols. (Washington, D.C.: Office of the Chief of Military History, 1955, 1959), I, 76–77; William L. Langer and S. Everett Gleason, *The Undeclared War, 1940–1941* (New York: Harper, 1953), p. 421; John M. Blum, *From the Morgenthau Diaries: Years of Urgency, 1938–1941* (Boston: Houghton Mifflin, 1965), pp. 229–231; FDR to Henry Stimson, Cordell Hull, HMJr, and Frank Knox, Feb. 25, 1941, in Elliott Roosevelt, ed., *FDR: His Personal Letters* (New York: Duell, Sloan, and Pearce, 1950), p. 1128; WSC to HLH, Feb. 28, 1941, PREM 3 224/1; Oscar Cox, diary, March 4, 1941, Cox Papers, Box 145.

3. Blum, *Urgency*, pp. 169, 231–232; Cox, diary, Feb. 28, 1941; Cox, interview with Joseph Alsop, March 25, 1941, Alsop Papers, Box 32, LC.

4. Mark Skinner Watson, *Chief of Staff: Prewar Plans and Preparations* (Washington, D.C.: Historical Division, Department of the Army, 1950), pp. 128, 169, 170–178, 182; Robert Sherwood, interview with General James H. Burns, Nov. 1, 1946, Sherwood Papers, Box 411; Civilian Production Administration, *Industrial Mobilization for War* (Washington, D.C.: Government Printing Office, 1947), pp. 51, 100.

5. Cox, diary, March 9, 10, 1941; James H. Burns to HLH, March 4,

1941, HHP, Box 305; Minutes of British Supply Council, March 5, 1941, CAB 115/33.

6. Memo, March 5, 1941, in folder titled "Hopkins 14 Points," S[ecretary of] W[ar] subject file 1940–1945, H-J, RG 107; General Henry H. Arnold to General George C. Marshall, March 5, 1941, HHP, Box 304.

7. Kingsley Wood to HLH, Feb. 1, 1941, with attached aide memoire, ibid., Box 305; Wood to WSC, March 15, 1941, PREM 4 17/2; "Takeout of All Old Contracts," in folder AB/15, materials prepared for L-L Hearings (1940), Assistant Secretary of the Treasury, RG 56.

8. HMJr, memo, March 15, 1941; Philip Young, memo of conversation with HMJr, March 15, 1941, HMJr, diary, vol. 382; HMJr, conference with Philip Young, Ed Foley, W. M. Cochran, D. W. Bell, and Oscar Cox, March 18, 1941, ibid., vol. 383; HMJr, meeting with British and Canadian representatives, March 19, 1941, Records of Assistant to the Secretary of the Treasury, ibid., folder AB/05, Conference Record Book; H. D. White to HMJr, June 2, 1941, ibid., folder AB/31, Treasury Chronicles, vol 5, item 161, RG 56; Colonel Henry Aurand, memo for General Eugene Reybold, March 20, 1941, Aurand Papers, Box 10; Cox, diary, March 18, 1941.

9. HMJr, conversation with Philip Young, March 17, 1941; HMJr, presidential diary, vol. 4; Blum, *Urgency,* p. 234; HMJr, memo, April 2, 1941, HMJr, diary, vol. 385.

10. Lord Halifax to WSC, March 13, 1941, PREM 4 27/9.

11. HLH TC HMJr, March 12, 1941, HMJr, diary, vol. 381.

12. HLH to James H. Burns, March 27, 1941, HHP, Box 325; FDR to HLH, March 27, 1941, OF 4117.

13. Philip Young to HLH, March 17, 1941, HHP, Box 307; Cox, diary, March 18, 1941.

14. "H.E.," memo, April 16, 1941, CAB 122/81.

15. Draft cable, British Supply Council, PURSA series, March 7, 1941, AVIA 38/35; Air Marshal J. C. Slessor to HLH, March 5, 1941; George C. Marshall to Henry Stimson, March 10, 1941, C/S Conferences, RG 165; HLH to WSC, April 4, 1941, HHP, Box 306.

16. British Supply Council, minutes showing contacts with HLH, CAB 115/33-34.

17. Blum, *Urgency,* p. 232; Joseph Alsop, interview with Oscar Cox, March 25, 1941, Alsop Papers, Box 32; Stimson, diary, Feb. 27, March 5, 1941.

18. George C. Marshall, interview with Robert Sherwood, July 23, 1947, Sherwood Papers, Box 411; Marshall to Louise Macy, July 3, 1942, George C. Marshall Papers, Box 71, GCML.

19. HLH to FDR, June 14, 1941; HLH to James H. Burns, June 20, 1941, HHP, Box 307; Herbert Feis to HLH, June 7, 1941; HLH to Feis,

June 7, 1941; HLH to Louis Johnson and WAH, June 7, 1941; HLH to Burns, June 7, 1941; HLH to H. L. Vickery, June 9, 1941; Burns to HLH, June 18, 1941, ibid., Box 326; Frank Knox to Philip Young, May 24, 1941; Burns to HLH, May 27, 1941; HLH to FDR, May 27, 1941; HLH to FDR, June 3, 1941, HLH to Senator Robert A. Taft, June 18, 1941, ibid., Box 307.

20. HLH to WAH, May 6, 1941, ibid., Box 305.

21. Blum, *Urgency,* pp. 242–243; Oscar Cox to HLH, memo, n.d., on execution of Lend-Lease, HHP, Box 305; Warren F. Kimball, *The Most Unsordid Act: Lend-Lease, 1939–1941* (Baltimore: Johns Hopkins Press, 1969), pp. 243–246; HLH TC HMJr, March 12, 1941, HMJr, diary, vol. 381.

22. J. M. Keynes to HMJr, May 16, 1941, in Donald Moggridge, ed., *The Collected Writings of John Maynard Keynes* (Cambridge: Cambridge University Press, 1979), XXIII, 73–78; conference with HLH, HMJr, et al., June 5, 1941, HMJr, diary, vol. 405; Keynes to Sir Horace Wilson, May 19, 1941, in Moggridge, *Keynes,* XXIII, 81; HLH TC HMJr, June 19, 1941, HMJr, diary, vol. 410. Keynes recommended that the administration ask Congress for a new Lend-Lease appropriation of $3 to $4 billion around July 1. Mr. [?] Adler to Miss [?] Meryel, May 14, 1941, Records of the Assistant Secretary of the Treasury, re aid to Great Britain, folder AB/31, Treasury Chronicles, vol. 4, item 153, RG 56.

23. J. M. Keynes to Sir Horace Wilson, June 8, 1941, in Moggridge, *Keynes,* XXIII, 114, 85–86, 90–91, 100; W. Merle Cochran to HMJr, May 21, 1941, Records of the Assistant Secretary of the Treasury, folder AB/31, RG 56; conference re aid to Britain, June 5, 1941, HMJr, diary, vol. 405.

24. Conference in D. W. Bell's office, May 29, 1941, Records of the Assistant Secretary of the Treasury, folder AB/05, Conference Record Book, RG 56; conference of June 5, 1941, HMJr, diary, vol. 405.

25. HLH TC HMJr, June 19, 1941, HMJr, diary, vol. 410.

26. J. M. Keynes to Sir Horace Wilson, July 2, 1941, in Moggridge, *Keynes,* XXIII, 149.

27. W. M. Cochran to HMJr, May 21, 1941, Records of the Assistant Secretary of the Treasury, folder AB/31, Treasury Chronicles, vol. 4, item 153, RG 56; James H. Burns to HLH, June 6, 1941, HHP, Box 324; the report itself is dated June 10, 1941, and alters the last part of the sentence; see *Senate Document* 66, 77th *Cong.,* 1st *Sess.,* 1941.

28. Admiral Richmond K. Turner to Director of War Plans Division and Chief of Naval Operations, April 29, 1941, reel 39, item 1587, GCML.

## 11. Supplies and Strategy

1. WSC to HLH, March 28, 1941, PREM 3 224/1.

2. HMJr, memo, March 16, 1941, HMJr, diary, vol. 382; HLH to FDR,

March 17, 1941; HLH to John G. Winant and WAH, March 28, 1941, HHP, Box 307.

3. Conference in the Office of the Chief of Staff, April 16, 1941, C/S Conferences, RG 165.

4. General Sir Frederick Beaumont-Nesbitt to Chief of the Imperial General Staff April 11, 1941; Lord Halifax to Anthony Eden, April 14, 1941; Beaumont-Nesbitt, memo of conversation with HLH, April 16, 1941, CAB 122/81.

5. Stimson, diary, April 15, 1941; conference in the Office of the Chief of Staff, April 16, 1941, C/S Conferences, RG 165; Forrest C. Pogue, *George C. Marshall: Ordeal and Hope* (New York: Viking Press, 1965), p. 134; Mark Skinner Watson, *Chief of Staff: Prewar Plans and Preparations* (Washington, D.C.: Historical Division, Department of the Army, 1950), pp. 376–377; Maurice Matloff and Edwin M. Snell, *Strategic Planning for Coalition Warfare,* 2 vols. (Washington, D.C.: Office of the Chief of Military History, 1953), I, 46–47.

6. Admiral Richmond K. Turner to Chief of Naval Operations, April 29, 1941, reel 39, item 1587 GCML. I have found no evidence that in this conversation Hopkins was speaking for President Roosevelt.

7. Lieutenant Colonel R. W. Crawford to General Harry Malony, April 30, 1941, ibid.; Robert J. Quinlan, "The United States Fleet: Diplomacy, Strategy and the Allocation of Ships (1940–1941)," in Harold Stein, ed., *American Civil-Military Decisions* (Birmingham: University of Alabama Press, 1963), pp. 181–185.

8. Frederic C. Lane, *Ships for Victory* (Baltimore: Johns Hopkins Press, 1951), p. vii; Emory S. Land to FDR and HLH, April 11, 1941; Land to FDR, March 20, 1941, HHP, Box 320.

9. Lane, *Ships,* p. 754; Joseph Alsop and Robert Kintner, *Washington Post,* May 14, 1941; HLH to H. H. Robson, May 12, 1941, HHP, Box 307; HLH, appointment diary, May 10, 1941, Hopkins microfilm, reel 5, HHP; HLH to Henry Stimson, May 15, 1941; Stimson to HLH, May 26, 1941, ibid., Box 303; HLH TC HMJr, June 19, 1941, HMJr, diary, vol. 410; HLH to J.H. Burns, June 19, 1941, HHP, Box 307.

10. Lane, *Ships,* pp. 42–45, 57–58, 61–62; HLH to Isadore Lubin, May 29, 1941; FDR to Emory S. Land, June 16, 1941, HHP, Box 320.

11. WSC to FDR, April 24 (two letters), May 4, 1941, in WSC, *The Grand Alliance* (Boston: Houghton, Mifflin, 1950), pp. 143–146, 235–236.

12. Oscar Cox to HLH, May 25, 1941, HHP, Box 304.

13. S. Shepard Jones and Denys P. Myers, eds., *Documents on American Foreign Relations,* vol. 3 (Boston: World Peace Foundation), pp. 417–419.

14. Lord Halifax to Anthony Eden, n.d., discussing Hopkins's and Benjamin Cohen's agreement to this strategy, Halifax microfilm, Churchill College,

Cambridge, reel 1, A 4.14; note given by Admiral Victor Danckwerts to HLH, June 12, 1941, ibid., reel 1, A 4.1; memo of meeting to compose a telegram to the prime minister, June 13, 1941, with Halifax's note, June 14, 1941, "These telegrams were drafted on June 12 . . . but suspended after a talk I had the same evening with Harry Hopkins," ibid., reel 1, A 4.410.4.4. Hopkins's diary notes meetings with Cohen on June 2 and 9, but no meeting with either Danckwerts or Halifax; Hopkins microfilm, reel 5.

15. HLH to FDR, June 14, 1941, in Sherwood, *Roosevelt and Hopkins*, p. 299; the original document is in PPF 4096.

16. Stimson, diary, June 23, July 6, 1941; Stimson to FDR, June 23, 1941, in Sherwood, *Roosevelt and Hopkins*, pp. 303–304.

17. HLH, appointment diary, April 29, May 1 [with FDR], 7, 1941, Hopkins microfilm, reel 5; Richard M. Leighton and Robert W. Coakley, *Global Logistics and Strategy*, 2 vols. (Washington, D.C.: Office of the Chief of Military History, 1955, 1959), I, 91, 94; Stimson, diary, May 6, 1941; FDR to WSC, July 12, 1941 in Francis L. Loewenheim, Harold D. Langley, and Manfred Jonas, eds., *Roosevelt and Churchill: Their Secret Wartime Correspondence* (New York: Saturday Review Press, 1975), p. 149; WAH, *Special Envoy to Churchill and Stalin, 1941–1946* (New York: Random House, 1975), pp. 62–71.

18. Sherwood, *Roosevelt and Hopkins*, pp. 311–312.

19. James Leutze, ed., *The London Journal of General Raymond E. Lee, 1940–1941* (Boston: Little, Brown, 1971), p. 343; Sherwood, *Roosevelt and Hopkins*, p. 314.

20. W[ar] M[inutes] (42) 71st conclusion, July 17, 1941, CAB 65.

21. WSC, *Grand Alliance*, pp. 424, 427.

22. Leutze, *Lee*, p. 344.

23. Ibid., p. 351–353; Hopkins also included Chief of Naval Operations Harold Stark to meet with Roosevelt and Marshall, but only after Lee had prompted him. Raymond Lee to George Marshall, July 27, 1941, verifax 683, item 2114, Research File, GCML.

24. War Cabinet Defense Committee (Supply), 6th mtg., July 22, 1941; 7th mtg., July 23, 1941; War Cabinet, July 24, 1941, HHP, Box 307; Leutze, *Lee*, p. 349.

25. Sherwood, *Roosevelt and Hopkins*, p. 318; HLH to FDR with notation by WSC that letter was drafted July 26, 1941, at Chequers but not sent, HHP, Box 307.

26. HLH to FDR, July 26, 1941 [not sent]; "Broadcast of Mr. Harry Hopkins," n.d., HHP, Box 307; Sherwood, *Roosevelt and Hopkins*, p. 320.

27. Sherwood, *Roosevelt and Hopkins*, pp. 248–249; H. V. Morton, *Atlantic Meeting* (New York: Dodd, Mead, 1943), pp. 28–29.

28. Theodore Wilson, *The First Summit: Roosevelt and Churchill at Placentia*

*Bay, 1941* (Boston: Houghton Mifflin, 1969), pp. 80, 83, 260; Sherwood, *Roosevelt and Hopkins,* p. 353.

29. HLH to FDR, on back of luncheon menu, PSF: Safe File: Atlantic Charter.

30. Sumner Welles, memorandum, Aug. 11, 1941, in *FRUS, 1941,* I, 361–362.

31. WSC, *Grand Alliance,* p. 24.

32. M. A. Gwyer, *Grand Strategy* (London: Her Majesty's Stationery Office, 1964), pp. 122, 364, 365, 368; WSC, *Grand Alliance,* p. 37.

33. Lord Moran, *Churchill: Taken from the Diaries of Lord Moran* (Boston: Houghton Mifflin, 1966), p. 22; Pogue, *Ordeal and Hope,* p. 143; Stimson, diary, Aug. 19, 1941; Wilson, *The First Summit,* p. 154, misinterprets this to be a joint Anglo-American organization and calls it the origin of the Combined Chiefs of Staff. Leighton and Coakley, *Logistics,* I, 95; General Henry Arnold, notes, Aug. 14, 1941, Arnold Papers, Box 181.

34. General Henry Arnold, notes on Argentia conference, Aug. 14, 1941, Arnold Papers, Box 181.

35. Stimson, diary, Aug. 19, 1941; Davies, diary, Aug. 30, 1941, Box 11; A. J. P. Taylor, *Beaverbrook* (London: Hamish Hamilton, 1972), p. 483.

36. WSC to HLH, Aug. 28, 1941, PREM 3 224/2.

37. HLH, handwritten note, n.d., HHP, Box 298.

38. Sherwood, *Roosevelt and Hopkins,* p. 372.

## 12. Ever So Confident

1. Jan Ciechanowski, *Defeat in Victory* (Garden City, N.Y.: Doubleday, 1947, pp. 25–26; Ciechanowski, memorandum, June 22, 1941, FO 371/29485.

2. WSC to HLH, June 26, 1941, HHP, Box 224; Stimson, diary, June 23, 1941.

3. Joseph Davies, *Mission to Moscow* (New York: Simon and Schuster, 1941), pp. 487–491; Davies, diary, July 8, 9, 1941, Box 11.

4. HLH to FDR, July 25, 1941, in Sherwood, *Roosevelt and Hopkins,* p. 318.

5. War Cabinet, "Record of a Meeting of the Prime Minister and Chiefs of Staff with United States Observers held at No. 10 Downing Street, at 10.0 P.M. on Thursday, 24th July, 1941," HHP, Box 307; Lord Halifax to FO, July 31, 1941, CAB 122/101; Supply Committee to British Supply Council, July 25, 1941, FO 115/3811; HLH to FDR, July 25, 1941, in Sherwood, *Roosevelt and Hopkins,* p. 318.

6. Forrest Davis and Ernest K. Lindley, *How War Came* (New York: Simon and Schuster, 1942), pp. 252–253; Ivan Maisky, *Memoirs of a Soviet*

*Ambassador* (New York: Scribner's, 1968), pp. 179–180; John Daniel Langer, "The Formulation of American Aid Policy Toward the Soviet Union, 1940–43: The Hopkins Shop and the Department of State" (Ph.D. diss., Yale University, 1975), pp. 72–73, admits that his interpretation is speculative; Sherwood, *Roosevelt and Hopkins,* p. 317.

7. HLH to FDR, July 25, 1941, ibid., p. 318.

8. HLH to FDR, n.d., but with a note by J. M. Martin, Churchill's private secretary: "This telegram was drafted by Mr. Harry Hopkins at Chequers 26.7.41; but not sent," HHP, Box 307.

9. FDR to HLH, July 26, 1941, in Sherwood, *Roosevelt and Hopkins,* p. 318; James Leutze, ed., *The London Journal of General Raymond E. Lee, 1940–1941* (Boston: Little, Brown, 1971), p. 357; HLH to FDR, July 27, 1941, HHP, Box 307; Sherwood, *Roosevelt and Hopkins,* p. 321; Maisky, *Memoirs,* p. 181.

10. Sherwood, *Roosevelt and Hopkins,* pp. 321–322.

11. D. C. McKinley, "Flight to Archangel with Mr. Harry Hopkins—July/August 1941," Hopkins microfilm, reel 19, HHP; Sherwood, *Roosevelt and Hopkins,* pp. 323–326.

12. *FRUS, 1941,* I, 802–813.

13. W[ar] M[inutes] (41) 72nd Conclusion, July 21, 1941, CAB 65/19; Supply Committee to British Supply Council, July 25, 1941, FO 115/3811; FO to Lord Halifax, July 24, 1941, CAB 122/101; WSC to Stalin, July 28, 1941, in *Stalin's Correspondence with Churchill, Attlee, Roosevelt, and Truman* (New York: E. P. Dutton, 1958), p. 16; Sherwood, *Roosevelt and Hopkins,* p. 331; *FRUS, 1941,* I, 822–823; WSC to Privy Seal, Aug. 12, 1941, in WSC, *The Grand Alliance* (Boston: Houghton Mifflin, 1950), p. 447.

14. Margaret Bourke-White, *Shooting the Russian War* (New York: Simon and Schuster, 1942), pp. 207–208.

15. HLH to FDR, Cordell Hull, and Sumner Welles, Aug. 1, 1941, *FRUS, 1941,* I, 814.

16. Davies, diary, Sept. 8, 10, 1941, Box 11; Sherwood, *Roosevelt and Hopkins,* pp. 343–344; Bourke-White, *Shooting,* pp. 213–214. "I would hardly call Uncle Joe a pleasant man," Hopkins wrote, "although he was interesting enough, and I think I got what I wanted, but you can never be sure about that"; HLH to Sir Hastings Ismay, Aug. 7, 1941, Hopkins microfilm, reel 19.

17. Alexander Werth, diary, July 31, 1941, in Werth, *Moscow War Diary* (New York: Knopf, 1942), pp. 108–109: Henry Cassidy, *Moscow Dateline* (Boston: Houghton Mifflin, 1943), p. 125; Bourke-White, *Shooting,* p. 210.

18. D. C. McKinley, "Flight . . . with Mr. Harry Hopkins"; HLH to Sir Charles Portal, Aug. 8, 1941, Hopkins microfilm, reel 19.

19. WSC to Privy Seal, Aug. 12, 1941, in WSC, *Grand Alliance,* pp. 446–

447; WAH, *Special Envoy to Churchill and Stalin, 1941–1946* (New York: Random House, 1975), p. 76.

20. Marvin D. Bernstein and Francis L. Loewenheim, "Aid to Russia: The First Year," in Harold Stein, ed., *American Civil-Military Decisions* (Birmingham: University of Alabama Press, 1963), p. 112; ERS, memo on meeting with HLH, Sept. 12, 1941, Stettinius Papers, Box 135; Davis and Lindley, *How War Came,* p. 212.

21. Bernstein and Loewenheim, "Aid to Russia," p. 112; HLH to ERS, n.d., in Sherwood, *Roosevelt and Hopkins,* p. 387.

22. James Burns to HLH, n.d. (Aug. 24–30, 1941), HHP, Box 306; Bernstein and Loewenheim, "Aid to Russia," pp. 114–116; R. Elberton Smith, *The Army and Economic Mobilization* (Washington, D.C.: Office of the Chief of Military History, 1959), pp. 136–137.

23. A. J. P. Taylor, *Beaverbrook* (London: Hamish Hamilton, 1972), p. 487; WSC to FDR, Sept. 5, 1941, in WSC, *Grand Alliance,* p. 460; HLH to WSC, Sept. 9, 1941, *FRUS, 1941,* I, 839–840; Langer, "Hopkins Shop," pp. 102–103; WAH, notes, Sept. 28, 29, 30, 1941, HHP, Box 306.

24. John M. Blum, *From The Morgenthau Diaries: Years of War, 1941–1945* (Boston: Houghton Mifflin, 1967), pp. 267–268; Raymond Dawson, *The Decision to Aid Russia* (Chapel Hill: University of North Carolina Press, 1959), pp. 245–246; Jesse Jones to Board of Directors, Federal Loan Agency, Oct. 1, 1941, HHP, Box 306; "Day Journal for Mr. John Hazard," Aug. 29, Sept, 17, 23, 24, 25, 26, 29, 30, Oct. 14, 21, 1941, John N. Hazard Papers, Box 8, Butler Library, Columbia University, New York City.

25. General R. C. Moore TC Colonel H. S. Aurand, Oct. 31, 1941, H. S. Aurand, diary, Aurand Papers, bk. 1; Dawson, *Decision,* pp. 266–269, 274–282.

26. HLH memo, Oct. 30, 1941, HHP, Box 309; FDR to Laurence Steinhardt, Nov. 5, 1941, *FRUS, 1941,* I, 852–853.

27. George C. Herring, Jr., *Aid to Russia, 1941–1946: Strategy, Diplomacy, the Origins of the Cold War* (New York: Columbia University Press, 1973), pp. 38–40, 42, 44–45; Philip Faymonville to HLH, Nov. 4, 1941, HHP, Box 306.

28. HLH to James Burns, Nov. 7, 1941, ibid.; HLH to Burns, Nov. 14, 1941, Soviet Protocol Committee Papers, Box 18, FDRL.

29. Sherwood, *Roosevelt and Hopkins,* p. 394.

## 13. The Long-Term–Short-Term Balance

1. General James Burns to HLH, March 4, 1941, HHP, Box 305.

2. Oscar Cox, diary, March 4, 1941, Cox Papers, Box 145; Richard V.

Gilbert to HLH, April 11, 1941, HHP, Box 158; Gilbert to HLH, April 12, 1941, ibid., Box 322.

3. R. Elberton Smith, *The Army and Economic Mobilization* (Washington, D.C.: Office of the Chief of Military History, 1959), pp. 134–135; Joseph Alsop and Robert Kintner, *Washington Post,* April 20, 1941; Mark Skinner Watson, *Chief of Staff: Prewar Plans and Preparations* (Washington, D.C.: Historical Division, Department of the Army, 1950), pp. 332–337.

4. Isadore Lubin to HLH, April 23, May 31, 1941, HHP, Box 307.

5. Conference in the offices of the chief of staff and the undersecretary of war, 11:00 A.M., May 17, 1941, C/S Conferences, RG 165.

6. HLH to John D. Biggers, May 2, 1941; HLH to James Burns, and attached documents, May 8, 1941; FDR to William Knudsen, drafted by HLH, May 28, 1941, HHP, Box 307.

7. FDR to Henry Stimson, drafted by HLH, May 29, 1941, ibid., Box 307; John Biggers to FDR, June 4, 1941, with note at top, "Not sent but discussed with Mr. Hopkins. He approved it and, in turn, read it to the President. JDB." War Production Board file 212, Production—Objectives—1941–1946, RG 179; Watson, *Chief of Staff,* pp. 338–339.

8. Civilian Production Administration, *Industrial Mobilization for War* (Washington, D.C.: Government Printing Office, 1947), pp. 190–192, 195; Oscar Cox, diary, July 11, 1941, Cox Papers, Box 145.

9. HLH, handwritten notes on Jesse Jones to HLH, June 4, 1941, with attached correspondence; HLH to Grace Tully, June 17, 1941, HHP, Box 307.

10. General Henry Arnold, notes, [Aug. 12, 1941], Arnold Papers, Box 181.

11. HLH to Robert Jackson, April 25, 1941, with attached telegram, HHP, Box 307; William Donovan to HLH, Oct. 28, 1941; HLH to Donovan, Nov. 2, 1941, ibid., Box 301.

12. Oscar Cox to HLH, June 20, 1941; HLH to Francis Biddle, July 1, 1941, HHP, Box 303.

13. HLH to FDR, Nov. 27, 1941; HLH to ERS, Oct. 20, 1941, ibid., Box 307; see also HLH to ERS, Nov. 27, 1941, ibid., Box 317.

14. Wayne Coy to FDR, Aug. 28, 1941, ibid., Box 323.

15. General L. T. Gerow to General George Marshall, Aug. 21, 1941; James Burns to HLH, Aug. 26, 1941, WPD 4576, RG 165; Richard M. Leighton and Robert W. Coakley, *Global Logistics and Strategy,* 2 vols. (Washington, D.C.: Office of the Chief of Military History, 1955, 1959), I, 23, 95; Stimson, diary, Aug. 19, 1941; Burns to HLH, n.d. (Aug. 26–28), HHP, Box 306; Civilian Production Administration, *Industrial Mobilization,* p. 110; FDR to Marshall and Admiral Harold Stark, Sept. 8, 1941, WPD 4576, RG 165.

16. Civilian Production Administration, *Industrial Mobilization,* pp. 139–140; Henry Stimson to FDR, Sept. 23, 1941, HHP, Box 304.

17. Sherwood, *Roosevelt and Hopkins,* pp. 410–418.

18. HLH to Isadore Lubin, Sept. 16, 1941, HHP, Box 327; HLH to Robert Patterson, Oct. 24, 1941, ibid., Box 323.

19. HLH to FDR, Nov. 3, 1941; Isadore Lubin to HLH, Oct. 10, 31, 1941, ibid.; HLH to James Forrestal, Nov. 14, 1941, ibid., Box 306; FDR to William Knudsen, drafted by HLH, Nov. 3, 1941; HLH to ERS, Nov. 2, 1941; Knudsen to FDR, Nov. 4, 1941; HLH to Patterson, Nov. 10, 1941, ibid., Box 323.

20. ERS, memo of meeting with HLH, Sept. 12, 1941, Stettinius Papers, Box 135; HLH, diary, Aug. 28–Sept. 12, Hopkins microfilm, reel 5, HHP; FDR to John D. Biggers, Aug. 29, 1941, OF 4117; HLH to James Burns, Aug. 20, 25, 1941; Biggers to HLH, William Knudsen, ERS, and [?] Whiteside, Sept. 16, 1941, HHP, Box 323; ERS, memo of meeting with HLH, Sept. 12, 1941, Stettinius Papers, Box 135.

21. Conference in the office of the secretary of war, July 21, 1941, C/S Conferences, RG 165; Henry Stimson to James Burns, Aug. 21, 1941, AVIA 38/1035; ERS to HLH, Nov. 26, 1941; HLH to ERS, Nov. 27, 1941, HHP, Box 314; HLH to FDR, Nov. 27, 1941, with FDR to Harold Smith on bottom, OF 25; ERS to HLH, Nov. 25, 1941; HLH to ERS, Nov. 26, 1941, HHP, Box 325.

22. HLH to Robert Patterson, Nov. 10, 1941; HLH to ERS, Nov. 10, 1941; James Burns to Henry Arnold, Nov. 14, 1941; E. P. Taylor to HLH, Nov. 8, 1941; HLH to Burns, Nov. 17, 1941; Burns to HLH, Nov. 19, 1941; HLH to Leon Henderson, Nov. 22, 1941; Henderson to HLH, Nov. 25, 1941, ibid., Box 328; Leighton and Coakley *Logistics,* I, 104, 139–140; HLH to FDR, Nov. 8, 1941, with draft of FDR to Henry Stimson, Nov. 8, 1941, PSF confidential file: Lend-Lease, Box 16; British Supply Council cables USLON 96, Nov. 7, 1941; USLON, 103, Nov. 11, 1941, FO 115/3811; Henry Stimson to FDR, Sept. 22, 1941, *Pearl Harbor Attack, Hearings before the Joint Committee on the Investigation of the Pearl Harbor Attack,* 79th Cong., pt. 10, pp. 4430–4435; HLH to FDR, Oct. 14, 1941, ibid., p. 4429.

23. HLH to WAH, Sept. 26, 1941; John D. Biggers to ERS and HLH, Sept. 18, 1941; HLH to Biggers, Sept. 18, 1941; HLH to ERS, Sept. 19, 1941; Philip Young to Secretary of State, Sept. 22, 1941, HHP, Box 317; HLH to Burns, Nov. 7, 1941, ibid., Box 326; ERS to HLH, Nov. 11, 1941, ibid., Box 306; HLH to Oscar Cox, Nov. 7, 1941, ibid., Box 307.

24. Admiral E. S. Land, press conference, Sept. 3, 1941, notes, ibid., Box 320; WSC, *The Grand Alliance* (Boston: Houghton Mifflin, 1950), pp. 516–519, 521–531, 782; Leighton and Coakley, *Logistics,* I, 741; Joint Board Report, Sept. 11, 1941, HHP, Box 304.

25. Memo in files of David Scoll, "Lend-Lease Activities—US Maritime Commission," Sept. 6, 1941; Sumner Welles to HLH, July 17, 1941; HLH to Secretary of War, July 12, 1941, HHP, Box 320; *FRUS, 1941,* I, 485–491; Oscar Cox, diary, July 10, 1941, Cox Papers, Box 145; W. K. Hancock and M. M. Gowing, *British War Economy* (London: His Majesty's Stationery Office, 1949), pp. 206, 267.

26. *FRUS, 1941,* I, 863; Philip Faymonville to S. P. Spalding, Nov. 14, 1941, HHP, Box 317.

27. Jerry Land to ERS, Nov. 27, 1941, forwarded to HLH with note by James Burns, Nov. 29, 1941; HLH to Burns, Nov. 21, 1941, ibid.; ERS, memo of meeting with HLH, Nov. 28, 1941, Stettinius Papers, Box 135; HLH to Burns, Nov. 18, 1941, Soviet Protocol Committee Papers, FDRL, Box 18; HLH to S. P. Spalding, Dec. 1, 1941, HHP, Box 316; HLH to WAH, Dec. 3, 1941, ibid., Box 317.

28. John G. Winant to Cordell Hull, Dec. 4, 1941; Hull to Winant, Dec. 5, 1941, *FRUS, 1941,* I, 192–195; HLH to WAH, Dec. 5, 1941, HHP, Box 317.

29. HLH to James Burns, Oct. 31, 1941, ibid., Box 194.

30. Civilian Production Administration, *Industrial Mobilization,* pp. 117–118; James Forrestal to HLH, Oct. 20, 1941, HHP, Box 322; HMJr, Oct. 28, 1941, HMJr, presidential diary, vol. 4; HLH to Forrestal, Oct. 27, 1941, attached to Forrestal to HLH, Oct. 20, 1941, HHP, Box 322; HLH, diary, Oct. 28, 1941, Hopkins microfilm, reel 5; "Wallace, Henry A.," Nov. 19, 1941, OF 4117.

31. ERS to HLH, Nov. 11, 1941, HHP, Box 306; HLH to Grace Tully, Nov. 22, 1941, PPF 4096; James Burns to Colonel Henry S. Aurand, Nov. 24, 1941, Aurand Papers, Box 10; ERS, conference with HLH, Nov. 28, 1941, Stettinius Papers, Box 134; HLH to FDR, Dec. 8, 1941, HHP, Box 312.

32. Letters from Hyde Park, Nov. 2, 3, 1941; HLH to Oscar Cox, Nov. 7, 1941; HLH to Betsey Roosevelt, Nov. 10, 1941, HHP, Box 307; HLH to Missy Lehand, Nov. 10, 1941, Hopkins microfilm, reel 12; Lois Berney to Adah Aime, Nov. 10, 1941, HHP, Box 299; HLH to Alfred E. Cohn, Dec. 3, 1941, ibid., Box 307.

33. On Henry S. Aurand, see Leighton and Coakley, *Logistics,* I, 78–81; ERS, memo of conference with HLH, Sept. 12, 1941, Stettinius Papers, Box 135.

34. ERS, memo of conference with HLH, Nov. 28, 1941, Stettinius Papers, Box 135.

35. Bruce Catton, *The War Lords of Washington* (New York: Harcourt, Brace, 1948), p. 8; Oscar Cox to Leon Henderson Nov. 6, 1941, HHP, Box 307; WAH, in Henry H. Adams, *Harry Hopkins, A Biography* (New York: G. P. Putnam's Sons, 1977), p. 20.

36. Stimson, diary, Dec. 1, 2, 1941; Sherwood, *Roosevelt and Hopkins,* pp. 426–427.

37. WAH, *Special Envoy to Churchill and Stalin, 1941–1946* (New York: Random House, 1975), pp. 111–112; WSC, *Grand Alliance,* p. 605.

38. WAH to HLH, Dec. 8, 1941, HHP, Box 320; WSC, *Grand Alliance,* pp. 606, 607–608.

39. Robert Sherwood, interview with Edward R. Murrow, Sept. 16, 1946, Sherwood Papers, Box 411.

## 14. Laying the Groundwork

1. Sherwood, *Roosevelt and Hopkins,* pp. 440–442; HLH to ERS, Dec. 12, 1941, HHP, Box 325; Robert Patterson to HLH, Dec. 22, 1941, ibid., Box 324.

2. ERS to HLH, Dec. 9, 1941, in *Foreign Relations of the United States: The Conferences at Washington and Casablanca* (Washington, D.C.: Government Printing Office, 1968), pp. 5–6, 10–11, 18–19, hereafter cited as *FRUS: Washington and Casablanca;* HLH to Lord Beaverbrook, Dec. 13, 1941, HHP, Box 306; HLH to FDR enclosing draft of FDR to William Batt, Dec. 17, 1941; HLH memo, Dec. 19, 1941, ibid., Box 320.

3. ERS, notes on meeting with HLH, Dec. 10, 1941, Stettinius Papers, Box 135; Henry Aurand, comments at Defense Aid Office meeting, Dec. 19, 1941, Aurand, diary, bk. 3, Aurand Papers.

4. HLH to FDR, Dec. 8, 1941, HHP, Box 312, italics in original; ERS, notes on conversation with HLH, Dec. 10, 1941, Stettinius Papers, Box 135; Oscar Cox, diary, Dec. 10, 1941, Cox Papers, Box 145; ERS to HLH, Dec. 17, 1941, HHP, Box 312; Richard M. Leighton and Robert W. Coakley, *Global Logistics and Strategy,* 2 vols. (Washington, D.C.: Office of the Chief of Military History, 1955, 1959), I, 216; ERS to HLH, Dec. 27, 1941; HLH to ERS, Dec. 29, 1941, HHP, Box 314; HLH, memo, Jan. 13, 1942, ibid., Box 298; Stimson, diary, Oct. 21, 23, 25, 30, Dec. 1, 2, 1941.

5. Colonel Charles Gross to General Brehon Somervell, Dec. 26, 1941, A.G. 400 (12-26-41), RG 407.

6. HLH to FDR, Dec. 17, 1941, PSF Safe: Hopkins, Box 4.

7. *FRUS: Washington and Casablanca,* pp. 22–25, 64–65; Lord Moran, *Churchill: Taken from the Diaries of Lord Moran* (Boston: Houghton Mifflin, 1966), p. 12.

8. M. A. Gwyer, *Grand Strategy* (London: Her Majesty's Stationery Office, 1964), p. 349; *FRUS: Washington and Casablanca,* p. 68.

9. Ibid., pp. 268, 95.

10. Ibid., pp. 91–93.

11. Forrest C. Pogue, *George C. Marshall: Ordeal and Hope* (New York:

Viking Press, 1965), pp. 277–279; Sherwood, *Roosvelt and Hopkins,* pp. 456–457; WSC, *The Grand Alliance* (Boston: Houghton Mifflin, 1950), p. 673; Gwyer, *Grand Strategy,* p. 370.

12. Pogue, *Ordeal and Hope,* pp. 280–281.

13. See *FRUS: Washington and Casablanca,* pp. 277–279, for facsimile with corrections.

14. HLH, memo, Dec. 30, 1941, in Sherwood, *Roosevelt and Hopkins,* p. 469.

15. Maurice Matloff and Edwin M. Snell, *Strategic Planning for Coalition Warfare,* 2 vols. (Washington, D.C.: Office of the Chief of Military History, 1953), I, 125, 126; *FRUS: Washington and Casablanca,* pp. 135, 138–139, 282; Sherwood, *Roosevelt and Hopkins,* p. 469.

16. Conference held at White House, 11:00 A.M., Sunday, Dec. 28, 1941, Xerox 1694, GCML; HLH, memo, Dec. 30, 1941, HHP, Box 311; *FRUS: Washington and Casablanca,* pp. 297, 300; HLH to FDR, Dec. 31, 1941, HHP, Box 321.

17. A. Salter to HLH, Dec. 23, 1941, ibid., Box 320; ERS to HLH, enclosing James Burns to ERS and S. P. Spalding to ERS, Dec. 26, 1941, ibid., Box 317.

18. FDR to Secretary of War, Dec. 28, 1941, in *FRUS, 1941,* I, 865. Hopkins's revisions of the Burns and Spalding draft are in HHP, Box 317.

19. *FRUS: Washington and Casablanca,* pp. 187–191, 193–194.

20. HLH, memo, Dec. 27, 1941, ibid., p. 368.

21. Joseph Lash, *Roosevelt and Churchill, 1939–1941: The Partnership that Saved the West* (New York: Norton, 1976), pp. 19–20.

22. *FRUS: Washington and Casablanca,* pp. 10, 327–328; William Batt TC Hopkins's office, Dec. 23, 1941, HHP, Box 314; Arthur Krock, memo of conversation with Lord Beaverbrook, Jan. 3, 1942, Krock Papers, Box 1, Princeton Library, Princeton University, Princeton, N.J.

23. Sherwood, *Roosevelt and Hopkins,* p. 476; Alexander Proudfit to HLH, Dec. 30, 1941; HLH to Proudfit, Jan. 21, 1942, HHP, Box 313.

24. Papers CR 31 and CR 32, Dec. 31, 1941, CAB 122/175; Gwyer, *Grand Strategy,* p. 395; L. C. Hollis to HLH, Jan. 9, 1942, in *FRUS: Washington and Casablanca,* pp. 349–352.

25. *FRUS: Washington and Casablanca,* pp. 198–199, 232, 352–353; Admiral R. C. Moore to General J. N. Macready, Jan. 12, 1942, HHP, Box 312.

26. Oscar Cox to ERS, Jan. 12, 1942, in *FRUS: Washington and Casablanca,* pp. 356–357, enclosed in ERS to HLH, Jan. 12, 1942, HHP, Box 312.

27. Conference at the White House, 9:30 A.M., Jan. 13, 1942, Harold Smith Papers, Box 13, FDRL; HLH, memo, Jan. 13, 1942, HHP, Box 298.

28. Notes on conference in the office of the chief of staff, 10:50 A.M., Jan.

14, 1942, C/S Conferences, RG 165; George Marshall to HLH, Jan. 14, 1942, Marshall Papers, Box 71; Sherwood, *Roosevelt and Hopkins,* pp. 471–472.

29. *FRUS: Washington and Casablanca,* pp. 204–207, 361.

30. Moran, *Churchill,* p. 22.

31. Pogue, *Ordeal and Hope,* pp. 299, 22–26, ellipses in original; Robert Sherwood, interview with General George Marshall, July 23, 1947, Sherwood Papers, Box 411; Colonel L. M. Guyer and Colonel C. H. Donnelly, interview with Marshall, Feb. 22, 1949, Xerox 2256, GCML.

32. George Marshall to HLH, Jan. 15, 1942, Aurand Papers, Box 10; HLH to Jean Monnet, Jan. 15, 1942, Hopkins microfilm, reel 12, HHP.

## 15. No Front Stairs in Washington

1. Sherwood, *Roosevelt and Hopkins,* pp. 473–474.

2. HLH to Donald Nelson, Dec. 17, 1941, HHP, Box 322; HLH to James Forrestal, Jan. 3, 1942, ibid., Box 323; HLH to Robert Lovett, Feb. 23, 1942, ibid., Box 311.

3. HMJr, conversation with FDR, Dec. 30, 1941, HMJr, presidential diary, vol. 4; Sherwood, *Roosevelt and Hopkins,* pp. 475–477, HLH, appointment diary, Jan. 13, 16, 1942, Hopkins microfilm, reel 5, HHP; conference at White House, 9:30 A.M., Jan. 13, 16, 1942, Harold Smith Papers, FDRL, Box 13; Civilian Production Administration, *Industrial Mobilization for War* (Washington, D.C.: Government Printing Office, 1947), pp. 206–211.

4. Sherwood, *Roosevelt and Hopkins,* p. 476.

5. Ibid., pp. 2–3.

6. Civilian Production Administration, *Industrial Mobilization,* pp. 208, 216–217; HLH to FDR, Jan. 13, Feb. 20, 1942, OF 3716.

7. British Supply Council minutes, Feb. 11, 1942, CAB 115/35; Admiral J. W. S. Dorling, memo to CCS, Feb. 17, 1942, CAB 88/85; Oliver Lyttelton to John Dill, Lord Halifax, and British Supply Council, April 22, 1942 (two letters); HLH to General Henry Arnold, April 28, 1942, HHP, Box 323; Halifax to Lyttelton, May 25, 1942, FO 954/29; Civilian Production Administration, *Industrial Mobilization,* pp. 218–219; minutes of Lyttelton meeting with British Supply Council, June 9, 1942, AVIA 38/908.

8. Richard M. Leighton and Robert W. Coakley, *Global Logistics and Strategy,* 2 vols. (Washington, D.C.: Office of the Chief of Military History, 1955, 1959), I, 205–211; A. Salter to WSC, Jan. 4, 9, 1942; WSC to HLH, Jan. 10, 1942, in *FRUS: Washington and Casablanca,* pp. 353–355; S. P. Spaulding to HLH, Jan. 14, 1942, Soviet Protocol Committee Papers, Box 18, FDRL; H. L. Vickery to HLH, Jan. 5, 1942 (two letters), HHP, Box 320; Vickery to HLH, Feb. 7, 1942, ibid., Box 321.

9. Sir Arthur Salter to WSC, Jan. 9, 1942, in *FRUS: Washington and*

*Casablanca,* pp. 353–354; Leighton and Coakley, *Logistics,* I, 216; George Marshall to Harold Stark, Dec. 31, 1941, HHP, Box 312; Anglo-American Shipping Adjustment Board, Jan. 14, 1942; Oscar Cox to HLH, Jan. 13, 1942, in *FRUS: Washington and Casablanca,* pp. 361–362, 358–359; Marshall to Stark and Ernest King, Jan. 9, 1942, Marshall Papers, Box 85; Henry Stimson and Frank Knox to FDR, Jan. 13, 1942, HHP, Box 320; H. L. Vickery to HLH, Jan. 12, 1942, ibid., Box 312; HLH to FDR, Jan. 22, 1942; H. Smith to FDR, Feb. 5, 1942, OF 4772.

10. Frederic C. Lane, *Ships for Victory* (Baltimore: Johns Hopkins University Press, 1951), pp. 754, 755; ERS, conversation with HLH, Nov. 28, 1941, Stettinius Papers, Box 135; HLH to WAH, Feb. 19, 1942, Map Room Papers, FDRL, Box 13.

11. LWD, memo for discussion with HLH, March 16, 1942, Douglas file: Notes on Conferences; LWD memo, Sept. 9, 1942, Douglas file: Hopkins folder, RG 248.

12. FDR to ERS, Donald Nelson, and Admiral Land, March 17, 1942, GCML, Research File, Xerox 1633; FDR to Secretaries of War and Navy and Office of Lend-Lease Administration, March 24, 1942, quoted in John Dill to COS, April 12, 1942, in *War Telegrams,* Hist. (F) 1 (Final), no. 9; HLH to George Marshall, Jan. 15, 1942, Marshall Papers, Box 71; HLH to FDR, March 24, 1942; HLH to Philip Faymonville, March 13, 1942; Faymonville to HLH, March 16, 1942, *FRUS, 1942,* pp. 697–698.

13. Admiralty to B.A.D., April 6, 1942, in *War Telegrams,* Hist. (F) 2 (Final), no. 24; COS to John Dill, April 4, 1942, ibid., no. 18; Sherwood, *Roosevelt and Hopkins,* p. 526.

14. David E. Scoll to LWD, April 24, 1942; LWD, notes on meeting with James Burns, April 23, 1942; LWD to HLH, April 24, 1942, Douglas file: Russian Shipping, RG 248; *FRUS, 1942,* III, 577–578, 707.

15. David Scoll to LWD, April 30, 1942, Douglas file: Russian Shipping, RG 248; LWD to HLH, May 25, 1942, Douglas file: Hopkins, RG 248; Sherwood, *Roosevelt and Hopkins,* pp. 568–569; HLH, appointment diary, 4:00 P.M., May 31, 1942, Hopkins microfilm, reel 5, HHP.

16. Josef Stalin to WSC, July 23, 1942, in WSC, *The Hinge of Fate* (Boston: Houghton Mifflin, 1950), p. 270; George C. Herring, Jr., *Aid to Russia, 1941–1946: Strategy, Diplomacy, the Origins of the Cold War* (New York: Columbia University Press, 1973), pp. 66–67.

17. Molotov conversations, May 29, 1942, HHP, Box 311; Sherwood, *Roosevelt and Hopkins,* p. 562; John Dill to WSC, July 20, 1942, CAB 105/39; W. B. Smith, notes of conference at the White House, 8:30 P.M., July 30, 1942, Arnold Papers, Box 39; James Burns to FDR, Aug. 3, 1942, Soviet Protocol Committee Papers, Box 11.

18. HLH to LWD, Aug. 25, 1942, Douglas file: Hopkins, RG 248.

19. E. S. Land, memo for files, Oct. 10, 1942, Douglas file: Hopkins, RG 248; HLH, appointment diary, Oct. 8, 1942, Hopkins microfilm, reel 5; LWD, memorandum statement, Oct. 9, 1942, and attached memo, Land and LWD to FDR, Douglas file: Construction, RG 248; conference with the president, HLH, and Admiral Land, LWD, diary, Oct. 21, 1942, Douglas file, ibid.; HLH to FDR, Oct. 29, 1942; and draft of memo from FDR to JCS, HHP, Box 219; notes on conference at the White House, Oct. 24, 1942, Douglas file: Construction, RG 248.

20. Minutes of Lyttelton mission, 6:00 P.M., Nov. 13, 1942, AVIA 38/908; LWD, memo, Oct. 31, 1942, Douglas file: Construction, RG 248.

21. JSM to AMSSO, April 19, 1945, CAB 109/48; Sherwood, *Roosevelt and Hopkins,* p. 472.

22. Sidney Hyman to Robert Sherwood, July 12, 1946, relating information from Roger W. Jones of the MAB statistical staff, Sherwood Papers, Box 411.

23. CCS, directive establishing MAB, filed as CCS 19/1, Feb. 4, 1942, HHP, Box 312.

24. Sidney Hyman to Robert Sherwood, July 12, 1946, Sherwood Papers, Box 411.

25. HLH to James Burns, Feb. 12, 1942, HHP, Box 312; Henry Aurand to Burns, Feb. 24, 1942, Aurand Papers, Box 6; MAB minutes, Feb. 16, 1942, HHP, Box 194.

26. See file [April 25–May 17, 1942], CAB 109/48.

27. Lord Halifax to Oliver Lyttelton, May 25, 1942, FO 954/29.

28. Combined Staff Planners, 9th meeting, March 19, 1942, HHP, Box 313; Joint Staff Planners Washington to Cabinet Office for Directors of Plans, March 21, 1942; James Burns for MAB to COS, April 13, 1942, CAB 122/170; Leighton and Coakley, *Logistics,* I, 272–274; Rafdel to Airwhit, May 23, 1942, CAB 122/171; T. H. Brand to Colonel Ian Jacob, May 16, 1942, CAB 109/47.

29. HLH, draft of FDR to George Marshall with copy to Ernest King, Aug. 24, 1942, HHP, Box 312; see also HLH to FDR, Aug. 25, 1942, PSF: War Department, Box 14; Donald Nelson to FDR, Aug. 25, 1942, WPB file 215, folder Production Programs—Joint Planning, RG 179; Isadore Lubin to HLH, Sept. 15, 1942, WPB file 203, Production—Military Strategy, RG 179; General Brehon Somervell to Marshall, Oct. 14, 1942, Office of the Commanding General, Army Service Forces, folder Chief of Staff (three letters), RG 160.

30. *War Telegrams,* Hist. (F) 3 (Final): John Dill to WSC, Oct. 7, 1942, no. 68; WSC to HLH, Oct. 9, 1942, HHP, Box 313; HLH to WSC, Oct. 13, 1942; HLH to WAH, Oct. 13, 1942, ibid., Box 312; War Papers (42) 486, Oct. 29, 1942, CAB 66/30.

31. Lord Halifax to Oliver Lyttelton, Oct. 27, 1942; Halifax to FO, Oct. 24, 1942, FO 954/29; Air Ministry to Britman, Oct. 30, 1942, in *War Telegrams*, Hist. (F) 3 (Final), no. 96; Minister of Production, meeting, 3:30 P.M., Nov. 5, 1942, and 6:00 P.M., Nov. 6, 1942, AVIA 38/908.

32. *War Telegrams*, Hist. (F) 3 (Final): WSC to Oliver Lyttelton, Nov. 9, 1942, no. 109; John Dill to WSC, Nov. 11, 1942, no. 112; meeting of Lyttelton mission, 6:00 P.M. Nov. 6, 1942, 3:30 P.M., Nov. 18, 1942, AVIA 38/908; Leighton and Coakley, *Logistics*, I, 282–284.

33. Rafdel to Airwhit, Sept. 24, 1942, CAB 122/172; HLH to Charles Portal, Dec. 18, 1942; D. C. S. Evill to HLH, Dec. 16, 1942, with attached memo, Dec. 15, 1942, HHP, Box 155.

34. ERS, meeting with HLH, Oct. 14, 1942, Stettinius Papers, Box 135.

## 16. The Man in the Middle

1. "American-British Grand Strategy," Dec. 31, 1941, in *FRUS: Washington and Casablanca,* pp. 214–217; "Operation Super-Gymnast," Jan. 14, 1942, ibid., pp. 262–265; Chief of the Imperial General Staff to John Dill, Feb. 9, 1942, enclosed in Dill to HLH, Feb. 11, 1942. Hopkins passed this to Roosevelt with the comment, "This is very interesting reading." HLH to FDR, Feb. 20, 1942; Raymond E. Lee to George Marshall, Feb. 12, 1942, HHP, Box 217. There are no indications that Hopkins forwarded Lee's letter to Roosevelt. Elisabeth Barker, *Churchill and Eden at War* (London: Macmillan, 1978), pp. 233–238; WSC to FDR, March 7, 1942, in Francis L. Loewenheim, Harold D. Langley, and Manfred Jonas, eds., *Roosevelt and Churchill: Their Secret Wartime Correspondence* (New York: Saturday Review Press, 1975), pp. 186–187; WAH to FDR, March 6, 1942, in WAH, *Special Envoy to Churchill and Stalin, 1941–1946* (New York: Random House, 1975), pp. 126–127; WAH to HLH, March 7, 1942, HHP, Box 308; Richard W. Steele, *The First Offensive, 1942* (Bloomington: University of Indiana Press, 1973), pp. 97–98; HLH, memo of conversation with John G. Winant, March 11, 1942, HHP, Box 154.

2. Steele, *First Offensive,* chaps. 1–3; HLH, memo, Jan. 24, 1942, in Sherwood, *Roosevelt and Hopkins,* p. 492; HLH to WAH, Feb. 19, 1942, Map Room Papers, FDRL, Box 13.

3. Steele, *First Offensive,* pp. 76–80.

4. HLH, diary, Feb. 12, 13, 14, 17, 20, 1942, Hopkins microfilm, reel 5, HHP; Stimson, diary, Feb. 18, 21, 25, 1942; Staff Conference at the White House, Feb. 14, 1942, CAB 122/583; Maurice Matloff and Edwin M. Snell, *Strategic Planning for Coalition Warfare,* 2 vols. (Washington, D.C.: Office of the Chief of Military History, 1953), I, 129.

5. Staff Conference at the White House, March 5, 1942, CAB 122/583;

JSM to COS, March 5, 1942, in *War Telegrams,* Hist. (F) 1 (Final), no. 237; Stimson, diary, March 5, 1942; Lord Moran, *Churchill: Taken from the Diaries of Lord Moran* (Boston: Houghton Mifflin, 1966), p. 29; WSC to FDR, March 4, 1942, in Loewenheim et al., *Correspondence,* p. 184; entries of Feb. 28, March 2–5, 1942, in David Dilks, ed., *The Diaries of Alexander Cadogan* (London: Cassell, 1971), pp. 439–440.

6. HLH to FDR, March 14, 1942, in Sherwood, *Roosevelt and Hopkins,* p. 519.

7. Stimson, diary, March 25, 1942.

8. Matloff and Snell, *Strategic Planning,* I, 210–211; Stimson, diary, April 1, 1942; General Henry Arnold, memos, April 1, 2, 3, 1942, Arnold Papers, Box 180; HLH, diary, April 1–4, 1942, Hopkins microfilm, reel 5; HLH to WSC, April 2, 1942, Map Room Papers, FDRL, Box 13.

9. See J. R. M. Butler, *Grand Strategy* (London: Her Majesty's Stationery Office, 1964), pp. 675–681, for one version of the American plan.

10. JSM to COS, April 1, 1942, no. 5; COS to JSM, April 6, 1942, no. 24; WSC to John Dill, March 14, 1942, no. 271, in *War Telegrams,* Hist. (F) 1 and Hist. (F) 2; WSC to FDR, April 1, 1942, WSC, *The Hinge of Fate* (Boston: Houghton Mifflin, 1950), pp. 201–203; Butler, *Grand Strategy,* pp. 572–573.

11. Arthur Bryant, *The Turn of the Tide* (Garden City, N.Y.: Doubleday, 1957), p. 284; Sherwood, *Roosevelt and Hopkins,* pp. 523–526.

12. Butler, *Grand Strategy,* pp. 576–579; Matloff and Snell, *Strategic Planning,* I, 187–190; Albert C. Wedemeyer, *Wedemeyer Reports!* (New York: Holt, 1958), pp. 112–113, 119–121.

13. Sherwood, *Roosevelt and Hopkins,* pp. 524, 530–531; HLH to FDR, April 11, 1942; HLH, handwritten memo, April 12, 1942, HHP, Box 308; FDR to HLH for WSC, April 12, 1942, in WSC, *Fate,* pp. 217–221.

14. WSC to FDR, April 12, 1942, ibid., pp. 316–317.

15. Minutes of meeting held on Tuesday, April 14, 1942, at 10:00 P.M., D.O. (42) 10th meeting, attached to Hastings Ismay to HLH, April 17, 1942, HHP, Box 308.

16. HLH, notes, in Sherwood, *Roosevelt and Hopkins,* p. 536; *London Evening Standard and News Chronicle,* April 9, 1942; *The Sunday Times,* April 19, 1942; *Liverpool Daily Post,* April 20, 1942, clippings in HHP, Box 308; Clementine Churchill to HLH, April 10, 1942, Hopkins microfilm, reel 11.

17. Sherwood, *Roosevelt and Hopkins,* p. 526; Alexander Cadogan, entry for April 9, 1942, in Dilks, *Cadogan,* p. 446.

18. Sherwood, *Roosevelt and Hopkins,* p. 540; Anthony Eden, *The Reckoning* (Boston: Houghton Mifflin, 1965), p. 378.

19. Wedemeyer, *Report,* p. 117; Sherwood, *Roosevelt and Hopkins,* p. 540; Gerald Pawle, *The War and Colonel Warden* (New York: Knopf, 1963), p.

161; HLH to Jacob Baker, April 22, 1942, in Sherwood, *Roosevelt and Hopkins,* p. 543; HLH to Clementine Churchill, April 21, 1942, Hopkins microfilm, reel 11.

20. Matloff and Snell, *Strategic Planning,* I, 192–194, 210–216, 218–219; Steele, *First Offensive,* pp. 125–126; Butler, *Grand Strategy,* pp. 619, 621; Bryant, *Tide,* pp. 288–290; Leighton and Coakley, *Logistics,* I, 378–382, 192–194; William Standley to Secretary of State, April 10, 1942, *FRUS, 1942,* III, 438.

21. FDR to Henry Stimson, George Marshall, H. H. Arnold, Frank Knox, Ernest King, and HLH, May 6, 1942, Verifax 650, item 2029, GCML; Matloff and Snell, *Strategic Planning,* I, 230–231; Leighton and Coakley, *Logistics,* I, 562.

22. HLH to Stafford Cripps, May 2, 1942, HHP, Box 314; Raymond Clapper, interviews with HLH, May 18, 19, 1942, Clapper Papers, Box 23; Lord Halifax to Oliver Lyttelton, May 25, 1942, FO 954/29; John Dill to COS, May 21, 22, 1942, in *War Telegrams,* Hist. (F) 2 (Final), nos. 160, 163.

23. James Burns to HLH, June 4, 1942, in Sherwood, *Roosevelt and Hopkins,* pp. 557–578; FDR to WSC, May 31, 1942, in Warren F. Kimball, ed., *Churchill and Roosevelt: the Complete Correspondence,* 3 vols. (Princeton, N.J.: Princeton University Press, 1984), I, 503–504.

24. HLH to John G. Winant, June 12, 1942, in Sherwood, *Roosevelt and Hopkins,* pp. 577–578.

25. WSC, *Fate,* p. 342; Lord Louis Mountbatten to FDR, June 15, 1942, in Sherwood, *Roosevelt and Hopkins,* pp. 582–583; Butler, *Grand Strategy,* pp. 621; HMJr, conversation with FDR, June 16, 1942, in HMJr, presidential diary, vol. 5; John Dill to COS, June 15, 1942, in *War Telegrams,* Hist. (G) Final, no. 228; Stimson, diary, June 15, 1942.

26. FDR to George Marshall and Ernest King, June 20, 1942, draft reproduced in Sherwood, *Roosevelt and Hopkins,* pp. 586–587; Hastings Ismay, memo, June 21, 1942, in *FRUS: Washington and Casablanca,* pp. 434–435; Matloff and Snell, *Strategic Planning,* I, 244.

27. Stimson, diary, July 10, 1942; WSC to John Dill, July 12, 1942, in *War Telegrams,* Hist. (F) 2 (Final), no. 291; JSM to COS, July 25, 1942, ibid., no. 314.

28. FDR to HLH, George Marshall, and Ernest King, July 16, 1942, in Sherwood, *Roosevelt and Hopkins,* pp. 603–605.

29. John Dill to WSC, July 15, 1942, in WSC, *Fate,* pp. 439–440.

30. Harry C. Butcher, diary, July 19, 1942, in Butcher, *My Three Years with Eisenhower* (New York: Simon and Schuster, 1946), p. 25; Sherwood, *Roosevelt and Hopkins,* p. 607.

31. "Prime Minister's Notes for a Meeting on July 20, 1942," in WSC, *Fate,* pp. 444–446; Sherwood, *Roosevelt and Hopkins,* p. 607.

32. Ibid., p. 609; minutes of Combined Staff Conference, No. 10 Downing Street, 3:00 P.M., July 22, 1942, HHP, Box 308.

33. General Dwight D. Eisenhower to General George Marshall, July 23, 1942, no. 389, in Alfred D. Chandler, ed., *The Papers of Dwight David Eisenhower: The War Years* (Baltimore: Johns Hopkins Press, 1970); Steele, *First Offensive,* pp. 174–175.

34. Sherwood, *Roosevelt and Hopkins,* p. 611; HLH to FDR, July 25, 1942, HHP, Box 308.

35. Roosevelt approved the word *opinion* but may not have originated it. See draft of FDR to HLH, George Marshall, and Ernest King, n.d., PSF, Box 5: Marshall. This draft contains the sentence using the word *opinion* in the handwriting of Admiral William Leahy.

36. WSC to FDR, July 27, 1942, in, Warren F. Kimball, ed., *Churchill and Roosevelt: the Complete Correspondence,* 3 vols. (Princeton, N.J.: Princeton University Press, 1984), I, 542.

37. HLH, note, March 20, 1943, HHP, Box 298. In this note Hopkins also says that the notes were for his April mission to London, a claim that the notes themselves clearly refute. Thus it appears that Hopkins was at least unconsciously trying to make himself out as something of a prophet in the matter, also contrary to the historical record.

## 17. The Third Card

1. HMJr, conversation with HLH, Sept. 9, 1942, HMJr, presidential diary, vol. 5.

2. WSC to FDR, Sept. 22, 1942, in WSC, *The Hinge of Fate* (Boston: Houghton Mifflin, 1950), p. 572.

3. HLH to FDR, Sept. 22, 1942, in Sherwood, *Roosevelt and Hopkins,* pp. 637–638.

4. FDR to WSC, Sept. 27, 1942, and WSC to FDR, Sept. 28, 1942, in WSC, *Hinge of Fate,* p. 573. Roosevelt's cable followed Hopkins's advice and was probably based on a draft that Hopkins sent him. HLH to FDR, Sept. 23, 1942, HHP, Box 278; General Follett Bradley to General George Marshall, Oct. 7, 1942, ibid., Box 235; John Dill to WSC, Oct. 7, 1942, in *War Telegrams,* Hist. (F) 3, no. 68; WSC to Josef Stalin, Oct. 9, 1942, in *Stalin's Correspondence with Churchill, Attlee, Roosevelt, and Truman* (New York: E. P. Dutton, 1958), I, 71–72; FDR to Stalin, Oct. 9, 1942, ibid., II, 36.

5. HLH to WAH, Oct. 9, 1942; HLH to LWD, Oct. 13, 1942; LWD, note on "HLH 10/16/42"; LWD, notes on conference with FDR, HLH, and E. S. Land, Oct. 21, 1942, Douglas file, folder: Russian Shipping 6/1–12/42, RG 248; HLH TC S. P. Spalding, Oct. 22, 1942, Soviet Protocol Committee Papers, FDRL, Box 18; HLH to George Marshall, Oct. 10, 1942, Arnold Papers, Box 39; Marshall to HLH, Oct. 10, 1942, ibid., Box 129.

6. Entries of Aug. 14, 15, 1942, in Lord Moran, *Churchill: Taken from the Diaries of Lord Moran* (Boston: Houghton Mifflin, 1966), pp. 64–70; WSC

to FDR, Oct. 24, 1942, in Francis L. Loewenheim, Harold D. Langley, and Manfred Jonas, eds., *Roosevelt and Churchill: Their Secret Wartime Correspondence* (New York: Saturday Review Press, 1975), pp. 258–259.

7. Davies, diary, Oct. 3, 29, 1942, Box 12.

8. For evidence of this attitude, see Raymond Clapper, interview with HLH, May 19, 1942, in Clapper papers, Box 23; Davies, diary, Oct. 29, 1942, Box 12.

9. Joseph Davies, report to Hopkins on Soviet Press on Stalin-Churchill Row, Oct. 3, 1942; "Davies Memorandum Prepared for . . . President Request and Questions of Harry Hopkins, Oct. 30, 1942," Davies Papers, Box 12; James Burns, memo, Dec. 1, 1942, in Sherwood, *Roosevelt and Hopkins,* pp. 641–643. Although Burns's memo is dated Dec. 1, Hopkins and Davies had seen an earlier version in October. Davies, note in file, "2/15, October, 1942," Davies Papers, Box 12.

10. William H. Standley and Arthur Ageton, *Admiral Ambassador to Russia* (Chicago: Henry Regnery Company, 1955), pp. 307–308; Lord Halifax to FO, Oct. 27, 1942, FO 954/29.

11. Standley and Ageton, *Ambassador,* pp. 314–315.

12. ERS, meeting with HLH, Oct. 14, 1942, Stettinius Papers, Box 135; FDR, memo for Lend-Lease Administrator, Oct. 30, 1942, HHP, Box 316.

13. Minutes of the meeting of the President's Soviet Protocol Committee, Nov. 25, 1942, HHP, Box 316.

14. HLH to John G. Winant, June 12, 1942, in Sherwood, *Roosevelt and Hopkins,* pp. 577–578; Raymond Clapper, interview with HLH, May 19, 1942, Clapper Papers, Box 23.

15. Lord Halifax to FO, Oct. 29, 1942, FO 954/29; Davies, diary, Nov. 29, 1942, Box 12; Oliver Lyttelton, "Notes on Meeting with the President," Nov. 24, 1942, FO 954/29.

16. Josef Stalin to FDR, Nov. 14, 27, 28, 1942, in *Stalin's Correspondence,* II, 39–42; Loy Henderson to Secretary of State, Nov. 8, Dec. 7, 1942, in *FRUS, 1942,* III, 475, 481–482; Llewellyn Thompson to Secretary of State, Nov. 15, 1942, ibid., p. 478.

17. "General Bradley's Conference with Mr. Harry Hopkins at 1700, December 8, 1942," Follett Bradley Papers, United States Air Force Academy Library, Colorado Springs, Colorado.

18. WSC to FDR, Nov. 26, Dec. 3, 1942, in WSC, *Hinge of Fate,* pp. 652–653, 662–663, 664–665; Josef Stalin to FDR, Dec. 6, 1942; FDR to Stalin, Dec. 8, 1942, in *Stalin's Correspondence,* II, 44; Maurice Matloff and Edwin M. Snell, *Strategic Planning for Coalition Warfare,* 2 vols. (Washington, D.C.: Office of the Chief of Military History, 1953), I, 335–336.

19. John M. Blum, ed., *The Price of Vision: The Diary of Henry A. Wallace* (Boston: Houghton Mifflin, 1973), pp. 147–149; Sherwood, *Roosevelt and*

*Hopkins,* pp. 653–654; Robert Dallek, *Franklin D. Roosevelt and American Foreign Policy* (New York: Oxford University Press, 1979), p. 366.

20. Richard M. Leighton and Robert W. Coakley, *Global Logistics and Strategy,* 2 vols. (Washington, D.C.: Office of the Chief of Military History, 1955, 1959), I, 677–679; LWD and E. S. Land, memorandum for the President, Oct. 8, 1942, HHP, Box 320; Minister of Production's Mission, meeting of Nov. 18, 1942, 3:30 P.M., AVIA 38/908; FDR to WSC, Nov. 30, 1942, draft with corrections by Hopkins, in HHP, Box 330; FDR to Land, Nov. 30, 1942, ibid., Box 321.

21. James Burns to HLH, Dec. 14, 1942, ibid., Box 316; HLH to LWD, Dec. 19, 1942; LWD to HLH, Dec. 21, 1942, ibid.; W.D.S., memo for General Somervell, Dec. 30, 1942, Office of Commanding General, Lieutenant General Somervell's Desk File, RG 160; Combined Military Transport Committee, 50th mtg., Dec. 31, 1942, CAB 122/102; JSM to War Cabinet Offices, Dec. 31, 1942, in *War Telegrams,* Hist. (F) 3, no. 194; HLH to WAH, Jan. 8, 1943, Map Room Papers, FDRL, Box 13.

22. Michael Howard, *Grand Strategy* (London: Her Majesty's Stationery Office, 1972), pp. 203–206; HMJr, conversation with HLH, Dec. 4, 1942, HMJr, presidential diary, vol. 5; LWD, Conference with Mr. H. L. Hopkins, Dec. 7, 1942, 10:30 A.M., Hopkins folder, Douglas File, RG 248.

23. JCS, minutes of a meeting at the White House, Jan. 7, 1942, in *FRUS: Washington and Casablanca,* p. 509; Sherwood, *Roosevelt and Hopkins,* p. 675.

24. Sherwood, *Roosevelt and Hopkins,* pp. 669–672.

25. Ibid., pp. 688, 691; *FRUS: Washington and Casablanca,* pp. 791–798.

26. On the morning of the day that General Somervell presented his report to the CCS, he conferred with Hopkins. Elliott Roosevelt, *As He Saw It* (New York: Duell, Sloan and Pearce, 1946), p. 100; CCS, minutes, Jan. 23, 1943, in *FRUS: Washington and Casablanca,* pp. 709–710.

27. Ibid., pp. 710–711.

28. CCS, minutes, Jan. 20, 1943, ibid., p. 657.

29. Sherwood, *Roosevelt and Hopkins,* pp. 684, 689–690; HLH, notes, Jan. 23, 1943, HHP, Box 330.

30. See "North Africa/Summary of Proposed Course of Action," Dec. 24, 1942, HHP, Box 330. The document has no identifying marks or names. Jean Monnet's claims of authorship are in his *Memoirs* (London: Collins, 1978), p. 181.

31. Sherwood, *Roosevelt and Hopkins,* pp. 682–683.

32. W. H. B. Mack, "Account of the Giraud-De Gaulle conversations at Anfa Camp," Jan. 28, 1943, PREM 3 442/16.

33. Sherwood, *Roosevelt and Hopkins,* p. 693. For other accounts, all of them conflicting with Hopkins's notes and with each other, see Llewellyn Woodward, *British Foreign Policy in the Second World War* (London: Her

Majesty's Stationery Office, 1971), II, 415–416; Harold Macmillan, *The Blast of War, 1939–1945* (New York: Harper and Row, 1968), pp. 202–203; Charles de Gaulle, *War Memoirs* (New York: Viking, 1955), I, 86–95.

34. *FRUS: Washington and Casablanca,* pp. 823–826. For the background of these memoranda, see Arthur Layton Funk, "The 'Anfa Memorandum': An Incident of the Casablanca Conference," *Journal of Modern History,* 26 (1954), 246–253; Air Ministry to Mideast, [Jan. 28, 1943], PREM 3 442/5.

35. Robert Murphy, *Diplomat Among Warriors* (New York: Pyramid Publications, 1965), p. 197; Hopkins-El Mokhri conversation, January 23, 1943, in *FRUS: Washington and Casablanca,* pp. 701–703.

36. Warren F. Kimball, ed., *Churchill and Roosevelt: the Complete Correspondence,* 3 vols. (Princeton, N.J.: Princeton University Press, 1984), II, 53–54; *FRUS: Washington and Casablanca,* p. 495.

37. Ibid., p. 727; FDR, address to Congress on the State of the Union, Jan. 7, 1943, in Samuel I. Rosenman, ed., *Public Papers and Addresses of Franklin D. Roosevelt,* 13 vols. (New York: Random House, 1950) XII, 32–34.

38. The question of whether Churchill knew that Roosevelt was going to announce the doctrine at the press conference is still unanswered. Churchill had discussed the issue with Roosevelt and had helped revise a draft of the communiqué containing language similar to that which Roosevelt used in his public statement. This suggests that Roosevelt simply announced the doctrine himself in order to accommodate Churchill's reservations about applying it to Italy. But Churchill maintained that Roosevelt's announcement took him by surprise. This and Churchill's reaction to Roosevelt's announcement cause me to credit Churchill's version. After Roosevelt had spoken, Churchill began by saying that he agreed "with everything the president had said" and emphasized that "nothing that may occur in this war will ever come between me and the president." He concluded that the Allies would continue to fight "until we have the unconditional surrender of the criminal forces who plunged the world into storm and ruin." These words do not sound like those of someone who was prepared to draw distinctions between the Germans and the Italians. Rather, they and the whole tone of Churchill's remarks suggest a man caught off guard, searching for the proper response, and concluding that it would be best to emphasize solidarity with the Americans. See *FRUS: Washington and Casablanca,* pp. 728–729, 835.

39. Ibid., p. 506.

40. WAH, *Special Envoy to Churchill and Stalin, 1941–1946* (New York: Random House, 1975), p. 190.

41. Sherwood, *Roosevelt and Hopkins,* p. 694; Kenneth Pendar, *Adventure in Diplomacy* (New York: Dodd, Mead, 1945), pp. 147–152.

42. Sherwood, *Roosevelt and Hopkins,* p. 694.

## 18. Lord Root of the Matter

1. Raymond Clapper, interview with HLH, Feb. 11, 1943, Clapper Papers, Box 23; HLH, memo for files, Feb. 11, 1943, HHP, Box 211; HLH, memo, March 10, 1943, in Sherwood, *Roosevelt and Hopkins,* pp. 707–708.

2. Richard M. Leighton, "U.S. Merchant Shipping and the British Import Crisis," in Kent Roberts Greenfield, ed., *Command Decisions* (Washington, D.C.: Office of the Chief of Military History, 1960), pp. 199–223; entries for Feb. 6, 19, 20, 21, 24, 27, March 1, 1943, CAB 105/31.

3. In the end, however, Roosevelt retreated in the face of predictions that taking the resolution to the Senate floor would provoke a fierce debate. Robert Divine, *Second Chance: the Triumph of Internationalism in America during World War II* (New York: Atheneum, 1967), pp. 92–97.

4. Anthony Eden to WSC, March 14, 1943, FO 954/30; Anthony Eden, *The Reckoning* (Boston: Houghton Mifflin, 1965), pp. 432–433, 437.

5. Sherwood, *Roosevelt and Hopkins,* pp. 714–715.

6. Anthony Eden, memo, produced as copy of a dispatch to Sir A. Clark Kerr, the British ambassador to the Soviet Union, March 10, 1943, HHP, Box 217; Sherwood, *Roosevelt and Hopkins,* p. 713; Raymond Clapper, interview with HLH, March 30, 1943, Clapper Papers, Box 23.

7. Eden, *Reckoning,* pp. 432–433; Sherwood, *Roosevelt and Hopkins,* pp. 717–718.

8. Leighton, "British Import Crisis," pp. 213–214.

9. Memo M.M. (S) 8, March 14, 1943, CAB 122/47; Anthony Eden to WSC, March 14, 1943, FO 954/30; General Lucius Clay to General W. D. Styer, March 20, 1943, WDSCA 570-1943, RG 407.

10. LWD, diary, lunch conference with HLH, March 19, 1943; conference with HLH at the White House, March 23, 1943, Douglas file: Hopkins folder, RG 248; LWD to WAH, March 27, 1943; LWD to HLH, March 26, 1943, LWD Reading File, RG 248; Richard M. Leighton and Robert W. Coakley, *Global Logistics and Strategy,* 2 vols. (Washington, D.C.: Office of the Chief of Military History, 1955, 1959), I, 616–623.

11. LWD, diary, Conference at the White House, March 29, 1943, Allocations General folder, Douglas file RG, 248; Leighton, "British Import Crisis," p. 220; LWD to WAH, March 27 (three letters), 1943, LWD Reading File, RG 248.

12. Lord Halifax to WSC, April 15, 1943, FO 954/32; JCS, special meeting with civilian chiefs of war agencies, March 30, 1943, RG 218.

13. HLH to LWD, May 5, 1943, HHP, Box 299; "Conference with Mr. Hopkins, Generals Somervell, Gross, and Admiral Smith," May 7, 1943; LWD TC HLH, May 10, 1943; LWD TC Brehon Somervell, May 10, 1943; LWD TC HLH, May 15, 1943; meeting with LWD, Admiral Horne, Admi-

ral Smith, General Somervell, General Gross, and others, May 22, 1943, JSC meeting, 11:00 A.M., CCS meeting 2:00 P.M., May 23, 1943, folder C.C.S. Requirements and Availables (1943), Granville Conway file, RG 248. Leighton and Coakley, *Logistics*, II, 86.

14. Martin Sherwin, *A World Destroyed: The Atomic Bomb and the Grand Alliance* (New York: Knopf, 1975), pp. 71ff; Richard G. Hewlett and Oscar E. Anderson, Jr., *The New World, 1939–1946*, (University Park, Pa.: Pennsylvania State University Press, 1962), chap. 8.

15. Lord Halifax to Anthony Eden, April 14, 1943, in Eden, *Reckoning*, pp. 657–658.

16. Vannevar Bush, memorandum, May 25, 1943, in *Foreign Relations of the United States: The Conferences at Washington and Quebec, 1943* (Washington, D.C.: Government Printing Office, 1970), pp. 209–211, hereafter cited as *FRUS: Washington and Quebec.*

17. Ibid., pp. 220–221; WSC to Lord President [Sir John Anderson], May 26, 1943, in WSC, *The Hinge of Fate* (Boston: Houghton Mifflin, 1950), p. 809.

18. Vannevar Bush, memorandum of conference with the president, June 24, 1943; WSC to FDR, July 9, 1943; FDR to HLH, July 14, 1943; HLH to FDR, July 20, 1943, in *FRUS: Washington and Quebec,* pp. 631–633.

19. Hewlett and Anderson, *New World,* pp. 275–280.

20. Charles F. Romanus and Riley Sunderland, *Stilwell's Mission to China* (Washington, D.C.: Office of the Chief of Military History, 1953), chaps. 5–8; Barbara Tuchman, *Stilwell and the American Experience in China, 1911–1945* (New York: MacMillan, 1971), chap. 13; Claire Chennault, *Way of a Fighter* (New York: Putnam, 1949).

21. HLH, memo, Nov. 30, 1942, in Sherwood, *Roosevelt and Hopkins,* pp. 660–661. Tuchman, *Stilwell,* p. 358; Joseph Alsop to HLH, Dec. 10, 22, 28, 1942, March 1, 3, 5, 1943, Hopkins Papers, Box 330; Sherwood, *Roosevelt and Hopkins,* pp. 681–682, 739.

22. Raymond Clapper, interview with HLH, Feb. 11, 1943, Clapper Papers, Box 23; HLH to Anthony Eden, April 23, 1943, HHP, Box 329.

23. Raymond Clapper, interview with HLH, Feb. 11, 1943, Clapper Papers, Box 23; Romanus and Sunderland, *Stilwell's Mission,* pp. 277–280.

24. HLH to George Marshall, May 19, 1943, Marshall Papers, Box 71.

25. Chin-tung Liang, *General Stilwell in China, 1942–1944: The Full Story* (New York: St. John's University Press, 1972), pp. 121–122.

26. Lauchlin Currie to HLH, May 28, June 10, 1943; HLH to Currie, June 9, 1943, HHP, Box 331. Theodore White's published story, which describes the famine without attributing blame for it, appeared under the introductory statement "How ageless are China's problems," *Time,* March 22, 1943.

## 19. Lining Up with the Russians

1. "Summary of Events Leading to Establishment of Hopkins Committee," April 5, 1943, CAB 122/48; British Supply Council, minutes, April 14, 1943, AVIA 38/966; HLH to WAH, April 15, 1943, Soviet Protocol Committee Papers, FDRL, Box 10; Bernard Knollenberg to ERS, April 19, 1943, Stettinius Papers, Box 135; Vojtech Mastny, "Stalin and the Prospects of a Separate Peace in World War II," *American Historical Review,* 77 (1972), 1373–1377; George C. Herring, Jr., *Aid to Russia, 1941–1946: Strategy, Diplomacy, the Origins of the Cold War* (New York: Columbia University Press, 1973), p. 97.

2. HLH, memo, March 10, 1943, HHP, Box 299; Davies, diary, March 12, 14, 1943, Box 12.

3. John Daniel Langer, "The Formulation of American Aid Policy Toward the Soviet Union, 1940–1943: The Hopkins Shop and the Department of State" (Ph.D. diss., Yale University, 1975), pp. 166–167, 193; Lord Halifax to FO, April 21, 1943, FO 954/30; Davies, diary, June 3, 1943, Box 13; *FRUS, 1943,* III, 704; James Burns to HLH, Aug. 10, 1943, in *FRUS: Washington and Quebec,* p. 626; Davies, journal, Sept. 25, 1943, Davies Papers, LC, Box 14. When Hopkins discussed the position with Stettinius, he was "quite emotional" about their past relationship and told him that he wanted to do all he could to improve liaison between the White House and State. He promised to keep State "closely advised" of any assignments he received from Roosevelt; ERS, memo, Sept. 28, 1943, Stettinius Papers, Box 237; ERS to Cordell Hull, Oct. 14, 1943, Cordell Hull Papers, LC, microfilm reel 50.

4. Davies, diary, April 19, 30, 1943, Box 13.

5. See "Revised Draft of Third Protocol," AVIA 38/1045; HLH to S.P. Spalding, April 30, 1943; Spalding TC HLH, May 3, 1943; Spalding to HLH, May 3, 11, 15, 17, 28, 1943; Spalding to JCS, May 17, 1943, Soviet Protocol Committee Papers, Box 2; minutes of British mission to Washington, Committee on Supplies to Russia, May 1, 18, 1943, CAB 122/103; British Supply Council, minutes, May 12, 1943, AVIA 38/966.

6. HLH TC LWD, May 10, 1943, LWD, diary, Conway File, folder C.C.S. Requirements and Availables (1943), RG 248.

7. Lord Moran, *Churchill: Taken from the Diaries of Lord Moran* (Boston: Houghton Mifflin, 1966), p. 102; Forrest Pogue, *George C. Marshall: Organizer of Victory* (New York: Viking, 1973), p. 205; WSC, *The Hinge of Fate* (Boston: Houghton Mifflin, 1950), p. 810. The British military chiefs were actually thankful for Hopkins's intervention; they had feared that Churchill might wreck what they considered a satisfactory compromise with the Americans; see Arthur Bryant, *The Turn of the Tide* (Garden City, N.Y.: Doubleday, 1957), p. 514.

8. Josef Stalin to FDR, May 26, June 11, 1943, in *Stalin's Correspondence with Churchill, Attlee, Roosevelt, and Truman* (New York: E. P. Dutton, 1958), II, 66, 70–71; Mastny, "Separate Peace," p. 1378; Sherwood, *Roosevelt and Hopkins,* p. 734.

9. Davies, diary, June 7, 1943, Box 13.

10. Henry Stimson to HLH, Aug. 4, 1943, with enclosed memorandum, in *FRUS: Washington and Quebec,* pp. 444–452; Stimson and McGeorge Bundy, *On Active Service in Peace and War* (New York: Harper and Brothers, 1948), pp. 434–435.

11. CCS, minutes, August 19, 1943, in *FRUS: Washington and Quebec,* pp. 895–896; entry for August 20, 1943, in Moran, *Churchill,* p. 117.

12. Raymond Clapper, interview with HLH, Sept. 20, 1943, Clapper Papers, Box 23.

13. Robert J. Quinlan, "The Italian Armistice," in Harold Stein, ed., *American Civil-Military Decisions* (Birmingham: University of Alabama Press, 1963), pp. 244–252.

14. Jean Monnet to HLH, May 6, 19, July 3, 1943; HLH to John G. Winant, July 17, 1943, HHP, Box 330. A few months later Hopkins wrote off Giraud as "dumb." Raymond Clapper, interview with HLH, Oct. 28, 1943, Clapper Papers, Box 23; William Leahy, diary, June 17, 1943, Leahy Papers, LC; HLH to George Marshall, n.d. (July 1943), Marshall Papers, Box 85; Robert Murphy to Cordell Hull, July 17, 1943, in *FRUS, 1943,* II, 172–173; WSC to FDR, July 8 (two letters), 1943, ibid., pp. 171–172, 173–175.

15. Draft identified by Robert Sherwood as State Department memo on establishing an Allied military government in Italy, n.d., in Sherwood, *Roosevelt and Hopkins,* pp. 721–724, also in HHP, Box 160. Earlier Hopkins had monitored efforts by Monnet to abrogate the Vichy laws that had restricted religious and civil rights in North Africa. Jean Monnet to HLH, March 11, 13, 1943, Eisenhower Pre-Presidential Papers, Eisenhower Library, Abilene, Kansas, Box 58; HLH, memo, Sept. 22, 1943, HHP, Box 160.

16. Raymond Clapper, interview with HLH, Sept. 20, 1943, Clapper Papers, Box 23; HLH to FDR, Oct. 4, 1943, in Sherwood, *Roosevelt and Hopkins,* p. 764.

17. Stimson, diary, Sept. 15, 1943; WSC to John Dill, Nov. 8, 1943, in WSC, *Closing the Ring* (Boston: Houghton Mifflin, 1951), p. 305; Dill to WSC, Nov. 9, 1943, CAB 105/85.

18. Lord Halifax to WSC, Oct. 30, 1943, FO 954/30.

19. WSC, *Closing the Ring,* pp. 210–215; HLH, memos of TC WSC, Oct. 7, 9, 1943, HHP, Box 299.

20. Davies, journal, Sept. 25, 1943, Davies Papers, Box 14.

21. Soviet Protocol Committee, minutes, Sept. 30, 1943, HHP, Box 316.

22. See War Cabinet Joint Intelligence Sub-Committee, "Probabilities of a German Collapse," Sept. 29, 1943, HHP, Box 328; Richard M. Leighton, "Overlord Versus the Mediterranean at the Cairo-Tehran Conferences," in Kent Roberts Greenfield, ed., *Command Decisions* (Washington, D.C.: Office of the Chief of Military History, 1960), pp. 262–263; George Marshall to HLH, Sept. 29, 1943, HHP, Box 328; HMJr, memo, Nov. 6, 1943, presidential diary, vol. 5; ERS to FDR, June 11, 1943, HHP, Box 176; Bernard Knollenberg to ERS, April 19, 1943, Stettinius Papers, Box 135; James Burns to HLH, Oct. 26 (two letters), 1943; General Boykin C. Wright to HLH, Oct. 25, 1943; General C. M. Wesson to Burns, Oct. 23, 1943, HHP, Box 176; Raymond Clapper, interview with HLH, Oct. 28, 1943, Clapper Papers, Box 23. The evidence on this last point is conflicting. The Russians reported Hopkins's proposal to Harriman in Moscow. Harriman expressed surprise and wired Washington. Stettinius replied that Hopkins knew "of no discussions on this subject." But on November 1 Stettinius reported that he and Hopkins had attended a dinner at the Soviet embassy where they had discussed various supply and shipping matters. Hopkins's appointment diary lists a luncheon meeting with Konstantin Lukashev of the Soviet Purchasing Commission on November 2. Furthermore, a few weeks later in *American Magazine* Hopkins wrote: "Recently I've been talking with some Russians in this country. From what they tell me, I estimate that in the first year after the war they will want to buy as much as $750,000,000 worth of goods from us." On this evidence I have cautiously accepted the Russian claim. ERS to Cordell Hull, Nov. 1, 1943, Cordell Hull Papers, LC, Box 86; HLH, diary, Nov. 2, 1943, Hopkins microfilm, reel 5, HHP; *FRUS, 1943,* III, 782–787; HLH "What Peace Will Bring Us," *American Magazine,* 137 (January 1944), 21. The issue of industrial equipment for Russia was not resolved and lingered into the fourth protocol negotiation and finally collapsed when the United States and Russia failed to agree on financial arrangements; Richard M. Leighton and Robert W. Coakley, *Global Logistics and Strategy,* 2 vols. (Washington, D.C.: Office of the Chief of Military History, 1955, 1959), II, 680.

23. Raymond Clapper, interview with HLH, Sept. 20, 1943, Clapper Papers, Box 23.

24. Ibid. and also Oct. 28, 1943.

25. Henry Arnold, notes, Nov. 13, 1943, Arnold Papers, Box 272.

26. *Foreign Relations of the United States: The Conferences at Cairo and Tehran, 1943* (Washington, D.C.: Government Printing Office, 1961), p. 280, hereafter cited as *FRUS: Cairo and Tehran;* Henry H. Arnold, *Global Mission* (New York: Harper and Brothers, 1949), p. 455; Sherwood, *Roosevelt and Hopkins,* p. 768.

27. *FRUS, 1943,* II, 407–414.

28. Ibid., pp. 253–256.

29. Draft reproduced in *FRUS: Cairo and Tehran,* pp. 399–404; Alexander Cadogan to Lord Halifax, Jan. 10, 1944, Halifax Papers, Churchill College, Cambridge, microfilm reel 2.

30. *FRUS: Cairo and Tehran,* pp. 367, 376.

31. Leighton, "Overlord," pp. 263–264.

32. Harry C. Butcher, *My Three Years with Eisenhower* (New York: Simon and Schuster, 1946), pp. 446–448.

33. Entry for Nov. 25, 1943, in Moran, *Churchill,* pp. 140–142.

34. According to the official log of the trip, Harriman accepted the possibility of a plot and urged acceptance of the Russians' invitation. Lord Ismay recalled that Harriman and Hopkins agreed with him that it was probably "a Russian trick" but thought that they could not take the risk. Harriman recalled that Hopkins, Patrick Hurley, and Pa Watson favored the move and Admiral Wilson Brown opposed it. After all had expressed their opinions, Hopkins left to see Roosevelt, who approved the change of plans. Churchill also favored the move. *FRUS: Cairo and Tehran,* p. 463; Hastings Ismay, *Memoirs* (New York: Viking Press, 1960), p. 337; WSC, *Closing the Ring,* p. 343; WAH, *Special Envoy to Churchill and Stalin, 1941–1946* (New York: Random House, 1975), p. 264.

35. Roosevelt-Stalin meeting, Nov. 28, 1943, in *FRUS: Cairo and Tehran,* pp. 482–486.

36. Entries for Nov. 28, 29, 1943, in Moran, *Churchill,* pp. 144–145, 146; WSC, *Closing the Ring,* pp. 385–386; WAH, *Envoy,* p. 277.

37. Entry of Nov. 29, 1943, in Moran, *Churchill,* p. 147; Charles E. Bohlen, *Witness to History* (New York: Norton, 1973), p. 148; *FRUS: Cairo and Tehran,* pp. 576–581; notes on Sextant, Nov. 30, 1943, Arnold Papers, Box 272.

38. Sherwood, *Roosevelt and Hopkins,* p. 799; WAH, foreword in Henry H. Adams, *Harry Hopkins: A Biography* (New York: G. P. Putnam's Sons, 1977), p. 17; Bohlen, *Witness,* p. 244.

39. Luncheon meeting, 1:30 P.M., Nov. 30, 1943, at the British embassy, in *FRUS: Cairo and Tehran,* pp. 568–575.

40. Ibid., pp. 586–587. Hopkins made a special effort to include his views in the minutes. Sherwood, *Roosevelt and Hopkins,* pp. 793–796.

41. Bohlen, *Witness,* p. 15.

42. *FRUS: Cairo and Tehran,* pp. 729–730.

43. Ibid., p. 732.

44. Ibid., p. 817.

45. Sherwood, *Roosevelt and Hopkins,* pp. 802–803.

46. Raymond Clapper, interview with HLH, Dec. 28, 1943, Clapper Papers, Box 23; Sherwood, *Roosevelt and Hopkins,* p. 804.

## 20. Where the Going Was Rough

1. John Harper to Lew Hopkins, Jan. 15, 1944, Lewis Hopkins Collection, Grinnell College Archives, Grinnell College; HLH to Fanny Hertz, Feb. 2, 1944, Hopkins microfilm, reel 11, HHP.

2. Lord Halifax to WSC, May 1, 1944, PREM 3 27/9.

3. George Marshall to HLH, March 29, 1944, HHP, Box 6.

4. General Brehon Somervell to HLH, May 10, 1944, Hopkins microfilm, reel 13.

5. Robert Sherwood, *Roosevelt and Hopkins,* p. 202.

6. S. McKee Rosen, *The Combined Boards of the Second World War* (New York: Columbia University Press, 1951), p. 205, n21; HLH, memo for files, Feb. 3, 1942; HLH to FDR, Feb. 26, 1942, HHP, Box 327; FDR to HLH with HLH reply, May 20, 1942, PSF Confidential File: Lend-Lease, Box 17; HLH to William Batt, March 13, 1942; HLH to FDR, March 13, 1942, HHP, Box 312; HLH to James Burns, Oct. 27, 1942, ibid., Box 316; HLH to General Malony, May 5, 1942, ibid., Box 322; HLH to Thomas McCabe, March 26, 1942, ibid., Box 235; HLH to WAH, March 20, 1942, Map Room Papers, FDRL, Box 13; George Marshall to Dwight Eisenhower, Feb. 14, 1942, Marshall Papers, Box 71; HLH to FDR, Dec. 13, 1941, HHP, Box 209; HLH to Burns, March 5, 1942, ibid., Box 325; HLH to ERS, Jan. 11, 1942, ibid., Box 160; HLH, memo for files, Jan. 13, 1942, ibid., Box 308; James Burns, memo for files, Sept. 24, 1942, Soviet Protocol Committee Papers, FDRL, Box 11; HLH to FDR, March 6, 1942; HLH to E. S. Land, March 6, 1942, HHP, Box 324. Hopkins's blocking the cable to Stalin is described in Sherwood, *Roosevelt and Hopkins,* p. 833.

7. HLH to Mr. and Mrs. Charles Claunch, Dec. 7, 1944, Hopkins microfilm, reel 11; HLH to General Wesson, Oct. 29, 1941, HHP, Box 322.

8. HLH to Leonard Lyons, March 18, 1942, Hopkins microfilm, reel 12.

9. HLH to Howard Hunter, Oct. 27, 1943, Hopkins microfilm, reel 11.

10. HLH to WSC, n.d. (1941), Hopkins microfilm, reel 11; HLH to WSC, Oct. 13, 1942, Map Room Papers, Box 13.

11. Earl of Birkenhead, *Halifax: The Life of Lord Halifax* (Boston: Houghton Mifflin, 1966), p. 501. Hopkins later compromised by addressing the ambassador as Edward. W. P. Crozier, *Off the Record: Political Interviews, 1933–1945,* ed. A. J. P. Taylor (London: Hutchinson, 1973), p. 231.

12. HLH to Steve Early, Sept. 5, 1941, HHP, Box 305; HLH to Leonard Lyons, Sept. 26, 1942, Hopkins microfilm, reel 12.

13. HLH to Captain John E. Gingrich, Oct. 23, 1944, Hopkins microfilm, reel 18; HLH to James Forrestal, March 27, 1944, Hopkins microfilm, reel 11.

14. FDR to HLH, May 18, 1944, in Sherwood, *Roosevelt and Hopkins,* p. 8; George Marshall to HLH, April 7, 1944, HHP, Box 6.

15. James Forrestal to Mr. [?] Gates, Nov. 27, 1943, HHP, Box 155; HLH to *South Bend Tribune,* June 30, 1943; bond purchase calculations by Dorothea E. Krauss, Hopkins microfilm, reel 18; HLH to Drew Pearson, Sept. 25, 1944; HLH, appointment diary, Hopkins microfilm, reel 5; Sherwood, *Roosevelt and Hopkins,* pp. 612–614.

16. HLH to Lowell Mellett, July 17, 1943, HHP, Box 182; HLH to Donald Comer, Aug. 16, 1943, Hopkins microfilm, reel 18; HLH to Joseph Davies, Sept. 17, 1943; Davies to HLH, Sept. 28, 1943, HHP, Box 137.

17. Felix Belair, "Harry L. Hopkins: Lender and Spender," *Life,* Sept. 22, 1941; Geoffrey Hellman, "House Guest," *New Yorker,* Aug. 7, 14, 1943; Leonard Lyons to HLH, Jan. 8, 1943, Hopkins microfilm, reel 12; Oscar Cox to HLH, Jan. 11, 12, Feb. 1, 13, 15, May 30, 1943, Cox Papers, Box 86.

18. Sherwood, *Roosevelt and Hopkins,* pp. 698–699. The columnist Damon Runyon commented: "If you have never enjoyed a solce [*sic*], you have not lived. Petit fors [*sic*] and the regulation demi tasse wound up the dinner, and my opinion of it as a whole may be indicated by the fact that when I finished reading the rundown, I was so hungry I went out and knocked off a batch of tamales." Clipping, Dec. 29, 1942, OF 4117; HLH to Captain John Hay Whitney, Dec. 19, 1942, Hopkins microfilm, reel 19.

19. Bill of sale, S. J. Phillips, London, July 24, 1942; Louise Hopkins to Lord Beaverbrook, n.d.; HLH to Beaverbrook, Sept. 26, 1942, Beaverbrook Papers, House of Lords Records Office, London.

20. Oscar Cox, draft of HLH to *Chicago Tribune* and *Washington Times-Herald,* March 2, 1943, Hopkins microfilm, reel 19.

21. James McGregor Burns and Michael Bechloss, "The Forgotten FDR," *The New Republic,* April 7, 1982.

22. Isadore Lubin to HLH, Feb. 12, 1942, HHP, Box 313.

23. HLH, memo, Jan. 26, 1942, ibid., Box 298.

24. HLH to Robert Sherwood, Jan. 30, 1942, ibid., Box 313; HLH to ERS, Dec. 4, 1941, ibid., Box 307.

25. JCS, special meeting with chairmen of civilian war agencies, Dec. 8, 1942, CCS 334, RG 218.

26. HLH to John Dingell (Democrat of Michigan), April 27, 1942, HHP, Box 314; John J. McCloy to HLH, Feb. 21, 1942; HLH to McCloy, Feb. 23, 1942, ibid., Box 313; Vere V. Loper to HLH, May 1, 1942; HLH to Steve Early, May 15, 1942; Early to HLH, n.d., ibid., Box 324.

27. HLH to Francis Biddle, Aug. 15, 1942. Biddle thought that Hopkins's proposal involved too many legal difficulties. Biddle to HLH, Aug. 25, 1942, ibid., Box 313. A few months later, when he did come up with a case that fit Hopkins's suggestion, he sent it along and Hopkins read it "with the greatest

of interest." Biddle to HLH, Nov. 28, 1942; HLH to Biddle, Dec. 1, 1942, ibid., Box 313; HLH to J. Edgar Hoover, Aug. 31, 1942, and other correspondence, ibid., Box 301.

28. Memorandum to the president, March 14, 1943, ibid., Box 324.

29. HLH to Frank Walker, Feb. 3, 23, 1942, ibid., Box 311; HLH to James Forrestal, Jan. 3, 1942, ibid., Box 323; HLH to Charles H. Strub, Dec. 19, 1941, ibid., Box 322.

30. Oscar Cox to HLH, June 3, 1943, ibid., Box 324; Cox to HLH, June 4, 1943, Cox Papers, Box 86; HLH to Laurence Steinhardt, June 22, 1943, HHP, Box 328.

31. Ronald Campbell to Richard Law for Secretary of State and Prime Minister, Oct. 7, 1943, FO 954/30; HLH, memo, Oct. 18, 1943, HHP, Box 322; Oscar Cox, diary, Oct. 10, 11, 1943, Cox Papers, Box 147.

32. HLH to FDR, Sept. 29, 1942, HHP, Box 298.

33. Sherwood, *Roosevelt and Hopkins,* p. 634.

34. HLH to James Byrnes, Nov. 19, 1942, HHP, Box 326.

35. Henry A. Wallace, diary, Feb. 5, 1943, COHC, p. 2301.

36. Jordan Schwartz, *The Speculator, Bernard M. Baruch in Washington, 1917–1965* (Chapel Hill: University of North Carolina Press, 1981), pp. 433–437. Byrnes told Roosevelt that Hopkins concurred "heartily" in recommending Baruch. But Hopkins was ill at the time and was not seeing anyone on a regular basis. This suggests that Byrnes may have caught Hopkins in a weak moment. See HLH, appointment diary, Feb. 1–5, 1943, Hopkins microfilm, reel 5.

37. Notes on talks with Bernard Baruch, Jan. 27–31, 1947, Sherwood Papers, Box 411; Schwartz, *The Speculator,* pp. 438–440, 625.

38. HLH TC ERS, Aug. 10, 1944, Stettinius Papers, Box 241; D. E. Krauss (secretary to HLH), "Given the President for his conference with Nelson," Aug. 24, 1944, HHP, Box 335.

39. HLH to FDR, Oct. 7, 1944, HHP, Box 335; ERS TC HLH, 11:45 A.M.; HLH TC ERS, 1:00 P.M.; ERS TC HLH, 3:45 P.M., Oct. 13, 1944; ERS TC HLH, 11:30 A.M.; HLH TC ERS, 4:45 P.M., Oct. 16, 1944, Stettinius Papers, Box 242.

40. Entry of Dec. 18, 1942, in John M. Blum, ed., *The Price of Vision: The Diary of Henry A. Wallace* (Boston: Houghton Mifflin, 1973), p. 148.

41. Henry A. Wallace, diary, Dec. 23, 1942, COHC, p. 2115; ibid., pp. 2639–2640.

42. Ibid., p. 2595; Hopkins's appointment diary does not support the rumor as Wallace reported it. See entry of July 14, 1943, Hopkins microfilm, reel 5; Blum, *Price of Vision,* pp. 375–376, 415; Henry A. Wallace, diary, COHC, pp. 3625–3626. See also ERS, calendar notes, Jan. 19, 1945, Stettinius Papers, Box 224.

43. HLH to Milo Perkins, June 3, 1943, HHP, Box 328.

44. HLH to James Rowe, July 5, 1941; HLH to Wayne Coy, June 9, 1941; HLH to Howard Drew, Feb. 28, 1941, ibid., Box 314; HLH to Robert Jackson, Feb. 28, 1941, ibid., Box 307; HLH to FDR, March 19, 1942, ibid., Box 209; HLH to Anna Rosenberg, Nov. 19, 1942, ibid., Box 154; Oscar Cox, diary, June 13, 1942 (emphasis added), Cox Papers, Box 145; HLH to Robert J. Watt, April 7, 1941, HHP, Box 307.

45. HLH to ER, Aug. 9, 1944, Eleanor Roosevelt Papers, FDRL, Box 1727; Sherwood, *Roosevelt and Hopkins,* p. 831.

46. HLH "Your Job After the War," *American Magazine,* 138 (November 1944), 20–21, 100–102, 104; HLH, "What Peace Will Bring Us," ibid., 137 (January 1944), 21, 87–88. Hopkins once encouraged Douglas to take an interest in postwar shipping "lest it fall into the hands of pure nationalists." LWD, memo, "Lunch with Mr. H. L. Hopkins at his office," June 9, 1943, Douglas file, Hopkins folder, WSA, RG 248; LWD to HLH, Jan. 23, 1944, HHP, Box 337.

47. Joseph P. Lash, *Eleanor and Franklin* (New York: Norton, 1971), p. 507; ER, *This I Remember* (New York: Harper and Brothers, 1949), pp. 172–173, 239; Lillian Rogers Parks, *The Roosevelts: A Family in Turmoil* (Englewood Cliffs, N.J.: Prentice-Hall, 1981), pp. 77–78; Joseph P. Lash, *Love Eleanor* (Garden City, N.Y.: Doubleday, 1982), pp. 399–400; Diana (Hopkins) Halsted, interview, May 15, 1979, Eleanor Roosevelt Oral History Project, FDRL, pp. 10–11.

48. Lash, *Love Eleanor,* pp. 354, 431, 451–498; ER, *This I Remember,* p. 261; ER to Mrs. Rome Hopkins, April 1, 1944, Eleanor Roosevelt Papers, Box 1727.

49. Harold Smith, memo, Feb. 16, 1944, Harold Smith Papers, FDRL, Box 14. When Hopkins returned to work, Roosevelt increased his salary to $15,000, commenting that Hopkins had incurred considerable expense: Smith, memo, July 13, 1944, ibid.

50. HMJr, Sept. 7, 1944, HMJr, presidential diary, vol. 6; Robert Sherwood, interview with Joseph Davies, March 6, 1947, Sherwood Papers, Box 411.

51. HLH to Donald Duncan, Sept. 10, 1943, Hopkins microfilm, reel 19; see remarks by Representative Alvin F. Weichel (Republican of Ohio), *Congressional Record,* Dec. 15, 1943. The owner of the house, who said she was a Republican, refuted the charge; Mrs. Harold L. Walker to Weichel, Dec. 16, 1943, HHP, Box 299.

52. HMJr, Sept. 7, 1944, HMJr, presidential diary, vol. 6; Lord Halifax to Anthony Eden and WSC, Jan. 7, 1945, FO 954/30; ERS, calendar notes, Nov. 15, 1944, Stettinius Papers, Box 243; Halifax to Eden, Dec. 5, 1944, FO 954/30.

53. Harold Ickes, diary excerpts, June 14, 1944, Harold Ickes Papers, LC

Box 25. In late 1943 Postmaster General Frank Walker traveled through the northern states and told Ickes that everywhere he found strong resentment against Hopkins; Ickes, diary excerpts, Dec. 11, 1943, ibid.

54. Lord Halifax to Anthony Eden, Feb. 14, 1944, PREM 4 27/9; Sir Ronald Campbell to Eden, Aug. 9, 1944, FO 954/30.

55. HLH to Edwin Pauley, Oct. 16, 1944, HHP, Box 138; Michael Wright, memo of conversation with HLH, [Nov. 7, 1944], PREM 4 27/7; HLH to WSC, Nov. 6, 1944, HHP, Box 136; HLH to Ross Fox, Nov. 2, 1944, ibid., Box 211.

56. HLH to Lord Beaverbrook, Nov. 15, 1944, Hopkins microfilm, reel 18; Ronald Campbell to Anthony Eden, Aug. 9, 1944, FO 954/30.

57. HLH to Lois Berney, May 3, 1943, Hopkins microfilm, reel 10; Diana (Hopkins) Halsted, interview, May 15, 1979, Eleanor Roosevelt Oral History Project, pp. 2–5, 18–19, 28–29, 31.

58. Louise Macy Hopkins to HLH, July 23, 1942, Hopkins microfilm, reel 21.

59. HLH to Henry Arnold, July 16, 1942, ibid., reel 3.

60. HLH to Donald B. Armstrong, Jr., May 21, 1942, HHP, Box 125.

61. HLH, "You and Your Family Will be Mobilized," *American Magazine,* 134 (December 1942), 18–19, 108–110; HLH, "But We Won't Go Hungry," ibid., 135 (May 1943), 32–33, 112–113.

62. Letters to HLH from John F. Raab, Feb. 3, 1943; Mrs. Charles M. Stack, Nov. 5, 1942; Ernest C. Adams, Nov. 5, 1942; Raymond C. Bendell, Nov. 9, 1942; Mrs. Anthony Rogers, Nov. 8, 1942; Fitzhugh Lundy, Nov. 9, 1942; Mrs. C. E. Cranston, Feb. 15, 1943; Ruth Abee Cuddington, Dec. 1, 1942, May 5, 1943; Ray Daugherty, Feb. 4, 1943; Mrs. Ivan E. Davidson, Feb. 3, 1943; Mary Falkner, March 24, 1943; Herbert Frank Gates, Feb. 4, 1943; Mrs. Mae Hall, Jan. 28, 1943; Florence Sweetwood, Feb. 3, 1943; Mrs. Gene Toomey, April 5, 1943; Hopkins microfilm, reel 17. The letter from the blind typist, with Hopkins's note to Lubin attached, is Herman Cox to HLH, April 3, 1943, ibid.

63. HLH to Mrs. L. E. LeBon, April 5, 1943, ibid. This response was drafted by A. M. Ross of the War Manpower Commission.

64. HLH to James I. Wendell, Oct. 16, 1942, Hopkins microfilm, reel 13; HLH to Tommy Dorsey, Sept. 26, 1942, HHP, Box 138.

65. HLH to Brigadier General W. E. Lauer, Feb. 2, 1943, HHP, Box 314; Patton also noted that Hopkins was "quite war-like and is in favor of discipline." When on one occasion Franklin, Jr., under the influence, slapped an admiral on the back and said, "How are you, you old S.O.B.?" Hopkins told the admiral to put him under arrest and confine him on his ship. Patton diary entries, Jan. 21, 23, 1943, in Martin Blumenson, ed., *The Patton Papers, 1940–1945* (Boston: Houghton Mifflin, 1974), pp. 157, 159.

66. HLH to Cecil Creel, May 21, 1942; HLH to Jane Hoey, Nov. 12,

1942, Hopkins microfilm, reel 18; HLH to John Carmody, Oct. 9, 1943, ibid., reel 11; HLH to Virginia Schoellkopf, Sept. 14, 1942; HLH to General Somervell, Jan. 26, 1942, ibid., reel 19; HLH to Marie Gerelli, Dec. 4, 1942, HHP, Box 154.

67. HLH to Harry Butcher, June 22, July 2, 1943, ibid., Box 329.

68. Items in folder "Hopkins, Stephen," Hopkins microfilm, reel 19.

69. George Marshall to HLH, Sunday, [Feb. 13, 1944], Hopkins microfilm, reel 19; HLH to Marshall, Feb. 16, 1944, Marshall Papers, Box 71.

70. HLH to Dwight Eisenhower, May 3, 1944, Eisenhower Pre-Presidential Papers, Eisenhower Library, Abilene, Kansas, Box 58.

## 21. Comeback

1. R. I. Campbell to Secretary of State, July 25, 1944; Campbell to Chancellor of the Exchequer, Aug. 2, 1944, FO 954/30; Isadore Lubin to HLH, Aug. 4, 1944, enclosing memorandum, July 20, 1944, HHP, Box 335; R. Brand to R. J. Hopkins, Aug. 12, 1944, AVIA 38/1022; HLH, memo, Aug. 18, 1944, in *Foreign Relations of the United States: The Conference at Quebec, 1944* (Washington, D.C.: Government Printing Office, 1972), pp. 160–161; hereafter cited as *FRUS: Quebec, 1944*.

2. Lord Halifax to WSC, Aug. 19, 1944; Halifax to Minister of Production, Aug. 26, 1944, FO 954/30.

3. Sherwood, *Roosevelt and Hopkins,* p. 814; Henry H. Adams, *Harry Hopkins: A Biography* (New York: G. P. Putnam's Sons, 1977), p. 359; WSC, *Triumph and Tragedy* (Boston: Houghton Mifflin, 1953), p. 161.

4. John M. Blum, *From the Morgenthau Diaries: Years of War, 1941–1945* (Boston: Houghton Mifflin, 1967), pp. 334–343; ERS TC HLH, summaries, Aug. 1, 4, 11, 1944, Stettinius Papers, Box 241; C.L.J. to General Roberts, Aug. 11, 1944, ABC 384 N.W. Europe (20 Aug 43) Sect. 1-B, RG 319; HLH to FDR, Aug. 3, 1944, HHP, Box 332; Stimson, diary, Aug. 21, 1944; *Morgenthau Diary (Germany)* Senate Committee on the Judiciary, 90th Cong., 1st Sess., (Washington, D.C.: Government Printing Office, 1967), pp. 426, 427–429.

5. Lord Halifax to Anthony Eden, Aug. 28, 1944, FO 954/30. Eden's marginal notes show that he agreed with Hopkins's interpretation of the Tehran minutes and with the idea of internationalizing the Ruhr; *Morgenthau Diary (Germany),* pp. 498, 500.

6. *FRUS: Quebec 1944,* p. 98; *Morgenthau Diary (Germany),* pp. 521–524, 528, 547–554.

7. Ibid., pp. 536–537.

8. Ibid., pp. 537, 545, 562–563, 605, 642, 648, 678.

9. Ibid., pp. 537, 648.

10. Ibid., p. 608; HLH, handwritten notes, n.d., filed with Sept. 20–30, 1944, HHP, Box 333; Paul Y. Hammond, "Directives for the Occupation of Germany: The Washington Controversy," in Harold Stein, ed., *American Civil-Military Decisions* (Birmingham: University of Alabama Press, 1963), pp. 367–368; *Morgenthau Diary (Germany)*, pp. 608–612.

11. Blum, *War,* pp. 378–379; *Morgenthau Diary (Germany)*, pp. 642–643, 647, 678–679.

12. ERS, conference with HLH, Sept. 26, 1944, Stettinius Papers, Box 242; HLH to FDR, Sept. 28, 1944, HHP, Box 333.

13. Lord Halifax to Anthony Eden, Sept. 29, 1944, FO 954/32; Colonel Lincoln, memo, Sept. 29, 1944, ABC 387 Germany (18 Dec 43) Sec. 4-B, RG 319; HLH to WSC, Sept. 29, 1944, HHP, Box 333.

14. WSC to HLH, Oct. 7, 1944, FO 954/32; Lord Halifax to Anthony Eden, Oct. 10, 1944, FO 954/32; HLH to FDR, Oct. 9, 1944, HHP, Box 333.

15. ERS, calendar notes, Dec. 3, 1944; HLH TC ERS, Dec. 2, 11, 1944, Stettinius Papers, Box 224.

16. ERS TC HLH, Dec. 3, 6, 1944; HLH TC ERS, Dec. 5, 11, 1944; ERS, calendar notes, Nov. 30, Dec. 5, 1944, Stettinius Papers, Box 224.

17. HLH to Murray D. Welch, Dec. 11, 1944, Hopkins microfilm, reel 19, HHP; *Congressional Record,* 78th Cong., 2d sess., 1944, pp. A4753-4; ERS, telephone summaries, Dec. 14, 1944, Stettinius Papers, Box 236.

18. HLH TC ERS, Dec. 16, 1944, Stettinius Papers, Box 236.

19. ERS, calendar notes, Nov. 27, 1944, in Thomas M. Campbell and George C. Herring, eds., *The Diaries of Edward R. Stettinius, Jr.* (New York: New Viewpoints, 1975), pp. 185–186; Charles E. Bohlen, *Witness to History* (New York: Norton, 1973), pp. 156, 162.

20. Lord Halifax to Anthony Eden, Nov. 27, Dec. 5, 1944, FO 954/30; James J. Dougherty, *The Politics of Wartime Aid* (Westport, Conn.: Greenwood Press, 1978), pp. 163–171.

21. Memos attached to HLH to FDR, Nov. 20, 1944, HHP, Box 336; items cited in Land, E.S., U.S. Maritime Commission, Nov. 23, 1944, OF 4117; Wilson Brown to HLH, Nov. 30, 1944, PSF Confidential: Joint Chiefs of Staff, Box 10.

22. FO to Washington, Dec. 8, 1944, PREM 4 29/2; JSM to COS, Dec. 4, 1944; Lord Halifax to FO, Dec. 5, 1944; JSM to COS, Dec. 8, 1944, AVIA 38/1204.

23. War Shipping Administration, memo "Recommendations of WSA Concerning Shipping for Liberated Areas," Dec. 4, 1944, attached to Granville Conway to HLH, Dec. 4, 1944, HHP, Box 336; FO to Washington,

Dec. 8, 1944, PREM 4 29/2; A. D. Marris, memo, Dec. 16, 1944, AVIA 38/ 1204.

24. Richard Law to HLH, [Dec. 17, 1944], HHP, Box 142; Law to Anthony Eden, Dec. 19, 1944, and draft of this message, AVIA 38/1204.

25. Minutes of meeting held Tuesday, Dec. 19, 1944, ibid.; Charles Bohlen, memorandum of meeting at the State Department, Dec. 20, 1944, HHP, Box 336.

26. Minutes of meeting held Dec. 22, 1944, AVIA 38/1204; minutes of meeting held in the White House, Jan. 5, 1945, Records of the Army Staff, ABC 560 (26 Feb 43) Ser. 1B, RG 319; minutes of meeting held at Blair Lee House, Jan. 6, 1945, AVIA 38/1204.

27. Lord Halifax to Anthony Eden, Jan. 15, 1945, and related material, ibid.

28. *Foreign Relations of the United States: The Conferences at Malta and Yalta, 1945* (Washington, D.C.: Government Printing Office, 1955), pp. 420–424; hereafter cited as *FRUS: Malta and Yalta.*

29. Record of meeting at the White House, Jan. 11, 1945, AVIA 38/ 1204.

## 22. Dawn of a New Day

1. Joseph Davies, journal, Oct. 11, 1944, Davies Papers, LC, Box 15.

2. Thomas M. Campbell and George C. Herring, eds., *The Diaries of Edward R. Stettinius, Jr.,* (New York: New Viewpoints, 1975), pp. 120, 124, 126.

3. ERS, conversation with HLH, Sept. 26, 1944, Stettinius Papers, Box 242; ERS, calendar notes, Sept. 7, 8, 1944, with attachment, Grace Tully to FDR, Sept. 8, 1944, HHP, Box 337; Campbell and Herring, *Stettinius,* pp. 129–131, 133–134.

4. George C. Herring, Jr., *Aid to Russia, 1941–1946: Strategy, Diplomacy, the Origins of the Cold War* (New York: Columbia University Press, 1973), pp. 112–113; WAH, *Special Envoy to Churchill and Stalin, 1941–1946* (New York: Random House, 1975), pp. 335–340.

5. WAH to HLH, Sept. 9, 1944, in *FRUS: Quebec, 1944,* pp. 198–200; WSC, *Triumph and Tragedy* (Boston: Houghton Mifflin, 1953), pp. 130– 140, 143.

6. Richard C. Lukas, *The Strange Allies: The United States and Poland, 1941–1945* (Knoxville: University of Tennessee Press, 1978), p. 72; Major General Fred Anderson, conference with HLH, Sept. 7, 1944, Carl Spaatz Papers, LC, Box 18.

7. HLH to John G. Winant, Sept. 4, 1944, HHP, Box 337.

8. HLH to FDR, Sept. 11, 1944, in *FRUS: Quebec, 1944,* pp. 396–397; Dorothea E. Krauss to Oscar Cox, Nov. 2, 1944; Foreign Economic Adminis-

tration news release, Nov. 5, 1944, HHP, Box 337; HLH to Pa Watson, noted in OF 4117.

9. HLH to Arnold, Oct. 17, 1944, HHP, Box 335.

10. Sherwood, *Roosevelt and Hopkins,* pp. 833–834; Charles E. Bohlen, *Witness to History* (New York: Norton, 1973), pp. 162–163; Bohlen to HLH, Oct. 3, 1944, HHP, Box 299.

11. Drew Pearson, column in *Philadelphia Record,* Dec. 12, 1944, clipping ibid., Box 337.

12. Lord Halifax to WSC, Dec. 8, 1944, in WSC, *Triumph and Tragedy,* p. 296; HLH, memo, Dec. 12, 1944, in Sherwood, *Roosevelt and Hopkins,* pp. 840–841.

13. *FRUS, 1944,* III, 1162.

14. *Parliamentary Debates,* House of Commons, 5th series, CCCCVI, 1478–1489, Dec. 15, 1944; HLH, memo, Dec. 12, 1944, in Sherwood, *Roosevelt and Hopkins,* pp. 840–841; Joseph Davies, journal, Dec. 22, 1944, Davies Papers, Box 15.

15. Josef Stalin to FDR, Oct. 19, 1944, *FRUS, 1944,* IV, 1016–1020.

16. Joseph Davies, journal, Dec. 22, 1944, Davies Papers, Box 15; Charles Bohlen, memo of conversation, Jan. 2, 1945, Stettinius Papers, Box 224; Kravchenko's book, *I Chose Freedom,* was published in 1946.

17. *FRUS: Malta and Yalta,* pp. 8–24; Sherwood, *Roosevelt and Hopkins,* pp. 844–845.

18. Sir N. Charles to FO, Feb. 1, 1945, FO 371/4951; Home Office to Harold Macmillan, Feb. 4, 1945; FO to Anthony Eden, Feb. 4, 1945; marginal notes to file ZM 762/1/22, FO 371/4952; Lord Halifax to FO, Feb. 5, 1945, FO 371/44535.

19. ERS, notes on conversation with HLH and others, Jan. 30, 1945, Stettinius Papers, Box 278.

20. Bohlen, *Witness,* p. 170; ERS, notes, Jan. 31, 1945, Stettinius Papers, Box 278; Joseph Grew to HLH, Feb. 3, 1945, HHP, Box 337.

21. Harry C. Butcher, *My Three Years with Eisenhower* (New York: Simon and Schuster, 1946), pp. 748–751; Butcher, diary, Jan. 27, 1945, folder 2, "Dictation Recopied," Butcher Papers, Eisenhower Library, Abilene, Kansas; ERS, notes on meeting with Anthony Eden et al., 10:30 A.M., Feb. 1, 1945, Stettinius Papers, Box 276.

22. ERS, *Roosevelt and the Russians* (Garden City, N.Y.: Doubleday, 1949), p. 57; Anna Roosevelt Boettiger, "Yalta Notes," Feb. 2, 1945, Anna Roosevelt Halsted Papers, FDRL, Box 21.

23. ERS to Walter Johnson, Oct. 10, Nov. 8, 1948; ERS, notes on conversation, [Jan. 31, 1945], Stettinius Papers, Box 278.

24. Anthony Eden, *The Reckoning* (Boston: Houghton Mifflin, 1965), p. 592; Anna Roosevelt Boettiger, notes, Feb. 2–3, 1945, Anna Roosevelt Halsted Papers, Box 15.

25. Lord Moran, *Churchill: Taken from the Diaries of Lord Moran* (Boston: Houghton Mifflin, 1966), p. 243; James F. Byrnes, *Speaking Frankly* (New York: Harper and Brothers, 1947), p. 23; ERS, notes, Feb. 10, 1945, Stettinius Papers, Box 279.

26. ERS, calendar notes, Feb. 6, 1945, Stettinius Papers, Box 278; *FRUS: Malta and Yalta,* pp. 660–677, 724, 729; Campbell and Herring, *Stettinius,* p. 246.

27. Moran, *Churchill,* p. 243; ERS, calendar notes, Feb. 8, 1945, Stettinius Papers, Box 278.

28. *FRUS: Malta and Yalta,* pp. 783, 791; ERS, calendar notes, n.d., [filed Feb. 8, 1945], Stettinius Papers, Box 278.

29. Bohlen, *Witness,* p. 188; Stettinius, *Roosevelt and the Russians,* pp. 157, 182; *FRUS: Malta and Yalta,* pp. 716–717, 720, 725; ERS, calendar notes, Feb. 8, 1945, Stettinius Papers, Box 278.

30. Stettinius, *Roosevelt and the Russians,* pp. 260, 270; *FRUS: Malta and Yalta,* pp. 907, 912. Molotov and Stalin had previously approved the boundary statement; ibid., pp. 899, 905, 907, 913, 917.

31. Ibid., pp. 634, 619, 629, 900.

32. Ibid., pp. 633, 614, 620, 626–627, 634, 808–809.

33. Stettinius, *Roosevelt and the Russians,* p. 265; *FRUS: Malta and Yalta,* p. 901. Hopkins's note suggests that there may have been an arrangement with the British to try to get the figure omitted. As the later discussion showed, this was a sound strategy, but the timing was wrong.

34. Sherwood, *Roosevelt and Hopkins,* p. 860.

35. Diane Shaver Clemens, *Yalta* (New York: Oxford University Press, 1970), pp. 280–287.

36. *FRUS: Malta and Yalta,* p. 790.

37. ERS to Walter Johnson, Oct. 10, 1948, Stettinius Papers, Box 278; Stettinius, *Roosevelt and the Russians,* pp. 284–285.

38. Sherwood, *Roosevelt and Hopkins,* p. 871; Henry H. Adams, *Harry Hopkins: A Biography* (New York: G. P. Putnam's Sons, 1977), p. 381.

39. Sherwood, *Roosevelt and Hopkins,* pp. 873–874; Bohlen, *Witness,* pp. 205–206.

40. Sherwood, *Roosevelt and Hopkins,* p. 870.

41. HLH to Russell Davenport, Feb. 26, 1945, HHP, Box 137.

## 23. On His Own Feet

1. Lord Halifax to WSC, March 2, 7, 16, 15, 1945, FO 954/30; Charles E. Bohlen, *Witness to History* (New York: Norton, 1973), p. 209.

2. HLH, messages to various people, April 13, 1945, HHP, Box 338.

3. Robert Sherwood, *Roosevelt and Hopkins,* pp. 880–881.

4. HST, *1945: Year of Decisions* (New York: New American Library,

1955), pp. 43–44; Lord Halifax to WSC, April 16, 1945, FO 954/30. Hopkins's remark that Roosevelt had not heard half of what was said at Yalta deserves some comment since it raises the issue of whether the president committed diplomatic blunders because of his bad health. Scholarly opinion overwhelmingly rejects such an interpretation, and I hope that the previous chapter indicates that I also reject it. Even if the president had been in poor form, Hopkins and the State Department team would have corrected his mistakes. Why, then, did Hopkins say this? First, because those who had been at Yalta recognized that Roosevelt's health and powers of concentration had failed. Second, because Hopkins was thinking of examples of the president's failure to proceed according to a previously arranged strategy, as when he stalled instead of opposing the Russians' request for additional votes in the General Assembly, or his failure to follow Hopkins's own advice, as when Hopkins suggested referring the reparations figure to the commission. At the plenary sessions Hopkins was involved in eight of these situations, and in three of them Roosevelt failed to follow through in this way. Third, because Hopkins wanted everyone to overcome the shock quickly and move on. He believed that Roosevelt had lost his powers and that it was a blessing that he had gone quickly. The sooner everyone accepted that, the sooner they could get on with the business at hand.

5. Sherwood, *Roosevelt and Hopkins,* pp. 881–882; Lord Halifax to WSC, April 16, 1945, FO 954/30; HLH, appointment diary, April 13–May 1, 1945, Hopkins microfilm, reel 5, HHP; JSM to AMSSO, April 12, 19, 25, 26, 1945, CAB 109/48.

6. For examples of Truman's anxieties, see Robert Ferrell, ed., *Off the Record: the Private Papers of Harry S Truman* (New York: Harper and Row, 1980), pp. 16, 23, 31–32, and Ferrell, ed., *Dear Bess: The Letters from Harry to Bess Truman, 1910–1959* (New York: W. W. Norton, 1983), pp. 516–519; Lord Halifax to WSC, April 16, 1945, FO 954/30; George C. Herring, Jr., *Aid to Russia, 1941–1946: Strategy, Diplomacy, the Origins of the Cold War* (New York: Columbia University Press, 1973), pp. 199–206.

7. Messages between WSC and HST, in *Foreign Relations of the United States: The Conference of Berlin (The Potsdam Conference), 1945* (Washington, D.C.: Government Printing Office), I, 3–12, hereafter cited as *FRUS: Potsdam.*

8. William D. Leahy, *I Was There* (New York: Whittlesey House, 1950), pp. 767–769; Forrest Pogue, *George C. Marshall: Organizer of Victory* (New York: Viking Press, 1973), pp. 579–581; Henry L. Stimson and McGeorge Bundy, *On Active Service in Peace and War* (New York: Harper and Brothers, 1948), pp. 609–611; Davies, diary, May 13, 1945, Box 16. Truman was already thinking along the lines Davies suggested. "I have been trying very carefully to keep all my engagements with the Russians," he wrote Eleanor Roosevelt, "because they are touchy and suspicious of us"; HST to ER, May 10, 1945, in Ferrell, *Off the Record,* pp. 21–22.

9. Bohlen, *Witness,* p. 215; WAH, *Special Envoy to Churchill and Stalin, 1941–1946* (New York: Random House, 1975), p. 459; Sherwood, *Roosevelt and Hopkins,* pp. 885, 887.

10. Ferrell, *Off the Record,* p. 31; Truman, *Decisions,* p. 287; Joseph Grew, memo of TC with ERS, May 21, 1945, *FRUS: Potsdam,* I, 22–23; ERS TC HST, May 21, 1945, Stettinius Papers, Box 244.

11. Davies, diary, May 22, 1945, Box 17; Ferrell, *Off the Record,* p. 31.

12. ERS, calendar notes, May 23, 1945, quoted in John Lewis Gaddis, *The United States and the Origins of the Cold War* (New York: Columbia University Press, 1972), p. 232; Thomas M. Campbell and George C. Herring, eds., *The Diaries of Edward R. Stettinius, Jr.,* (New York: New Viewpoints, 1975), p. 378. See also WAH, *America and Russia in a Changing World* (Garden City, N.Y.: Doubleday, 1971), pp. 37, 44.

13. Davies, journal, May 21, 22, 1945, Box 17; HST, *Decisions,* p. 289.

14. Davies, diary, May 22, 1945, Box 17; Walter Millis, ed., *The Forrestal Diaries* (New York: Viking Press, 1951), p. 58.

15. *FRUS, 1945,* III, 318; HLH to HST, May 28, 1945, HHP, Box 338.

16. Ibid.

17. Charles Bohlen, notes, May 30, 1945, ibid.

18. HLH to HST, May 31, 1945, ibid.

19. Ibid., June 1, 1945.

20. Ibid., June 3, 1945; HLH to WSC, June 5, 1945, in WSC, *Triumph and Tragedy* (Boston: Houghton Mifflin, 1953), p. 583.

21. WSC to HST, June 4, 1945, in HHP, Box 338.

22. HLH to HST, June 5, 1945; HST to HLH, June 5, 1945, ibid.

23. HLH to HST, June 6, 1945, ibid.

24. Diane Shaver Clemens, *Yalta* (New York: Oxford University Press, 1970), pp. 192, 226; Sherwood, *Roosevelt and Hopkins,* pp. 911–912.

25. Ibid., pp. 922, 924.

26. G. K. Zhukov, *The Memoirs of Marshal Zhukov* (New York: Delacorte Press, 1971), p. 667; HLH to HST, n.d., HHP, Box 338; Sherwood, *Roosevelt and Hopkins,* p. 914; WSC, *Triumph and Tragedy* (Boston: Houghton Mifflin, 1953), pp. 606–608; Robert Murphy, *Diplomat among Warriors* (New York: Pyramid Publications, 1965), pp. 292–293; *FRUS, 1945,* III, 333–334.

27. Sherwood, *Roosevelt and Hopkins,* pp. 913–914; Joseph Davies, journal, June 13, 1945, Joseph Davies Papers, LC Box 17.

28. Sherwood, *Roosevelt and Hopkins,* p. 913; Clark Kerr to FO, telegrams 2104, 2122, 2176, 2177, CAB 122/613; Davies, journal, June 14, 1945, Box 17.

29. Davies, journal, June 13, 1945, ibid.

30. WAH to HST, June 8, 1945, *FRUS: Potsdam,* I, 61–62; Joseph Grew,

conversation with HST, June 7, 1945, Records of the Department of State, 860.01; John G. Winant to Secretary of State, June 13, 1945, 860C.01, RG 59; *The Times,* June 14, 1945.

31. Raymond Gram Swing, broadcast script, June 13, 1945, HHP, Box 224.

32. HLH to Lord Beaverbrook, June 21, 1945, Beaverbrook Papers, House of Lords Records Office, London, Box C/175.

33. Sherwood, *Roosevelt and Hopkins,* pp. 915–916; HLH to Lord Beaverbrook, July 6, 1945, Beaverbrook Papers, Box C/175.

34. Charles Payne to HLH, July 7, 1945; HLH to Payne, July 10, 1945, Hopkins microfilm, reel 12; HLH to Felix Frankfurter, July 26, 1945, Frankfurter Papers, LC, Box 67.

35. HLH to Hastings Ismay, July 28, 1945, Hopkins microfilm, reel 11; HLH to Lord Beaverbrook, July 28, 1945, Beaverbrook Papers, Box C/172.

36. HLH to Charles Payne, July 10, 1945, Hopkins microfilm, reel 12; HLH to Lord Beaverbrook, July 6, 1945, Beaverbrook Papers, Box C/175.

37. HLH to George Marshall, Sept. 10, 1945, Marshall Papers, Box 71.

38. HLH to Lord Beaverbrook, Sept. 19, 1945, Hopkins microfilm, reel 10.

39. HLH to HST, Sept. 7, 1945, OF 220-C, Harry S Truman Library, Independence, Missouri; HLH to Colonel Roger W. Jones, Sept. 14, 1945, HHP, Box 160; Sherwood, *Roosevelt and Hopkins,* pp. 921, 925–926.

40. HLH to Lord Beaverbrook, Oct. 10, 1945, Beaverbrook Papers, Box C/175.

41. Sherwood, *Roosevelt and Hopkins,* pp. 921–927.

42. Bohlen, *Witness,* p. 273; Joseph Lash, *Eleanor: The Years Alone* (New York: Norton, 1972), p. 83.

43. James Halsted, interview with Mount Vernon and Fannie Lewis, Feb. 3, 1977, courtesy of Dr. Halsted; HLH to Dr. Frank Leahy, Nov. 17, 1945, Hopkins microfilm, reel 12.

44. HLH to ERS, Nov. 9, 1945, Stettinius Papers, Box 694; Lord Halifax to WSC, Dec. 3, 1945, Halifax Papers, Churchill College, Cambridge, microfilm reel 1; James A. Halsted, "Severe Malnutrition in a Public Servant," *Transactions of the American Clinical and Climatological Association,* 86 (1974), 29.

45. Lord Halifax to WSC, Dec. 3, 1945, Halifax Papers, microfilm reel 1; Henry H. Adams, *Harry Hopkins: A Biography* (New York: G. P. Putnam's Sons, 1977), p. 401.

46. HLH to WSC, Jan. 22, 1946, Sherwood, *Roosevelt and Hopkins,* pp. 930–931.

47. James Halsted, interview with Mount Vernon and Fannie Lewis, Feb. 3, 1977.

# Index